Ada 95
From the Beginning

INTERNATIONAL COMPUTER SCIENCE SERIES

Consulting Editor   A D McGettrick   University of Strathclyde

SELECTED TITLES IN THE SERIES

JAN SKANSHOLM

Ada 95
From the Beginning

THIRD EDITION

ADDISON-WESLEY

Harlow, England · Reading, Massachusetts · Menlo Park, California · New York
Don Mills, Ontario · Amsterdam · Bonn · Sydney · Singapore
Tokyo · Madrid · San Juan · Milan · Mexico City · Seoul · Taipei

© Addison Wesley Longman 1997

Addison Wesley Longman Limited
Edinburgh Gate
Harlow
Essex CM20 2JE
England

and Associated Companies throughout the World.

Published in the United States of America by Addison Wesley Longman Inc.,
New York.

The right of Jan Skansholm to be identified as author of the Work has been asserted by
him in accordance with the Copyright, Designs and Patents Act 1988.

The programs in this book have been included for their instructional value. They have
been tested with care but are not guaranteed for any particular purpose. The publisher
does not offer any warranties or representations, nor does it accept any liabilities with
respect to the programs.

Many of the designations used by manufacturers and sellers to distinguish their
products are claimed as trademarks. Addison-Wesley has made every attempt to supply
trademark information about manufacturers and their products mentioned in this book.
A list of the trademark designations and their owners appears on page xiii.

Cover design by Chris Eley
Typeset by Meridian Colour Repro, Pangbourne
Printed and bound in the United States of America

First edition printed 1988. Reprinted 1989 (twice), 1990, 1991 (twice), 1992 and 1993.
Second edition printed 1994.
Third edition printed 1996.
Reprinted 1997.

ISBN 0–201–40376–5

British Library Cataloguing in Publication Data
A catalogue record for this book is available from the British Library.

Library of Congress Cataloging-in-Publication Data is available.

Preface

To construct computer programs – programming – can be an exciting task,
marked by creativity and professional know-how. To see a well-structured and
efficient program take shape in one's hands can actually give the programmer
the same sort of pleasure that an artist feels when he creates a new work, or that
a mathematician gets from developing an elegant proof. But programming can
also mean an endless searching for errors in badly composed and incomprehensible program code. The difference lies, of course, in the programmer's skill and
knowledge. No one is born a clever programmer. Just as a craftsman can learn
his trade, so can a programmer learn by studying the work of others, by practis-
ing and by acquiring different techniques.

   This book will teach the craft of programming and is intended to be used
in introductory courses in programming. The reader needs no earlier experience
of programming, although the book can be used by those who have used another
language (such as Basic, Pascal or FORTRAN) and want an easy introduction
to Ada.

   The main aim of the book is to teach the basics of constructing computer
programs. For that reason, concepts such as algorithms, data abstraction and
data representation, abstract data types, breaking programs into subprograms,
concealing inessential details, modular program development, generic program
units and object-oriented programming are discussed. In particular, a number
of examples are given where the technique of stepwise refinement is used to
construct algorithms.

   Every craftsman can confirm the importance of having good tools. The
programmer's most important tool is the programming language he or she uses.
In this book the programming language Ada is used, because it is an excellent
programming tool. Even if it is the fundamental principles for the construction
of programs which are the most important thing in a first programming course,
it is known that the first language one meets has a lasting effect on one's thinking. Therefore it is vital that the first language is a 'good' language. It should

have support for the basic principles of programming and the language should have a good structure. The previous editions of this book have now been in use for some years, and Ada has been used as an introductory programming language at a number of universities and colleges all over the world. Experience shows clearly that Ada is a language suitable for beginners. It contains all the constructs necessary for putting programs together in a way that is both well structured and comprehensible. It supports program construction based on algorithms, and its types offer the possibility of data abstraction and representation of data objects. The concept of packages supports modular programming, and the revised standard now proposed also provides support for object-oriented programming.

Ada builds on experience from the normal conventional languages. The basic constructs of Ada are very similar to those of the other common languages, such as Pascal. Therefore, it is no great task for those who have learnt Ada as their first language to rather quickly learn to write programs in other languages.

Ada is a modern language with a broad field of use, appropriate for both technical and administrative applications. Furthermore, Ada is a standardized language (ANSI and ISO) with strong support internationally; most other languages are found in different versions and dialects for different computers. For Ada there is only one standard, Ada 95 (International Standard ISO/IEC 8652:1995(E), Information Technology – Programming Languages – Ada) which replaces the original standard (Reference Manual for the Ada Programming Language. ANSI/MIL-STD-1815A-1983) from 1983, called Ada 83.

Ada is a language with a wide range of possibilities. Apart from the 'ordinary' constructs there are a number of constructs intended for more sophisticated programming. For example, it is possible to write programs at machine level (programs that work directly with the computer's hardware), real-time programs (programs with parallel execution) and distributed programs (programs that are executed in several processors at the same time). One advantage of this is that you can grow with the language: when you want to progress and study more advanced types of programming you can still use Ada, as the concepts you need are to be found there. There is no need, as with other simpler first languages, to study special dialects and additions, or go over to another language completely.

Just because Ada has many possibilities, it does not mean that it is a difficult language. There is no need to learn all the fine detail in order to be able to use it: to start with you can stick with a restricted part of the language. If you, for example, have no knowledge about constructing real-time programs there is no risk of getting into that part of the language by accident.

This book deals with all those parts of Ada that are not to do with machine-level programming, real-time programming and distributed programming. Chapter 1 gives an overview of how a computer is constructed, and how compilation, linking and execution of programs take place. There is also a résumé of the most common programming languages. Chapter 2 gives an introduction to software engineering and the place of programming in the process of developing programs. It also contains a broad presentation of the most basic programming constructs in Ada and a number of simple examples which demonstrate how they are used in writing a program. The chapters that follow go into these various constructs in greater detail. The basics of Ada, such as control statements, different data types and subprograms, are covered in Chapters 3–7. In Chapters 8–14 more advanced constructs of the language are dealt with, including packages, handling exceptional events, dynamic data structures, files, generic program units and object-oriented programming. At the end of each chapter there are a number of exercises.

A textbook in programming must have two functions: it has to present its material in a way that is easily understood when you read it for the first time, and it must act as a reference book when you are sitting writing a program and need to check on constructs and examples. This latter function has been attended to by gathering similar aspects into single chapters. This means that you might meet a construct in part of a chapter that does not seem necessary to learn on the first reading: you can look at it briefly and pass on to the next section.

The parts of the language that are unique to Ada 95 have been indicated by a clear mark in the margin, to indicate that these are not applicable if you have only an Ada 83 compiler:

▼   A section marked like this is only applicable to Ada 95.
▲

The first edition of this book dealt with Ada 83. The second edition was published while the final work with the new standard was taking place, consequently that edition was based on a draft standard. In the second edition the new constructs of Ada 95 were included. A new chapter dealing with object-oriented programming was added, and descriptions of pointers to subprograms and of child packages were included in Chapters 11 and 8 respectively. Apart from this, minor pedagogical changes were made.

This edition, the third, is based on the final, approved version of the standard. Some minor changes have been made to the book as a result of this. The major difference, compared to the previous edition, is that two new sections have been added: one describing how to give arguments to the main program, and one dealing with generic child packages. Furthermore, Chapter 14, dealing with object-oriented programming, has been revised. For instance, the idea of iterators is demonstrated in a couple of new examples. Another new feature of this edition is that, on request, a table index with summaries has been added in order to make it easier to find a certain table when you use the book as a reference book.

All the programs written in Ada 83 have been tested using either Verdix or Telesoft's Ada compiler under the Unix operating system, or with Meridian's Ada compiler under MS-DOS. All the program examples written in Ada 95 have been syntax checked using Gnat Ada 95 compiler. The compiler can be obtained free of charge by using the file transfer program ftp and opening up a connection to cs.nyu.edu and logging in as an anonymous user.

Finally, I wish to extend warm thanks to the colleagues and students at the Department of Computer Science at Chalmers University of Technology who have contributed useful points of view on the book's content and format. Special thanks are due to Erland Holmström and Hans Lindström, who read the proofs of the first edition, and Shirley Booth, who translated it into English.

Jan Skansholm
November 1995

Contents

1 An Introduction to Computers and Programming Languages

Computers are found everywhere in modern society and, for better or worse, we are becoming more and more dependent on them. Most large administrative systems, such as those dealing with wages, bank accounts, inventory control and sales, are now computerized. The computer is an indispensable work tool for the engineer, who needs to make calculations of many kinds. In fact, some calculations would be impossible without some help from a computer. Computers have also come to play a greater and greater role as components in engineering systems, as a result of developments in the field of microelectronics, where it has become possible to manufacture powerful electronic units in large quantities and at low cost. Computers can be found as components in everything from kitchen stoves and sewing machines to space shuttles and satellites. Furthermore, in recent years, developments in personal computers have brought computers nearer to the man in the street.

This first chapter will give an introduction to the structure of the computer, its most important components and their function. The role of programs is explained, how they are translated and how the computer carries them out. Finally, an overview is given of the most important programming languages and their historic development.

1.1   A computer's structure and operation

A computer can be described as a 'machine' that can store and process information. A simplified representation of what apparently happens when a computer program is run is shown in Figure 1.1.

This shows that a computer can be seen as a unit into which certain data can be fed – the input. The computer manipulates these data and produces the output. The input and output data can take different forms – electric signals, light or sound. To start with, the computer may be thought of as communicating with people, and then it is natural that the input and output should take the form of written text. But computers are also used in many other situations where communication is not primarily with people: in manufacturing processes, for example, or as components of engineering systems such as aeroplanes and cars. Here the input generally consists of signals from monitoring devices that feed information to the computer about the current state of the system, for instance temperature or speed. The output from the computer might be control signals to relays or motors, perhaps to change the flow of fuel or initiate transfers in the system.

One very important thing to understand from the diagram is that the computer's behaviour is controlled by a program inside it. The computer can be made to do other things by changing the program. It is this that distinguishes a modern computer from an 'ordinary' machine which is only designed to do certain preordained tasks. There are, however, computers that are intended to perform only one particular task, in other words, to run only one particular program. These are known as dedicated computers. One example is the computer found in a computer or video game. However, this still does not contradict the principle that a computer is always controlled by a program and that the program is replaceable.

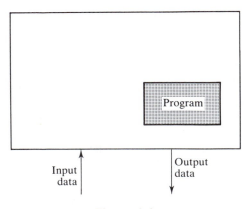

Figure 1.1

Computers compared with ordinary machines

A computer differs from an ordinary machine in that its actions are controlled by a *program*.

Figure 1.2 shows the central parts of a computer in a little more detail. The computer's 'brain' consists of a **central processing unit** (CPU). In the CPU there is a **control unit** (CU) that controls and coordinates all the computer's activities. Decisions are made in the control unit regarding the operations to be executed and the order in which these should be undertaken. The control unit also sends out control signals, which regulate all the other units of the computer. In the CPU there is also an **arithmetic logic unit** (ALU) containing electronic circuits that can carry out various operations on the data being manipulated, such as addition, subtraction, multiplication and division.

Another very important unit in the computer is the **primary memory**, which stores, among other things, the program that the computer is running or executing at any given time. Various data and temporary storage spaces needed for the executing program to function properly are also found in the primary memory.

Execution

When a program is run in a computer, it is said to be *executed*.

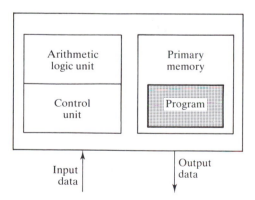

Figure 1.2

Primary memory can be thought of as a series of **memory cells**, sometimes called **words** (although they have nothing to do with ordinary spoken words). Each memory cell has a certain **address**, which specifies its position in the memory. The number of memory cells in a computer can vary, depending on type and model, but it is usually a question of millions of cells. Each memory cell consists of a certain number of bits, usually 8, 16, 32 or 64. Each bit contains a **binary digit**, i.e. zero or one.

A group of 8 bits is usually called a **byte**. The size of memory is usually expressed in the unit **kilobyte**, shortened to **Kb**, which is 1024 (2^{10}) bytes. Memory can also be expressed as a number of **megabytes** (Mb) (million bytes) or **gigabytes** (Gb) (billions of bytes).

A program that is being executed, and is therefore in primary memory, occupies a number of connected memory cells. A memory cell, or a group of cells, contains one **instruction** from the program. Different instructions can be represented by different combinations of bits in the memory cells. Thus a program consists of a series of instructions. An instruction tells the computer that it should perform a particular task, for example, move the contents of a memory cell from primary memory to the CPU, or add two numbers in the ALU. When a program is executed, the control unit reads the instructions one by one from primary memory and makes sure that they are carried out in the same order.

An instruction can thus be thought of as a particular combination of zeros and ones. These combinations look different for different models of computer. The program must be stored in primary memory in this form so that it can be executed in the computer, and then it is said to be in the form of **machine code**. Machine code is very 'unfriendly' in the sense that it is difficult to read and write. In the early days of computers, when the principle of a stored program was first applied, programs had to be written directly in machine code. Fortunately, this area has developed and today the programmer does not generally need to worry about the computer's machine code. As we will see, programs are written in what are known as **high-level languages** (for example, Ada and Pascal), which are much more 'friendly'. Special translator programs are used to translate from high-level language to the machine code, so that the program can be run in the computer.

In Figure 1.3 our computer system is extended with some very common units. To be able to communicate with its environment a computer must have one or more **input** and **output units**. The drawing shows the most common input/output units used to communicate with people, namely a **screen** and a **keyboard**. There are other units people use to communicate with the computer, the most common being a mouse, which is used to point with, and output units such as line printers and plotters.

We saw that the primary memory is used partly to store the program being executed, but in general a computer must also be able to store programs that are not being executed. The various data used as input to different programs must also be stored. Such data, which will be saved more permanently, are stored in **secondary storage**. Common types of secondary storage include the

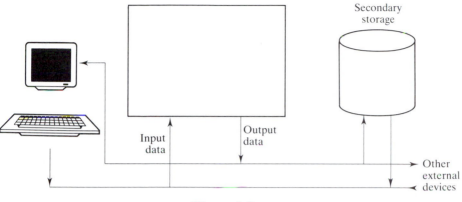

Figure 1.3

disk and **magnetic tape** (Figure 1.3 shows a disk). As a rule, secondary storage has considerably greater capacity than primary memory.

The data in secondary storage is usually organized into **files**. A file is a collection of data that belong together in some way; it might contain, for example, a program or the input data for a particular program. A file can be thought of as an envelope into which related data can be put. Each file is given its own name so that it can easily be referred to. It is possible to create new files, remove files and make changes in files.

The units in a computer that do not belong to the central parts are usually called **external units** or **peripherals**.

Important units of a computer

- *Central processing unit* (CPU) controls the computer and processes data.
- In *primary memory*, the program being executed and the data needed by that program are stored.
- *Peripheral units* are used for reading and writing data (input and output units) or for storing data more permanently (secondary storage).

1.2   How the program gets into the computer

In a programming language such as Ada or Pascal, what form does a computer program take? Because the program is written by an ordinary person, it has the form of normal written text. The program can even be written on ordinary paper. In this section we shall see what happens when this original **program text**, or **source code**, is translated into the machine's own machine code and loaded into the computer.

The program is an ordinary text, so it can be written in at the keyboard. Computers are generally delivered with a number of support programs, and one that is almost always supplied is a **text-editing program**, or **text editor**. Figure 1.4 shows what happens when this program is run.

Using the text editor, any text can be fed into the computer or stored in a file in secondary storage. A file containing text is usually called a **text file**. Using the text editor, it is easy to revise, erase, change, shift or insert text. It is normally possible to see a section of text on the screen, and then the parts of the text that are to be revised can be selected using the keyboard, a light-pen or a mouse. The details of how a text editor works and which commands it understands vary a lot from system to system. Note that the text editor pays no heed to what the text is about, whether it is an Ada program or a chapter from a book.

In the next stage the program text is translated from ordinary text to machine code, which is done, as indicated in Figure 1.5, with a special translation program called a **compiler**. Each compiler is designed to handle a specific programming language. Thus, to translate an Ada program you must have access to and use an Ada compiler. A computer system usually has compilers for several different languages.

Every programming language has special rules regarding the form of different program constructions; this can be likened to the rules for sentence structure in natural languages. It is said that each language has a certain **syntax**. The compiler reads the program from the text file created earlier and checks first that it obeys the rules of the language, i.e. that it is syntactically correct. If the compiler discovers faults it displays an error message on the screen. Sometimes the compiler attempts to correct errors if they are not too serious, but

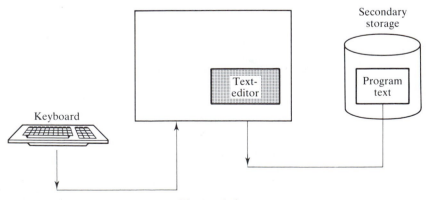

Figure 1.4

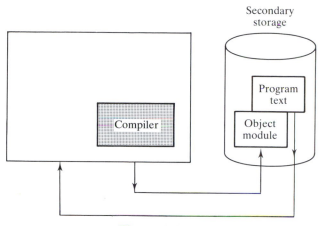

Figure 1.5

normally compilation stops when errors are found. The programmer then has to go back a stage and use the text editor to revise the program and correct the errors. A new attempt to compile the program can then be made. Sometimes this process has to be repeated several times before the program is free of syntax errors.

If no errors are found in this first stage, the compiler goes on to translate the program from text to machine code. The machine code so produced is generally called the **object module** and it is saved in a file in secondary storage.

Note that, because different models of computer have different machine codes, a compiler designed for one computer will not work on another. Different compilers are needed for different computers. This is no problem for the programmer, because an Ada compiler always requires an Ada program as input, irrespective of the computer being used. The text of an Ada program that is developed for a particular computer can thus easily be transferred to another computer and run there. Thus the programs are said to be **portable**. One of the advantages of high-level languages is the possibility of writing portable programs, which is not possible using machine code.

The compilation of a fairly simple program may give rise to an object module that can be loaded directly into the primary memory and executed, but normally a **linking** stage is needed before this. Figure 1.6 illustrates this stage. A special link program must be run. When a large program is designed it is usually divided into different parts that are written, developed and compiled separately. The link program gathers together the different object modules from these separate compilations into a single entity called the **load module**. This is saved in a file in secondary storage. Even if the program has not been divided, linking might still be necessary because the program needs access to existing system routines, for example, routines for input and output or mathematical routines.

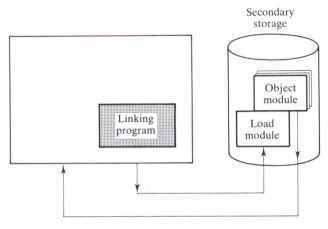

Figure 1.6

Only the final stage now remains – to get the load module into the primary memory so that the program can be run. This brings us to the question: how does the computer know which program it should run? For the answer to this, study Figure 1.7.

In the earlier figures we have only shown one program at a time in the primary memory – the program that is currently being run. In actual fact there is always one more program permanently stored in the primary memory. That is the **operating system**, abbreviated to OS. The operating system is the program that is always running when no 'ordinary' program is being run. It operates automatically when the ordinary program has finished or stopped for some

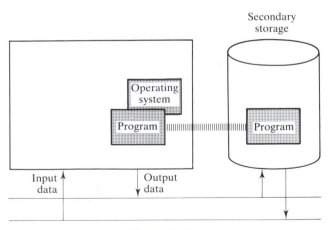

Figure 1.7

reason. The computer is also designed to put the operating system directly into operation when the computer starts.

The operating system usually communicates with the user via the screen, keyboard and mouse. The user can write commands using the keyboard, or point and click using the mouse. One command is the instruction to load and execute a particular program. The operating system searches for the required module in secondary storage and copies it into primary memory, as indicated in the diagram. Control is then passed to the loaded program, which is then executed until it is finished, or until it is stopped.

The operating system performs many other tasks in a computer. For example, it checks that the computer's contacts with the peripherals are working and keeps track of all the files stored in secondary storage. The operating system is often a very advanced program and computer manufacturers generally provide one when a computer is delivered.

Now we have seen how a program is written, and how it is loaded and run. This process can often be simplified so that the programmer does not need to be aware of the separate stages, by using, for example, a program that combines the compiling and linking stages.

The stages of making a working program

- The program text (source code) is created using the text editor.
- The compiler translates the program text into an object module.
- The linker puts several object modules together to form an executable load module.
- The operating system puts the load module into primary memory and the program is executed.

There is another way of running programs written in a high-level language, distinctly different from the one just described. Instead of a compiler, a special program, called an **interpreter**, is used. This is shown in Figure 1.8.

The program text is created using the text editor, exactly as before. The interpreter is then run with the program text in secondary storage as input data. Just like the compiler, the interpreter reads the text and checks that the program has no syntax errors. The difference is that the interpreter never translates the program into machine code. Instead, it interprets the program step by step and carries out the tasks of the program. From the user's point of view, it appears as

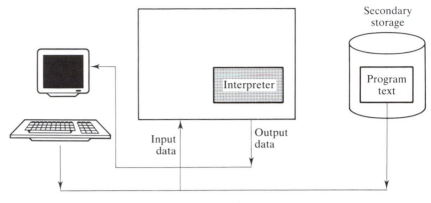

Figure 1.8

if the program he or she has written is being executed. This often provides a faster and easier way of test running small and simple programs. The disadvantage is that the program runs much more slowly. It is thus not a method to be used in the everyday running of working programs.

In some systems even the text editor and the interpreter have been combined in one program; then, using just this one program, a user's program can be both edited and run.

1.3   Programming languages

As mentioned earlier, the earliest computers had to be programmed in machine code. Part of such a program might have looked like this:

```
0111000100001111
1001110110110001
1110000100111110
```

It is easy to understand that it was seen as a tremendous advance when **assembler languages** started to be used. Then the above fragment of program might have been rewritten as:

```
LOAD   A
ADD    B
STORE  C
```

In the assembler language each line of the program corresponds to one instruction in machine code. Thus the little program above has three instructions. For a program written in assembler language to be run in the computer, a translating program is required – an **assembler** – that translates the program into machine code. Such a translator does not have to be too complicated because the assembler language lies so close to the structure of the machine code.

In spite of the considerable advance provided by assembler languages, they still have enormous disadvantages. One disadvantage is that each model of computer has its own unique assembler language, naturally enough, because the language is so close to the machine code. An assembler programmer is thus forced to learn many different assembler languages, which can differ considerably in their details. Another disadvantage is that the assembler language is extremely detailed. Each individual instruction must be given to the computer, which means it is time-consuming to use an assembler language. Furthermore, the error risk is high, so a program may contain many errors that may be difficult to detect.

With the development of high-level languages in the 1950s, programming changed radically. A program written in a high-level language is more adapted to human modes of expression than to the computer's set of instructions. Programs are expressed in 'half-English' and arithmetic calculations are written in a way familiar in mathematics. The above fragment of program may now be written as:

```
C := A + B
```

The programmer can concentrate on the problem to be solved rather than a mass of detail about how the computer works. In principle, it is also possible to write a program in a high-level language with the intention of running it on different computers. There is no need to learn a new language for each computer.

The first high-level language was **FORTRAN** (FORmula TRANslator), which was introduced in 1954. It was originally intended to simplify writing programs that made calculations using arithmetic expressions. The language's great weakness, however, is its poor structure, which means that FORTRAN programs often become muddled and difficult to see as a whole. In addition, the language has poor facilities for describing data and handling input and output. FORTRAN had something of a facelift with the more recent versions, FORTRAN 77 and FORTRAN 90.

In 1959 a new programming language, **COBOL**, was introduced, designed for programming in the areas of finance and administration. A few years later the language was standardized and it has become, and remains, one of the most used languages. COBOL programs are very readable in that they resemble ordinary English. The disadvantage of this is that programs in the language are sometimes considered wordy and awkward. What was new about COBOL, compared to FORTRAN, was its better ways of describing the data a program had to handle.

A language that came to be very significant for subsequent developments was **ALGOL**, which was presented in 1960. The big advantage of the language is that it has good structure. It is possible to write a program so that the way it works is reflected in its appearance. Despite these advances, ALGOL never had any great commercial success. A completely new version, ALGOL68, was presented in 1968, but even that never achieved any real breakthrough.

A language that has been significant for later language developments was **SIMULA**, the first version of which appeared in 1967, a direct extension of ALGOL. The language is used primarily, as its names implies, to write simulation programs. SIMULA is significant for being the first programming language that enabled **object-oriented** programs to be written. All of today's so-called object-oriented languages are based on SIMULA.

The language **Pascal** was presented in 1971. The aim was for Pascal to be a simple programming language, suitable for use in teaching, and it has achieved wide usage in this field. The reason is that it has good program structure, which makes it easier for beginners to acquire a good 'programming style'. The language is based directly on ALGOL and ALGOL68, with some ideas from SIMULA, although several constructs have been deliberately simplified. An important feature of the language is that data can be described well and new data types can be introduced by the programmer. Pascal is standardized, both as an American standard (ANSI) and as an international standard (ISO). Even so, variants of the language have appeared in which certain additions have been made, for example UCSD Pascal and TurboPascal. The greatest weakness of the language is that it lacks constructs for enabling larger programs to be built up in a modular way. Further, it is limited in its handling of text, and in its input and output facilities.

C is a language that has become very popular in spite of its age (it was developed at the start of the 1970s). It is a language which can be said to be a 'high-level language at a low level'. It gives the programmer great freedom to control the computer in detail, and has therefore come largely to replace the assembler in the development of system programs. Most of today's operating systems and other system programs, such as those for handling windows and menus, are written in C. The language is relatively small, but it demands a lot of the programmer since monitoring is lax and it is easy to make mistakes.

The most widely used of the object-oriented languages is **C++**, the first commercial version of which came out in 1985. C++ is a pure extension of C, a number of constructs to facilitate the handling of what are called classes and objects having been added. These constructs are largely taken from SIMULA. C++ is not an easy language to learn as first you have to master ordinary C, followed by the object-oriented constructs.

Remarkably fast developments in the field of electronics, in that more and more powerful components can be produced more and more cheaply, led many to believe that it would similarly be possible to construct ever larger and more complex programs. In the event, this assumption was quite wrong. All too many programs either failed to be ready on time, greatly exceeded their budget, contained many errors or did not fulfil the customers' specifications. This phenomenon became known as the **software crisis**. Among the reasons for this crisis was poor project management, and the fact that the programmer often considered the program to be his or her own property. Many individual and curious programming styles developed and it proved difficult to create error-free programs. In order to remedy this, the concept of **structured programming** was introduced, with the aim that a program should be written in such a way that it is both easily understood and free from errors. Structured programming can be said to be a set of rules and recommendations for how 'good' programs should be written. Such programming needs the support of a suitable program-ming language, and it was this need for well-structured programs that was behind the development of what became known as structured languages, such as Pascal.

During the 1970s it became clear that even well-structured programs were not enough for mastering the complexity involved in developing a large program system. It was also recognized that it was necessary to support the divi-sion of the program into well-defined parts, or **modules**, that could be developed and tested independently of one another, so that several people could work together within one large programming project.

One way to divide a program into modules is to use so-called **objects** as building blocks in the program. An object in the program can be thought of as a representation of a real or conceptual thing in the program's environment. This idea originated from the language SIMULA but was further elaborated in a pro-ject at Xerox, where a brand new language, **Smalltalk**, was constructed. The first available version of Smalltalk was presented in 1980 and the concept of **object-oriented** program development was introduced in connection to this pro-ject. Many of the special words which are used in the object-oriented programming languages, **messages** and **methods** for instance, come from Smalltalk. In Smalltalk the concept of object is particularly emphasized. There are no data types in the language and all data in a program are just objects. The syntax of Smalltalk is also somewhat particular; that is, the language looks very different compared to other languages. A Smalltalk system is an integrated interactive environment with a window-oriented user interface. A drawback of Smalltalk that is often mentioned is that the interactive environment demands large computer resources and that the programs produced usually execute slowly. The latter is due to that fact that the program code is not compiled, but *interpreted*, at execution.

The US Department of Defense was an important customer for systems of programs, which were supplied by a large number of independent companies and written in a large number of different languages. The cost of development and maintenance increased steadily. In 1975, in response to the software crisis, the Department of Defense published a list of requirements that should be met by any programming language before its use would be accepted. It turned out that none of the existing languages met these requirements and a competition was announced for the design of a modern, general, programming language. The winning entry was named **Ada**, and was accepted in 1983 as a standard in the USA, later to become an ISO standard as well. Since all compilers must follow the standard, each compiler must go through a special validation test before it can be called an Ada compiler.

Apart from being a well-structured language, Ada also supports the modular development of programs. The concept of the **package** has been introduced and it is possible to build up libraries of packages which can be put together to make large programs. One thing that distinguishes Ada from most other programming languages is that it can be used to write **parallel programs**, that is, programs that are to be executed simultaneously and interact with one another. Such programs are encountered in applications for computer control of technical systems.

After a few years of use it was decided to revise the standard. The work was started in 1988 and the new standard was officially approved in 1995; hence it is called Ada 95. One important innovation compared with the old standard (called Ada 83) is that of object-oriented language constructs. Another important addition is that of child libraries, which further simplify the construction of large programs. Furthermore, a number of minor aspects of the language have been improved (international character sets, pointers to subprograms, etc.), and a number of changes have taken place in the part of the language to do with parallel programming. A number of **annexes** have also been brought into the standard, which contain descriptions of the parts of the language which are special and are not necessary in every implementation. These annexes and their contents are: **system programming** (machine-level programming, such as interrupt handling), **real-time systems** (control of the priority of different processes, etc.), **distributed systems** (program execution on several processors at the same time), **information systems** (decimal arithmetic, text handling, etc.), **security** (discusses the special problems involved in writing programs that must be secure), and **numerical computation** (mathematical functions, etc.).

Finally, there are a few programming languages which are based, in part at least, on different principles from those we have discussed so far. **LISP** is a language developed as early as 1958, intended to manipulate symbols of various kinds, such as characters and words. Programs are built up using lists of symbols and have a very special appearance. LISP has been used extensively, especially in the area generally known as artificial intelligence.

Research is going on all the time into developing new programming languages which are based on new ideas, and the language **PROLOG** and the so-called **functional programming** languages are examples of these.

2 The Construction of Programs

We will start this chapter by discussing what is known as software engineering and the place of programming in the process of developing programs. The two important concepts of algorithms and stepwise refinement will be introduced. Then a number of simple programs will be presented to give the reader a first idea of what an Ada program looks like. We do not want to get caught up in a mass of details at this stage, so this chapter will give only an outline description of the different program constructions, and more detailed descriptions will follow in later chapters.

2.1   The process of developing programs

This book is all about programming or, in other words, how one builds or constructs a program. However, developing a program is not only a question of programming. It might be compared with what happens when a house is built – it is not just a case of going ahead and laying the bricks. A good deal of careful preparation is needed. First, you have to decide how the house will be used, then the plans can be drawn, and after that all the calculations have to be made before the actual building can commence. And even when the house is completely built it cannot be left to itself: it needs to be maintained. The work of building a house can thus be divided into a number of phases – from the decision about its future usage to its maintenance. This is quite similar to what has to happen if you are going to develop a computer program: the programming, corresponding to the actual carpentry and bricklaying, is only *one* phase of the whole process.

This is where a useful distinction can be made between **programming in the small** and **programming in the large**. Programming in the small means that you work alone and produce a little program of a temporary nature. Programming in the large means that you work with the development of a larger program and that the work is often the joint effort of a group of programmers. Most programming in educational settings is on the small scale, but on occasion it can also be large-scale, for example in project-based courses and the sort of applied project work incorporated in many educational programmes. In the case of commercial and industrial program development, it is almost always a question of programming in the large.

When there is a program to be written, it happens all too often that someone sits down and starts to write it at once – one could call this the direct-programming method. In the case of professional programming, in the large, this practice leads to greater costs and it is questionable whether a functioning and usable program can ever be produced in this way. It is generally admitted that such direct programming brought about the software crisis that was discussed in the previous chapter. It is less serious to use the direct-programming approach for programming in the small, but even then it is worthwhile to decide in advance *what* the program should do and *how* it should do it.

The overall goal when developing a professional program is to produce a high-quality program within given constraints of time and cost. A program should match the demands of the user, be reliable, well documented and easy to maintain. To achieve these ends the program has to be developed with a well-structured approach; just as with building a house, this calls for engineer-like work in accordance with a clear plan. The term **software engineering** is often used to refer to such a well-structured approach.

In order to draw up a work plan you need a model for the way in which program development proceeds, and there are several models to choose from. The most widely used is what is known as the **waterfall model**, of which there are several variants. The **program development process** is here divided up into the following phases:

- Requirements analysis and specification
- Design
- Implementation
- Test and installation
- Operation and maintenance.

The reason for calling this the waterfall method is that each phase results in a set of documents that run down to the next phase.

During the first phase, **requirements analysis** and **specification**, the goal is to determine *what* has to be done. You have to try to understand the environment in which the desired program will have to function. You should specify what the program is required to do, what different functions it should be capable of, and the principles for its communication with the user. Such questions as the sort of computers it should be run on should also be addressed now. This work should result in a written **requirements specification**, which clearly states all these demands. The specification is the document which defines the program that is to be constructed and it has to be accepted both by the customer and by the program developer(s). The specifications might include a **preliminary user manual** and it can also prescribe **trial procedures**, which state how the final program will be tested.

In the second phase, that of **design**, the question being addressed is how should the program meet the demands now specified? You could say that this is producing a blueprint for the program. You decide what different parts should go to make up the program, what each of these should do, how they should interface and how they should communicate with one another. This is done first in outline and then in greater detail. The detailed design really means that you have decided how the program is to be implemented. For example, it is now that decisions are made about suitable algorithms (see the next section) and data structures. The details of the interface with the user are worked out – what it should look like, how commands will be given to the program, what the menus should include, and so on. The documents which are produced during the design phase are firstly a detailed **system description**, laying out the program's design, and secondly a **user manual**, which gives directions for how the program should be used.

It is only in the third phase, **implementation**, that any programming starts to be done, when there is already a detailed system specification and user manual to adhere to. This phase also sees the testing of the parts of the program, one by one, as they are completed. The result of the implementation phase is, naturally, the **program code**, but there might also be **test protocols** resulting from the tests carried out on parts of the program.

In the fourth phase of development, **test and installation**, all the parts of the program are now put together for a check that everything works. If the program is to be installed at a particular site, that is also done now. Testing is carried out according to the prescribed test procedures which were defined earlier. This phase results in a test protocol, and it is only after this has been found acceptable that the program developer gets paid in full by the customer.

The final phase, **operation and maintenance**, is the longest phase in the life of the product. Now the program is in full use, but errors that were missed in earlier tests have to be put right and the program might have to be adjusted to cope with new demands, for example to work in a more modern hardware environment.

There is criticism of the waterfall model in that it is too static: if one should happen upon a mistake made in an earlier phase it cannot be corrected. Of course, the waterfall model is not in reality used so strictly: some degree of feedback is allowed. There is, after all, no point in implementing something known to be incorrect or unsuitable. For example, one might discover during the design phase that some of the demands made in the first phase are impossible, or very expensive, to implement, and then it is only natural to relax the demands.

The specifications which are drawn up during the program development process should be as clear as possible, so that there is no possibility of misunderstanding. There are no generally recognized formal methods for writing specifications. The most common method is to use **graphic notation**, **ordinary text**, or a **program description language**. In the case of using normal text it is usual to make it as formal as possible, by filling in sets of prespecified forms, for example. Program description languages (PDL) are simplified programming languages which contain certain simple language constructs and which enable one to include explanatory text. There are progam description languages which are based on Ada.

2.2   Algorithms

When designing a program the problem has to be faced of deciding on suitable methods of solving the different partial problems of the whole program. A description of how a particular problem is solved – a computational method – is called an **algorithm**. An algorithm consists of a number of elementary operations and instructions about the order in which these operations should be carried out. Certain demands can be made of an algorithm:

- it should solve the given problem;
- it should be unambiguous;
- if the program has an end in view, such as computing a certain value, then the algorithm should terminate after a finite number of steps.

Note: Not all algorithms have to terminate. For instance, the algorithm that describes the control program for a nuclear power plant should certainly not terminate.

We come across algorithms every day. One example is a recipe: the problem is to prepare a particular dish and the algorithm gives us the solution. Another example is the assembly instructions we get when we buy furniture in kit form; and then there are all the different kinds of instruction manuals. And knitters will recognize that a knitting pattern is nothing other than an algorithm.

Algorithms can be expressed in many different ways. One common way is in natural language. Pictures and symbols can also be used, as in a knitting pattern; so can formal languages like mathematical notation. Flow charts have also been popular. Here we are dealing with programming, so it is naturally of interest to us that algorithms can be expressed in programming languages. The programming language ALGOL, which lies at the roots of most of today's conventional programming languages, was designed specifically so that it could be made to express algorithms, hence the name.

Algorithms

Description of how a particular problem should be solved.

Let us look at an example. We shall describe an algorithm that shows how the sum $1 + 2 + 3 + \ldots + N$ can be evaluated, if N is a given whole number > 0. One way of describing the algorithm in natural language is:

(1) Set SUM equal to 0 and the counter K equal to 1.
(2) Repeat the following steps until K is greater than N:
    (2.1) Calculate the sum of SUM and K and save the result in SUM.
    (2.2) Increase the value of K by 1.
(3) The result required is now the number in SUM.

Expressed as an Ada program, the algorithm looks like this:

```
GET (N);
SUM := 0;
K := 1;
while K <= N loop
    SUM := SUM + K;
    K := K + 1;
end loop;
PUT (SUM);
```

These lines of program read in the number N from the terminal keyboard and display the required result at the terminal.

To describe general algorithms the description method must be able to express the following three constructs:

(1)   **Sequence**   A sequence is a series of steps that are carried out sequentially in the order in which they are written. Each step is carried out only once. An example is the assembly instructions for book-shelves:

> (1)   Put the side pieces in position.
> (2)   Screw the back piece on to the sides.
> (3)   Put the shelves into the frame.

(2)   **Selection**   Selection means that one of two or more alternatives should be chosen. Calculating the absolute value of a number T can be taken as an example:

> If $T > 0$ then the result is T, otherwise the result is $-T$.

(3)   **Iteration**   Part of the algorithm should be capable of repetition, either a defined number of times or until a certain condition has been met. An example of the latter repetition could be:

> Whisk the egg whites vigorously, until they become fluffy.

The most important algorithmic constructs

- Sequence: series of steps.
- Selection: choice between alternative paths.
- Iteration: repetition.

Another kind of construct that is commonly used in algorithms, and which can sometimes replace iteration, is **recursion**. This construct seldom occurs in 'everyday' algorithms and may therefore feel a little strange. The principle is to break down the original problem into smaller, but structurally similar, problems. The smaller problems can then be solved by reapplying the same algorithm. The previous example, calculating the sum of the first N positive integers, can be solved with recursion in the following manner:

(1)   If $N = 0$ set the result to 0.
(2)   Otherwise:
> (2.1)   Compute the sum $1 + 2 + 3 + \ldots + (N-1)$ using this algorithm.
> (2.2)   The required result is obtained by adding N to the result from step (2.1).

> **Problem solving with computers**
>
> (1) Specify the problem.
>
> (2) Design an algorithm for solving the problem.
>
> (3) Express the algorithm as a program in a pro-
>   gramming language.
>
> (4) Compile and run the program on the computer.

2.3   Top-down design

When a complicated problem has to be solved it is helpful to split it into smaller
subproblems and solve them separately. The subproblems can then be split into
further subproblems, and so on. This is a very important technique in algorithm
and program design and is known as top-down design, or stepwise refinement.
We shall use it extensively in the rest of the book. Let us look at a real-world
algorithm that describes how to wash a car. A first, rough algorithm may be
simply:

    (1)   Wash car.

This can quickly be expanded to:

    (1.1)   If you are feeling lazy:
                (1.1.1)   Wash it at a car wash.
    (1.2)   Otherwise:
                (1.2.1)   Wash it by hand.

Step (1.1.1) can be refined to:

    (1.1.1.1)   Drive to the nearest car wash.
    (1.1.1.2)   Buy a token.
    (1.1.1.3)   Wait in line.
    (1.1.1.4)   Have the car washed.

Step (1.1.1.4) can be refined further:

    (1.1.1.4.1)   Drive into the car wash.
    (1.1.1.4.2)   Check that all the doors and windows are closed.
    (1.1.1.4.3)   Get out of the car.

(1.1.1.4.4)   Put the token into the machine.
(1.1.1.4.5)   Wait until the car wash is finished.
(1.1.1.4.6)   Get into the car.
(1.1.1.4.7)   Drive away.

In this way, different parts of an algorithm can be refined until a level is reached where the solution is trivially simple.

Top-down design

- Divide a problem into subproblems.
- Solve the subproblems individually.
- Divide the subproblems into further subproblems.
- Continue in this way until all the subproblems are easily solvable.

Let us look at another example where iteration is also involved. Imagine the following situation. In your bookcase you have a cassette holder for ordinary music cassettes. You keep your cassettes there, neatly arranged alphabetically according to the name of the composer. (For simplicity, assume that you only have classical music.) The holder is made of small slots, each large enough for one cassette, so that they cannot move sideways. We assume that the cassettes are kept in the left part of the holder, so there are no gaps or empty slots on the left, but at least five empty ones on the right.

Now suppose you have bought five new cassettes that need to be put in the holder in their correct positions, so that alphabetical order is maintained. Assume also that the bookshelves are so full that there is nowhere to put the cassettes, so you have to hold them in your hands while you shift them around. To avoid the risk of dropping any, you cannot have more than one cassette in your hand at a time. The five new cassettes are on the floor and you pick them up one after the other and position them in the holder.

We can make up a crude algorithm:

(1)   Sort the new cassettes into the holder.

The first refinement is:

(1.1)   For each new cassette:
      (1.1.1)   Lift the cassette from the floor in your left hand.
      (1.1.2)   Sort it into its correct place.

The way we have written points (1.1.1) and (1.1.2) inset on the line shows that they have to be repeated several times (once per new cassette). Thus iteration has been introduced into the algorithm. Point (1.1.1) needs no further refinement so we can expand point (1.1.2):

(1.1.2.1)   Locate the slot in the holder where the new cassette should be placed.
(1.1.2.2)   Shift all the cassettes to the right of (and including) the located slot one place to the right, so that the located one becomes empty.
(1.1.2.3)   Put the new cassette into the empty slot.

Refining point (1.1.2.1) gives:

(1.1.2.1.1)   Place your left index finger on the leftmost slot of the cassette holder. (You can do this even though you have the new cassette in that hand.)
(1.1.2.1.2)   Repeat the following point until the located slot is empty or the composer's name on the cassette in the located slot comes alphabetically after the composer's name on the new cassette.
  (1.1.2.1.2.1)   Move the left index finger one place to the right.
(1.1.2.1.3)   The left index finger has now located the slot where the new cassette should be inserted.

Point (1.1.2.2) becomes:

(1.1.2.2.1)   Place your right hand on the cassette on the extreme righthand side and repeat the following steps until the slot pointed to by your left index finger is empty:
  (1.1.2.2.1.1)   Move the cassette held in your right hand one place to the right.
  (1.1.2.2.1.2)   Move your right hand to the nearest cassette on the left.

If we now put all the expanded steps together, we get the following complete algorithm:

For each of the newly bought cassettes:
  Lift the cassette from the floor with your left hand.
  Put your left index finger on the slot on the extreme left of the holder. (You can do this even though you are holding the new cassette.)
  Repeat the following step until the slot pointed to is either empty or contains a cassette with a composer whose name comes alphabetically after the name of the composer of the new cassette.
    Move your left index finger one slot to the right.
  Your left index finger has now located the slot where the new cassette should be placed.

Put your right hand on the rightmost cassette and repeat the following steps until the located slot is empty.
   Move the cassette held in your right hand one place to the right.
   Move your right hand to the nearest cassette on the left.
Put the new cassette in the located slot.

The numbering has been removed to make it look neater. Note that the lines that are inset are repeated a number of times.

We have just seen an example of what is known as a **sort algorithm**. This is not the only algorithm that could be used for sorting the cassettes into position. You can think of several other ways of doing it. Sort algorithms often occur in programming and many computers are used extensively for sorting different kinds of data.

There are usually several alternative algorithms for solving a particular problem. In general, it is sensible to design an algorithm that is as simple and easily understood as possible, because there is a better chance that it will work as it was intended.

2.4 Simple programming examples

We shall now look at some simple examples of programs and become familiar with a number of the constructs of Ada. As mentioned previously, a more thorough treatment of the different constructs will be given in later chapters. Therefore there is no need to pay attention to all the details at this first reading.

2.4.1 Simple output

The first program looks like this;

```
with TEXT_IO;
use TEXT-IO;
procedure HELLO is
begin
   PUT ("Hellow! This is your computer speaking.");
end HELLO;
```

When the program is run, it prints the text:

Hello! This is your computer speaking.

at the terminal. In the program, certain words are written in bold type. These are called **reserved words**, words that have special meanings. When writing a program, it is not necessary to emphasize different words in this way. It will only be done here so that the programs are clearer. If desired, everything can be written with ordinary small or capital letters.

An Ada program consists of a **procedure**. The procedure in the program above starts on the third line and has been given the name HELLO. The name is repeated on the last line so that it is easy to see where the procedure ends.

In the program there is a printout of text (the line starting PUT). Ada is designed for use in many different working environments, so it cannot always be taken for granted that a program should write to a terminal as this one does. If we want to read or write to a terminal, this must be stated, as seen here in the first line. The line says that the program needs the help of a **package** called TEXT_IO which is accessible on all Ada implementations. The package contains several tools, including PUT, which enable us to read and write text at a terminal. (A complete specification of the package is given in Appendix A.)

When we want to use PUT in our program we must inform the compiler that PUT is to be found in the package TEXT_IO. We can do this by writing TEXT_IO.PUT in the program. This is a bit cumbersome to write, especially if we want to use PUT many times. There is a more convenient way, as shown in our example. On the second line we have written:

use TEXT_IO;

This causes the compiler automatically to search in the package TEXT_IO. Therefore we can continue by writing only PUT instead of TEXT_IO.PUT.

In fact, PUT is a procedure just like HELLO. The line:

PUT ("Hello! This is your computer speaking.";

means that our program **calls** PUT. This means that the procedure PUT will be carried out, or **executed**. The text in brackets is a **parameter** to PUT. We can say that this parameter is input data to PUT. This parameter is a **text string**, seen from the quotation marks around it. The procedure PUT is designed so that it expects a text string as input. When it is called it will write out the text between the quotation marks, but not the quotation marks themselves.

Printing text

PUT ("the text to be printed");

2.4.2   Reading and writing numbers

The next example shows a program that both reads from and writes to a terminal.

```
with TEXT_IO, BASIC_NUM_IO;
use TEXT_IO, BASIC_NUM_IO;
procedure SUM_AND_PROD is
   NUMBER1, NUMBER2 : INTEGER;
begin
   PUT_LINE ("Give two whole numbers!");
   GET (NUMBER1);
   GET (NUMBER2);
   PUT ("The sum of the numbers is:");
   PUT (NUMBER1+NUMBER2); NEW_LINE;
   PUT ("The product of the numbers is:");
   PUT (NUMBER1*NUMBER2); NEW_LINE;
end SUM_AND_PROD;
```

When the program is run the output looks like this:

```
Give two whole numbers!
4
12
The sum of the numbers is:        16
The product of the numbers is:        48
```

The second and third lines were written by the user and the rest by the program.

Another package has been introduced in this example, BASIC_NUM_IO. This package contains all the facilities needed for reading and writing numbers at the terminal. In Ada, as will be shown later, it is possible to work with many different kinds of numbers, and there is a general mechanism for creating packages of facilities for reading and writing them. The non-standard package BASIC_NUM_IO has been used here instead, to avoid complicating things unnecessarily, even though it is not available on all implementations of Ada. (Appendix B shows how to create this package using TEXT_IO.) The resources in BASIC_NUM_IO are called in exactly the same way as those in Ada's standardized, general packages. Therefore it will look exactly the same as if we had used such packages.†

---

† If you do not have access to a package like BASIC_NUM_IO you can start your program as follows (see Chapter 5.5):

```
with TEXT_IO;
use  TEXT_IO;
procedure program_name is
   package INTEGER_INOUT is new INTEGER_IO(INTEGER);
   package FLOAT_INOUT is new FLOAT_IO(FLOAT);
   use INTEGER_INOUT, FLOAT_INOUT;
    : the rest of the program
    :
```

To put it simply, an Ada program can be thought of as a cake recipe. First comes the name of the cake, then the list of ingredients to be used. Finally there is the part stating how the ingredients should be mixed. First in an Ada procedure comes the procedure specification, giving, among other things, the name of the procedure. The procedure's name in the example above is SUM_AND_PROD. This is followed by a part of the procedure where **declarations** can be made. In our example, two objects are declared, the variables NUMBER1 and NUMBER2:

NUMBER1, NUMBER2 : INTEGER;

A variable can be thought of as a storage box into which values may be placed. Each box, or store, can only contain values of a certain type. The word INTEGER states that the variables NUMBER1 and NUMBER2 can contain only whole numbers, called integers in mathematics. They are said to have type INTEGER. This can be illustrated as in Figure 2.1. The contents of the stores are not yet defined. Last in the procedure, between the words **begin** and **end**, is the part that describes what it does when it is executed. This part contains a series of **statements**. Each statement is terminated by a semicolon. It is useful to write one statement per line.

Program structure

with   ... ;

use   ... ;

procedure *program name* **is**

    declarations (including variables)

begin

    statements

end *program name;*

NUMBER 1

NUMBER 2

Figure 2.1

The first statement in the program:

PUT_LINE ("Give two whole numbers!");

makes the program begin by printing at the terminal:

Give two whole numbers!

when it is run. The procedure PUT_LINE in TEXT_IO has been used here. This works in exactly the same way as PUT in the previous example, but with the difference that a new line is automatically started *after* the text has been printed.
When the program comes to the statement:

GET(NUMBER1);

which contains a call to the procedure GET in BASIC_NUM_IO, it will stop and wait until the user has entered a whole number at the terminal. Assume the user types the number 4, as shown in the example output. Then the procedure GET places the value 4 in the variable NUMBER1, as illustrated in Figure 2.2.
The next statement:

GET(NUMBER2);

works in the same way, but this time the number read is placed in the variable NUMBER2. If we assume that the user has written 12, then the variable NUMBER2 will contain the value 12.

Input of numbers

GET *(variable name)*;

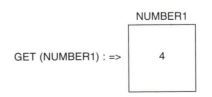

Figure 2.2

The following lines:

```
PUT ("The sum of the numbers is:");
PUT (NUMBER1+NUMBER2); NEW_LINE;
```

contain three statements which together produce a line of output at the terminal. First comes a call to the procedure PUT in the package TEXT_IO. This call causes the text:

```
The sum of the numbers is:
```

to be written out. Then comes a fresh call to the procedure PUT, but this time it is not PUT in TEXT_IO that is called but the procedure with the same name in the package BASIC_NUM_IO. This procedure expects a whole number as parameter. The parameter is the expression:

```
NUMBER1+NUMBER2
```

The value of this expression is computed. In our example it has the value 4 + 12, thus PUT gets the value 16 as parameter and writes out this value at the terminal. The compiler sees to it that the correct version of the procedure PUT is chosen. When an integer is given as parameter, it is 'understood' that we mean PUT in BASIC_NUM_IO, and when a text string is given as parameter it is 'understood' that we mean PUT in TEXT_IO to be used.

The procedure NEW_LINE, called in the last line, causes a new line to be started in the output at the terminal. Why is PUT_LINE not used here as well? The answer is that PUT_LINE only exists for text strings, not for numbers.

Getting new lines in output

```
        NEW_LINE;
```
or:
```
        PUT_LINE ("the text that is to be written");
```
The new line is generated after the text is written.

The output:

```
The sum of the numbers is:      16
The product of the numbers is:      48
```

may not look so neat. If we want the output to look as follows:

```
The sum of the numbers is:      16
The product of the numbers is:      48
```

then we can change the program:

```
PUT ("The sum of the numbers is:");
PUT (NUMBER1+NUMBER2, WIDTH => 7); NEW_LINE;

PUT ("The product of the numbers is:");
PUT (NUMBER1*NUMBER2, WIDTH => 3); NEW_LINE;
```

The parameter WIDTH tells PUT how many positions are to be used in the output, the width of the output field. If the number to be written requires fewer positions than stated (as in our example), PUT fills the field in with spaces to the left of the number. When the width of the field is decided, one position should be allowed for a possible minus sign if the number could be negative.

If the number requires more positions than stated, then it is not an error but the number is output using as many positions as needed. If we had written for example:

```
PUT ("The sum of the numbers is:");
PUT (NUMBER1+NUMBER2, WIDTH => 1); NEW_LINE;
```

and the sum had been 16, then the output would have been:

```
The sum of the numbers is:16
```

If no WIDTH parameter is specified in PUT, then the number of positions needed to write out the greatest whole number that can be stored in the computer is assumed. This is the reason for the original appearance of the output in our example.

Output of whole numbers

> PUT (the value to be output);

or:

> PUT (the value to be output, WIDTH => N);

where N specifies the width of the output field.

2.4.3 Writing an invoice

Now we shall look at an example in which the technique of top-down design will be used in designing and writing a program. Our program will be used in general sales situations and we can imagine that it is intended for use as follows. A customer buys a number of items of the same kind and should receive an invoice stating their product code, the number of items bought, the price per item excluding value added tax (VAT) and the total price for all the goods, including VAT. The invoice should also state what part of the total cost is VAT.

Our task is to write a program to produce such an invoice. Input to the program should be the product code (comprising six letters and numerals), the number of items sold, and the item price, excluding VAT. We assume that the VAT rate is a known percentage that is fixed.

First we write a very rough algorithm:

(1) Read input data.
(2) Make the computations.
(3) Print the invoice.

Step (1) can be split into substeps:

(1.1) Read in the product code.
(1.2) Read in the number of items sold.
(1.3) Read in the unit price (excluding VAT).

For simplicity we shall start with step (1.2) and expand it:

(1.2.1) Ask the operator to enter the number of items sold.
(1.2.2) Read what the operator has written.

Step (1.2.1) can be written in Ada as follows:

```
PUT_LINE ("Enter number of items sold");
```

Step (1.2.2) becomes in Ada:

```
GET (NUMBER_OF_ITEMS);
```

Now we have introduced a variable NUMBER_OF_ITEMS which must be declared:

```
NUMBER_OF_ITEMS : INTEGER;
```

We can continue with step (1.3), 'Read in the unit price', and expand it:

(1.3.1) Ask the operator to enter the price per unit.
(1.3.2) Read what the operator has written.

Step (1.3.1) is in Ada:

PUT_LINE ("Enter price per unit");

and step (1.3.2) becomes:

GET (ITEM_PRICE);

We have introduced a second variable, ITEM_PRICE. Obviously, this cannot be an integer variable, that is, have type INTEGER. It is unlikely that the items cost a whole number of monetary units, whether pounds sterling, US dollars or Swiss francs. What we need is another kind of store that can contain real numbers. If we imagine that the user writes 13.0 at the terminal we can picture the situation after the GET call has been executed, as in Figure 2.3.

In Ada there is a standard type called FLOAT, and this can be used to declare variables that have to hold real numbers, that is, numbers that are not integers. We let the variable ITEM_PRICE have this type. The declaration is then:

ITEM_PRICE : FLOAT;

In the package BASIC_NUM_IO there is a version of GET that can be used for reading in variables of type FLOAT. There is also a version of PUT for output of numbers of type FLOAT.

Now we can deal with step (1.1), 'Read in the product code'. We can start by subdividing:

(1.1.1) Ask the operator to enter the product code.
(1.1.2) Read what the operator has written.

Step (1.1.1) is easy:

PUT_LINE ("Enter product code (6 characters)")

ITEM_PRICE

13.0

Figure 2.3

Step (1.1.2) is then:

    GET (PRODUCT_CODE);

How should the variable PRODUCT_CODE be declared? It is neither an integer nor a real number, so neither INTEGER nor FLOAT, as used earlier, will do. In fact the variable PRODUCT_CODE is a text string, exactly the same as the text strings we have written in several places. It must be possible to store an arbitrary code of six characters in the variable, so we need yet another kind of store. If we assume that the user writes the code a1bX67 at the terminal, after the call to GET, we have the situation illustrated in Figure 2.4. Ada has a standard type STRING that can be used. The declaration is:

    PRODUCT_CODE : STRING(1..6);

The expression in brackets states that the text string will consist of six characters, numbered from 1 to 6.

Now we can go on to step (2), 'Make the computations', which can be subdivided directly:

    (2.1)   Calculate the total price (excluding VAT).
    (2.2)   Calculate the total VAT.
    (2.3)   Calculate the net price (including VAT).

For step (2.1) we can immediately write the Ada statement:

    PRICE := ITEM_PRICE * FLOAT (NUMBER_OF_ITEMS);

This statement contains a few new things. The expression:

    ITEM_PRICE* FLOAT (NUMBER_OF_ITEMS)

means that the values of the variables ITEM_PRICE and NUMBER_OF_ITEMS should be multiplied together. Ada does not permit different types to be mixed

PRODUCT_CODE

a	1	b	X	6	7

Figure 2.4

in expressions of this kind. Since ITEM_PRICE has type FLOAT and
NUMBER_OF_ITEMS has type INTEGER, they cannot be mixed without doing
something first. We want the final result of the expression to have type FLOAT,
and therefore we take the value of NUMBER_OF_ITEMS and convert it to a value
of type FLOAT. This is achieved with the construct:

FLOAT (NUMBER_OF_ITEMS)

We then get a temporary store containing a real number. If, for example, NUM-
BER_OF_ITEMS has value 100, then the temporary store will hold the value
100.0. This is shown in Figure 2.5. Note that the variable NUMBER_OF_ITEMS
and the value it holds are in no way changed by this.

> **Mixing types**
>
> It is *not* allowed to mix different types (for example
> INTEGER and FLOAT) in expressions.

It might seem clumsy that all this is necessary, but one of the advantages of Ada, as will be shown later, is that different types are carefully watched
and kept apart. It is not possible to mix apples and pears by accident, so to
speak.
The effect of the expression:

ITEM_PRICE * FLOAT (NUMBER_OF_ITEMS)

is that we get a new temporary store to hold the result of the multiplication.
Step (2.1) also introduced a new variable PRICE with the type FLOAT.
This variable should therefore be declared as:

PRICE : FLOAT;

NUMBER_OF_ITEMS   Temporary storage

100   FLOAT(NUMBER_OF_ITEMS) =>   100.0

Figure 2.5

We shall save the result of the calculation in this variable. This is achieved using an **assignment**. The compound symbol := is called the assignment symbol and is used to denote assignment. Assignment means that whatever is on the right-hand side of the assignment symbol is placed in the variable on the left-hand side. The variable must be of the same type as whatever is on the right of the symbol. Note that any variables that may appear on the right-hand side are not affected by the assignment. Their values are unchanged.

Assignment

variable_name := expression;

- The value of the right-hand side is evaluated first.
- This value is placed in the variable that appears on the left-hand side.
- The previous value of the variable will be destroyed.
- The expression on the right-hand side must be of the same type as the variable on the left.

We can now continue with step (2.2), 'Calculate the total VAT'. We make the assumption that the rate of VAT is a known and constant percentage. Clearly it has to be of type FLOAT because it does not necessarily have to have an integral value. It is possible to declare constants in Ada, using a declaration that looks like a variable declaration. If we assume that the VAT rate is 15.0%, we can declare a constant VAT_PERCENT:

    VAT_PERCENT : **constant** := 15.0;

We can then use this to calculate the total VAT due:

    VAT := PRICE * VAT_PERCENT / 100.0;

The statement simply means that the values of PRICE and VAT_PERCENT are multiplied together and the result is then divided by 100. Note that 100 must be written as a real number, 100.0. If we had written 100 it would have been interpreted as an integer. The final result is saved in a new variable VAT which should be declared:

    VAT : FLOAT;

Step (2.3), 'Calculate the net price (including VAT)' is now easy:

NET_PRICE := PRICE + VAT;

where the variable NET_PRICE has the following declaration:

NET_PRICE : FLOAT;

We finish with step (3), 'Print the invoice', which we can split into the following steps:

(3.1) Print a heading.
(3.2) Print the product's code.
(3.3) Print the number of items sold.
(3.4) Print the unit price.
(3.5) Print the net price (including VAT).
(3.6) Print the VAT.

We assume that the program will be run from a terminal with printer output. We want the invoice to look like Figure 2.6.

We can deal with step (3.1), 'Write a heading'. For simplicity we will split it into smaller steps:

(3.1.1) Start a new page.
(3.1.2) Set the output position so that the heading starts in column 20 of the page.
(3.1.3) Print the word "INVOICE".
(3.1.4) Skip the next two lines.

INVOICE
Product code: A1BX67
Number of items: 100
Pice per item: 13.00
Total price (incl. VAT):   1495.00
Of which VAT is: 195.00

Figure 2.6

We make use of the facilities offered by TEXT_IO. The four steps become the four corresponding statements:

```
NEW_PAGE;
SET_COL (20); PUT ("INVOICE"); NEW_LINE (2);
```

Two useful output facilities

```
        NEW_PAGE;
```

The next output starts on a new page (useful when the terminal output is to paper).

```
        SET_COL(N);
```

The next output starts in position N on the current line. (If output is already beyond position N, a new line is started.)

The next step, 'Print the product's code', can be split further:

(3.2.1)   Set the output position so that the text starts at column 10.
(3.2.2)   Print the text "Product code:".
(3.2.3)   Print the product code.
(3.2.4)   Move on one line.

We have the corresponding Ada statements:

```
SET_COL (10);
PUT ("Product code:        ");
PUT (PRODUCT_CODE); NEW_LINE;
```

Note the six extra spaces at the end of the text in the second statement. These have been added to provide adequate space between the colon and the code.

Similarly, the next step, 'Print the number of items sold', is:

```
SET_COL (10);
PUT ("Number of items:");
PUT (NUMBER_OF_ITEMS, WIDTH => 9); NEW_LINE;
```

Here the WIDTH parameter to PUT is used to get the right edge of NUMBER_OF_ITEMS directly under the right edge of the product code on the line above.

The step 'Print the unit price' is:

```
SET_COL (10);
PUT ("Price per item:");
PUT (ITEM_PRICE, FORE => 7, AFT => 2, EXP => 0);
NEW_LINE;
```

The variable ITEM_PRICE contains a real number. There are two alternative forms for writing out real numbers. The number 125.7, for example, can be written either:

125.7

or:

1.257E+02

The latter is called **exponent form** and should be read as 1.257 times 10 to the power 2. If we had had the simple statement:

```
PUT (ITEM_PRICE);
```

in the program, PUT would have written ITEM_PRICE in exponent form. But we do not want this, so we make use of the possibility of assigning further parameters to PUT when real numbers are to be output. Instead, we write:

```
PUT (ITEM_PRICE, FORE => 7, AFT => 2, EXP => 0);
```

The parameters FORE and AFT state the number of positions required in the output before and after the decimal point, respectively. Allowance should be made for a possible minus sign among the positions before the decimal point. If the number that is printed does not fill all the positions before the decimal point (as in our example), PUT will place blanks there instead. The parameter EXP gives the number of positions that we want the exponent to be given. Since we have decided not to have an exponent at all, we set EXP to 0.

If we were to give FORE a smaller value than the number of positions actually needed, no error would result, but PUT would use as many positions before the point as required. If, for example, the variable ITEM_PRICE had the value 13.00 and we had the statements:

```
PUT ("Price per item:");
PUT (ITEM_PRICE, FORE => 1, AFT => 2, EXP => 0);
```

in the program, then the output would be:

Price per item:13.00

Output of real numbers

   PUT (real value);

or:

   PUT (real value, FORE => N, AFT => M,
     EXP => 0);

where N and M give the number of figures before and
after the decimal point, respectively.

Now we can go on to the next step, 'Print the net price'. This is analogous to the previous steps and so are the statements:

```
SET_COL (10);
PUT ("Total price (incl. VAT):");
PUT (NET_PRICE, FORE => 7, AFT => 2, EXP => 0);
NEW_LINE;
```

The last step, 'Print the VAT', is:

```
SET_COL (10);
PUT ("Of which VAT is:");
PUT (VAT, FORE => 6, AFT => 2, EXP => 0);
```

We finish this example by putting the whole program together. We have several variables of type FLOAT, and their declarations can be put together as shown in the program.

```
with TEXT_IO, BASIC_NUM_IO;
use TEXT_IO, BASIC_NUM_IO;
procedure WRITEINVOICE is
    NUMBER_of_ITEMS : INTEGER;
    ITEM_PRICE, PRICE, VAT,.NET_PRICE : FLOAT;
    VAT_PERCENT     : constant := 15.0;
    PRODUCT_CODE : STRING (1..6);

begin
    PUTUNE("Enter: product code (6 characters)");
```

```
GET(PRODUCT_CODE);

PUT_LINE ("Enter  number of items sold");
GET(NUMBER_OF_ITEMS);
PUT_LINE("Enter price per unit");
GET(ITEM_PRICE);

PRICE =: ITEM_PRICE * FLOAT (NUMBER_OF_ITEMS);
VAT := PRICE * VAT_PERCENT / 100.0;
NET_PRICE := PRICE + VAT;

NEW_PAGE;
SET_COL(20); PUT("INVOICE"); NEW_LINE(2);

SET_COL(10); PUT("Product code:          ");
PUT(PRODUCT_CODE); NEW_LINE;

SET_COL(10); PUT("Number of items:");
PUT(NUMBER_OF_ITEMS, WIDTH => 9); NEW_LINE;

SET_COL(10); PUT("Price per item:");
PUT(ITEM_PRICE, FORE => 7, AFT => 2, EXP => 0);
NEW_LINE;

SET_COL(10); PUT("Total price (incl. VAT):");
PUT(NET_PRICE, FORE => 7, AFT => 2, EXP => 0);
NEW_LINE;

SET_COL(10); PUT("Of which VAT is:");
PUT(VAT, FORE => 6, AFT => 2, EXP => 0);
NEW_LINE;

end WRITE_INVOICE;
```

2.4.4   Drawing outsize letters

By displaying the character * appropriately at the terminal an outsize letter can be written. A giant A, for example, can be written thus:

Now we shall write a (slightly useless) program to draw the three letters A D A, under each other, in this giant format. So the program should produce the output shown in Figure 2.7.

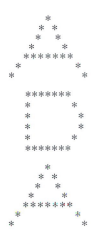

Figure 2.7

The ability to make **comments** will be made use of in this program. The compound symbol -- (double hyphen) introduces a comment and everything written after it on a line will be interpreted as a comment, which means that the compiler does not try to translate it.

Comments are used to make a program clearer to understand and to provide support in writing a program.

Comments

 -- *this is a comment*
- Makes a program clearer.
- Simplifies program design and writing.

Using the top-down design technique we make a first sketch of the program using comments:

```
procedure GIANT_ADA is
begin
    -- draw a giant A
    -- draw a giant D
    -- draw a giant A
end GIANT_ADA;
```

Drawing on our experience from earlier examples, we can refine the three steps directly and come up with a first version of the program:

```
with TEXT_IO;
use TEXT_IO;
procedure GIANT_ADA is
begin
    -- draw a giant A
    NEW_LINE;
    PUT_LINE("    *");
    PUT_LINE("   * *");
    PUT_LINE("  *   *");
    PUT_LINE("  *******");
    PUT_LINE(" *     *");
    PUT_LINE("*       *");
    NEW_LINE;

    -- draw a giant D
    NEW_LINE;
    PUT_LINE(" *******");
    PUT_LINE(" *     *");
    PUT_LINE(" *     *");
    PUT_LINE(" *     *");
    PUT_LINE(" *     *");
    PUT_LINE(" *******");
    NEW_LINE;

    -- draw a giant A
    NEW_LINE;
    PUT_LINE("    *");
    PUT_LINE("   * *");
    PUT_LINE("  *   *");
    PUT_LINE("  *******");
    PUT_LINE(" *     *");
    PUT_LINE("*       *");
    NEW_LINE;

end GIANT_ADA;
```

Each giant letter starts and ends with an empty line so that the letters are not too crowded. Since PUT and NEW_LINE are needed from the package TEXT_IO, we have organized access to this package, as before. The comments can remain in the program because they make it clearer.

Note that the step 'draw a giant A' in our program has been repeated and all the statements in it have been written out twice. This is clumsy and makes the program unnecessarily long – imagine what it would be like if we wanted to write DADDA instead of ADA. To set this right we shall create a new procedure DRAW_GIANT_A:

```
procedure DRAW_GIANT_A is
-- this procedure draws a giant A
begin
   NEW_LINE;
   PUT_LINE("    *");
   PUT_LINE("   * *");
   PUT_LINE("  *   *");
   PUT_LINE(" *******");
   PUT_LINE(" *     *");
   PUT_LINE("*       *");
   NEW_LINE;
end DRAW_GIANT_A;
```

We have placed an explanatory comment at the start of the procedure. For the sake of symmetry we will write a corresponding procedure DRAW_GIANT_D, in the same way:

```
procedure DRAW_GIANT_D is
-- this procedure draws a giant D
begin
   NEW_LINE;
   PUT_LINE(" *******");
   PUT_LINE(" *     *");
   PUT_LINE(" *     *");
   PUT_LINE(" *     *");
   PUT_LINE(" *     *");
   PUT_LINE(" *******");
   NEW_LINE;
end DRAW_GIANT_D;
```

Now we can change our program so that the outsize letters are drawn by making **calls** to the new procedures. The central part of the program then becomes:

```
DRAW_GIANT_A;

DRAW_GIANT_D;

DRAW_GIANT_A;
```

Note that the calls to our procedures **DRAW_GIANT_A** and **DRAW_GIANT_D** look exactly like calls to the built-in procedures in Ada's standard packages.

Compare them with the call to, for example, the procedure NEW_LINE in the package TEXT_IO.

It is worth noting that by choosing good names for our procedures we have made the program so clear that the comments are superfluous. It is always important to choose good names for everything in a program. You should not be concerned about using long names, even if it seems a bit tedious while you are actually writing the program – in the long run there is much to be gained. After all, the program is only written once but it is read many times during development, debugging and maintenance.

Choosing names

- Use clear names within your program.
- Do not be afraid of using long names.

Now comes the question: where should our procedures be placed in the program? We can picture our procedures as 'ingredients' in the program (recall the earlier comparison with the cake recipe) in the same way as variables are 'ingredients'. So our procedures must be declared in the program, just like the variables. In fact, the procedures texts are declarations and we can place them in the declarative part of the program. We then get a new version of our program:

```
with TEXT_IO;
use TEXT_IO;
procedure GIANT_ADA is

    procedure DRAW_GIANT_A is
    -- this procedure draws a giant A
    begin
        NEW_LINE;
        PUT_LINE("     *");
        PUT_LINE("    * *");
        PUT_LINE("   *   *");
        PUT_LINE("  *******");
        PUT_LINE(" *     *");
        PUT_LINE("*       *");
        NEW_LINE;
    end DRAW_GIANT_A;

    procedure DRAW_GIANT_D is
    -- this procedure draws a giant D
    begin
```

```
        NEW_LINE;
        PUT_LINE(" *******");
        PUT_LINE(" *       *");
        PUT_LINE(" *       *");
        PUT_LINE(" *       *");
        PUT_LINE(" *       *");
        PUT_LINE(" *******");
        NEW_LINE;
    end DRAW_GIANT_D;
    begin
        DRAW_GIANT_A;          --execution begins here
        DRAW_GIANT_D;
        DRAW_GIANT_A;
    end GIANT_ADA;
```

The procedures DRAW_GIANT_A and DRAW_GIANT_D have been declared in
the procedure DRAW_GIANT_ADA. So that this is seen clearly, their text is written a little further to the right on the line. This method of organizing the appearance of a program by shifting parts of the text over is called **indentation**. It
is very important that you indent your programs properly, a skill that will be
developed by studying the various example programs as they are presented.

Indentation

- A program is made much easier to read if the text
  is indented in such a way that it reflects the structure of the program.
- A well-structured program is always indented.
- Indenting should be used in all program writing.

When the program (the procedure DRAW_GIANT_ADA) is run, the three
statements between **begin** and **end**, namely:

```
DRAW_GIANT_A;
DRAW_GIANT_D;
DRAW_GIANT_A;
```

will be executed in order. The first line in the program:

```
DRAW_GIANT_A;
```

for example, means that the statements in the procedure DRAW_GIANT_A are executed. These statements cause a big A to be drawn at the terminal. When this is done and we have reached the line:

end DRAW_GIANT_A;

we return to the end of the first line in the procedure DRAW_GIANT_ADA. The first statement in that procedure has now been executed and execution can continue with the next statement:

DRAW_GIANT_D;

This statement is also a call to a procedure and is executed in the same way.

What we have actually done is to divide our original program into a main program and two subprograms. We have broken down the problem of writing the outsize text ADA into two simpler problems: writing an outsize A and writing an outsize D. What has been gained is an increase in the overall clarity of the program and avoidance of the need to repeat identical sequences of statements. This technique of refining problems, breaking them down into subproblems and then using subprograms, is very important. There will be much work with subprograms in the chapters to come.

Suppose we have been given the task of writing another similar program that will print out the giant text DADDA at the terminal. We realize that we should be able to make use of the procedures DRAW_GIANT_A and DRAW_GIANT_D here as well. But these procedures exist only as internal 'ingredients' in the procedure DRAW_GIANT_ADA and are not available to other programs (unless we write them again). Compare this with using the procedure NEW_LINE – a useful procedure that finds uses in many different programs. This is possible because it has been put into a package, TEXT_IO. As we have seen, this package can be accessed so that NEW_LINE can be used without the need to write it out and declare it in every program.

Let us now make the procedures DRAW_GIANT_A and DRAW_GIANT_D generally accessible by placing them in a package. We will create a package called GIANT_LETTER.

A package in Ada can be compared to a meal in a restaurant. The guest sees brief descriptions on the menu. This is all the guest needs to be able to decide whether he or she will order a dish. To prepare the dish, however, a more detailed description is needed – a recipe – but this is needed only by the cook. The guest is not normally interested in the recipe, and even if he or she wanted to see it, it is possible that the restaurant would not agree to it.

Similarly, a package in Ada consists of two parts:

(1)   A **specification** (menu) to inform the programs that want to use it what resources are to be found in the package – for example, procedures – and how they are used.

(2)   A **body** (recipes) where the resources are described in detail. The programs that use the package do not see this part of the package. It can be thought of as the contents of the package's 'black box' and concerns only its designer.

Packages

Two parts:

(1)   *Specification:* gives the user information about the resources contained and how they are used.

(2)   *Package body:* details the resources. Not visible to the user.

We shall start by writing the specification of the new package, GIANT_LETTER:

```
package GIANT_LETTER is

    procedure DRAW_GIANT_A;
    -- this procedure draws a giant A

    procedure DRAW_GIANT_D;
    -- this procedure draws a giant D

end GIANT_LETTER;
```

This specification informs the program that is going to use the package that the package is called GIANT_LETTER and that it contains two procedures, DRAW_GIANT_A and DRAW_GIANT_D (neither of which has parameters). To make this clearer we have put in a comment for each procedure. This specification can now be used by the program that will write the outsize text DADDA:

```
with GIANT_LETTER;
procedure GIANT_DADDA is
begin
    GIANT_LETTER.DRAW_GIANT_D;
    GIANT_LETTER.DRAW_GIANT_A;
    GIANT_LETTER.DRAW_GIANT_D;
    GIANT_LETTER.DRAW_GIANT_D;
    GIANT_LETTER.DRAW_GIANT_A;
end GIANT_DADDA;
```

As before, we can insert a **use** clause and get:

```
with GIANT_LETTER;
use GIANT_LETTER;
procedure GIANT_DADDA is
begin
    DRAW_GIANT_D;
    DRAW_GIANT_A;
    DRAW_GIANT_D;
    DRAW_GIANT_A;
end GIANT_DADDA;
```

The first version is often preferred for packages other than Ada's standard packages, because it states specifically which procedures are meant.

The first line means that the procedure DRAW_GIANT_DADDA gets
access to the package GIANT_LETTER. Note that since DRAW_GIANT_DADDA
does not use the facilities in TEXT_IO directly, TEXT_IO does not need to be
included in the first line.

Now we can rewrite DRAW_GIANT_ADA in a similar manner. The internal procedures are no longer needed and so the procedure becomes very simple:

```
with GIANT_LETTER;
procedure GIANT_ADA is
begin
    GIANT_LETTER.DRAW_GIANT_A;
    GIANT_LETTER.DRAW_GIANT_D;
    GIANT_LETTER.DRAW_GIANT_A;
end GIANT_ADA;
```

It only remains to write the body of the package GIANT_LETTER:

```
with TEXT_IO;
use TEXT_IO;
package body GIANT_LETTER is

    procedure DRAW_GIANT_A is
    begin
        NEW_LINE;
        PUT_LINE("    *");
        PUT_LINE("   * *");
        PUT_LINE("  *   *");
        PUT_LINE("  *******");
        PUT_LINE(" *     *");
        PUT_LINE("*       *");
        NEW_LINE;
    end DRAW_GIANT_A;
```

```
procedure DRAW_GIANT_D is
begin
    NEW_LINE;
    PUT_LINE(" *******");
    PUT_LINE(" *     *");
    PUT_LINE(" *      *");
    PUT_LINE(" *      *");
    PUT_LINE(" *     *");
    PUT_LINE(" *******");
    NEW_LINE;
end DRAW_GIANT_D;

end GIANT_LETTER;
```

Access to TEXT_IO is needed here because the procedures PUT and NEW_LINE are used in the package body.

By creating a package we have thus made our routines generally accessible as resources for other programs. It would be natural now to extend the package with procedures for drawing large versions of all the letters, not only A and D. The use of packages is one of the fundamental concepts in Ada.

Advantages of packages

- The use of packages provides convenient access to resources that the programmer (or another) has written.

- Programming becomes more efficient and the quality of programs improves.

2.4.5   Comparing numbers

In foregoing example programs we have looked at sequential algorithms – algorithms consisting of a number of stages executed one after the other. Now we shall study a program where there is a choice between different possible actions:

```
with TEXT_IO, BASIC_NUM_IO;
use TEXT_IO, BASIC_NUM_IO;
procedure BIGGER_NUMBER is
    FIRST_NUMBER, SECOND_NUMBER : INTEGER;
begin
    PUT("Give the first whole number:  ");
    GET(FIRST_NUMBER);
```

```
PUT("Give the second whole number: ");
GET(SECOND_NUMBER);

if FIRST_NUMBER > SECOND_NUMBER then
    PUT("The first number is bigger.");
else
    PUT("The second number is bigger.");
end if;
end BIGGER_NUMBER;
```

The program asks for two whole numbers. When the user has entered them from the terminal, the program states which is the larger. An example of output from the program is:

```
Give the first whole number:     12300
Give the second whole number: 13200
The second number is bigger.
```

One small detail in the output from the program that might puzzle us is how the second and third lines manage to start on new lines, despite the fact that neither PUT_LINE nor NEW_LINE has been used in the program? The answer is simple. The two numbers, 12300 and 13200, are written by the user at the terminal. When input is written to a program, a number is usually terminated by pressing the terminal's RETURN (ENTER) key. This means that the output at the terminal moves on a line. So the answer to the question is that in this case it is the user who has made the output move on a line and not the program.

The more interesting part of the program is a construct that we have not met before – the **if** statement, which starts with the word **if** and ends with **end if**. The first line of the statement:

if FIRST_NUMBER > SECOND_NUMBER **then**

means that the values of the variables FIRST_NUMBER and SECOND_NUMBER will be compared when the program is executed. If the expression:

FIRST_NUMBER > SECOND_NUMBER

is true, that is, FIRST_NUMBER is larger than SECOND_NUMBER, then the statements that appear after the word **then** will be executed. In this case, the statement:

PUT("The first number is bigger.");

will be executed. If, instead, the expression:

FIRST_NUMBER > SECOND_NUMBER

is false, that is, the SECOND_NUMBER is greater than (or equal to) the FIRST_NUMBER, then the statements following **else** will be executed, in this case the statement:

```
PUT("The second number is bigger.");
```

Observe that *either* the statements following **then** *or* those following **else** are carried out. Only one alternative is chosen when the **if** statement is executed. The use of the **if** statement in Ada is one way to formulate algorithms where a choice has to be made.

Note that several statements may appear after the words **then** and **else**. For example, we can alter the program a little:

```
with TEXT_IO, BASIC_NUM_IO;
use TEXT_IO, BASIC_NUM_IO;
procedure BIGGER_NUMBER is
    FIRST_NUMBER, SECOND_NUMBER : INTEGER;

begin
    PUT("Give the first whole number:  ");
    GET(FIRST_NUMBER);
    PUT("Give the second whole number: ");
    GET(SECOND_NUMBER);

    if FIRST_NUMBER > SECOND_NUMBER then
        PUT("The first number, ");
        PUT(FIRST_NUMBER, WIDTH => 1);
        PUT (", is bigger.");
    else
        PUT("The second number, ");
        PUT (SECOND_NUMBER, WIDTH => 1);
        PUT(", is bigger.");
    end if;
end BIGGER_NUMBER;
```

When this program is run, the following output is typical of what may appear at the terminal:

```
Give the first whole number:     12300
Give the second whole number:  13200
The second number, 13200, is bigger.
```

The last line has been obtained using three statements in the program. In the second of these the WIDTH parameter has deliberately been given a value that is too small. This means that the procedure PUT chooses to allow exactly as many positions as needed and we get the output of the bigger number exactly as we want it, without unnecessary blanks in front of it. The single blank results from the blank after the comma in the text string that precedes the number.

We need to make one more change to the program. What would happen if the user entered the same number twice? Since the expression

FIRST_NUMBER > SECOND_NUMBER

is then false, our original program would carry out the statements following **else** and say:

The second number is bigger.

This, of course, is wrong.

We can make use of another option of the **if** statement, and rewrite our program thus:

```
with TEXT_IO, BASIC_NUM_IO;
use TEXT_IO, BASIC_NUM_IO;
procedure BIGGER_NUMBER is
    FIRST_NUMBER, SECOND_NUMBER : INTEGER;
begin
    PUT("Give the first whole number:     ");
    GET(FIRST_NUMBER);
    PUT("Give the second whole number:     ");
    GET(SECOND_NUMBER);

    if FIRST_NUMBER > SECOND_NUMBER then
        PUT("The first number is bigger.");
    elsif SECOND_NUMBER > FIRST_NUMBER then
        PUT("The second number is bigger.");
    else
        PUT("The numbers are equal.");
    end if;
end BIGGER_NUMBER;
```

Now the **if** statement has been augmented: there is a new part starting with the word **elsif**. When the program is executed the following will occur. If the expression after **if**, that is:

FIRST_NUMBER > SECOND_NUMBER

is true, then the statement:

PUT("The first number is bigger.");

will be executed, as before. If the expression is not true then the expression that comes after **elsif**:

SECOND_NUMBER > FIRST_NUMBER

will be examined. If this second expression is true, then the statement:

PUT("The second number is bigger.");

will be carried out. If this is also false, as when the two numbers are the same, then the statement that follows **else** will be carried out, namely:

PUT("The numbers are equal.");

Just as in the simpler type of **if** statement, only *one* alternative is chosen when the statement is executed.

In fact, the **if** statement can be generalized even further; there can be as many **elseif** alternatives as necessary.

Selection

- Can be made by using an **if** statement.
- Only one alternative can be chosen.

2.4.6   Calculating a selling price

We can look at another program that uses selection:

```
with TEXT_IO, BASIC_NUM_IO;
use TEXT_IO, BASIC_NUM_IO;
procedure CALCULATE_PRICE is
    DISCOUNT_PERCENT : constant := 10.0;
    DISCOUNT_LIMIT      : constant := 1000.0;
    NUMBER_OF_ITEMS  : INTEGER;
    ITEM_PRICE, PRICE, DISCOUNT : FLOAT;
begin
    -- read input data
    PUT("Enter the number of items sold: ");
    GET(NUMBER_OF_ITEMS);
    PUT("Enter the cost per item: ");
    GET(ITEM_PRICE);

    -- do calculations
    PRICE := ITEM_PRICE * FLOAT(NUMBER_OF_ITEMS);
    if PRICE > DISCOUNT_LIMIT then
        DISCOUNT := PRICE * DISCOUNT_PERCENT/100.0;
```

```
            PRICE := PRICE - DISCOUNT;
        end if;

            -- print result
            PUT("Final price is ");
            PUT(PRICE, FORE => 1, AFT => 2, EXP => 0);
        end CALCULATE_PRICE;
```

The program is designed for calculating a selling price. The input required is the number of items sold and the price per item. The program calculates and displays the total price to the customer. If the total price is above a certain amount, in this case £1000, the customer gets a quantity discount of 10%. In this example, for the sake of simplicity, we shall ignore the problems of VAT and sales tax – they can be assumed to be included in the price from the start. When the program is executed the output may look like this:

```
Enter the number of items sold:  25
Enter the cost per item:  45.50
Final price is 1023.75
```

There is an **if** statement in the program, but note that it has no **else** part. This is quite legal. What happens is that the statements following **then** are carried out if the expression in the **if** statement is true. If the expression is false then nothing is done. In our example, therefore, the two statements:

```
DISCOUNT := PRICE * DISCOUNT_PERCENT/100.0;
PRICE := PRICE - DISCOUNT;
```

are executed only if PRICE is greater than 1000.

Two constants, DISCOUNT_PERCENT and DISCOUNT_LIMIT, have been used. In the statements in the program these have then been used instead of the corresponding numerical values. For example, instead of writing:

if PRICE > 1000.0 **then**

we have written:

if PRICE > DISCOUNT_LIMIT **then**

It is sensible to try to avoid numerical values in the statements of a program. Suppose at a later date the discount is lowered to 8% and the minimum discount sale is lowered to £900. Then the only things to be changed are the constant declarations in the program. If the numerical values 10 and 1000 had been written, maybe in several places, it might have been difficult to find all the places requiring change, and something could well have been changed by mistake. Another important reason for using constant declarations is that the program gains clarity. The name DISCOUNT_PERCENT used in the program tells us much more than the number 10.

Using constants

- Avoid numerical values in a program.
- Declare and use constants instead.

2.4.7   Producing tables

Now we have seen examples of programs that use sequences of statements and selection. The third important algorithmic construct is iteration, or the repetition of groups of statements. A couple of programs that use iteration are now presented. The first will produce a table of integers and their squares. Output from the program should look like that in Figure 2.8. It can be seen from this figure that when the program is run the user has to enter the size of the table, that is, how many numbers starting from 1 are to be squared. In the example the user has written 12.

```
with TEXT_IO, BASIC_NUM_IO;
use TEXT_IO, BASIC_NUM_IO;
procedure TABLE_OF_SQUARES is
    TABLE_SIZE : INTEGER;
begin
    PUT_LINE("Give the size of the table:");
```

```
Give the size of the table:
12
    Number   Square
      1        1
      2        4
      3        9
      4       16
      5       25
      6       36
      7       49
      8       64
      9       81
     10      100
     11      121
     12      144
```

Figure 2.8

```
GET(TABLE_SIZE);
NEW_LINE;
PUT_LINE("Number            Square"); NEW_LINE;
for NUMBER in 1..TABLE_SIZE loop
    PUT(NUMBER, WIDTH => 4);
    PUT(NUMBER * NUMBER, WIDTH => 10); NEW_LINE;
end loop;
end TABLE_OF_SQUARES;
```

There is an iteration statement in the program that starts with the word **for**. The statements that appear between the words **loop** and **end loop** will be repeated a certain number of times. Note that these lines have been indented. The line:

for NUMBER **in** 1..TABLE_SIZE **loop**

states the number of times the repetition should occur, in this case the number of times given by TABLE_SIZE, which has been given the value 12 in our example. The variable NUMBER introduced on this line is the loop parameter: it counts the number of iterations made. The first time through the loop, NUMBER automatically gets the value 1; on the second loop it becomes 2, the third 3, and so on, until it finally becomes 12. Note that the variable NUMBER should not be declared explicitly. It is declared automatically because it appears after **for**. In this case it is of type INTEGER. Each time through the loop the program will write one line at the terminal.

Iteration a known number of times

When the number of times an iteration should occur is known before it starts, a construct using **for** is used.

2.4.8   How long before I'm a millionaire?

In the final example in this chapter we will look at what may be unrealistic conditions of employment. Imagine you have been offered a very dangerous job, filled with all sorts of risks. If you take the job, the chances of surviving long are slight. The pay is a bit unusual. On the first day you will receive £0.01, £0.02 for the second day, £0.04 for the third, and so on. The pay is doubled daily. Although you are anxious about your health and safety, you are still prepared to consider taking a few risks if it means riches, so you decide to see what the offer really means. The question you want an answer to is simply: how many days must you work in order to become a millionaire? To get an answer you could use this program:

```
with TEXT_IO, BASIC_NUM_IO;
use TEXT_IO, BASIC_NUM_IO;
procedure RICH is
   NUMBER_OF_DAYS    : INTEGER := 1;
   DAYS_WAGE         : FLOAT := 0.01;
   TOTAL_EARNINGS    : FLOAT := 0.01;
   DESIRED_EARNINGS : constant := 1000000.0;
begin

   while TOTAL_EARNINGS < DESIRED_EARNINGS loop
      NUMBER_OF_DAYS := NUMBER_OF_DAYS + 1;
      DAYS_WAGE := DAYS_WAGE * 2.0;
      TOTAL_EARNINGS := TOTAL_EARNINGS+DAYS_WAGE;
   end loop;

   PUT("You will be a millionaire in ");
   PUT(NUMBER_OF_DAYS, WIDTH => 1);
   PUT_LINE(" days.");
end RICH;
```

Three variables are used in this program: NUMBER_OF_DAYS, DAYS_WAGE and TOTAL_EARNINGS. In the declarations we have made use of the option to **initialize** the variables. The declaration:

```
NUMBER_OF_DAYS : INTEGER := 1;
```

for example, means that the variable NUMBER_OF_DAYS automatically gets the initial value 1 when the program is run. (If a variable is not initialized, as in our previous examples, the variable's value is normally undefined when the program starts. This means that the variable contains 'garbage' and should not be used until it has been given a proper value.)

The three variables in our program have been given initial values that represent the situation after one day's work, namely that NUMBER_OF_DAYS is 1, DAYS_WAGE is 0.01, and TOTAL_EARNINGS is also 0.01. DESIRED_EARNINGS contains the amount you want to earn to be rich, in this case £1,000,000.

The iteration statement in this program starts with **while**. The three statements:

```
NUMBER_OF_DAYS := NUMBER_OF_DAYS + 1;
DAYS_WAGE := DAYS_WAGE * 2.0;
TOTAL_EARNINGS := TOTAL_EARNINGS + DAYS_WAGE;
```

will be repeated a certain number of times: actually once for every day worked except the first day. We see that every day we increase the day counter NUMBER_OF_DAYS by 1; work out DAYS_WAGE, the current day's wage (which is double the previous one) and add the latter quantity to the running total, TOTAL_EARNINGS. After two days (after the first time through the loop) NUMBER_OF_DAYS will thus be 2, DAYS_WAGE will be 0.02, and TOTAL_EARNINGS will be 0.03. After three days (after the second loop) they will be 3, 0.04, and 0.07, respectively.

How many iterations are needed? We do not know. Each iteration represents one day worked, and it is precisely the number of days to be worked that the program is intended to find out. To control the iteration therefore we do not use the construct with **for** as in the previous example, but a version of the **loop** statement where **while** is used. This works as follows. Each time a new iteration begins, the expression after **while** is investigated first. If this expression is true then one iteration of the three statements in the loop is carried out. If it is not true, then the **loop** statement terminates; the loop is not repeated and the program continues with the statement after **end** loop. When the **loop** statement is finished, the program will display the number of days you must work to become a millionaire. The output will be:

You will be a millionaire in 27 days.

Iteration an undetermined number of times

When the number of times an iteration should be carried out is not known in advance, but a condition is known for the iteration to terminate, a construct with **while** is used.

The difference between using constructs with **if** and **while** should be noted. The lines of program:

```
N := 0;
if N < 10 then
   PUT(N, WIDTH => 1); NEW_LINE;
   N := N + 1;
end if;
```

assuming that the variable N has type INTEGER, would give the output:

0

when run. The statements between **then** and **end** if would therefore be executed once only. This can be compared with the lines:

```
N := 0;
while N < 10 loop
    PUT(N, WIDTH => 1); NEW_LINE;
    N := N + 1;
end loop;
```

which would give the output:

```
0
1
2
3
4
5
6
7
8
9
```

Here, then, the corresponding statements are executed 10 times.

EXERCISES

2.1   Give an algorithm for evaluating the sum:

$$\sum_{i=1}^{n} i^2$$

2.2   Specify an algorithm, using any method, to calculate:

$$N! = 1 \; 2 \times 3 \times \ldots \times N \qquad (N > 0)$$

2.3   A table contains N different numbers. Design an algorithm that looks through the table to find the smallest number. The algorithm should give the position of the smallest number in the table as its result (an index between 1 and N).

2.4   A table contains N different numbers. Design an algorithm that changes the table so that the numbers are in order, from smallest to largest. Use a method that starts by putting the smallest number in the first position, then puts the second smallest in the second position, and so on. (*Hint*: Use the algorithm developed in the previous question.)

2.5   Write an Ada program that will write your name and address at the terminal.

2.6   Write a program that works out and displays the number of miles a car has been driven over the past year. When the program is run it should request the current mileometer reading and that of a year ago. The two mileages should be given as whole numbers of miles.

2.7   Add to the program in Exercise 2.6 so that it will also calculate the car's average petrol consumption in litres per mile. In addition to the two mileages, the program should read in from the terminal the number of litres of petrol used during the year (stated as a real number). The program should also read in the car's registration number so that it can produce output in the following format:

Registration number:	ABC123X
Total mileage:	9290
Total petrol consumption in litres:	1234.5
Consumption in litres per mile:	0.13

2.8   When a car is to be insured it is common to choose 'full cover' in the case of a new car (less than 5 years old, say). If the car is older it is often thought that 'third party' insurance is adequate.

(a)   Write a program that tells you whether to choose full or third-party insurance. The program should receive as input data the current year and the car's year of manufacture. One of the messages:

Choose full cover
Choose third party insurance

should be displayed, depending on whether the car is less than or more than 5 years old.

(b)   A number of insurance companies offer special insurance policies for veteran cars, that is, cars more than 25 years old. Add to the program so that it can also display the message:

Choose a veteran car policy

if the car is at least 25 years old.

2.9   Write a program that produces a table for all the integers in the interval n_1 to n_2. For each integer k, k^2 and k^3 should be written. The two integers n_1 and n_2 should be read from the terminal.

2.10   A bank gives interest at a rate of 9.25% on money deposited in a deposit account. Suppose you put in £X at the start of a year. Write a program to calculate how many years it will take before the balance in the deposit account exceeds £100,000 if no deposits or withdrawals are made. The amount deposited, X, should be read in from the terminal.

2.11 (a)   Write a program that draws two circles and two triangles at the terminal.

(b)   Rewrite the program so that the circle and triangle are drawn using separate sub-programs.

(c)   Construct a package containing the two subprograms that draw a circle and a triangle.

(d)   Show what the program from part (a) would look like if the package from part (c) is used.

The Basics of Ada

This chapter presents some of the basic concepts behind Ada. The built-in standard types, INTEGER, FLOAT, CHARACTER, STRING and BOOLEAN are described. A brief discussion is also presented about how data is stored in a computer using binary code.

The rules for stating different values and expressions are given, and Ada's standard operators are described. Finally, the various errors that can occur in the programming process are discussed.

3.1 Standard types

The task of a computer program is to manipulate data objects of various kinds. A data object in a program often represents something that occurs in the real world. In Chapter 2, for example, we saw how a variable, ITEM_PRICE, could represent a real selling price, and how another variable, PRODUCT_CODE, could represent the product's actual code.

Different objects have different properties. For example, the value of the variable ITEM_PRICE could be increased by 10%, but it would be meaningless to talk about increasing PRODUCT_CODE by 10%. Conversely, you can imagine changing all the upper-case letters in PRODUCT_CODE to lower case, whereas trying to change a letter in a selling price would be nonsense. In Ada, we say that objects that have different properties have different **types**. Each object that is to be used in a program must be declared before it is used and its type is stated in the declaration. For example, the variables ITEM_PRICE and PRODUCT_CODE were declared in the following way:

```
ITEM_PRICE : FLOAT;
PRODUCT_CODE : STRING(1 .. 6);
```

Data objects

- A program manipulates data objects.
- An object represents something that occurs in the real world.
- Objects with different properties have different *types*.

A type is characterized by:

(1) the **values** that can be taken by objects belonging to the type; and

(2) the **operations** that can be performed on them.

For example, for the type FLOAT the possible values are, in principle, all the real numbers, and the operations are the normal mathematical operations such as addition and multiplication. (In reality, for each implementation of Ada the values possible are limited by the way in which the computer stores numbers in its memory.)

> **Types**
>
> Are characterized by:
>
> (1) the values that can be taken by objects of the type; and
>
> (2) the operations that can be carried out on objects of the type.

Ada is a language that keeps careful check on the types of different objects, that is, objects of a certain type can only take values that are acceptable for that type. For example, it would be impossible to store a product code in the variable ITEM_PRICE. One great advantage of keeping different types separate in this way is that it leads to better and more reliable programs. If you try to mix different types in a program, it is often a sign that there is an error in the logic of the program design. The compiler detects forbidden confusion of types and gives an error message; this can be helpful in finding certain logic faults.

In Ada, as we shall see later, there is enormous scope for the programmer to construct types of varying complexity to represent real phenomena. For example, a type can be created to describe a car in a car-hire company's file, or a line of customers in a bank. In Ada there are some basic standard types that can be used to describe objects or to build up more complex types; we shall study some of these in this chapter. The standard types are defined in a special package STANDARD, which is included in all implementations of Ada. All Ada programs automatically have access to the STANDARD packages; thus **with** and **use** clauses are not used to access it.

3.1.1   The numeric types *INTEGER* and *FLOAT*

In earlier programs we have seen the standard types INTEGER and FLOAT. The type INTEGER can be used to describe objects that can take only integral values, such as counters and numbers of things. The type FLOAT can be used for other numerical values, for example, physical properties such as temperature and length. The standard types INTEGER and FLOAT exist in all implementations of Ada.

> **INTEGER and FLOAT**
>
> - INTEGER represents the mathematical concept 'integer', that is, only whole numbers are possible.
> - FLOAT represents the mathematical concept 'real number'.

To the question 'Would it be enough just to have the standard type FLOAT, which could then be used for all numerical quantities?' the answer is 'Yes, in principle.' The reason why INTEGER is still included is that most computers handle integers more quickly and more simply than real numbers. Moreover, integers can always be stored exactly in the computer, whereas real numbers often can be stored only in an approximate form.

To help with understanding the properties of the types INTEGER and FLOAT there follows a short description of the principles of storing numerical values in a computer. It is not absolutely essential for the programmer to know this in detail, so those who want to can leave this section for later reading.

The computer's memory comprises a number of memory cells, as mentioned in Chapter 1. Each cell consists of a certain number of bits and each bit can contain one binary digit (a zero or a one). This means that numbers are naturally stored in binary form in memory and we shall therefore start by looking at the **binary number system**.

In our culture the decimal system dominates completely (presumably because we have ten fingers). So if we write a number, such as 158.32, we assume automatically that it is expressed in the decimal system where the base is 10. This means that we interpret 158.32 as:

$$1 \times 10^2 + 5 \times 10^1 + 8 \times 10^0 + 3 \times 10^{-1} + 2 \times 10^{-2}$$

Expressing this more generally, we can say that a decimal number:

$$a_n a_{n-1} \ldots a_1 a_0 . d_1 d_2 \ldots d_m$$

(where the as denote the integral part and the ds the decimal part) really means:

$$a_n \times 10^n + a_{n-1} \times 10^{n-1} + \ldots + a_1 \times 10^1 + a_0 \times 10^0 + d_1 \times 10^{-1} + d_2 \times 10^{-2} + \ldots + d_m \times 10^{-m}$$

Using base 2 instead of base 10, the binary number:

$$b_n b_{n-1} \ldots b_1 b_0 . c_1 c_2 \ldots c_m$$

is interpreted as:

$$b_n \times 2^n + b_{n-1} \times 2^{n-1} + \ldots + b_1 \times 2^1 + b_0 \times 2^0 + c_1 \times 2^{-1} + c_2 \times 2^{-2} + \ldots + c_m \times 2^{-m}$$

Here, the bs denote the integral part and the cs denote what is sometimes called the bicimal part. For example, the binary number 10111.101 can be interpreted as:

$$1 \times 2^4 + 0 \times 2^3 + 1 \times 2^2 + 1 \times 2^1 + 1 \times 2^0 + 1 \times 2^{-1} + 0 \times 2^{-2} + 1 \times 2^{-3}$$

or:

$$16 + 0 + 4 + 2 + 1 + 0.5 + 0 + 0.125 = 23.625$$

When an integer is stored in a computer a certain number of bits are used. The actual number of bits varies from computer to computer, but it is commonly either 16 or 32. If, for example, the integer 23 has to be stored in 16 bits, we get the binary pattern:

0000000000010111

The bit on the extreme left usually gives the number's sign, zero and one indicating a positive and a negative number, respectively. The greatest positive number that can be stored in 16 bits is therefore:

0111111111111111

This is actually $2^{15} - 1 = 32\ 767$. For storing negative numbers it is usual to employ a form known as **two's complement**. In this, the number -1 is stored in 16 bits as:

1111111111111111

The number -2 is obtained by subtracting 1 from this, thus getting:

1111111111111110

The number -3 is:

1111111111111101

By continuing to subtract one at a time we see that the least number (that is, the most negative number) that can be stored in 16 bits is:

1000000000000000

This has the value $-2^{15} = -32\ 768$. In general, it can be stated that if integers are stored in N bits, the least number that can be stored is -2^{N-1}, and the greatest is $2^{N-1}-1$.

Variables of type INTEGER will be stored in this, or some similar, way in the computer. The programmer does not need to know exactly how the storage works; the compiler takes care of this.

There is a certain risk attached to using the type INTEGER. Because the size of the numbers that can be stored depends on the design of the particular computer being used, the type INTEGER will not have the same properties in all implementations of Ada. Suppose we develop a program in a computer that uses 32 bits for storing integers of the type INTEGER. Now suppose a variable of type INTEGER at some point in the program takes the value 100 000. This is fine because there is room in 32 bits to store 100 000. But if we want to transfer our program to another computer that uses 16 bits to store integers we shall have a problem. When it is run, the program will be terminated because there is not enough space for the value 100 000.

To determine the least and greatest numbers of the type INTEGER that can be stored in the computer, another feature of Ada can be used – an **attribute**. For each type there are a number of attributes that give information about particular properties of the type. For INTEGER, for example, there are the two attributes:

> INTEGER'FIRST
> INTEGER'LAST

These give, respectively, the least and greatest numbers (that is, the most negative and the most positive numbers) of type INTEGER that can be stored. A test program could be written to see which numbers can be stored in the computer in use, including the statements:

> PUT(" The least INTEGER is: ");   PUT(INTEGER'FIRST);
> PUT(" The greatest INTEGER is: ");   PUT(INTEGER'LAST);

Attributes for the type INTEGER

INTEGER'FIRST
  gives the least possible integer that can be stored (the most negative number).

INTEGER'LAST
  gives the greatest possible integer that can be stored.

To be on the safe side and to ensure that programs are portable, that is, that they can be used on any computer, do not use the type INTEGER, but declare a new integer type where it is explicitly stated how big and how small the numbers involved will be. How to do this will be dealt with later.

In addition to the standard type INTEGER, an Ada implementation may also have the standard types SHORT_INTEGER and LONG_INTEGER. SHORT_INTEGER is then used to store only small integers while LONG_INTEGER is used for integers that cannot be stored as INTEGER. The attributes FIRST and LAST can also be used for these types.

In science and engineering, to avoid using too many zeros in a number, standard notation is often used for writing very large and very small numbers. In standard notation the numbers 350 000 000 and 0.000 000 73, for example, are written as:

$$0.35 \times 10^9 \qquad 0.73 \times 10^{-6}$$

The same technique is used for storing real numbers in a computer, but the base 2 is used instead of 10. The decimal number 10.5 can first be translated into binary form, giving the binary number 1010.1, and this can be written as:

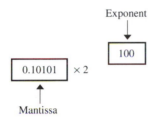

The first part, 0.10101, is usually called the mantissa and the second part, 100, the exponent. Both the mantissa and exponent are written as binary numbers (the exponent 100 meaning 4 in base 10).

When a real number is stored in a computer its mantissa and exponent can each use a certain number of bits, the numbers varying from computer to computer. In addition, one bit is used to store the sign of the number.

The principle of storing real numbers is demonstrated in the following example, where we assume that the decimal number 10.5 is stored in a computer that uses 32 bits to store real numbers; the first of the 32 bits holds the sign (0 for plus, 1 for minus), the next 8 bits are used for the exponent, and the remaining 23 bits are used to store the mantissa. The integral part of the mantissa does not need to be stored because it is always 0. (Sometimes, the first digit in the mantissa is not stored either because it is always possible to adjust the number so that this digit is 1.)

```
s exponent        mantissa
0 00000100 10101000000000000000000
```

It must be noted that the details of storing real numbers vary considerably from computer to computer. This example merely shows the general principles.

Note that the exponent can also be negative, when a small number is stored. For example, the number 0.06125 (= 1/16) would be stored as follows, using the same format as the previous example:

```
0 11111 101 10000000000000000000000
```

Here, the value of the exponent (–3) is expressed in the two's complement form.

This method of storing real numbers means that some numbers, such as the example of 10.5 above, can be stored exactly, whereas others, such as 0.6, cannot. If the number –0.6 is to be stored in the computer using the form outlined above, the pattern of bits would look like:

1 00000000 10011001100110011001100

The bit pattern 1001 in the mantissa should be repeated infinitely many times, but only 23 bits are available.

The number of significant decimal figures obtained depends on the number of bits used to store the mantissa. (It takes, on average, 3.2 bits per decimal figure.) The number of bits used for the exponent determines the largest and smallest numbers (excluding zero) that can be stored. The number zero is usually handled specially, and stored exactly using a particular pattern of bits.

The type FLOAT uses the foregoing technique to store real numbers. This means that the number of significant figures is the same over the whole range of possible numbers, and that the position of the decimal point 'floats'. It is said the numbers are stored as **floating point numbers** and that FLOAT is a **floating point type**. (Note there is also another technique for storing real numbers in Ada, using a fixed decimal point. 'Fixed point types' are used in this latter situation, but we shall not study these here.)

There are also a number of attributes for the type FLOAT that can be used to determine the properties of the type in the computer being used. The most common attributes are FLOAT'DIGITS, FLOAT'FIRST, and FLOAT'LAST. An Ada implementation may also have the standard types SHORT_FLOAT and LONG_FLOAT which are, respectively, less and more accurate than the type FLOAT. The attributes described above can also be used for these types.

Attributes for the type FLOAT

FLOAT'DIGITS
  gives the number of significant figures one has.

FLOAT'FIRST
  gives the smallest positive number (apart from zero) that can be stored.

FLOAT'LAST
  gives the largest positive number that can be stored.

Storing real numbers is therefore complicated, but it is reassuring to know that a programmer does not need to worry about the details of what is happening. However, the programmer should be aware of the accuracy that the decimal numbers retain. Furthermore, the programmer should remember that real numbers are not always stored in their exact form, that is, care must be taken when determining whether two real numbers are equal. Even if they are equal in principle, they can still differ by one bit in their mantissas and the computer will then see them as unequal. Such problems do not arise with numbers of the type INTEGER because all numbers are stored exactly.

Comparing real numbers

Avoid comparisons such as:

$$X = Y \quad \text{or} \quad X = 2.37$$

The numbers may be 'equal' but they can still be considered unequal by the computer.

3.1.2 The type *CHARACTER*

Most of the data handled by computers is probably not numerical at all, but text, characters and symbols. In the programs studied earlier we saw how to read in and print out a product code using the type STRING. We shall start by describing a more basic standard type, namely the type CHARACTER. This type is used for handling only single characters, such as letters, digits, special symbols (for example, question mark, full stop or colon), or non-printing control characters. Non-printing control characters can be used for communication tasks when the computer needs to make a terminal do certain things, for example, begin a new line, clear the screen or make a bell ring.

Let us write a short program to read a character from the terminal keyboard and write it on the screen.

```
with TEXT_IO;
use TEXT_IO;
procedure CHARACTER_DEMO is
    CHAR : CHARACTER;
begin
    PUT_LINE("Type any character!");
    GET(CHAR);
    PUT(CHAR);
end CHARACTER_DEMO;
```

In the program we have declared a variable CHAR of type CHARACTER. The package TEXT_IO contains versions of the procedures PUT and GET which can be used to read and write values of type CHARACTER. The statement:

GET(CHAR);

results in the character that the user types at the keyboard occupying the variable CHAR. We can think of CHAR as a storage box, or store, for characters. If, for instance, the user types a percentage sign, the situation after the GET statement has been executed could be illustrated by Figure 3.1. Observe that CHAR can contain only *one* character; if the user types in several characters at the keyboard only the first one will land in CHAR.

Values of characters are written enclosed by apostrophes. If, for example, we want to put a plus sign in CHAR we can write the assignment statement:

CHAR := '+';

If we want to put an apostrophe in CHAR instead, we would write:

CHAR := '''';

To store a character in a computer, a group of eight bits – a byte – is most often used. In Ada 83 only seven of these bits are used; the eighth bit, called the **parity bit**, is reserved for purposes of checking. The parity bit is usually the first bit of a byte; the other seven can be combined in 128 different ways, which means that there are 128 different character codes.

There is a generally accepted standard, called the ASCII standard, which determines which characters can be coded with the seven available bits, and for each pattern of seven bits there is one character designated in the standard. For example, '%', '9' and 'A' are represented by, respectively,

00100101
00111001
01000001

These patterns of bits can be interpreted as binary integers, called **character codes**. The codes start with 0, which means that the character codes lie between 0 and 127; the characters '%', '9' and 'A' thus have character codes 37, 57 and 65, respectively.

CHAR

Figure 3.1

The type CHARACTER in Ada 83 is made to follow the ASCII standard, which means that a variable of this type can contain any of the 128 characters defined in the standard. It also means that the different characters are represented in the computer in precisely the pattern that the ASCII standard specifies. In our example above, then, the variable CHAR will contain the bit-pattern 00100101 if the user types a percentage sign at the terminal.

The type CHARACTER is an **enumeration type**. It is actually defined within the package STANDARD, where all the values that a variable of type CHARACTER can take are enumerated; a list of all the ASCII codes and characters is given in Appendix F.

In an enumeration type there is a relative ordering defined between the possible values, determined by the order in which the values are given in the definition. Of two values, the one listed first is considered to be the lesser value. Values of type CHARACTER are ordered in just this way: first come 32 non-printing characters, and then 95 printable characters in the order given in Appendix F. Note that the first printable character is a blank, which corresponds to 'space' on the terminal keyboard.

Below we have amended our earlier program so that it reads in two characters and prints them out in order (as defined by the ASCII standard).

```
with TEXT_IO;
use TEXT_IO;
procedure CHARACTER_DEMO2 is
    CHAR1, CHAR2 : CHARACTER;
begin
    PUT_LINE("Type two characters!");
    GET(CHAR1);
    GET(CHAR2);
    if CHAR1 < CHAR2 then
        PUT(CHAR1);
        PUT(CHAR2);
    else
        PUT(CHAR2);
        PUT(CHAR1);
    end if;
end CHARACTER_DEMO2;
```

We see that the two variables CHAR1 and CHAR2 can simply be compared by using an **if** statement.

The printable characters can easily be given using apostrophes, as shown earlier, but not so for the non-printing characters. Instead, they have been given special symbolic names which are defined in a package ASCII, which is included in the package STANDARD. For example, the character which tells the terminal to move on a line (linefeed) can be placed in the variable CHAR as follows:

```
CHAR := ASCII.LF;
```

▼

The ASCII standard is an American standard which was developed on the assumption that the language in use is English. 'The English alphabet has 26 letters derived from the Latin alphabet. This set of letters suffices for English, Swahili and Hawaiian; all other living languages use either the Latin alphabet plus other characters, or other, non-Latin alphabets, or syllabaries.'† The ASCII standard, on the other hand, is spread throughout the world. The fact that the ASCII standard has only the letters a–z has been a problem and a constant source of irritation for all who work in the sphere of programming in countries with languages other than English. The languages of western Europe, for example, are based on the Latin alphabet but have various diacritical marks (accents, umlauts, circles and so on) on some of their letters. Sometimes such a mark gives a special stress or pronunciation to a letter: the meaning of a word can even be changed accordingly. For example, in Italian the word *e* means *and*, but the word *è* means *is*. In other cases such a mark gives an entirely new letter. In Swedish, for example, the letters å, ä and ö are quite different letters from a and o (for example, *kö* in Swedish means *queue* while *ko* means *cow*, and å, ä and ö come last in the Swedish alphabet, without reference to a and o).

The solution to the problem is naturally to allow for more characters in the standard. If we drop the use of the first bit in each byte as a parity bit we can make use of eight bits instead of seven, and can, as a consequence, represent 256 different characters instead of 128. Then the numbers from 128 to 255 can be used to represent new letters, and even other characters. This has been done, for example, in Macintosh and PC computers (but unfortunately, codes have been assigned inconsistently).

In Ada 95 the type **CHARACTER** has been extended to use eight bits and can thus represent 256 different characters. There is an international standard (ISO 8859) specifying which characters are defined by which codes, and Ada 95 adheres to it. For the character codes from 0 to 127 ISO 8859 agrees with the ASCII standard, so it is no different from Ada 83 for those who only use characters from the ASCII standard. The character codes between 128 and 255 are used partly for non-printing control characters and partly for a set of printable characters. The set of printable characters which are used in Ada 95 and which are included in the ISO 8859 is called **LATIN_1**. (Ada 95 does, however, allow sets of characters other than **LATIN_1** to be used.) Among the characters of **LATIN_1** are to be found the letters with diacritics which are used in the languages of western Europe, for example à, å, è, æ, ö, ü, ñ, and ç, in both lower- and upper-case variants. (The only exceptions are the letter β, German double s, and the letter ÿ, which are only defined as lower-case letters.) Apart from the letters with diacritical marks, **LATIN_1** also contains various graphical characters such as §, £, ±, and ¹/₂. The printable characters of **LATIN_1** are given in Appendix F. In Ada 95, the following, for example, are allowed:

---

† *Rationale for Draft Proposal ANSI-standard, Programming Language C.*

```
CHAR := 'ê';
CHAR := '¿';
```

There are symbolic names for the non-printing control characters in just the same way as there are in the ASCII standard. These are defined in the package ADA.CHARACTERS.LATIN_1 (see Appendix F).

In order to handle languages which are not based on the Latin alphabet, Ada 95 has yet another standard type, called WIDE_CHARACTER. This makes use of 16 bits, which means that 65336 different characters can be represented, and these are specified in another international standard (ISO 10646 BMP). The printable characters can be referred to in the same way as for ordinary CHARACTER, by using apostrophes. If the variable WCHAR is of type WIDE_CHARACTER, then one could write, for example:

```
WCHAR := 'Σ';
WCHAR := '∀';
WCHAR := 'ϰ';
WCHAR := '↑';
```

In practice, however, it can be difficult to refer to a printable character in this way, because it might not be included on the keyboard in use, or a graphics character might not be included in the set of characters available for the program text. In such cases, the symbolic names of the characters might be available for use, but they are dependent on the implementation; if there is no symbolic name, then the attribute VAL can be used (see below).

There is a standard package ADA.WIDE_TEXT_IO, which includes the procedures GET and PUT for reading and writing characters of type WIDE_CHARACTER. This package contains the same procedures as TEXT_IO but the type CHARACTER is replaced by the type WIDE_CHARACTER.

A number of functions which can be used for testing and converting different characters are defined in the package ADA.CHARACTERS.HANDLING (see Appendix G).

If in a program you need to know which character code a particular character has, you can use an attribute which exists for the type CHARACTER. For example:

```
CHARACTER'POS('A')
```

gives the order number for A, which is 65. The parameter in the parentheses can also be a variable. For example, one can write:

```
CHARACTER'POS(CHAR)
```

and get as a result the order number of the character which is stored in variable CHAR. If you need to go in the other direction, there is another attribute to use.

CHARACTER'VAL(65)

will give the 65th character, namely A. Note that this attribute gives a result of type CHARACTER.

The attributes POS and VAL can also be used for the type WIDE_CHARACTER. The following expression gives the character code for the symbol ∞:

WIDE_CHARACTER'POS('∞')

and if you want the character with character code 10517 you write:

▲   WIDE_CHARACTER'VAL(10517)

Attributes for CHARACTER

CHARACTER'POS(C)
gives the character code of C (where C has type CHARACTER).

CHARACTER'VAL(N)
gives the character that has character code N.

3.1.3   The text type *STRING*

The standard type CHARACTER can only be used to describe one character at a time. For an object that contains several characters, the standard type STRING must be used instead. We saw an example of this in the invoicing program of Chapter 2. A declaration of a variable of type STRING, a **text string variable**, might appear as follows:

NAME : STRING(1 .. 5);

The number of characters to be stored in the variable and how they are to be numbered are stated in the brackets. In this case, NAME will hold five characters, numbered from 1 to 5.

A text string variable can, just like other sorts of variable, be given a value by assignment. If the statement:

NAME := "Tommy";

appears in the program, then after execution NAME will be as in Figure 3.2. Note that the text string on the right-hand side of the statement must contain the

NAME

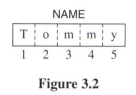

Figure 3.2

same number of characters as the variable on the left-hand side has space for; in Figure 3.2 this is five. To write 'Thomas' or 'Tom' on the right, for example, is not allowed, but 'padding out' with blanks and writing 'Tom ' is permitted. Also note that double quotation marks are used to enclose text strings in a program. In the example in Chapter 2, we saw that it is also possible to give a value to a text string variable by reading it in from the terminal using the GET procedure. The situation in Figure 3.2 could also be achieved if the program contained the statements:

```
PUT_LINE("Give a name with 5 letters!");
GET(NAME);
```

and if the user typed the name Tommy at the terminal keyboard.

When a text string variable is declared, the two quantities in the brackets do not need to be constants. It is possible to use simple expressions that may themselves contain variables. What is essential is that the expressions should have integer values and that the first expression is greater than zero.

```
MY_WORD : STRING(2 .. 10*N);
ADDRESS  : STRING(K .. K+10);
```

The type STRING is called a **composite type**. An object of type STRING is actually composed of a number of objects of type CHARACTER. The variable NAME, for example, consists of a collection of five CHARACTER objects, numbered from 1 to 5. It is possible to access the individual parts of a variable of type STRING. If, for example, the content of the variable NAME is to be changed to Tammy, the statement:

```
NAME(2) := 'a';
```

can be written. The expression NAME(2) is an example of **indexing**. The 2 specifies that it is the second element of the variable NAME that is meant. This element has type CHARACTER, not type STRING. This is the reason for the apostrophes around the letter a on the right-hand side of the statement: they are used, as we saw earlier, for the type CHARACTER. Figure 3.3 shows the state of NAME after this assignment statement has been executed.

NAME

T	a	m	m	y
1	2	3	4	5

Figure 3.3

In the following example, indexing is used to print out the last character in the variable NAME:

    PUT(NAME(5));

With indexing, the expression in brackets need not have a constant value. The index for a text string can be any expression at all, provided it has type INTEGER and its value lies within the declared range, as shown in the following examples:

    NAME(2+3)
    NAME(J+1)   -- correct if 0 <= J <= 4
    NAME(2*K);   -- correct if 1 <= K <= 2

Indexing in a variable of type STRING

   S(*integer expression*)

where S has type STRING and the value of the integer expression must lie within the index range for S.

The result of indexing is a single component of type CHARACTER.

Using indexing it is thus possible to select a particular element of a text string. It is also possible to choose a number of contiguous elements simultaneously, by creating a **slice** – a part of a string. For example, the variable NAME can be changed so that it contains the name Jimmy instead of Tammy:

    NAME(1 .. 2)   "Ji";

A slice has type STRING and therefore quotation marks are needed on the right-hand side (even if the slice that is cut consists of a single element). The following statement will print the second, third and fourth elements of NAME:

```
PUT( NAME(2 .. 4) );
```

As with indexing, more general expressions are allowed as index limits. When a slice of a text string is taken, the two indexes must have type INTEGER and they must lie within the index range of the text string. An exception is made of the **empty slice** – a slice whose second index number is lower than the first. The index is then allowed to fall outside the range of the text string's index. Here are some examples of slices of the text string NAME:

```
NAME(2 .. 2+1);
NAME(J–3 .. J) --OK if J has, for example, the value 4
NAME(1 .. 0)    -- empty slice
NAME(3 .. K)    -- slice if 2 < K < 6, empty slice if K < 3, error if K > 5
```

Slices of text strings

S(N1 .. N2)

where S has type STRING. N1 and N2 are integer expressions.

- If N2 < N1 we get an empty slice.

- Otherwise, N1 and N2 must lie within the index range of S.

- The result has type STRING.

It is possible to join strings together in sequence – to **catenate** strings – using an operator denoted by the symbol &. Here are a few examples:

```
NAME := "Tom" & "my";          -- result is "Tommy"
NAME := "Ji" & NAME(3 .. 5);   -- result is "Jimmy"
PUT( NAME & " Johnson");        -- "Jimmy Johnson" is printed
NAME := NAME(1 .. 4) & 'o';    -- result is "Jimmo"
SYMB := 'A'                     -- SYMB has type CHARACTER
PUT( SYMB & "-team");           -- "A-team" is printed
```

The last three lines show that it is also possible to add a CHARACTER on to a text string (either at the beginning or at the end).

Catenation of text strings

SI & S2

where S1 and S2 can be either variables of type STRING or constant text strings.

- It is also possible for one (or both) of S1 and S2 to have type CHARACTER.

- The result has type STRING.

The next example program shows how catenation and slices can be used. The method used to write the date is different in different countries and can sometimes be a little confusing. For example, the American way of writing 26th March 1996 is 03/26/96, whereas in Britain it would be written 26/03/96. The day and the month have swapped places. According to the ISO standard, the same date should be written 1996-03-26. Let us look at a program that can read in a date in the American format and translate it into the equivalent British and ISO formats. When the program is run the conversation at the terminal would appear as:

```
Give the date in the form mm/dd/yy
03126/96
The British form of the date is:
26/03/96
The ISO form of the date is:
1996-03-26
```

Our first version of the program looks like this:

```
with TEXT_IO;
use TEXT_IO;
procedure TRANSLATE–DATE is
    AMERICAN_DATE : STRING(1 .. 8);
    BRITISH_DATE    : STRING(1 8)       := " / / ";
    ISO_DATE          : STR1NG(1 .. 10) := "19 - - ";
begin
    PUT_LINE("Give the date in the form mm/dd/yy'");

    GET(AMERICAN_DATE);
    BRITISH_DATE(1 .. 2)  := AMERICAN_DATE(4 .. 5);
    BRITISH_DATE(4 .. 5)  := AMERICAN_DATE(1 .. 2);
    BRITISH_DATE(7 .. 8)  := AMERICAN_DATE(7 .. 8);
    PUT_LINE("The British form of the date is:");
    PUT_L1NE(BRITISH_DATE);
```

```
ISO–DATE(3 .. 4)   := AMERICAN_DATE(7 .. 8);
ISO–DATE(6 .. 7)   := AMERICAN_DATE(1 .. 2);
ISO–DATE(9 .. 10) := AMERICAN_DATE(4 .. 5);
PUT_LINE("The ISO form of the date is:");
PUT_LINE(ISO_DATE);
end TRANSLATE_DATE;
```

In the program, the variables BRITI5H_DATE and ISO_DATE have been initialized at the same time as being declared. The spaces for the year, month and day
numbers have been filled with blanks that are changed later in the program.

We can write a more compact version of the program by constructing the
text string for printing directly in the output statement. We then need only one
variable, DATE:

```
with TEXT_IO;
use TEXT_IO;
procedure TRANSLATE_DATE is
   DATE : STRING(1 .. 8);
begin
   PUT_LINE("Give the date in the form mm/dd/yy");
   GET(DATE);
   PUT_LINE("The British form of the date is:");
   PUT_LINE(DATE(4 .. 5) & "/" & DATE(1 .. 2) & "/" & DATE(7 .. 8));
PUT_LINE("The ISO form of the date is:");
PUT_LINE("19" & DATE(7.. 8) & "-" & DATE(1 .. 2) & "-" &
            DATE(4 .. 5));
end TRANSLATE_DATE
```

Text strings can easily be compared with one another:

```
if NAME = "Clare" then
   PUT("Hi Clare");
end if;
```

The text 'Hi Clare' will be printed out only if the variable NAME contains the
text string 'Clare'. It is also possible to compare alphabetically, and compare
strings of different lengths:

```
NAME < "Diana"
"Betty" < "Peter"       -- True
"Jill" > "Jack"         -- True
"Liz" > "Elizabeth"     -- True
"Adam" < "Eve"          -- True
"Victor" /= "Victoria"  -- True (/= "not equal to")
"Victor" < "Victoria"   -- True
"Rose" < "rose"         -- True
```

When making comparisons the normal alphabetical order applies, but note that it does not hold for the additional letters of Ada 95, such as á, à, â, ä, ã, and å. Another thing to be aware of is that, for purposes of comparison, lower- and upper-case letters are not identical; somewhat paradoxically, the upper-case letters have lower values than the lower-case letters (see Appendix F).

Comparing text strings

- There are normal comparing operations.

- Text strings of different lengths can be compared.

- Ordinary alphabetical order is used, except for the additional letters with diacritical marks.

- Upper- and lower-case letters are considered to be different.

This section concludes with a useful method for reading text of variable length from the terminal. We have seen that it is possible to read text into a variable of type STRING, using GET. For example, in the date program above we had the line:

```
GET(DATE);
```

The disadvantage of GET, however, is that the text typed at the keyboard must contain exactly the same number of characters as there are places in the variable. Since the variable DATE has eight places, in this example, the user must type in eight characters at the terminal. This poses no problem when reading in a date because we know that it always has exactly eight characters; in many other cases, however, it is not possible to decide in advance just how many characters to expect.

As an example, we can look at a program that reads in two lines from the terminal. Each line ends when the user presses the end-of-line key, the RETURN key in most systems. Assume that each line contains a name, and the program's job is to sort them into alphabetical order.

```
with TEXT_IO;
use TEXT_IO;
procedure DEMONSTRATE_LINE is
    LINE1, LINE2 STRING(1 .. 100);
    L1, L2      : INTEGER;
begin
    PUT_LINE("Enter first name");
```

```
            GET_LINE(LINE1, L1);
            PUT_LINE("Enter second name");
            GET_LINE(LINE2, L2);
            if LINE1(1 .. L1) < LINE2(1 .. L2) then
                PUT_LINE( LINE1(1 .. L1));
                PUT_LINE( LINE2(1 .. L2)
            else
                PUT_LINE( LINE2(1 .. L2)
                PUT_LINE( LINE1(1 .. L1));
            end if;
        end DEMONSTRATE_LINE;
```

In the program we have declared two text string variables, LINE1 and LINE2, where the two lines will be placed. We assume that no line will be more than 100 characters long and, therefore, we let both variables have room for 100 characters. The integer variables L1 and L2 will be used to keep track of how many characters the user writes in the two respective lines.

For the actual reading we use a procedure GET_LINE from the package TEXT_IO. The first line is read with:

```
    GET_LINE(LINE1, L1);
```

What happens here is that the characters the user writes at the terminal for the first line are read in and placed in the variable LINE1, from left to right, starting at position 1. The variable L1 will get as its value the number of characters read in the first line. To return to an earlier example, if the user writes 'Tommy' for the first line, the text 'Tommy' will appear in elements 1–5 of LINE1 and L1 will automatically get the value 5. The remaining elements of LINE1 (elements 6-100) are not defined.

The second line is read in in the same way:

```
    GET_LINE(LINE2, L2);
```

If the user should write 'Catherine' for the second line, the text 'Catherine' would appear in elements 1–9 of the variable LINE2 and the variable L2 would have the value 9.

The two names can now be compared easily. We cut two slices that contain only the two names and write:

```
    if LINE1(1 .. L1) LINE2(1 .. L2) then
```

If the user writes 'Tommy' and 'Catherine' for the two lines, the text strings 'Tommy' and 'Catherine' will thus be compared with one another. (The remaining elements of LINE1 and LINE2 are of no significance.)

The name is then written out using PUT_LINE, and here we also cut out the slice that contains the name read in.

Reading in text of variable length

(1)   Declare a variable S of type STRING that is long enough to hold a text of the maximum length.

(2)   Declare an integer variable N.

(3)   Read a line at the terminal using:

   GET_LINE(S,N);

(The user ends a line by pressing the end-of-line key.)

The variable N will contain the number of characters in the line read, and the characters themselves will be in elements 1–N of S.

▼

In Ada 95 there are a number of predefined utility routines to handle text strings – fixed length strings as well as unbounded strings. These utility routines are defined in the standard package ADA.STRINGS and its child packages MAPS, FIXED, BOUNDED and UNBOUNDED. There is also a standard type WIDE_STRING which works in the same way as type STRING, except for the difference that the individual characters in a string of type WIDE_STRING are of type WIDE_CHARACTER rather than of type CHARACTER. This type is used for describing texts written in characters other than those to be found in the set LATIN_1. The standard package ADA.WIDE_TEXT_IO contains procedures for reading and writing characters of type WIDE_STRING.

▲

3.1.4   The logical type *BOOLEAN*

In Ada, the comparison:

   NUMBER_OF_ITEMS > 0

is considered as much an expression as:

   NUMBER_OF_ITEMS + 1

The second expression has type INTEGER, but what type does the first one have? If you make the claim:

   NUMBER_OF_ITEMS > 0

it can be either true or false. In other words, we can say that the expression can take **the value true** or **the value false**. It is quite normal to think of values as numerical, for example, 14 or 68.24. When we discussed the types CHARACTER and STRING, we saw that characters could also be seen as values, but of another kind. Now we have met a third sort of value, logical values, known as **Boolean values** after the mathematician Boole. In Ada there is a standard type BOOLEAN that can be used for handling such values. For example, variables of the type BOOLEAN can be declared:

ACTIVE : BOOLEAN;

The variable ACTIVE can only contain the values TRUE or FALSE. We can make an assignment:

ACTIVE := TRUE;

and then we have the situation depicted in Figure 3.4.

In the same way as other variables, we have thought of ACTIVE as a storage box, but now a store that can only contain the values FALSE or TRUE. If we want to, we can assign the result of a comparison to a BOOLEAN variable:

ACTIVE := NAME = "Tommy";

This may look a little strange to start with, but note the difference between := and =. The assignment symbol := means that what is on its right, that is, the logical expression:

NAME = "Tommy"

should be evaluated first and then the result should be placed in the variable ACTIVE. In the expression on the right-hand side the operator = appears; this is an operator concerned with comparing and has nothing to do with assignment.

ACTIVE

Figure 3.4

> **The type BOOLEAN**
>
> - The only values allowed are FALSE and TRUE.
>
> - Expressions of type BOOLEAN are called Boolean expressions.

If in a program we want to test the value of a BOOLEAN variable, we could do so as follows:

```
if ACTIVE = TRUE then
   PUT("In action!");
end if;
```

Since ACTIVE already contains a value of type BOOLEAN, it is more elegant to write simply:

```
if ACTIVE then
   PUT("In action!");
end if;
```

BOOLEAN is actually an enumeration type, like the type CHARACTER. It is also defined in the STANDARD package where the two possible values, FALSE and TRUE, have been listed (such that FALSE < TRUE, but this is not normally significant).

3.2 Identifiers

The concept of an **identifier** is found in most programming languages, and Ada is no exception. An identifier can be used as a **name** for different components in a program, such as a procedure or variable. Identifiers are also used to denote **reserved words**. GIANT_ADA, PUT, **begin**, and **if** are all examples of identifiers. There are strict rules governing the appearance of identifiers. In Ada, the rules are as follows:

- An identifier consists of a series of one or more characters. The number of characters permitted in an identifier is, in principle, limitless (at least 200, according to the standard) and all characters are significant.
- The first character must be a letter (a letter being, in Ada 83, one of the characters a–z).

- The remaining characters may be a letter or the underline symbol _, or one of the numerals 0, 1, …, 8, 9. The underline symbol is significant, which means that, for example, NR_1 and NR1 are interpreted as two different identifiers. More than one underline symbol in sequence is not allowed, nor is an underline symbol at the end of an identifier. Blank characters (spaces) are not allowed in an identifier, so that, for example, NUMBER NR1 is interpreted as two identifiers.

- Lower-case letters are also permitted. They are interpreted in the same way as the corresponding upper-case letter, so that, for example, PUT, puT and put are taken to be the same.

Here are some examples of identifiers:

```
TOMMY          Smallest_Number   x      P_1
NUMBER_NR1     PageNumber        x1
```

In Ada 95, all the characters which are interpreted as letters in the ISO standard (for example, á, à, â, ä, æ, é, è, í, ì, ó, ò, ö and ü) are permitted in identifiers, whereas in Ada 83 and all other common programming languages, only the letters a–z are permitted. Thus the following identifiers are valid in Ada 95 but not in Ada 83:

```
CITTÀ     Noël   Straße   año
Garçon    ØL     pâte     smörgåsbord
```

Here are some examples of invalid identifiers:

```
1X                    -- first character may not be a numeral

max%                  -- the character % is not permitted

_post                 -- the first character may not be _

ID–NUMBER             -- the minus sign may not be used

ID Number             -- interpreted as two identifiers

km/hr                 -- / symbol not allowed
```

There are a number of so-called **reserved** words which have special meanings, and it is therefore not permitted to use these words as names in a program. For example, you may not declare a variable with the name END. To show the reserved words clearly, they are always given in our examples in bold print. (When writing programs, there is no need to mark the reserved words in any special way.) A list of all reserved words in Ada is given in Figure 3.5; **abstract, aliased, protected, requeue, tagged** and **until** were introduced in Ada 95.

abort	abs	abstract	accept
access	aliased	all	and
array	at	begin	body
case	constant	declare	delay
delta	digits	do	else
elsif	end	entry	exception
exit	for	function	generic
goto	if	in	is
limited	loop	mod	new
not	null	of	or
others	out	package	pragma
private	procedure	protected	raise
range	record	rem	renames
requeue	return	reverse	select
separate	subtype	tagged	task
terminate	then	type	until
use	when	while	with
xor			

Figure 3.5

3.3   Literals

Sometimes actual values are needed in a program, such as 12, 34.5 or 'Hello'. In programming, actual values such as these are called **literals**. Numeric literals are used to give numeric values and can be either integer literals or real literals. It is most common to give numeric literals as decimal numbers, as in the following examples:

13	0	4598	-- integer literals
1E7	15e5	1E0	-- integer literals
13.0	0.0	0.379	-- real literals
1.0e7	43.2E–12	3.2E+8	-- real literals

The exponent form is interpreted as the number before the 'e' multiplied by 10 to the power of the integer after the 'e'. (Both upper- and lower-case e can be used.) 1.234e2 is therefore interpreted as 123.4, while 1.4E–3 is 0.0014. The integer after e can be preceded by a plus or a minus sign.

Zeros can be written at the start if desired, for example 0028 or 002.35. There must be at least one figure before the decimal point in a real number, for example .34 is illegal and should be written 0.34. Spaces are not allowed in a literal, so that 1.4e –3 is not allowed, but underline symbols may be inserted for grouping digits. For example, 1_245_000 would be interpreted as 1 245 000, and 1.356_491 is taken as 1.356 491.

These format rules for numeric literals also apply when numbers are read into a program using the procedure GET. This means that the user must follow the same rules at the terminal. Note that if an integer is to be read in, the rules for integers apply; if a real number is to be read in then the rules for real numbers apply. For example, if the variable TEMPERATURE has the type FLOAT and the statements:

```
PUT_LINE("Enter the temperature!");
GET(TEMPERATURE);
```

are in the program, then the user must type a real literal at the terminal. This could be 12.0 or 1.2e1, for example. If the user only types 12, then this is an error because 12 is an integer literal, not a real literal. In Ada, the user will be given a DATA_ERROR. If the statements:

```
PUT_LINE("Give the number of items!");
GET(NUMBER_OF_ITEMS);
```

appear in a program and the variable NUMBER_OF_ITEMS is declared as an INTEGER, then the user must type an integer literal at the terminal, for example, 123, 25_000 or 1e3. The program will malfunction if the user types a real literal such as 1.0e3 or 123.0.

We saw character literals when we discussed the character type CHARACTER. A character literal consists of any of the printable characters enclosed in apostrophes. Some examples are:

'z'   'B'   '7'   '?'   '('   ' '   '''

The last of these shows how the apostrophe is given as a character literal.

We have also seen several examples of text string literals. These comprise a number of printable characters (or possibly none) enclosed in quotation marks, for example:

```
"This is a text string literal"
"       "
"abx'+%"
"  "
```

In Ada 95 the characters of a character literal or a text string literal do not have to be ASCII characters. For example, the letters with diacritical marks in LATIN_1 can be used:

'É'   'Ò'   'ä'   'ì'   'â'   'ç'
"à la carte"   "più forte"   "Dido and Æneas"

The types of character and text string literals are determined by the context, or in other words, how they are used in the program. In the majority of cases, character literals are of the type CHARACTER and text string literals are of type STRING, but they might well be of other types. For example, a character literal might be of type WIDE_CHARACTER, and a text string literal could be of type WIDE_STRING, as is the case in this example:

```
WTEXT : WIDE_STRING := "The letter '?' is strange";
...
WTEXT(13) := 'Ξ';
```

▲

(In this example there is no need to specify an index range in the declaration of WTEXT since the length of the text is given when it is initiated.)

The citation marks in a text string literal are not part of the text itself – they are only delimiters. If you want to have a quotation mark in a text string, you can get it by writing two quotation marks, as in this example:

```
"Americans call a ""lift"" an ""elevator""."
```

This example is interpreted as a single text string literal and not as five.

A text string literal must appear on a single line in a program. If it is too long for one line, then the catenation operator can be used:

```
"This is a text string literal that is so long that " &
"we shall have to write it on two lines."
```

When the user has to type in a value for a variable of type CHARACTER or STRING from the terminal, then the apostrophes or quotation marks should not be typed. Suppose the variable NAME is declared as a STRING(1 .. 5) and the following two statements are in a program:

```
PUT_LINE("Enter a name with 5 letters!");
GET(NAME);
```

If the user now types the word Tommy (without quotation marks), the variable NAME will take the value 'Tommy'.

The final type of literal we have met is the literal of type BOOLEAN. Since there are only two values in the type BOOLEAN, there are only two literals:

```
FALSE    TRUE
```

It is also possible to read in values to BOOLEAN variables, and then these literals are used. We shall return to this in a later chapter.

Literals

- Constant values, such as numeric values.

- Exist for all types.

3.4 Expressions

Expressions can be constructed in a program to calculate new values from literals and the names of objects. NUMBER_OF_ITEMS * 2 is an example of an expression. Note that every expression is of a particular type which is determined by how it is constructed and the components included in it. The expression NUMBER_OF_ITEMS * 2 has type INTEGER if NUMBER_OF_ITEMS has type INTEGER.

The simplest form of expression comprises only one literal or the name of an object:

```
3.14
ID_NUMBER
VAT_PERCENT
TRUE
"Hello!"
```

More complicated expressions can be built using **operators**. The symbol *, for example, denotes the multiplication operator in the expression NUMBER_OF_ITEMS * 2. A set of basic operators is defined in Ada. (It is also possible for the programmer to define new operators, as will be discussed in Section 6.9.) Some operators exist only for certain types, for example, multiplication is defined for two integers but not for two text strings.

Expressions

- Simplest form: literal or name of an object.

- More complicated expressions are constructed using operators and simpler expressions.

3.4.1 Numeric expressions

Expressions that calculate with ordinary numbers are called **numeric** or **arithmetic expressions**. In arithmetic expressions the normal operations of mathematics can be used: addition, subtraction, multiplication and division. In addition, there are operators to find the remainder after integer division; to find the absolute value of a number; and to carry out exponentiation.

Ada is careful to separate the different types. As we have seen, different types may not be mixed in an arithmetic expression at will. We shall see later that it is possible for the programmer to define new numeric types other than the standard types INTEGER and FLOAT. Therefore, when the term 'integer type' is used in future it will refer not only to the type INTEGER but also to all other integer types: for example, SHORT_INTEGER and integer types defined by the programmer. In the same way, the term 'floating number type' refers not only to FLOAT, but also to SHORT_FLOAT and all other defined types that are related to the type FLOAT. 'Numeric type' means any integer type or float type at all.

Numeric expressions

- Expressions constructed of ordinary mathematical numbers.

- Different types, for example, INTEGER and FLOAT, may not be mixed at will in an expression.

We begin with a discussion of the types of numeric literals. Each expression has a particular resulting type depending on how it is put together. As we saw above, a numeric literal is the simplest form of expression, but what is its type? What are the types of the expressions 28 and 25.84? If 28 has the type INTEGER and the variable SMALL_NUMBER has the type SHORT_INTEGER, then the assignment:

    SMALL_NUMBER := 28;

would not be permitted, because the two sides have different types. This would be impracticable. Clearly an integer literal does not have the type INTEGER. This problem, and all similar problems, have been solved in Ada by introducing an anonymous type called *universal_integer,* and all integer literals are said to be of this type. A value of the type *universal_integer,* is converted automatically to a suitable integer type when it is used. In the assignment statement above, therefore, the value 28 is converted automatically into type SHORT_INTEGER in connection with the assignment. If instead we have the statement:

    BIG_NUMBER := 28;

where BIG_NUMBER has type LONG_INTEGER, then 28 is converted automatically into type LONG_INTEGER. This means that an integer literal can always be regarded as having the 'right' integer type and there is no need to worry about converting it to a particular type.

In a similar way, there is also an anonymous real type called *universal_real* and all real literals can be regarded as having this type and being converted automatically into the 'right' float type.

Literals in numeric expressions

- Integer literals may be used anywhere an integer type is required.

- Conversion to the right integer type occurs automatically.

- Real literals may be used anywhere a real type is required.

- Conversion to the right real type occurs automatically.

Let us examine the different operations that can be performed in an arithmetic expression. Addition, subtraction, multiplication and division can be performed with the operators +, −, * and /. For example:

```
NUMBER + 1        NO_1 + VALUE     3.8 + MEAN_TEMP
SALARY − 378.50   34.8 − 185.3     NUMBER − 8
5 * NUMBER        NO_1 * NO_2      VALUE * 1.3E3
NUMBER / 3        12 / 5           VALUE / 3.76
```

The quantities before and after the operator are called the **operands**. It is essential that both operands have the same type. For example, if NO_1 has type INTEGER, then so must VALUE; if VALUE had another type, such as SHORT_INTEGER or FLOAT, the expression would be faulty. The whole expression has the same type as the operands involved. If NUMBER has type INTEGER, the whole expression NUMBER + 1 also has type INTEGER. The expression 34.8 − 185.3 has the type *universal_real* and the expression 12 / 5 the type *universal_integer*.

There are also **unary** variants of the plus and minus operators. These variants have an operand on the right but none on the left. The unary minus is of use in constructs such as:

```
K := −1;     K * (−3)   PUT( −K);     K := −K;
```

Division requires a little more explanation. If the operands are of floating point type, there is no problem: ordinary division takes place and the result is of the same type as the operands. If, however, the operands are of integer type, the result is also of integer type: so-called integer division takes place. This means that we see how many times the right-hand operand 'goes into' the left-hand operand. For example, the expression 12 / 5 gives the result 2 because there are 2 whole 5s in 12. The result is *not* 2.4. As a further example, the expression (–7) / 4 gives the result –1, 12 / (–3) gives –4, and (–12) / (–5) gives 2.

The operator **rem** (remainder) can be used to find the remainder after integer division. This needs two integer parameters of the same type. The expression:

> 12 **rem** 5

for example, gives the result 2, the remainder when 12 is divided by 5. There is another operator **mod** (modulus operator) that works in almost the same way. The expression:

> 12 **mod** 5

also gives the value 2. If one of the operands to **rem** or **mod** is less than zero, then it is a little more complicated. The next few lines can be omitted by readers who are not interested in the details.

A mathematical definition is necessary. A and B below denote arbitrary integers. Integer division and the operator **rem** are defined by:

> A = (A/B)∗B + (A **rem** B)
> (–A)/B = –(A/B) = A/(–B)

where (A **rem** B) has the same sign as A and an absolute value less than the absolute value of B.

For the operator **mod:**

> A = B∗N + (A **mod** B)   for some integer N.

(A **mod** B) has the same sign as B and an absolute value less than B. Figure 3.6 illustrates the similarities and differences. If the second operand to one of the operators /, **rem** or **mod** is 0, an error occurs in the program. In Ada, the user is given a NUMERIC_ERROR.

There is an **exponentiation operator** denoted by ******. Its first operand can either be integer or floating point type. The second operand is the exponent and must always be of integer type. If the first operand is of integer type, the result will also be of integer type; if the first operand is a floating point type then so will be the result. Here are a few examples:

```
NUMBER ** 2    2 ** NUMBER      5 ** 4
VALUE ** 3     MAX_TEMP ** K   5.78 ** 7
VALUE ** (–3)  MAX_TEMP ** 0
```

A	B	A/B	A rem B	A mod B
10	5	2	0	0
12	5	2	2	2
14	5	2	4	4
10	−5	−2	0	0
12	−5	−2	2	−3
14	−5	−2	4	−1
−10	5	−2	0	0
−12	5	−2	−2	3
−14	5	−2	−4	1
−10	−5	2	0	0
−12	−5	2	−2	−2
−14	−5	2	−4	−4

Figure 3.6

The operation that takes place is ordinary exponentiation. The expression N ** 5, for example, is interpreted as N * N * N * N * N. If the second operand is 0, the result is always 1. If the first operand has floating point type, then a negative exponent is also permitted. The expression X ** (−4), for example, is interpreted as 1/(X * X * X * X).

The final standard numeric operator is **abs.** This operator has only one operand and that can be of arbitrary numeric type. The operator calculates the absolute value of the operand: in other words, the operand itself if it is positive and the negated operand if it is negative. The result is of the same type as the operand.

    abs K   **abs** MEAN_VALUE   **abs** (−23.4)

More complicated expressions can be created by combining several operators. For example, expressions such as the following are possible:

    NUMBER * 5 + 37

    VALUE / FACTOR + 14.3 − CORR

    NUMBER **rem** 8 − K

    abs VALUE / 5.78 * FACTOR

    TEMPERATURE ** 3 * PRESSURE + CORR

The result of one operation is a value that, in turn, is one operand in a new operation. The question of ordering the different operations arises in a complicated expression. In the expression:

    2 + 4 / 2 * 3

the result could be completely different, depending on the order of addition, division and multiplication.

Each operator in Ada has a certain **precedence**. The evaluation of a complicated expression occurs in such a way that the operator with the highest precedence is the first to be executed, followed by the one with next highest precedence, and so on, until finally the operator with lowest precedence is executed. If several operators have the same precedence, they are executed from left to right. Of the operators we have seen, **abs** and ∗∗ have the highest precedence; next are ∗, /, and **mod**; and then the unary operators + and −. The ordinary + and − operators have the lowest precedence.

If we apply these evaluation rules to the expression above, we see that the operators / and ∗ have higher precedence than + and should therefore be performed first. Since / and ∗ have the same precedence they are carried out from left to right, so that the division 4 / 2 is carried out first. The result of this division, 2, then becomes the left operand to the operator ∗, which is now executed. The result of the multiplication is 6 and this makes the right operand to the operator +, which is carried out last. Thus, the result of the whole expression is 8.

It is possible to control the order of execution of the various operators using parentheses. The expression:

(2 + 4) / 2 ∗ 3

has the value 9, for example, and:

(2 + 4) / (2 ∗ 3)

has the value 1.

Order of evaluation in expressions

- Is determined by the precedence of the operators.
- Can be controlled by the use of parentheses.

In the invoice example of Chapter 2, we saw that sometimes we are forced to mix types. We wanted to multiply a FLOAT variable, ITEM_PRICE, with an INTEGER, NUMBER_OF_ITEMS. It is illegal to write ITEM_PRICE ∗ NUMBER_OF_ITEMS because the two operands are of different types. We must use **type conversion** and write:

ITEM_PRICE ∗ FLOAT(NUMBER_OF_ITEMS)

The value of the variable NUMBER_OF_ITEMS is converted to a value of type FLOAT and this converted value becomes the right-hand operand to the operator *. Conversion between all the numeric types is allowed, and is achieved simply by writing the required type followed by a numeric expression in brackets. The numeric expression is then converted to the type requested. If a real expression is converted to an integer expression, then **rounding** to the nearest whole number occurs. Here are a few examples:

```
MEAN_VALUE := SUM / FLOAT(NUMBER_OF_MEASUREMENTS);
5 * SHORT_INTEGER(2.85)      -- Result is 15
X * SHORT_FLOAT(N1 + N2)
```

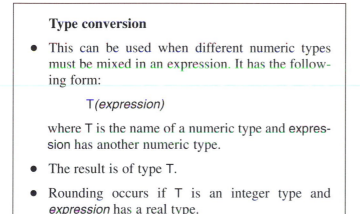

Type conversion

- This can be used when different numeric types must be mixed in an expression. It has the following form:

    T*(expression)*

    where T is the name of a numeric type and expression has another numeric type.

- The result is of type T.

- Rounding occurs if T is an integer type and *expression* has a real type.

The following program can be used for converting a weight in pounds (lb) and ounces (oz) to the equivalent in kilograms (kg) (1 lb = 0.4536 kg and there are 16 oz in 1 lb). Output from the program may look like:

```
Give weight in pounds and ounces
(integers, separated by spaces)
11 9
This is 5.245 kg.
```

The program is as follows:

```
with TEXT_IO, BASIC_NUM_IO;
use TEXT_IO, BASIC_NUM_IO;
procedure WEIGHT_CONVERSION is
```

```
OZ_PER_LB          : constant := 16.0;
KG_PER_LB          : constant := 0.4536;
NO_LBS, NO_OZ      : INTEGER;
WEIGHT             : FLOAT;      -- expressed in kg
begin
    PUT_LINE("Give weight in pounds and ounces");
    PUT_LINE("(integers, separated by spaces)");
    GET(NO_LBS);
    GET(NO_OZ);
    WEIGHT := (FLOAT(NO_LBS)+FLOAT(NO_OZ)/OZ_PER_LB)
                                    * KG_PER_LB;
    PUT("This is ");
    PUT(WEIGHT, FORE => 1, AFT => 3, EXP => 0);
    PUT_LINE(" kg.");
end WEIGHT_CONVERSION;
```

The variables NO_LBS and NO_OZ are declared as INTEGER, so that the user can enter the data in a simple way and not have to type in real numbers. The weight in kg will be a real number and therefore NO_LBS and NO_OZ must be converted to the type FLOAT in the arithmetic expression.

The result of an expression that only contains operands of the type *universal_integer* (or *universal_real*) has the type *universal_integer* (or *universal_real*), depending on the operands involved. The types *universal_integer* and *universal_real* may actually be mixed in multiplication. Also, an operand of type *universal_real* may be divided by an operand of type *universal_integer*. In both cases the result is *universal_real*. Here are a few examples:

```
1 + 2          -- has type universal_integer
1.2 + 5.3      -- has type universal_real
2 ** 8         -- has type universal_integer
2.0 ** 8       -- has type universal_real
5 ** 2.8       -- has type universal_real
4 / 9          -- has type universal_integer
3.74 / 9       -- has type universal_real
```

On an ordinary calculator there are often several mathematical functions for evaluating logarithms and trigonometric functions, for example. Which mathematical functions are accessible with Ada, and how do you use them?

In the Ada 95 standard, there is a standard package called ADA. NUMERICS.GENERIC_ELEMENTARY_FUNCTIONS, which contains various useful mathematical functions. (The package's specification is given in Appendix E.) If you are using Ada 83 it is most likely that there is a similar package, but its name has not been standardized in Ada 83.

If you need to use mathematical functions in a program you must ensure that the program has access to the mathematical package, by placing at the start of the program a **with** clause specifying the name of the package. Because it should be possible to use mathematical functions for all floating point types, the package GENERIC_ELEMENTARY_FUNCTIONS in Ada 95 is not a complete package in itself but rather a template for a package, known in Ada as a **generic** package. Therefore, you do not have a **use** clause for the package in the program, but first have to make a new 'complete' package with the help of the template, by stating what type of floating point type you want to use. This is demonstrated by the following program, which reads in the lengths of the shorter sides of a right-angled triangle and writes out the length of the hypotenuse. The floating point type FLOAT is used in the program, so a new package is created for the type FLOAT, called MATH_FUNC:

```
with TEXT_IO, BASIC_NUM_IO,
     ADA.NUMERICS.GENERIC_ELEMENTARY_FUNCTIONS;
use TEXT_IO, BASIC_NUM_IO, ADA.NUMERICS;
procedure HYPOTENUSE is
   A, B : FLOAT;
   package MATH_FUNC is new
   GENERIC_ELEMENTARY_FUNCTIONS (FLOAT);
   use MATH_FUNC;
begin
   PUT_LINE ("Enter the lengths of the shorter sides");
   GET(A);
   GET(B);
   PUT("The hypotenuse has length: ");
   PUT( SQRT(A**2 + B**2), FORE => 1, AFT => 2, EXP => 0 );
   NEW_LINE;
end HYPOTENUSE;
```

The expression:

```
SQRT(A ** 2 + B ** 2)
```

is evaluated in the program, and we make use of the mathematical function SQRT to calculate a square root. The expression in brackets is a parameter to the function: it is evaluated first, and its value is then passed to the function as input data. In Ada, a function call is considered to be an expression, and a function call therefore has a particular value and type, which is the same as saying that the function returns output data of a particular value and type. The result of the function SQRT here has type FLOAT and its value depends, of course, on the value of the parameter. If the parameter has value 25.0, for example, then the result will be 5.0. We do not need to worry about how the square root is actually calculated in SQRT: only the people who write the package GENERIC_ELEMENTARY_FUNCTIONS need be concerned about that.

Standard mathematical functions

In Ada 83, these can be found in a special package whose name is not standardized.
In Ada 95, these are found in the package ADA. NUMERICS.GENERIC_ELEMENTARY_FUNCTIONS. Use **with** and **use** clauses in the following way:

   with ADA.NUMERICS.GENERIC_ELEMENTARY_

      FUNCTIONS;

   use ADA.NUMERICS;

   procedure *program_name* **is**

     package *name* **is new**

       GENERIC_ELEMENTARY_FUNCTIONS

            (FLOAT);

     use *name*;

     ...

In the generic package GENERIC_ELEMENTARY_FUNCTIONS, as well as the square root function there are also functions for exponentials, logarithms and various trigonometric functions. The package also contains a further version of the exponentiation operator **, a version which permits the second operand to be a real number. It can also be mentioned here that in the numeric annex to Ada 95 there are packages specified which enable calculations to be made with complex numbers. For reasons of tradition, many programs involving calculations are written in FORTRAN, and for that reason there are a large number of mathematical functions already written in that language. The numeric annex to Ada 95 contains various aids to assist in making use of these FORTRAN functions in an Ada program.

3.4.2 Boolean expressions

Section 3.1.4 showed how to assign values and declare variables of the type BOOLEAN. It is also possible to build an expression whose value has the type BOOLEAN, that is, the result of the expression can have the value either TRUE or FALSE. We call such an expression a **Boolean expression**. In fact, we have already met several examples of Boolean expressions, most often in **if** statements, such as:

```
if K > 5 then
    PUT(K);
end if;
```

The expression K > 5 can be either false or true: it can have the value either FALSE or TRUE. Thus the expression has the type BOOLEAN. The operator > has been used and the integer expressions K and 5 are its operands.

In Ada there is a set of **relational operators** that can be used for making a comparison, for example in **if** statements. The two operands of a relational operator must be of the same type. For example, the expressions TEMPERA-TURE < 5 and CHAR = 78 are wrong if we assume that TEMPERATURE has type FLOAT and CHAR has type CHARACTER. The two operands may be expressions, such as:

```
5 * N > K ** 3 + N
3.45 * SIN(ALPHA) / FACTOR <= 0.35
NAME1 & NAME2 = "PeggySue"
```

Relational operators

=	-- equal to
/=	-- not equal to
<	-- less than
<=	-- less than or equal to
>	-- greater than
>=	-- greater than or equal to

Note that real numbers should be compared with caution because they are not always stored in an exact form. Expressions such as:

```
X = Y
Z = 0.87
```

are dangerous and should be avoided. The variables X and Y may be 'virtually' equal but the computer still interprets them as unequal if they are not stored in exactly the same way. Z might be 'virtually' equal to 0.87 but the two operands may still be seen as unequal by the computer. It is safer to use comparisons such as:

```
abs(X – Y) < 1.0e–9
abs(Z – 0.87) < 0.5–4
```

The small quantity that should be used on the right-hand side is a matter of judgement: it depends on the order of magnitude of the operands on the left-hand side. Comparing integers, however, is straightforward because they are always stored in an exact form.

The operators **in** and **not in** can be used to test whether a value lies in a given interval:

```
K in 1 .. N
TEMPERATURE not in MIN_TEMP .. MAX_TEMP
CHAR in 'a' .. 'z'
5 in 3 .. 5              --true!
3.75 not in 1.5 .. 3.5 --true!
'H' in 'D' .. 'J'        --true!
```

The second operand has to be an interval defined by its first and last values. The left-hand operand and the limits of the interval should be of the same type. The operators **in** and **not in** exist for all types.

A set of operators exists for which both the operands and the result are of the type BOOLEAN. These operators are:

not

and

or

xor

and then

or else

The operator **not** is the simplest. It takes only one operand and performs logical negation, that is, it changes TRUE to FALSE and vice versa.

```
not ACTIVE
not K > 74
not TRUE        -- gives the value FALSE
```

The remaining operators are called Boolean operators and all have two operands. Figure 3.7 shows how they work.

A	B	A **and** B	A **or** B	A **xor** B
TRUE	TRUE	TRUE	TRUE	FALSE
TRUE	FALSE	FALSE	TRUE	TRUE
FALSE	TRUE	FALSE	TRUE	TRUE
FALSE	FALSE	FALSE	FALSE	FALSE

Figure 3.7

The operators **and** and **or** have their natural logical meanings. The operator **xor** is generally called 'exclusive or' and is not used very often. Here are two examples:

ACTIVE **or** TEMPERATURE > 17.6

100 < K **and** K < 500

Note the way of writing the second example. To write the expression:

100 < K < 500   -- MISTAKE

is not allowed.

The operators **and then** and **or else** give exactly the same results as **and** and **or**, respectively. The difference is in the way the operands are evaluated. In expressions such as:

expression1 **and** *expression2*

expression1 **or** *expression2*

there is no way of telling whether *expression1* or *expression2* is evaluated first. Normally it makes no difference, but under certain circumstances it is essential to determine the order of evaluation. In particular, it is sometimes necessary to avoid the evaluation of *expression2; t*his is when the operators **and then** and **or else** are valuable. If we look at how the operator **and** works, we notice that it is not necessary to evaluate the second operand if the first operand is FALSE. The result of the **and** will be FALSE regardless of the value of the second operand. In the same way, it is unnecessary to evaluate the second operand of an **or** operator if the first operand is TRUE. The result will be TRUE anyway, regardless of the value of the second operand.

The operator **and then** is defined so that the left operand is evaluated first. If this is FALSE then the right operand is *not* evaluated, and the result of the **and then** operator is FALSE. If the left operand is TRUE the right operand is also evaluated. The result obtained is then the same as using the **and** operator.

For the operator **or else**, the left operator is also evaluated first. If this is TRUE the right operand is *not* evaluated and the result of the **or else** operator is TRUE. If the left operand is FALSE, the right operand is evaluated, and the same result is obtained as if the **or** operator had been used.

For example, the program fragment below determines whether a variable of type STRING(1 .. 10) contains any space characters. If it has no spaces, the message:

No spaces

is printed. Otherwise, the message:

First space is in position X

is printed, where X is in the interval 1–10. We assume that the variable K has type INTEGER. The section of program is:

```
K := 1;
while K <= 10 and then TEXT(K) /= ' ' loop
    K := K + 1;
end loop;
if K = 11 then
    PUT("No spaces");
else
    PUT("First space is in position ");
    PUT(K, WIDTH => 1);
end if;
```

In the Boolean expression:

```
K <= 10 and then TEXT(K) /= ' '
```

it is essential that the operator **and then** is used rather than **and.** If TEXT does not contain any spaces, then after 10 iterations of the loop the variable K takes the value 11. If the **and** operator had been used, there would have been an attempt to evaluate TEXT(11). This would be an illegal index because TEXT has only 10 elements, and the program would stop with an error message. Using the operator **and then** ensures that this cannot happen.

3.4.3 Operator precedence

We have now seen all the standard operators in Ada, namely: numeric operators, operators that are used in Boolean expressions, and the operator & that is used to catenate strings. Complex expressions containing several of these expressions may be constructed:

```
N – J < 100 and K ** 2 < 50 or I = 10
SIN(X) > 0.0 or abs COS(Y) + DELTA < 0.5
TEMPERATURE > 25.3 or PRESSURE > 2.6 and not ACTIVE
NAME & "Smith" & "25 Elm Terrace" & "Newtown"
        = PERSONAL_DATA
```

When complicated expressions such as these are constructed, it is important to know the order in which component expressions will be evaluated.

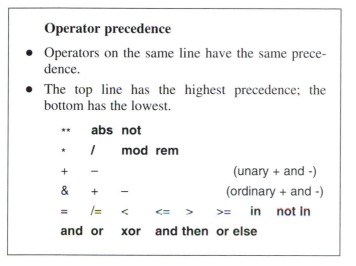

Operator precedence

- Operators on the same line have the same precedence.
- The top line has the highest precedence; the bottom has the lowest.

**	**abs**	**not**					
*	**/**	**mod**	**rem**				
+	–				(unary + and -)		
&	+	–			(ordinary + and -)		
=	/=	<	<=	>	>=	**in**	**not in**
and	**or**	**xor**	**and then**	**or else**			

Earlier we saw that operators with the highest precedence were evaluated first and those with equal precedence were evaluated from left to right. We have also seen that control over the order of evaluation in a complicated expression can be achieved by using brackets. For example, the Boolean operators **and** and **or** have the same precedence, and it may sometimes be necessary to use brackets to evaluate an expression in the correct order, such as:

not (A **and** (B **or** C))

3.5   Variables and constants

In Ada, variables and constants are called **objects.** Objects have a name and a value. In the case of variables, we illustrated this with our storage boxes, or stores. Before a variable or constant can be used in a program it must be declared.

Objects

- Variables and constants.
- Have a name and value.
- Must be declared.

In our programs we have already seen several examples of how variables and constants are declared. We have seen how such declarations are made in the declaration section of a procedure; as we shall see later, they can also be made in a similar way in functions and packages that we write ourselves. The simplest form of variable declaration is:

```
NUMBER_OF_ITEMS      : INTEGER;
TEMPERATURE          : FLOAT;
WEIGHT_PER_PERSON  : SHORT_FLOAT;
ADDRESS              : STRING(1 .. 30);
ACTIVE               : BOOLEAN;
SYMBOL               : CHARACTER;
```

First the variable's name is stated and then its type.† If there are several variables of the same type they can be declared in a shortened form:

```
MEAN_TEMP, MAX_TEMP, MIN_TEMP : FLOAT;
```

This is equivalent to:

```
MEAN_TEMP   : FLOAT;
MAX_TEMP    : FLOAT;
MIN_TEMP    : FLOAT;
```

Variable declarations

> *variable_name* : *type*;

or:

> *variable_name1, variable_name2, ... : type*;

(all the variables listed are given the same type).

---

† If we are to be absolutely strict, it is not the variable's type that is given but rather its **subtype**. In Ada 95 all types are actually unnamed, only subtypes have names. INTEGER, for example, is a subtype of a predefined anonymous integer type and INTEGER has exactly the same characteristics as this anonymous type. The split into types and subtypes is done so that the language's syntax can be described in a correct way. In everyday usage this split can be ignored without risk of ambiguity, and one says quite simply that a variable has a particular type. To avoid unnecessary complication, we will also use this simplified terminology.

What value does a variable have when it is declared like this? Normally, a variable's value is undefined. Certain compilers set numerical variables to zero, but this cannot be relied on absolutely. In most cases the value of a variable is undefined until it is given a value in the program. In Ada it is possible to initialize variables, giving them a starting value at the same time as they are declared:

```
BALANCE  : FLOAT := 0.0;
SYMB     : CHARACTER := '%';
NAME     : STRING(1..5) := "David";
PRESSURE : FLOAT := 1.5;
K, N, M  : INTEGER := 0;
```

The last of these declarations is equivalent to:

```
K : INTEGER := 0;
N : INTEGER := 0;
M : INTEGER := 0;
```

The initial value can be a complicated expression but it must be of the same type as the variable being initialized:

```
VOLUME     : FLOAT := 37.9;
COEFF      : FLOAT := SQRT(LOG(VOLUME));
MIN_TEMP   : FLOAT := 10.0;
MAX_TEMP   : FLOAT := 100.0;
MEAN_TEMP  : FLOAT := (MIN_TEMP + MAX_TEMP) / 2.0;
```

Note that the order of declarations is important. In the above example, the variable VOLUME had to be declared before it could appear on the second line.

Initializing variables

> variable_name : type := expression;

or:

> variable_name1, variable_name2, ... : type :=
> expression;

(all the variables listed are given the same initial value).

▼

In Ada 83, index limits must always be stated when a variable of type STRING is being declared. In Ada 95 this is not necessary if the variable is initialized, for example:

▲

NAME : STRING := "David";

The compiler will allow the variable to be just long enough for the initializing value to be held.

Constants can also be declared. As with variables, constants can be regarded as storage boxes of a certain type that contain a certain value. The difference is that the value received by the constant at the time of declaration cannot be changed later in the program. Constant declarations look like variable declarations, but the word **constant** is added. In the declaration, the constant must be given a value.

```
END_CHAR    : constant CHARACTER := '*';
MAX_NO      : constant INTEGER := 500;
START_TEMP  : constant FLOAT := MIN_TEMP – 5.0;
```

For constants of type STRING, no index limits need be given in the declaration:

HEADING : **constant** STRING := "Report for first quarter";

In addition to the sorts of constants discussed so far, there is a special form of constant declaration in Ada called a **number declaration**. A number declaration looks much like an ordinary constant declaration, but no type is stated:

```
PI        : constant := 3.1415926536;
TWO_PI  : constant := 2 * PI;
MIN       : constant := 5;
TWO_16  : constant :=2 ** 16;
```

Number declarations can only be made for numeric values. A constant takes one of the types *universal_integer* or *universal_real*, depending on the initialization. The initializing value must be of one of these types, that is, it can only be an expression containing numeric literals and other constants that have been declared in number declarations. It can be an advantage to use this type of constant instead of an ordinary constant when the object to be declared is a mathematical constant that should be usable in association with several numeric types.

> **Constant declarations**
>
> > *constant_name* : **constant** *type* := *expression;*
>
> or:
>
> > *constant_name* : **constant** := *numeric*
> > > *expression;*
>
> (in the second case, the constant takes the type *universal_integer* or *universal_real*).

3.6   Errors in programs

Writing a computer program is not a trivial task and it is normal to make a number of mistakes. Even an experienced programmer falls into traps of various kinds. It is therefore important when learning to program that we also learn how to find and correct errors in the program. This can only be done by designing and writing programs, running tests and correcting any errors found, which is why practical work is necessary.

When writing a computer program, three kinds of error can occur:

(1) **Compile-time error**   This is an error indicating that the rules of the language have not been followed. This type of error is detected by the compiler during compilation of the program. A printed listing of the program is usually provided in which the mistake is marked. Examples of compile-time errors are misspelling a variable name, forgetting an **end**, losing a semicolon, or pressing a wrong key when typing the program.

(2) **Run-time error**   Such errors do not occur until the program is run. The program may be syntactically correct – the language rules have been obeyed – but it still contains mistakes that prevent it from continuing normally when executed. Examples of such mistakes are trying to index outside the limits in a STRING variable, and attempting to enter a value of the wrong type from the terminal. A common error is 'overflow', when a value is calculated that is too large for the intended variable. This can happen, for example, if an attempt is made to divide by 0 or some other extremely small number. Normally the program halts when an error occurs and an error message is given. Errors can be trapped by the programmer, however, and as we shall see in Chapter 10, this facility allows the program to continue in execution.

(3) **Errors of logic**   Such errors are caused simply by faulty thinking when the program was written: a faulty algorithm has been used. It is difficult to find this kind of error because it is possible to compile and run the program without getting any error messages. An error in the logic of a

program only shows when a test is run and the result obtained. If there is no verified data available for testing the program, it can be hard to be quite certain that the program is free from logic errors. Even if the program works correctly for a particular set of input data, it can be faulty for another set.

Different kinds of error

- *Compile-time error*
  Rules of the language have been broken. Detected during compilation.
- *Run-time error*
  Illegal values occur when the program is run, for example, incorrect indexing. Detected during execution.
- *Errors of logic*
  Algorithm is incorrect. The program works out wrong values. Detected (hopefully) during test runs.

We shall demonstrate the different types of error by looking at an example. The program that will be written is to evaluate N!, that is, the product:

$$1 * 2 * 3 * 4 * \ldots * N$$

We start by writing the program with the help of the text editor:

```
with TEXT_IO, BASIC_NUM_IO;
use TEXT_IO, BASIC_NUM_IO;
procedure FACTORIAL is
    PRODUCT : INTEGER := 0;
    N_VALUE  : INTEGER;
begin
    PUT("Enter value of N: ");
    GET(N_VALU);
    for I in 1 .. N_VALUE loop
        PRODUCT := PRODUCT * I;
    end loop;
    PUT("Result is: "); PUT_LINE(PRODUCT);
end FACTORIAL;
```

The next step is to try to compile the program using the Ada compiler. We then get the listing:

```
with TEXT_IO, BASIC_NUM_IO;
use TEXT_IO, BASIC_NUM_IO;
procedure FACTORIAL is
    PRODUCT : INTEGER := 0;
    N_VALUE  : INTEGER;
begin
    PUT("Enter value of N: ");
    GET(N_VALU);
  _____^
-- error: identifier undefined
    for I in 1 .. N_VALUE loop
  _____^
-- warning: high bound may not yet have a value
        PRODUCT := PRODUCT * I;
    end loop;
    PUT("Result is: "); PUT_LINE(PRODUCT);
  _____^
-- error: types of formal and actual parameter do not match
    end FACTORIAL;
```

Here we see that the compiler has marked certain lines in the program and written error messages. For each error, the compiler tries to point out the line where the error occurs. The first faulty line is:

```
GET(N_VALU);
```

The message from the compiler points to the identifier N_VALU and says that this identifier is undefined. We see that we have left off the last letter of the identifier – it should be N_VALUE.

The next line marked is:

```
for I in 1 .. N_VALUE loop
```

The compiler has not found any real error here, but just a line that may be incorrect; it gives us a warning that we should watch out for this line. What may lead to problems is that the upper limit in the expression:

```
1 .. N_VALUE
```

in other words N_VALUE, might not be given a value when the program is run later on. This would mean a run-time error. The reason for this potential error is that earlier in the program we wrote:

```
GET(N_VALU);
```

If this had been correct, the variable N_VALUE would always be given a value and we would not have had a warning from the compiler. Therefore we do not need to change the line:

for I **in** 1 .. N_VALUE **loop**

It is correct and the warning is only the result of our earlier error.

The final line to be marked faulty is:

```
PUT("Result is: "); PUT_LINE(PRODUCT);
```

Here the compiler is complaining that the parameter to the procedure PUT_LINE does not have the type that it should have formally. The variable PRODUCT has type INTEGER. If we look at the package TEXT_IO we see that the procedure PUT_LINE is only specified in one place in the package and that it requires a parameter of type STRING. We have mistakenly assumed that the procedure PUT_LINE, just like PUT, also exists for the type INTEGER. The solution is to use PUT and NEW_LINE instead:

```
PUT("Result is: "); PUT(PRODUCT); NEW_LINE;
```

Now we use the text editor again to correct the mistakes in the program, and we get:

```
with TEXT_IO, BASIC_NUM_IO;
use TEXT_IO, BASIC_NUM_IO;
procedure FACTORIAL is
    PRODUCT : INTEGER := 0;
    N_VALUE  : INTEGER;
begin
    PUT("Enter value of N: ");
    GET(N_VALUE);
    for I in 1 .. N_VALUE loop
        PRODUCT := PRODUCT * I;
    end loop;
    PUT("Result is: "); PUT(PRODUCT); NEW_LINE;
end FACTORIAL;
```

This program compiles well; no error messages this time. We shall go on to run some tests on it. The program prints the message:

```
Enter value of N:
```

We shall try to calculate 4!, which we know should be 24; therefore we type a 4 at the terminal. The program answers, to our surprise:

Result is: 0

We run another test, this time giving another value of N as input. Whatever value of N we give, we find that we always get the answer 0. Of course, this is wrong. There is an error of logic in the program.

Now we must look carefully at the program to find out where the fault lies. In the program we have a counter I which counts from 1 to the value of N, and at each count PRODUCT is multiplied by I. At the first count we multiply by 1, at the second by 2, and so on. This seems right, but what was the value of PRODUCT at the start? The declaration shows that at the start PRODUCT had the value 0. That is the mistake! When any number is multiplied by 0 the result is 0. Of course, the variable PRODUCT should be initialized to 1. The text editor enables us to correct this so that PRODUCT is initialized properly:

PRODUCT: INTEGER := 1;

We compile the program again. (This must be done; it is not enough to make corrections only in the text.) A fresh test run shows that we now get the result 24 if we enter the number 4. The program appears to be working correctly. If, for example, we enter 12, we get the result 479001600. We can try with 13, but then we get the following strange output:

Enter value of N: 13
** EXCEPTION "numeric_error" RAISED, line 10.

We have got an execution error. A numeric error has occurred on line 10. On this line we have the statement:

PRODUCT := PRODUCT * I;

The result of the expression on the right-hand side has become so great that it is bigger than the greatest whole number that can be stored in a variable of type INTEGER in our system. The program cannot continue in the normal way and so it stops running.

If we want our program to calculate N! for values of N greater than 12 we must change the program. The best way is to change PRODUCT to a variable of type FLOAT. Such a variable can hold considerably larger numbers than an integer variable. We now use the text editor to make the necessary changes:

```
with TEXT_IO, BASIC_NUM_IO;
use TEXT_IO, BASIC_NUM_IO;
procedure FACTORIAL is
    PRODUCT : FLOAT := 1.0;
    N_VALUE  : INTEGER;
begin
    PUT("Enter value of N: ");
    GET(N_VALUE);
    for I in 1 .. N_VALUE loop
        PRODUCT := PRODUCT * FLOAT(I);
    end loop;
    PUT("Result is: "); PUT(PRODUCT); NEW_LINE;
end FACTORIAL;
```

In addition to changing the declaration of PRODUCT we must also make a change so that I is converted to a floating number on each multiplication:

```
PRODUCT := PRODUCT * FLOAT(I);
```

We may not mix INTEGER and FLOAT in a multiplication. After a further compilation we can run a test of the corrected program. If we now try to calculate 13! we get:

```
Enter value of N: 13
Result is: 6.22702080E+09
```

Looking for errors in a program and correcting them has come to be known, lightheartedly, as 'debugging' the program. In some systems there are excellent aids for debugging. For example, it may be possible to test run a program step by step, or stop at particular points in the program, study the values of the various variables and change them. Such debugging aids are very valuable when errors have to be found in more complicated programs.

If there is no access to such debugging aids, the values of the variables can still be studied at given points in the program by inserting temporary test printouts, and using them to find possible errors.

In general, if a program is well-written from the start, is well-structured and has suitable names for variables, types, subprograms and packages, and if it uses clear and well-thought-out algorithms, it will contain fewer errors and be easier to debug than a less well-written program. Well-written programs, therefore, are also more reliable and require less maintenance than programs that are poorly conceived from the start. Therefore, with program design, the rule is to think first and write later.

Testing programs

- Use debuggers or insert temporary test printing routines in the program.
- Well-written and well-structured programs are easier to rid of errors.

EXERCISES

3.1 Which of the following are allowed as identifiers in Ada? Which are allowed as the names of variables, types and constants?

MY_CAR	CAR_3	"Tommy"
NUMBER1	number1	ADAM&EVE
IN	%VAT	Number_5
3_DIGIT	car-number	identifier

3.2 State for each of the following whether it is an integer literal, a real literal, a text string literal, a character literal or a literal of type BOOLEAN.

167	167.0	'x'
"true"	16.4e3	16e5
7	'7'	"7"
false	1_000	0.000_005

What type do the integer and real literals really have?

3.3 Assume the following declarations have been made:

```
I : INTEGER := 2;
J : INTEGER := 3;
X : FLOAT := 4.0;
Y : FLOAT := 5.0;
```

Evaluate the following expressions and state the type for each value.

(a)	I + J	(b)	I + 5	(c)	2 + 3
(d)	X − 1.5	(e)	2.0 * 2.5	(f)	Y / X
(g)	J / I	(h)	14 **rem** 4	(i)	J **mod** I
(j)	X ** I	(k)	Y ** (−1)	(l)	I ** J
(m)	I + J * 2	(n)	X * Y ** 2	(o)	**abs** X−Y
(p)	X / Y * 2.0	(q)	2.0 * FLOAT(J)		

3.4 Make a suitable variable declaration to describe the following:
- the number of goals scored in a football match
- winning time in the 110 m hurdles
- an identity number
- a shoe size
- the size of fine for a parking offence
- the information relating to whether a person has a driving licence
- an address
- a type of vitamin (A, B, C, D or E)

3.5 Write a program to calculate the volume and area of a sphere. The radius of the sphere is to be given as input. The following formulae are given:

$$V = \frac{4\pi r^3}{3} \qquad A = 4\pi r^2$$

3.6 In Europe, a car's fuel consumption is usually given in litres per kilometre. Write a program to read in petrol consumption in this format and translate it into the form more common in Britain, miles per gallon. The following conversion factors apply:

$$1 \text{ mile} = 1.609 \text{ km} \qquad 1 \text{ gallon} = 3.785 \text{ litres}$$

3.7 A car-hire firm takes £30 per day plus a fee of £0.55 per mile for a particular car. In addition there is the cost of the fuel. Assume the car does, on average, 26 miles per gallon and that the price of fuel is £1.75 per gallon.

Write a program to calculate the total cost of hiring the car. The input should be the distance driven and the number of days' hire.

3.8 A running competition consists of two separate races. The winner of the competition is the one with the shortest total time for the two races. Write a program to calculate the total time for a competitor. The input should be the times for the two separate races. These times are given in hours, minutes and seconds in the format hh mm ss and the result is given in the same format.

3.9 Write a program to calculate how much change should be received after making a purchase, and in which notes and coins the change should be given. Input to the program should be the price to be paid and the amount given in payment. For the sake of simplicity, assume that no transactions involve coins smaller than 10p or notes greater than £20. For example, if a person bought goods for £62.10 and paid with four £20 notes, the program should print out that the change should be one £10 note, one £5 note, two £1 coins, one 50p coin, and four 10p coins.

3.10 The distance between two points (x_1, y_1) and (x_2, y_2) in a coordinate system is given by the formula:

$$s = \sqrt{(x_1 - x_2)^2 + (y_1 - y_2)^2}$$

Write a program to read in the coordinates of two points and write out the distance between them.

3.11 For radioactive decomposition, the amount of radioactive material, n, remaining after a certain time, t, can be calculated using the formula:

$$n = n_0 \, e^{-\lambda t}$$

where n_0 is the amount of radioactive material at time $t = 0$. λ is a constant for the material. This is usually given as a half-life (the time taken for half the radioactive material to decompose). If the half-life is denoted by T, it is easy to calculate that:

$$\lambda = \frac{0.693}{T}$$

The half-life for the isotope ^{14}C is 5730 years. Write a program to print out what percentage of this isotope is left after S years. S is the input to the program.

3.12 Write a program which reads in an angle (given in degrees) and prints out the values of its sine and cosine. The functions SIN and COS in the generic package ADA.NUMERICS.GENERIC_ELEMENTARY_FUNCTIONS expect a parameter expressed in radians. The conversion between degrees and radians uses the formula:

$$radians = degrees * \frac{2\pi}{360}$$

3.13 Evaluate the following Boolean expressions:

(a) TRUE **and** 10 > 8
(b) 5.0 >= 10.3 **or** 'a' > 'b'
(c) 3 **not in** 1 .. 7
(d) I /= 0 **and then** 14 / I > 3   -- assume I = 3
(e) 3 > 3 **or else** "hello" /= "HELLO"

3.14 Evaluate the following expressions:

(a) CHARACTER'POS('~')
(b) CHARACTER'VAL(32)

3.15 Assume the CHARACTER variable C contains one of the lower-case letters 'a' to 'z'. Write a statement that changes C to hold the corresponding upper-case letter instead.

3.16 Assume the CHARACTER variable T has a value in the interval '0' to '9'. Write a statement to convert T's value to an integer in the interval 0 to 9 and assign the integer to the variable I of type INTEGER.

3.17 In Sweden, every resident has a personal identification number made up of a six-figure date of birth followed by a four-figure code. The last but one figure is odd for a male and even for a female.

Write a program to read in a Swedish identification number and determine if the person concerned is male or female.

4 Control Statements

Chapter 3 dealt with the basic building blocks of Ada. It showed how to use the standard types in expressions and in declarations of data objects. This chapter concentrates on the part of an Ada program that describes what the program does, in other words, the part of the program that describes algorithms.

The chapter deals with the most common statements that can be used to control the behaviour of a program. It shows how to put statements together into a program sequence and how alternative paths through a program can be achieved in various ways. Programming iterative sequences, that is, making certain parts of a program execute repeatedly, is also covered.

In an interactive program – a program that, while running, communicates with a user via a terminal – the user often wants to feed data to the program in stages and decide how long the program should run. Iteration is used in this kind of program; Section 4.8 deals with iteration in the context of interactive programs.

4.1   Sequential program structure

In simple terms, an Ada program or subprogram consists of a specification part, a declarative part and a statement part.

Program and subprogram structure

subprogram_specification **is**
   declarative part
begin
   statement1;
   statement2;

     ⋮

   statementN;
end subprogram_name;

The specification of a subprogram contains its name and a description of possible parameters to the subprogram. We shall come back to this in Chapter 6. In the declarative part, variables, constants and other parameters can be declared. It is possible also to make other declarations, for example, declarations of internal subprograms, as seen in one of the example programs in Chapter 2. In Chapter 5 we shall see that programmers can also declare their own types in the declarative part of the program.

Here we shall concentrate on the part of the program between **begin** and **end**. This part of the program should contain a sequence of one or more **statements**. When the program is executed, these statements are executed one at a time, from top to bottom. Each statement is executed once.

Every statement ends with a semicolon. The rules of the language do not specify that statements should be written on special lines or that they should start in particular positions on the line. To write well-structured programs, however, it is important to apply certain rules. Each statement should start on a fresh line. (Exceptions can be made if a number of statements together produce output at a terminal; in this case these statements can be written on the same line.) The statements should be indented on the line; statements which belong to the same sequence (such as statement1, statement2, ... , statementN above) should be indented by the same amount.

There are two kinds of statement, **simple statements** and **compound statements**. The most common simple statements are **assignment statements** and **procedure calls**; we have already seen examples of these. Here is another example showing a sequence of simple statements. The sequence reads in two real numbers and calculates their mean.

```
PUT_LINE("Enter two real numbers");
GET(X1);
GET(X2);
MEAN_VALUE := (X1 + X2) / 2.0;
PUT("The mean is: ");
PUT(MEAN_VALUE);
```

The statement:

```
MEAN_VALUE := (X1 + X2) / 2.0;
```

is an assignment statement and the others are procedure calls. Procedure calls will be discussed more fully in Chapter 6.

There is a very simple statement which is written as follows:

```
null;
```

This is called a **null** statement. When this statement is executed nothing at all happens. This statement exists because the syntax sometimes demands that a statement should be found at a particular place in a program. If there is nothing to do at this place, a **null** statement can be used.

The most common compound statements are **if** and **loop** statements. A compound statement can contain several statements. Using these, statements can be structured hierarchically.

4.2 Assignment statements

An assignment statement consists of two parts. On the left-hand side (the term on the left of the assignment symbol, :=) there can be the name of a variable, while to the right there should be an expression. The expression and the variable must be of the same type. When an assignment statement is executed the expression on the right is evaluated and that value is given to the variable on the left, replacing its previous value. There may be only *one* variable on the left-hand side. If the same value is to be given to several variables, several assignment statements must be written. Here are a few examples:

```
K := I + 15;
X1 := 23.8;
ALARM := TEMP > 200.0; -- ALARM has type BOOLEAN
HEAD := "INVOICE";      -- HEAD has type STRING(1 .. 7)
```

If the variable is of type STRING, as in the last example, both sides must have the same number of components. However, the components do not need to be numbered in the same way. A slice may also appear in the left-hand side. In the following examples, we start by assuming that S has type STRING(1 .. 15) and that T has type STRING(26 .. 40);

```
S := T;                        -- same number of components
S(7 .. 11) := "HELLO";
T(31 .. 33) := S(4 .. 6);
```

The left- and right-hand sides may even overlap, as shown in the following example:

```
S(1 .. 3) := "Ada";
S(3 .. 5) := S(1 .. 3);        -- S(1 .. 5) becomes "AdAda"
```

4.3   Selection: the *if* statement

The most common way of achieving selection in a program, that is, a choice between two or more different paths in a program, is to use an **if** statement. An **if** statement starts with the reserved word **if** and terminates with the reserved words **end if**. An **if** statement comprises a **then** part followed by a number (possibly zero) of **elsif** parts, ending possibly with an **else** part.

The if statement, the simplest form

if *Boolean expression* **then**
    sequence_of_statements
end if;

The sequences of statements within the **then**, **elsif** and **else** parts of an **if** statement should be inset a little on the line, to show clearly where the **if** statement begins and ends, and which parts belong to it.

When the statement is executed, the Boolean expressions that follow the words **if** and **elsif** are evaluated in order from the top down. If any of these Boolean expressions are true, the sequence of statements in the corresponding part of the **if** statement is executed, and control then passes to the first statement after the words **end if**.

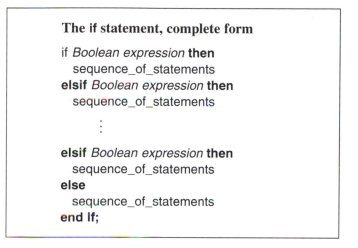

The Boolean expressions following the first true expression will not be evaluated. If all the Boolean expressions are false, but there is an **else** part, then the sequence of statements contained therein will be executed. If all the Boolean expressions are false and there is no **else** part, then the **if** statement terminates without any of the sequences of statements being executed. Observe that, at most, *one* sequence in an **if** statement is executed. Some examples of **if** statements are:

```
if K > 5 or J < 4 then
    K := K + J;
    J := J + 1;
end if;

-- ACTIVE, CLOSED, and PASSIVE have type BOOLEAN
if ACTIVE and not CLOSED then
    PUT_LINE("System is in operation");
else
    PUT_LINE("System is down");
    PASSIVE := TRUE;
end if;

if TEMPERATURE < 15.0 then
    PUT_LINE("Emergency!");
    RAD_SET := RAD_SET + 5.0;
elsif TEMPERATURE < 18.0 then
    PUT_LINE("Too cold.");
    RAD_SET := RAD_SET + 1.0;
elsif TEMPERATURE < 21.0 then
    PUT_LINE("OK.");
```

```
    else
        PUT_LINE("Too hot.");
        RAD_SET := RAD_SET - 1.0;
    end if;
```

Any statements are allowed in a sequence of statements, even compound statements as in:

```
if TEMPERATURE < 15.0 then
    PUT_LINE("Emergency!");
    RAD_SET := RAD_SET + 5.0;
elsif TEMPERATURE < 18.0 then
    if NIGHT then
        PUT_LINE("OK.");
    else
        PUT_LINE("Too cold.");
        RAD_SET := RAD_SET + 1.0;
    end if;
end if;
```

Here, the **elsif** part consists of a single statement – a new **if** statement. When one **if** statement is contained within another, they are usually said to be nested. Note that it is particularly important to indent the text clearly in the case of nested statements. It is essential to see the structure underlying the statements.

We can now look at a couple of variants of a program that reads in three (different) integers from the terminal and writes them out in order of increasing size. The first version is:

```
with TEXT_IO, BASIC_NUM_IO;
use TEXT_IO, BASIC_NUM_IO;
procedure SORT_3 is
    A, B, C : INTEGER;
begin
    PUT_LINE("Enter three different integers");
    GET(A); GET(B); GET(C);
    if A < B then
        if B < C then
            PUT(A); PUT(B); PUT(C);
        elsif A < C then
            PUT(A); PUT(C); PUT(B);
        else
            PUT(C); PUT(A); PUT(B);
        end if;
    else
        if A < C then
```

```
      PUT(B); PUT(A); PUT(C);
   elsif B < C then
      PUT(B); PUT(C); PUT(A);
   else
   end if;
end SORT_3;
```

In this version of the program there are two levels of **if** statement. We obtain a somewhat simpler program structure if we employ more complex Boolean expressions.

```
with TEXT_IO, BASIC_NUM_IO;
use TEXT_IO, BASIC_NUM_IO;
procedure SORT_3 is
   A, B, C : INTEGER;
begin
   PUT_LINE("Enter three different integers");
   GET(A); GET(B); GET(C);
   if A < B and B < C then
      PUT(A); PUT(B); PUT(C);
   elsif A < C and C < B then
      PUT(A); PUT(C); PUT(B);
   elsif C < A and A < B then
      PUT(C); PUT(A); PUT(B);
   elsif B < A and A < C then
      PUT(B); PUT(A); PUT(C);
   elsif B < C and C < A then
      PUT(B); PUT(C); PUT(A);
   else
      PUT(C); PUT(B); PUT(A);
   end if;
end SORT_3;
```

4.4   Selection: the *case* statement

We have seen how the **if** statement can be used to make a selection. In Ada there is also a **case** statement that can be used if a choice has to be made between several different paths in a program. If there are several alternatives, a **case** statement is often preferable to an **if** statement because it gives a clearer program.

A **case** statement starts with the reserved word **case** and ends with the reserved words **end case**. After the word **case** appears an expression whose value determines the choice of one of several alternatives.

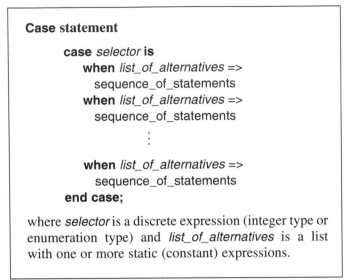

Case statement

    case *selector* **is**
        when *list_of_alternatives* =>
          sequence_of_statements
        when *list_of_alternatives* =>
          sequence_of_statements

              ⋮

        when *list_of_alternatives* =>
          sequence_of_statements
    end case;

where *selector* is a discrete expression (integer type or enumeration type) and *list_of_alternatives* is a list with one or more static (constant) expressions.

The selector should be a **discrete expression**. In Ada, the notion **discrete type** covers integer types and enumeration types. A discrete expression is an expression whose value is of a discrete type, that is, the expression is either an integer type (for example, INTEGER) or some enumeration type (for example, CHARACTER). Examples of discrete expressions are:

    NUMBER_OF_ITEMS   N + 8   I ** 3   CHAR

Note that the selector may not be a real type.

A list of alternatives following the word **when** in a **case** statement is a list of one or several possible discrete values that the selector can assume. (Since the selector is a discrete expression, it is possible to name all possible values.) When the **case** statement is executed, the selector is evaluated. If the value found appears among the values enumerated in a particular list of alternatives, then the sequence of statements following the list is executed. Note that only *one* sequence of statements is executed.

In the following example the simplest form of list of alternatives is used, that has only one possible value. The variable MONTH_NUMBER is assumed to have the type INTEGER.

```
case MONTH_NUMBER is
   when 1 =>
      PUT("January");
   when 2 =>
      PUT("February");
   when 3 =>
```

```
      PUT("March");
   when 4 =>
      PUT("April");
   when 5 =>
      PUT("May");
   when 6 =>
      PUT("June");
   when 7 =>
      PUT("July");
   when 8 =>
      PUT("August");
   when 9 =>
      PUT("September");
   when 10 =>
      PUT("October");
   when 11 =>
      PUT("November");
   when 12 =>
      PUT("December");
   when others =>
      PUT("Error in month number");
end case;
```

This **case** statement writes out the name of a month. The particular name written depends on the value of a variable, MONTH_NUMBER. If it has value 1, 'January' is written, if 2 then 'February' is written, and so on. If MONTH_NUMBER has a value that lies outside the interval 1–12, then the message 'Error in month number' is written.

The values in a list of alternatives must be **static expressions** – expressions made only of constant parts. Often the values in a list of alternatives are simply constant values (literals), as in this example.

If any possible values are omitted from the lists of alternatives, there must be a special **others** alternative. (In our example, INTEGER can take values other than 1–12, of course.) The **others** alternative must come last in the **case** statement, so that when the **case** statement is executed, the **others** alternative is reached only if the selector has a value other than those already enumerated in the earlier alternatives.

The example is now changed a little to show how it appears when several possible alternatives are enumerated in one list of alternatives:

```
case MONTH_NUMBER is
   when 1 | 2 | 12 =>
      PUT("Winter");
   when 3 | 4 | 5 =>
      PUT("Spring");
```

```
      when 6 | 7 | 8 =>
        PUT("Summer");
      when 9 | 10 | 11 =>
        PUT("Autumn");
      when others =>
        PUT("Error in month number");
    end case;
```

This **case** statement writes the season of the year according to the value of the variable MONTH_NUMBER. If MONTH_NUMBER has one of the values 1, 2 or 12, the text 'Winter' is written; if it has one of the values 3, 4 or 5, 'Spring' is written; if it is 6, 7 or 8, 'Summer' is written; and if MONTH_NUMBER is 9, 10 or 11, then 'Autumn' is written. As before, the **others** alternative has to appear, to trap illegal month numbers. The different alternatives in the list of alternatives are enumerated with a vertical line (|) or an exclamation mark (!) between them. To avoid enumerating all alternatives in a list, the interval containing them may be stated. We can rewrite our last example to take advantage of this option:

```
case MONTH_NUMBER is
    when 1 .. 2 | 12 =>
      PUT("Winter");
    when 3 .. 5 =>
      PUT("Spring");
    when 6 .. 8 =>
      PUT("Summer");
    when 9 .. 11 =>
      PUT("Autumn");
    when others =>
      PUT("Error in month number");
end case;
```

Alternative list in a case statement

- Examples of different forms:

  ```
  when 5 =>
  when 5 | 8 | 23 =>
  when 100 .. 125 =>
  when 50 | 60 | 70 .. 75 | 80 .. 85 =>
  when others =>
  ```

- Reference must be made to all possible values.
- If there is an **others** alternative, it must come last.

The selector can also be an expression of an enumeration type. The following example is a section of program designed to read in a character C of type CHARACTER from the terminal and determine whether it is a letter, a figure or some other symbol. We assume that we have already declared three integer variables, LETTER_COUNT, FIGURE_COUNT and OTHERS_COUNT. If the character is a letter, the variable LETTER_COUNT is increased by one and the text 'Letter' is displayed at the terminal; similar actions are taken if the character is a figure or one of the remaining symbols.

```
GET(C);
case C is
    when 'a' .. 'z' | 'A' .. 'Z' =>
        LETTER_COUNT := LETTER_COUNT + 1;
        PUT_LINE("Letter");
    when '0' .. '9' =>
        FIGURE_COUNT := FIGURE_COUNT + 1;
        PUT_LINE("Figure");
    when others =>
        OTHERS_COUNT := OTHERS_COUNT + 1;
        PUT_LINE("Other");
end case;
```

We shall show one further example of the use of a **case** statement, in a program that simulates a simple calculator. When the program is run it expects the user to type at the terminal a simple arithmetic expression, such as:

```
63*35
```

The program calculates the value of the expression and displays it at the terminal. To simplify matters, we shall allow the user to write the expression only in the form:

```
NoM
```

where the operands N and M are whole numbers and o is one of the operators +, −, * or /. We shall not allow spaces between the operands and the operator. Here is the program:

```
with TEXT_IO, BASIC_NUM_IO;
use TEXT_IO, BASIC_NUM_IO;
procedure CALCULATOR is
    OPERAND_1, OPERAND_2 : INTEGER;
    OPERATOR : CHARACTER;
begin
    PUT_LINE("Write a simple arithmetic expression");
```

```
                GET(OPERAND_1);
                GET(OPERATOR);
                GET(OPERAND_2);
                case OPERATOR is
                  when '+' =>
                     PUT(OPERAND_1 + OPERAND_2, WIDTH => 1);
                  when '-' =>
                     PUT(OPERAND_1 - OPERAND_2, WIDTH => 1);
                  when '*' =>
                     PUT(OPERAND_1 * OPERAND_2, WIDTH => 1);
                  when '/' =>
                     if OPERAND_2 /= 0 then
                        PUT(OPERAND_1 / OPERAND_2, WIDTH => 1);
                     else
                        PUT("Division by zero not allowed");
                     end if;
                  when others =>
                     PUT("Faulty operator");
                end case;
              end CALCULATOR;
```

In the program, checks are made for division by zero and attempts to use an undefined operator. An appropriate error message is sent to the user in either case. The following display shows the output from four separate runs of the program:

```
Write a simple arithmetic expression
63*35
2205

Write a simple arithmetic expression
17/6
2

Write a simple arithmetic expression
17/0
Division by zero not allowed

Write a simple arithmetic expression
3%67
Faulty operator
```

4.5 Iteration: the *loop* statement

To perform iteration in Ada, that is, to execute one or several statements a number of times, a **loop** statement is used. There are three variants of this:

(1)　a simple **loop** statement for writing part of a program that is to be executed an infinite number of times;

(2)　a **loop** statement with **for** for writing part of a program that is to be executed a fixed number of times;

(3)　a **loop** statement with **while** for writing part of a program that is to be executed until a certain condition is met.

4.5.1　Simple *loop* statement

We shall start with the simple **loop** statement.

Simple loop statement

loop
    sequence_of_statements
end loop;

Between the reserved words **loop** and **end loop** there is a sequence of statements that is executed endlessly, repeated time after time. (The **loop** statement can be stopped using the operating system to stop it 'by force'. This can usually be done by pressing a **break** key or a **delete** key at the terminal.) For example:

```
loop
    PUT_LINE("HELP! I can't stop");
end loop;
```

Figure 4.1 shows the output from the **loop** statement. The program has to be stopped 'by force'.

In the next program, the intention is really that the program should run without interruption. It is part of a simple supervision program ensuring that a temperature is kept within certain permitted values. We assume that TAKE_TEMPERATURE, INCREASE_TEMPERATURE and DECREASE_TEMPERATURE are procedures that we have already written and that MIN_TEMPERATURE and MAX_TEMPERATURE are two constants.

```
loop
    TAKE_TEMPERATURE(TEMPERATURE);
    if TEMPERATURE < MIN_TEMPERATURE then
      INCREASE_TEMPERATURE;
    elsif TEMPERATURE > MAX_TEMPERATURE then
      DECREASE_TEMPERATURE;
    end if;
end loop;
```

HELP! I can't stop
HELP! I can't stop
HELP! I can't stop
HELP! I can't stop
HELP! I can't stop
HELP! I can't stop
HELP! I can't stop
HELP! I can't stop
HELP! I can't stop
HELP! I can't stop
HELP! I can't stop
.
.
.
etc.

Figure 4.1

4.5.2 The *loop* statement with *for*

Here is an example of the second variant of the **loop** statement, where the repetition occurs a specified number of times. The statements in the example write out the 12 times table, from 1×12 to 12×12.

```
for I in 1 .. 12 loop
    PUT(I * 12); NEW_LINE;
end loop;
```

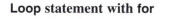

Loop statement with for

```
for loop_parameter in start_value .. end_value loop
sequence_of_statements
end loop;
```

- *start_value* and *end_value* should be discrete expressions (integer type or enumeration type).

- *loop_parameter* is an identifier that is declared automatically (treated as a constant in the sequence of statements). Its type depends on *start_value* and *end_value*.

There must be start and end values for the iteration after the word **in** (1 and 12 in the foregoing example). These should be discrete expressions, that is, expressions of an integer type or an enumeration type. Note that floating point types are not allowed. The start and end values must be of the same type, except that one may be of integer type and the other of type *universal_integer* (for example, a constant numeric value).

The loop parameter can be seen as a constant that is declared automatically because it occurs in a **for** construct. Thus it should not be declared in the program's declarative part with the other declarations. (In the foregoing example the loop parameter is called I.)

The type of the loop parameter depends on the type of *start_value* and *end_value*. (The rules are a little complicated, so it may not be necessary to go into these in detail at first reading.)

If *start_value* and *end_value* are of the same type, then the **loop parameter** also takes that type, as long as they are not both constant values, in which case the **loop parameter** is of type INTEGER. If *start_value* is of an integer type and *end_value* is a constant value, then the **loop parameter** is of the same type as *start_value* and if *start_value* is a constant value but *end_value* is of an integer type, then the **loop parameter** is of the same type as *end_value*. (In Ada 83, these rules unfortunately led to constructions of the form

for I **in** −1 .. 10 **loop**

being incorrect. Instead one had to write

for I **in** INTEGER **range** −1 .. 10 **loop**

In Ada 95, this is not a problem.)

We will show some examples where N is assumed to be of type INTEGER and S is of type SHORT_INTEGER.

```
for I in 1 .. 10 loop            -- I is INTEGER
for J in 1 .. N loop             -- J is INTEGER
for K in S .. 15 loop            -- K is SHORT_INTEGER
for L in S + 10 .. 2 * S loop    -- L is SHORT_INTEGER
for T in 'A' .. 'C' loop         -- T is CHARACTER
for B in FALSE .. TRUE loop  -- B is BOOLEAN
```

It should be mentioned here that it is possible to control the type of the loop parameter by explicitly stating it. If, for instance, the loop parameter in the first example above should be of type SHORT_INTEGER, then it could be written instead:

for I **in** SHORT_INTEGER **range** 1 .. 10 **loop**

If the loop parameter is intended to run through all possible values for a certain type, the **range** expression can be omitted and only the name of the type stated. In the following example the loop parameter will run through all possible values of the type CHARACTER:

> **for** C **in** CHARACTER **loop**

When the **loop** statement is executed, the *start_value* and *end_value* are evaluated first. If *start_value* is greater than *end_value* the **loop** statement terminates immediately: the sequence of statements is not executed. If *start_value* is less than or equal to *end_value*, the loop parameter is initialized to *start_value*. The sequence of statements is then executed once. The loop parameter may be used as a constant within the sequence of statements in the normal way, in expressions for example. To attempt to change the value of the loop parameter by assignment or in any other way is not allowed – it is, after all, a constant.

When the sequence of statements has been executed once, the value of the loop parameter is automatically changed. If it has an integer type it is increased by one; if it has an enumeration type it takes the next value in the series. Then the loop parameter is compared with *end_value*. (Note that *end_value* is not evaluated again: the program 'remembers' the value that it found the first time through the **loop** statement.) If the loop parameter is less than or equal to *end_value*, the sequence is executed once again, otherwise the loop statement terminates. This process is repeated until the loop statement terminates. The number of times the sequence of statements is repeated depends, therefore, on the *start_value* and *end_value*.

It should be noted that the loop parameter is only defined within the **loop** statement: it cannot be used either before or after the **loop** statement.

Consider a few more examples. The first is part of a program that reads in an integer N and then displays N * N lines at the terminal with a plus sign on every line. If, for example, the user gives the number 4 at the terminal, 16 lines will be displayed with a plus sign on every line.

```
GET(N);
for LINE_NUMBER in 1 .. N * N loop
    PUT_LINE("+");
end loop;
```

The next example involves a loop parameter that is not an integer type but an enumeration type. In the **loop** statement, the alphabet is written out in small letters.

```
for CHAR in 'a' .. 'z' loop
    PUT(CHAR);
end loop;
```

Here *start_value* and *end_value* have the enumeration type CHARACTER and the loop parameter CHAR also takes this type. The first time through, CHAR has value 'a', the second time 'b', the third time 'c', and so on, until the final time it has the value 'z'. (This is because the lower-case letters 'a' to 'z' are next to each other in the ASCII code, as we saw earlier.) The display appears:

abcdefghijklmnopqrstuvwxyz

The repetition can be made to go backwards, that is, the loop parameter can count down instead of up, if the word **reverse** is added. For example, the statement:

```
for NUMBER in reverse 1 .. 5 loop
    PUT(NUMBER);
end loop;
```

gives the output:

5 4 3 2 1

Reverse

In a **loop** statement with **for**, the loop parameter can run through its values backwards if the word **reverse** is added.

Note that a loop parameter of integer type will always increase (or decrease) by one, each time it goes through the loop. If another step length is required, it can be achieved as shown in the next example. First two integers, FIRST_NUMBER and LAST_NUMBER are read from the terminal. Then every tenth number in the interval between FIRST_NUMBER and LAST_NUMBER is displayed at the terminal.

```
GET(FIRST_NUMBER);
GET(LAST_NUMBER);
for I in 0 .. (LAST_NUMBER – FIRST_NUMBER) / 10 loop
    PUT(FIRST_NUMBER + I * 10);
end loop;
```

If the user types in 200 and 250, for example, the output is:

200   210   220   230   240   250

4.5.3   The *loop* statement with *while*

The third variant of the **loop** statement can be used when the number of times the repetition will be made is not known in advance. What is known, however, is that it will be obeyed provided a certain condition is true. When the condition becomes false, the repetition stops.

Loop statement with while

while *Boolean expression* **loop**
    sequence_of_statements
end loop;

The statement is executed as follows. First the Boolean expression following the word **while** is evaluated. If this expression is false nothing more is done: the **loop** statement has been executed. If, however, the Boolean expression is true, the sequence of statements within the **loop** statement is executed once. After that, the Boolean expression is evaluated anew. If it is false, the **loop** statement terminates; if it is true it is executed once more, and so on.

Thus, execution continues until the Boolean expression finally becomes false. If the expression never becomes false, the sequence of statements will be executed endlessly, or until the program is terminated 'by force'. It is very common for an error to be made during programming such that the Boolean expression never becomes false: the program is said to have gone into a loop, meaning an endless loop. It is therefore important to ensure that the values used in the Boolean expression that follow **while** are changed by the statements between **loop** and **end loop**.

Here are a couple of simple examples. The lines of program:

```
J := 0;
while J < 6 loop
    PUT(J);
    J := J + 2;
end loop;
```

give the output:

```
0    2    4
```

Before the first time through, J has the value 0 and the Boolean expression J < 6 is therefore true. This means that the two statements between the words **loop** and **end loop** will be executed once: the number 0 is written and J's value is increased to 2. The expression J < 6 is evaluated a second time and this time it is also true. The sequence of statements is executed again. The number 2 is written, and J is increased to 4. The expression J < 6 is still true and so the statements are executed a third time. The number 4 is written and J is increased to 6. When the Boolean expression J < 6 is evaluated this time it is false, which means that the **loop** statement terminates. Execution continues with the next statement after the **loop** statement. Note that the variable J in this example is an ordinary integer variable that is declared in the normal way. It should not be confused with a loop parameter that is used in a **loop** statement with **for**. Such a loop parameter may not be used outside the **loop** statement.

In the next example, it is presumed that the variable X has type FLOAT. The lines of program:

```
X := 10.0;
while X > 1.0 loop
    PUT(X, FORE => 6, AFT => 2, EXP => 0);
    X := X / 2.0;
end loop;
```

when executed, give the output:

```
10.00     5.00     2.50     1.25
```

After the **loop** statement has been executed the variable X has value 0.625.

We shall now look at a more complicated example. We shall write a program to calculate the sum of the mathematical series:

$$\frac{1}{1 \times 1} - \frac{1}{2 \times 2} + \frac{1}{3 \times 3} - \frac{1}{4 \times 4} + \frac{1}{5 \times 5} - \frac{1}{6 \times 6} \cdots$$

The series has an infinite number of terms, so it is impossible to take account of them all in the program. The signs of the terms alternate between plus and minus and the absolute value of the terms decreases with each new term. The sum of the series therefore approaches a certain limit: the series is said to be convergent. We take the decision to ignore terms that are insignificantly small with respect to the final result. If the result is to be written with 5 decimal figures, terms with absolute value less than 0.000 001 can be ignored without any effect.

We make up an algorithm:

(1)   Initialize the sum to 0 and the first term to 1.
(2)   If the absolute value of the next term >= 0.000 001, carry out the following two steps:
      (2.1)   Add the next term to the sum.
      (2.2)   Evaluate a new next term.
(3)   Write out the sum.

We can refine step (1):

```
SUM := 0.0;
NEXT_TERM := 1.0;
```

Here we have introduced two variables, SUM and NEXT_TERM. They are both real types since the sum and its terms are real numbers. The second variable is called NEXT_TERM, even if it gives the value of the first term at this stage, because it can then be used in the rest of the program when calculating the values of the remaining terms. (And anyway, before starting, the first term is the same as the next term.) We can initialize the variables directly, at the same time as declaring them:

```
SUM : FLOAT := 0.0;
NEXT_TERM : FLOAT := 1.0;
```

Then the assignment statements above are not needed.
Step (2) becomes a **loop** statement:

```
while abs(NEXT_TERM) >= EPSILON loop
    -- (2.1) Add the next term to the sum
    -- (2.2) Evaluate a new next term
end loop;
```

We have introduced a constant EPSILON here to avoid having a constant value within the program. EPSILON is declared as follows:

```
EPSILON : constant := 10.0 ** (−DEC_FIGS − 1);
```

We have initialized EPSILON in terms of another constant DEC_FIGS which is declared:

```
DEC_FIGS : constant := 5;
```

This is practical. If another time we want to have another number of figures after the decimal point we only need to change the constant DEC_FIGS. EPSILON does not need changing.
Step (2.1) becomes quite simply:

```
SUM := SUM + NEXT_TERM;
```

Step (2.2), 'Evaluate a new next term', requires some thought. A particular term in the series, let us call it the kth term, should have the form:

```
1.0/FLOAT(K * K)
```

To work out its value, therefore, we need a counter K to keep track of the number of the term. It is best to make this counter an integer initialized to 1 and then increase it by 1 each time a new term is calculated. Thus we have the declaration:

```
K : INTEGER := 1;
```

and the statement:

```
K := K + 1;
```

which will be executed first in step (2.2).

Having alternate terms that are positive and negative presents a complication. It can be resolved by introducing a variable SIGN which takes alternate values + and −. If the calculated terms are multiplied by SIGN, they will become alternately positive and negative. For simplicity, we shall let SIGN be a real variable. Since term number 1 should be positive, we initialize SIGN to +1, using the declaration:

```
SIGN : FLOAT := 1.0;
```

By including the statement:

```
SIGN := − SIGN;
```

in step (2.2), we make SIGN alternate between +1 and −1 each time a new term is calculated. The actual calculation of the next term is then:

```
NEXT_TERM := SIGN / FLOAT (K * K);
```

NEXT_TERM has type FLOAT, so the right-hand side must also have this type for the assignment to be made. SIGN has type FLOAT, but because K has type INTEGER the expression K * K also has type INTEGER. This expression must therefore be converted to type FLOAT before the division can be performed. Note that if we had declared SIGN to be an integer, then the expression SIGN / (K * K) would have been allowed. However, that would have meant integer division, the result of which would always have been an integer and that would be incorrect. NEXT_TERM should not be an integer.

If we put the three statements in step (2.2) together we get:

```
K := K + 1;
SIGN := − SIGN;
NEXT_TERM := SIGN / FLOAT (K * K);
```

Step (3), 'Write out the sum', becomes:

```
PUT("The sum of the series is: ");
PUT(SUM, FORE => 1, AFT => DEC_FIGS, EXP => 0);
```

Now we can assemble all the steps into a complete program:

```
with TEXT_IO, BASIC_NUM_IO;
use TEXT_IO, BASIC_NUM_IO;
procedure SUM_SERIES is
    SUM                    : FLOAT := 0.0;
    NEXT_TERM, SIGN : FLOAT := 1.0;
    K                      : INTEGER := 1;
    DEC_FIGS : constant := 5;
    EPSILON   : constant := 10.0 ** (EC_FIGS – 1);
begin
    while abs(NEXT_TERM) >= EPSILON loop
        -- Add the next term to the sum
        SUM := SUM + NEXT_TERM;
        -- Evaluate a new next term
        K := K + 1;
        SIGN := – SIGN;
        NEXT_TERM := SIGN / FLOAT(K * K);
    end loop;
    PUT("The sum of the series is: ");
    PUT(SUM, FORE => 1, AFT => DEC_FIGS, EXP => 0);
end SUM_SERIES;
```

When the program is run, the output:

```
The sum of the series is: 0.82247
```

is obtained.

4.6   *Exit* statement

There is a special **exit** statement that can be used in conjunction with the **loop** statement. There are two variants, the first of which is simply:

exit;

This statement must lie within a **loop** statement. When it is executed the iteration is terminated and control passes out of the **loop** statement to the first statement after **end loop**.

The second variant of the **exit** statement is conditional:

exit when *Boolean_expression*;

On execution, the Boolean expression is evaluated first. If this is true, then a jump out of the **loop** statement takes place, just as in the simple **exit** described above. If the Boolean statement is not true, execution continues with the next statement within the **loop** statement: no jump takes place.

For example:

```
loop
    PUT("Enter data");
    GET(X);
    exit when X < 0.0;
    -- Do calculations
        ⋮

    -- Display result
        ⋮

end loop;
-- This is where you come if a number < 0 is entered.
        ⋮
```

> **Exit statement**
>
> Two forms:
>
> (1)   **exit;**
> (2)   **exit when** *Boolean_expression;*

Care must be taken when **exit** statements are used because they can easily lead to a program that is unclear and difficult to understand. Normally, a **loop** statement with **while** can be used instead, with the advantage that the condition for termination is stated at the start. If an **exit** statement is used, this condition is hidden within the **loop** statement and it can be difficult to see it. However, it is sometimes practical to use the **exit** statement in connection with interactive data input, as in the foregoing example, and as we shall see later.

4.7   Nested *loop* statements

Since the sequence of statements within a **loop** statement can be built up of arbitrary statements, there may well be one **loop** statement within another. Such program constructs are common.

Let us look at a simple example. We shall write a few lines of program to print *N* rows of plus signs at the terminal. On the first row there will be one +, two +s on the second, and so on. The number *N* will be read as input from the terminal. If, for example, the number 5 is entered, these lines of program will produce the following output:

```
+
++
+++
++++
+++++
```

Using the top-down method we get:

(1) Read in number *N*.
(2) Repeat the following step for each number *K* from 1 to *N*.
    (2.1) Print a row of *K* plus signs.

Step (1) is simple:

```
PUT_LINE("Enter the number of rows to be printed.");
GET(N);
```

Step (2) is:

```
for K in 1 .. N loop
   -- (2.1) Print a row of K plus signs.
end loop;
```

Finally we have step (2.1):

```
for J in 1 .. K loop
   PUT('+');
end loop;
NEW_LINE;
```

If we put them all together we get:

```
PUT_LINE("Enter the number of rows to be printed");
GET(N);
for K in 1 .. N loop
   for J in 1 .. K loop
      PUT('+');
   end loop;
   NEW_LINE;
end loop;
```

If we want the following output instead:

```
+++++
++++
+++
++
+
```

we only need to add the word **reverse** to the outer loop statement:

for K **in reverse** 1 .. N **loop**

As a further example, let us write a program that reads in 10 lines and counts the number of lower-case letters they contain. The 10 lines can be of different length but we shall assume that no line is longer than 100 characters. We can use the algorithm:

(1)   Set N_SMALL_LETTERS to 0.
(2)   Repeat the following for each of the ten lines.
    (2.1)   Read in the current line.
    (2.2)   Repeat the following for each character in the line.
        (2.2.1)   If the current character is between 'a' and 'z', increase the value of N_SMALL_LETTERS by one.
(3)   Print N_SMALL_LETTERS.

This algorithm can be translated into the Ada program:

```
with TEXT_IO, BASIC_NUM_IO;
use TEXT_IO, BASIC_NUM_IO;
procedure COUNT_SMALL_LETTERS is
    CURRENT_LINE        : STRING(1 .. 100);
    LENGTH              : INTEGER;
    N_SMALL_LETTERS     : INTEGER := 0;
begin
    PUT_LINE("Write 10 lines");
    for LINE_NUMBER in 1 .. 10 loop
      GET_LINE(CURRENT_LINE, LENGTH);
      for CHAR_NUMBER in 1 .. LENGTH loop
        if CURRENT_LINE(CHAR_NUMBER) in 'a' .. 'z' then
          N_SMALL_LETTERS := N_SMALL_LETTERS + 1;
        end if;
      end loop;
    end loop;
    PUT("There are ");
```

```
                PUT(N_SMALL_LETTERS, WIDTH => 1);
                PUT(" small letters");
        end COUNT_SMALL_LETTERS;
```

Here the procedure GET_LINE is used to read in the current line.

4.8   Interactive input

Programs that communicate with a user at a terminal while being executed are called **interactive programs**. Such programs ask the user for input data and compute the output data, which is then displayed to the user at the terminal. Interactive programs are very common so we shall make a special study of how such programs can be written.

All the examples shown so far have been interactive programs. We have seen that it is important that there is a message telling the user what data he or she should write before each input of data. A program halts when it comes to an input statement and will not continue until the user has entered data. If there is no message before the input statement, the user will not notice that the program is waiting for input.

Interactive programs

- Programs that communicate with the user at the terminal.
- Input from the terminal to the program should be preceded by a request for the user to input data.

A computation of any sort has the following general form:

- Read input data.
- Perform computations.
- Write out the result.

Frequently, a program should be able to carry out a computation several times in a row without having to be restarted each time. The program should then act according to the following model:

- Repeat the following three steps time after time until the user wants to stop.

- Read input data.
- Carry out computations.
- Write out result.

This clearly involves iteration. We shall now look at some different ways of producing this type of program.

As an example, we shall use a program that was shown in Section 3.4.1 to calculate the length of the hypotenuse in a right-angled triangle. The input data required are the lengths of the two shorter sides. The program in Section 3.4.1 does only one calculation. We shall now modify the program so that it can be used to carry out several calculations in a row, as in the foregoing model.

In the first version, we make it easy for ourselves as programmers. We simply ask the user to state how many calculations are required at the beginning of the program. Thus we use a **loop** statement with **for** and get the program:

```
-- VERSION 1

with TEXT_IO, BASIC_NUM_IO,
     ADA.NUMERICS.GENERIC_ELEMENTARY_FUNCTIONS;
use TEXT_IO, BASIC_NUM_IO, ADA.NUMERICS;
procedure HYPOTENUSE is
   A, B : FLOAT;
   N_CALCULATIONS : INTEGER;
   package M_FUNC is new GENERIC_ELEMENTARY_FUNCTIONS(FLOAT);
   use M_FUNC;
begin
   PUT_LINE ("How many calculations do you want to make?");
   GET(N_CALCULATIONS);
   for I in 1 .. N_CALCULATIONS loop
      PUT_LINE ("Enter lengths of the two shorter sides:");
      GET(A); GET(B);
      PUT("The hypotenuse has length: ");
      PUT(SQRT(A**2 + B**2), FORE => 1, AFT => 2, EXP => 0);
      NEW_LINE;
   end loop;
end HYPOTENUSE;
```

Of course, this is inconvenient for the user, who often wants to try out different input data and see how the results vary. In this case the number of times the calculation should be repeated is generally not known in advance.

What the user wants is to be able to terminate the program at any time. This can be achieved by the program asking the user if further calculations are to be made each time a calculation is completed:

```
-- VERSION 2

with  TEXT_IO, BASIC_NUM_IO,
        ADA.NUMERICS.GENERIC_ELEMENTARY_FUNCTIONS;
use  TEXT_IO, BASIC_NUM_IO, ADA.NUMERICS;
procedure HYPOTENUSE is
   A, B      : FLOAT;
   ANSWER  : CHARACTER := 'y';
package M_FUNC is new GENERIC_ELEMENTARY_FUNCTIONS(FLOAT);
use M_FUNC;
begin
   while ANSWER = 'y' loop
      PUT_LINE ("Enter lengths of the two shorter sides:");
      GET(A); GET(B);
      PUT("The hypotenuse has length: ");
      PUT(SQRT(A**2 + B**2), FORE => 1, AFT => 2, EXP => 0);
      NEW_LINE;
      PUT_LINE("Are there more calculations?");
      PUT_LINE("Enter y or n");
      GET(ANSWER);
   end loop;
end HYPOTENUSE;
```

In this version we have introduced a character variable, ANSWER. The user is asked if the program should continue, and then the first character entered in reply (a 'y' or an 'n') is read to the variable ANSWER. We have assumed that the user will want to carry out the calculation at least once, and have initialized ANSWER to 'y'. This makes the expression after **while** always true the first time through.

The disadvantage of this second version is that the user must arswer a question after each calculation. There is a common trick that can be used to avoid this: a particular value of input can be taken to mean that the program should terminate. This should be a value that would not normally occur. It is not always possible to find such a value. Consider, for example, a program that reads in and adds together an arbitrary number of real numbers. There is no particular real number that may not appear in such a sum and therefore the method cannot be used.

In our hypotenuse example, the input data are the lengths of the shorter sides, which must be greater than 0. We can therefore use a value <= 0 to denote that the program should terminate. If we use a **loop** statement with **while** we get the following program:

```
-- VERSION 3

with  TEXT_IO, BASIC_NUM_IO,
        ADA.NUMERICS.GENERICELEMENTARYFUNCTIONS;
```

```
use  TEXT_IO, BASIC_NUM_IO, ADA.NUMERICS;
procedure HYPOTENUSE is
   A, B : FLOAT;
   package M_FUNC is new GENERIC_ELEMENTARY_FUNCTIONS(FLOAT);
   use M_FUNC;
begin
   PUT_LINE ("Enter lengths of the two shorter sides:""");
   PUT_LINE ("Terminate by giving a negative length.");
   GET(A); GET(B);
   while A > 0.0 and B > 0.0 loop
      PUT("The hypotenuse has length: ");
      PUT( SQRT(A**2 + B**2), FORE => 1, AFT => 2, EXP => 0);
      NEW_LINE;
      PUT_LINE; ("Enter lengths of the two shorter sides:");
      PUT_LINE ("Terminate by giving a negative length.");
      GET(A); GET(B);
   end loop;
end HYPOTENUSE;
```

In this method, the calculation must come first in the loop and the input last, because on the final go through, the negative values are read into variables A and B. If we had the input first, as before, the program would try to carry out the calculation using the negative values, which, of course, it should not do. We must put the first input outside the **loop** statement. This is a bit clumsy because the same statements have to be written in two places in the program.

To make the program less clumsy we can use an **exit** statement. Then the input does not need to be written in several places and the **loop** statement becomes:

```
-- VERSION 4

loop
   PUT_LINE ("Enter lengths of the two shorter sides:");
   PUT_LINE ("Terminate by giving a negative length.");
   GET(A); GET(B);
   exit when A <= 0.0 or B <= 0.0;
   PUT("The hypotenuse has length: ");
   PUT( SQRT(A**2 + B**2), FORE => 1, AFT => 2, EXP => 0);
   NEW_LINE;
end loop;
```

Here the statements appear in an order that might be closer to the natural way of thinking.

In the two final versions of the hypotenuse program we shall use a function in the TEXT_IO package that we have not seen before, called END_OF_FILE. When the function END_OF_FILE is called in a program, a value of type BOOLEAN is returned, in other words a value that is either TRUE or FALSE. The value TRUE is obtained if the user states that he or she does not intend to give more data to the program, and the value FALSE is obtained if the user continues to input data in the normal way.

How does the user state that he does not intend to input more data? If, for example, the program requests:

Enter the lengths of the shorter sides

and the user wants the program to continue, he writes in data in the normal way, for example:

25.7 11.3

If, on the other hand, there is no further input data, a special combination of keys should be pressed at the terminal. The combination varies from system to system, but it is common to use the key that says CTRL on it together with another key. (The D key or the Z key is used in some common systems.) In future, we shall assume that the CTRL key and the D key should be pressed simultaneously.

If we use a **loop** statement with **while**, the statements in the program appear:

```
-- VERSION 5
PUT_LINE("Enter lengths of the two shorter sides:");
PUT_LINE("Terminate by typing CTRL-D.");
while not END_OF_FILE loop
   GET(A); GET(B);
   PUT("The hypotenuse has length: ");
   PUT( SQRT(A**2 + B**2), FORE => 1, AFT => 2, EXP => 0);
   NEW_LINE;
   PUT_LINE ("Enter lengths of the two shorter sides:");
   PUT_LINE("Terminate by typing CTRL-D.");
end loop;
```

As we already know, there should be an expression of type BOOLEAN after the word **while**. The program can be written as it is because a call to the function END_OF_FILE gives just such a BOOLEAN value as result. As in version 3 of the program, we have been forced to change the order of the reading and calculation within the loop. On the final go through, after the user has pressed the CTRL and D keys, no calculation should be made. Note that the call to END_OF_FILE should occur after the user has been asked to give the input data and before the program tries to read in what the user has written.

In the last version we use an **exit** statement and avoid turning round the order of the statements in the loop and repeating statements before the first **loop** statement. This gives the most compact solution:

```
-- VERSION 6

loop
    PUT_LINE ("Enter the lengths of the two shorter sides:");
    PUT_LINE("Terminate by typing CTRL-D.");
    exit when END_OF_FILE;
    GET(A); GET(B);
    PUT("The hypotenuse has length: ");
    PUT( SQRT(A**2 + B**2), FORE => 1, AFT => 2, EXP => 0);
    NEW_LINE;
end loop;
```

The question arises: 'Which of these methods is best?' This depends partly on the application. If it is known that a definite number of input data will be read (for example, that the results from a fixed number of measurements will be input), the first method with a **for** statement might be preferable.

The second version, in which the user is asked if further calculations are to be made, is a bit clumsy, and the user may find it tedious to answer the question over and over. This version may be useful if written for an inexperienced user who needs accurate and easily understood instructions.

Version 3 has the advantage that the condition for continuing with the calculations is seen at the very beginning of the **loop** statement. The disadvantages are clearly that certain lines of program must be repeated and that the statements come in an unnatural order. In this respect, version 4 with its **exit** statement is preferable. This version avoids repeating part of the program and the statements come in a natural order. It can be disadvantageous that the program contains a jump out of a loop. It is usually said that no jumps should occur in a well-structured program. Even so, the jump brought about by this **exit** statement can be said to be well-controlled and, therefore, does not offend the principles of structured programming.

In certain computer systems it may be standard to terminate the input data to certain types of program using END_OF_FILE. Also, if there is no natural 'end value' for input, END_OF_FILE is useful. Then versions 5 or 6 could be used. If these two versions are compared, version 6 might be preferred, for the same reasons as version 4 was preferred to version 3.

EXERCISES

4.1 In an examination it is possible to get a maximum of 60 points. To pass requires 28 points and to get honours requires at least 48 points. Write a program that reads in the marks obtained by a student and writes out one of the comments: *fail, pass* or *honours.*

(a)   Use an **if** statement.

(b)   Use a **case** statement.

4.2   The sides of a triangle can be denoted a, b and c. If the lengths of sides a and b, and the size of the angle γ between them are known then the length of the third side c can be calculated using the formula:

$$c = \sqrt{a^2 + b^2 - 2ab \cos \gamma}$$

Write a program that reads in the lengths of two sides of a triangle and the angle between them (in radians) and determines if the triangle is equilateral (all sides equal length), isosceles (two sides equal), or scalene (no sides equal). The program should print one of the comments: *equilateral, isosceles* or *scalene.* Remember to be careful when comparing real numbers.

4.3   In Sweden, everyone has a personal identification number of 10 digits. The first six denote the person's date of birth in the format *yymmdd*, and the last four are a code (described in Exercise 4.9).

Write a program that reads in the day's date in international ISO format, namely *19yy–mm–dd*, including the dashes. The program then reads in a person's 10-digit identification number (no dashes) and prints the message:

Congratulations!

if it is his or her birthday.

4.4   A Swedish postal code consists of five digits; the first two denote the district to which the code belongs. If these digits lie in the range 20–62 inclusive, or are 65 or 66, then the code belongs somewhere in the southern part of Sweden (Götaland). If the digits are greater than or equal to 80, the code refers to somewhere in northern Sweden (Norrland), and all others denote central areas (Svealand).

Write a program that reads in an address consisting of two lines: street (number and street name) and town (postal code and town name). Each line can be up to 20 characters long and will be padded with spaces when read in. The program should output one of the messages:

To southern Sweden
To central Sweden
To northern Sweden

depending on the postal code in the first five characters in the second line of the address.

4.5   Write a program that draws up a neat table of values for the following function:

$$f(x) = 3x^3 - 5x^2 + 2x - 20$$

(a)   Make the program write out values of $f(x)$ for all integers in the interval -10 to $+10$.

(b) Make the program write out values of $f(x)$ for all x-values in the interval -2 to $+2$ in steps of 0.1, that is, for the values $-2.0, -1.9, -1.8, \ldots, 1.9, 2.0$.

4.6 A borough has made the following prognosis for the changes in population over the next few years:

- At the start of 1994 there were 26 000 inhabitants.

- The rates of births and deaths are estimated at 0.7% and 0.6% of the population, respectively.

- The number of people moving in and out of the borough annually is estimated at 300 and 325, respectively.

Write a program to calculate the borough's estimated number of inhabitants at the beginning of a particular year. The year in question is to be read in as input.

4.7 Write a program that will print out all the printable ASCII characters and their corresponding ASCII codes.

4.8 A Caesar cipher is a very simple coding method in which each letter in the message to be coded is replaced by the letter a fixed number of places further on in the alphabet. If, for example, a displacement of two places is chosen, then A is replaced by C, B by D, C by E, ... , X by Z, Y by A, and Z by B. The message:

SEND MORE MONEY

is thus coded to:

UGPF OQTG OQPGA

(a) Write a program that reads in a message (maximum 80 characters), codes the message and prints it out. Use a displacement of three for coding. Assume that only uppercase letters are used. If any character other than an uppercase letter appears in the message, do not replace it.

(b) Write a program that will read in a secret message, coded with a displacement of three, and translate the message back to a readable form.

(c) Write a program that will read in a secret coded message where the displacement used is unknown. The program should write out all possible solutions, so that the original message can be found among them.

4.9 Referring again to the Swedish 10-digit identification number (see Exercise 4.3) write a program to check that a given number is correct. If it is incorrect, the text:

Incorrect identification number

should be output.

(a)   Make the program check that all characters are numerals.

(b)   Make the program also check that the control figure (the final digit) is correct. The control figure is calculated as follows:

  (1)   Add digits in positions 2, 4, 6 and 8.

  (2)   Multiply the digits in positions 1, 3, 5, 7 and 9 in the identification number by 2 and add the digits in the result.

  (3)   Add the results of steps 1 and 2.

  (4)   The control figure can now be determined because the sum of the control figure and the sum from step (3) should be exactly divisible by 10.

4.10   A palindrome is a text that reads the same forwards as backwards. For example, '*Ada*' and '*Able was I ere I saw Elba*'. Write a program that reads in a word (no more than 20 characters) and decides whether the word is a palindrome.

4.11   Write a program to write out a multiplication table as in the following example:

1	2	3	4	5
2	4	6	8	10
3	6	9	12	15
4	8	12	16	20
5	10	15	20	25

The upper limit of the table should be read in as input.

4.12   Write a program to compute the least integer k such that:

$$\sum_{i=1}^{k} i^2 > n$$

The number n should be read in from the terminal.

4.13   If there is no accessible package with mathematical functions, Maclaurin series can be used to calculate the values of certain common functions. For example, the function 'sin' can be evaluated with the following series:

$$\sin x = x - \frac{x^3}{3!} + \frac{x^5}{5!} - \frac{x^7}{7!} + \frac{x^9}{9!} \cdots$$

Write a program that reads in a value of x and writes out $\sin x$ using this series. The result should be written correct to four decimal places. Neglect any terms in the series that are less than 10^{-5}.

4.14   Write a program that reads in a certain number of real numbers and writes out at the terminal:

- The largest number.

- The smallest number.

- Their mean value.

Formulate the reading in of input data in a suitable way for the following cases:

(a)   The number of numbers to be read in is always known (for example, 100).

(b)   The number of numbers is arbitrary but it is known that all the numbers are greater than zero.

(c)   The number of numbers is arbitrary and any real number can occur.

4.15   Write a program that calculates the value of the sum:

$$H_n = \sum_{i=1}^{n} \frac{1}{i}$$

for different values of n. The program should be designed so that it repeatedly writes out the text:

Enter the value of n

and calculates and writes out the value of H_n. There should be some suitable way of indicating that no further calculations are to be made.

4.16   Write a program that reads a line from the terminal comprising a number of words separated by one or more spaces (80 characters maximum). The program should write out the line of text such that only one space comes between each pair of words.

5 Types

In earlier chapters use has been made of Ada's predefined types as declared in the package STANDARD. This chapter will show how it is possible to declare new types. The concepts of abstraction and representation will be discussed, that is, how types can be introduced in order to describe and represent phenomena from the real world. The ways of declaring new numeric types will also be reviewed. The use of enumeration types to describe the kind of real phenomena that cannot be expressed as numerical quantities will be studied further. In Section 5.5 a number of useful attributes for scalar types are presented.

So far a non-standard package, BASIC_NUM_IO, has been used to access the tools for input and output of values of the types INTEGER and FLOAT. In Ada there is a general mechanism for creating new input/output packages for all numeric types and enumeration types, even those declared by the programmer. In Section 5.6 the use of this mechanism is explained.

The use of so-called subtypes in Ada will also be described, showing how these can be used to describe objects that belong to a subgroup of a larger, more general, group. Sections 5.8 and 5.9 deal with types that consist of several components of the same sort and which can be used to represent tables, texts and other data.

5.1   Data abstraction

In Chapter 3 we discussed the concept that the task of a computer program is to manipulate data, and that data objects in a program often represent some phenomenon in the real world. When we talk about phenomena in the real world, we nearly always use a technique known as **abstraction**. Abstraction means creating a concept of something so that it can be talked about and described. The word 'truck', for example, is an abstraction for a vehicle that can be used for transporting things. We can talk about a truck and say that it has certain properties, such as capacity, length, running cost and so on.

The abstraction can be made at different levels. For a maintenance mechanic it is natural to think of a truck as consisting of many components, such as a gear box, brake system and so on. To go down another level, it can be said that the gear box is made up of many parts, axles, gear wheels, etc. This level is appropriate for the design or repair of a gear box. The level of abstraction chosen, therefore, depends on the context in which the phenomenon is to be studied.

The advantage of deliberately choosing an abstraction is that it allows inessential details to be ignored in favour of those properties important for the study in hand. The driver of a truck is not interested in how the different gear wheels inside the gear box are moving. He or she only needs to know how to use the gear lever.

Abstraction

- A 'model' or 'concept' of a real-world phenomenon is created.

- Abstraction is made at such a level that inessential details can be ignored.

Because the data objects in a program should represent a phenomenon in the real world, we must also be able to use abstractions when we create different data objects. This is possible in Ada. Using types and packages that we declare ourselves, we can build up complicated types with particular properties. It can actually be said that we have already met abstraction of data. A variable of the built-in type INTEGER, for example, is a representation of a mathematical whole number. If we prefer, we do not need to study the underlying level of abstraction that describes how an INTEGER is represented in binary form with ones and zeros. We only need to know which operations can be performed on an object of the type INTEGER.

There are several advantages to be gained by setting up new types that specifically represent the properties of a phenomenon. The program becomes clearer because it is more closely linked with reality. The program also becomes safer: the compiler checks that we are not illegally mixing different types and that we are not giving variables illegal values. The program becomes less complex because we can choose a suitable level of abstraction and ignore unnecessary details.

There is a distinction in Ada between **scalar types** and **composite types**. (There are also types called 'access types' and 'private types', but we shall not consider these yet.) Scalar types are used to describe things that can be expressed in a single value, for example, a temperature, a printable character, or the score in a test. Earlier we illustrated scalar data objects as storage boxes containing only a single value. The **numeric types** (integer and real types) and **enumeration types** are among the scalar types.

The composite types are used to build up more complex descriptions of data objects. Descriptions can be built up that contain several component elements of the same sort, for example, text strings or tables, or descriptions that contain component elements of different kinds, for example, the description of a person in a hospital register.

Scalar types

The object can be expressed as *one* single value (for example, a number or a character).

Composite types

The objects are composed of several individual values (for example, a text).

The declarations of types should be placed alongside other declarations in an Ada program. It is the ways of defining different types that will be discussed in the rest of this chapter.

Type declaration

> **type** *typename* **is** *type definition*;

where *type definition* depends on the type being declared.

- A type declaration is placed among the other declarations in the program.
- No objects of the type are created by the type declaration: they are created when an object declaration is given.

The name of a type can be used in the same way as the names of Ada's standard types. This includes being able to declare objects (variables and constants) using the name. If we have the following type declaration, without worrying how the declaration itself continues:

type TEMPERATURE **is** ... ;

then the following object declarations can be made:

MEAN_TEMPERATURE : TEMPERATURE;

LIMITING_TEMPERATURE : **constant** TEMPERATURE := 100.0;

Note that no objects are created when the type is declared. The type (or the idea of) TEMPERATURE is only introduced so that it can be used later. It is only when an object declaration is made that an object is created. Type declarations and object declarations may appear in arbitrary order in the declaration section of a program, but a type must be declared before it is used in another declaration.†

When both types and objects are declared in a program it can be a problem to find suitable names. It is all too easy to decide on names in a program that make it difficult to tell types and objects apart, making the program both confusing and hard to understand. It can, therefore, be useful to devise a principle for allocating names. One common principle for differentiating between the names of types and other quantities is to let all type names end in TYPE, for example, TEMPERATURE_TYPE and PERSON_TYPE.

---

† It has been pointed out before that in Ada 95 all types are without name. TEMPERATURE is actually a subtype. The type declaration above is in fact two things: first, an anonymous type is declared and second, a subtype, TEMPERATURE, of this anonymous type is declared. The subtype will have exactly the same characteristics as the anonymous type.

5.2   Integer types

When an integer type is declared, the least and greatest possible integer values that objects of the type can take are stated. A few examples to illustrate this are:

type LINE_NUMBER **is range** 1 .. 72;

type SCORE **is range** 0 .. 100;

type NEGATIVE_INTEGER **is range** –100_000 .. –1;

Declaration of integer types

   type *typename* **is range** *min_value .. max_value;*

where *min_value* and *max_value* are static (constant) integer expressions.

Condition: *min_value* <= *max_value*

Here LINE_NUMBER, for example, describes a type whose possible values are whole numbers in the interval 1–72. The permissible limits depend on how integers are stored in the particular Ada implementation. If limits are requested that the Ada implementation cannot cope with, the compiler will give an error message. In the majority of implementations, it would probably not be permitted to declare the following type, for instance:

type GIANT_INTEGER **is range** 0 .. 100_000_000_000_000_000;

In every Ada implementation, as we know, there is a predefined type INTEGER which is declared in the package STANDARD. The declaration of INTEGER can be considered as:

type INTEGER **is range** *least_integer .. greatest_integer;*

where the limits *least_integer* and *greatest_integer* can be different for different implementations of Ada.

The standard type INTEGER

- The least possible and greatest possible values can be different in different implementations of Ada.
- To include all desired values, the programmer should declare a new specific integer type.

The two limits in a declaration of an integer type do not necessarily have to be simple literals as above. Static expressions, that is, expressions consisting of constant components, are also allowed:

```
MAX_LINE : constant := 72;
MAX_COL  : constant := 17;
type ELEMENT_NUMBER is range 1 .. (MAX_LINE * MAX_COL);
```

Facts from the real world can be represented using specifically declared integer types. For example, a variable MY_SCORE can be created by making the object declaration:

```
MY_SCORE : SCORE;
```

The variable is thus an object that can only take integral values between 0 and 100. It represents a genuine score in, for example, a test. If an attempt is made to assign a value to MY_SCORE that lies outside the limits 0 and 100, there is a run-time error and an error message is output. This gives valuable assistance in tracing errors of logic in a program. If MY_SCORE were simply declared as an INTEGER, this help would not be available: all the integers included in the type INTEGER would then be allowed. The type INTEGER can be considered as representing the concept of whole numbers in a general mathematical sense, that is, having no connection with any particular real object, but this is too vague a model for a real test score.

All the operations that can be performed on objects of type INTEGER (for example, assignment, addition, comparison) can also be performed with other integer types, but mixing different types is not allowed. Assume, for example, we have the following object declarations:

```
CURRENT_LINE, NEXT_LINE : LINE_NUMBER;
MY_SCORE : SCORE;
K : INTEGER;
```

Then the following assignments are not permitted:

```
CURRENT_LINE := MY_SCORE;      -- Error!
K := NEXT_LINE;                -- Error!
MY_SCORE := K;                 -- Error!
```

Nor is it permitted to mix types in expressions:

```
CURRENT_LINE + K      -- Error!
MY_SCORE * K          -- Error!
```

However, the following are allowed:

```
CURRENT_LINE := NEXT_LINE;           -- Same type
CURRENT_LINE := LINE_NUMBER(K)       -- Type conversion
MY_SCORE * SCORE(K)                  -- Type conversion
```

In the second example we have used explicit type conversion and converted the value of K, which is of type INTEGER, into a value of type LINE_NUMBER. In the expression in the third example, K's value has been turned into the type SCORE. Type conversion is allowed between all numeric types.

If we have the following declarations:

```
type PAGE_NUMBER  is range 1 .. 500;
type INDEX           is range 1 .. 500;
PAGE : PAGE_NUMBER;
I      : INDEX;
```

then PAGE_NUMBER and INDEX are different types in spite of being declared in the same way. Therefore the variables PAGE and I have different types and may not be mixed.

Operations on integer types

- The normal operations that exist for INTEGER (for example, +, –) also exist for other integer types.
- Different integer types may not be mixed.
- Explicit type conversion is permitted.

As discussed earlier, integer literals have the type *universal_integer* and are automatically converted into the 'right' integer type. Therefore, the following, for example, are allowed:

```
CURRENT_LINE := 1;
MY_SCORE + 5
K * 27
```

5.3   Real types

In Ada there are two categories of real types, namely floating point types and fixed point types, as mentioned in Section 3.1.1. Only floating point types will be treated here. Floating point types are used to represent real values with a certain precision, that is, with an accuracy of a certain number of digits after the decimal point. As we saw earlier, an Ada implementation uses a binary representation to store floating point numbers internally. Therefore only certain real numbers can be stored exactly. The rest are stored in an approximate form.

Declaration of floating point types

> **type** *typename* **is digits** *number_of_sig_figs;*

where *number_of_sig_figs* expresses the accuracy as the number of significant figures following the decimal point, and is a static (constant) expression.

When a floating point type is declared, the accuracy required is simply stated in terms of the number of figures following the decimal point. The compiler then chooses a suitable form of binary representation, namely, how many bits should be used to store the mantissa and the exponent. The number of digits accuracy varies from implementation to implementation. If the number of digits accuracy requested is greater than can be stored in the implementation in use, the compiler will give an error message. (It should be noted that when the compiler accepts a declaration of a floating point type, it also guarantees that a minimum number of bits will be used to store the exponent, which determines the range of numbers that can be stored. The greater the accuracy requested, the greater the number of bits devoted to storing the exponent.) Some examples are:

> **type** TEMPERATURE **is digits** 4;
>
> **type** PRECISION_MEASUREMENT **is digits** 15;

Following the word **digits** there must be a static integer expression. An integer literal is most often used, as in these examples.

We have already met the standard type FLOAT, which can be thought of as being declared in the following manner in the package STANDARD:

> **type** FLOAT **is digits** *figure_dependent_on_implementation;*

Thus the number of digits' accuracy obtained when the type FLOAT is used can vary from implementation to implementation. It can, therefore, be dangerous to use this type when writing a program that is intended to be portable (usable on all Ada implementations), because it is not possible to be sure of the accuracy of the results computed by the program. It is thus recommended that the programmer declares his or her own floating point types so that he or she can state the desired precision. If it is not possible to obtain that precision, the compiler will detect it as an error, output an error message and the program will not be compiled. Thus the programmer can be assured of getting the desired accuracy if a program can be compiled without error.

The standard type FLOAT

- The number of digits accuracy can be different in different implementations of Ada.
- To be sure of obtaining a certain number of digits accuracy, the programmer should declare a specific floating point type.

It is possible to state the bounds within which the numbers belonging to the type may lie:

type PERCENTAGE **is digits** 4 **range** 0.0 .. 100.0;

type ERROR_PROBABILITY **is digits** 6 **range** 0.0 .. 1.0;

This ensures a check that, while the program is running, variables of the particular type never assume values that lie outside its limits. It also offers assistance with tracking down possible errors in the program's logic. The limits that appear after the word **range** must be static real expressions.

In the same way as for integer types, all the operations that exist for the type FLOAT also exist for programmer-declared floating point types, but again, mixing different floating point types in an expression is not allowed. If this is necessary, type conversion can be used. Real literals present no problem because they have the type *universal_real* and automatically take the 'right' type. If, for example, we have the declarations:

MAX_PERCENT : PERCENTAGE;

MAX_PROB   : ERROR_PROBABILITY;

the following assignment is incorrect:

MAX_PROB := MAX_PERCENT / 100.0;   -- Error!

because the expression on the right of the assignment has type PERCENTAGE and that on the left has type ERROR_PROBABILITY. However, the following is correct:

MAX_PROB := ERROR_PROBABILITY(MAX_PERCENT / 100.0);

> **Operations on floating point types**
>
> - The normal operations that exist for FLOAT (for example, +, –) also exist for other floating point types.
> - Different floating point types may not be mixed.
> - Explicit type conversion is allowed.

5.4 Enumeration types

There are many phenomena in the real world that are described in words rather than numbers, for example, the days of the week. The second day of the week is usually called Tuesday rather than day number 2. In the same way, the suits in a pack of cards are not numbered but have names: hearts, clubs, diamonds and spades. To describe the state of something it is also common to use different terms rather than numbers, such as the state of an elevator being 'going up', 'going down' or 'stationary'. If phenomena like these are to be represented in a program, numeric types will not suffice. Instead, there is the opportunity to use **enumeration types**. When an enumeration type is declared, the possible values are simply enumerated or listed.

Let us look at the three examples already mentioned: the days of the week, the suits in a pack of cards and the state of an elevator. We can make the following type declarations:

```
type DAY_OF_THE_WEEK is (MONDAY, TUESDAY, WEDNESDAY,
                         THURSDAY, FRIDAY, SATURDAY,
                         SUNDAY);
type SUIT is (CLUBS, DIAMONDS, HEARTS, SPADES);
type ELEVATOR_STATUS_TYPE is (GOING_UP, GOING_DOWN,
                              STATIONARY);
```

We can then declare variables of these types:

```
TODAY, TOMORROW : DAY_OF_THE_WEEK;
CURRENT_TRUMP_SUIT, SUIT_PLAYED : SUIT;
ELEVATOR_1_STATUS : ELEVATOR_STATUS_TYPE;
```

The variable CURRENT_TRUMP_SUIT can then take any of the values CLUBS, DIAMONDS, HEARTS or SPADES, but no other value. Although values are usually considered numeric, CLUBS must also be thought of as a *value* of type SUIT in the same way as 257 is a value of type INTEGER. Here are a few examples of permitted statements:

```
SUIT_PLAYED := DIAMONDS;
CURRENT_TRUMP_SUIT := SUIT_PLAYED;
if ELEVATOR_1_STATUS = STATIONARY then
  PUT_LINE("Elevator is free");
end if;
```

It is also possible to initialize variables of enumeration types when they are declared, as in:

```
ELEVATOR_1_STATUS : ELEVATOR_STATUS_TYPE := STATIONARY;
```

Of course, to mix types is not allowed. The following are incorrect:

```
CURRENT_TRUMP_SUIT := FRIDAY;               -- Error!
TODAY := 2;                                 -- Error!
if CURRENT_TRUMP_SUIT = TOMORROW then       -- Error!
```

The values that are listed when an enumeration type is declared can, as in the example above, be identifiers like TUESDAY, but it is also possible to use character literals, as in the following example:

```
type HEX_DIGITS is ('0',  '1',  '2',  '3',  '4',  '5',  '6',  '7',
                    '8',  '9',  'A',  'B',  'C',  'D',  'E',  'F');
```

Identifiers and character literals can be mixed in the same type declaration if necessary. This has been done in the declaration of the enumeration type CHARACTER in the package STANDARD.

Declaration of enumeration types

- **type** *typename* **is** (*value_1, value_2, ... value_N*);
  where *value_1, value_2*, etc. are either identifiers or character literals (can be mixed in the same declaration).
- The values in the type are ordered in such a way that *value_1* < *value_2* < *value_3*, etc.

The values in an enumeration type are **ordered** so that the value listed first is least and the one that is listed last is greatest. The following logic expressions, therefore, have the value TRUE:

```
TUESDAY < SUNDAY
CLUBS <= HEARTS
STATIONARY > GOING_UP
```

This can be used in constructs such as:

```
if TODAY >= SATURDAY then
    PUT_LINE("Free day");
end if;
if ELEVATOR_1_STATUS in GOING_UP .. GOING_DOWN then
    PUT_LINE("Elevator in motion");
end if;
```

It is common to use the **case** statement in conjunction with enumeration types, often leading to readable programs as in the following example:

```
case TODAY is
    when MONDAY .. THURSDAY =>
        PUT("Only work");
    when FRIDAY =>
        PUT("Out on the town tonight");
    when SATURDAY.. SUNDAY =>
        PUT("Free day");
end case;
```

No **others** alternative is needed here because all the possible values are listed.

It is also very useful to use enumeration types to control the iteration in a **loop** statement with **for**. The total number of hours worked in a week is calculated in the following program. When the program is run, the operator gives for each day of the week how many hours have been worked.

```
with TEXT_IO, BASIC_NUM_IO;
use TEXT_IO, BASIC_NUM_IO;
procedure COMPUTE_HOURS_WORKED is
    type DAY_OF_THE_WEEK is (MONDAY, TUESDAY,
                             WEDNESDAY, THURSDAY,
                             FRIDAY, SATURDAY, SUNDAY);
    TOTAL_HOURS        : INTEGER := 0;
    NUMBER_OF_HOURS : INTEGER;
begin
    PUT_LINE("Enter hours worked on each day of the week");
    for DAY in MONDAY .. SUNDAY loop
        GET(NUMBER_OF_HOURS);
        TOTAL_HOURS := TOTAL_HOURS + NUMBER_OF_HOURS;
```

```
      end loop;
      PUT("The total number of hours worked is: ");
      PUT(TOTAL_HOURS, WIDTH => 1);
   end COMPUTE_HOURS_WORKED;
```

The loop parameter here automatically takes the type DAY_OF_THE_WEEK. The first time through the loop, DAY will have the value MONDAY, the second time it will have TUESDAY, and so on, until, on the final time through, DAY has the value SUNDAY.

In general, using enumeration types increases the clarity of programs. Therefore one should try to use enumeration types and avoid 'coding' information in programs, such as representing a Wednesday by the number 3.

Using enumeration types

- Makes programs clear.
- Avoids 'coding' information with numbers.
- Combines well with **case** statements.

5.5   Attributes for scalar types

When we discussed the standard types INTEGER, FLOAT and CHARACTER in Chapter 3 we introduced the notion of an attribute. In this section we will describe the most common attributes for scalar types, in other words for integer types, real types and enumeration types. Attributes have the following form: there is always a prefix first, which is the name of the type in question; that is followed by a single apostrophe; then comes the name of the attribute. Attributes can be divided into two categories. The first of these consists of attributes which give information about the current type, for example, INTEGER'FIRST and FLOAT'DIGITS. The second category consists of attributes which are a sort of function, and they always have a parameter following the attribute name. An example is CHARACTER'POS(C), where the variable C is here a parameter to the attribute.

We will start with attributes of the first category. The most common are the following (where the identifier T specifies a type):

T'FIRST   States the least possible value for objects of type T.

T'LAST   States the greatest possible value for objects of type T.

T'DIGITS States the number of decimal figures accuracy for floating point type T.

T'WIDTH   Gives an integer which states how long a text string must be in order that all values of type T can be printed in it. In Ada 83 the attribute WIDTH is found only for integer types and enumeration types. This attribute is often used in conjunction with the attribute IMAGE (see below).

We can look at some examples. If we assume that an enumeration type DAY_OF_THE_WEEK has been declared, as in the previous section, then the expressions DAY_OF_THE_WEEK'FIRST and DAY_OF_THE_WEEK'LAST have values MONDAY and SUNDAY, respectively. If we want to know the number of possible values which exist for the type SHORT_INTEGER we can use the expression:

SHORT_INTEGER'LAST – SHORT_INTEGER'FIRST + 1

Assume that the following declaration is in force:

```
type TEMPERATURE is digits 4;
TEMP_1 : TEMPERATURE;
```

If we want to find out the largest number that can be stored as type TEMPERATURE we can make use of the attribute TEMPERATURE'LAST. As an example of using the attribute DIGITS, we can look at a statement that writes out the value in the variable TEMP_1 with as many digits accuracy as is suitable:

PUT(TEMP_1, EXP => 0, FORE => 1, AFT => TEMPERATURE'DIGITS);

The attribute WIDTH can be used in connection with declarations of text string variables. If, for example, we want to declare a variable NUMBER_STRING which is sufficiently long to allow all integers of type SHORT_INTEGER to be 'written' in it, we can write the following:

NUMBER_STRING : STRING(1 .. SHORT_INTEGER'WIDTH);

In the second category of attributes, those which are functions, the following are most common. As before, T is the type in question, and now one or more parameters are found in brackets.

T'POS(*value*)   Gives the order (enumeration number) of *value*. The parameter *value* must be of type T. This attribute does not exist for real types.

T'VAL(*number*)   Gives the value of type T which has order *number*. The parameter *number* must be an integer. This attribute does not exist for real types.

T'PRED(*value_n*)   Gives *value_n–1* (the predecessor) of type T. The parameter *value_n* must be of type T. In Ada 83 this type does not exist for real types.

T'SUCC(*value_n*)   Gives *value_n+1* (the successor) of type T. The parameter *value_n* must be of type T. In Ada 83 this type does not exist for real types.

T'IMAGE(*value*)   The parameter *value* must be of type T. It returns as result a text string in which is 'written' the value of the parameter. Integers are written without leading zeros but with a leading sign which can be a blank or a minus sign. No trailing blanks are given. Values of enumeration types are 'written' in upper-case letters with neither leading nor trailing blanks. This attribute does not exist for real types in Ada 83.

T'VALUE(*text*)   This is the inverse of IMAGE. The parameter text must be of type STRING and contain text which can be interpreted as a literal of type T. Leading and trailing blanks are allowed. It returns as result a value of type T.

T'MIN(*x,y*)   Both parameters must be of type T. It returns as result the lesser of *x* and *y*. This attribute exists only in Ada 95.

T'MAX(*x,y*)   Both parameters must be of type T. It returns as result the greater of *x* and *y*. This attribute exists only in Ada 95.

We can look at some examples of these attributes. The expression DAY_OF_THE_WEEK'POS(TUESDAY) returns the value 1 since enumeration types are numbered from 0. CHARACTER'VAL(119) gives the character which has order number 119 in the ASCII code, namely the character 'w'.

The attributes PRED and SUCC can be used to obtain, respectively, the predecessor and successor of a value of an enumeration type, thus:

```
DAY_OF_THE_WEEK'PRED(FRIDAY)      -- returns value THURSDAY
TOMORROW := DAY_OF_THE_WEEK'SUCC(TODAY);
```

The last of these examples indicates that the content of the brackets does not need to be a constant value. For an enumeration type, the first value has no predecessor and the last value has no successor; if an attempt is made to get either such value the result will be an execution error when the program is run.

The following example shows how the attribute IMAGE might be used. Suppose we have a procedure DRAW_STRING which can write text at a specified point on a graphics screen. The procedure will have three parameters, the first two giving the x and y coordinates of the point on the screen where the text will start and the third, of type STRING, being the text to be written out. Assume now that we have calculated a value of type INTEGER and that its value is in variable N. If we want to write on the screen, "The final result is: xxx", where xxx means the value in variable N, we make the following call:

DRAW_STRING(X, Y, "The final result is: " & INTEGER'IMAGE(N));

▼

The attributes PRED and SUCC are defined in Ada 95 for floating point types as well. For example, in Ada 95 the expression FLOAT'SUCC(0.0) returns the smallest number greater than zero which can be represented.

A number of further attributes are defined for floating point types, some of which are given below. For all those shown here, T is a floating point type and the parameters and result are of type T.

T'ROUNDING(x)	Returns the rounded value of x.
T'TRUNCATION(x)	Gives the value of x with the decimal figures dropped.
T'FLOOR(x)	Gives the largest integer which is not larger than x.
T'CEILING(x)	Gives the smallest integer which is not smaller than x.

▲

5.6   The tools for input and output

In our programs we have used the resources in the standardized package TEXT_IO to access read and write values of the types STRING and CHARACTER. To read and write values of the types INTEGER and FLOAT we have so far used a 'home-made' package, BASIC_NUM_IO that is not standardized. We have used it to simplify input and output in the early stages of learning Ada. If we have numeric types other than INTEGER and FLOAT, the package BASIC_NUM_IO will not do. We shall, therefore, look at how to use a general, standardized method to create the resources needed for reading and writing any sort of numeric type. We shall also look at how to read and write values of enumeration types.

Contained in TEXT_IO, as well as the procedures for reading and writing text, there are some templates that can be used to create new input/output packages. One template is called INTEGER_IO, and with its help new packages containing procedures for reading and writing integer types can be created. The way this is used in a program is illustrated by the following example, where a package is created enabling values of the type INTEGER to be read and written without using BASIC_NUM_IO.

```
with TEXT_IO;
use TEXT_IO;
procedure INOUT_DEMO_1 is
   package INTEGER_INOUT is new INTEGER_IO(INTEGER);
   use INTEGER_INOUT;

   N : INTEGER;
begin
   GET(N);
   PUT(N);
   NEW_LINE;
end INOUT_DEMO_1;
```

The first **with** statement gives access to the package TEXT_IO and all its resources. The first **use** statement makes it easy to refer to the contents of the package TEXT_IO. For example, we can write NEW_LINE, avoiding writing the longer form TEXT_IO.NEW_LINE as we would have to if the **use** statement were not there.

Within the procedure we use the template INTEGER_IO (which is in the package TEXT_IO) to create a new package that we name INTEGER_INOUT. Since we want our package to contain the resources to enable values of the type INTEGER to be read and written, we write this type name in brackets after the template's name. (The template INTEGER_IO has all that is needed for a complete package to be created; the only thing missing is the name of the type and we must therefore state this.)

The second **use** statement makes it easy for us to refer to the routines in the new package INTEGER_INOUT. For example, we can write PUT instead of INTEGER_INOUT.PUT.

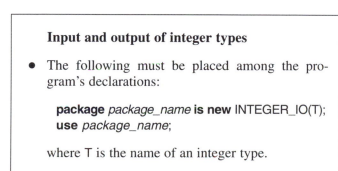

Input and output of integer types

- The following must be placed among the program's declarations:

   package *package_name* **is new** INTEGER_IO(T);
   use *package_name*;

   where T is the name of an integer type.

- The procedures PUT and GET can then be used.

If we also want to be able to read and write values of the integer type LINE_NUMBER, we can create another package of routines:

```
with TEXT_IO;
use TEXT_IO;
procedure INOUT_DEMO_2 is
   type LINE_NUMBER is range 1 .. 72;
   package LINE_NO_INOUT is new INTEGER_IO(LINE_NUMBER);
   package INTEGER_INOUT is new INTEGER_IO(INTEGER);
   use INTEGER_INOUT, LINE_NO_INOUT;

   N    : INTEGER;
   LINE : LINE_NUMBER;
begin
   GET(N);
   PUT(N);
   NEW_LINE;
   GET(LINE);
   PUT(LINE);
end INOUT_DEMO_2;
```

The new package is called LINE_NO_INOUT and is created in the same way as the package INTEGER_INOUT. Both of these packages thus contain exactly the same resources for their respective types. The procedures GET and PUT will be found in two versions, one for the type INTEGER and one for the type LINE_NUMBER.

The template FLOAT_IO in the package TEXT_IO can be used in the same way to create new packages for input and output of floating point values. If we want to be able to read and write values of type FLOAT without using the package BASIC_NUM_IO, we can write in our program:

```
package FLOAT_INOUT is new FLOAT_IO(FLOAT);
use FLOAT_INOUT;
```

Then we get direct access to procedures, including PUT and GET, in versions which can handle values of the type FLOAT.

Input and output packages for other floating point types can be created in an analogous way. If we want to be able to read and write values of the type TEMPERATURE directly, we can add the following lines to a program:

```
type TEMPERATURE is digits 4;
package TEMPERATURE_INOUT is new FLOAT_IO(TEMPERATURE);
use TEMPERATURE_INOUT;
```

> **Input and output of floating point types**
>
> - The following must be placed among the program's declarations:
>
>   > **package** *package_name* **is new** FLOAT_IO(T);
>   > **use** *package_name*;
>
>   where T is the name of a floating point type.
>
> - The procedures PUT and GET can then be used.

As shown previously, it is good to use enumeration types because they make a program clearer to understand. But to be really useful, there has to be a simple way of reading and writing their values. In TEXT_IO there is a template ENUMERATION_IO that can be used to achieve this. The following program illustrates how a package of resources for reading and writing values of the type SUIT is created.

```
with TEXT_IO;
use TEXT_IO;
procedure INOUT_DEMO_3 is
   type SUIT is (CLUBS, DIAMONDS, HEARTS, SPADES);
   package SUIT_INOUT is new ENUMERATION_IO(SUIT);
   use SUIT_INOUT;
   TRUMP : SUIT;
begin
   GET(TRUMP);
   PUT(TRUMP);
end INOUT_DEMO_3;
```

The template ENUMERATION_IO is used to create a new package SUIT_INOUT. Writing SUIT in brackets states that the new package will contain resources tailored for the type SUIT. In the package there are new versions of the procedures PUT and GET that can be used as in the program above. The statement:

> GET(TRUMP);

makes the program halt and wait for the operator to write a value of the type SUIT at the terminal. The operator can then type one of the words CLUBS, DIAMONDS, HEARTS or SPADES. (Both upper- and lower-case letters are acceptable.) Anything else is wrong and gives a run-time error.

The statement:

PUT(TRUMP);

means that one of the words CLUBS, DIAMONDS, HEARTS or SPADES will be displayed at the terminal, depending on the value of the variable TRUMP.

It is possible for the programmer to control whether the output is in upper- or lower-case letters. If lower-case letters are wanted, the statement:

SUIT_INOUT.DEFAULT_SETTING := LOWER_CASE;

can be inserted near the start of the program. If upper-case letters are wanted, then the statement:

SUIT_INOUT.DEFAULT_SETTING := UPPER_CASE;

should be inserted instead. If no such statement is made, output will be in upper-case letters.

Input and output of enumeration types

- The following must be placed among the program's declarations:

  package *package_name* **is new**
          ENUMERATION_IO(T);
  use *package_name*;

  where T is the name of an enumeration type.

- The procedures GET and PUT can then be used to write and read values of type T.

The standard type BOOLEAN is an enumeration type and thus values of type BOOLEAN can be read in and written if a new package is declared:

package BOOLEAN_INOUT **is new** ENUMERATION_IO(BOOLEAN);
use BOOLEAN_INOUT;

This makes it possible to use PUT and GET as in the following examples:

GET(ACTIVE);   -- ACTIVE is a variable of type BOOLEAN
PUT(ACTIVE);
PUT(A > B);

In the first example, the operator must type one of the words TRUE or FALSE at the terminal, while in the other two examples either TRUE or FALSE is displayed at the terminal.

This section ends by studying a program that reads in a date in the form:

28 OCTOBER 1996

and computes the number of the day in the year, the day number. The program will take leap years into account. A year is a leap year if it is exactly divisible by four but not by 100, or if it is exactly divisible by 400.

We introduce three types of our own into the program. We let the numbers of the days hav type DAY_NUMBER_TYPE. years have type YEAR_TYPE, and the months have the type MONTH_TYPE. We will confine our interest to the years between 2000 BC and 2100 AD. To be able to read and write values of these types, we shall create new input and output packages using the templates in TEXT_IO. The program looks like this:

```
with TEXT_IO;
use TEXT_IO;
procedure COMPUT_DAY_NUMBER is
  type YEAR_TYPE is range -2000 .. 2100;
  type MONTH_TYPE is (JANUARY, FEBRUARY, MARCH,
                      APRIL, MAY, JUNE, JULY,
                      AUGUST, SEPTEMBER, OCTOBER,
                      NOVEMBER, DECEMBER);
  type DAY_NUMBER_TYPE is range 1 .. 366;
  package YEAR_INOUT is new INTEGER_IO(YEAR_TYPE);
  package MONTH_INOUT is new ENUMERATION_IO(MONTH_TYPE);
  package DAY_NUMBER_INOUT is new
                     INTEGER_IO(DAY_NUMBER_TYPE);
  use YEAR_INOUT, MONTH_INOUT, DAY_NUMBER_INOUT;
     YEAR         : YEAR_TYPE;
     MONTH        : MONTH_TYPE;
     DAY, DAY_NO  : DAY_NUMBER_TYPE;
begin
     PUT_LINE("Enter date in form: day month year,");
     GET(DAY); GET(MONTH); GET(YEAR);

case MONTH is
     when JANUARY     => DAY_NO := DAY;
     when FEBRUARY    => DAY_NO := 31  + DAY;
     when MARCH       => DAY_NO := 59  + DAY;
     when APRIL       => DAY_NO := 90  + DAY;
     when MAY         => DAY_NO := 121 + DAY;
     when JUNE        => DAY_NO := 151 + DAY;
     when JULY        => DAY_NO := 182 + DAY;
```

```
      when AUGUST      => DAY_NO := 212 + DAY;
      when SEPTEMBER   => DAY_NO := 242 + DAY;
      when OCTOBER     => DAY_NO := 273 + DAY;
      when NOVEMBER    => DAY_NO := 303 + DAY;
      when DECEMBER    => DAY_NO := 334 + DAY;
   end case;
   if (YEAR mod 4 = 0 and YEAR mod 100 /= 0)
      or YEAR mod 400 = 0 then
      -- leap year
      if MONTH >= MARCH then
         DAY_NO := DAY_NO + 1;
      end if;
   end if;

   PUT("The day's number in the year is ");
   PUT(DAY_NO, WIDTH => 1);
end COMPUTE_DAY_NUMBER;
```

The program should contain a check that DAY is not greater than the number of days in MONTH, but to simplify the program we shall ignore this potential problem. However, there is no risk of the program accepting incorrect years or months. If incorrect data is typed in for these, a run-time error will result.

Ada's input/output mechanism may at first appear a little complicated. This is only because it is so general and works for all possible numeric types and enumeration types. There can be much to write in a program if you are working with several types. Sometimes it is tempting to avoid declaring your own types and adhere to the standard types INTEGER and FLOAT. Then access is only needed to the input/output packages for these two types. In spite of this, an attempt should still be made to use Ada's facilities for working with different types. It increases the clarity and reliability of the program. Ada's facilities are better equipped to represent the phenomena required, and these are automatically checked so that variables contain only permitted values. Furthermore, the program is made more easily transferable from one implementation of Ada to another.

Using your own types

- Clearer and more reliable programs.
- Better representation of reality.
- Automatic checks on values.
- Easier to transfer programs.

5.7   Subtypes

When a real-world phenomenon is described, it is sometimes useful to introduce a concept that denotes a subset of a more general concept. For example, 'work-day' denotes a subset of the concept 'days of the week', and 'positive integers' is a subset of the concept 'integers'. In Ada, such subsets of concepts can be represented by using **subtypes**. Declarations of subtypes appear much like the ordinary type declarations and are placed in the same part of the program. A declaration of a subtype begins with the reserved word **subtype**.

For example, suppose we have already declared the enumeration type DAY_OF_THE_WEEK:

```
type DAY_OF_THE_WEEK is (MONDAY, TUESDAY, WEDNESDAY,
                         THURSDAY, FRIDAY,
                         SATURDAY, SUNDAY);
```

Now we can declare a subtype of DAY_OF_THE_WEEK that we shall call WORKDAY:

```
subtype WORKDAY is DAY_OF_THE_WEEK range MONDAY .. FRIDAY;
```

In the declaration of the subtype we state that the base type is DAY_OF_THE_WEEK† and that the permitted values for the new subtype should lie in the interval MONDAY to FRIDAY.

Now it is possible to declare objects of either the type DAY_OF_THE_WEEK or the subtype WORKDAY:

```
TODAY            : DAY_OF_THE_WEEK;
NEXT_WORKDAY : WORKDAY;
```

The declaration of a subtype does *not* mean that a new type has been created. It simply means that a name has been introduced for a subset of a base type. In our example we can express it thus: the variables TODAY and NEXT_WORKDAY belong to the same type, namely DAY_OF_THE_WEEK, but NEXT_WORKDAY is specified further in that it belongs to the subtype WORKDAY. This means that the following assignment is permitted:

```
TODAY := NEXT_WORKDAY;
```

---

† As we have mentioned before, types in Ada 95 are actually nameless. In fact, DAY_OF_THE_WEEK is itself a subtype, with an anonymous base type. This means that the base type of WORKDAY is not DAY_OF_THE_WEEK but its anonymous base type.

Both variables are simply of the same type. The assignment may also be turned round:

NEXT_WORKDAY := TODAY;

However, this assignment could lead to a run-time error when the program is executed; this would happen if TODAY contained some value outside the interval MONDAY .. FRIDAY (that is, either of the values SATURDAY or SUNDAY).

The good thing about using subtypes, then, is that they provide extra support in finding errors in the logic of a program. Furthermore, they allow a better representation of the facts, which again increases the clarity of a program.

The limits stated in a declaration do not need to be static. Arbitrary expressions may be used:

START   : INTEGER := ... ;

N   : INTEGER := ... ;

type NUMBER_TYPE **is range** 1 .. 1000;

subtype CERTAIN_NUMBERS **is** NUMBER_TYPE
                          range START .. START + N − 1;

Here we assume that the variables START and N are initialized to some values. If the values are such that one of the limits lies outside the interval 1–1000, or if the second limit is lower than the first, we shall get a run-time error.

In the package STANDARD two subtypes of the type INTEGER are declared:

subtype NATURAL   **is** INTEGER **range** 0 .. INTEGER'LAST;

subtype POSITIVE   **is** INTEGER **range** 1 .. INTEGER'LAST;

These represent the mathematical concepts of 'natural numbers' and 'positive integers' and it is appropriate to use them instead of INTEGER for work with general integral values that are known to be ≥ 0 or ≥ 1, respectively.

If we have the following object declarations:

N   : NATURAL;

P   : POSITIVE;

I   : INTEGER;

then the following statements are allowed because all the variables actually have the same type, INTEGER:

P   := N + P;

I   := P − N;

Types other than enumeration and integer types may have subtypes. For example, subtypes of floating point types can be constructed:

> **type** MEASUREMENT **is digits** 10;
>
> **subtype** PRESSURE **is** MEASUREMENT **range** 0.0 .. 3.0;

If a numeric object has to be described, then either a completely new type can be declared, as we did earlier, or a subtype of a numeric type already in existence, such as FLOAT or INTEGER, can be used. When is one better than the other? The choice of method should be guided by the actual objects to be represented. To represent things that have nothing to do with one another, use completely new types and not subtypes. Then, of course, it is possible to check that they are not mixed by mistake in the program. Otherwise, subtypes can be used. This can be particularly practical when carrying out many computations with closely related objects, because then it is not necessary to make explicit type conversions throughout the computations.

Declaring subtypes

> **subtype** U **is** T **range** *min_value .. max_value*;

where U is the name of the subtype and T is the name of a type. T can be a numeric type or an enumeration type. The smallest and greatest possible values for objects of subtype U are given by *min_value* and *max_value*.

- U becomes a subtype of T. No new type is created.
- Objects of subtype U will have type T.

Using subtypes

- When closely related objects are in use and many computations are to be made using them.
- Good representation of reality.
- Provide help with tracing errors of logic.
- For real objects that are not closely related, completely new types should be used in preference to subtypes.

Let us look at a program where it is natural to use subtypes. The program asks the user to choose two of the colours red, yellow and blue, and then it writes out the name of the colour obtained by mixing them. A type COLOUR is introduced that describes all possible colours and mixtures. We then let the three primary colours make up a subtype of COLOUR, called PRIMARY_COLOUR.

```
with TEXT_IO;
use TEXT_IO;
procedure MIX_COLOURS is
  type COLOUR is (RED, YELLOW, BLUE,
                         ORANGE, GREEN, PURPLE);
  subtype PRIMARY_COLOUR is COLOUR range RED .. BLUE;
  package COLOUR_INOUT is new ENUMERATION_IO(COLOUR);
  use COLOUR_INOUT;

  COLOUR1, COLOUR2  : PRIMARY_COLOUR;
  COLOUR_MI              : COLOUR;

begin
  PUT_LINE("Welcome to the colour mixing program!");
  PUT_LINE("The primary colours are RED, YELLOW and BLUE");
  PUT_LINE("The colour mixes are ORANGE, GREEN and PURPLE");
  PUT_LINE("Terminate the run with CTRL-D.");

loop
  NEW_LINE;        -- extra blank line
  PUT_LINE("Enter two of the primary colours");
  exit when END_OF_FILE;
  GET(COLOUR1); GET(COLOUR2);

  if (COLOUR1 = RED and COLOUR2 = YELLOW) or
     (COLOUR2 = RED and COLOUR1 = YELLOW) then
     COLOUR_MIX := ORANGE;
  elsif  (COLOUR1 = YELLOW and COLOUR2 = BLUE) or
         (COLOUR2 = YELLOW and COLOUR1 = BLUE) then
    COLOUR_MIX := GREEN;
  elsif  (COLOUR1 = RED and COLOUR2 = BLUE) or
         (COLOUR2 = RED and COLOUR1 = BLUE) then
     COLOUR_MIX := PURPLE;
  else – same colours
     COLOUR_MIX := COLOUR1;
  end if;

  PUT("The colour mixture will be ");
  PUT(COLOUR_MIX); NEW_LINE;
 end loop;
end MIX_COLOURS;
```

The two input colours are of the subtype PRIMARY_COLOUR, thus automatically checking that no values other than the permitted ones, RED, YELLOW and BLUE, are input. We can use the same input/output package, COLOUR_INOUT, for reading and writing all the colours, both primary colours and mixtures, because they all belong to the same type, COLOUR.

The program is designed so that it repeatedly reads in the primary colours and displays the name of the mixture, until the user wants to stop. The termination variant with END_OF_FILE and an **exit** statement is used in the program, as described in Section 4.8. Below is shown the output from the program:

```
Welcome to the colour mixing program!
The primary colours are RED, YELLOW and BLUE
The colour mixes are ORANGE, GREEN and PURPLE
Terminate the run with CTRL-D.

Enter two of the primary colours
yellow blue
The colour mix will be GREEN

Enter two of the primary colours
blue red
The colour mix will be PURPLE

Enter two of the primary colours
yellow yellow
The colour mix will be YELLOW

Enter two of the primary colours
Now the user types CTRL-D at the terminal
```

5.8 Array types

The scalar types we have declared so far have been simple types where each object of the type assumes only one single value. Now we shall study **array types**. In an array type, an object consists of a numbered collection of similar components. It can also be said that an object of an array type is a kind of table in which each element has a particular number associated with it.

5.8.1 Constrained array types

We shall start by looking at **constrained array types**. When a constrained array type is declared, both the numbering of the components and the types of the individual components must be specified. Let us look at an example:

```
type SERIES_OF_MEASUREMENTS is array (1 .. 10) of FLOAT;
```

The idea is that the type SERIES_OF_MEASUREMENTS should represent a series of 10 measurements of some sort, in which each single measurement is represented by a real number. The reserved word **array** states that the declaration involves an array type. After this word, the numbering of the components is specified. In this example, they will be numbered using the integers 1–10, inclusive. Finally, the type of the individual components is given, here FLOAT because each measurement consists of a real number. We can declare variables of this new type:

> SERIES_A, SERIES_B : SERIES_OF_MEASUREMENTS;

Figure 5.1 illustrates the variable SERIES_A. The variable can be likened to 10 'compartments', each holding a value of the type FLOAT. The first compartment is numbered 1, the second is 2 and so on. The contents of the compartments are not yet defined: the value of a variable is normally undefined after declaration unless deliberately initialized. (It is possible to initialize array variables at the same time as they are declared in exactly the same way as simple variables. We will return to this soon.)

To enable access to a particular component of an array, **indexing** is used; we have already seen this in operation in connection with the type STRING. For example, to give the second component of the variable SERIES_A the value 1.5, we can write:

> SERIES_A(2) := 1.5;

Then we get the SERIES_A shown in Figure 5.2. A component that is selected by indexing can be used in the same way as a normal scalar variable, as in the expression:

> SERIES_B(1) := 2.0 * SERIES_A(7);

When the type SERIES_OF_MEASUREMENTS was declared, the interval:

> (1 .. 10)

was specified as the way in which the individual components should be numbered. What this really means is that the component numbers should have type INTEGER and lie in the interval 1–10. When an individual component is

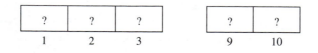

Figure 5.1

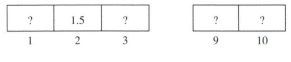

Figure 5.2

selected by indexing, the index expression in the brackets can be a normal expression. It does not need to be a constant value as in the example above. However, the expression must have the same type as the numbers of the components of the array and its value must lie in the specified interval. Thus for the variables SERIES_A and SERIES_B, index expressions must have the type INTEGER and be in the interval 1–10.

We shall look at a simple example of a program that uses an array. The program will read from the terminal 10 real numbers that make up a series of measurements. Then it will calculate the mean value of the measurements and display it. Finally, the program will write out all the measurements that are larger than the calculated mean. We shall use the type SERIES_OF_MEASUREMENTS, but in the declaration we have used a constant SERIES_LENGTH instead of writing the literal 10. This constant is also used in the program itself, so the program can be changed easily if the size of the series should change. It is a good rule to use constants in this way. The program is:

```
with TEXT_IO, BASIC_NUM_IO;
use TEXT_IO, BASIC_NUM_IO;
procedure INVESTIGATE_MEASUREMENTS is
   SERIES_LENGTH : constant := 10;
   type SERIES_OF_MEASUREMENTS is array
                   (1 .. SERIES_LENGTH) of FLOAT;

   SERIES  : SERIES_OF_MEASUREMENTS;
   SUM     : FLOAT := 0.0;
   MEAN    : FLOAT;

begin
   PUT_LINE("Enter the measurements");
   for I in 1 .. SERIES_LENGTH loop
      GET(SERIES(I));
      SUM := SUM + SERIES(I);
   end loop;

   MEAN := SUM / FLOAT(SERIES_LENGTH);
   PUT("The mean is "); PUT(MEAN); NEW_LINE;

   PUT_LINE("Measurements greater than the mean: ");
   for I in 1 .. SERIES_LENGTH loop
```

```
    if SERIES(I) > MEAN then
       PUT("Measurement no. ");
       PUT(I, WIDTH => 2);
       PUT(" is ");
       PUT(SERIES(I)); NEW_LINE;
    end if;
  end loop;
end INVESTIGATE_MEASUREMENTS;
```

It is very common to use **loop** statements with **for** when arrays are involved. In the first **loop** statement we make the loop parameter run from 1 to 10, that is, through all the components of the array SERIES. Each time, one measurement is read and stored in one of the components of the array SERIES. The statement:

```
GET(SERIES(I));
```

causes one measurement to be stored in the component numbered I. Thus, the first time round a value is read to component 1, the second time to component 2, and so on.

While measurements are being read in, the program also calculates the sum of all the components. The mean is obtained by dividing this sum by the length of the series. The constant SERIES_LENGTH has type *universal_integer* and must therefore be converted to type FLOAT in the calculation.

The second **loop** statement runs, again, through all the components in the array SERIES. Each component now holds the result of one measurement. If a measurement is larger than the mean, the number of the measurement and the measurement itself are displayed at the terminal. Figure 5.3 shows the output for one run of this program.

There is much freedom in specifying how the individual components should be indexed when an array type is declared. They do not have to be numbered with integers starting from 1, as we did when we declared the type

---

Enter the measurements
4.3 6.5 3.8 3.9 5.2 5.0 3.9 4.4 6.1 5.5
The mean is 4.86000000E+00
Measurements greater than the mean:
Measurement no.   2 is 6.5000000E+00
Measurement no.   5 is 5.2000000E+00
Measurement no.   6 is 5.0000000E+00
Measurement no.   9 is 6.1000000E+00
Measurement no. 10 is 5.50000000E+00

Figure 5.3

SERIES_OF_MEASUREMENTS. For example, we can choose to start the numbering with –100:

> **type** LIST **is array** (–100 .. 100) **of** INTEGER;

Here we have declared a list type in which each component is a whole number of type INTEGER. The list is indexed with integers –100 to 100, so that the first component is numbered –100, the second –99, and so on.

In fact, values of any discrete type (integer type or enumeration type) can be used for indexing. Here are a few examples where enumeration types are used:

> **type** WORKING_HOURS **is array** (MONDAY .. FRIDAY) **of** FLOAT;
> **type** COLOUR_NUMBER **is array** (RED .. PURPLE) **of** INTEGER;
> **type** NO_OF_DAYS   **is array** (JANUARY .. DECEMBER) **of**
>   INTEGER;

We have assumed that the types DAY_OF_THE_WEEK, COLOUR and MONTH_TYPE have been declared as earlier in the chapter. If we declare the variables:

> MY_WORKING_HOURS : WORKING_HOURS;
> NO_OF_DAYS_1   : NO_OF_DAYS;

then the first components of the variable MY_WORKING_HOURS has the index 'number' MONDAY, and the first component in the variable NO_OF_DAYS_1 has the index 'number' JANUARY. To illustrate this, we can represent the variable MY_WORKING_HOURS as in Figure 5.4.

In the program, if a particular component is to be chosen by using indexing, then the enumeration values are used as 'numbers':

> MY_WORKING_HOURS(WEDNESDAY) := 8.5;
> GET(MY_WORKING_HOURS(FRIDAY));
> NO_OF_DAYS_1(MARCH) := 31;
> **if** NO_OF_DAYS_1(FEBRUARY) = 29 **then**
>   PUT("Leap year");
> **end if**;

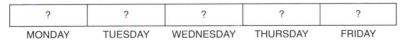

?	?	?	?	?
MONDAY	TUESDAY	WEDNESDAY	THURSDAY	FRIDAY

Figure 5.4

> **Indexing in arrays**
>
> A(N)
>
> where N is an expression of the same type as the index type of A.
>
> N's value must lie within the index constraints of A.

The type of the index expressions and the constraints on their values depend on the index specification in the declaration. To make the type of the index obvious, it is recommended that the following alternative form of array declaration is used:

type SERIES_OF_MEASUREMENTS **is array**
                (INTEGER **range** 1 ..10) **of** FLOAT;

type WORKING_HOURS **is array**
                (DAY_OF_THE_WEEK **range** MONDAY .. FRIDAY)
                of FLOAT;

type LETTER_COUNT **is array** (CHARACTER **range** 'a' .. 'z')
                        of INTEGER;

type COLOUR_NUMBER **is** array (COLOUR **range** RED .. PURPLE)
                        of INTEGER;

In this alternative, the type of the index is stated in the brackets as well as the interval to be used. In the third example we have used CHARACTER as index type, CHARACTER being an enumeration type which can therefore also be used. The first element in an object of type LETTER_COUNTS is 'numbered' 'a' and the last element is 'numbered' 'z'.

The range expression in the brackets may be left out, meaning that all the values of the given type should be used as index values. The declaration of COLOUR_NUMBER and NO_OF_DAYS can thus be written as follows:

type COLOUR_NUMBER   **is array** (COLOUR) **of** INTEGER;

type NO_OF_DAYS   **is array** (MONTH_TYPE) **of** INTEGER;

It is often appropriate to introduce a new type or subtype for the index using a special declaration. This often makes the program clearer and, in addition, it is then possible to declare variables of the index type. These variables can then be used for indexing purposes. For example:

type LINE_NUMBER   **is range** 1 .. 72;

type LINE_TABLE   **is array** (LINE_NUMBER) **of** INTEGER;

subtype LC_LETTER   **is** CHARACTER **range** 'a' .. 'z';

type LC_LETTER_COUNT **is array** (LC_LETTER) **of** INTEGER;

Ordinary expressions may be used for stating the index constraints in a declaration of an array type: it is not necessary to use constant values as in the examples so far. An expression that specifies a constraint on an index may thus contain variables whose values are unknown until the program is run. The size of the array, therefore, does not need to be known when the program is compiled; this applies irrespective of the form chosen for stating the constraints:

type TABLE **is array** (N .. 2 * N) **of** FLOAT;

type VECTOR **is array** (INTEGER **range** 1 .. N) **of** FLOAT;

subtype LIST_INDEX **is** INTEGER **range** 100 .. 100 + N;

type LIST **is array** (LIST_INDEX) **of** CHARACTER;

N is assumed to be an integer variable. If the first index expression takes a value which is greater than the second, the declaration is of an array with no components. If such an object is declared, it is called an **empty array**.

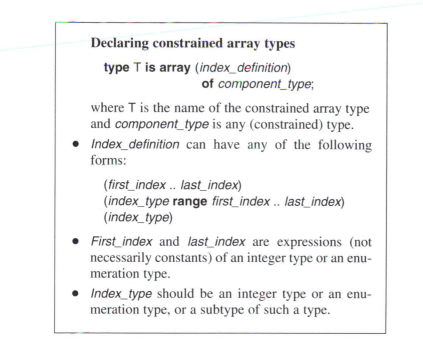

Declaring constrained array types

> **type** T **is array** (*index_definition*)
>   **of** *component_type*;

where T is the name of the constrained array type and *component_type* is any (constrained) type.

- *Index_definition* can have any of the following forms:

  > (*first_index* .. *last_index*)
  > (*index_type* **range** *first_index* .. *last_index*)
  > (*index_type*)

- *First_index* and *last_index* are expressions (not necessarily constants) of an integer type or an enumeration type.

- *Index_type* should be an integer type or an enumeration type, or a subtype of such a type.

5.8.2   Array aggregates

It has been shown that values can be assigned to the individual components of an array by indexing. If values are to be given to several components in one array, there is a more convenient method than assigning values component by component, and that is by making use of **array aggregates**. Then the values of all components are given at once. A few examples will explain what this means. The following statement means that the first, second and third components of array SERIES_A (declared earlier) are assigned the value 1.0, the fourth is assigned the value 0.5 and the rest of the elements in the array (that is, components 5–10) are assigned the value 0.0:

```
SERIES_A := (1.0, 1.0, 1.0, 0.5, 0.0,
                 0.0, 0.0, 0.0, 0.0, 0.0);
```

When there is a large array where several components are to be given the same value the reserved word **others** can be used. The statement above can be written:

```
SERIES_A := (1.0, 1.0, 1.0, 0.5, others => 0.0);
```

It is very common to set all the components of an array to zero. Then we write:

```
SERIES_B := (others => 0.0);
```

Using aggregates, array variables can be initialized when they are declared. The variable DAYS_IN_MONTH can, for example, be declared in the following way:

```
DAYS_IN_MONTH : NO_OF_DAYS := (31, 28, 31, 30, 31, 30,
                                   31, 31, 30, 31, 30, 31);
```

There is an alternative form of aggregate that has some similarities with the **case** statement. One example is:

```
SERIES_A := SERIES_OF_MEASUREMENTS'(1 .. 3 => 1.0,
                                        4 => 0.5,
                                        others => 0.0);
```

Before the apostrophe the type of the aggregate is given. In some cases when the reserved word **others** is used it is difficult for the compiler to decide the length of the aggregate. In those cases a **qualified expression** including the type name must be given, as in this example. Another example of the alternative form of an aggregate is:

```
DAYS_IN_MONTH : NO_OF_DAYS :=
NO_OF_DAYS'(APRIL | JUNE | SEPTEMBER | NOVEMBER => 30,
                FEBRUARY => 28, others => 31);
```

In an aggregate there must be exactly one value for each component. This is most easily arranged using an **others** alternative. If **others** is used it must come last.

> **Array aggregates**
>
> - A list where the values of all the components of an array are stated at the same time.
> - Can be used, for example, in assignments and comparisons.
> - Alternative forms:
>
>   (*value_1, value_2, ... , value_N*)
>   (*index_i* => *value_i, index_j* => *value_j, ... *)
>   (*index_k* | *index_m* => *value, ... *)
>   (*index_a .. index_b* => *value, ... *)
>   (... **others** => *value*)
>
>   *Value* can be a general expression.

In the following example program, all the components of an array are set to zero when the array is declared. The program's task is to read a text from the terminal and count how many times each of the lower-case letters 'a' to 'z' occurs in the text. To keep count of the different letters, an array COUNT is used whose components have the standardized subtype NATURAL, that is, they are integers ≥ 0. In the array COUNT there is a component for each of the lower-case letters 'a' to 'z', and so the components of the array are 'numbered' with the lower-case letters. COUNT has type COUNT_TABLE in the declaration of which the subtype LC_LETTER has been used as index type. LC_LETTER is a subtype of CHARACTER in which the only permitted values are the letters 'a' to 'z'.

In the program, one character at a time is read from the terminal to the variable CHAR. This continues until the user says that the text is finished by typing CTRL-D. If the character read is one of the lower-case letters, the corresponding component in the array COUNT is increased by one. The program ends by printing the contents of the array COUNT.

```
with TEXT_IO, BASIC_NUM_IO;
use TEXT_IO, BASIC_NUM_IO;
procedure LC_LETTER_FREQUENCY is
    subtype LC_LETTER is CHARACTER range 'a' .. 'z';
    type COUNT_TABLE is array (LC_LETTER) of NATURAL;

    COUNT : COUNT_TABLE := (others => 0);
    CHAR  : CHARACTER;

begin
    PUT_LINE("Enter the text; terminate with CTRL-D");
    while not END_OF_FILE loop
```

```
      GET(CHAR);
      if CHAR in 'a' .. 'z' then
         COUNT(CHAR) := COUNT(CHAR) + 1;
      end if;
   end loop;

   -- Write how many times each letter has occurred

   NEW_LINE;
   PUT_LINE("Letter      Frequency");
   NEW_LINE;
   for T in 'a' .. 'z' loop
      SET_COL(4); PUT(T); PUT(COUNT(T), WIDTH => 11);
      NEW_LINE;
   end loop;
end LC_LETTER_FREQUENCY;
```

The statement:

```
COUNT(CHAR) := COUNT(CHAR) + 1;
```

means that if the variable CHAR contains, for example, the letter 'g', the component with index 'number' 'g' is increased by one. Figure 5.5 illustrates the output from a run of the program.

5.8.3 Unconstrained array types

The array types we have studied so far have all been **constrained array types**. They are so called because the index constraints (and hence the number of components) are specified in the type declaration. If we declare objects of such a constrained array type, they will all have the same index constraints and number of components. In certain situations it is undesirable to specify the constraints on the index numbers. If, for instance, a part of a program is to be written that will sort the elements of a list into order of magnitude, or one that will carry out mathematical operations on vectors, then it is desirable that it should work for all lists or vectors, irrespective of the number of elements in the list or the number of components in the vectors. To cope with such a situation Ada offers the possibility of declaring **unconstrained array types**. When an unconstrained array type is declared, the index type is specified but there is no need to state limits for the index. Instead, the symbol < > is used:

```
type VECTOR      is array (INTEGER range < >) of FLOAT;
type INDEX_TYPE   is range 1 .. 100;
type NUMBER_LIST is array (INDEX_TYPE range < >) of INTEGER;
type CHAR_COUNT  is array (CHARACTER range < >) of INTEGER;
```

Enter the text; terminate with CTRL-D
ada is a registered trademark of the us government
ada joint program office

Letter	Frequency
a	8
b	0
c	1
d	4
e	8
f	3
g	3
h	1
i	4
j	1
k	1
l	0
m	3
n	3
o	5
p	1
q	0
r	7
s	3
t	5
u	1
v	1
w	0
x	0
y	0
z	0

Figure 5.5

When an object of an unconstrained array type is declared, then the index constraints must be stated:

```
VECTOR_1            : VECTOR(-10 .. 10);
VECTOR_2            : VECTOR(1 .. N);          -- N is a variable
MY_LIST             : NUMBER_LIST(I .. 2 * I) -- expressions OK
YOUR_LIST           : NUMBER_LIST(90 .. 100);
UC_LETTER_COUNT : CHAR_COUNT('A' .. 'Z');
DIGIT_COUNT         : CHAR_COUNT('0' .. '9');
```

In these examples, the variables VECTOR_1 and VECTOR_2 have the same type but different index constraints.

▼
▲

In Ada 95 the index constraints may be left out if the object is initialized. In that case the index constraints are fixed by the initial value.

It is also possible to declare subtypes of an unconstrained array type. Then the index constraints are stated in the subtype declaration:

subtype LITTLE_VECTOR **is** VECTOR(1 .. 3);
POINT : LITTLE_VECTOR;

Unconstrained array types

> **type** T **is array** (*index_type* **range** < >)
> > **of** *component_type;*

where *index_type* is an integer type or an enumeration type.

The index constraints must be stated when an object of type T, or a subtype of T, is declared.

With unconstrained array types, as with constrained array types, it is possible to give the value of an entire array at once, by assignment or at initialization, using aggregates:

VECTOR_1 := (0.0, 0.0, 0.0, **others** => 1.0);
VECTOR_2 := (**others** => 0.0);

In fact, we have already used an unconstrained array type on several occasions – the standard type STRING that is defined in the package STANDARD:

type STRING **is array** (POSITIVE **range** < >) **of** CHARACTER;

The declarations of variables of type STRING that we have used, for example:

PRODUCT_CODE : STRING(1 .. 6);

are thus nothing more than declarations of variables of an unconstrained array type. For the type STRING there is, as we have seen, a special short way of writing an aggregate, namely by enclosing the values of the components in quotation marks:

PRODUCT_CODE := "xWy98k";

5.8.4 Assignment and comparison

When assigning values to an array, instead of an aggregate on the right-hand side, it is possible to have another array of the same type and with the same number of components as that on the left-hand side. (Two arrays that belong to the same constrained array type always fulfil these demands.) We can, for example, make the assignments:

```
SERIES_A     := SERIES_B;    -- constrained array types, always OK
VECTOR_1     := VECTOR_2;    -- OK if same number of components
```

> **Array assignments**
>
>   A1 := A2;
>
> where A1 and A2 have the same type and an equal number of components.
>
> It is not necessary for the components to have the same numbering.

It is also possible to compare two entire arrays if they have the same type. (They may even have different numbers of components if they belong to the same unconstrained array type.)

```
if SERIES_A = SERIES_B then
while SERIES_A /= SERIES_B then
```

Aggregates can also be used in comparisons:

```
if SERIES_A = SERIES_OF_MEASUREMENTS'(others => 0.0) then
```

For making comparisons, the operators = and /= are defined for all array types. Two arrays are equal if they have the same number of components and all their corresponding components are equal. Otherwise, they are unequal. The bounds of the array do not have to be the same. If, for example, A has an index range 1 .. 5 and B an index range 0 .. 4, then A(1) and B(0) are corresponding components, as well as A(2) and B(1), etc. For array types where the individual components are of a discrete type (that is, integer type or enumeration type) the comparison operators <, >, <= and >= are also defined. It is thus possible to write:

```
if MY_LIST > YOUR_LIST then
```

In such a case the comparison occurs in the same way as it does for alphabetical order: if the first element in MY_LIST is greater than the first element of YOUR_LIST (element number 90) then MY_LIST is considered to be bigger and the Boolean expression above is true. If, however, the first element of MY_LIST is less than the first element of YOUR_LIST, then YOUR_LIST is the bigger and the expression is false. If the two first elements are equal, then the comparison continues to the two second elements. If the arrays have the same number of elements and all corresponding elements turn out to be equal, then the two arrays are equal and the Boolean expression above is false. If the arrays have different numbers of components and all the elements in the shorter array are the same as the corresponding elements in the longer array, then the shorter one is determined to be the lesser of the two.

Comparing arrays

- The operators = and /= exist for all arrays which have the same type (even if the numbers of components are not the same).

- The operators <, <=, > and >= also exist if the components are of an integer type or an enumeration type. Comparison is made on the same principles as sorting into alphabetical order.

In assignments and comparisons, **slices** can be used, in the same way as they were earlier for the type STRING.

```
VECTOR_1 := VECTOR_2(N − 20..N);  -- N is a variable
VECTOR_1 (0 .. 5) := VECTOR_2(1 .. 6);
if VECTOR_1(−10 .. N − 11) = VECTOR_2 then
```

Slices of arrays

A(N1 .. N2)

where A is an array type. N1 and N2 are expressions whose type is the same as the index type for A.

- If N2 < N1, the result is an empty slice.

- Otherwise N1 and N2 must lie within the index constraints for A.

- The result has the same type as A.

5.8.5 Attributes

We have seen that when an array is declared there are many possible ways of indexing it. The index constraints do not even need to be known at compilation time, but they can be determined by expressions that are only evaluated when the program is run. It is sometimes impossible to use constant values in a program to refer to different values of an index, for example, to state the first and last index numbers for an array. Then some of the attributes that are defined for array types can be used. The most useful are FIRST, LAST, RANGE and LENGTH.

FIRST and LAST are used to find the first and last index numbers in an array. VECTOR_1'FIRST, for example, gives the first index value for the array VECTOR_1. FIRST and LAST can be used, for instance, to make a loop run through all the index values for an array:

```
for I in VECTOR_1'FIRST .. VECTOR_1'LAST loop
    ...
end loop;
```

It is more elegant, maybe, to make use of the RANGE attribute instead, giving the index interval for the array. Using RANGE we can rewrite the above **loop** statement:

```
for I in VECTOR_1'RANGE loop
    ...
end loop;
```

Here the loop parameter will run through all the index values for the array VECTOR_1.

The attribute LENGTH is used to find the number of components in an array:

```
PUT("Number of components in the vector: ");
PUT(VECTOR_1'LENGTH);
```

In front of the apostrophe can appear either a name of an array object (variable or constant) or a type name, but not the name of an unconstrained array type. Here are a few further examples:

```
NO_OF_DAYS'LAST        -- gives the value DECEMBER
NO_OF_DAYS_1'FIRST     -- gives the value JANUARY
NO_OF_DAYS_1'LENGTH    -- gives the value 12
NO_OF_DAYS'RANGE       -- gives JANUARY .. DECEMBER
```

Attributes for array types

T'FIRST   – gives first index value for array type T

T'LAST   – gives last index value for array type T

T'LENGTH – gives number of components in array
              type T

T'RANGE – gives the index interval for array type T

where T is the name of a constrained array type.

Instead of a type name, the name of an object of an
array type can be used:

A'FIRST   – gives first index value for array A

A'LAST   – gives last index value for array A

A'LENGTH – gives number of components in array A

A'RANGE – gives the index interval for array A

It is a good habit to try to use these attributes instead of stating index limits as constant values in programs, for example, in **loop** statements. Programs then become much more general and can more easily be changed if the constraints on an array are changed.

5.8.6   Catenating arrays

Just as for text strings, the operator & can be used for **catenating** arrays. If the type VECTOR has been declared, as earlier, to be:

type VECTOR **is array** (INTEGER **range** < >) **of** FLOAT;

and we have the variables:

```
V2 : VECTOR(1 .. 2);
V3 : VECTOR(101 .. 103);
V5 : VECTOR(0 .. 4);
```

then we can join V2 and V3 together:

```
V5 := V2 & V3;
```

It is also possible to join a component onto an array as in the following examples:

```
V3 := 27.0 & V2;
V3 := V2 & 8.0;
```

5.9   Searching and sorting

To be able to search for a piece of information in tables or lists is a very common requirement of a computer program. Arrays are naturally used in such programs. As an example of searching we shall study a program that produces the selling price of an article from a catalogue. As input, the user types in the article number at the terminal when the program is run. Assume that there are only seven different articles with the numbers and selling prices shown in Figure 5.6. The program should work like this: if the user types, for example, article number 123 at the terminal, then the program should write out the price £9.15. If the user gives an article number that is not in the table, the program should print out the message "Price details missing". We use two constant arrays in the program, ART_NUMBER_TABLE and ART_PRICE_TABLE, both with seven components. In ART_NUMBER_TABLE the seven article numbers are stored, one number to each component. The first component, ART_ NUMBER_TABLE(1), thus holds the number 56, ART_NUMBER_TABLE(2) holds 81, and so on (see Figure 5.7).

If we want to make it easy we can let the components of array ART_ NUMBER_TABLE have type INTEGER. If, however, we want to write a program that more closely represents reality, we should declare an integer type of our own, ARTICLE_NUMBER, and let the components have this type. We can assume that the article numbers lie between 1 and 999.

In the array ART_PRICE_TABLE are stored, in the same way, 3.50 in the first component, ART_PRICE_TABLE(1), 1.75 in the second, ART_PRICE_ TABLE(2), and so on. We shall declare a floating point type ARTICLE_PRICE and let the components of ART_PRICE_TABLE have this type, assuming that no prices are higher than £99.99.

Both arrays are initialized when they are declared. Note that the arrays are declared as constants. A constant has been introduced into the program, called TAB_SIZE, with the value 7, which is made use of both in the declarations of the array types and in the program itself. It is a good idea to use a constant in this way because the size of the tables can then easily be changed.

Article number	Price
56	3.50
81	1.75
123	9.15
379	20.00
505	0.50
811	31.45
944	5.95

Figure 5.6

56	81	123	379	505	811	944
1	2	3	4	5	6	7

Figure 5.7

There are several methods available for searching in arrays, and these methods have varying degrees of efficiency. In this program the simplest form of searching, **linear searching**, is employed. This involves going through the array ART_NUMBER_TABLE from the beginning until the component containing the required article number is found, or until the whole array has been searched unsuccessfully. To indicate whether the article number has been found, a variable FOUND of type BOOLEAN is used. This is given the initial value FALSE. Another variable I, initialized to 1, is used to run through all possible values of the index of the array ART_NUMBER_TABLE. The first version of the program looks like this:

```
with TEXT_IO;
use TEXT_IO;
procedure LOOK_UP_PRICE is
   type ARTICLE_NUMBER  is range 1 .. 999;
   type ARTICLE_PRICE     is digits 4 range 0.00 .. 99.99;

   package ART_NO_INOUT is new INTEGER_IO(ARTICLE_NUMBER);
   package ART_PRICE_INOUT is new FLOAT_IO(ARTICLE_PRICE);
   use ART_NO_INOUT, ART_PRICE_INOUT;

   TAB_SIZE : constant := 7;
   type ART_NO_TAB_TYPE      is array(1 .. TAB_SIZE)
                               ARTICLE_NUMBER;
   type ART_PRICE_TAB_TYPE is array(1 .. TAB_SIZE)
                               of ARTICLE_PRICE;

   ART_NUMBER_TABLE : constant ART_NO_TAB_TYPE :=
                     (56, 81, 123, 379, 505, 811, 944);
   ART_PRICE_TABLE :   constant ART_PRICE_TAB_TYPE :=
                     (3.50, 1.75, 9.15, 20.00,
                      0.50, 31.45, 5.95);
   I : INTEGER := 1;
   FOUND : BOOLEAN := FALSE;
   WANTED_ART_NO : ARTICLE_NUMBER;

begin
   PUT_LINE("Enter the article number");
   GET(WANTED_ART_NO);
```

```
   while I < TAB_SIZE and not FOUND loop
      if ART_NUMBER_TABLE(I) = WANTED_ART_NO then
         FOUND := TRUE;
      else
         I := I + 1;
      end if;
   end loop;

   if FOUND then
      PUT("Its price is ");
      PUT(ART_PRICE_TABLE(I), EXP => 0, FORE => 1, AFT => 2);
   else
      PUT("Price details missing");
   end if;
end LOOK_UP_PRICE;
```

First we shall comment on the declarations of the constant arrays ART_
NUMBER_TABLE and ART_PRICE_TABLE. These have been given the types
ART_NO_TAB_TYPE and ART_PRICE_TAB_TYPE. When an array is to be
declared, it sometimes seems clumsy to have to declare its type explicitly before
the array itself can be declared, especially if the array type is not used elsewhere
in the program. A shorter way is to declare the array's type directly in the object
declaration instead. In our program, the declarations of ART_NUMBER_TABLE
and ART_PRICE_TABLE could look like this:

```
ART_NUMBER_TABLE : constant array(1 .. TAB_SIZE)
                                     of ARTICLE_NUMBER
                       := (56, 81, 123, 379, 505, 811, 944);
ART_PRICE_TABLE    : constant array(1 .. TAB_SIZE)
                                     of ARTICLE_PRICE
                       := (3.50, 1.75, 9.15, 20.00, 0.50, 31.45, 5.95);
```

and the declarations of the types ART_NO_TAB_TYPE and ART_PRICE_
TAB_TYPE could be omitted.

We have created our own input/output packages in the program for the
types ARTICLE_NUMBER and ARTICLE_PRICE. The search itself takes place
in the **loop** statement. Each time through, one component of the array
ART_NUMBER_TABLE is looked at, and if it is the same as the required article
number the variable FOUND is set to TRUE. Otherwise, I is increased by 1 so
that the next component will be examined the next time through. This is
repeated until I has become greater than the size of the table, or until the required
article number is found.

When the loop ends, if the required article number has been found in
ART_NUMBER_TABLE the variable FOUND has the value TRUE and the
variable I contains the number of the relevant component. The corresponding

component in the array ART_PRICE_TABLE contains the price of the required article and this is printed in the **if** statement's **then** part. If, however, FOUND has the value FALSE, the message "Price details missing" is printed.

If we make the Boolean expressions after **while** a little more complicated we can manage without the variable FOUND and we can simplify what is written in the **loop** statement. The last part of the program could be written:

```
while I <= TAB_SIZE
      and then ART_NUMBER_TABLE(I) /= WANTED_ART_NO loop
   I := I + 1;
end loop;

if I <= TAB_SIZE then
   PUT("The price is ");
   PUT(ART_PRICE_TABLE(I), EXP => 0, FORE => 1, AFT => 2);
else
   PUT("Price details missing");
end if;
```

The condition for the search to continue another time is that I is not too large and that the component that I points to does not contain the required article number. That is, the **loop** statement is terminated if I is greater than TAB_SIZE or if the required article number has been found. Note that the **and then** operator must be used here instead of **and**. Otherwise there would be an error on the last time through the loop if the required article number is not found in the array, because the program would attempt to evaluate ART_NUMBER_TABLE(8), which does not exist. (Compare this with the argument presented in Section 3.4.2.)

The variable I can be used in the if statement to determine whether the article number sought has been found. If I has a value that is less than or equal to TAB_SIZE then the **loop** statement must have terminated because the Boolean expression after **and then** was false, that is, because the article number has been found in the table, and I points to the component holding it.

If we look at the table of article numbers we see that it is organized in numerical order. This can be exploited to make the program more efficient. If we look for an article number that is not in the table, for example, 250, we can stop looking when we reach a number greater than it, 379 in this case. We then know that all the remaining entries in the table are greater than 250 and hence 250 is not in the table. We can change the program thus:

```
while I <= TAB_SIZE
      and then ART_NUMBER_TABLE(I) < WANTED_ART_NO loop
   I := I + 1;
end loop;
```

```
if I <= TAB_size
  and then ART_NUMBER_TABLE(I) = WANTED_ART_NO then
  PUT("The price is ");
  PUT(ART_PRICE_TABLE(I), EXP => 0, FORE => 1, AFT => 2);
else
  PUT("Price details missing");
end if;
```

In the **loop** statement we have changed only the second Boolean expression, so that the search is only continued if the article number we are looking at is less than the one required. Thus the loop terminates as soon as we find a component that is greater than or equal to the one we are looking for. A test is made in the **if** statement to see if the required article number has been found in the table. If it has, I must be less than or equal to TAB_SIZE and, in addition, the **loop** statement must have stopped because the article number pointed to is the same as the one required. Note that we must have the **and then** operator here as well, so that there is no error if I has the value 8.

Because ART_NUMBER_TABLE was sorted into order, we were able to make the search more efficient. For work with sorted arrays, there are, in fact, much more efficient methods of searching than the linear method used in this example. (No one looking for a name in a telephone directory starts from the beginning and works through until he or she finds the name required!) So it is worthwhile having arrays sorted if they have to be searched. Therefore, in addition to searching arrays, it is important to be able to sort them if so required. There are many common algorithms to describe ways of sorting. We have already met one in Section 2.2 when we put cassettes into a cassette holder. We shall now study another algorithm for sorting arrays of integers.

We shall write a program which first reads in a maximum of 100 integers and puts them into an array. Input ends by the user typing CTRL-D at the terminal. Then the program sorts the array into numerical order so that the smallest integer comes first and the largest comes last. Finally, the program prints out the numbers in the array. To do the sort we shall use an algorithm based on the following principle: the smallest number is found first and swapped into the array's first 'compartment', then the next smallest element is found and swapped into the second 'compartment', and so on. The sort algorithm can be described as follows:

(1)   Set K to 1.
(2)   While K is less than the number of elements in the array:
    (2.1)   Search for the smallest element in that part of the array that starts at the Kth position and ends with the last element in the array.
    (2.2)   Swap the smallest element (from step (2.1)) and the element in position K.
    (2.3)   Increase K by 1.

Step (2.1) can be expanded to:

> (2.1.1) Set *M* to *K*.
>
> (2.1.2) Let *I* run from *K* + 1 to the number of the last element in the array:
>
> > (2.1.2.1) If the *I*th element is less than the *M*th element, then set *M* to *I*.
>
> (2.1.3) The smallest element is now the *M*th element.

Step (2.2) can be expanded to:

> (2.2.1) Move the *K*th element to a temporary store.
>
> (2.2.2) Move the *M*th element to position *K*.
>
> (2.2.3) Move the element in the temporary store to position *M*.

Using this we can now put the program together and also include reading in the numbers to the array and printing out the array.

```
with TEXT_IO, BASIC_NUM_IO;
use TEXT_IO, BASIC_NUM_IO;
procedure SORT is
  MAX_NO_OF_ELTS : constant := 100;
  subtype INDEX is INTEGER range
                            1 .. MAX_NO_OF_ELTS;
  type INTEGER_ARRAY is array (INDEX) of INTEGER;

  A             : INTEGER_ARRAY;
  NO_OF_ELTS  : NATURAL := 0;
  M             : INDEX;
  TEMP          : INTEGER;

begin
  -- Read numbers into the array
  PUT_LINE("Enter at most 100 whole numbers");
  PUT_LINE("Terminate by typing CTRL-D");

  while not END_OF_FILE and
                    NO_OF_ELTS < MAX_NO_OF_ELTS loop
    NO_OF_ELTS := NO_OF_ELTS + 1;
    GET(A(NO_OF_ELTS));
  end loop;

  -- Sort array
  for K in 1 .. NO_OF_ELTS loop
    -- Find the smallest element between
    -- the (K + 1)th and the last, inclusive
    M := K;
    for I in K + 1 .. NO_OF_ELTS loop
```

```
    if A(I) < A(M) then
       M := I;
    end if;
    end loop;

    -- Swap Kth and Mth elements
    TEMP := A(K);
    A(K) := A(M);
    A(M) := TEMP;
 end loop;

    -- Write out the sorted array
    NEW_LINE;
    for K in 1 .. NO_OF_ELTS loop
       PUT(A(K));
    end loop;
 end SORT;
```

The output from a run of the program is as follows:

```
Enter at most 100 whole numbers
Terminate by typing CTRL-D
16 –8 34 0 –500
      –500    –8      0     16      34
```

EXERCISES

5.1   Write type declarations for the following:

(a)   A measurement of numbers of traffic accidents.

(b)   The average hourly pay of an industrial worker.

(c)   A bank's rate of interest, expressed as a percentage.

(d)   A type of bank account. (Assume that there are *current account, savings account, capital account, checking account* and *house account.*)

(e)   A table of information about the rates of interest on these different bank accounts.

(f)   The countries of the European Union (EU).

(g)   A table of the average hourly wage of industrial workers in the countries of the EU.

5.2   A department store has five different departments numbered 1–5. Write a program that reads in the takings of each department for the past week. The output from the program should be a table that shows the percentage share of the total sales that each department is responsible for.

What changes would have to be made to the program if the departments, instead of being numbered, had the names *women, men, children, sport* and *perfume*?

5.3 Write a program to read in a maximum of 1000 integers from the terminal and print them out in the same order, but any given integer should only be printed once. If it has already been printed it should not be printed again.

For example, if the following numbers are read from the terminal:

| 45 | 77 | −22 | 3 | 45 | 0 | 21 | −1 | 3 |

the program should output the following:

| 45 | 77 | −22 | 3 | 0 | 21 | −1 |

5.4 Assume that the enumeration type DAY_OF_THE_WEEK is declared as earlier in the chapter. Declare a table TOMORROW that can be used to find out which day comes after a particular given day. For example, TOMORROW(TUESDAY) should have the value WEDNESDAY, and the value of TOMORROW(SUNDAY) should be MONDAY.

5.5 The Swedish administrative counties are denoted for many purposes by the set of letter codes: *AB, C, D, E, F, G, H, I, K, L, M, N, O, P, R, S, T, U, W, X, Y, Z, AC* and *BD*. Statistics for all traffic accidents that occurred in each county in a particular year have been examined. Additional information is available on how many cars are registered in each county. Write a program to read in the information about the accidents and the numbers of registered cars, county by county. The program should print out which county had the greatest number of accidents, which county had the most registered cars and which county had the highest accident frequency in terms of accidents per registered car.

5.6 The Roman numerals are indicated by the letters I, V, X, L, C, D and M, standing for 1, 5, 10, 50, 100, 500 and 1000, respectively.

(a) Declare a table that can be used for translating a Roman numeral into an ordinary number (for example, L to 50). Use an enumeration type to describe the Roman numerals.

(b) Write a program to read in a Roman number and translate it into an integer. The Roman number is to be read as input to the program. Terminate input by using the character combination for END_OF_FILE. For simplicity, it can be assumed that when a Roman number is input at least one space is left between the numerals. The user can write, for instance, *M X M V I* at the terminal. The program should then print out: 1996.

In a Roman number, if the Roman numeral *P* stands immediately to the left of another Roman numeral *Q* and if *P* denotes a smaller number than *Q*, then the value of *P* is subtracted from the total number (for example, LIX means 59), otherwise *P* is added to the total number (for example, LXI means 61).

5.7 A number can be shown to be a prime number if it is not exactly divisible by any smaller prime number. Use this fact to write a program that computes the first 50 prime numbers and puts them into a table. (When you want to determine whether a certain number k is a prime, you can thus find out if k is exactly divisible by one of those already saved in the table.) The program should end when the table of 50 prime numbers has been printed.

5.8 A travel agency at a tourist resort organizes bus tours. There is one tour on each day of the week, and each tour has 40 places. Customers are able to reserve places on a tour no more than one week in advance.

Write a program for the agency to look after the reservation of places. The program should repeatedly read in the name of a day and one of the following commands: *book*, *cancel* or *new*.

When the command *book* is given the program should see if there is a place free for the given day. If there is, the program should 'remember' that one more place has been reserved for that day. Otherwise the program should print the message *No places left*.

If the command *cancel* is given, the program should cancel one reservation for the given day and 'remember' that there is one more place free. If no places were reserved for that day, an error message should be printed.

The command *new* is given when there is one week until a tour should take place. Then, the program should note that there are 40 free places.

5.9 Write a program to read in a maximum of 100 integers and place them in an array, sorted into ascending numerical order. The program should be designed so that one number at a time is read in and placed in the array. Before each new number is read, the numbers read in so far should be sorted.

5.10 Statistics of the rainfall for a certain location have been collected over the past 20 years. Write a program that reads in the information for the 20 years and presents the results in the form of a histogram. Assume the annual rainfall lies in the interval 0–3000 mm.

(a) Present the result as a horizontal histogram in the format:

```
            0      1      2      3    (× 1000 mm)
                                        rainfall


    Year
      1        ***************
      2        ************************
      3        *************
      :           :
      :           :
```

(b) Present the result as a vertical histogram in the format:

Rainfall (mm)

```
3000
                        *

                        *

2000                    *

                        *

                        *

              *         *

              *         *

              *         *         *

1000          *         *         *

              *         *         *

              *         *         *

              *         *         *

              *         *         *

              *         *         *

   0          *         *         *

              1         2         3    .    .    .    Year
```

5.11 Write a program that first reads in an integer k from the terminal. Then the program should read in a maximum of 500 integers from the terminal and place them in an array. The numbers in the array should then be rearranged to form two groups in the array. The left-hand group should contain all the numbers $\leq k$ and the right-hand group all the numbers $> k$. (The number of numbers in each group and where the boundary between the two groups lies depends on the numbers read into the array and the value of k.)

For example, if k is 20 and the array consists of the numbers:

    23   16   27   3   11   34   25   20   8

then one permissible rearrangement of the array is:

    8   16   20   3   11   34   25   27   23

Several other arrangements would be allowed. Note that it is not necessary to sort the array (even if it is a possible way of solving the problem).

6 Subprograms

It has been shown that a program consists of two parts: a declarative part where the data objects used in the program are described, and a statement section where the actions that the program will perform are described. The statement section describes the algorithm that the program will carry out. Algorithms have been expressed using the statements available in Ada (assignment statements, **if** statements, **loop** statements, etc.). In constructing an algorithm, it is often useful to express certain steps on a 'higher level' than is possible with Ada's basic statements. Steps at such a higher level include, for example, 'calculate the logarithm of X', 'sort the table T', 'print a heading at the terminal' and 'calculate the mean of the measurements'. As we have seen, higher-level steps in an algorithm occur naturally when the technique of top-down design is applied to a programming problem. The advantage of using this higher level is that inessential details can be ignored while the algorithm is made the focus of attention.

In Ada it is possible to define **subprograms** that are made up of several basic Ada statements. Calls to subprograms can be used as higher-level algorithmic steps when an algorithm is under construction.

The use of subprograms is a very important technique when mastering the complexity of program design. A program should normally be assembled from several subprograms, each of which describes a particular calculation or stage of the program. In a large program there might even be subprograms written in different programming languages. Subprograms can be thought of as building blocks that are used to construct a whole program. It is because of the support given by subprograms that the top-down design method can be used.

In Ada there are two kinds of subprogram: **functions** and **procedures**. A function is used to describe the computation of a particular value (for example, the calculation of the mean of a series of measurements) and a procedure is used to describe an action that the program has to perform but that does not result in a direct value (for example, printing a heading at the terminal).

Examples have already been given of the use of both functions and procedures that have come in ready-written packages, mostly in connection with input and output. This chapter will deal with how to design subprograms and how to use them.

6.1   Functions

A function can be regarded as a 'black box' into which one or more values can be placed. Out of the box comes a result, whose value depends on the input values. We have used functions before. In the example for calculating the hypotenuse we used the supplied function SQRT which, as its name suggests, calculates the square root of a number. The SQRT black box is illustrated in Figure 6.1. When a supplied function is used, there is no need to worry about its internal looks: it is sufficient to know how it should be used.

Now we shall look at how to write new functions. As the first simple example we shall study a function MEAN_VALUE that calculates the mean of two floating point numbers. From the point of view of the programmer who will use it, the function will look like Figure 6.2.

In Ada, the function MEAN_VALUE appears as:

```
function MEAN_VALUE (X1, X2 : FLOAT) return FLOAT is
begin
    return (X1 + X2) / 2.0;
end MEAN_VALUE;
```

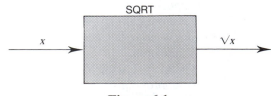

Figure 6.1

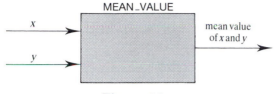

Figure 6.2

This is called a **function body**.

Function body

function *function_name* (*parameter_list*)
                   return *result_type* **is**
    declarative part
begin
      statement_1;
      statement_2;

        .
        .
        .

      statement_N;
end *function_name*;

After the function's name, the data that has to be entered to the function is specified by writing a list of the function's **formal parameters**. Two values of type FLOAT will be entered to the function MEAN_VALUE, so we have written in brackets:

    X1, X2 : FLOAT

We have given the function two formal parameters, called X1 and X2, both with type FLOAT. This is very similar to the declaration of two variables. When the function is called, X1 and X2 will contain the two values that are entered to the function.

Formal parameters to functions

- Contain the values to be entered to the function.
- Exist only within the function.
- Are treated as constants in the function.

After the reserved word **return**, the type of the result that will be returned by the function is specified. We have stated that the value returned by the function MEAN_VALUE will have type FLOAT.

Thus the first line of the function, usually called the function's **specification**, tells the programmer how to use it.

Function specification

- First part of the function body.
- Contains the function name, its formal parameters and the type of its result.

The rest of the function body describes what is inside the 'black box', and the user of the function does not normally need to bother with this. This part of the function looks like the programs we have seen already: first comes a declarative part and then a sequence of statements. The body of our 'box' is only one statement:

return (X1 + X2) / 2.0;

This is a new sort of statement that we have not met before, a **return** statement, in which an expression follows the word **return**. This expression should have the same type as specified after the word **return** in the function specification. In the function MEAN_VALUE, therefore, the expression must have the type FLOAT. When the **return** statement is executed, the expression will be evaluated. Then execution of the function terminates and the result of the function will be the value of the expression. That is, when the **return** statement is executed, the computations in the 'box' terminate and what comes out of the 'box' is the value of the expression in the **return** statement. There can be several **return** statements in a function, but it is most common to have only one and for that to be the last statement in the function.

Return statement

   return *expression*;

The type of the expression should be the same as the type of the function's result.

A function is only a description of how a particular computation works, telling us what we can put into the 'box' and what we will get out as a result. To invoke a computation, we have to put something into the 'box'; we must **call** the function. In the example that follows, we have put our function MEAN_VALUE into a complete program that reads in two numbers from the terminal, calculates their mean and displays it at the terminal:

```
with TEXT_IO, BASIC_NUM_IO;
use TEXT_IO, BASIC_NUM_IO;
procedure EVALUATE_MEAN is
    NUMBER1, NUMBER2, MEAN : FLOAT;

    function MEAN_VALUE (X1, X2 : FLOAT) return FLOAT is
    begin
        return (X1 + X2) / 2.0;
    end MEAN_VALUE;

begin
    PUT_LINE("Enter two real numbers");
    GET(NUMBER1); GET(NUMBER2);
    MEAN := MEAN_VALUE(NUMBER1, NUMBER2);
    PUT("The mean is:"); PUT(MEAN);
end EVALUATE_MEAN;
```

Note that the function body has been placed in the program's declaration section. In Ada 83, subprogram bodies should be placed *after* any declarations of types, subtypes, variables and constants.

In Ada 95 the various declarations can be placed in any order. For example, the declarations of subprograms can be put before the declarations of variables if appropriate.

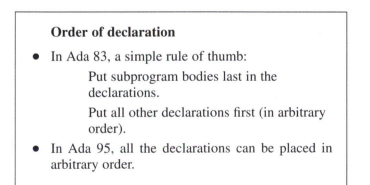

> **Order of declaration**
>
> - In Ada 83, a simple rule of thumb:
>
>   > Put subprogram bodies last in the declarations.
>   >
>   > Put all other declarations first (in arbitrary order).
>
> - In Ada 95, all the declarations can be placed in arbitrary order.

When the program is executed, the first statement in the program's statement part is carried out as usual, in this case the first input statement. Suppose the user types the values 2.0 and 2.5 at the terminal. After the program has read these

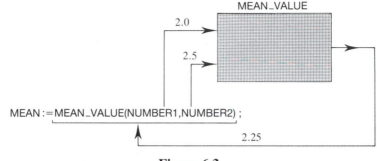

Figure 6.3

values into the variables **NUMBER1** and **NUMBER2**, there follows, on the third line of the statement part, a call to the function **MEAN_VALUE**. What happens is illustrated in Figure 6.3.

The expression:

MEAN_VALUE(NUMBER1, NUMBER2)

is the actual function call. First there is the name of the function being called, and then, in brackets, there is a list of the **actual parameters** to the function. When the call is executed, the values of the actual parameters are calculated first. (In this case, no calculation is necessary because the values are already in the variables **NUMBER1** and **NUMBER2**.) The values of the actual parameters are then passed to the function. Thus, here the values 2.0 and 2.5 are entered to the function **MEAN_VALUE**. Figure 6.4 illustrates the function.

The two formal parameters **X1** and **X2** can be thought of as 'temporary storage boxes' that are created in connection with the call to **MEAN_VALUE** and which only exist while the function call is in operation. When the function is called, the values of the first and second actual parameters are stored in **X1** and

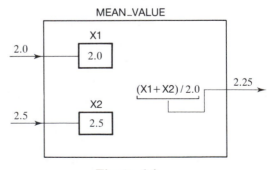

Figure 6.4

X2, respectively. Thus here, X1 takes the value 2.0 and X2 takes the value 2.5. Note that neither NUMBER1 nor NUMBER2 is affected by this: their values are only copied into X1 and X2, respectively.

When the actual parameters have been copied, execution of the program EVALUATE_MEAN stops temporarily while the statements in the function MEAN_VALUE are executed. In this case the only statement, the **return** statement, is executed. The expression:

(X1 + X2) / 2.0

means that the values in X1 and X2 are added and the result is divided by 2. Thus we get the result 2.25, the same result we would have got if we had calculated the mean of NUMBER1 and NUMBER2 directly. The value calculated in the **return** statement becomes the value which leaves the function. The function call:

MEAN_VALUE(NUMBER1, NUMBER2)

will thus take the value 2.25.

When execution of the statements in the function MEAN_VALUE is finished, the call to the function MEAN_VALUE terminates and normal execution of the program EVALUATE_MEAN is resumed. The value of the function call is assigned to the variable MEAN, thus here MEAN takes the value 2.25. Note that when the function call terminates, the 'storage boxes' X1 and X2 no longer exist. They are only temporary, for the duration of the call to MEAN_VALUE.

Within a function, the formal parameters are considered to be constants that are initialized at the time of the call. They can be used as ordinary constants within the statement section of the function. In the function MEAN_VALUE, for example, they are used in an expression. Just as the value of a constant may not be changed, it is not permitted for a function to try and change the value of a formal parameter.

A call to a function is considered to be an expression. The type of the expression is the same as the type given after the word **return** in the function specification. Thus a call to the function MEAN_VALUE is considered as an expression of type FLOAT. This means that a function call can be used in the same way as other expressions in a program. In the program EVALUATE_ MEAN, for example, a call to MEAN_VALUE was placed on the right-hand side of an assignment. We could also use a function call in a bigger expression, such as:

MEAN_VALUE(NUMBER1, NUMBER2) / NUMBER1 * 100.0

Since a function call is an expression, it can also be used as a parameter to the output statement PUT. If we make use of this, we can manage without the variable MEAN in our program:

```
begin
    PUT_LINE("Enter two real numbers");
    GET(NUMBER1); GET(NUMBER2);
    PUT("The mean is:"); PUT( MEAN_VALUE(NUMBER1, NUMBER2) );
end EVALUATE_MEAN;
```

In this version, the execution of the last statement is such that the function MEAN_VALUE is called first. It returns a value of type FLOAT and the procedure PUT is then called with this value as parameter.

The **actual** parameters to a function can be expressions: they do not have to be simple variables of the kind used so far. What is essential is that an actual parameter has the same type as the corresponding **formal** parameter in the function specification. For example, the following function call would be permissible:

```
MEAN_VALUE(NUMBER1 * NUMBER2, NUMBER1 + 10.0)
```

The first actual parameter is the expression:

```
NUMBER1 * NUMBER2
```

and the second is the expression:

```
NUMBER1 + 10.0
```

When a function call is executed, first the values of the actual parameters are evaluated. If we assume the same values for NUMBER1 and NUMBER2 as before, 2.0 and 2.5, respectively, then the first actual parameter has the value 5.0 and the second has the value 12.0.

A common misunderstanding regarding functions is that the values that are entered to and returned by a function should be read from or written to the terminal. Note that a function does not need to have anything at all to do with terminal input and output. The values that enter the function come from the calling program and are entered via the formal parameters (thus the values are not read from the terminal), and the result of the function is returned to the calling program using the return statement (it is not written at the terminal).

> **Function calls**
>
> function_name(*a1*, *a2*, ... *an*)
>
> *a1, a2, ... an* are *actual* parameters
> - They may be expressions.
> - Their types must agree with those of the corresponding formal parameters.
> - A function call is considered to be an *expression*.
>
>   The following occur:
> (1)   The values of *a1, a2, ... an* are computed.
> (2)   The value of *a1* is copied to the first formal parameter, that of *a2* to the second, and so on.
> (3)   The statements in the function are executed.
> (4)   The function terminates on execution of a return statement.
> (5)   The value of the function call is the value in the return statement.
> (6)   Execution continues after the function call.

Let us look at another example. This time we shall write a function MAX that finds the larger of two integers. Two values of type INTEGER are entered to the function, and the function returns one value, also of type INTEGER. Here is the function:

```
function MAX (X, Y : INTEGER) return INTEGER is
begin
    if X > Y then
        return X;
    else
        return Y;
    end if;
end MAX;
```

The function's statement part consists of a single **if** statement, but we have used two **return** statements. If the formal parameter X contains the bigger of the two values, that is returned as the resulting value; otherwise the result is the other formal parameter, Y.

The following program is an example of the use of the function MAX:

```
with TEXT_IO, BASIC_NUM_IO;
use  TEXT_IO, BASIC_NUM_IO;
```

```
procedure MAX_DEMO is
    A, B, C, M : INTEGER;

    function MAX (X, Y : INTEGER) return INTEGER is
    begin
    if X > Y then
        return X;
    else
        return Y;
    end if;
    end MAX;

begin
    loop
        PUT_LINE("Enter three whole numbers");
        exit when END_OF_FILE;
        GET(A); GET(B); GET(C);
        M := MAX(A, B);
        M := MAX(M, C);
        PUT("The biggest of them is");
        PUT(M); NEW_LINE;
    end loop;
end MAX_DEMO;
```

Note that the function MAX is called in two places in the program. It is quite permissible to call the same function from several places in one program and use different parameters for different calls. Note also that, when the program is executed, the function will be repeated many times because the calls are both in a **loop** statement. In the statement:

```
M := MAX(A, B);
```

the values of the variables A and B are used as actual parameters in the function call. When the call is executed, 'temporary stores' X and Y will be created and the values of A and B will be copied into them. If, say, A has the value 6 and B the value 2, then X and Y will contain the values 6 and 2, respectively. This means that the **then** part of the **if** statement will be carried out. The statement:

```
return X;
```

is thus carried out and this means that the value of X is given as the result of the function. In our case, it means that the function call has the value 6 and this value is assigned to the variable M.

In the next statement:

```
M := MAX(M, C);
```

the values of M and C are used as actual parameters. New 'temporary stores' X and Y are created: the previous ones no longer exist. If C has the value 9, then the values 6 and 9 will be copied to X and Y. This time, the **else** part of the **if** statement will be executed, and the function returns the value of C, 9, as its result. This becomes the right-hand side of the assignment statement, and the value 9 is assigned to the variable M. (Thus the value of M changes from 6 to 9.) Now M contains the biggest of the three numbers.

We can manage without the variable M if we write a more complicated expression as parameter to the last PUT statement:

```
loop
    PUT_LINE("Enter three whole numbers");
    exit when END_OF_FILE;
    GET(A); GET(B); GET(C);
    PUT("The biggest of them is");
    PUT(MAX( MAX(A,B), C)); NEW_LINE;
end loop;
```

The statement:

```
PUT( MAX( MAX(A,B), C) );
```

means that the procedure PUT is called with the expression:

```
MAX( MAX(A,B), C)
```

as parameter. This expression consists of a call of the function MAX with the two actual parameters MAX(A,B) and C. The first of these is in turn a call of the function MAX with the actual parameters A and B. When the statement is executed, the expressions are evaluated from the innermost level, that is, the expressions A and B are evaluated first (which is easy since they are simple variables). Then the expression MAX(A,B) is evaluated (which will take the larger of the two values of A and B) and the expression C. When that is done, the expression:

```
MAX( MAX(A,B), C)
```

is evaluated, which thus gives the largest of the three values as a result. This value is passed to the procedure PUT and will be printed.

A function can have parameters of different types, as demonstrated by the following example which deals with the calculation of interest. Assume that £b is placed in a bank with an annual interest rate of $r\%$. The capital that accrues if the money remains invested for n years can be calculated from the formula $b(1 + 0.01r)^n$.

A function for calculating the capital can take the following form:

```
function COMPOUND_INTEREST(B, R : NAT_FLOAT; N : NATURAL)
                                      return NAT_FLOAT is
begin
    return B * (1.0 + 0.01 * R) ** N;
end COMPOUND_INTEREST;
```

The function has three formal parameters B, R and N. The first two are of subtype NAT_FLOAT, which we declare thus:

```
subtype NAT_FLOAT is FLOAT range 0.0 .. FLOAT'LAST;
```

The values belonging to this subtype are thus non-negative and of type FLOAT. By making B and R take the subtype NAT_FLOAT we are guaranteeing that they are always greater than or equal to zero. In like manner we let the third parameter N be of subtype NATURAL, which guarantees that N never goes negative. If the function is called in a program and one of the parameters happens to be negative, then an execution error occurs.

In the function specification we see how to specify the formal parameters when they are of different types and subtypes: the various parameters are specified, separated by semicolons. If there are several formal parameters of the same type or subtype then they can be written in the shorter way, as in the example above: the parameters are listed, separated by commas, but the type name need only be written once. Thus the rules for writing formal parameters are like the rules that apply for writing several variable declarations one after another in a program.

Specifying formal parameters

Rules similar to variable declaration.

For example:

(X1, X2. ... Xn : *type1*; Y1, Y2, ... Yn : *type2*)

The functions we have studied so far have all had parameters and have returned values of numeric types. Such functions are very common. However, a function can have parameters and return results of any type. We shall look at some functions that have parameters and results of types other than numeric. The first example shows a function LETTER that determines whether a particular character (of type CHARACTER) is a letter. The character for investigation is a parameter to the function and as a result the function returns a BOOLEAN value. The result of the function can be either FALSE or TRUE. The function can be written:

```
function LETTER (CHAR : CHARACTER) return BOOLEAN is
begin
case CHAR is
    when 'a' .. 'z' | 'A' .. 'Z' =>
        return TRUE;
    when others =>
        return FALSE;
end case;
end LETTER;
```

In the function specification we can see that the formal parameter CHAR has type CHARACTER and that the result type is BOOLEAN. The statement part of the program consists of only one **case** statement. If CHAR contains a lower- or upper-case letter the statement:

```
return TRUE;
```

will be executed. Otherwise the statement:

```
return FALSE;
```

will be executed.

The function can be called as in the following example, assuming the variable C has type CHARACTER:

```
GET(C);
if LETTER(C) then
    PUT_LINE("letter");
else
    PUT_LINE("not a letter");
end if;
```

In an **if** statement, an expression of type BOOLEAN should appear immediately after the reserved word **if**, and the call of the function LETTER is just such an expression.

We can make the function LETTER a little more elegant if we write an expression of type BOOLEAN directly after **return** instead of using a **case** statement:

```
function LETTER(CHAR : CHARACTER) return BOOLEAN is
begin
    return CHAR in 'a' .. 'z' or CHAR in 'A' .. 'Z';
end LETTER;
```

The way of calling the function is not affected by this, since we have not changed the function specification.

Result type

A function may return results of any type.

The next example is a function that calculates the sum of the components of a vector. A vector can be regarded as a list of numbers, such as:

(2.0, 1.5, −1.0)

In an Ada program we can represent a vector by an array. A vector with three components can be described by the type:

type THREE_VECTOR **is array** (1 .. 3) **of** FLOAT;

We can now write a function SUM that has a parameter of type THREE_VECTOR and which returns a result of type FLOAT:

```
function SUM(V : THREE_VECTOR) return FLOAT is
    S : FLOAT := 0.0;
begin
    for I in 1 .. 3 loop
        S := S + V(I);
    end loop;
    return S;
end SUM;
```

Within the function the formal parameter can be treated as an ordinary constant array. For example, we can pick out the individual components of V by indexing.

There is something else new in this function. We use a variable S to calculate the sum, and this variable is declared in a declarative part of the function. A variable that is declared within a subprogram like this is usually called a **local variable** because it can only be used locally, within the subprogram. A local variable can be regarded in exactly the same way as a formal parameter, that is, as a 'temporary store', which is created when the function is called and only exists while the call is in operation. After a function has finished execution, the local variables no longer exist. A local variable is something that exists only within the 'black box' of the function. It is one of the things that a programmer who is going to use the function need never know about.

Local variables

- Are declared within a subprogram.
- Exist only within the subprogram.

Let us see how a call to SUM may appear. If we assume that a program has the following variable declaration:

A : THREE_VECTOR := (2.0, 1.5, −1.0);

then our new function could be called, for example, like this:

PUT(SUM(A));

The value 2.5 would be written out.

The function SUM as we have written it so far has one great weakness. It can only be used for calculating the sum of the components of a three-dimensional vector in which the components are numbered from 1 to 3. If on another occasion we want to calculate the sum of the components of, say, a four-dimensional vector, this function cannot be used. We shall now see how, with a few small changes, the function can be made so general that it can be used for vectors of arbitrary length and index constraints. To do this we shall use an unconstrained array type. We declare a type VECTOR:

type VECTOR **is array** (INTEGER **range** < >) **of** FLOAT;

We shall now give the function's formal parameters this type instead of the type THREE_VECTOR. This means that the number of components in V is not pre-determined. The number of components can change from call to call and is determined by the number of components in the actual parameter.

One more detail of the function must be changed. We can no longer let the loop parameter go from 1 to 3 in the **loop** statement. The number of times through the loop and the indexing now depend on the number of components in V and the index constraints on V. The solution to this problem is to use the attribute V'RANGE, which gives the interval between V's first and last index. With these amendments, the general version of the function SUM is as follows:

```
function SUM(V : VECTOR) return FLOAT is
    S : FLOAT := 0.0;
begin
    for I in V'RANGE loop
        S := S + V(I);
    end loop;
    return S;
end SUM;
```

Let us look at how to call this general function. If we have a variable declaration:

A : VECTOR(1 .. 3) := (2.0, 1.5, −1.0);

then the function can be called as before, using:

    PUT(SUM(A));

and we get 2.5 written out. On this call, the formal parameter V takes length 3 and index limits 1 and 3. However, if we also have the following declarations in the same program:

    X : VECTOR(0 .. 3) := (1.0, 2.0, 6.5, −4.0);
    Y : VECTOR(5 .. 6) := (3.5, 2.5);

we can also have the statements:

    PUT(SUM(X));   -- returns the result 5.5
    PUT(SUM(Y));   -- returns the result 6.0

On the first call the formal parameter V will take the length 4 and have index limits of 0 and 3. On the second call V's length will be 2 and it will have index limits 5 and 6.

An array aggregate or a slice is also allowed as an actual parameter. For example, we can make the calls:

    SUM((1.4, 0.3)) -- returns the result 1.7
    SUM(X(1 .. 2)) -- returns the result 8.5

Writing subprograms that are as general as possible is a worthwhile habit: they can be used in several contexts, and the risk of having to change them when circumstances change is reduced. The use of unconstrained array types, as in this example, is therefore highly recommended.

Subprograms and unconstrained array types

It is advantageous to make subprograms general by using unconstrained array types for formal parameters and the result.

The next example will show that a function in Ada can return a value of a composite type as its result. We shall write a function ADD that calculates the sum of two vectors, which is a new vector with the same number of components as the original vectors. The first component of the new vector is the sum of the two first components of the original vectors, the second is the sum of the second components, and so on. For example, the sum of the two vectors:

(1.0, 2.5, 4.3)
(3.1, –1.0, 0.0)

is the vector:

(4.1, 1.5, 4.3)

One condition is that the two vectors to be added have the same number of components. First we shall write a version of the function with the limitation that it can only add two vectors of dimension 3. Both the formal parameters of the function and the result have type THREE_VECTOR. This first version looks like this:

```
function ADD(V1, V2 : THREE_VECTOR) return THREE_VECTOR is
    TEMP : THREE_VECTOR;
begin
    for I in 1 .. 3 loop
        TEMP(I) := V1(I) + V2(I);
    end loop;
    return TEMP;
end ADD;
```

In the function we have used a local array variable TEMP which also has type THREE_VECTOR. The three components of TEMP are calculated in the **loop** statement, one component per loop. The statement:

```
return TEMP;
```

means that we return the value of TEMP as result, TEMP having the type THREE_VECTOR.
    If we have the declarations:

```
A : THREE_VECTOR := (1.0, 2.5, 4.3);
B : THREE_VECTOR := (3.1, –1.0, 0.0);
C : THREE_VECTOR;
```

in a program, then the following statement is allowed:

```
C := ADD(A,B);
```

The value of the right-hand side of the statement will be (4.1, 1.5, 4.3) and it will have type THREE_VECTOR. The array variable C will thus be assigned the value (4.1, 1.5, 4.3).
    Of course, the function ADD should be formulated generally instead, so that it can deal with vectors of arbitrary length, and only a few minor changes

are needed. Instead of the type THREE_VECTOR we can let the parameters and result of the function have unconstrained array type VECTOR, as declared earlier. The declaration of the local array variable TEMP must be changed, to have the same number of components as the parameters V1 and V2. (We assume that V1 and V2 have the same lengths.) We can achieve this using the attribute V1'RANGE in the declaration of TEMP:

```
TEMP : VECTOR(V1'RANGE);
```

In the brackets is an interval with the same limits as the index limits for V1. If, for example, V1 is indexed from 1 to 4, then TEMP will also be indexed from 1 to 4. In the **loop** statement we have used V1'RANGE in the same way as in the function SUM, to let the loop parameter I run through the required index values. With these amendments, the following general version of ADD is obtained:

```
function ADD(V1, V2 : VECTOR) return VECTOR is
    TEMP : VECTOR(V1'RANGE);
begin
    for I in V1'RANGE loop
        TEMP(I) := V1(I) + V2(I);
    end loop;
    return TEMP;
end ADD;
```

If we have the following declarations in a program:

```
X : VECTOR(1 .. 4)  :=  (1.0, 1.0, 1.0, 1.0);
Y : VECTOR(1 .. 4)  :=  (2.5, 3.5, 4.5, 5.5);
Z : VECTOR(0 .. 1)  :=  (0.5, 0.5);
```

then the following calls, as examples, are allowed:

```
ADD(X, Y)      -- gives (3.5, 4.5, 5.5, 6.5)
ADD(Z, Z)      -- gives (1.0, 1.0)
ADD( (2.7, 3.8), (1.0, 2.0) )      -- gives (3.7, 5.8)
```

To be able to add two vectors they must have the same length, but it is not necessary for them to be indexed in the same way. For example, it should be possible to add a vector indexed from 0 to 3 to another vector indexed from 1 to 4. This version of ADD cannot manage it. It demands that both vectors are indexed in the same way. If we were to call it with vectors with different indexing we would get a run-time error. (This is because when V2(I) is executed in the **loop** statement, the loop parameter I will sometimes lie outside the range of V2's index values.)

It is possible to make further amendments to the function so that it can cope with vectors with different index limits. (But the lengths of the vectors must always be the same.) When the local variable TEMP is declared, it can be initialized so that its components will contain the same values as those of V2. (This is always possible since TEMP and V2 have the same number of components.) In the **loop** statement we can then add V1's components to TEMP's components. Since VI and TEMP have the same index limits we shall not meet problems with indexing. With this final amendment the function ADD becomes:

```
function ADD(V1, V2 : VECTOR) return VECTOR is
   TEMP : VECTOR(V1'RANGE) := V2;
begin
   for I in V1'RANGE loop
      TEMP(I) := TEMP(I) + V1(I);
   end loop;
   return TEMP;
end ADD;
```

There are also functions without parameters. We have already seen an example of these – the function END_OF_FILE in the package TEXT_IO. When such a function is called it is enough to write simply the name of the function without brackets afterwards. One example of the use of the function END_OF_FILE is:

```
exit when END_OF_FILE;
```

Thus a call to a function without parameters looks exactly as if the function were a normal variable.

To write a function without parameters, we leave out the brackets and the list of formal parameters in the function specification:

```
function MY_RANDOM_NO return FLOAT is
      ⋮
end MY_RANDOM_NO;
```

How should we name functions that we write ourselves? It is best to try to make the function name specific, in the same way as ordinary variables. If the function performs some mathematical operation and the parameters can be regarded as operands to the operation, then an appropriate name will describe the operation, for example, EXPONENTIATE and ADD. Functions that return a BOOLEAN result can be given names in the style of a question, for example, END_OF_FILE, END_OF_INPUT and PERMITTED_VALUE. In these cases it helps to imagine a question mark following the function name.

6.2 Procedures

The other subprogram is the **procedure**. A procedure differs from a function in that it does not return a result when it is called. When a procedure is called, its sequence of statements is put into action.

A procedure has exactly the same form as a function. The only differences are that the reserved word **procedure** is used instead of **function**, and that no result type is given in the procedure specification, its first line.

Since a procedure does not return any value as a result, there need not be a **return** statement in the procedure. A procedure normally terminates when execution reaches the final **end**.

For example, let us write a procedure HEAD_NEW_PAGE that can be used when a new page of output is to be started with a page number written at the top. The page number should be written in the middle of the top line as follows:

$$- 34 -$$

We shall assume that the terminal produces printed output and a line of output has at most 80 characters. We shall make use of the existing procedures NEW_PAGE and SET_COL in the package TEXT_IO. NEW_PAGE ensures that

---

Procedure specification

- The first part of the procedure body.
- Contains the name of the procedure and its formal parameters.

Procedure body

procedure *procedure_name* (*parameter_list*) **is**

declarative part

begin
    statement_1;
    statement_2;

      ⋮

    statement_N;
end *procedure_name*;

a new page is fed and SET_COL allows a particular position on the current line of output to be chosen for printing. The procedure is as follows:

```
procedure HEAD_NEW_PAGE (PAGE_NUM : INTEGER) is
begin
   NEW_PAGE;
   SET_COL(38);
   PUT("– "); PUT(PAGE_NUM, WIDTH => 1); PUT(" –");
end HEAD_NEW_PAGE;
```

Procedures, like functions, can take parameters: HEAD_NEW_PAGE has the formal parameter PAGE_NUM with type INTEGER.

We shall now examine this procedure when it is used in a program that writes the page number at the top of three pages, numbers 34, 50 and 51.

```
with TEXT_IO, BASIC_NUM_IO;
use  TEXT_IO, BASIC_NUM_IO;
procedure PAGE_DEMO is
   N : INTEGER := 50;
   procedure HEAD_NEW_PAGE (PAGE_NUM : INTEGER) is
   begin
      NEW_PAGE;
      SET_COL(38);
      PUT("– "); PUT(PAGE_NUM, WIDTH=>1); PUT(" –");
   end HEAD_NEW_PAGE;
begin
   HEAD_NEW_PAGE(34);
   HEAD_NEW_PAGE(N);
   HEAD_NEW_PAGE(N+1);
end PAGE_DEMO;
```

We notice that a procedure body, like a function body, should be located in the declarative part of the program.

The program PAGE_DEMO has three calls to the procedure HEAD_NEW_PAGE. A procedure call works in much the same way as a function call. A 'temporary store' PAGE_NUM is created in the procedure and the value of the actual parameter is copied to it. In this example, the first call copies the value 34 to PAGE_NUM. Then the execution of PAGE_DEMO is halted while the statements in HEAD_NEW_PAGE are carried out. When their execution is complete, the execution of PAGE_DEMO is resumed and the next statement after the procedure call is executed.

Note that the procedure does not return any value to the calling program. This is what distinguishes a procedure from a function. A procedure call is considered to be an entire **statement** in the calling program, whereas a function call, as shown in the foregoing section, is considered to be an **expression**. A call to a procedure is written as in the example above. It is terminated with a semi-colon. A function call, however, is written in the same places in a program as ordinary expressions, and the calling program must deal with the result. The following subprogram calls are therefore in error:

```
PUT( HEAD_NEW_PAGE(N) );   -- ERROR! HEAD_NEW_PAGE is a
                                         procedure
N := HEAD_NEW_PAGE(45);    -- ERROR! HEAD_NEW_PAGE is a
                                         procedure
SQRT(X);                   -- ERROR! SQRT is a function
END_OF_FILE;               -- ERROR! END_OF_FILE is a function
```

Procedure call

> *procedure_name(a1, a2, ... an)*;

a1, a2, ... an are *actual* parameters.

- Their types must agree with those of the corresponding formal parameters.
- A procedure call is considered to be a *statement*.

As the next example, we shall write a procedure PRINT_CENTRED that will print any piece of text in the centre of the line. A procedure, exactly like a function, can have parameters of any types at all. The procedure we shall write now will have a parameter of type STRING that gives the text to be output:

```
procedure PRINT_CENTRED (TEXT : STRING) is
    LINE_LENGTH : constant := 80;
begin
    SET_COL((LINE_LENGTH – TEXT'LENGTH) / 2);
    PUT(TEXT);
end PRINT_CENTRED;
```

For simplicity, we have assumed that the output has room for only 80 characters. To avoid having numbers in the statements, we have declared a local constant LINE_LENGTH in the procedure. The type STRING is an unconstrained array type and, therefore, the procedure's parameter can be text of arbitrary length. To refer to the length of the text within the procedure, we use the attribute TEXT'LENGTH. If the text is 80 characters long or longer, we shall get a run-time error when the program is executed.

We shall look at a program that uses PRINT_CENTRED to print out the text:

Hello
Ada
is my
name!

The program looks like this:

```
with TEXT_IO;
use  TEXT_IO;
procedure PRINT_GREETING is
   procedure PRINT_CENTRED (TEXT : STRING) is
      LINE_LENGTH : constant := 80;
   begin
      SET_COL(LINE_LENGTH – TEXT'LENGTH) / 2);
      PUT(TEXT);
   end PRINT_CENTRED;
begin
   NEW_LINE;
   PRINT_CENTRED("Hello");  NEW_LINE;
   PRINT_CENTRED("Ada");    NEW_LINE;
   PRINT_CENTRED("is my");  NEW_LINE;
   PRINT_CENTRED("name!"); NEW_LINE;
end PRINT_GREETING;
```

6.3   Parameter association

The two procedures we have studied so far in this chapter have both been used for special printing. They, too, can be thought of as 'black boxes'; we put values into them but they return no result value to the calling program.

However, procedures can be used in a much more general way. Transferring parameters between the calling program and the procedure can actually be carried out in more ways than we have seen so far. This is best explained from a simple example. We shall write a procedure NONSENSE that does nothing of any use, but illustrates how **parameter association** works.

```
procedure NONSENSE (A : in      INTEGER;
                    B : in out  INTEGER;
                    C : out     INTEGER) is
begin
   B := B + A;
   C := 0;
end NONSENSE;
```

The procedure NONSENSE has three formal parameters, A, B and C, written on separate lines only for the sake of clarity. What is new is that the reserved words **in** and **out** appear in the parameter specifications.

In Ada, a parameter can be either a **parameter of mode in**, a **parameter of mode in out** or a **parameter of mode out**. In the procedure NONSENSE, these are exemplified by A, B and C, respectively. We can say that A is used to put values into the NONSENSE 'box', B is used both to put values in and get them out, and C is used only to get values out of the NONSENSE 'box'.

The parameters we have seen in our earlier examples, of both functions and procedures, have all been **in** parameters. If neither **in** nor **out** are used in a parameter specification, the parameter is automatically an **in** parameter: that is, the specification **in** is assumed.

We shall put NONSENSE into a program that calls the procedure:

```
with TEXT_IO, BASIC_NUM_IO;
use  TEXT_IO, BASIC_NUM_IO;
procedure PARA_DEMO is
   X, Y, Z: INTEGER;

   procedure NONSENSE (A :  in      INTEGER;
                       B :  in out  INTEGER;
                       C :  out     INTEGER) is

   begin
      B := B + A;
      C := 0;
   end NONSENSE;

begin
   X := 1; Y := 5; Z := 10;
   PUT(X); PUT(Y); PUT(Z); NEW_LINE;
   NONSENSE(X, Y, Z);
   PUT(X); PUT(Y); PUT(Z); NEW_LINE;
end PARA_DEMO;
```

To see what happens we shall study a couple of diagrams. The variables X, Y and Z in the main program can be illustrated, as usual, by three storage boxes in the program PARA_DEMO. At the start of the call:

```
NONSENSE(X, Y, Z);
```

three temporary storage boxes, A, B and C, are created in the procedure NON-SENSE. They only exist while the call is in progress. At the start of the call the situation is as in Figure 6.5. The formal parameter A is an **in** parameter. The formal parameters we saw in our earlier examples were also **in** parameters, so the result with A is exactly what we are used to. First the value of the corresponding actual parameter is calculated. This is already done here: X already has the value 1.

This value is then copied to the formal variable A which thus also gets the value 1. The copying does not affect the variable X at all.

The formal parameter B is an **in out** parameter. As with an **in** parameter, the value of the actual parameter corresponding to an **in out** parameter is copied to the formal parameter at the start of the call. In our example, the value 5 which is in the variable Y is copied to B.

The third formal parameter is an **out** parameter. There is *no* copying for an **out** parameter when the procedure is called. The value in the temporary store C will thus be undefined at the start of the call, as shown in Figure 6.5.

When the temporary stores have been created and those associated with **in** or **in out** parameters have been initialized, execution continues with the procedure's sequence of statements. First, the statement:

```
B := B + A;
```

is executed. This statement means, as usual, that the value in store B is changed to 5 + 1, that is, 6. The next statement:

```
C := 0;
```

means, of course, that the store called C is given the value 0.

Within the procedure NONSENSE the **in** parameter A is considered to be a constant. Therefore no attempt may be made to change its value. If we were to try, for example, to add the statement:

```
A := 0;      -- ERROR!
```

we would get a compile-time error.

An **in out** parameter is considered to be a normal variable within the procedure. Therefore, we can change the value of B and put it into expressions in the normal way.

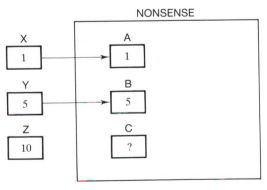

Figure 6.5

The value of an **out** parameter is undefined at the start of procedure execution. Therefore in Ada 83 it is not possible to refer to the value of an **out** parameter within a procedure. For example, the parameter C is not allowed to appear in the right-hand side of an assignment statement or in an expression. The following statements would result in compilation errors:

```
B := C;        -- ERROR in Ada 83!
B := B + C;    -- ERROR in Ada 83!
```

The only thing you can do with **out** parameters is give them values, which is often done with assignment statements, as in NONSENSE.

▼ It is also true of Ada 95 that the value of an **out** parameter is undefined when the procedure starts execution. However, Ada 95 does allow reference to the value of an **out** parameter. This change has been implemented for the practical reason of avoiding the need to declare an extra local variable when the value of the **out** parameter is derived in stages. The following is allowed in Ada 95, for example:

```
C := 0;
C := C + 1;
```
▲

When the two statements in the procedure NONSENSE have been executed the procedure call terminates. The result is shown in Figure 6.6. The parameter A is an **in** parameter and its value cannot have changed in the procedure. Thus it must still contain the same value as when the procedure was called. *No* copying of the value of an **in** parameter occurs when a procedure terminates. The variable X can thus never be changed by the procedure call.

For an **in out** parameter, the value it has at the end of the procedure call is copied back to the actual parameter. In this case, the value 6 will be copied to the variable Y. Thus Y's value is changed by the procedure call.

For an **out** parameter, its value is also copied to the corresponding actual parameter at the end of the call. The variable Z will thus have been changed by the procedure call and get the value 0.

When the program PARA_DEMO is run, it will give the output:

```
1    5    10
1    6    0
```

We have seen before that an expression can be used as an actual parameter to a call. This is only allowed when the corresponding formal parameter is an **in** parameter. If the corresponding formal parameter is an **in out** parameter or an **out** parameter the actual parameter must be a variable. Otherwise, it would be impossible to copy the value of the formal parameter to the actual parameter at the end of the call – a value cannot be copied to an expression. The calls:

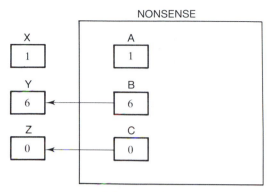

Figure 6.6

```
NONSENSE(X, 2 * Y, Z);    -- ERROR! The second parameter is an
                          -- in out parameter
NONSENSE(X, Y, Z + 1);    -- ERROR! The third parameter is an
                          -- out parameter
```

are thus in error. However, the following is allowed:

```
NONSENSE(X * 3, Y, Z);    -- CORRECT! The first parameter is an
                          -- in parameter
```

We can now summarize the rules for the different types of parameter. If we look at them first from the point of view of the **calling program**, we can say:

in   The actual parameter can be a variable or an expression and it must have a legal value at the time of the call. If the actual parameter is a variable, its value may never be changed during the call to the subprogram. It will always have the same value after the call as before it.

in out   The actual parameter must be a variable and the variable must have a legal value at the time of the call. The value of the variable can change during the procedure call, so that it has a different value at the end.

out   The actual parameter must be a variable. Its value at the time of the call is of no interest, because the procedure ignores it. At the end of the procedure call, the actual parameter will have taken a value other than it had before.

If we look at them from the point of view of the **called subprogram**, the different parameters have the following consequences:

in   When execution of the subprogram starts, the formal parameter has a value. Within the subprogram the formal parameter is treated like a constant: it can be used but its value cannot be changed.

in out When execution of the procedure starts, the formal parameter has a value. Within the procedure the parameter can be used as an ordinary variable: its value can be both used and changed.

out   When execution of the procedure starts, the value of the formal parameter is undefined. In Ada 83 the value of the formal parameter may not be used within the procedure: for example, the formal parameter may not be used in expressions. (In Ada 95, on the other hand, one can also make use of the value of a formal **out** parameter.) In the procedure the formal parameter must be *given* a value in the procedure, through assignment, for example. The value that the formal parameter is given will also be given to the corresponding actual parameter in the program which called the procedure.

The figures shown earlier in the text illustrate how parameters are copied in a purely logical way. If there are parameters of compound types, large arrays for example, it might be inefficient to copy values to and fro. The Ada implementation being used might implement parameter association in a more efficient way. However, pay no attention to this and try not to make use of the fact. A program should always be written so that parameter association occurs as described here.

The three modes of parameter can be used freely in procedures. In functions, however, only **in** parameters may be used. The reason for this limitation is that functions should be clear of **side-effects**. A side-effect means a subprogram which, during execution, affects a variable that is not local to the subprogram but which occurs in another part of the program. When a function is called the values of actual parameters should not be changed. For example, when the function SQRT is called to calculate the square root of a variable W:

SQRT(W)

it would be very strange if the value of W could be changed by the call. Thanks to the fact that functions only have **in** parameters, there is no risk of this happening: the actual parameters to a function can never be changed by calling the function.

The procedures in the previous section had **in** parameters. As a simple example of **in out** parameters we shall look at a procedure that can be used to swap the values of two variables:

```
procedure SWAP (NUMBER1, NUMBER2 : in out INTEGER) is
   TEMP : INTEGER;
begin
   TEMP    := NUMBER1;
   NUMBER1 := NUMBER2;
   NUMBER2 := TEMP;
end SWAP;
```

Formal parameters to procedures

- Handle communication between the procedure and other subprograms.
- Exist only within the procedure.
- Are three different types:
    - **in** parameters. Have values at the time of call. Treated as constants. May not be changed within the procedure.
    - **in out** parameters. Have values at the time of call. Can be both used and changed within the procedure.
    - **out** parameters. Values undefined at time of call. In Ada 83 they may not be used in the procedure. Must be *given* values.

If we assume that in some program there are two variables P and Q with type INTEGER and values 1 and 2, respectively, then the call:

SWAP(P, Q);

from the program will result in the variables P and Q swapping values, thus taking values 2 and 1, respectively. It is essential that the formal parameters to SWAP are **in out** parameters: **in** parameters would not have worked, because they may not be changed. Nor would it have been possible to specify **out** parameters, because then it would not have been possible to use the values of P and Q in the procedure.

When a subprogram has to be written to compute a certain value dependent on certain input values it is, as we have seen, natural to write it as a function rather than as a procedure. If, for example, we want a subprogram that will search for the smallest element in an array of floating point numbers and return it as the result, we will make the subprogram a function. Sometimes we want more than one result from a subprogram and then a function cannot be used. In our example, if we wanted to know both the smallest element in the array and where in the array it occurred, we would have to write a procedure in which the required results were **out** parameters.

Let us look at such a procedure, for finding details of the smallest element in an array of floating point numbers. Input to the procedure is the array itself, which we will give as an **in** parameter, because the array should not be altered. We have two **out** parameters, the smallest element and its index in the array. We shall formulate the procedure to be general and useful for all arrays of floating point numbers, irrespective of the index constraints. We use the same declaration of the type VECTOR as before:

```
            type VECTOR is array (INTEGER range < >) of FLOAT;
```

The procedure looks like this:

```
procedure FIND_SMALLEST (V                              : in VECTOR;
                         SMALLEST_VALUE  : out FLOAT;
                         SMALLEST_PLACE  : out INTEGER) is
    SMALLEST_SO_FAR   : FLOAT      := V(V'FIRST);
    PLACE                    : INTEGER  := V'FIRST;
begin
    for I in V'FIRST + 1 .. V'LAST loop
        if V(I) < SMALLEST_SO_FAR then
            SMALLEST_SO_FAR := V(I);
            PLACE := I;
        end if;
    end loop;
    SMALLEST_VALUE := SMALLEST_SO_FAR;
    SMALLEST_PLACE := PLACE;
end FIND_SMALLEST;
```

The algorithm we are using is based on looking right through the array, from start to end, and always remembering the least element found so far and its index. At the start we remember the first number and the first index. We use the local variable SMALLEST_SO_FAR to hold the smallest element found so far, and the local variable PLACE to remember its index. When we find in the course of the search an element smaller than the smallest found so far, we have found a new smallest number and we change the variables SMALLEST_SO_FAR and PLACE accordingly. When the whole array has been searched SMALLEST_SO_FAR contains the smallest element of the array and PLACE contains its index. The procedure finishes by assigning these values to the procedure's **out** parameters.

When a subprogram is designed to carry out some particular calculation, it is often the case that the calculation can only be achieved for certain input data: some input data will not work. Then the subprogram should take the form of a procedure, with the calculated value as an **out** parameter, and a further **out** parameter should be introduced with type BOOLEAN. This is given the value TRUE in the subprogram if the calculation can be carried out in the normal way, and FALSE if not. The calling program can then, using this parameter, know whether the calculation has been carried out or not.

For example, let us write a procedure COMPUT_ROOTS that computes the two real roots of a second-order equation of the form:

$$x^2 + px + q = 0$$

the roots of which are given by the formula:

$$x = \frac{-p}{2} \pm \sqrt{\left(\frac{p^2}{4} - q\right)}$$

The expression under the square root sign, the discriminant, must be greater than or equal to zero if the equation has real roots. Our procedure can thus only calculate the roots if that is the case.

```
procedure COMPUTE_ROOTS (P, Q                : in FLOAT;
                         ROOT1, ROOT2 : out FLOAT;
                         REAL_ROOTS    : out BOOLEAN) is
     D : FLOAT;
begin
     D := P ** 2 / 4.0 – Q;
     if D < 0.0 then
          REAL_ROOTS := FALSE;
     else
          REAL_ROOTS := TRUE;
          ROOT1 := / 2.0 + SQRT(D);
          ROOT2 := / 2.0 – SQRT(D);
     end if;
end COMPUTE_ROOTS;
```

The procedure takes the two coefficients P and Q as **in** parameters, and it has three **out** parameters, the two calculated roots and a parameter REAL_ROOTS of type BOOLEAN. In the procedure, the parameter REAL_ROOTS is given the value TRUE if the equation has real roots, and otherwise is FALSE. If we assume that the variables A, B, R1 and R2 have type FLOAT and the variable OK has type BOOLEAN, the procedure can be called as follows:

```
PUT_LINE("Enter coefficients P and Q");
GET(A); GET(B);
COMPUTE_ROOTS(A, B, R1, R2, OK);
if OK then
     PUT("The equation has roots ");
     PUT(R1); PUT(" and "); PUT(R2);
else
     PUT("The equation has no real roots");
end if;
```

If OK has the value FALSE after the call, the values of variables R1 and R2 are undefined (they presumably contain rubbish).

What is the best way of naming a procedure? Since a procedure is a program unit that describes how something is done, it is generally appropriate to give them names that specify that something. Suitable names may be, for example, COMPUTE_ROOTS, WRITE_HEADING and CHECK_STATE.

6.4 Top-down design with subprograms

In this section we shall see how subprograms come into use when the technique of top-down design is used. We will also discuss how different subprograms can be placed in text files and compiled separately.

6.4.1 Example: Binomial coefficients

As a first example we will design and write a program to calculate and print the binomial coefficients. These are defined for non-negative integers, n and k, as follows:

$$\binom{n}{k} = \frac{n!}{k! \times (n-k)!}$$

where $n!$ is the factorial of n and is given by:

$$n! = \begin{cases} 1 & \text{if } n = 0 \\ 1 \times 2 \times 3 \times \dots \times n & \text{if } n > 0 \end{cases}$$

In future this binomial coefficient will be written in the form $(n{:}k)$.

We can specify that the program should work as follows. Input to the program should be a value of n and the first step is to read this from the terminal. The program should then calculate all the binomial coefficients for this value of n, that is $(n{:}k)$ for all values of k between 0 and n. Finally, the calculated binomial coefficients should be printed as a table. If, for example, the value of n is 4, then the program should print the table in Figure 6.7. The program should be written so that it can be repeated an arbitrary number of times with different values of n.

A first, rough sketch of the program is:

(1)   Repeat the following an arbitrary number of times:
     (1.1)   Read the input (terminate calculations if no more input given).
     (1.2)   Print the table of values.

We shall try to translate this directly into Ada, making use of calls to subprograms. Step (1.1) can be carried out using a procedure READ_INPUT that can have two **out** parameters, the value of n read and a Boolean parameter that says whether data has been input. We will not worry about how to indicate that input is finished when the program is run. To write step (1.1), therefore, we must assume that the procedure READ_INPUT exists, or will exist. Then step (1.1) can be written:

```
READ_INPUT(N_VALUE, INPUT_COMPLETE);
exit when INPUT_COMPLETE;
```

k	(4:k)
0	1
1	4
2	6
3	4
4	1

Figure 6.7

We have introduced two variables that are used as actual parameters in the procedure call. These variables must, of course, be declared in our program. Since the values of n must be whole numbers that are greater than or equal to 0, NATURAL is a suitable subtype for N_VALUE. The variable INPUT_COMPLETE is of type BOOLEAN.

In step (1.2) we can introduce another procedure, PRINT_TABLE, that takes the value of n as an **in** parameter. This step can be written as:

```
PRINT_TABLE(N_VALUE);
```

Now we can put the algorithm steps into a program where we can include the necessary variable declarations. The specifications of the two procedures we are going to use can also be included, but their details are unimportant for the moment. The program has the following structure:

```
procedure COMPUTE_BINOMIAL_COEFFICIENTS is
    N_VALUE               : NATURAL;
    INPUT_COMPLETE : BOOLEAN;
    procedure READ_INPUT (N_INPUT     : out NATURAL;
                          END_INPUT : out BOOLEAN) is

        ⋮

    end READ_INPUT;
    procedure PRINT_TABLE (N : in NATURAL) is

        ⋮

    end PRINT_TABLE;
begin
    loop
        READ_INPUT(N_VALUE, INPUT_COMPLETE);
        exit when INPUT_COMPLETE;
        PRINT_TABLE(N_VALUE);
    end loop;
end COMPUTE_BINOMIAL_COEFFICIENTS;
```

Now we have finished at the top level of the algorithm. By using the top-down technique combined with calls to subprograms, the program has the correct structure right from the start, without any worry about the technical details of reading the input, or about how the calculations or table output should be done. The procedure at the highest level, here the procedure COMPUTE_BINO-MIAL_COEFFICIENTS, is usually called the **main program**. It is enough for the main program to have only a few statements, mostly subprogram calls, which outline its main structure. Except for *very* trivial programs, where no sub-programs are used, no calculations should be made in the main program. Even in the earlier programs, it would have been better to introduce subprograms and avoid doing everything in the main program.

In the foregoing program we have indicated where to place the body of the subprograms READ_INPUT and PRINT_TABLE, and before the program can be compiled, these procedures must be completed.

The next stage of program development is to write the procedures READ_INPUT and PRINT_TABLE. We shall take them one at a time. It does not matter which we take first: their internal appearance should have nothing to do with the order in which they are written. We can start with READ_INPUT because that should be simpler.

The procedure specification for READ_INPUT is already given:

```
procedure READ_INPUT (N_INPUT    : out NATURAL;
                      END_INPUT : out BOOLEAN)
```

The procedure has to read an integer greater than or equal to 0 from the termi-nal. This integer will be returned from the procedure as the **out** parameter N_INPUT. In the usual case, when a number is read from the terminal, the sec-ond **out** parameter END_INPUT has the value FALSE, but when the operator states that the input is finished it will be given the value TRUE. Now we have to decide how the operator should indicate that the input is over. There are two nat-ural alternatives. One is to make use of the END_OF_FILE, that is, to let the operator note the end of input by writing a special combination of characters, the combination depending on the system, for example, CTRL-D. The other possibility is to let the operator enter a negative number to mark the end of input, because binomial coefficients are not defined for negative values of *n*. Here we choose the first alternative, END_OF_FILE. The algorithm can be very simple:

(1) Request user to type in data.
(2) If the user indicates END_OF_FILE, then set END_INPUT to TRUE. Otherwise, set the out parameter N_INPUT to the number read and set END_INPUT to FALSE.

If we translate this algorithm to Ada and put it together with the procedure's specification, the whole procedure will be as follows:

```
procedure READ_INPUT (N_INPUT     : out NATURAL;
                      END_INPUT : out BOOLEAN) is
begin
   PUT_LINE("Enter N. Terminate with CTRL-D");
   if END_OF_FILE then
      END_INPUT := TRUE;
   else
      END_INPUT := FALSE;
      GET(N_INPUT);
   end if;
end READ_INPUT;
```

Now the procedure READ_INPUT is ready and can be put into the program text written earlier.

The next step is to write the procedure PRINT_TABLE. The procedure specification is already written. The procedure takes the current value of n as **in** parameter, and its task is to write out the table in Figure 6.7, with the binomial coefficients $(n:k)$ for all values of k between 0 and n. We start, as usual, with a rough algorithm:

(1)   Write table heading.
(2)   For each value of k in the interval 0 to n:
     (2.1)   Write a line of the table.

Step (2.1) can be refined to:

(2.1.1)   Write the value of k.
(2.1.2)   Calculate $(n:k)$.
(2.1.3)   Write the calculated value.

Should any of these steps be formulated as a subprogram call? The decision as to whether to do this is always a matter for judgement, but here it is obvious that step (2.1.2), 'Calculate $(n:k)$', should be written as a subprogram; the reason is that it is a well-defined calculation. From two input values, n and k, a result is obtained, $(n:k)$. It is always appropriate to carry out a well-defined calculation of this sort in a subprogram, and the subprogram should be a function. Thus we can assume that we have a function BIN_COEFF that is specified as follows:

```
function BIN_COEFF (P, Q : NATURAL) return POSITIVE is

   ⋮

end BIN_COEFF;
```

The function takes two **in** parameters, P and Q, and returns the binary coefficient $(p:q)$.

We choose to translate the other steps in the algorithm directly into Ada without using subprograms. Step (1), 'Write table heading' could well be performed in a subprogram but, because the step is not complicated, we have chosen not to do that.

We can translate our algorithm to Ada:

```
-- print table heading
PUT(" k");
PUT("    ("); PUT(N, WIDTH => 1); PUT_LINE(":k)");
NEW_LINE;
for K in 0 .. N loop
    -- print a line of the table
    PUT(K, WIDTH => 3); PUT(BIN_COEFF(N,K), WIDTH => 10);
    NEW_LINE;
end loop;
```

The statements contain a good deal of technical detail to make the output look as we want it to. Step (2.1.2), the calculation of (*n:k*), is translated as a call to BIN_COEFF. By placing this call inside the call to PUT, we avoid introducing extra variables for saving the calculated values.

If suitable names are chosen for subprograms and an algorithm has steps that are carried out by calls to subprograms, it is often clear what the steps and the algorithm are doing; thus extra comments are not always necessary. If, however, a subprogram is not used to perform a step in the program, it is sensible to add some comments to explain what is happening.

Now we can put together the entire procedure PRINT_TABLE:

```
procedure PRINT_TABLE (N : In NATURAL) is
    function BIN_COEFF (P, Q : NATURAL) return POSITIVE is

        ⋮

    end BIN_COEFF;
begin
    -- print table heading
    PUT(" k");
    PUT("    (");PUT(N, WIDTH => 1); PUT_LINE(":k)");
    NEW_LINE;

    for K in 0 .. N loop
        -- print a line of the table
        PUT(K, WIDTH  =>  3); PUT(BIN_COEFF(N,K), WIDTH => 10);
        NEW_LINE;
    end loop;
    NEW_LINE'
end PRINT_TABLE;
```

We have placed the specification of the function BIN_COEFF in the right place in the procedure, but we do not yet need to worry about the inside of the function. Note that we can have several levels of subprogram defined within one another. Here we have three levels because the procedure PRINT_TABLE is defined inside COMPUTE_BINOMIAL_COEFFICIENTS.

Now we can go on and construct the function BIN_COEFF that will take the numbers p and q as **in** parameters and return the value $(p:q)$ as its result. Direct from the definition of the binomial coefficients we can write the following very simple algorithm:

(1)   Calculate and return as result $p!/(q! * (p - q)!)$

We see that three different factorials are calculated, so it makes sense to introduce a special function FACTORIAL to calculate the factorial of a given number. Then we can write the function BIN_COEFF as follows:

```
function BIN_COEFF (P, Q : NATURAL) return POSITIVE is
    function FACTORIAL (NUMBER : NATURAL) return POSITIVE is
        .
        .
        .
    end FACTORIAL;
begin
    return FACTORIAL(P) / ( FACTORIAL(Q) * FACTORIAL(P – Q) );
end BIN_COEFF;
```

The function FACTORIAL is at the fourth level inside BIN_COEFF. The only remaining step is to write the function FACTORIAL. We have already discussed (Section 3.6) how a factorial can be calculated. Using this we get:

```
function FACTORIAL (NUMBER : NATURAL) return POSITIVE is
    RESULT : POSITIVE := 1;
begin
    for J in 2 .. NUMBER loop
        RESULT := RESULT * J;
    end loop;
    return RESULT;
end FACTORIAL;
```

For the sake of clarity, we have given the result the type POSITIVE, but we know that we can have problems with the calculation if the value of n is not relatively small, because there may be insufficient room in an integer type. The solution to the problem, as we saw earlier, would be to let the result have the type FLOAT instead.

Now all the subprograms of the program have been written and we can assemble them together as a complete program:

```
with TEXT_IO, BASIC_NUM_IO;
use  TEXT_IO, BASIC_NUM_IO;
procedure COMPUTE_BINOMIAL_COEFFICIENTS is
   N_VALUE          : NATURAL;
   INPUT_COMPLETE : BOOLEAN;

   procedure READ_INPUT (N_INPUT    : out NATURAL;
                         END_INPUT : out BOOLEAN) is
   begin
      PUT_LINE("Enter N. Terminate with CTRL-D");
      if END_OF_FILE then
        END_INPUT := TRUE;
      else
         END_INPUT := FALSE;
         GET(N_INPUT);
      end if;
   end READ_INPUT;

   procedure PRINT_TABLE (N : in NATURAL) is
      function BIN_COEFF (P, Q : NATURAL) return POSITIVE is
         function FACTORIAL (NUMBER : NATURAL) return
            POSITIVE is RESULT : POSITIVE := 1;
         begin
            for J in 2 .. NUMBER loop
               RESULT := RESULT * J;
            end loop;
            return RESULT;
         end FACTORIAL;
      begin
         return FACTORIAL(P) / ( FACTORIAL(Q) * FACTORIAL
                  (P – Q) );
      end BIN_COEFF;
   begin
      -- print table heading
      PUT(" k");
      PUT("   ("); PUT(N, WIDTH => 1);
      PUT_LINE(":k)");
      NEW_LINE;

      for K in 0 .. N loop
         -- print a line of the table
         PUT(K, WIDTH => 3);
         PUT(BIN_COEFF(N,K), WIDTH => 10);
         NEW_LINE;
      end loop;
      NEW_LINE;
   end PRINT_TABLE;
```

```
  begin
    loop
        READ_INPUT(N_VALUE, INPUT_COMPLETE);
        exit when INPUT_COMPLETE;
        PRINT_TABLE(N_VALUE);
    end loop;
  end COMPUTE_BINOMIAL_COEFFICIENTS;
```

When we assemble the program we must make sure that we also have access to the packages TEXT_IO and BASIC_NUM_IO, because these are used in READ_INPUT and PRINT_TABLE.

This exercise has shown that using the technique of top-down design with subprograms allows one step to be in focus at a time. In the procedure PRINT_TABLE, for example, we could concentrate on how the table should be printed and not worry about how the input should be read or how the binomial coefficients should be calculated.

Division into subprograms

- A program should always be divided into several subprograms.

- A well-defined calculation or operation (that is, a 'high-level step' of an algorithm) is carried out in a subprogram.

- A subprogram should be no longer than can be easily understood. If it becomes too long it should be divided into further subprograms.

6.4.2   Separate compilation

When a largish program is to be written it can be of advantage to divide the program text up and compile the parts separately. Then, no program text need be too big and it is easier to keep a grasp of the program as a whole. It also becomes possible to compile a program before all the subprograms are ready, and thus check that it is free from compilation errors. It is even possible to run tests on a program and check that its main features work correctly by including very simple test versions of the separate parts; these can subsequently be replaced by complete versions when the program as a whole is running well. The option of writing the various parts of a program separately is of great advantage when several programmers are jointly developing a large program. They no longer need to work on one and the same program text, but the work can be divided up so that they can work independently of one another and develop separate parts of the program.

In Ada there are two main methods for compiling different parts of a program separately. One makes use of **subunits** and the other of **library units**. The technique of working with subunits is used naturally in connection with top-down design, so we will study it first. In the program for binomial coefficients we placed subprograms within other subprograms. For example, READ_INPUT and PRINT_TABLE were placed within COMPUTE_BINOMIAL_COEFFICIENTS. The program was not complete until these subprograms had been written. When the technique of subunits is used, you tell the Ada compiler that you are going to write and compile the body of a subprogram by itself later, and you do this by writing the word **separate** after the subprogram specification instead of writing the body of the subprogram. The program COMPUTE_BINOMIAL_ COEFFICIENTS, for example, could be written as follows:

```
procedure COMPUTE_BINOMIAL_COEFFICIENTS is
    N_VALUE           : NATURAL;
    INPUT_COMPLETE : BOOLEAN;
    procedure READ_INPUT (N_INPUT      : out NATURAL;
                          END_INPUT : out BOOLEAN)
                          is separate;
    procedure PRINT_TABLE (N : in NATURAL) is separate;
begin
    loop
        READ_INPUT(N_VALUE, INPUT_COMPLETE);
        exit when INPUT_COMPLETE;
        PRINT_TABLE(N_VALUE);
    end loop;
end COMPUTE_BINOMIAL_COEFFICIENTS:
```

The declarations of READ_INPUT and PRINT_TABLE are known as **procedure stubs**. This program is now complete and can be compiled. Of course, it cannot be run and tested until READ_INPUT and PRINT_TABLE have been written and compiled separately. Note that the packages TEXT_IO and BASIC_NUM_IO do not need to be present: they are not used in the procedure COMPUTE_BINOMIAL_ COEFFICIENTS itself.

The subprograms that have been omitted can be compiled separately and are then called **subunits**. When a subunit is going to be compiled separately the name of the subprogram into which it is to be inserted has to be stated, so a subunit is not an independent item but belongs to some other part of a program. The word **separate** has to be written in front of the subunit and the name of the subprogram into which it is to be inserted is written in brackets. The procedure READ_INPUT will thus appear as follows:

```
with  TEXT_IO, BASIC_NUM_IO;
use   TEXT_IO, BASIC_NUM_IO;
separate (COMPUTE_BINOMIAL_COEFFICIENTS)
```

```
procedure READ_INPUT (N_INPUT    : out NATURAL
                      END_INPUT : out BOOLEAN) is separate;
begin
    PUT_LINE("Enter N. Terminate with CTRL-D");
    if END_OF_FILE then
        END_INPUT := TRUE;
    else
        END_INPUT := FALSE;
        GET(N_INPUT);
    end if;
end READ_INPUT;
```

Since READ_INPUT is to be inserted into the procedure COMPUTE_BINOMIAL_ COEFFICIENTS, COMPUTE_BINOMIAL_COEFFICIENTS is written in brackets after the word **separate**. The packages TEXT_IO and BASIC_NUM_IO also have to be included since they are used by the procedure READ_INPUT.

When a program is being developed, just as with any other construction work, it is an advantage if it can be built of ready-made standard parts. As we have seen, the method of top-down design, or stepwise refinement as it is more fittingly known in this context, leads to a problem being broken down into smaller and smaller parts, each of which becomes a subprogram. Subprograms thus become components of the construction. The problem with this sort of successive refinement is that the subprograms you arrive at are often much too specialized to be used in other contexts. In practice, therefore, this method is not applied too strictly. There is often an element of 'bottom-up' design as well. For example, if there are existing subprograms that do a particular job, then you might try to design your program to make use of them. In the example which writes out the binomial coefficients, for instance, it is quite likely that a function to calculate the coefficients already exists.

Separate compilation using subunits

Where the subprogram body would normally be placed (in another subprogram A, for instance) is written:

> **function** *name*(*parameters*) **return** *result_type*
> **is separate**;

or

> **procedure** *name*(*parameters*) **is separate**;

When the body of the subprogram is later compiled separately, where it would normally be placed must be specified. If the body would normally be in another subprogram A, the following would be written:

> **separate** (A)
> *subprogram_body*

Now we will look at the second method for separate compilation, using **library units**. First we have to ensure that there is a function BIN_COEFF which is ready to be used. We do this by putting the following program text into a file of its own and compiling it:

```
function BIN_COEFF(P, Q : NATURAL) return POSITIVE is
    function FACTORIAL(NUMBER : NATURAL) return POSITIVE is
        RESULT : POSITIVE := 1;
    begin
        for J in 2 .. NUMBER loop
            RESULT := RESULT * J;
        end loop;
        return RESULT;
    end FACTORIAL;
begin
    return FACTORIAL(P)/FACTORIAL(Q) * FACTORIAL(P);
end BIN_COEFF;
```

We have now compiled BIN_COEFF as a free-standing library unit, which is quite independent of the program COMPUTE_BINARY_COEFFICIENTS; the word **separate** is not used.

The next stage is to compile the program COMPUTE_BINARY_COEFFICIENTS, making use of a **with** clause to allow access to the function BIN_COEFF:

```
with TEXT_IO, BASIC_NUM_IO, BIN_COEFF;
use  TEXT_IO, BASIC_NUM_IO;
procedure COMPUTE_BINARY_COEFFICIENTS is
    N_VALUE          : NATURAL;
    INPUT_COMPLETE : BOOLEAN;
    procedure READ_INPUT (N_INPUT     : out NATURAL;
                          END_INPUT : out BOOLEAN) is
    begin

        :

    end READ_INPUT;
    procedure PRINT_TABLE(N : in NATURAL) is
    begin
        -- print table heading
        PUT(" k");
        PUT("        ("); PUT(N, WIDTH => 1);
        PUT_LINE(":K)");
        PUT_LINE("===============");
```

```
        for K in 0 ..N loop
            -- print in a line of the table
            PUT(K, WIDTH => 3);
            PUT(BIN_COEFF(N,K), WIDTH => 10);
            NEW_LINE;
        end loop;
        NEW_LINE;
    end PRINT_TABLE;
begin
        .
        .
        .

end COMPUTE_BINARY_COEFFICIENTS;
```

Note two things. First, BIN_COEFF is not stated in the **use** clause, since **use** clauses are only used for packages. Secondly, there is no declaration of BIN_COEFF anywhere in the program: it is entirely free-standing.

In general, ready-written subprograms are to be found in packages, and not alone as BIN_COEFF is in the example we have been looking at. In fact, we have already seen several examples of the technique of using library units in connection with packages, such as using standard procedures from the package TEXT_IO and standard functions from the generic package GENERIC_ELEMENTARY_FUNCTIONS. Constructing packages and more about using them will be the subject of Chapter 8.

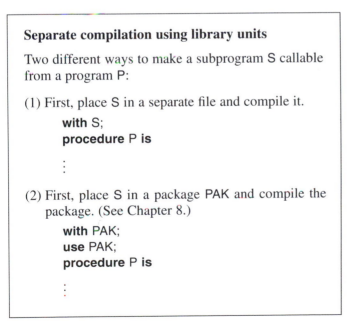

Separate compilation using library units

Two different ways to make a subprogram S callable from a program P:

(1) First, place S in a separate file and compile it.

> **with** S;
> **procedure** P **is**
>
> .
> .
> .

(2) First, place S in a package PAK and compile the package. (See Chapter 8.)

> **with** PAK;
> **use** PAK;
> **procedure** P **is**
>
> .
> .
> .

6.4.3   Example: Sorting

Let us now look at another program using the technique of top-down design with subprograms. We shall write a new version of the sort program in Section 5.9. The program's job was to read a number of integers from the terminal and then print them out in numerical order. A rough algorithm is:

    (1)   Read in the numbers.
    (2)   Sort the numbers.
    (3)   Print the sorted numbers.

This can easily be translated to Ada if we assume that we have three sub-programs, READ, SORT and WRITE. READ can be a procedure with two **out** parameters: an integer array of the numbers read and an integer which gives the number of numbers read and placed in the array. If we assume that we have the declarations:

```
MAX_NO_ELTS : constant := 100;
subtype INDEX is INTEGER range 1 .. MAX_NO_ELTS;
type INTEGER_ARRAY is array (INDEX range < >) of INTEGER;
```

then the specification of the procedure READ can be written:

```
procedure READ (S     : out INTEGER_ARRAY;
                SIZE : out NATURAL)
```

Now step (1) in the algorithm is:

```
READ (A, N_ELTS);
```

Here we have used two variables, A and N_ELTS, as the actual parameters to READ. They are declared as follows:

```
A       : INTEGER_ARRAY(1 .. MAX_NO_ELTS);
N_ELTS : NATURAL;
```

The variable A is an integer array. The number of places in the array is determined by the constant MAX_NO_ELTS, which has the value 100 in this example. When the procedure READ is called it fills the array A with the numbers that are entered from the terminal. If the user enters fewer numbers than there is room for, then the whole array is not filled. The number of places used is given by the parameter N_ELTS. We assume that the procedure checks that there are no more numbers than the array has room for.

    Step (2) in the algorithm is now simple. We start by writing a specification for a subprogram SORT:

      procedure SORT (S : **in out** INTEGER_ARRAY)

The procedure thus has only one parameter, an **in out** parameter, which is an integer array. When the procedure is called the array is sorted so that the elements are in ascending numerical order. Using it, step (2) can be written:

      SORT (A(1 .. N_ELTS));

As parameter, we have not given the entire array, A, but only the part of it that is being used.

      Step (3) is also simple. First we specify a procedure WRITE:

      procedure WRITE(S : **in** INTEGER_ARRAY)

The procedure takes the array to be written as an **in** parameter. Step (3) is:

      WRITE(A(1 .. N_ELTS));

Here, too, we only give the part of the array that is in use.

      Now the three steps of the program can be assembled, with the resulting structure:

```
procedure SORT_EXAMPLE is
    MAX_NO_ELTS : constant := 100;
    subtype INDEX is INTEGER range 1 .. MAX_NO_ELTS;
    type INTEGER_ARRAY is array (INDEX range < >) of INTEGER;
    A        : INTEGER_ARRAY(1 .. MAX_NO_ELTS);
    N_ELTS : NATURAL;
    procedure READ (S     : out INTEGER_ARRAY;
                    SIZE : out NATURAL) is

        ⋮

    end READ;
    procedure SORT (S : in out INTEGER_ARRAY) is

        ⋮

    end SORT;
    procedure WRITE(S : in INTEGER_ARRAY) is

        ⋮

    end WRITE;
begin
```

```
                    READ (A, N_ELTS);
                    SORT (A(1 .. N_ELTS));
                    WRITE(A(1 .. N_ELTS));
                end SORT_EXAMPLE;
```

Now the three subprograms have to be written. We shall start with WRITE, which is the simplest and uses the algorithm:

(1)   Write heading.
(2)   For all the numbers in the array S:
      (2.1)   Write out the number.

This is easily translated to Ada:

```
        procedure WRITE(S : in INTEGER_ARRAY) is
        begin
            NEWLINE;
            PUT_LINE("The numbers are:");
            for K in S'RANGE loop
                PUT( S(K) );
            end loop;
            NEW_LINE;
        end WRITE;
```

Here we have used the attribute S'RANGE to state the index range for S.
    The algorithm for what should be done in the procedure READ is:

(1)   Set the number of elements read to zero and ARRAY_FULL to FALSE.
(2)   Request the user to enter the array.
(3)   Repeat the following until the user states that nothing more will be entered, or until ARRAY_FULL is TRUE.
      (3.1)   If the array is full, output an error message and set ARRAY_FULL to TRUE. Otherwise, read a number into the next vacant place and increase the number of elements read by 1.
(4)   Give the number of elements read as result.

We choose to use the END_OF_FILE technique for the user to notify the end of input. The algorithm can be translated to Ada:

```
        procedure READ (S      : out INTEGER_ARRAY;
                         SIZE  : out NATURAL) is
            N_ELTS_READ : NATURAL  := 0;
            ARRAY_FULL   : BOOLEAN := FALSE;
        begin
            PUT_LINE("Enter the integers to be sorted.");
```

```
        PUT_LINE("Terminate input with CTRL-D");
        while not END_OF_FILE and not ARRAY_FULL loop
            if N_ELTS_READ = S'LENGTH then
                PUT_LINE("Too many!");
                ARRAY_FULL := TRUE;
            else
                N_ELTS_READ := N_ELTS_READ + 1;
                GET( S(N_ELTS_READ) );
            end if;
        end loop;
        SIZE := N_ELTS_READ;
    end READ;
```

We use a local variable N_ELTS_READ to count the numbers read in. If the entire array is full and another number is input at the terminal, the procedure gives the error message:

Too many!

We have already given the algorithm for the procedure SORT in Section 5.9:

(1)   Set K to 1.
(2)   While K is less than the number of elements in the array:
    (2.1)   Search for the smallest element in that part of the array that starts at the Kth position and ends with the last element in the array.
    (2.2)   Swap the smallest element (from step (2.1)) and the element in position K.
    (2.3)   Increase K by 1.

To achieve step (2.1) we specify a function SMALLEST as follows:

function SMALLEST (T : INTEGER_ARRAY) **return** INDEX

The function takes an integer array as an **in** parameter. As result it returns the index of the smallest number in the array. Step (2.1) can now be written:

SMALLEST_POSN := SMALLEST(S(K .. S'LAST));

We have introduced the variable SMALLEST_POSN with type INDEX in which we save the result of the call. S is, as we can see in the specification of SORT, the array to be sorted. As parameter to the function SMALLEST we give the part of the array that starts at index K. SMALLEST will thus give the index of the smallest element of that part of the array as result.

Step (2.2) can be carried out using a procedure SWAP, which we specify as follows:

```
procedure SWAP (I, J  : in INDEX;
                T    : in out INTEGER_ARRAY)
```

When this procedure is called, elements number I and J in array T will swap places.

The remaining steps in the algorithm can be achieved with a **for** construct. The procedure SORT can then be written:

```
procedure SORT (S : in out INTEGER_ARRAY) is
    SMALLEST_POSN : INDEX;

    function SMALLEST (T : INTEGER_ARRAY) return INDEX is
    -- gives the index number for the smallest element in T

        ⋮

    end SMALLEST;

    procedure SWAP (I, J : in      INDEX;
                    T   : in out INTEGER_ARRAY) is
    -- swap the Ith and Jth elements in array T

        ⋮

    end SWAP;
begin
    for K in S'RANGE loop
        SMALLEST_POSN := SMALLEST(S(K .. S'LAST));
        SWAP(K, SMALLEST_POSN, S);
    end loop;
end SORT;
```

Now it remains to write the subprograms SMALLEST and SWAP. Algorithms for these were given in Section 5.9. The algorithm for SMALLEST can, with some amendment, be written:

(1)   Set M to the first index in T.
(2)   Let I run from the second to the last index in T.
    (2.1)   If element number I is less than element number M then set M to I.
(3)   The smallest element is now element number M. Give M as result.

Translation to Ada gives:

```
function SMALLEST (T : INTEGER_ARRAY) return INDEX is
-- gives the index number for the smallest element in T
   M : INDEX := T'FIRST;
begin
   for I in T'FIRST + 1 .. T'LAST loop
      if T(I) < T(M) then
         M := I;
      end if;
   end loop;
   return M;
end SMALLEST;
```

The algorithm for the final procedure, SWAP, was also given in Section 5.9.

(1)   Move the *I*th element to a temporary store.
(2)   Move the *J*th element to position *I*.
(3)   Move the element in the temporary store to position *J*.

The procedure is in Ada:

```
procedure SWAP (I, J : in INDEX;
                     T    : in out INTEGER_ARRAY) is
-- swap the Ith and Jth elements in array T
   TEMP : INTEGER;
begin
   TEMP := T(I);
   T(I)    := T(J);
   T(J)    := TEMP;
end SWAP;
```

All the different parts can now be assembled to make a complete program, when we also ensure that the packages TEXT_IO and BASIC_NUM_IO are accessible:

```
with TEXT_IO, BASIC_NUM_IO;
use  TEXT_IO, BASIC_NUM_IO;
procedure SORT_EXAMPLE is
   MAX_NO_ELTS : constant := 100;
   subtype INDEX is INTEGER range 1 .. MAX_NO_ELTS;
   type INTEGER_ARRAY is array (INDEX range < >) of INTEGER;
   A         : INTEGER_ARRAY(1 .. MAX_NO_ELTS);
   N_ELTS : NATURAL;
   procedure READ (S : out INTEGER_ARRAY;
                      SIZE : out NATURAL) is
      N_ELTS_READ : NATURAL     := 0;
      ARRAY_FULL  : BOOLEAN := FALSE;
```

```
begin
    PUT_LINE("Enter the integers to be sorted.");
    PUT_LINE("Terminate input with CTRL-D");
    while not END_OF_FILE and not ARRAY_FULL loop
        if N_ELTS_READ = S'LENGTH then
            PUT_LINE("Too many!");
            ARRAY_FULL := TRUE;
        else
            N_ELTS_READ := N_ELTS_READ + 1;
            GET( S(N_ELTS_READ) );
        end if;
    end loop;
    SIZE := N_ELTS_READ;
end READ;
procedure SORT (S   : in out INTEGER_ARRAY) is
    SMALLEST_POSN : INDEX;

    function SMALLEST (T : INTEGER_ARRAY) return INDEX is
    -- gives the index number for the smallest element in T
        M : INDEX := T'FIRST;
    begin
        for I in T'FIRST + 1 .. T'LAST loop
            if T(I) < T(M) then
                M := I;
            end if;
        end loop;
        return M;
    end SMALLEST;

    procedure SWAP (I, J : in INDEX;
                            T   : in out INTEGER_ARRAY) is
    -- swap the Ith and Jth elements in array T
        TEMP : INTEGER;
    begin
        TEMP := T(I);
        T(I)    := T(J);
        T(J)    := TEMP;
    end SWAP;
begin
    for K in S'RANGE loop
        SMALLEST_POSN := SMALLEST(S(K .. S'LAST));
        SWAP(K, SMALLEST_POSN, S);
    end loop;
end SORT;

procedure WRITE(S : in INTEGER_ARRAY) is
begin
```

```
            NEW_LINE;
            PUT_LINE("The numbers are:");
            for K in S'RANGE loop
                PUT( S(K) );
            end loop;
            NEW_LINE;
        end WRITE;
    begin
        READ    (A, N_ELTS);
        SORT    (A(1 .. N_ELTS));
        WRITE   (A(1 .. N_ELTS));
    end SORT_EXAMPLE;
```

Clearly, this program is longer (with regard to the number of lines) than the program we wrote in Section 5.9. However, it is not always the case that a short program is a 'good' program. The clarity of a program is determined by its structure. In general a program that is developed from the top down with subprograms has a better structure: it does not matter that it is a few lines longer than it would be without subprograms.

6.5   The scope of a declaration

It has been shown that a local variable in a subprogram can be considered as a temporary store that exists only while the subprogram is called. That is, the declaration of the local variable has only a certain **scope**, which extends over the subprogram in which it is declared. It is not only the declarations of variables that have a particular scope; all sorts of declarations, such as those of types, constants and subprograms, have an associated scope so that what has been declared is only known and only used in a certain part of the program: it is said that they are only **visible** in that part of the program. There are well-specified rules in Ada for declaration scope; these are analogous to the corresponding rules in other closely related languages such as Pascal.

To explain the rules we use the outline nonsense program:

```
procedure P1 is
    type T is  ... ;
    A : constant INTEGER := 100;
    B : INTEGER := 2 * A;

    procedure P2 (X: INTEGER) is
        A : FLOAT;

        procedure P3 (C : T) is
            X : FLOAT;
        begin
```

$\vdots$

  end P3;

 begin

  $\vdots$

 end P2;

 procedure P4 (I : INTEGER) **is**

  Q : T;

 begin

  $\vdots$

 P2(... , ...);   -- call of P2

  $\vdots$

 end P4;

 begin

  $\vdots$

 end P1;

In the program there are procedures P1, P2, P3 and P4. P1 is the main program and is the outermost procedure. The declarations of P2 and P4 are within P1 and the declaration of P3 is within P2.

  The main rule is that the scope of a declaration extends from the place where it is made to the end of the subprogram it is in. This means, in our example, that the variable Q and the formal parameter I are only known in the procedure P4. If attempts are made to use Q or I outside P4 a compile-time error will result. The fact that a declaration's scope begins where the declaration is made means that reference may not be made to something that is declared later in the program, even if it is declared in the same subprogram. In the example, it is important that A's declaration comes before that of B because A is used in the declaration of B.

The scope of a declaration

A declaration applies from the place where it is made to the end of the subprogram in which it is made.

  The next rule states that something declared in a subprogram P is also visible in all subprograms declared within P. The type T in our example is thus visible not only in P1 but also in P2 (and therefore also in P3) and in P4, because P2 and P4 are declared within P1. Another example is that P2 is visible in P4 and can be called there, because both P2 and P4 are declared in P1, and P2 is declared before P4.

Global declarations

A declaration that applies in a subprogram P also applies in all the subprograms to P.

The two rules can also be expressed thus: from the outside it is impossible to 'see into' a subprogram and get at the declarations that are made there; it is possible, however, to 'see out from the inside' of a subprogram and get at declarations made outside it.

These rules mean that in a subprogram it is possible to access variables that are declared in an enclosing subprogram. For example, the variable B in P1 is accessible from P4. The variable B is a **global variable** to P4. When programming, it is often very tempting to use global variables in a subprogram and change them, thereby avoiding the use of parameters to the subprogram. The use of global variables is, however, contrary to the ideals of good programming style, because using them leads to programs being confused and difficult to understand. Then the risk of errors in the program increases and, at the same time, it becomes more difficult to find the errors in a program. From the calling program it is impossible to see that variables might be changed within a subprogram. Unexpected and elusive side effects can result. The rule is therefore: *never use global variables*. (As with all rules, there have to be exceptions. If subprograms are written in a package, under certain circumstances global variables can be used without offending the rules of good programming style.)

In Ada 95, as we have already seen, declarations can be placed in arbitrary order: the declarations of variables do not have to be placed before declarations of subprograms. This can be used to eliminate the risk associated with global variables. If, for example, variable B is declared after the declaration of P4 in the example, then none of the procedures P2, P3 or P4 can mistakenly get at B.

▼

▲

Global variables

In a well-structured program, *never*, or virtually never, use global variables.

It is forbidden to declare several items with the same name in a particular subprogram (except for subprograms and enumeration literals). However, the same names may be used in declarations that are in different subprograms. In the foregoing example, the name A appeared in both P1 and P2 and the name X in both P2 and P3. If the same name is used in two declarations in different subprograms the two declared quantities have nothing to do with one another: they only have the same name. The name A, in our example, is used to denote an integer constant in procedure P1 but a floating point variable in P2.

Even if the scope of a declaration extends to the end of the subprogram in which it is declared, the declared quantity can be 'covered' in an enclosed subprogram, if this subprogram contains a declaration where the same name is used. In P2 (and P3), for example, the constant A in P1 cannot be accessed. If the name A is written in P2 or P3 it is the variable A that is declared in P2 that matters. In the same way, P2's formal parameter X cannot be reached within P3 because there it is 'covered' by the floating point variable X.

Using the same names

- Quantities that are declared in the *same* subprogram must have different names (with the exception of subprograms and enumeration literals).
- Quantities that are declared in *different* subprograms may have the same name.

The rules mean that if global variables are avoided then each subprogram can be considered as a separate 'building block' in the total program. Contact between each 'building block' and its surroundings (that is, the other subprograms) occurs through the subprogram's specification. Within the subprogram, any name can be used for declared quantities: it makes no difference whether the name appears in another subprogram. Subprograms can thus be developed independently of one another.

For example, in the program we wrote to compute the binomial coefficients, we could have used the names N and K for the formal parameters to the function BIN_COEFF; this might have been more natural than calling the parameters P and Q. This would not have been affected by the fact that the names N and K were also used in the procedure PRINT_TABLE. N and K within BIN_COEFF would be considered different from N and K in PRINT_TABLE.

6.6   Overloaded subprograms

To declare several quantities with the same name in a subprogram is normally forbidden, but in Ada, to declare several subprograms with the same name in the same subprogram is allowed, and they are known as **overloaded subprograms**.

To explain when this is allowed, we first need some definitions. (In Ada 95 a different terminology is used, but the meaning of the rules is the same.)

- By **base type** of a subtype we mean the type from which this subtype is derived. (For example, the base type of NATURAL is INTEGER.) The base type of an ordinary type that is not a subtype is the type itself. (For example, the base type of INTEGER is INTEGER.)
- If two subprograms have the same number of parameters, and if the corresponding parameters have the same base types, we say that the two subprograms have the same **parameter type profile**.
- Two subprograms have the same **profile** (parameter and result type profile) if they are both procedures with the same parameter type profile, or if they are both functions with the same parameter type profile and, in addition, their results have the same base type.

If we write the following subprogram specifications, for example:

```
procedure A (P1 : in FLOAT; P2 : in out INTEGER)
procedure B (X: in out FLOAT; Y: out INTEGER)
function C (U : POSITIVE) return CHARACTER
function D (V : INTEGER) return CHARACTER
```

then A has the same profile as B, and C has the same profile as D. Note that the two formal parameters do not need the same names for the two subprograms to have the same profiles. Nor does it matter whether the corresponding parameters are of the same kind in the sense of **in, in out** or **out**.

Several subprograms may have the same name in a subprogram (or a package) if these subprograms have different profiles:

```
type VECTOR is array (INTEGER range < > ) of FLOAT;

function MEAN (X1, X2 : FLOAT) return FLOAT is
begin
    return (X1 + X2) / 2.0;
end MEAN;

function MEAN (V : VECTOR) return FLOAT is
    SUM : FLOAT := 0.0;
begin
    for I in V'RANGE loop
        SUM := SUM + V(I);
    end loop;
    return SUM / FLOAT(V'LENGTH);
end MEAN;
```

Here we have two different functions with the same name: the two functions are overloaded. The functions have different profiles, in that the first takes two parameters of type FLOAT and the second takes one parameter of type VECTOR. If we assume the variables MV, X, Y and W are declared as follows:

```
MV  : FLOAT;
X   : FLOAT := 6.5;
Y   : FLOAT := 4.5;
W   : VECTOR (1 .. 3) := (0.5, 3.0, 1.0);
```

then we can call the function MEAN:

```
MV := MEAN(X, Y);          -- MV takes the value 5.5
MV := MEAN(0.0, 1.0);      -- MV takes the value 0.5
MV := MEAN(W);             -- MV takes the value 1.5
MV := MEAN( (1.1, 1.3) );  -- MV takes the value 1.2
```

In the first call there are two actual parameters, X and Y, which both have type FLOAT. These actual parameters match with the formal parameters for the first function MEAN, but not with the formal parameter of the second. The compiler 'understands' that we intend to call the first of the subroutines MEAN. The second call also matches with the first function but not with the second. The last two calls, however, do not match with the first function. They suit the second instead, and that will be called.

Overloaded subprograms

Two subprograms that are in the same subprogram may have the same name (the name may be overloaded) if they have different profiles, that is, different base types for parameters, and for the result in the case of functions.

The reason why overloaded subprograms must have different profiles is that the compiler must be able to choose which subprogram is intended for use every time a call is made. Only one subprogram can be suitable, otherwise the program would be ambiguous. (If none of the subprograms with the same name fit the bill, then the program is in error and an error message will be given during compilation.)

We have already called overloaded subprograms many times. In the package TEXT_IO and BASIC_NUM_IO there are several procedures with the name PUT, for example. There are several procedures PUT with different profiles: output of text does not use the same procedure as output of a floating point number, to give one example. In the following statements four different procedures are being called:

```
PUT("Hello'.");  -- The parameter has type STRING
PUT('a');        -- The parameter has type CHARACTER
```

```
PUT(I);          -- The parameter has type INTEGER
PUT(X);          -- The parameter has type FLOAT
```

Because the compiler has always chosen the correct PUT procedure we have not needed to worry that there are several versions. In the same way, TEXT_IO and BASIC_NUM_IO have several subprograms called GET.

The use of overloaded subprograms is thus a convenient way of carrying out similar operations on objects with different types. It is still possible to use the same name for the operation rather than inventing different names for the subprograms for each type.

6.7   Named parameter association

The normal procedure for calling a subprogram is to list all the actual parameters, separated by commas. The first actual parameter is associated with the first formal parameter, the second actual parameter is associated with the second formal parameter and so on. Let us now write a procedure MULTIPLE_WRITE that has the task of writing out a particular character a number of times at the terminal, each time on a new line. As parameters, MULTIPLE_WRITE will have the character to be printed and an integer that specifies the number of times it should be written:

```
procedure MULTIPLE_WRITE (CHAR: CHARACTER;
                          N      : INTEGER) is
begin
    for I in 1 .. N loop
        PUT(CHAR); NEW_LINE;
    end loop;
end MULTIPLE_WRITE;
```

If we want to write the character 'x' three times, we would use the procedure call:

```
MULTIPLE_WRITE('x', 3);
```

Then the first actual parameter 'x' will be associated with the formal parameter CHAR and the second actual parameter, 3, will be associated with the second formal parameter N. This can be called **positional parameter association** because the position of an actual parameter in a procedure call determines the formal parameter with which it is associated.

> ### Positional parameter association
>
> - The call appears thus:
>
>   *subprogram_name*(*a1, a2, ... an*)
> - The actual parameters are listed in the call.
> - Normally, all the actual parameters are listed.
> - The first actual parameter is associated with the first formal parameter, the second actual parameter with the second formal parameter, etc.

In Ada there is another method of associating the actual parameters with the formal parameters in a subprogram call. It is possible to state the name of a formal parameter the actual parameter is to be associated to. We call this **named parameter association**. How it works is shown in the following call to MULTIPLE_WRITE:

MULTIPLE_WRITE(CHAR => 'x', N => 3);

The term:

CHAR => 'x'

means that the actual parameter 'x' should be associated with the formal parameter CHAR. Similarly,

N => 3

means that the actual parameter 3 should be associated with the formal parameter N. One thing gained by writing a call in this way is that it is clearer (if the formal parameters have good names). Someone reading the program later does not need to know exactly the formal parameters used or the order in which they appear, before being able to understand the significance of the call.

When named parameter association is used the parameters do not need to be listed in any special order. The previous call could have been written:

MULTIPLE_WRITE(N => 3, CHAR => 'x');

and this would have been equally correct.

In addition, positional and named parameter association can be mixed. Our call could also be written, for example:

MULTIPLE_WRITE('x', N => 3);

Named parameter association

The call appears thus:

  subprogram_name(*name* => a1, name => *a2*, ...);

The parameters may be listed in any order.

When the two parameter associations are mixed in a call, the positional associations must be written first in their correct order. Named parameters can then be written in arbitrary order. When one named parameter association has been used in a call, all the remaining parameters in the call must also be named. For example, it is wrong to write:

    MULTIPLE_WRITE(CHAR => 'x', 3);   -- ERROR!

One question that arises is whether all the parameters must be listed in a call and what happens if they are not. First, we can state that in the case of **out** and **in out** parameters they must all be listed in a call. At the end of the call copying to the actual parameters, which must be variables, will occur and this cannot happen if actual parameters are missing.

In the case of **in** parameters, however, it is possible in Ada to omit actual **in** parameters. The condition allowing this to be possible is that a value is given in the subprogram that can be used if no actual parameter is given. To show how this works we can make a simple amendment to the procedure MULTIPLE_WRITE:

    procedure MULTIPLE_WRITE (CHAR : CHARACTER;
                         N   : INTEGER := 2) **is**
    begin
    for I **in** 1 .. N **loop**
       PUT(CHAR); NEW_LINE;
    end loop;
    end MULTIPLE_WRITE;

Here we have given the formal parameter N a value which is to be used if there is no actual parameter in a call. Such a value, used if no explicit value is stated, is called a **default value**. Thus the formal parameter N has a default value of 2.

Now the actual parameter that is to be associated with the formal parameter N may be omitted. We can write, for example:

    MULTIPLE_WRITE(CHAR => '+');

This call means that two plus signs will be written. The call could also be written:

```
MULTIPLE_WRITE('+');
```

and again two plus signs will be written.

Of course, an actual parameter can still be associated explicitly with N if necessary. The call:

```
MULTIPLE_WRITE(CHAR => '+', N => 10);
```

will write out 10 plus signs and the default value, the formal parameter N, is of no significance.

Parameters with default values

- An **in** parameter to a subprogram may be given a default value when the formal parameter is specified:

  (... ; *parameter_name* : **in** *type* := *default_value*; ...)

- Parameters with default values may be omitted from calls. Then the formal parameter is given the default value.

- **In out** parameters and **out** parameters may *not* have default values.

An **in** parameter may not be omitted from a call if there is no default value for the corresponding formal parameter. For example, it is wrong to write:

```
MULTIPLE_WRITE(N => 5);      -- ERROR!
```

When we have called the procedures PUT in the packages TEXT_IO and BASIC_NUM_IO we have made frequent use of named parameter association. We have also made use of the fact that certain **in** parameters to PUT have default values. For example, we have written calls such as:

```
PUT(I, WIDTH => 5);
```

where we have used positional parameter association for the first formal parameter and named parameter association for the formal parameter WIDTH. This call could also have been written:

```
PUT(ITEM => I, WIDTH => 5);
```

because the first formal parameter to all the PUT procedures is called ITEM.

When we have written a simple call, such as:

PUT(I);

we have made use of the fact that there is a default value of WIDTH in PUT. In the same way, the formal parameters EXP, FORE and AFT also have default values in the version of PUT that is used to write out floating point numbers. When we make a call such as:

PUT(X);

these default values will be used.

6.8   Recursive subprograms

It has been shown that one subprogram can call another. Furthermore, a subprogram can call itself, and such a subprogram is called a **recursive subprogram**.
   It is appropriate to use recursive subprograms to solve certain types of problem. The problems for which recursion is most useful are those which are defined from the start in a recursive way: this occurs often in mathematical calculations. The most common example of a recursive subprogram – an example that occurs in almost all books about programming – is a function to calculate the factorial of a number n. This is a problem we have studied a couple of times already. We then used iteration to solve the problem but now we shall see how recursion can be used instead. The factorial of a number n, written $n!$, can be defined by:

$$n! = \begin{cases} 1 & \text{if } n = 0 \\ 1 \times 2 \times 3 \times \ldots \times n & \text{if } n > 0 \end{cases}$$

Another way of writing the definition is:

$$n! = \begin{cases} 1 & \text{if } n = 0 \\ n(n-1)! & \text{if } n > 0 \end{cases}$$

There is one case where the value is given (that is, $0! = 1$) and one case where induction is used to express the solution in terms of values already defined.
   This second definition leads naturally to the following Ada function:

```
function FACTORIAL (N : NATURAL) return POSITIVE is
begin
    if N = 0 then
        return 1;
```

```
        else
            return N * FACTORIAL(N − 1);
        end if;
    end FACTORIAL;
```

The parameter N with subtype NATURAL ensures that the case $N < 0$ can never occur. If the function is called with an actual parameter that is less than 0, a run-time error will result at the call.

We see that on the sixth line the function calls itself. To see what happens when the function is called, assume we have a program with the statement:

```
M := FACTORIAL(3);
```

where the variable M has type POSITIVE. Figure 6.8 shows the situation at the start of the call. As before, the formal parameter N can be thought of as a temporary store and the value 3 is copied to it.

Because N is not 0, the second of the two **return** statements will be executed. Here a new call to the function FACTORIAL occurs and the actual parameter takes the value 2, as illustrated in Figure 6.9. We get a new instance of the function FACTORIAL and in it a new temporary store is created, also called N. When the new instance of FACTORIAL is called, the value 2 is copied to the new store. Note that we now have two different stores N with different values. When the new instance of FACTORIAL is called, execution of the first instance is temporarily suspended waiting for the new instance to finish execution and return a result. It works like an entirely normal function call.

When the second instance of FACTORIAL is executed it will again be the **else** part of the **if** statement that is executed, because N in the second instance of FACTORIAL has the value 2. This results in a third call to FACTORIAL. A further instance of the function is generated and it creates a third temporary store called N, this time the value 1 being placed in it. When the call occurs, execution in the second instance is temporarily suspended in the normal way, until execution of the third instance is finished and has given a result value. Figure 6.10 illustrates the situation.

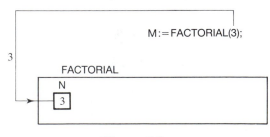

Figure 6.8

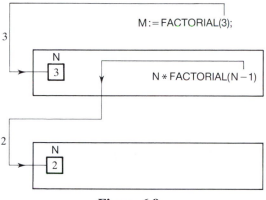

Figure 6.9

Now the third instance of FACTORIAL will be executed. Again, the second of the **return** statements will be executed because N here has the value 1. Thus we get a fourth call to FACTORIAL, a fourth instance of the function is made and a fourth temporary store with the name N is created. When the call to the fourth instance of the function occurs the value 0 will be copied into this N. Execution of the third instance will, as with the two earlier instances of FACTORIAL, be temporarily suspended.

Execution now continues in the fourth instance of the function FACTORIAL, as illustrated in Figure 6.11. Since the formal parameter N has the value 0, this

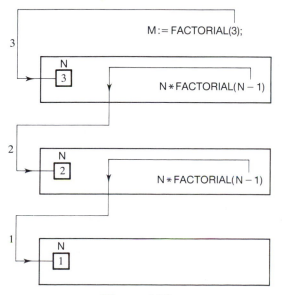

Figure 6.10

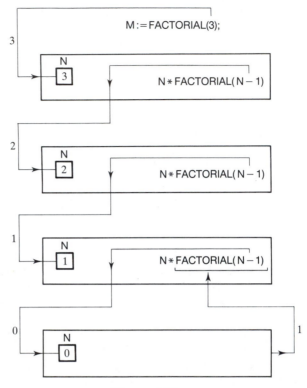

Figure 6.11

time the first **return** statement will be executed. As a result the function will give the value 1. This value is returned to the third instance of the function FACTORIAL.

In the third instance of FACTORIAL the function call:

FACTORIAL(N−1)

now has the value 1. Execution of the third instance can continue and the multiplication:

N ∗ FACTORIAL(N−1)

is performed. The result is 1 because N has the value 1 in this instance. Thus the result given by the third instance of FACTORIAL will have the value 1. This value is returned to the calling subprogram, that is, to the second instance of FACTORIAL, as shown in Figure 6.12. Now execution of the second instance can be completed. The function call:

FACTORIAL(N−1)

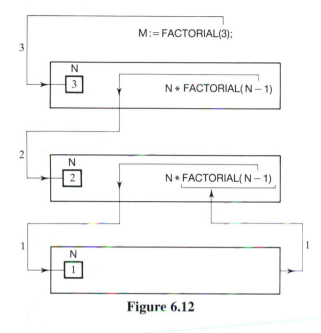

Figure 6.12

gets the value 1 and the expression:

    N * FACTORIAL(N–1)

takes the value 2 since N has the value 2 in the second instance. Thus the second instance of FACTORIAL returns the value 2 to the first instance (see Figure 6.13).

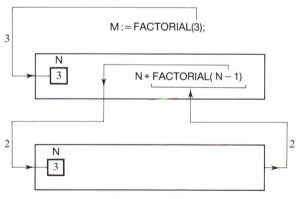

Figure 6.13

Finally, the first instance of FACTORIAL can be resumed. The function call:

FACTORIAL(N−1)

gets the value 6 since N has the value 3. Thus the first instance of the function FACTORIAL will give the calling program the value 6 as its result. This means that the variable M in our original statement:

M := FACTORIAL(3);

takes the value 6, as shown in Figure 6.14.

In this way we are able to visualize what happens in a call to a recursive subprogram. The important thing to note is that several instances of the subprogram will exist and that each instance will have its own temporary stores for its formal parameters and any local variables.

We shall now consider a function FIBONACCI that calculates so-called Fibonacci numbers. These are a series of numbers that were originally used in a model to describe the growth of a population of rabbits. The first numbers in the series are 1, 1, 2, 3, 5, 8, 13, 21, 34, ... They are defined as follows:

$$f_n = \begin{cases} 1 & \text{if } n = 1 \text{ or } n = 2 \\ f_{n-2} + f_{n-1} & \text{if } n > 2 \end{cases}$$

Recursive subprograms

- A subprogram that directly or indirectly calls itself.
- During execution there are as many instances of the subprogram as the number of calls made.
- Each instance has its own unique stores for formal parameters and local variables.

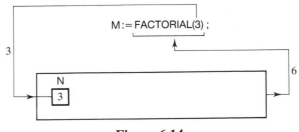

Figure 6.14

It is easy to write a recursive function for calculating the Nth Fibonacci number based on this definition. The number N is given to the function as a parameter:

```
function FIBONACCI (N : POSITIVE) return POSITIVE is
begin
    if N = 1 or N = 2 then
        return 1;
    else
        return FIBONACCI(N−2) + FIBONACCI(N−1);
    end if;
end FIBONACCI;
```

We see that this function contains two recursive calls. If it would help, we could make drawings as before to show what is happening, but even for small values of N there are many instances of the function FIBONACCI and there would be much to draw. This function does not evaluate a Fibonacci number in the most efficient way but it illustrates nicely the fact that a problem specified recursively from the start can easily be solved using a recursive subprogram. Writing the function FIBONACCI is largely a question of rewriting the definition.

Even certain problems that are not initially defined in a recursive way can be solved easily with recursion. But first, the problem has to be reformulated recursively. It can best be demonstrated by the problem of calculating the sum of the components of a vector of floating point numbers. We have already solved this problem using iteration in Section 6.1, where we wrote a function SUM, but here we shall show how the problem can be solved using recursion.

The sum of the components of a vector V with N components can be defined in the following way:

$$\text{sum} = \begin{cases} 0, \text{ if the vector has no components (that is, } N = 0) \\ V(1) + \text{ the sum of the components of the vector } V(2 \dots N) \end{cases}$$

This definition provides a direct basis for writing the function:

```
function SUM(V : VECTOR) return FLOAT is
begin
    if V'LENGTH = 0 then
        return 0.0;
    else
        return V(V'FIRST) + SUM( V(V'FIRST + 1 .. V'LAST) );
    end if;
end SUM;
```

In the second **return** statement a recursive call to SUM is made. The actual parameter to this call is the vector formed from the components 2 to N, inclusive, of V.

When the function is called we will get N + 1 instances of the function, all in existence at the same time. Each new instance will get as parameter a vector that is one component shorter than that of the previous instance. If we suppose that the original vector had 100 components, for example, we shall get 101 instances of the function SUM. The final instance (number 101) will get an empty vector as its parameter, that is, V will have no components. Instance 101 of SUM will thus return its result, the value 0.0, to instance number 100. Then instance 100 can complete its execution and return as result the sum of component 100 and 0.0, that is, the value of component 100. This result is returned to instance 99 which can then complete its execution. This will give as result the sum of components 99 and 100, that is, the sum of the two last components. Instance 98 will then give, in an analogous manner, the sum of the last three components. This continues until finally instance 1 is reached, and that will give the sum of all the components as its result.

It is not only functions that can be recursive: recursive procedures can also be written. For example, we shall show a little procedure that reads text from the terminal and writes it out backwards. To solve this problem we use the following recursive idea:

(1)   If there is any text to read, do the following:
    (1.1)   Read and remember the first character in the text.
    (1.2)   Read in the rest of the text and write it out backwards.
    (1.3)   Write out the first character of the text.

Step (1) is simple. The user can indicate the end of the text by giving an END_OF_FILE sign. Steps (1.1) and (1.3) are also simple. The character read in step (1.1) can be remembered in a variable of type CHARACTER and this variable can then be written out in step (1.3). Step (1.2) is more troublesome. How can we read in the rest of the text and write it out backwards? We observe that it is exactly the same problem as the original one. The only difference is that the text that has to be read in and written out is one character shorter than the original text. Therefore we should be able to use the same algorithm to solve this problem as to solve the whole problem. We can achieve this by placing a recursive call to the procedure which solves the whole problem. Since the first character is already read in, the text that remains to be read from the terminal will consist of the rest of the text, precisely as we want.

It is easy to translate this algorithm into Ada. We get the procedure:

```
procedure BACKWARDS is
    CHAR : CHARACTER;
begin
    if not END_OF_FILE then
        GET(CHAR);
        BACKWARDS;
        PUT(CHAR);
```

```
      end if;
   end BACKWARDS;
```

The same number of instances of this procedure will exist as there are characters in the text, plus one. The first instance of the procedure reads in the text's first character and saves it in the local variable CHAR. Its execution will then be suspended temporarily while it makes its recursive call. Execution will not be resumed until all the other instances of the procedure have finished being executed.

When execution reaches the last instance of the procedure BACKWARDS, the whole text has been read in. This last instance will observe that there is no more text to read (END_OF_FILE is TRUE) and will therefore do nothing but return immediately to the last but one instance of the procedure. The last but one instance of the procedure has read the final character of the text and writes it out. Thus the last character read in is written out first.

Eventually, control is returned to the first instance of the procedure BACKWARDS, which will write out the character that it saved. This means that the first character in the text will always be written out last.

In the examples we have looked at, recursion has always occurred because a subprogram called itself. It is also possible to have **indirect recursion.** A subprogram A can call another subprogram B which, in turn, calls A. Then A and B are said to be **mutually recursive.** (It is even possible for recursion to occur through several stages, for example, A calls B which calls C which calls A.)

We can illustrate mutual recursion with the example of two subprograms that determine whether a positive number is odd or even. This problem can, of course, easily be solved in Ada by writing the Boolean expression:

N **mod** 2 = 1

which has the value TRUE if the integer variable N is odd. To demonstrate mutual recursion, however, we shall assume that we do not have access to the operators /, **rem** or **mod**. The solution to the problem is then obtained with the algorithm:

(1)   If N is equal to 0 then N is not odd.
(2)   Otherwise, N is odd if $N - 1$ is even.

If we assume access to a function EVEN that determines whether a number is even or not, we can make a direct translation into Ada:

```
   function ODD (NUMBER : NATURAL) return BOOLEAN is
   begin
      if NUMBER = 0 then
         return FALSE;
```

```
        else
            return EVEN(NUMBER – 1);
        end if;
end ODD;
```

The function EVEN is, in structure, like the function ODD and can easily be written:

```
function EVEN (NUMBER : NATURAL) return BOOLEAN is
begin
    if NUMBER = 0 then
        return TRUE;
    else
        return ODD(NUMBER – 1);
    end if;
end EVEN;
```

As we see, this function uses the function ODD. The question remains: 'How should the two functions be placed in relation to one another?' If the function ODD is placed before the function EVEN it is possible to call ODD from EVEN. But then, it is not possible to call EVEN from ODD because ODD has not yet been declared when the call is made. If the functions are written in the other order, the same problem arises but the opposite way round.

The solution lies in first writing a **separate subprogram specification** for one of the functions. If we start by declaring a separate subprogram specification for ODD our declarations will look like this:

```
function ODD (NUMBER : NATURAL) return BOOLEAN;

function EVEN (NUMBER : NATURAL) return BOOLEAN is
begin
    if NUMBER = 0 then
        return TRUE;
    else
        return ODD(NUMBER – 1);
    end if;
end EVEN;

function ODD (NUMBER : NATURAL) return BOOLEAN is
begin
    if NUMBER = 0 then
        return FALSE;
    else
        return EVEN(NUMBER – 1);
    end if;
end ODD;
```

On the first line the specification for ODD is given. In Ada, this permits the body of a subprogram to be left until later. The complete declaration must be made later, and note that the specification must then be repeated. Since ODD is specified on the first line it is now known by EVEN and can be called from within EVEN.

Separate subprogram specification

> **procedure** *name(parameters);*

or:

> **function** *name(parameters)* **return** *result_type;*

- May appear anywhere among the declarations.
- The complete subprogram body (including the specification) must be written later.

Separate subprogram specifications are always allowed, not only for recursive subprograms. Their specifications can be put anywhere among the declarations.

6.9   Functions as operators

In Ada, as we have seen, there are many built-in operators. The operator + exists for both integer and floating point types, for example, and the operator = is defined for all types met so far. When we declare our own, more complicated, types we may also like to define operators for them. Let us take, as example, the type VECTOR which we have already used:

type VECTOR **is array** (INTEGER **range** < >) **of** FLOAT;

We can declare variables of type VECTOR:

X, Y, Z : VECTOR(1 .. 5);

In Section 6.1 we wrote a function ADD that could be used to add two vectors. The following statement, for example, adds the vectors X and Y and the result is assigned to the vector Z:

Z := ADD(X, Y);

The meaning is quite clear, but how much more elegant it would be to write:

```
Z := X + Y;
```

This is not immediately possible because the operator + is not defined for the type VECTOR, but it is possible in Ada to define operators for any type. This is achieved using functions that, instead of having ordinary identifiers as names, are given operator names.

For example, we shall alter the function ADD so that it is called "+" instead:

```
function "+" (V1, V2 : VECTOR) return VECTOR is
    TEMP : VECTOR(V1'RANGE) := V2;
begin
    for I in V1'RANGE loop
        TEMP(I) := TEMP(I) + V1 (1);
    end loop;
    return TEMP;
end "+";
```

The function "+" is now called in the same way as if it were an operator. Instead of writing, as before:

```
ADD(X, Y)
```

we can now write:

```
X + Y
```

Note that the two parameters are written before and after the function's name. Here are some examples of different ways in which the function "+" can be called:

```
Z := X + Y;
Z := X + Y + Z;              -- the function is called twice
X := X + (1.0, 2.0, 3.0, 0.0, 1.5);
Y := (1.3, 3.5, 6.7, 0.8, −3.4) + (0.3, 5.6, 1.2, 0.0, 4.5);
```

The third and fourth examples show that the parameters can also be array aggregates. The compiler 'understands' that we do not mean the 'ordinary' plus operator but the one we declared ourselves because the operands have type VECTOR. We can say that we have overloaded operators in exactly the same sense as the overloaded subprograms we discussed earlier. If we write the expression:

```
I + J
```

where I and J are integer types the compiler would choose the 'ordinary' plus operator, in spite of the fact that we have defined another. As many operators as necessary may be declared with the same name, provided their profiles are different (see Section 6.6).

There are only certain operator names that can be used as declared operators, and they are the normal operator names we studied in Chapter 3, namely:

and	**or**	**xor**		
=	<	<=	>	>=
+	–	&		-- normal + and –
+	–			-- unary + and –
*	/	**mod**	**rem**	
**	**abs**	**not**		

The operators that normally have two operands, for example *, **and** and the ordinary + operator, must also have two operands if new versions are declared; that is, the operator functions must have two parameters. The operators **abs**, **not** and the unary versions of + and – should have one operand.

Note that the operator /= is missing from the set of operators shown above. In Ada 83 it is actually not permitted to declare this operator explicitly because it is declared automatically if an equality operator, =, is declared. Since the equality operator exists automatically for all normal types, it may not normally be declared in Ada 83: it is only allowed for limited private types that are used in conjunction with packages (see Section 8.8).

In Ada 95 an explicit declaration of an equality operator, =, is permitted for all types, not only for private types. If such an equality operator is explicitly declared and its result type is BOOLEAN, then a corresponding inequality operator, /=, is automatically defined. If, on the other hand, an equality operator has been explicitly declared but its result is not of type BOOLEAN, then no inequality operator is automatically defined, but it is permitted to declare one explicitly.

▼

▲

6.10   Interface to other languages

From an Ada program it is possible to call a subprogram written in another programming language. Furthermore, in Ada 95 it is possible to construct functions and procedures that can be called from a program written in a foreign language.

First we shall demonstrate how a subprogram written in another language can be called from an Ada program. To accomplish this we use a so-called **pragma**. An example will show the details. Suppose that we want to call the function EXP, which is written in the programming language FORTRAN. Then we would give the following declaration in the Ada 83 program:

```
function EXP (X:FLOAT) return FLOAT;
pragma IMPORT(FORTRAN, EXP);
```

The function EXP can now be called in the normal way. For instance we can make the call EXP(Y).

An extra parameter can be given to the IMPORT pragma. This parameter is a text string containing a so-called *external name*. The external name is the name of the foreign subprogram in its own language. If, for example, we want to call a function FC, written in the C language, and the true name of the function is fun, then we can write:

```
function FC (I:INTEGER) return INTEGER;
pragma IMPORT(C, FC, "fun");
```

If no external name is given, the name is assumed to be the same as the name in the Ada program.

In Ada 83 the pragma INTERFACE should be used instead of IMPORT.

The pragma IMPORT can also be used to get access to a variable declared in a module written in a foreign language. If, for example, we want to use a global variable ERRNO, declared in a C module, we could give the declaration:

```
ERRNO: INTEGER;
pragma IMPORT(C, ERRNO, "errno");
```

▼   In Ada 95 there is also a pragma EXPORT, which can be used to make Ada subprograms accessible from programs written in other languages. If we want to write a procedure ADA_PROC, for example, which should be callable from a C program, we can declare it as follows:

```
procedure ADA_PROC(I:INTEGER);
▲   pragma EXPORT(C, ADA_PROC, "ada_proc");
```

When mixing different languages we must be very careful and make sure that the types of the parameters match. In Ada 95 there is a standard package INTERFACES. This package has child packages which include type declarations that simplify the interface to various foreign languages. The package INTERFACES.C is perhaps of special interest. It contains declarations of all standard types in C and functions that convert between these types and Ada's types. There are also the packages INTERFACES.C.STRINGS, with type declarations and utility functions allowing an Ada program to handle text strings in C format, and INTERFACES.C.POINTERS, which makes it possible to handle pointers in the same way as in C. To be safe, the examples presented here should have used the type int, which is declared in the package INTERFACE.C, instead of the type INTEGER.

6.11   Arguments to the main program

When we start a program from a terminal or a command window, we normally type the name of the program. Some operating systems, MS-DOS and UNIX for instance, also allow parameters, or **arguments** as they are usually called, to be given to the program. These arguments are typed after the program name. The command

    > demo -x /r file1

for instance, means that the program with the name demo shall be run and that the program shall be given the three arguments -x, /r and file1.

In Ada 95 there is a standard package ADA.COMMAND_LINE which makes it possible to get access to the arguments in the main program. Three functions are declared in this package. The function COMMAND_NAME returns the program name (a STRING), ARGUMENT_COUNT returns the number of arguments, and ARGUMENT, which shall have an argument number as parameter, returns the corresponding argument (a STRING). As an example, the following program prints its name and its arguments:

```
with TEXT_IO, ADA.COMMAND_LINE;
use TEXT_IO, ADA.COMMAND_LINE;
procedure DEMO is
begin
    PUT_LINE("Program name: " & COMMAND_NAME);
    for I in 1..ARGUMENT_COUNT loop
        PUT_LINE(ARGUMENT(I));
    end loop;
end DEMO;
```

EXERCISES

6.1   Write a function to evaluate the sign of an integer in the following way. The function should return as its result the value 1 if the integer is greater than 0, the value 0 if the integer is equal to 0, and the value −1 if the integer is less than 0.

6.2   Write a function that receives a character in the interval 'A'..'Z' as parameter. As its result the function should give the corresponding lower-case letter.

6.3   Write a function that uses the following Maclaurin series to calculate the value of e^x.

$$e^x = 1 + \frac{x}{1!} + \frac{x^2}{2!} + \frac{x^3}{3!} + \frac{x^4}{4!} + \cdots$$

Exclude terms that are less than 10^{-7} from the sum.

6.4   (a)   **Euclid's algorithm** for evaluating the greatest common divisor of two positive integers m and n can be described as follows:

  (1)   Divide m by n and denote the remainder by r.

  (2)   If $r = 0$ the evaluation is finished and the result is in n.

  (3)   Otherwise, set the value of m to that of n and the value of n to that of r, and return to step 1.

  Use this algorithm to write a function GCD that evaluates the greatest common divisor of two positive integers.

  (b)   Write a program that reads in an arbitrary number of pairs of positive integers and writes out the greatest common divisor for each pair. Use the function GCD.

6.5   To calculate the square root of a number x we can use **Newton's method** as follows. Start by guessing a number $g \geq 0$. When we guess g, we know that there must be a number h such that $g \times h = x$. (The number h can thus be written as $h = x/g$.) If we are very lucky and made a good guess, g and h are approximately equal and we have found the solution. In general, however, guesses are not that good. A new better guess is the mean of g and h:

$$\text{new guess} = \frac{g + \dfrac{x}{g}}{2}$$

Now we can replace g by the new guess and calculate a new value of h. By taking the mean of the new values of g and h we can get a still better guess, and so on.

  Use this method to write a function that evaluates the square root of x. Use $x/2$ for the first guess and let the guesses continue until the difference between two consecutive guesses is less than 10^{-6}.

6.6   The amplitude of a vector $(v_1, v_2, \ldots, v_n)$ can be calculated using the formula:

$$l = \sqrt{v_1^2 + v_2^2 + v_3^2 + \ldots + v_n^2}$$

Write a function that can be used to calculate the amplitude of a vector whose components are real numbers.

  (a)   Assume the vector has four components.

  (b)   Write the function so that it can calculate the amplitude of a vector with an arbitrary number of components.

6.7   Two vectors $(u_1, u_2, \ldots, u_n)$ and $(v_1, v_2, \ldots, v_n)$ are said to be **orthogonal** if the sum:

$$\sum_{i=1}^{n} u_i v_i$$

is equal to zero. Write a function that determines whether two integer vectors are orthogonal. The function may assume that the vectors have the same number of components, but the actual number should be arbitrary and they need not be numbered in the same way.

6.8 (a) Write a function that checks that a given text string contains an identifier according to Ada's definition (see Section 3.2). The function should give one of the results TRUE or FALSE.

(b) Use the function to write a program that reads in a line with a number of words from the terminal and writes out how many of the words are allowed identifiers. The words in the line are separated by one or more spaces.

6.9 Write a function that takes two text strings, T1 and T2, as parameters. The function should determine whether T1 is a substring of T2. If this is true, the function should return as a result the index of the start of the substring in T2. If T1 is not a substring of T2 the function should return the value 0.

Hint: If T1 has the value 'ada' and T2 has the value 'Time enough to be a gadabout when you have finished studying', the function would give the value 22 as its result, assuming that T2 is indexed from 1.

6.10 In an array of integers, 'rotation to the right' can be defined as an operation that moves each element one place to the right and the last element into the first position. Write a subprogram that rotates an array an arbitrary number of places to the right. The subprogram should have two parameters, the array to be rotated and an integer that gives the number of places to be rotated.

6.11 A **list** can be defined as a series of objects all of which are of the same type. A list can have an arbitrary number of objects and can also be a null list, an empty list. Examples of integer lists are:

(−1,−8,0,326)   (15)   ()

The last example is of an empty list. A list can be represented in Ada by an unconstrained array type.

(a) Construct a subprogram that writes out an integer list in the same format as the examples above, that is, enclosed in brackets and with the objects separated by commas. There should be no spaces in the output. The list to be written is given as a parameter to the subprogram.

(b) The **head** of a list can be defined as the first object in the list, and its **tail** is the list that is formed if the head is removed. The list (17, −3,8), for example, has head 17 and tail (−3,8). Note that the head is a single object and not a list. The head and tail are not defined for an empty list. A list with only one object has the empty list as tail.

   Write two functions HEAD and TAIL that return the head and tail of a list, respectively. Both functions should have a list of integers as parameter. If the parameter is the empty list both functions should give a suitable error message.

(c) Write a function SECOND that gets a list of integers as its parameter and as its result returns the second object in the list. Make use of the functions HEAD and TAIL from part (b).

6.12 When wage statistics are presented, a **median value** is often quoted. The median is the 'central' value of a collection of values; the number of values less than the median is the same as the number of values that are greater. One way to evaluate the median is to sort all the values into numerical order and then select the value in the middle. If there is an even number of values, the median is the mean of the two central values.

Write a program to read in a maximum of 1000 monthly wages and calculate and print their median value.

6.13 A numerically controlled drilling machine drills a large number of holes in a piece to be machined. A large part of the machine's time is spent moving from one hole to another. It is, therefore, desirable to minimize the moving time by making the machine drill holes in an appropriate order. It is practically impossible to find the optimal solution to the problem, even for a small number of holes, but here it is enough to find an 'acceptably' good method rather than the optimal one. One such method is that each time a hole has been drilled the next hole for drilling is the one that is nearest (and still needs to be drilled).

Write a program that reads in the coordinates of the holes to be drilled and then writes them out in the 'acceptable' order, according to the algorithm outlined above. The positions of the holes can be given as points in a two-dimensional coordinate system and can be stored in two arrays, one for each of the x and y coordinates.

Thus the program should start with an arbitrary point and then choose the next point by determining the one that lies closest and has not yet been dealt with, etc. The coordinates of the points should be written out in the order they are to be drilled. The distance between two points (x_1, y_1) and (x_2, y_2) is given by:

$$s = \sqrt{(x_1 - x_2)^2 + (y_1 - y_2)^2}$$

Assume that the coordinates of the points do not exceed a 'reasonable' size, say 100.

Hint: to avoid moving to a hole that has already been drilled, replace the x and y coordinates for each hole visited by a large number, for example, 10^{10}, so that such a point is so far away from the rest that it will not be chosen again.

6.14 A trade union makes the following offer for a long-term wage agreement:

- The first year (year number 1) each employee will receive a monthly wage of £790.

- In the following years (years number 2, 3, 4 and so on) there will be an increase of 4% over the previous year's wage, and an additional general rise of £30 per month.

Write a recursive function that will calculate the monthly wage for a particular year according to the scheme presented here. The only input parameter is to be the year number.

6.15 One way of finding the greatest common divisor of two positive integers is to use the definition:

$$gcd(m,n) = \begin{cases} m & \text{if } m = n \\ gcd(m - n, n) & \text{if } m > n \\ gcd(m, n - m) & \text{otherwise} \end{cases}$$

Write a recursive function GCD that evaluates the greatest common divisor of two positive integers based on this definition.

6.16 The binomial coefficients can be defined in the following way:

$$\binom{n}{0} = 1$$

$$\binom{n}{n} = 1$$

$$\binom{n}{k} = \binom{n-1}{k-1} + \binom{n-1}{k} \qquad 0 < k < n$$

Write a recursive function to evaluate the binomial coefficient $\binom{i}{j}$.

Assume that $0 \leq j \leq i$.

6.17 An efficient way of sorting the elements of an array goes under the name of **quicksort**. The method can be described by the following recursive algorithm:

(1)   If the array has no elements or only one element, then it is sorted. Otherwise, perform the following steps:

(2)   Choose an arbitrary element in the array and call it k.

(3)   Move the elements around in the array so that two groups are formed. The element k should be placed between the two groups. All the elements that are $\leq k$ should be placed in the group to the left of k and all the rest in the group to the right.

(4)   Sort the part of the array to the left of k using this algorithm.

(5)   Sort the part of the array to the right of k using this algorithm.

Use the algorithm to write a procedure that sorts an array of integers. (Compare with Exercise 5.11.)

6.18 Suppose you need to calculate the value of expressions of the form p^q, where both p and q are real numbers. (If q were an integer there would be no problem because the operator ** could be used from the standard definition of Ada.) If you are running under Ada 95 then it is simple, since in the generic package ADA.GENERIC_ELEMENTARY_ FUNCTIONS there is an operator, **, which permits the second operand to be a real number.

Let us assume, however, that there is no available operator ** to use, but that there is access to a mathematics package containing the basic functions EXP and LN. The task is to use them to construct an operator ** of your own, where both operands are of type FLOAT.

Hint: The normal mathematical formula for calculating logarithms involves: $p^q = e^{q \ln(p)}$.

7 Data Structures

In Chapter 5 we saw how Ada's simple types could be used to describe simple data objects – objects that can be represented by a single value, such as a temperature measurement. We also saw that array types can be used to describe a series of simple objects, such as text and lists. This chapter describes two opportunities offered by Ada which enable more complicated data structures to be described. First array types with several dimensions will be used to describe tables and arrays of numbers; then record types will be used to represent objects comprising several different components.

7.1 Multidimensional array types

In the array types studied so far there has been an index that could be used to select particular components from an array. When the array type has been declared the type of the index has also been stated: either integer or enumeration types are allowed. In this section we shall see how array type declarations can be generalized so that an array type can have several indexes.

7.1.1 Constrained array types

Data is often presented in the form of a table. One example is the distance tables found in road atlases, such as the one in Figure 7.1. The types studied so far are not adequate for describing a data structure of this kind. Using an array type, it is possible to describe a row or a column of such a table, but not the whole table.

It is possible to describe this sort of data structure in Ada with a **multi-dimensional array type**. To illustrate this we shall make a type declaration to describe the table in Figure 7.1. The distance between two cities is expressed as a whole number of kilometres, which can never be negative, so one possibility is to use the type NATURAL to describe a distance. Because this type represents natural numbers in the abstract sense, however, it is rather too general; it is better to declare a new integer type DISTANCE_TYPE:

> **type** DISTANCE_TYPE **is range** 0 .. 40077;   -- expressed in km

(The upper limit for possible distances has been chosen as the equatorial circumference.)

The rows and columns of the distance table are named by cities, so we declare an enumeration type CITY that 'numbers' them:

> **type** CITY **is** (AMSTERDAM, BERLIN, LONDON, MADRID,
> PARIS, ROME, STOCKHOLM);

	Amster-dam	Berlin	London	Madrid	Paris	Rome	Stock-holm
Amsterdam	0	648	494	1752	495	1735	1417
Berlin	648	0	1101	2349	1092	1588	1032
London	494	1101	0	1661	404	1870	1807
Madrid	1752	2349	1661	0	1257	2001	3138
Paris	495	1092	404	1257	0	1466	1881
Rome	1735	1588	1870	2001	1466	0	2620
Stockholm	1417	1032	1807	3138	1881	2620	0

Figure 7.1

Now the declaration of a type DISTANCE_TABLE can be made:

    type DISTANCE_TABLE **is array** (CITY, CITY) **of** DISTANCE_TYPE;

This is a two-dimensional array type. It differs from the one-dimensional array types seen earlier in that two index types have to be stated. The term:

    (CITY, CITY)

states that the array will have two indexes, both of type CITY.

Multidimensional array types

        type A **is array** (*index1, index2, ... indexN*)
                of *element_type*;

Index1, index2, ... are intervals of the form *first_value .. last_value*, or the names of discrete types.

Element_type is any (constrained) type.

Now a variable of type DISTANCE_TABLE can be declared:

    DISTANCE : DISTANCE_TABLE;

This variable comprises a table, as above, with seven rows and seven columns. Both columns and rows are 'numbered' with the enumeration type CITY. Each element in the table is an integer of type DISTANCE_TYPE. If we make the definitions as above, the contents of the variable DISTANCE are still undefined. Assignment can be used to give a particular value to each element, by indexing, exactly as in a one-dimensional array. For example, to insert the distance from Berlin to Rome in the table, we could write:

    DISTANCE(BERLIN, ROME) := 1588;

If we want to write out this distance we can use the statement:

    PUT((DISTANCE(BERLIN, ROME));

Thus indexing for multidimensional arrays works in exactly the same way as for one-dimensional arrays, the only difference being that more than one index must be given.

Indexing in multidimensional arrays

A(*value1*, *value2*, ... , *valueN*)

where *value1* has *index_type1*, etc.

In a one-dimensional array it is possible to cut a slice, for example:

NAME(2 .. 5)

This is not possible in multidimensional arrays. Thus constructs such as:

DISTANCE(BERLIN .. ROME, AMSTERDAM)   -- ERROR!
DISTANCE(PARIS, LONDON .. STOCKHOLM)   -- ERROR!

are wrong.

It may be practical to give values to the whole distance table at once, and to do this a two-dimensional array aggregate can be used. If the table is to be initialized at the same time as it is declared, we can write:

```
DISTANCE : DISTANCE_TABLE :=
            ((    0,  648,   494, 1752,   495, 1735, 1417),
             ( 648,     0, 1101, 2349, 1092, 1588, 1032),
             ( 494, 1101,     0, 1661,   404, 1870, 1807),
             (1752, 2349, 1661,     0, 1257, 2001, 3138),
             ( 495, 1092,   404, 1257,     0, 1466, 1881),
             (1735, 1588, 1870, 2001, 1466,     0, 2620),
             (1417, 1032, 1807, 3138, 1881, 2620,     0));
```

In the two-dimensional aggregate each row has been stated as an ordinary one-dimensional aggregate. The expression:

(494, 1101,   0, 1661,   404, 1870, 1807)

for example, states the value of 'London's' row in the table. The rules for writing aggregates are the same as those we studied earlier. If, for example, we want to set the whole table to zero we can write one of the following alternatives:

```
DISTANCE := ( (0, 0, 0, 0, 0, 0, 0),
              (0, 0, 0, 0, 0, 0, 0),
              (0, 0, 0, 0, 0, 0, 0),
              (0, 0, 0, 0, 0, 0, 0),
              (0, 0, 0, 0, 0, 0, 0),
              (0, 0, 0, 0, 0, 0, 0),
              (0, 0, 0, 0, 0, 0, 0) );
```

```
DISTANCE := ( AMSTERDAM    => (0, 0, 0, 0, 0, 0, 0),
              BERLIN       => (0, 0, 0, 0, 0, 0, 0),
              LONDON       => (0, 0, 0, 0, 0, 0, 0),
              MADRID       => (0, 0, 0, 0, 0, 0, 0),
              PARIS        => (0, 0, 0, 0, 0, 0, 0),
              ROME         => (0, 0, 0, 0, 0, 0, 0),
              STOCKHOLM    => (0, 0, 0, 0, 0, 0, 0));

DISTANCE := ( (others => 0),
              (others => 0),
              (others => 0),
              (others => 0),
              (others => 0),
              (others => 0),
              (others => 0) );

DISTANCE := (others => (others => 0) );
```

As with one-dimensional arrays, sometimes the compiler must be given help in the form of a qualified expression giving the type of the aggregate:

```
DISTANCE := DISTANCE_TABLE'
            (MADRID => (1752, 2349, 1661, 0, 1257, 2001, 3138),
             others  => (0, 0, 0, 0, 0, 0, 0) );
```

It is very common for nested **loop** statements to be used in connection with multidimensional arrays. The following lines of program show how a distance table can be printed at the terminal:

```
-- write out the table
for FROM in AMSTERDAM .. STOCKHOLM loop
  -- write a line of the table
  for TO in AMSTERDAM .. STOCKHOLM loop
    -- write a distance in the current line
    PUT(DISTANCE(FROM, TO), WIDTH => 6);
  end loop;
  NEW_LINE;
end loop;
```

The outer **loop** statement is run through once per row of table. On the first loop the iteration counter FROM has the value AMSTERDAM, on the second it is BERLIN, etc. Each time round, the outer **loop** statement writes out a line at the terminal, the line being terminated by NEW_LINE. The inner **loop** statement is executed once for each time through the outer loop. Each execution of the inner **loop** statement involves seven iterations, the iteration counter TO having the value AMSTERDAM the first time round, BERLIN the second, and so on. This means that the call to PUT will occur for each possible combination of FROM and TO, that is, 49 times.

When a multidimensional array type is declared, in the same way as for one-dimensional arrays, any discrete type, integer or enumeration type can be used as the index types. The same rules apply. It is probably most common to number the rows and columns in a two-dimensional array type with figures. For example, we shall look at the simple game of noughts and crosses, played on a 3 × 3 board. One player has crosses and the other has noughts. They take it in turn to place a piece on the board and the player who gets three of his pieces in a line – a row, a column or a diagonal – is the winner. The game continues until one player wins or the board is full. During the game a square on the board can either be empty or contain a cross or a nought. A square can thus be described by the type declaration:

```
type  SQUARE is (EMPTY, X, O);
```

and the board can be described by the two-dimensional array type:

```
type GAMES_BOARD is array (1 .. 3, 1 .. 3) of SQUARE;
```

If we wanted to, we could introduce special index types and write instead:

```
subtype ROW_NUMBER is INTEGER range 1 .. 3;
subtype COL_NUMBER is INTEGER range 1 .. 3;
type GAMES_BOARD is array (ROW_NUMBER, COL_NUMBER) of
                         SQUARE;
```

Now variables of type GAMES_BOARD can be declared, such as:

```
P : GAMES_BOARD := ( others => ( others => EMPTY) );
```

Here P has been initialized so that all the squares are empty when the game starts. Individual elements of P can be selected by indexing. If, for example, we want to put a cross in the centre square we can write:

```
P(2,2) := X;
```

We shall study a function that determines whether the games board is full:

```
function FULL(BOARD : GAMES_BOARD) return BOOLEAN is
begin
   -- find out if board has any empty squares
   for R in 1 .. 3 loop
     -- find out if row R has any empty squares
```

```
      if BOARD(R,C) = EMPTY then
         return FALSE;
      end if;
    end loop;
  end loop;
  -- no empty square has been found
  return TRUE;
end FULL;
```

The function gets a board as parameter and returns a BOOLEAN value as its result. If the board is full, that is, all the squares contain either a cross or a nought, the function returns the value TRUE, but otherwise it returns FALSE.

The function contains two nested **loop** statements. The outer one goes through all the rows and the inner one, which is performed once for each row, goes through all the columns. If a square is reached that has the value EMPTY the statement:

return FALSE;

is executed, which means that execution of the function ceases and the value FALSE is returned. Thus if an empty square is found, the remaining squares are not looked at. If none of the squares are empty then, eventually, the function's last statement:

return TRUE;

is executed and the function returns the value TRUE.

In a multidimensional array type the index types do not need to be the same, as they have been in the examples seen so far. In the next example we assume that we have measured the temperature of the air every hour for a whole week. We shall write a program that reads in the temperature measurements made and then calculates and writes out the mean hourly temperatures for the week.

We start by declaring an enumeration type DAY:

type DAY **is** (MONDAY, TUESDAY, WEDNESDAY,
            THURSDAY, FRIDAY, SATURDAY, SUNDAY);

We can also declare an integer type HOUR to describe the 24 hours of the day:

type HOUR **is range** 0 .. 23;

If the temperature measurements have been made with an accuracy of one decimal figure, the following type can be used to describe them:

type TEMP **is digits** 3 **range** −99.9 .. 99.9;

Now we can construct a two-dimensional array type that describes a whole week's measurements:

type MEASUREMENT_TABLE **is array** (DAY, HOUR) **of** TEMP;

The two indexes here are of different types. If we declare a variable of type MEASUREMENT_TABLE:

MEASUREMENTS : MEASUREMENT_TABLE;

then we can, for example, give the Thursday 7 pm measurement the value 11.3 by writing the statement:

MEASUREMENTS(THURSDAY, 19) := 11.3;

Now we write a procedure that reads values into a measurement table. The user has to be requested to input 24 hourly measurements for each day. The procedure will have a measurement table as an out parameter. When execution of the procedure is complete this table should be filled with the week's measurements.

```
procedure READ_MEASUREMENTS
                (TAB : out MEASUREMENT_TABLE) is
begin
  -- Read values into table
  for D in DAY loop
    PUT("Enter the temperatures for ");
    PUT(D); NEW_LINE;

    -- Read values into a line of the table
    for H in HOUR loop
      GET( TAB(D, H) );
    end loop;
  end loop;
end READ_MEASUREMENTS;
```

The elements of the table are run through and filled in *row by row*. First the elements in the Monday row get their values in order (for 00.00, 01.00, and so on). Then the elements of the Tuesday row get theirs, then the Wednesday row, and so on. At this point, we assume that packages have been created in the main program to handle reading and writing the types DAY and TEMP.

Note the construct:

for H **in** HOUR **loop**

This ensures that the loop parameter H has the type HOUR and that it will run through all the values of the type HOUR, namely 0–23. It would have been wrong to write:

> **for** H **in** 0 .. 23 **loop**   — ERROR!

because then H would have had type INTEGER and it would not have been possible to use H as index in the array TAB. If we did not want to run through all the hours but only certain ones, for example, 0–11 am, we would have to state the type and write:

> **for** H **in** HOUR **range** 0 .. 11 **loop**

The next procedure we shall write receives a completed measurement table as **in** parameter. Its job is to calculate and write out the mean of all the week's measurements for each hour of the day. The output should look like that in Figure 7.2.

We use the algorithm:

(1)   Write the heading.
(2)   Carry out the following for each hour:
    (2.1)   Calculate the mean for the current hour.
    (2.2)   Write out the calculated mean.

Step (2.1) can be expanded to:

(2.1.1)   Add all the measurements made during the week for the current hour.
(2.1.2)   Divide the sum obtained by the number of measurements, that is, by 7.

A further refinement can be made for step (2.1.1):

(2.1.1.1)   Set MV to 0.
(2.1.1.2)   Run through all the days of the week and add the temperatures measured to MV.

hr	mean temp
0	5.2
1	5.0
2	5.0
3	4.9
.	.
.	.
.	.
22	5.7
23	5.3

Figure 7.2

The algorithm can now be translated to Ada, giving the procedure:

```
procedure WRITE_MEAN (M_TAB : MEASUREMENT_TABLE) is
   MEAN : TEMP;
begin

   -- Write heading
   PUT_LINE("hr        mean temp");
   NEW_LINE;
   for H in HOUR loop

      -- Add all the measurements for this hour
      MEAN := 0.0;
      for D in DAY loop
         MEAN := MEAN + M_TAB(D, H);
      end loop;

      -- Divide by the number of measurements
      MEAN := MEAN / 7.0;

      -- Print the calculated mean value
      PUT(H, WIDTH => 2);
      PUT(MEAN, EXP => 0, FORE => 7, AFT => 1);
      NEW_LINE;
   end loop;
end WRITE_MEAN;
```

In this procedure there is an outer **loop** statement which runs through all the hours. Each time round, this **loop** statement calculates the mean value of the week's measurements at a particular hour of the day. This means that the elements of the table are run through *column by column*. Compare this with the procedure READ_MEASUREMENTS, where the elements were run through row by row.

Running through a table row by row

```
for ROW in first_row_no .. last_row_no loop
   for COL in first_col_no .. last_col_no loop
      ... A(ROW, COL) ...
   end loop;
end loop;
```

Running through a table column by column

```
for COL in first_col_no .. last_col_no loop
  for ROW in first_row_no .. last_row_no loop
    ... A(ROW, COL) ...
  end loop;
end loop;
```

Now we can put these two procedures into a main program where we have also included the necessary type declarations and declared the packages for reading and writing the types DAY, HOUR and TEMP. When the program is run it will first call the procedure READ_MEASUREMENTS to get the week's temperature measurements. Then the procedure WRITE_MEAN is called, to calculate and write out the hourly means of the temperatures.

```
with TEXT_IO;
use TEXT_IO;
procedure MEASUREMENTS_EXAMPLE is
  type DAY is (MONDAY, TUESDAY, WEDNESDAY,
               THURSDAY, FRIDAY, SATURDAY, SUNDAY);
  type HOUR is range 0 .. 23;
  type TEMP is digits 3 range -99.9 .. 99.9;
  type MEASUREMENT_TABLE is array (DAY, HOUR) of TEMP;
package DAY_INOUT is new ENUMERATION_IO(DAY);
package HOUR_INOUT is new INTEGER_IO(HOUR);
package TEMP_INOUT is new FLOAT_IO(TEMP);
use DAY_INOUT, HOUR_INOUT, TEMP_INOUT;

MEASUREMENTS : MEASUREMENT_TABLE;

procedure READ_MEASUREMENTS
                (TAB : out MEASUREMENT_TABLE) is
  begin
    -- Read values into table
    for D in DAY loop
      PUT("Enter the temperatures for ");
      PUT(D); NEW_LINE;

      -- Read values into a line of the table
      for H in HOUR loop
        GET( TAB(D, H) );
      end loop;
    end loop;
  end READ_MEASUREMENTS;
```

```
procedure WRITE_MEAN (M_TAB : MEASUREMENT_TABLE) is
  MEAN : TEMP;
begin

  -- Write heading
  PUT_LINE("hr      mean temp");
  NEW_LINE;

  for H in HOUR loop

    -- Add all the measurements for this hour
    MEAN := 0.0;
    for D in DAY loop
      MEAN := MEAN + M_TAB(D, H);
    end loop;

    -- Divide by the number of measurements
    MEAN := MEAN / 7.0;

    -- Print the calculated mean value
    PUT(H, WIDTH => 2);
    PUT(MEAN, EXP => 0, FORE => 7, AFT => 1);
    NEW_LINE;
  end loop;
end WRITE_MEAN;

begin
  READ_MEASUREMENTS(MEASUREMENTS);
  WRITE_MEAN(MEASUREMENTS);
end MEASUREMENTS_EXAMPLE;
```

The examples we have seen so far (distance tables, games boards, tables of measurements) have all been arrays with two dimensions. Even if two-dimensional arrays are the most common among multidimensional arrays, in Ada there are no limits as to the number of dimensions allowed. For example, we can look at the sales of various goods in a supermarket with 10 check-outs. The goods in the store are divided into five categories: food, confectionery, household goods, tobacco and miscellaneous goods. There are statistics concerning the sales for a whole year. For each month the value of the goods sold at each check-out have been collected, classified according to the five categories above. A suitable type for describing the sales statistics is:

```
type STATISTICS is array (MONTH, CHECK_OUT, GOODS) of FLOAT;
```

where the types MONTH, CHECK_OUT and GOODS are declared as follows:

```
type MONTH is (JANUARY, FEBRUARY, MARCH, APRIL,
               MAY, JUNE, JULY, AUGUST,
```

SEPTEMBER, OCTOBER, NOVEMBER, DECEMBER);
type CHECK_OUT **is range** 1 .. 10;
type GOODS **is** (FOOD, CONFECTIONERY, HOUSEHOLD_GOODS,
TOBACCO, MISCELLANEOUS);

Suppose we want to know which check-out had the best total sales during the year. We write a function BEST_CHECK_OUT to look into it. As **in** parameter to the function we shall give the current year's sales statistics, that is, a multi-dimensional array of type STATISTICS. As its result the function will return a check-out number, of type CHECK_OUT.

```
function BEST_CHECK_OUT (SALES : STATISTICS)
                                        return CHECK_OUT is
    CURRENT_BIGGEST  : FLOAT       := 0.0;
    CURRENT_BEST        : CHECK_OUT    := 1;
    SUM : FLOAT;
begin
    -- look for the best check-out
    for C in CHECK_OUT loop

        -- calculate the total sales at check-out C
        SUM := 0.0;
        for M in MONTH loop
          for G in GOODS loop
            SUM := SUM + SALES(M, C, G);
          end loop;
        end loop;

        if SUM > CURRENT_BIGGEST then
          -- check_out C is the best so far
          CURRENT_BIGGEST := SUM;
          CURRENT_BEST    := C;
        end if;
    end loop;
    return CURRENT_BEST;
end BEST_CHECK_OUT;
```

In the function there are three nested **loop** statements. The outermost runs through all the check-outs. For each check-out the total sales of all kinds of goods during the year is calculated and placed in the local variable SUM. In order to do this, it must sum over all the months and all the categories of goods. Then it looks at whether the current check-out has a better sales result than the best of those already investigated. If so, the variables CURRENT_BIGGEST and CURRENT_BEST are updated. When all the check-outs have been examined, CURRENT_BEST contains the number of the check-out with the largest total sales. This number is returned by the function as its result.

7.1.2   Matrices and unconstrained arrays

In mathematics a set of numbers arranged in M rows and N columns is called an M × N **matrix**. As an example, here is a 3 × 4 matrix:

$$\begin{pmatrix} 11 & 45 & -5 & 0 \\ 4 & 10 & 26 & 32 \\ -1 & 0 & 2 & 16 \end{pmatrix}$$

It is possible to define mathematical operations. For example, addition of two matrices, A and B, can be defined if they have the same numbers of rows and columns. Their sum is then a new matrix in which each element is the sum of the corresponding elements in A and B. Here is an example:

$$\begin{pmatrix} 0 & 3 & 5 & 1 \\ 1 & 2 & 2 & -1 \\ 4 & 8 & 3 & 0 \end{pmatrix} + \begin{pmatrix} 1 & 1 & 1 & 1 \\ 0 & 4 & 5 & 0 \\ 0 & 2 & 1 & 0 \end{pmatrix} = \begin{pmatrix} 1 & 4 & 6 & 2 \\ 1 & 6 & 7 & -1 \\ 4 & 10 & 4 & 0 \end{pmatrix}$$

A matrix is naturally represented in Ada by a two-dimensional array of either integers or real numbers. The indexes are integers and row and column numbering usually starts from 1. For example, a 3 × 4 matrix of integers can be described by this type:

```
type MATRIX34 is array (1 .. 3, 1 .. 4) of INTEGER;
```

Here is a function that adds two 3 × 4 matrices and gives a new 3 × 4 matrix as its result.

```
function ADD (A, B : MATRIX34) return MATRIX34 is
   C : MATRIX34;
begin
   -- Calculate elements of matrix C
   for I in 1 .. 3 loop

      -- Calculate elements of row I of matrix C
      for J in 1 .. 4 loop
         -- Calculate element in column J of row I
         C(I,J) := A(I,J) + B(I,J);
      end loop;
   end loop;
   return C;
end ADD;
```

The function runs through the two matrices, element by element, adding pairs from corresponding positions and placing the result in the local variable C, another 3 × 4 matrix. Then C is returned from the function as its result.

We saw earlier that unconstrained array types may be used to write general subprograms that work for all sizes of array. This is also possible in the case of multidimensional arrays. We can declare a type MATRIX that denotes matrices with arbitrary numbers of rows and columns:

```
type MATRIX is array (POSITIVE range < >,
                      POSITIVE range < >) of INTEGER;
```

The constructs:

```
POSITIVE range < >
```

state that both index types should be of the subtype POSITIVE and that their exact limits can vary. As for a one-dimensional array, the index constraints must be stated when a variable of the type is declared:

```
P35, Q35 : MATRIX(1 .. 3, 1 .. 5);
X24, Y24 : MATRIX(1 .. 2, 1 .. 4);
```

Here P35 and Q35 are 3×5 matrices and X24 and Y24 are 2×4 matrices.

Unconstructed multidimensional array types

type A **is array** (T1 **range** < >, T2 **range** < >, ...)
                           of *element_type;*

T1, T2, etc. are discrete types.

- Index constraints must be given when an object is declared but unconstrained types may be used in declaring formal parameters to subprograms.

- *Element_type* can be any (constrained) type.

Now we can write a general version of the function ADD that will work for all matrices, irrespective of the numbers of rows and columns. However, the elements must be of the same type and the two matrices must have the same numbers of rows and columns.

```
function ADD(A, B : MATRIX) return MATRIX is
   C : MATRIX(A'RANGE(1), A'RANGE(2));
begin

   -- Calculate elements of matrix C
   for I in A'RANGE(1) loop
```

```
        -- Calculate elements in row I
        for J in A'RANGE(2) loop
            -- Calculate element in column J of row I
            C(I,J) := A(I,J) + B(I,J);
        end loop;
    end loop;
    return C;
end ADD;
```

A generalized form of the RANGE attribute, valid for multidimensional arrays, has been used here.

A'RANGE(1)

gives the interval for the first index of A, and

A'RANGE(2)

gives the interval for its second index. The declaration:

C : MATRIX(A'RANGE(1), A'RANGE(2));

thus means that C gets the same numbers of rows and columns as A. For example, if we call the function with:

ADD(X24, Y24)

then A'RANGE(1) is the equivalent of:

1 .. 2

and A'RANGE(2) is the equivalent of:

1 .. 4

If X24 has the value:

```
1   3   0   7
2   4   6   1
```

and Y24 has the value:

```
1   1   2   0
1   0   1   1
```

then the function will return:

2 4 2 7
3 4 7 2

as the result of being called.

We could also call ADD in the following way:

ADD(P35, Q35)

Then it would return the 3×5 matrix which is the sum of P35 and Q35.

The attributes FIRST, LAST, LENGTH and RANGE exist in generalized forms for multidimensional arrays, as is seen from these examples:

X24'FIRST(1)   gives the value 1
X24'FIRST(2)   gives the value 1
X24'LAST(1)   gives the value 2
X24'LAST(2)   gives the value 4
X24'LENGTH(1) gives the value 2
X24'LENGTH(2) gives the value 4
X24'RANGE(2)   gives the range 1 .. 4

Attributes for multidimensional arrays

- FIRST(N) gives the first index value for index number N.

- LAST(N) gives the last index value for index number N.

- LENGTH(N) gives the number of index values for index number N.

- RANGE(N) gives the index interval for index number N.

7.2 Arrays of arrays

When one-dimensional arrays were used earlier we saw that they had components of scalar types, that is, simple objects such as INTEGER or FLOAT. In Ada, however, there is nothing to stop the components being compound types. For example, the components of an array could actually be of array type.

For example, we shall study an alternative way of representing matrices. Instead of considering a matrix as a two-dimensional arrangement of numbers we can see it as a number of rows, each consisting of a number of simple elements. A 4×5 matrix can then be described thus:

> **type** ROW5 **is array** (1 .. 5) **of** INTEGER;
> **type** MATRIX45 **is array** (1 .. 4) **of** ROW5;

Now variables of type MATRIX45 can be declared, such as:

> X : MATRIX45;

X is a one-dimensional array where each component is in turn a one-dimensional array. To get at individual components in the array, indexing can be used, as normal. The expression:

> X(2)

for example, means that element number 2 in X, that is, the second row, is selected. Since a row is in itself an array, it can also be indexed. To select the third component of the second row we write:

> X(2) (3)

Note that this has a different form from that used to describe a matrix using two-dimensional arrays.

One disadvantage of using arrays of arrays rather than two-dimensional arrays is that unconstrained types may not be used for the rows. When an array is declared its component types must be constrained. Thus it is *not* permitted to make the declarations:

> **type** ROW **is array** (POSITIVE **range** < >) **of** INTEGER;
> **type** MATRIX **is array** (POSITIVE **range** < >) **of** ROW;   -- ERROR!

ROW is an unconstrained type and is not allowed to be a component type in the declaration of MATRIX. However, there is nothing against MATRIX being an unconstrained array type. If we amend the row type to be a constrained type, with five components for example, the following declarations are allowed:

> **type** ROW5 **is array** (1 .. 5) **of** INTEGER;
> **type** MATRIX **is array** (POSITIVE **range** < >) **of** ROW5;

The number of rows in the matrix can thus be indeterminate when an array of arrays is used, but the number of columns must be specified.

> **Arrays of arrays**
>
> > **type** ROW **is array** (*index2*) **of** *element_type*;
> >
> > **type** A **is array** (*index1*) **of** ROW;
>
> - *Index1* and *index2* are intervals of the form *first_value* .. *last_value* or the name of a discrete type.
> - *Index1* (but *not* index2) can also be an unconstrained expression of the form:
>
> > *discrete_type_name* **range** < >

> **Indexing in arrays of arrays**
>
> > A(*value1*) (*value2*)
>
> where *value1* is of *index_type1* and *value2* is of *index_type2*.

One advantage of using an array of arrays instead of a two-dimensional array is that it is possible to cut slices, since we have two one-dimensional array types. If the variable X of type MATRIX45 has the value:

```
 1    2    3    4    5
 6    7    8    9   10
11   12   13   14   15
16   17   18   19   20
```

then the expression X(2 .. 4) means rows 2–4, that is:

```
 6    7    8    9   10
11   12   13   14   15
16   17   18   19   20
```

Indexing can be used in this part matrix, or further slices can be cut. The rows retain their original numbering, so the first row has number 2. The expression X(2 .. 4) (2) therefore means the first row of the part matrix, which is to say the row

```
 6   7   8   9   10
```

and the expression X(2 .. 4) (3 .. 4) means rows 3–4 of the part matrix, or:

> 11   12   13   14   15
> 16   17   18   19   20

We can also cut slices from rows. The expression X(4) means the fourth row:

> 16   17   18   19   20

and X(4) (2 .. 4) is then the part row:

> 17   18   19

Slices in an array of arrays

- It is permitted to cut out slices.
- A(*j* .. *k*) means row *j* to row *k* in A.
- A(*n*) (*p* .. *g*) means elements *p* to *g* in row *n* of A.

Whether or not to use a two-dimensional array or an array of arrays to describe a two-dimensional data structure is a matter of judgement. In many cases it is most natural to use a two-dimensional array. Then there is the advantage of being able to use unconstrained arrays. Sometimes it is necessary to be able to cut slices and then an array of arrays should be used, since slices are not permitted in two-dimensional arrays.

As an example of a case when it is appropriate to use an array of arrays we shall study a very simple membership list for a club of some sort. We shall assume that each member has a particular membership number. A register is kept of all the members, an entry consisting of the membership number and the member's surname. There is no fixed upper limit for the number of members the club can have. Each time a new person joins, he or she is allocated the next available membership number and the number and name are entered at the end of the list. This means that the members are not listed in alphabetical order but according to the length of time they have held membership.

A member's name can be described by the type:

```
MAXLENGTH : constant := 20;
subtype NAME is STRING(1 .. MAXLENGTH);
```

Thus we store only the first 20 letters of a member's name, and if the name is shorter than that we pad it with blanks.

The membership list can now be described by an unconstrained array type, with room for an arbitrary number of members:

type REGISTER_TYPE **is array** (POSITIVE **range** < >) **of** NAME;

Since the type NAME is an array type (an array of 20 characters of type CHARACTER) the type REGISTER_TYPE is an array of arrays.

Now we can declare a variable of the type REGISTER_TYPE:

MEMBERS : REGISTER_TYPE (1 .. 5);

If we want to initialize the variable, we can use a two-dimensional array aggregate:

```
MEMBERS : REGISTER_TYPE := ("Ponsonby           ",
                            "Tomlinson          ",
                            "Donaldson          ",
                            "Ellis              ",
                            "Hall               ");
```

Note that an expression of the form:

```
"Ellis              "
```

is a special aggregate that is used for the array type STRING.

We shall look at a function whose job is to see whether a certain person is in the membership list. The function will have two **in** parameters. The first is the name of the person sought. We shall let this parameter have the unconstrained type STRING. The second parameter is the membership register itself. If the person in question is a member of the club then the function will return the membership number as its result; otherwise it will return the value 0.

```
function FIND_NUMBER (REQUIRED_NAME : STRING;
                      REGISTER : REGISTER_TYPE)
                      return NATURAL is
   LENGTH        : NATURAL;
   TEMP_NAME     : NAME := (others => ' ');
begin
   -- Set LENGTH to the lesser of the
   -- required name length and MAXLENGTH
   if REQUIRED_NAME'LENGTH <= MAXLENGTH then
      LENGTH := REQUIRED_NAME'LENGTH;
   else
```

```
              LENGTH := MAXLENGTH;
          end if;
          TEMP_NAME (1 .. LENGTH) :=
                                   REQUIRED_NAME (1 .. LENGTH);

          -- Look for the name in the register
          for N in REGISTER'RANGE loop
            if REGISTER(N) = TEMP_NAME then
               -- The name is present in the register
               return N;
            end if;
          end loop;
          -- The name is not present
          return 0;
        end FIND_NUMBER;
```

If the name sought contains more than 20 characters the local variable LENGTH is set to 20; otherwise it is set to the actual length of the name. Then the number of characters specified by LENGTH are copied from REQUIRED_NAME to the local variable TEMP_NAME. Since TEMP_NAME is initialized to a blank character string it will contain the required name either shortened to 20 characters or padded with blanks. In the **loop** statement the membership register is run through. Each entry in the register is examined for the name required. If it is found the function terminates and the value N – the membership number – is returned as its result. If the whole list is examined without finding the name, the value 0 is returned as result.

The following are examples of ways of calling the function:

```
FIND_NUMBER("Tomlinson", MEMBERS)    -- gives the value 2
FIND_NUMBER("Hall", MEMBERS)         -- gives the value 5
FIND_NUMBER("Ponsonby", MEMBERS)     -- gives the value 1
```

7.3   Record types

We have seen that by using array types we can describe complicated data objects with many components. One limitation of array types is that all the components of an array must be of the same kind. Therefore array types cannot be used to describe compound data objects where the components of an object are of different types. Instead, we use **record** types.

As an example we shall study the description of a car in a hypothetical register of cars. A car can be characterized by many things, such as its registration number, make, year of manufacture, weight and engine capacity. If we have the type declarations:

```
type YEAR_TYPE      is range 1900 .. 2000;
type WEIGHT_TYPE is range 100 .. 10000;  -- measured in kg
type POWER_TYPE  is digits 4;            -- measured in kW
```

the information can be put together using the record type declaration:

```
type CAR_TYPE is
   record
      REG_NUMBER : STRING(1 .. 7);
      MAKE           : STRING(1 .. 20);
      MODEL_YEAR  : YEAR_TYPE;
      WEIGHT         : WEIGHT_TYPE;
      POWER          : POWER_TYPE;
   end record;
```

A definition of a record type starts with the reserved word **record** and ends
with **end record**. Between these words are declarations of the record type's
components.

Declaration of a record type

```
type T is
   record
      component_name_1 : type_1;
      component_name_2 : type_2;

            ⋮

      component_name_N : type_N;
   end record;
```

If there are several components with the same type, it
is possible to write instead:

```
component_name_i, ... component_name_j : type_ij;
```

Now we can declare variables of type CAR_TYPE:

```
MY_CAR : CAR_TYPE;
```

The variable MY_CAR comprises five different components, as shown in
Figure 7.3. (The contents of the different fields are still undefined.)

When we worked with arrays we used indexing to get at the individual
components in an array. Each component in the array had a unique number (of

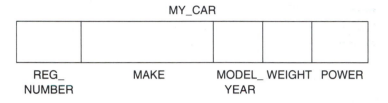

REG_   MAKE   MODEL_ WEIGHT POWER
NUMBER   YEAR

Figure 7.3

integer or enumeration type) that could be specified as an index. In a record the components have no numbers, but they do have explicit names. To access a particular component of a record, **selection** is used. A stop is written after the name of the record, followed by the name of the component. If, for example, we want to give the component WEIGHT in the variable MY_CAR the value 920, we can write the assignment:

    MY_CAR.WEIGHT := 920;

The following are some more examples of selection:

    MY_CAR.POWER := MY_CAR.POWER + 10.0;
    if MY_CAR.POWER > 100.0 then
        PUT_LINE("Tuned");
    end if;
    PUT(MY_CAR.MAKE);

A component that is selected in this way can be used in the same way as normal simple variables, in expressions for example.

Selection in record variables

record_variable_name.component_name

The declarations of the components in a record type have exactly the same form as variable declarations, but it is important to note that no object is created in connection with the declaration of a record type. As before, a type declaration is only a description of what the objects will look like if some are created later. Objects are only created when there is an object declaration, such as the declaration of the variable MY_CAR.

Selection is thus used for accessing the individual components of a record, but the whole record can also be handled at once. We could declare another variable of type CAR_TYPE:

```
YOUR_CAR : CAR_TYPE;
```

Now we can make assignments and comparisons, as for example:

```
YOUR_CAR := MY_CAR;
if YOUR_CAR = MY_CAR then
```

Only the comparison operators = and /= are defined. Thus it is not possible to see whether one record is 'greater than' or 'less than' another.

Assignment of records

```
R1 := R2;
```

where R1 is a record variable and R2 is a variable or a constant of the same type as R1.

Comparing records

```
R1 = R2 or R1 /= R2
```

where R1 and R2 are objects of the same record type.

In the case of arrays, we could use array aggregates to give values to all the components at once. There is a corresponding construct for records, also called an aggregate. If, for example, we want to initialize the variable MY_CAR at the same time as declaring it, we write:

```
MY_CAR : CAR_TYPE := ("C123XYZ", "Ford Escort 1.8    ",
                       1994, 840, 30.0);
```

We can also use record aggregates in assignments and comparisons, such as:

```
YOUR_CAR := ("ABD_544", "Volvo 850 GLT     ",
             1994, 1400, 70.0);
if YOUR_CAR = ("12BN123", "Volvo 850 GLT     ",
             1994, 1400, 70.0) then
```

In these record aggregates we have simply listed the values of the individual components in their proper order. We have used positional association between the values and the components. Named association can also be used by stating the name of the component and its corresponding value. In that case it is not necessary to give the values of the components in the same order as they appear in the record. For example, we can write:

```
YOUR_CAR := (REG_NUMBER => "ABD_544",
             MODEL_YEAR => 1994,
             MAKE => "Volvo 850 GLT     ",
             POWER => 70.0,
             WEIGHT => 1400);
```

Record aggregates

- A specification where the values of all the components of a record can be stated at once.
- Alternative forms:

  (*value_for_comp_1, value_for_comp_2, …*)

  or:

  (*component_name => corresponding_value,
  component_name => corresponding_value,*

  $\vdots$

  component_name => corresponding_value)

- The values in a record aggregate can be arbitrary expressions which must have the same types as the corresponding components.

The individual components of a record can have any type. If we declare a new record type PERSON:

```
type PERSON is
   record
      NAME        : STRING(1 .. 20);
      ID_NUMBER  : STRING(1 .. 10);
   end record;
```

then we can extend the record type CAR_TYPE with a further component, OWNER:

```
type CAR_TYPE is
  record
    REG_NUMBER   : STRING(1 .. 7);
    MAKE         : STRING(1 .. 20);
    MODEL_YEAR   : YEAR_TYPE;
    WEIGHT       : WEIGHT_TYPE;
    POWER        : POWER_TYPE;
    OWNER        : PERSON;
  end record;
```

If the owner's identification number has to be found for printing, it can be achieved in two stages:

```
PUT(MY_CAR.OWNER.ID_NUMBER);
```

Using record types it is possible to build up several levels of data description. The type PERSON could well have another component, ADDRESS, which in turn could have a record type, and so on. In this way it is possible to make the kind of data abstraction discussed in Chapter 5. A record type can describe a phenomenon in the real world, as for example, the phenomenon of a 'car'. In studying the concept of a 'car', there is naturally no interest in the detailed description of the 'owner'. Then it becomes natural to introduce a new record type to describe a 'person', and this new record type can then be studied separately if needed.

Since record types can be used to describe phenomena they are commonly used as parameters and results of subprograms. Let us study, as an example, the phenomenon of a 'point' in a two-dimensional coordinate system. A particular point in the system can be defined by an x and a y coordinate. The concept of a point can then be described by the record type:

```
type POINT is
  record
    X, Y : FLOAT;
  end record;
```

The formula:

$$d = \sqrt{(x_1 - x_2)^2 + (y_1 - y_2)^2}$$

gives the distance d between two points (x_1, y_1) and (x_2, y_2), and this can be used to construct a function DISTANCE. The function will take two points as **in** parameters and give the distance between them, a real quantity, as result.

```
function DISTANCE (P1, P2 : POINT) return FLOAT is
begin
   return SQRT((P1.X – P2.X) ** 2 + (P1.Y – P2.Y) ** 2);
end DISTANCE;
```

If we declare the variables A and B thus:

```
A  : POINT := (1.0, 2.0);
B  : POINT := (–3.0, –1.0);
```

then the statement:

```
PUT( DISTANCE(A, B) );
```

will print out the resulting value 5.0.

We can also have record aggregates as parameters to the function. The call:

```
DISTANCE( (6.0, 8.0), (0.0, 0.0) )
```

for example, will give the result 10.0.

A function can return a result of a record type. A function that finds the mid-point of a line joining two points P1 and P2 could look like this:

```
function MIDPOINT (P1, P2 : POINT) return POINT is
begin
   return ((P1.X + P2.X) / 2.0, (P1.Y + P2.Y) / 2.0);
end MIDPOINT;
```

If we declare a new variable C:

```
C : POINT;
```

and execute the statement:

```
C := MIDPOINT(A, B);
```

then C will get the value (–1.0, 0.5), assuming that A and B still have their earlier values.

The call:

```
MIDPOINT( (1.0, 1.0), (2.0, 2.0) )
```

returns the point (1.5, 1.5) as result.

As discussed earlier, the value of a variable is undefined at the time of declaration unless it is explicitly initialized. Record types have a special feature that does not exist for other types. At the time of type declaration, initial values for the components of the record type can be stated. If this is done, all the variables of that record type that are later declared will automatically be initialized to these values, unless the variable declaration itself gives specific initial values. To illustrate this, let us amend the declaration of the type POINT:

```
type POINT is
  record
    X, Y : FLOAT := 0.0;
  end record;
```

If we now declare a variable START_POINT:

```
START_POINT : POINT;
```

Then this will have the value (0.0, 0.0) after the declaration. If we had not had the initialization expression in the type declaration, the variable START_POINT would have been undefined.

An ordinary initialization when the variable is declared would override the automatic initialization. After the declaration:

```
END_POINT : POINT := (10.0, 5.0);
```

the variable END_POINT will, in the usual way, have the value (10.0, 5.0). It is not necessary to give all the components of a record type the same automatic initialization values, nor do all the components have to have them. As an example, we can rewrite the declaration of CAR_TYPE:

```
type CAR_TYPE is
  record
    REG_NUMBER  : STRING(1 .. 7) := "       ";
    MAKE        : STRING(1 .. 20);
    MODEL_YEAR  : YEAR_TYPE := CURRENT_YEAR;
    WEIGHT      : WEIGHT_TYPE;
    POWER       : POWER_TYPE;
  end record;
```

where CURRENT_YEAR is a constant:

```
CURRENT_YEAR : constant := 1994;
```

If we now declare a variable NEW_CAR:

```
NEW_CAR : CAR_TYPE;
```

then the component MODEL_YEAR in NEW_CAR will have the value 1994 and REG_NUMBER will have the value "   ". The other components are undefined.

Ordinary scalar variables cannot be automatically initialized on declaration, except by using the trick of enclosing the scalar type in a record type. For example, assume we have a type SCORE_TYPE:

type SCORE-TYPE **is range** 0.. 100;

If we declare a variable S:

S : SCORE-TYPE;

then S's value is undefined. If, however, we introduce the type SCORE_RECORD_TYPE instead:

type SCORERECORDTYPE **is**
  record
    SR SCORE-TYPE := 0;
  end record;

and make the variable declaration:

S : SCORE_RECORD_TYPE;

then S will automatically be initialized to the value 0 on declaration. A disadvantage of this is, of course, that every time S is referred to, S.SR must be written instead of S.

Automatic initialization of components of records

- When a record type is declared, initial values can be given for individual components.
- When a variable of the type is later declared, such components will automatically be initialized to these values.
- An initializing value can be a general expression and should have the same type as the record component.

7.4 Arrays of records

It is very common in real life to have a number of objects with the same properties. One example is a telephone directory with many subscribers, each entry specifying a telephone number, name, title and address. Another example is the result list from a sporting event. For each competitor, his or her number, name, club and result are given. The natural data structure to use in Ada to describe such a real thing is an array of records. The result list from the sporting event could be described using the type RESULT_LIST below:

```
type NUMBER  is range 1 .. 1000;
type TIME       is digits 7 range 0.0 .. 600.0;
type COMPETITOR is
  record
    ID_NUMBER  : NUMBER;
    NAME        : STRING(1 .. 10);
    CLUB        : STRING(1 .. 20);
    RUN_TIME   : TIME;
  end record;
type RESULT_LIST is array (1 .. 500) of COMPETITOR;
```

We have assumed that there are at most 500 competitors but that they can have identifying numbers in the range 1–1000, so that not all available numbers are used. We have also assumed that the competition is one where all results are given as times, for example, swimming or cross-country skiing. The times are given in minutes and it is assumed that none are more than 10 hours.

Of course, it is also possible to have an unconstrained array of records, where the number of records is not decided in advance. As an example of this we can take the telephone directory:

```
type TELEPHONE_NUMBER is range 0 .. 9999999;
type SUBSCRIBER is
  record
    NAME     : STRING(1 .. 20);
    TITLE    : STRING(1 .. 15);
    ADDRESS  : STRING(1 .. 20);
    NUMBER   : TELEPHONE_NUMBER;
  end record;
type TELEPHONE_CATALOGUE is array (INTEGER range < >)
                                   of SUBSCRIBER;
```

The number of subscribers must then be stated when a variable is declared, such as:

```
NEWTOWN_CATALOGUE : TELEPHONE_CATALOGUE(1 .. 50000);
```

In the rest of this section we shall assume that we have a car hire firm and a list of all its cars. To describe such a list we can use the type CAR_TYPE that we declared earlier:

```
type CAR_TYPE is
  record
    REG_NUMBER   : STRING(1 .. 7);
    MAKE         : STRING(1 .. 20);
    MODEL_YEAR   : YEAR_TYPE;
    WEIGHT       : WEIGHT_TYPE;
    POWER        : POWER_TYPE;
    CLIENT       : PERSON;
  end record;
```

We have added a component CLIENT, which states who is currently hiring the car in question. The type PERSON is declared as follows:

```
type PERSON is
  record
    NAME            : STRING(1 .. 20);
    CLIENT_NUMBER   : STRING(1 .. 10);
    ADDRESS         : STRING(1 .. 30);
  end record;
```

Then we can declare a type CAR_LIST:

```
type CAR_LIST is array (POSITIVE range < >) of CAR_TYPE;
```

If we assume that the firm has at most 100 cars we can declare a variable CARS_OWNED:

```
CARS_OWNED : CAR_LIST(1 .. 100);
```

Data about the firm's cars can now be entered in the array. For example, to give values to car number 23 we can use indexing and write the assignment statement:

```
CARS_OWNED(23) := ("D135ADG", "Opel Vectra 2.0 iGLS          ",
                   1993, 1320, 70.0,
                   ("Frederick Smith          ", "100121PRIV",
                    "13, High St, Granton              "));
```

Note that the right-hand side contains one record aggregate within another, since the component CLIENT in type CAR_TYPE is itself of a record type.

If we want to write out the name of the customer who hired car number 23 we can use indexing and selection:

```
PUT(CARS_OWNED(23).CLIENT.NAME);
```

Assume that values have been assigned to all the components in the array of descriptions of the firm's cars. The following lines of program read in a registration number from the terminal and investigate whether there is a car with that registration number. If there is such a car, the name and address of the client who has hired the car will be written out. If the car is not hired out, the message "The car is not hired out" is written.

```
PUT_LINE("Enter registration number.");
GET(REG_NR);

P := SEARCH(CARS_OWNED, REG_NR);

if P = 0 then
   PUT_LINE("No car with this registration number.");
elsif CARS_OWNED(P).CLIENT.NAME = (others =>' ') then
   PUT_LINE("The car is not hired out");
else
   PUT_LINE("The car is hired out to:");
   PUT_LINE(CARS_OWNED(P).CLIENT.NAME);
   PUT_LINE(CARS_OWNED(P).CLIENT.ADDRESS);
end if;
```

We assume that the variable REG_NR has type STRING(1 .. 7) and that the variable P has the type INTEGER. In these lines we have called a function SEARCH which searches the array for the record containing a particular registration number. As a result, the function returns the index of the record in the array. If it finds no such record, the function returns the value 0. The function SEARCH has two **in** parameters – the array to be searched and the registration number of interest.

Now we have to write the function SEARCH. The simplest way is to use a **linear search**, as discussed in connection with arrays in Chapter 5. We simply search through the whole array, until either the array is finished or the record we are looking for is found. The function SEARCH is:

```
-- LINEAR SEARCH
function SEARCH (C : CAR_LIST; REQ_REG_NR : STRING)
                     return NATURAL is

   I : POSITIVE := C'FIRST;
begin
```

```
-- search until the array is finished or
-- the required registration number is found
while I <= C'LAST and then
        C(I).REG_NUMBER /= REQ_REG_NR loop
    I := I + 1;
end loop;

if I <= C'LAST then
    -- Required registration number has been found
    return I;
else
    -- Required registration number not found
    return 0;
end if;
end SEARCH;
```

This method of finding something in an array is not particularly efficient. In the worst case, we must search through the whole array. If the array were sorted we would be able to find a more efficient method, so we shall start by sorting the array according to registration number.

We studied one simple sort method in Section 5.9. Here we shall demonstrate another common and simple (but not particularly efficient) method that is usually called **bubble sort**, which is based on ordering neighbouring pairs. In this method the array is run through time and again. As soon as two neighbouring components of the array are found that are not in correct order, they are swapped. In this way the 'lighter' components (those with smaller values) 'rise up' to the 'surface', while the 'heavier' ones 'sink' to the 'bottom', hence the name.

We can devise a rough algorithm for the bubble sort:

(1) Repeat the following until the array is sorted, that is, until the array has been run right through without any swap taking place:
    (1.1) Run through the array and investigate each pair of consecutive components. If the components in a pair are in the wrong order, swap them.

We can refine step (1.1) of the algorithm:

(1.1.1) Set SWAP_HAS_OCCURRED to FALSE.
        (No swap has yet occurred in this run through the array.)
(1.1.2) Let I run from the first to the last but one index in the array.
    (1.1.2.1) If component I is greater than component I+1:
        (1.1.2.1.1) Swap components I and I+1.
        (1.1.2.1.2) Set SWAP_HAS_OCCURRED to TRUE.

By making a number of adjustments to this algorithm it can be made more efficient; for example, it is not necessary to run through the whole array each time, since the largest unsorted element ends up in the right place each time. Here we shall not worry about this.

Everything is now ready to translate the algorithm to Ada, and we can write a procedure SORT, whose only parameter is the array to be sorted. The parameter must be an **in out** parameter because the procedure must be able to both read and change components in the array. The array CARS_OWNED can then be sorted by making the call:

```
SORT(CARS_OWNED);
```

We consider component I to be bigger than component J if component I contains a 'bigger' registration number than component J, that is, if I's registration number comes after J's in alphabetical/numerical order.

So that the first run through takes place, we initialize SWAP_HAS_ OCCURRED to TRUE. The procedure is as follows:

```
-- BUBBLE SORT
procedure SORT(C : in out CAR_LIST) is
   SWAP_HAS_OCCURRED : BOOLEAN := TRUE;
   TEMP : CAR_TYPE;                      -- used during swap
   begin
      while SWAP_HAS_OCCURRED loop
      -- run through array anew
      SWAP_HAS_OCCURRED := FALSE;

      for I in C'FIRST .. C'LAST - 1 loop
        if C(I).REG_NUMBER > C(I+1).REG_NUMBER then
           -- in wrong order - swap places
           TEMP := C(I);
           C(I)    := C(I+1);
           C(I+1) := TEMP;
           SWAP_HAS_OCCURRED := TRUE;
        end if;
      end loop;
   end loop;
end SORT;
```

This section closes by giving a more efficient version of the function SEARCH to find the record in the array that contains a particular registration number. In the new version of SEARCH we shall make use of the fact that the array is sorted to speed up the search. We use the following concept, assuming the array to be sorted into ascending order, from left to right.

First we look at the component in the middle of the array. If this component holds the required registration number then we are lucky and need look no further. If the middle component has a registration number that is greater than the one we want, we know that the required registration number is in the left half of the array, because the array is sorted. Likewise, if the middle component contains a registration number that is less than the one we want, we know that it must be in the right half of the array. When we have looked at the middle component, therefore, we have either found the required component or we know which half we should continue to search.

When we continue the search we can consider the half-array as a new array, smaller than the original. Now we have exactly the same problem as when we started, only this time the new array is smaller. We can thus use the same idea as before, namely, look at the middle component of the new array. If the required component is not the middle component we can determine whether we should continue the search in the left or the right half of the array. We can then apply the same technique once more on the even smaller array left to look in.

This process is continued with decreasingly small arrays until we find the component we are looking for or until the array we are searching is empty. In the latter case the required component is not in the array at all.

What we have discussed here is a recursive search method that is usually known as a **binary search**, that is, the size of the array to be searched is halved at every stage. We can formulate the algorithm, assuming the array ordered from left to right in ascending order:

(1) Evaluate the index of the middle component.
(2) If the array is empty (length is zero) then the required component is not in the array.
(3) If the middle component is the one we want, the algorithm terminates with the index of the middle component as result.
(4) If the middle component is greater than the one we are looking for, we continue our search in the left half of the array, that is, the array that includes the first component up to and including the component to the left of the middle component.
     Use this algorithm to continue the search.
(5) Otherwise the middle component is smaller than the one we are looking for. Then continue the search in the right half of the array, that is, the array that includes the component to the right of middle, up to and including the last component.
     Use this algorithm to continue the search.

This search technique is much more efficient than the simple linear search that we looked at before. If, for example, we have an array with 100 elements, the binary search algorithm needs to look at a maximum of seven elements to determine whether a particular element is in the array. If a linear search were used instead, in the worst case we would have to look at all 100 elements. In an array of 1000 elements, binary searching would require in the worst case 10 elements to be investigated while linear searching would, in the worst case, require 1000 elements to be investigated.

The algorithm can be translated directly into a recursive Ada function. Steps (4) and (5) in the algorithm are made up of recursive calls of the function itself, with a subarray as parameter.

```
-- BINARY SEARCH

function SEARCH (C: CAR_LIST; REQ_REG_NR : STRING)
                     return NATURAL is

   MIDDLE : INTEGER := (C'FIRST + C'LAST) / 2;
begin
   if C'LENGTH = 0 then
      -- required registration number does not exist
      return 0;
   elsif C(MIDDLE).REG_NUMBER = REQ_REG_NR then
      -- we have found the required reg number
      return MIDDLE;
   elsif C(MIDDLE).REG_NUMBER > REQ_REG_NR then
      -- search the left half of the array
      return SEARCH (C(FIRST .. MIDDLE – 1), REQ_REG_NR);
   else
      -- search the right half of the array
      return SEARCH (C(MIDDLE + 1 .. C'LAST), REQ_REG_NR);
   end if;
end SEARCH;
```

7.5   Records with variants

It sometimes happens that you want to describe data where all the data objects have certain common properties, but where there are also variants. One example could be when you want to describe a group of people who belong to different categories (for example, teachers, students, administrative staff, etc.). All these people share the property of having a name and address, but different types of information might be of interest for the different categories. For a teacher we might want to know about the conditions of their employment, while for a student it is the courses they have passed which are of interest. To describe data of this kind in Ada we can use what are called **records with variants**.

To take a concrete example, let us return to the car hire firm from the previous section. Assume that the firm hires out other kinds of vehicles as well as cars, such as vans and buses. We start by declaring an enumeration type for the different kinds of vehicle:

```
type VEHICLE_TYPE is (PRIVATE_CAR, VAN, BUS, UNKNOWN);
```

Instead of using the type CAR_TYPE that we declared earlier, we will introduce a type which we will call VEHICLE:

```
type VEHICLE(KIND : VEHICLE_TYPE := UNKNOWN) is
  record
    REG_NUMBER        : STRING(1 .. 7);
    CHARGE_PER_DAY  : POSITIVE;
    case KIND is
      when PRIVATE_CAR =>
        NUMBER_OF_SEATS  : POSITIVE;
        MODEL                  : CAR_MODEL;
      when VAN =>
        MAX_LOAD : POSITIVE;
      when BUS =>
        NUMBER_OF_PASSENGERS : POSITIVE;
        AIR_CONDITIONING        : BOOLEAN;
      when UNKNOWN =>
        null;
    end case;
  end record;
```

The enumeration type CAR_MODEL which is used in the record declaration might be declared as follows:

```
type CAR_MODEL is (SALOON, HATCH, ESTATE, CONVERTIBLE);
```

In the first row of the declaration of VEHICLE there is a special component called KIND. A component like this is called a **discriminant**, which is in a sense a parameter to a type. When a record with variants is declared, a discriminant is used to state which variant of the record is being dealt with. A discriminant has a name, a type and, possibly, as in this example, a default value. Here the discriminant is called KIND, is of type VEHICLE_TYPE and has default value UNKNOWN.

The part of the declaration that immediately follows the word **record** is called the record's **fixed part**, and there you declare the components that are common to all variants. In our example, there is a registration number and a daily hire charge for all the types of vehicle. These are given as the components REG_NUMBER and CHARGE_PER_DAY.

The part of the declaration that starts with the word **case** is called the **variant part**, and the components which are different for different variants are stated there. There must be an entry for each possible variant in the variant part. If a particular variant has no special components at all, then the word **null** is used to declare that. In our example, the variant part gives information that is special for the different types of vehicle, for example the number of passengers a bus can have, and the maximum load allowed for a van.

When there is a data object of a record type with variants, there is only sufficient memory to store information for a single variant at a time. For example, if you have a data object of type VEHICLE, and the vehicle in question is a private car, then it has components KIND, REG_NUMBER, CHARGE_ PER_DAY, NUMBER_OF_SEATS, and MODEL. If the vehicle were a van instead, then there would be components KIND, REG_NUMBER, CHARGE_ PER_DAY and MAX_LOAD. Using records with variants is thus a way to save memory, since there is no need to have space for all of a record with variants' components at once.

Now we can look at how to declare variables of a record type with variants. When such a variable is declared you can choose to let it be **constrained** or **unconstrained**. When a constrained variable is declared, its variant is stated as a parameter on declaration. The following are examples of constrained variables:

```
MY_CAR   : VEHICLE(PRIVATE_CAR);
COACH_1 : VEHICLE(BUS);
```

The special thing about constrained variables is that they will always be of the same variant as they were declared to be. For example, the variable MY_CAR can never contain data other than about a private car.

An unconstrained variable, in contrast, can change variant during execution. If no specific variant is stated on declaration, then the variable will be unconstrained, as the variables F1 and F2 in the following declaration:

```
F1, F2 : VEHICLE;
```

When a variable is declared and is unconstrained, to start with it will have the variant given by the discriminant's default value: thus F1 and F2 will be of variant UNKNOWN. An important condition for being able to declare unconstrained variables is that the record type has a default value – otherwise a compilation error will occur. On the other hand, if only constrained variables are going to be declared, the discriminant does not require a default value. These rules ensure that it is impossible to declare a variable which is of an undetermined variant.

There are rules that specify how the components of a variable may be read and changed. These are to ensure that a variable is of a well-specified variant at all times, and that the information in the variant part of a variable will be in agreement with the current variant. The components of the fixed part of a variable must exist for all variants, and they may be read and changed in any way whatever. For example, we can write:

```
MY_CAR.CHARGE_PER_DAY := 30;
F1.REG_NUMBER :="A789XYZ";
```

The rule for the components in the variant part of a variable is that they exist only for the current variant. The following, for example, is allowed:

```
COACH_1.AIR_CONDITIONING := TRUE;
PUT(MY_CAR.NUMBER_OF_SEATS);
```

The following, however, are not allowed because the variants do not agree:

```
PUT(COACH_1.MAX_LOAD);    -- ERROR. COACH_1 is not a VAN
F1.MODEL := CONVERTIBLE;  -- ERROR. F1 is not a PRIVATE_CAR
```

The rule for a discriminant itself is that it can always be read. For example, the following can be written:

```
if F1.KIND = BUS then
```

The discriminant of a constrained variable may never be changed. For an unconstrained variable the discriminant may be changed, but only if the whole record is given a completely new value at one time. For example, we can write:

```
F1 := (PRIVATE_CAR, "F123ACB", 30, 5, HATCH);
F2 := F1;
F1 := COACH_1;
```

It is naturally permitted to declare arrays in which the components are records with variants, such as the following declaration:

```
type VEHICLE_TABLE is array (POSITIVE range < >) of VEHICLE;
COMPANY_VEHICLES : VEHICLE_TABLE(1 .. 100);
```

The elements of the array will be unconstrained, and the following statement, for example, would be permitted:

```
COMPANY_VEHICLES(8) := (VAN, "333XYZC", 75, 5000);
```

The following program extract could be used to print information from the array COMPANY_VEHICLES:

```
for I in COMPANY_VEHICLES'RANGE loop
  PRINT_INFO(COMPANY_VEHICLES(I));
end loop;
```

Here we have called a procedure called PRINT_INFO which could be:

```
procedure PRINT_INFO (V : VEHICLE) is
begin
  if V.KIND /= UNKNOWN then
```

```
PUT_LINE(V.REG_NUMBER);
PUT(V.KIND); NEW_LINE;
PUT(V.CHARGE_PER_DAY, WIDTH => 1);
PUT_LINE(" £/day");
case V.KIND is
  when PRIVATE_CAR =>
    PUT(V.NUMBER_OF_SEATS, WIDTH => 1);
    PUT_LINE(" seats");
    PUT(V.MODEL); NEW_LINE;
  when VAN =>
    PUT(V.MAX_LOAD, WIDTH => 1);
    PUT_LINE(" kg maximum load");
  when BUS =>
    PUT(V.NUMBER_OF_PASSENGERS, WIDTH => 1);
    PUT_LINE(" passengers");
    if V.AIR_CONDITIONING then
      PUT_LINE("With air-conditioning");
    end if;
  when others => null;
  end case;
end if;
end PRINT_INFO;
```

This procedure prints the contents of the elements of the array, when their variant is not of kind UNKNOWN. It is typical, as in this example, to use a case statement in connection with records of variants.

EXERCISES

7.1 A table can be drawn to show how different countries border one another. Part of such a table could be:

	Belgium	France	Italy
Belgium	–	yes	no
France	yes	–	yes
Italy	no	yes	–

(a) Make a suitable type declaration in Ada to represent such a table, including some arbitrary countries. Declare the table and initialize it appropriately.

(b) Write a function NUMBER_OF_NEIGHBOURS that takes a country and a table similar to the above as parameters. The function should return the number of countries that border the given country. For an appropriate table, a call NUMBER_OF_NEIGHBOURS(SWEDEN, TABLE), for example, should return the value 2, since its only neighbours joined by land are Norway and Finland.

7.2 A chess board has 64 squares. The columns are usually denoted by the letters a, b, c, d, e, f, g and h, and the rows by the numbers 1–8. The different pieces are *king*, *queen*, *bishop*, *knight*, *rook* and *pawn*, and black pieces and white pieces are used. Write a type declaration that describes the appearance of an arrangement of pieces on the chess board.

7.3 Write a function to determine whether an $n \times n$ matrix is symmetric. In a symmetric matrix A, $a_{ij} = a_{ji}$ for all i and j.

7.4 A magic square is an arrangement of numbers with n rows and n columns. The sums of the values in each row, column and diagonal are the same. The following square is a magic square, for example:

$$\begin{pmatrix} 16 & 9 & 2 & 7 \\ 6 & 3 & 12 & 13 \\ 11 & 14 & 5 & 4 \\ 1 & 8 & 15 & 10 \end{pmatrix}$$

(a) Write a function that takes such an arrangement as parameter and determines whether it is a magic square. The number of rows and columns is arbitrary.

(b) Another condition for an arrangement of numbers with n rows and columns to be a true magic square is that it contains all the integers 1, 2, ... n^2. Amend the function so that it also checks for this condition.

7.5 (a) Write a function that takes an $n \times n$ matrix of integers as parameter. As a result, the function should return the same matrix turned through a quarter-turn anticlockwise. For example, if the function is given the matrix:

$$\begin{pmatrix} 1 & 2 & 3 \\ 4 & 5 & 6 \\ 7 & 8 & 9 \end{pmatrix}$$

as parameter it should return the matrix:

$$\begin{pmatrix} 3 & 6 & 9 \\ 2 & 5 & 8 \\ 1 & 4 & 7 \end{pmatrix}$$

(b) Use the function in a program to read in a 4×4 matrix from the terminal. The matrix is read in row by row. The program should write out the matrix turned first through a quarter-turn anticlockwise and then through a half-turn anticlockwise. In the output, each row of the resulting matrices should be written out as a row at the terminal.

7.6 **Matrix multiplication** can be defined for two matrices A and B with dimensions $m \times n$ and $n \times p$, respectively. (Note that the number of columns in A must be the same as the number of rows in B.) The result of the matrix multiplication is a new matrix with dimension $m \times p$. If we call the resulting matrix C, a particular element c_{ij} in C is calculated as the sum:

$$c_{ij} = \sum_{k=1}^{n} a_{ik} \times b_{kj}$$

For example:

$$\begin{pmatrix} 1 & 2 \\ 4 & 7 \\ 8 & 3 \end{pmatrix} \times \begin{pmatrix} 1 & 2 & 0 & 2 \\ 3 & 4 & 3 & 1 \end{pmatrix} = \begin{pmatrix} 7 & 10 & 6 & 4 \\ 25 & 36 & 21 & 15 \\ 17 & 28 & 9 & 19 \end{pmatrix}$$

Use this to construct a function that gets two matrices as parameters. In the result, the function should give the matrix that results from multiplying them together.

7.7 (a) Write two functions ROW and COL that can be used to select a particular row or column from a matrix. Both should take a matrix as parameter. In addition, ROW should get a row number as parameter and the function COL should get a column number. If matrix M is, for example:

$$\begin{pmatrix} 1 & 4 & 7 & 9 \\ 3 & 0 & 2 & 5 \\ 8 & 7 & 0 & 2 \end{pmatrix}$$

then the call ROW(M,2) should return the vector (3, 0, 2, 5) and the call COL(M,4) should return the vector (9, 5, 2).

(b) The **scalar product u·v** of two vectors $u = (u_1, u_2, \ldots, u_n)$ and $v = (v_1, v_2, \ldots, v_n)$ can be defined as the sum:

$$\sum_{i=1}^{n} u_i \times v_i$$

The scalar product of the vectors (1, 2, 3) and (3, 4, 5), for example, is 26. A condition for forming the scalar product is that the two vectors have the same number of elements. Write a function that forms the scalar product of two vectors.

(c) Multiplication of two matrices A and B with dimensions $m \times n$ and $n \times p$ can now be defined as an operation which gives a new matrix C with dimensions $m \times p$. A particular element c_{ij} of C has as its value the scalar product of row i from A and column j from B. Using this definition, write a function that multiplies two matrices, making use of the functions written in parts (a) and (b) of this question. Compare this function with that of the previous question.

7.8 The Morse code for the alphabet is shown in the following table, where dots and dashes are used to represent short and long signals, respectively.

A	·—	H	····	O	———	U	··—
B	—···	I	··	P	·——·	V	···—
C	—·—·	J	·———	Q	——·—	W	·——
D	—··	K	—·—	R	·—·	X	—··—
E	·	L	·—··	S	···	Y	—·——
F	··—·	M	——	T	—	Z	——··
G	——·	N	—·				

(a)   Write a program that reads in a message and codes it into Morse code.

(b)   Write a program that reads in a message in Morse code, decodes it and writes out the decoded message. In the Morse message letters are separated by one space and words are separated by two spaces.

7.9   Declare a record type that is appropriate for describing a card in an ordinary pack of cards.

7.10   To define a point in a two-dimensional coordinate system it is most common to use the form (x,y), called **rectangular coordinates**. An alternative way of defining it is to use **polar coordinates** (r,θ). r is the distance of the point from the origin and θ is the angle between the straight line joining the point to the origin and the x-axis. Transformation from polar coordinates to ordinary rectangular coordinates can be effected with the formulae:

$$x = r \cos \theta$$
$$y = r \sin \theta$$

Write a function that takes a point described in polar coordinates as input parameter and returns it expressed in rectangular coordinates.

7.11   A rational number can be written as a fraction in which both numerator and denominator are integers.

(a)   Make an appropriate type declaration to describe a rational number.

(b)   Write a function that takes two rational numbers as parameters and returns a new rational number that is the sum of the two parameters.

(c)   Add to the function above so that it always returns a rational number where the numerator and the denominator have no common factor. (Compare with Exercises 6.4 and 6.15.)

7.12   A company has a warehouse where it stores several kinds of articles. There are a number of articles of each kind and a computer program is required to keep track of them all. For each kind of article the following are important:

●   The article identification (a code of four characters).

●   Article description (a text with at most 30 characters).

●   The number of this article in store.

●   The selling price.

Write a program that first reads in this information from the terminal for all the kinds of article and saves it using a suitable data structure. Assume that there are no more than 1000 kinds of article in the warehouse. Input can terminate when, for example, the article identification "0000" is given. The program will then repeatedly read commands from the terminal and perform the tasks required. The different commands are, where xxxx stands for an article identification code:

INFO xxxx	Write out all current information about article xxxx.
SOLD xxxx N	Register that N items of article xxxx have been removed from the store.
BOUGHT xxxx N	Register that N items of article xxxx have been put into the store.

7.13 There are a number of chemical elements – for example, carbon, hydrogen, mercury and gold – and for each element there is a symbol comprising one or two letters, in these cases C, H, Hg and Au, respectively. The first letter is always upper case and the second, if there is one, is lower case. Each element has a certain atomic weight.

(a) Declare and initialize a table that contains the symbols for a number of elements and the corresponding atomic weights. Information can be found in any chemistry textbook, but here are some examples:

H	1.0079	O	15.999	F	18.9984
He	4.0026	Na	22.9898	Au	196.9665
Be	9.0122	S	32.06	Hg	200.5
C	12.011	Cl	35.453	Ra	226.0254

(b) A common problem is to calculate a molecular weight. Write a program that reads in a chemical formula and, using the table formulated in part (a), calculates and writes out the corresponding molecular weight. Examples of chemical formulae are:

$$NaCl \qquad H_2O \qquad H_2SO_4$$

The subscript n after an element symbol means that there are n atoms of the corresponding element in the molecule. If no figure is given, it means that there is only one atom of that element. As input to the program a chemical formula can be given in the following format:

NaCl   H2O   H2SO4

7.14 Using a record type with variants, declare a type FIGURE which describes geometric figures in some suitable way. The figures to be described are circles, rectangles and triangles, and each kind of figure should have its own variant in a record type. For each figure, the position of the centre has to be stated, giving where on the screen it should be drawn, and this can be given as two Cartesian coordinates. Then write a function AREA which calculates the area of a figure of type FIGURE.

8 Packages

It has been shown that it is possible to solve problems by breaking them down into smaller subproblems which are then solved one by one. This process can be repeated for each subproblem until all the subproblems are so simple that they can easily be solved. Chapter 6 showed that subprograms helped us to apply this strategy – a call to a subprogram described the solution to a more complicated subproblem, and subprograms could then be written separately, one by one. The advantage of subprograms is that they hide inessential details that the programmer does not need to know, and allows him or her to concentrate on one problem at a time. A subprogram is thus a construction that can be used to bring together a number of statements into a logical unit with a defined interface with the other parts of the program.

In Ada there is another construction for bringing together related parts of a program into a logical unit, and this is called a **package**. Subprograms, types and objects that logically belong together in some way can be brought together in a package. When a package is constructed, its interface with the rest of the program or, in other words, the part of the package that will be visible to the program, has to be specified. Details that are inessential to the user of the package can then be concealed within the package. A package can be developed and compiled alone.

When a complicated product such as a car is being built, it is necessary to make the different parts separately in order to prevent the work from becoming too complex. Eventually, the separate parts are assembled into a complete product. To fit the parts together successfully, a specification of how the parts fit must have been carefully made during the design phase.

Ada is a language that is designed not only to handle small problems, but also to be used in large programming projects where large complicated programs or systems of programs are developed, and where many people are involved. As with building a car, it is necessary that all the parts are written separately and put together later. Ada's package facility allows a program to be built up in the form of several separate modules, each of which forms a logical unit. With the help of a **package specification** it can be stated how a package should be put together with the other parts of the program. Working with large unmanageable programs is thus avoided: one subproblem can be tackled at a time. Most of the common programming languages, such as Pascal and BASIC, lack these features for building up programs in the form of separate packages.

It is also possible to build up a library of general packages that may be used in several contexts within different programs. These could include a package of different mathematical functions or a package of tools for presenting results in a graphic form. These packages may have been written by the individual programmer, or be standard packages in an implementation of Ada, or have been obtained from some other source.

In Ada 95 there are so-called **child packages**. These can be used to extend existing packages without recompilation, or to divide a large complex system into subsystems.

8.1 Package specification

Each package has a **specification**. This can be regarded as the package's 'shop-window', which says what the package has to offer the potential user. The specification specifies the package's interface with the other parts of programs. A package specification is introduced with the word **package** followed by the name of the package. Within the specification, declarations of types, objects and subprogram specifications may appear, but the bodies of subprograms may not be given in a package specification.

Let us look at an example. Suppose we want to work with ordinary two-dimensional geometric figures such as rectangles, circles and triangles. It may then be appropriate to construct a package containing the tools for performing various calculations on these figures. We can call the package PLANIMETRY and write a specification for it. In the specification we shall declare types LENGTH and AREA which describe, obviously, lengths and areas associated with the geometric figures. In addition we declare functions that calculate the

---

Package specification

> **package** *package_name* **is**
>   declarations
> **end** *package_name*;

Subprograms can have their specifications but not
their bodies among the declarations.

---

areas of rectangles, circles and triangles. The specification of the package
PLANIMETRY is then:

```
package PLANIMETRY is
   type LENGTH  is digits 5 range 0.0 .. 1.0E10;
   type AREA      is digits 5 range 0.0 .. 1.0E20;
   function AREA_RECTANGLE (L, H : LENGTH) return AREA;
   function AREA_CIRCLE        (R : LENGTH) return AREA;
   function CIRCUMF_CIRCLE  (R : LENGTH) return LENGTH;
   function AREA_TRIANGLE    (B, H : LENGTH) return AREA;
end PLANIMETRY;
```

This is the 'shop-window' for the package PLANIMETRY. Note that we have not
yet said anything about what it will look like within the package, that is, what
the function bodies will be. We shall state this later by writing a package body.

8.2   The Ada programming environment

Before we go on to see how a package can be used and what a package body
looks like, a few words must be said about the programming environment in
Ada. When a program or a part of a program is compiled a compiler is used. The
compiler reads the program text and gives as a result the program translated into
machine code. Compilers of all kinds work in this way, not only the Ada compiler.

An Ada compiler differs from most other language compilers, however,
in that it not only produces machine code but also keeps track of all the compilation that is performed. The compiler maintains what is called the **Ada library**.
When a compilation is complete, the Ada compiler puts a description of the
program (or part of a program) that has been compiled into the Ada library.

This means that it is possible to refer to what has been compiled earlier
in a program. The compiler goes into the Ada library and searches for information about the relevant item, making it feasible to build up large complicated
programs gradually.

An Ada environment thus contains not only an Ada compiler but also an Ada library. There are also utility programs for creating new Ada libraries and for removing information from a library.

The Ada programming environment

- Ada library with information about all the compilations performed.
- Ada compiler that translates to machine code and places information into the Ada library.
- Utility programs for handling Ada libraries, for example, creating new libraries and removing information from a library.

For compilation, a **compilation unit** is fed into the compiler (or a sequence of several compilation units may be fed in at one time). A compilation unit contains a program component which is to be compiled, and this might be a procedure (as we have seen in many examples) but it can also be a program component other than a procedure, such as a package specification or a package body. Thus the specifications and bodies of packages may be compiled separately.

As we saw in Chapter 6, when we studied top-down design with subprograms, Ada distinguishes between what are known as **library units** and **subunits**. A library unit is a free-standing program component whereas a subunit is logically included in another surrounding component. (A subunit is always introduced with the word **separate**.)

In a compilation unit you can refer to program components that have been compiled earlier (but only library units and not subunits). This is achieved by placing a **with** clause first in the compilation unit.

With clause

    with *name1, name2 ... nameN;*

Placed first in a compilation unit. States that the current compilation unit requires access to program components called *name1, name2 ... nameN.*

If we are compiling a procedure P, for example, we can have the clause:

with Q, R;

as the first line, where Q and R are the names of other program components that we refer to and which therefore need to be accessible in P. The Ada compiler then searches the Ada library for information about Q and R. If the compiler cannot find Q and R in the library there is an error and compilation terminates. This means that Q and R should have been compiled earlier.

The specification of a package must be compiled before the body. However, it is not necessary to compile the body of a package before compiling a procedure that uses that package. Naturally, however, all parts of the program must be compiled before the program can be executed.

Compilation order for packages

- Compile the package specification first.
- Then compile, in any order, the package body and the compilation units that refer to the package in question.

If the body of a package is recompiled there is no need to recompile the procedures that use the package. If, on the other hand, the specification of a package is recompiled then both the package body and the program components which use the package must be recompiled. Information is stored in the Ada library stating when each program component was compiled; the Ada compiler can thus monitor that the different parts of a program were compiled in the correct order.

8.3   Using packages

A package whose specification has been compiled can be used in programs, or parts of programs, that are compiled later. If, for example, we write a program COMPUTE_AREAS and we want to use the procedures contained in the package PLANIMETRY, we write at the start of the program:

with PLANIMETRY;

The compiler will search for the package PLANIMETRY in the Ada library and we can use the package in our program. We can use everything that is declared in the package's specification, but what exists within the package body is not known to the procedure COMPUTE_AREAS.

One way to refer to the items declared in the specification of PLANI-METRY is to use selection, or dot notation. For example, we can declare a variable of type AREA:

A : PLANIMETRY.AREA;

Here PLANIMETRY.AREA refers to the type AREA in the package PLANI-METRY. Similarly, we can declare a variable R:

R : PLANIMETRY.LENGTH;

If we now want to read in the radius of a circle in our program and calculate its area, we can write the lines:

PUT_LINE("Enter the radius of the circle");
GET(R);
A := PLANIMETRY.AREA_CIRCLE(R);

The expression on the right of the last line means that we call the function AREA_CIRCLE in the package PLANIMETRY. The variable A will then be assigned the value of the area of the circle requested.

Selection

> P.N

where P is the name of a package and N is the name of something that is declared in the specification of the package.

This notation, where the name of the package is followed by a dot, is clear. Each time something from a package is used it is obvious which package is being referred to. In one program several different packages may be in use and one name in the declarations of one package may also occur in another package, but under a different name. If selection is used this causes no problems since the intended package is always explicitly stated.

If the contents of a package are used in many places in a program it is clumsy to state the package name every time. In most programs so far, we have used the package TEXT_IO. It would have been inconvenient to write TEXT_IO.PUT every time we wanted to write something out at the terminal. It is more convenient to refer to the items declared in a package specification if a **use** clause is introduced. If we put into our program:

use PLANIMETRY;

for example, the declarations of A and R can simply be written:

    A : AREA;
    R : LENGTH;

We no longer need to state the name of the package. The call to the function AREA_CIRCLE can be written:

    A := AREA_CIRCLE(R);

A **use** clause can either be placed directly after the **with** clause at the start of the compilation unit, or anywhere among the declarations in a subprogram. If the **use** clause is put at the start of the compilation unit, it is valid for the whole compilation unit. Thus it is possible to access the contents of the package everywhere, without using selection. If the **use** clause is placed among the declarations in a subprogram, it is only valid in that subprogram.

Use clause

> **use** *PI, P2, ... , PN*;

where *PI, P2, ... , PN* are names of packages.

Can be placed after **with** clause or among the declarations in a subprogram.

The disadvantage of a **use** clause is that the program can become less clear; names of quantities can occur that are declared in the packages being used. Since these packages have been compiled separately, it is not possible to see from the program how the quantities are declared. Nor is it possible to see the package from which they come. If, for example, we had also used a package SOLID_GEOMETRY and had put the following **use** clause in our program:

    use SOLID_GEOMETRY, PLANIMETRY;

then in the declaration:

    A : AREA;

we would not be able to see if AREA exists in the package SOLID_GEOMETRY or in the package PLANIMETRY.

It is recommended that **use** clauses are employed with caution and are not habitually placed first in compilation units. (This is acceptable in the case of TEXT_IO because it is used so commonly and we know that it contains the procedures GET and PUT.) An alternative to using selection, which can be a little clumsy, is to have a local **use** clause for each package and place it within the subprogram where the contents of the package are actually used.

8.4 Package bodies

Now we shall look at how to construct a package body – the part of the package that is concealed from the user. Details that the user does not need to know are placed in the package body, for example, the subprogram bodies and internal data.

A package body is introduced with the reserved words **package body**. The rest of the package body has the same structure as a subprogram body. First comes a declarative part and then a sequence of statements. This latter section can be omitted, and this is most common.

Package bodies

package body *package_name* **is**
  declarations
[begin
   statements]
end *package_name*;

- All kinds of declaration are allowed in the package body.
- The quantities that are declared in the body are not accessible from outside the package.
- The section within square brackets [ ] can be omitted.
- If there is a statement section, the statements are only executed once, when the program using the package starts.

For example, we shall look at how the body of our package PLANI-METRY may appear:

```
package body PLANIMETRY is

PI : constant := 3.1415926536;

function AREA_RECTANGLE(L, H : LENGTH) return AREA is
begin
   return AREA(L) * AREA(H);
end AREA_RECTANGLE;
```

```
function AREA_CIRCLE (R : LENGTH) return AREA is
begin
    return PI * AREA(R) ** 2;
end AREA_CIRCLE;
```

```
function CIRCUMF_CIRCLE (R : LENGTH) return LENGTH is
begin
    return 2.0 * PI * R;
end CIRCUMF_CIRCLE;
```

```
function AREA_TRIANGLE (B, H : LENGTH) return AREA is
begin
    return AREA(B) * AREA(H) / 2.0;
end AREA_TRIANGLE;
```

```
end PLANIMETRY;
```

Within the package body are the complete function bodies for the functions that were declared in the package specification. There is also a constant PI and this is known only within the package body. Thus in a program that uses the package it is not permitted to write:

```
PLANIMETRY.PI      -- ERROR! PI is only known
                   -- in the package body
```

It is only the items from the package specification that are known outside.

In the functions that calculate areas we have used type conversion so that the results of the functions have type AREA. The expression:

```
B * H
```

would have type LENGTH since both operands have that type. The expression:

```
AREA(B) * AREA(H)
```

however, has the type AREA.

The body of the package PLANIMETRY has no statement section. A section of statements in a package body is used when something has to be initialized within the package body before the package can be used. The constant PI needs to be initialized in the body of PLANIMETRY but we manage with a simple initialization in its declaration and, therefore, no statement part is needed. We shall look at an example of a package with a statement section later.

A package body must be compiled after its specification has been compiled. In the specification we talk about what the package will be able to do and in the body we state how to do what we have promised. It is possible to compile the specification and body separately on separate occasions or, if the texts are to remain together, to compile them as two compilation units but fed to the compiler together. In the latter case the specification should come before the body. It is recommended that the two parts should be compiled separately; since the package body contains whole subprograms it is likely that they will have to be amended and the body recompiled many times during program development. It is then advantageous not to have to recompile the package specification at the same time, since if the specification is recompiled all the programs using the package must also be recompiled.

8.5   Different categories of package

Packages can be used for different purposes in an Ada program. To clarify this idea it may be useful to try to classify the different kinds of package. Generalizing a little, it can be said that there are four different categories of package:

(1)   Packages with a collection of types and constants, for example, a package of mathematical constants.

(2)   Packages with a group of subprograms that logically belong together, for example, a package of standard mathematical functions.

(3)   Packages with 'memory' that can be used to represent complicated objects in different states.

(4)   Packages which construct abstract data types.

(In Ada 95 there are child packages, as will be described in Section 8.9, which make packages even more useful. For example, large subsystems can be built up consisting of several packages.)

We have already seen examples of packages from category (2): our package PLANIMETRY for example. Subprograms in the package belong together logically because they all perform calculations on geometrical figures. Packages with mathematic functions also belong to category (2).

8.6   Packages of types and constants

As an example of a package of category (1) we shall study a package ATOMIC_CONSTANTS which contains various constants:

```
package ATOMIC_CONSTANTS is
   ELECTRON_CHARGE : constant := 1.602E–19;    -- coul
   ELECTRON_MASS    : constant := 0.9108E–30;   -- kg
   NEUTRON_MASS     : constant := 1674.7E–30;   -- kg
   PROTON_MASS      : constant := 1672.4E–30;   -- kg
end ATOMIC_CONSTANTS;
```

There are no subprograms in the package, only constants. If the **with** clause:

```
with ATOMIC_CONSTANTS;
```

is placed first in a program, then the package can be accessed and the mass of the proton, for example, can be accessed by writing:

```
ATOMIC_CONSTANTS.PROTON_MASS
```

Of course, a **use** clause can also be inserted in the program:

```
use ATOMIC_CONSTANTS;
```

Then the mass of the proton can simply be referred to by:

```
PROTON_MASS
```

In Ada 83, packages belonging to category (1) are somewhat special, in that they do not need to have a body. Since such a package contains only constants and types there is no special substance to the package that needs further description.

In Ada 95 packages in this category are not allowed to have a body.

▼
▲

8.7   Packages with memory

Now we shall study packages that belong to category (3). This kind of package can be used to build up a description of a complex real object – an object that can be in different states. For example, when a program is written to control an engineering system, for example an aeroplane, a program design method can be used based on representing each physical component of the system by an Ada package, a package of category (3). For example, it should be possible to represent a fuel valve by an Ada package.

The special thing about packages of category (3) is that they can be in different states. Each time the package is used, its state changes. Therefore the package must be able to 'remember' its state between uses.

The standard package TEXT_IO can be said to belong to category (3). It represents the real object – the 'terminal'. The package must remember how long a line of output can be and how many lines there can be on a page of output. When printing output, between calls to PUT, PUT_LINE and NEW_LINE the package must 'remember' which page is being printed, which line it is on and how much of the output has already been printed.

As another example of a package of category (3) we shall construct a package that can be used to generate random numbers. It will represent a random number generator. In some programs, such as games programs and simulation programs, access to a source of random numbers is necessary.

To obtain random numbers from a computer, the concept used is based on generating a series of numbers that appear to be random. Let us call this series:

$$u_0 \quad u_1 \quad u_2 \quad u_3 \quad \ldots$$

It is most common to use the formula:

$$u_{n+1} = Ku_n \bmod M$$

to generate a particular term in the series, where mod means the modulo operator (see Section 3.4.1). If the nth term is known, the $(n+1)$th can be evaluated using the formula. Term number 0 is given a particular start value and thereafter the formula can be applied repeatedly to generate an arbitrary number of terms of the series. The numbers in the series will all lie in the interval 0 to $M-1$.

For the numbers to appear random, K and M must be chosen in a special way, as must the start value of term number 0. (For example, if we gave K the value 3, M the value 10 and the start value 5, then all terms in the series would be 5 – not particularly random.) There are theories that provide suitable values of K and M and the start value. Such suitable values for K and M can be, for example:

$$K = 5^5 \qquad M = 2^{13}$$

Then the start value for the series should be an odd number in the range 1 to $M-1$.

We shall use the formula above, with the suggested values for K and M, to construct a package for generating random numbers. We want the package to contain a function NEXT_NUMBER that will return a random number when called, and each time it should be a new random number. It is useful if the random numbers obtained lie in a particular fixed interval: the interval 0–1 is generally chosen. Thus the random numbers will be real numbers. To be able to generate different series of random numbers the user must be able to specify what start value will be used; if the same start value is always used the same series of random numbers will always be generated. We can solve this by using a procedure INITIALIZE with an **in** parameter that is the start value – known as the seed – to the random number generator.

Now we are in a position to write a specification of the package RANDOM:

> **package** RANDOM **is**
>
> M : **constant :=** 2 ** 13;
>
> **subtype** NUMBER **is** FLOAT **range** 0.0.. 1.0;
> **subtype** SEED is INTEGER **range** 1 .. M –1;
>
> **procedure** INITIALIZE (START_VALUE : **in** SEED);
> -- initialize random number generator
> -- START_VALUE should be an odd integer
>
> **function** NEXT_NUMBER **return** NUMBER;
> -- gives a random number that is greater
> -- than or equal to 0 and less than 1
>
> **end** RANDOM;

In addition to the subprograms NEXT_NUMBER and INITIALIZE we have declared two subtypes, NUMBER and SEED. The subtype NUMBER describes a floating point number in the interval 0–1, a number of the kind that the function NEXT_NUMBER returns as its result. The subtype SEED describes how a start value, the seed, may look. The parameter to the procedure INITIALIZE will be of this subtype. The next step is to construct the body of the package. In the body we must state what the bodies of the subprograms NEXT_NUMBER and INITIALIZE should look like. Let us start with the function NEXT_NUMBER. To evaluate the next number in the series we use the statement:

> U := U * K **mod** M;

where K and M are constants with values 5^5 and 2^{13}, respectively. U is a variable that we initialize at the start to the first number in the series, the seed. Each time the above statement is executed, U will take the next value in the series. U will take integer values in the interval 1 to $2^{13} - 1$. However, for the result of the function NEXT_NUMBER we want a floating point number in the interval 0–1, which can easily be achieved by dividing U by M:

> **return** FLOAT(U) / FLOAT(M);

(Observe that we must convert U and M to floating point numbers. Had we not done so the result would always have been 0.)

The package body is:

```
package body RANDOM is

  U : NATURAL;
  K : constant := 5 ** 5;

  procedure INITIALIZE (START_VALUE : in SEED) is
  begin
    U := START_VALUE;
  end INITIALIZE;

  function NEXT_NUMBER return NUMBER is
  begin
    U := U * K mod M;
    return FLOAT(U) / FLOAT (M);
  end NEXT_NUMBER;
end RANDOM;
```

The important thing to note here is the positioning of the declaration of the variable U. U may not be declared as a local variable in the function NEXT_NUMBER for two reasons:

(1)   U must be accessible to the procedure INITIALIZE, whose job is to give U a starting value. If the declaration had been placed in NEXT_NUMBER, U would not have been known outside NEXT_NUMBER.

(2)   U must 'remember' its value between calls to NEXT_NUMBER. If U had been declared as a local variable inside NEXT_NUMBER it would not have existed between calls. As a consequence, U's value would have been undefined at each new call to NEXT_NUMBER.

The solution to the problem is to place the declaration of U directly in the package body, as above, outside INITIALIZE and NEXT_NUMBER. It is then accessible to both subprograms and, moreover, it will not be spoiled between calls.

Thus U is a global variable to INITIALIZE and NEXT_NUMBER. In normal cases global variables must not be used, but this is one of the few exceptions, mentioned earlier, where it is allowed. In packages of category (3), global variables are used in the package body to give the package a 'memory'. In the other categories of package, which lack this 'memory', such global variables are not to be used.

Now we shall look at the use of RANDOM in a program. We shall write a short program to test whether the random number generator is 'good'. The program will start with the user entering a start value for the random number generator, which will then be used to generate 100 random numbers. These numbers will be written out. Finally the program calculates the mean of the 100 numbers and writes it out. If the mean is not close to 0.5 then either the random number generator is not good or we have chosen an unsuitable start value. (To

---

Packages with 'memory'

- By using global variables in the package body, a package can be created that has 'memory' so that it can exist in different states.

- The state can be changed by calls to subprograms in the package.

- This is one of the few occasions where it is 'allowed' to use global variables.

---

determine whether a random number generator is 'good' in a more correct statistical sense requires more extensive tests. The random number obtained should have an appropriate standard deviation and the periodicity of the series of random numbers, that is, how long it takes before the same sequence of random numbers is repeated, should be adequately large.)

```
with TEXT_IO, BASIC_NUM_IO, RANDOM;
use TEXT_IO, BASIC_NUM_IO;
procedure TEST_RANDOM is
   S : RANDOM.SEED;
   X : RANDOM.NUMBER;
   SUM : FLOAT := 0.0;
begin
   -- Initialize random number generator
   PUT_LINE("Enter seed for random number generator");
   PUT("An odd integer in the interval ");
   PUT(RANDOM.SEED'FIRST, WIDTH => 1); PUT(" to ");
   PUT(RANDOM.SEED'LAST, WIDTH => 1); NEW_LINE;
   GET(S);
   RANDOM.INITIALIZE(S);

   -- Generate 100 random numbers
   for I in 1 .. 100 loop
      X := RANDOM.NEXT_NUMBER;
      PUT(X); NEW_LINE;
      SUM := SUM + X;
   end loop;

   -- evaluate and print mean of the random numbers
   PUT("Mean: "); PUT(SUM / 100.0); NEW_LINE;
end TEST_RANDOM;
```

In the program, we have made the random number generator in the package RANDOM accessible by including RANDOM in the **with** clause in the first line of the program. We have no **use** clause for the package RANDOM but use selection with the dot notation for clarity.

The variables S and X are given, respectively, the types SEED and NUMBER, which are declared in the specification of RANDOM. In the message that requests a seed from the user, we have used RANDOM.SEED'FIRST and RANDOM.SEED'LAST instead of the numbers 1 and 8191 ($2^{13} - 1$). In this way the program is made more general and would not need to be changed if the value of the constant M, and hence the subtype SEED, were changed in the random number generator. The start value is given to the random number generator by making the procedure call:

```
RANDOM.INITIALIZE(S);
```

The 100 random numbers are generated by 100 calls to the function NEXT_NUMBER:

```
X := RANDOM.NEXT_NUMBER;
```

After each call the variable U in the body of RANDOM will change in value, but we do not need to worry about how things are working within the package because this program is only using the facilities. (In fact, we do not even know that there is a variable U.)

We see that if the random number generator were initialized automatically our program would be much simpler. We would not need to enter the seed, the variable S would not be necessary and we would not need to know about the subtype SEED.

```
with TEXT_IO, BASIC_NUM_IO, RANDOM;
use TEXT_IO, BASIC_NUM_IO;
procedure TEST_RANDOM is

  X : RANDOM.NUMBER;
  SUM : FLOAT := 0.0;
begin

  -- Generate 100 random numbers
  for I in 1 .. 100 loop
    X := RANDOM.NEXT_NUMBER;
    PUT(X); NEW_LINE;
    SUM := SUM + X;
  end loop;

  -- evaluate and print mean of the random numbers
  PUT("Mean: "); PUT(SUM / 100.0); NEW_LINE;
end TEST_RANDOM;
```

Furthermore, we could simplify the specification of the package RANDOM since neither the subtype SEED nor the procedure INITIALIZE would be needed. Instead the specification of RANDOM would be:

```
package RANDOM is

   subtype NUMBER is FLOAT range 0.0 .. 1.0;

   function NEXT_NUMBER return NUMBER;
   -- gives a random number that is greater
   -- than or equal to 0 and less than 1

end RANDOM;
```

How can we get the random number generator to be initialized automatically? One simple way, of course, is that when the variable U is declared in the body of the package RANDOM it is given a suitable initial value. However, this has one big disadvantage. Since U would then always be initialized to the same number, the random number package would generate the same sequence of random numbers each time it was used. This would mean that every time we ran a program that made use of the package RANDOM the program would behave in the same way. The program would not be particularly random.

We shall therefore make use of the possibility offered by having a sequence of statements in the package. Statements can be placed there to read a start value from the terminal. The body of the package RANDOM now looks like this:

```
with TEXT_IO, BASIC_NUM_IO;
use TEXT_IO, BASIC_NUM_IO;
package body RANDOM is

   U : NATURAL;
   K : constant := 5 ** 5;
   M : constant := 2 ** 13;

   function NEXT_NUMBER return NUMBER is
   begin
      U := U * K mod M;
      return FLOAT(U) / FLOAT(M);
   end NEXT_NUMBER;

begin
   PUT_LINE("Enter seed for random number generator");
   PUT_LINE("An odd number in the interval 1 to ");
   PUT(M - 1, WIDTH => 1); NEW_LINE;
   GET(U);
end RANDOM;
```

Observe that the package now needs access to the packages TEXT_IO and BASIC_NUM_IO. Therefore the **with** and **use** clauses for these are placed first. The main difference from the earlier version is that INITIALIZE is no longer there. Instead, there are statements in the package that read in a start value of the variable U. The question is 'When will these statements be executed?' A package body looks more or less like that of a subprogram. The statements in the body of a subprogram are, as we know, executed each time the subprogram is called. A package body is never called: all that can be called are those subprograms in the package that are declared in the package specification. Therefore a package body must work in a different way from a subprogram body. In fact, the statements in a package body are executed only once and this occurs when the program using the package is started. We can picture it in connection with the program's **with** clause.

This means that if we run the program TEST_RANDOM, the first thing that occurs is that the statements in the statement part of RANDOM will be executed. The program thus begins by writing out at the terminal:

Enter seed for random number generator
An odd number in the interval 1 to 8191

The user then writes the value at the terminal and this is entered to the variable U in the body of RANDOM. Thereafter execution in RANDOM's body terminates and the statements in the procedure TEST_RANDOM will be executed in the normal way.

▼

It should be pointed out that in Ada 95 there is a standard package ADA.NUMERICS.FLOAT_RANDOM, which contains a function, RANDOM, giving random numbers in the interval 0–1. There is also a generic standard package ADA.NUMERICS.DISCRETE_RANDOM which can generate random numbers of discrete types.

▲

8.8   Abstract data types

Earlier, we talked about a data type being characterized by the values that its objects can assume and by the operations that can be carried out on them. The allowed values for a particular type are decided when the type declaration is made, and there are also some standard types, such as CHARACTER and INTEGER, for which the allowed values are specified. As for possible operations, we have seen that for the simple types there are a number of standard operations, such as addition and multiplication. For more complicated types that we construct ourselves, such as array types and record types of various kinds, only comparison operators are normally automatically defined, but we can create new operators for such types by writing subprograms. For example, we have already made functions that add vectors and matrices. It is thus possible, using type declarations and subprograms, to build up whole new types where the permitted values are defined by type declarations and the possible operations are defined by subprograms. Such a type, built up by the programmer, is called an **abstract data type**.

When an abstract data type is constructed, the type declarations and the subprograms that can operate on objects of the type belong together logically; together they define the abstract data type. It is therefore appropriate to combine them into a unit in the program. A package can be constructed containing everything that describes the abstract data type.

In mathematics we often work with sets. As a first example we can construct an abstract data type which describes sets of characters. We want to be able to perform the usual operations on sets, namely: insert an element into a set, remove an element from a set, see if a set contains a particular element, construct the intersection and the union of two sets, and determine if one set is a subset of another set.

Let us start by seeing how a set can be represented in Ada. We will be looking only at sets of characters (that is, having type CHARACTER), and if we consider a particular set, then it is true of each character that either it belongs to the set or it does not belong to the set. Thus we can represent a set by an array of components of type BOOLEAN, with one component for every character, using an array indexed with type CHARACTER. If we call the type SET we can make the declaration:

```
type SET is array (CHARACTER) of BOOLEAH;
```

If we declare a variable S of type SET:

```
S : SET;
```

the component for a specific character in S will state if that character is a member of S or not. The empty set (the set with no elements) is represented by an array in which all elements have the value FALSE.

Now we can specify a package SET_PACKAGE which describes the abstract data type for sets of characters:

```
package SET_PACKAGE is
   type SET is private;

   function EMPTY_SET return SET;
   -- returns the empty set

   function "+" (C : CHARACTER; S : SET) return SET;
   function "+" (S : SET; C : CHARACTER) return SET;
   -- inserts C into the set S
```

```
            function "–" (C : CHARACTER; S : SET) return SET;
            function "–" (S : SET; C : CHARACTER) return SET;
            -- removes C from set S

            function MEMBER (C : CHARACTER; S : SET) return BOOLEAN;
            -- determines if C is a member of S

            function "+" (S1, S2 : SET) return SET;
            -- returns the union of sets S1 and S2

            function "*" (S1, S2 : SET) return SET;
            -- returns the intersection of sets S1 and S2

            function "<=" (S1, S2 : SET) return BOOLEAN;
            -- determines if S1 is a subset (improper) of S2

            procedure PUT (M : in SET);
        -- prints all characters which are members of set S
        private
            type SET is array (CHARACTER) of BOOLEAN;
        end SET_PACKAGE;
```

In addition to the operations we have already mentioned we have specified a function which will give us an empty set and a procedure which will enable us to print out the characters which are members of a given set. Most of the operations have been specified as operators. Note that several of them are overloaded (see Section 6.6); there are three different "+" operators, the first two of which are used for inserting an element into a set, while the third is used for building the union of two sets.

There is a construct in this specification that has not been seen before. The type declaration:

```
        type SET is private;
```

makes SET into what is known as a **private type**. This means that a user of the package knows that SET is a type, but will not know *how* the type is implemented in the package. The user can declare variables and parameters of a private type, and is able to write, for example:

```
        S1, S2 : SET;
```

It is not allowed, however, for the user to specify operations that need knowledge of the exact structure of the private type. For example, it is not permitted to write:

```
        S1('X') := TRUE;      -- ERROR!
```

since that needs the knowledge that S1 is an array. The idea of abstract data types is that the package's user should only use the operations that are specified in the package specification. If the user were allowed to poke around in the variables of the abstract data type it would no longer be sure to work as intended. In the body of the package, on the other hand, the private type is completely known and may be used in any way.

Apart from the operations given in the package specification, there are just two more operations a user can apply, namely **assignment** and **comparison** for equality or inequality. A user can write, for example:

```
S1 := S2;
S1 := EMPTY_SET;
if S1 = S2 then
```

Using private types

- Variables may be declared of a private type, or parameters to a subprogram may be of a private type.
- Outside the body of the package, only the operations defined in the package specification may be used, and the operations of assignment and comparison for equality or inequality.
- Within the body of a package the package's private types may be used freely.

In the specification of SET_PACKAGE we wrote at the end what is called the **private part**:

```
private
    type SET is array (CHARACTER) of BOOLEAN;
```

In a private part, the private types that have been specified in the package are described. The private part of the package is not visible to the user's program (even though the user can, of course, read what is written there). The reason for having the private part in the package specification is that the compiler must know what the private type looks like when the user's program is compiled. (When a variable of a private type is declared, space has to be saved for it in the computer's memory, for instance.)

It should be added that it would have been possible to avoid using a private type: we could have put the complete declaration of SET into the specification of the package and not had a private part. The disadvantage of that would

---

Declaration of private data types

    package P **is**
      type T **is private**;

      ...

    private
      type T **is** *normal type specification*;

      ...

    end P;

---

be that the user would have got to know how the type SET was implemented, and would have been able to manipulate the data type directly, without employing the operations given in the package specification.

Let us look at constructing the body of the package SET_PACKAGE. First, we observe that an empty set can be described by an array in which all components have the value FALSE, and which can be expressed using the aggregate:

(**others** => FALSE)

To insert an element into a set S we just need simple assignment. The statement:

S('*') := TRUE;

for example, inserts the character '∗' into the set S. An element can be removed from a set in a similar way; to remove the character '8' from a set S we write:

S('8') := FALSE;
‘

It is easy to determine if a particular character is a member of a set S. If, for example, the expression

S('A')

has value TRUE, it means that the character 'A' is a member of S; if it has value FALSE, then 'A' is not a member of S.

In constructing the union and intersections of two sets we can make use of the fact that the logical operators **and** and **or** are more general than we have hitherto seen. These operators do not only apply for simple scalar operands of type BOOLEAN, but both operands can also be arrays with the same number of components of type BOOLEAN. The result of an operation is a new array with the same number of components, also of type BOOLEAN, as the original arrays. A couple of examples will demonstrate this best. If we have declarations:

```
type LOGIC_ARRAY is array (1 .. 4) of BOOLEAN;
LA : LOGIC_ARRAY := (TRUE, FALSE, TRUE, FALSE);
LB : LOGIC_ARRAY := (TRUE, TRUE, FALSE, FALSE);
LC, LD : LOGIC_ARRAY;
```

then we can write the statements:

```
LC := LA and LB;      -- LC will be (TRUE, FALSE, FALSE, FALSE)
LD := LA or LB;       -- LD will be (TRUE, TRUE, TRUE, FALSE)
```

It is worth noting that the logical operators **not** and **xor** are also defined for arrays with components of type BOOLEAN.

Now back to our sets of characters. The union of two sets S1 and S2 is the set comprising all the elements to be found either in S1 or in S2. The intersection of S1 and S2 is the set comprising all the elements to be found in both S1 and S2. If S1 and S2 have type SET, it is simple to construct their union and intersection:

```
S1 or S2     --gives a set which is the union of S1 and S2
S1 and S2    --gives a set which is the intersection of S1 and S2
```

To determine whether a set S1 is a subset of another set S2 we can construct the intersection of the two sets. If the intersection is equal to S1 it means that S1 contains only elements which are also in S2, and therefore S1 is a subset (an improper subset) of S2.

Now we are ready to write the body of SET_PACKAGE:

```
with TEXT_IO;
package_body SET_PACKAGE is

  function EMPTY_SET return SET is
  begin
    return (others =>  FALSE);
  end EMPTY_SET;

  function "+" (C : CHARACTER; S SET) return SET is
    R : SET:=S;
  begin
    R(C) := TRUE; return R;
  end "+";

  function "+" (S : SET; C : CHARACTER) return SET is
  begin
    return C + S;
  end "+";
```

```
function "–" (C : CHARACTER; S : SET) return SET is
  R : SET := S;
begin
  R(C) := FALSE; return R;
end "–";

function "–" (S : SET; C : CHARACTER) return SET is
begin
  return C – S;
end "–";

function MEMBER (C : CHARACTER; S : SET) return BOOLEAN is
begin
  return S(C);
end MEMBER;

function "+" (S1, S2 : SET) return SET is
begin
  return S1 or S2;
end "+";

function "*" (S1, S2 : SET) return SET is
begin
  return S1 and S2;
end "*";

function "<=" (S1, S2 : SET) return BOOLEAN is
begin
  return S1 * S2 = S1;
end "<=";

procedure PUT (S : in SET) is
begin
  for C in CHARACTER loop
    if S(C) then
      TEXT_IO.PUT(C);
    end if;
  end loop;
end PUT;
end SET_PACKAGE;
```

Now we can look at how to use the abstract data type SET in a program. Let us suppose the following clauses are at the start of the program:

```
with SET_PACKAGE, TEXT_IO;
use SET_PACKAGE, TEXT_IO;
```

We can declare the sets LETTERS and OPS:

```
LETTERS, OPS : SET := EMPTY_SET;
```

We have called the function EMPTY_SET from the package SET_PACKAGE to initialize these variables, and suitable values can be given to them by using the following statements:

```
for CHAR in 'a' .. 'z' loop
   LETTERS := LETTERS + CHAR;
end loop;
for CHAR in 'A' .. 'Z' loop
   LETTERS := LETTERS + CHAR;
end loop;
OPS := OPS + '+'; OPS := OPS + '-';
OPS := OPS + '*'; OPS := OPS + '/';
```

We are now able to read a character from the terminal and determine whether it is a letter or an operator symbol:

```
GET(T);
if MEMBER(T, LETTERS) then
   -- the character was a letter
elsif MEMBER(T, OPS) then
   -- the character was an operator symbol
else
   -- some other character
end if;
```

Finally, we will look at a program that reads two lines of text from the terminal and prints all the characters that appear in either the first or the second line, and all the characters that appear in both lines.

Input takes place using the procedure GET_LINE and the two lines that are read are placed in variables LINE1 and LINE2. We declare two sets, IN_LINE1 and IN_LINE2, where we will store all the characters from the respective lines. The program constructs the union and the intersection of the sets IN_LINE1 and IN_LINE2 and prints out the resulting sets using the procedure PUT from the package SET_PACKAGE:

```
with TEXT_IO, BASIC_NUM_IO, SET_PACKAGE;
use TEXT_IO, BASIC_NUM_IO, SET_PACKAGE;
procedure COMPARE_LINES is
   LINE1,    LINE2      : STRING(1 .. 200);
   LENGTH1, LENGTH2 : NATURAL;
   IN_LINE1, IN_LINE2   : SET := EMPTY_SET;
begin
   -- read in the two lines
```

```
            PUT_LINE ("Write two lines of text");
            GET_LINE(LINE1, LENGTH1);
            GET_LINE(LINE2, LENGTH2);
            -- Construct a set of all characters in line 1
            for I in 1 .. LENGTH1 loop
               IN_LINE1 := LINE1(I) + IN_LINE1;
            end loop;

            -- Construct a set of all characters in line 2
            for I in 1 .. LENGTH2 loop
               IN_LINE2 := LINE2(I) + IN_LINE2;
            end loop;

            PUT("The following characters appear");
            PUT(IN_LINE1 + IN_LINE2); NEW_LINE;
            PUT("The following characters appear in both the lines");
            PUT(IN_LINE1 * IN_LINE2); NEW_LINE;
         end COMPARE_LINES;
```

▼

In most situations it is natural to allow a package to contain only one abstract data type and its operations, as in our example. However, it is possible to place several declarations in one and the same package. For example, several abstract data types which belong together in some way can be put into a single package, and a package can even contain other sorts of declaration. If a **use** clause for a package is used in a program, then, as we have seen, everything in the package becomes visible in the program without having to use point notation. This is sometimes undesirable: you sometimes want to retain point notation for clarity. In Ada 95 it is possible to make only a certain abstract data type and its operations visible. If, for example, there is a package MY_PACKAGE, which contains, among other things, definitions of an abstract data type ABS_TYPE, then the following clauses can be given:

```
      with MY_PACKAGE;
      use type MY_PACKAGE.ABS_TYPE;
```

Then only the type ABS_TYPE and its operations will be directly visible in the program; if anything else defined in MY_PACKAGE is to be used then it has to
▲   be referred to using point notation.

For the next example of an abstract data type we will study a **queue**, or more precisely a queue of characters. You should be able to insert characters into a queue and remove them in the order they were inserted. We will also want to determine whether a queue is empty. Thus the operations we will want for the abstract data type QUEUE are PUT_IN, TAKE_OUT and EMPTY.

To implement a queue we will use a character array inside the package, that is, an array of type STRING. The simplest way to implement a queue is by

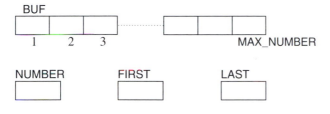

Figure 8.1

using an array and putting the first element of the queue in the first position in the array, the second element in the second position and so on. It is rather inefficient, however, because you have to shift all the elements one place to the left each time an element is removed. For this reason we will employ an alternative technique, usually known as the **circular buffer**. We will use an array BUF where the elements of the queue are stored. Apart from this array we will have three integers, NUMBER, FIRST and LAST, to store the current number of elements in the queue, and the indexes of the elements of the array holding the first and the last elements in the queue, respectively. Figure 8.1 illustrates this.

Thus the implementation of a queue consists of four components, an array and three integers, and we can put them in a record:

```
type QUEUE is
      record
          BUF        : STRING(1 .. MAX_NUMBER);
          NUMBER  : NATURAL     := 0;
          FIRST      : POSITIVE    := 1;
          LAST       : POSITIVE    := MAX_NUMBER;
      end record;
```

We have also given initial values to the components in this record declaration, so that a variable of type QUEUE will always be initialized on declaration.

Now we are able to specify a package, QUEUE_PACKAGE, which describes the abstract data type QUEUE:

```
package QUEUE_PACKAGE is
   type QUEUE is limited private;
   procedure PUT_IN      (Q : in out QUEUE; C : in CHARACTER);
   procedure TAKE_OUT (Q : in out QUEUE; C : in CHARACTER);
   function EMPTY        (Q in QUEUE) return BOOLEAN;
private
   MAX_NUMBER : constant := 1000;
   type QUEUE is
     record
```

```
            BUF         : STRING(1 .. MAX_NUMBER);
            NUMBER      : NATURAL := 0;
            FIRST       : POSITIVE := 1;
            LAST        : POSITIVE := MAX_NUMBER;
        end record;
    end QUEUE_PACKAGE;
```

The exact declaration of the type has been placed in the private part of the package. Observe that further declarations can be put in the package's private part if required. The type QUEUE is private, as was the type SET in the previous example. There is, however, a small but important difference. As the word **limited** implies, its presence in the declaration makes the type QUEUE into a limited private type. From the SET example, we saw that in a normal private type the only operations the user can do are assignment and comparison, and limited private types differ from these in that not even assignment and comparison are allowed. (Of course, for both kinds of private type the user is allowed to use the operations which are defined in the package specification.)

Limited private types

    type T is limited private;

For such a type, neither assignment nor comparison is permitted outside the body of the package.

Assume that the user has declared two variables Q1 and Q2 of type QUEUE. The statements

```
    Q1 := Q2;          -- ERROR! limited private type
    if Q1 = Q2 then    -- ERROR! limited private type
```

are not allowed. The reason we have chosen to make the type QUEUE limited private is that, if comparison were allowed, it would give incorrect results. That two queues are equal means, logically, that they are of the same length and contain the same elements. Two queues which are logically equal can, however, be stored differently in the abstract data type QUEUE. To demonstrate this, assume that Q1 and Q2 have the same lengths and contain identical elements but are shifted with respect to one another so that the first elements do not lie in the same positions in the arrays. If Q1 and Q2 were compared, they would be found to be different, in spite of their logical equality.

When you construct an abstract data type you can give your own equality operator (see Section 6.9). In QUEUE_PACKAGE, for example, the operation = can be added:

```
function "=" (Q1, Q2 : QUEUE) return BOOLEAN;
```

But note that you may not declare your own inequality operator /=; this is declared automatically as a result of declaring the operator =.

Let us look at the body of the QUEUE package.

```
with TEXT_IO;
use TEXT_IO;
package body QUEUE_PACKAGE is
  procedure PUT_IN(Q : in out QUEUE; C : in CHARACTER) is
  begin
    if Q.NUMBER < MAX_NUMBER then
      Q.LAST := Q.LAST mod MAX_NUMBER + 1;
      Q.BUF(Q.LAST) := C;
      Q.NUMBER := Q.NUMBER + 1;
    else
      PUT_LINE("The queue is full!");
    end if;
  end PUT_IN;

  procedure TAKE_OUT(Q : in out QUEUE; C : out CHARACTER);
  begin
    if Q.NUMBER > 0 then
      C := Q.BUF(Q.FIRST);
      Q.FIRST := Q.FIRST mod MAX_NUMBER + 1;
      Q.NUMBER := Q.NUMBER - 1;
    else
      PUT_LINE("The queue is empty!");
    end if;
  end TAKE_OUT;

  function EMPTY(Q : in QUEUE) return BOOLEAN;
  begin
    return Q.NUMBER = 0;
  end EMPTY;
end QUEUE_PACKAGE;
```

The function EMPTY is simplest: a queue is empty if the number of elements in it is zero. The procedures PUT_IN and TAKE_OUT take a bit more thought. Both procedures have an error check so that a message is returned if you try to add an element to a full queue or remove an element from an empty queue. When an element is to be added to a queue, the statement:

```
Q.LAST := Q.LAST mod MAX_NUMBER + 1;
```

is executed in the procedure PUT_IN. If Q.LAST has a value which is less than MAX_NUMBER, then this statement simply means that Q.LAST is increased by

1, and if Q.LAST has the value MAX_NUMBER, then Q.LAST will take the value 1. Note that the initial value of Q.LAST is MAX_NUMBER, so that the first time an element is put into the queue, Q.LAST will take the value 1. There is a corresponding statement in the procedure TAKE_OUT which ensures that Q.FIRST also lies within the permitted interval.

There follows an example of a program which uses the abstract data type QUEUE, first to read in 100 characters from the keyboard and then to write them out in the same order:

```
with TEXT_IO, QUEUE_PACKAGE;
use TEXT_IO, QUEUE_PACKAGE;
procedure QUEUE_EXAMPLE is
   CHAR_QUEUE : QUEUE;
   CH              : CHARACTER;
begin
   for I in 1 .. 100 loop
      GET(CH);
      PUT_IN(CHAR_QUEUE, CH);
   end loop;
   NEW_L1NE(2);
   for I in 1 .. 100 loop
      TAKE_OUT(CHARQUEUE, CH);
      PUT(CH);
   end loop;
end QUEUE_EXAMPLE;
```

Now we have constructed two abstract data types, SET and QUEUE, and we should look at an interesting difference of principle between them. If we consider the operations that exist for the data type SET we see that, apart from the printing operation PUT, there are only functions and no procedures. There are no operations which can *change* an existing set. We can look at the example of adding the character 'a' to a set S by writing the statement:

```
S := S + 'a';
```

The function "+" does not change S; what it does is to work out a new set S and return the new set as the result. (The fact that S changes anyway is a result of the assignment operation in the user's program.) We can call this a **functional** approach to abstract data types. All operations get *values* of the abstract data type as arguments and produce as results *new* values of the abstract data type. There are no operators that can *change* a variable of the abstract data type. This is analogous to the view of ordinary mathematics. If, for example, a and b are two numbers, then the expression $a + b$ means that a new number is computed and that the value of the new number is equal to the sum of a's value and b's value; a and b do not change.

This functional approach is elegant and well suited to data types of a mathematical nature. On the other hand, it is not always so efficient. If we look again at the statement:

```
S := S + 'a';
```

we can see that two copies must be made of the whole array we are using in order to implement the type SET. The first copy is made when the function "+" is called, when it gets a copy of the value of S as argument, and the second copy is made when the variable S is assigned to the result. (A clever compiler, however, can avoid making the first of these copies by sending a reference to S as parameter to "+".)

Instead of copying the values of abstract data types in and out of functions it is often more natural to employ an alternative approach, which we can call an **object-oriented** approach. Now variables of a particular abstract data type are considered as objects – things – which have certain properties and at any instant have a particular internal state. The operations for an abstract data type are allowed to *affect* an object so that its internal state changes. This approach leads to more efficient programs.

Our abstract data type QUEUE is implemented with an object-oriented approach. When we want to add an element to a queue Q we make the call:

```
PUT_IN(Q, 'a');
```

What happens is that the procedure PUT_IN gets a reference to the object Q as argument. Then the procedure makes a change directly in Q so that its internal state changes. We no longer need to make copies of the whole queue.

As a final example of abstract data types we will discuss the type TIME, which is defined as a package called CALENDAR. It is included in the Ada standard and is to be found in all installations of Ada. The package looks like this:

```
package CALENDAR is
  type TIME is private;
  subtype YEAR_NUMBER   is INTEGER   range 1901 .. 2099;
  subtype MONTH_NUMBER  is INTEGER   range 1 .. 12;
  subtype DAY_NUMBER    is INTEGER   range 1 .. 31;
  subtype DAY_DURATION  is DURATION  range 0.0 .. 86_400.00;

  function CLOCK return TIME;
  function YEAR      (DATE : TIME) return YEAR_NUMBER;
  function MONTH     (DATE : TIME) return MONTH_NUMBER;
  function DAY       (DATE : TIME) return DAY_NUMBER;
  function SECONDS   (DATE : TIME) return DAY_DURATION;
```

```
procedure SPLIT (DATE      : in TIME;
                 YEAR      : out YEAR_NUMBER;
                 MONTH     : out MONTH_NUMBER;
                 DAY       : out DAY_NUMBER;
                 SECONDS   : out DAY_DURATION);

function TIME_OF (YEAR     : YEAR_NUMBER;
                  MONTH    : MONTH_NUMBER;
                  DAY      : DAY_NUMBER;


function "+"(LEFT : TIME;       RIGHT : DURATION) return TIME;
function "+"(LEFT : DURATION; RIGHT : TIME)       return TIME;
function "−"(LEFT : TIME;       RIGHT : DURATION) return TIME;
function "−"(LEFT : TIME;       RIGHT : TIME)     return
                                                  DURATION;

function "<"  (LEFT, RIGHT : TIME) return BOOLEAN;
function "<=" (LEFT, RIGHT : TIME) return BOOLEAN;
function ">"  (LEFT, RIGHT : TIME) return BOOLEAN;
function ">=" (LEFT, RIGHT : TIME) return BOOLEAN;

TIME_ERROR : exception;
-- can be raised by TIME_OF, "+" and "−"
private
-- implementation-dependent
end CALENDAR;
```

TIME is an abstract data type which gives the current moment in time, consisting of both the date and the time of day. You can get the current moment of time, both date and time, by calling the function CLOCK:

```
NOW : TIME := CLOCK;
```

If you want only a particular part of it you can use any of the functions YEAR, MONTH, DAY or SECONDS, as in:

```
PUT("This year is "); PUT(YEAR(NOW));
```

The function SECONDS gives the number of seconds that have passed since midnight. The type DURATION is a standard type, defined in the package STANDARD: it is a fixed-point type and is used in the CALENDAR package to give intervals of time, expressed in whole seconds. The time is measured with an accuracy of at least 20 milliseconds.

Alternatively, the function SPLIT can be used to pick out all of the parts of the time and date at once. It is also possible to construct a new date and time using the function TIME_OF:

```
NEXT_YEAR : TIME := TIME_OF(YEAR(NOW) + 1, 1, 1);
```

The operator "+" can be used for adding a time interval to the date and time, and the operator "−" can be used either to remove an interval of time from a date and time or to calculate the length of an interval. There are also operators for comparing dates and times.

The following program writes out the current date and time. The date is printed in the form 19YY-MM-DD and the time in the form HH:MM:SS.

```
with TEXT_IO, BASIC_NUM_IO, CALENDAR;
use TEXT_IO, BASIC_NUM_IO, CALENDAR;
procedure TIME_EX is
  NOW : TIME := CLOCK;
begin
  PUT(YEAR(NOW),      WIDTH => 4); PUT('_');
  PUT(MONTH(NOW),     WIDTH => 2); PUT('-');
  PUT(DAY(NOW),       WIDTH => 2); NEW_LINE;
  PUT(INTEGER(SECONDS(NOW)) / 3600,      WIDTH => 2); PUT(':');
  PUT(INTEGER(SECONDS(NOW)) rem 3600 / 60, WIDTH => 2); PUT(':');
  PUT(INTEGER(SECONDS(NOW)) rem 60 ,     WIDTH => 2);
                                         NEW_LINE;
end TIME_EX;
```

8.9 Child packages

In Ada 95, a hierarchical library structure has been adopted that makes it possible to define packages and subprograms which are children to packages defined earlier. Here we will discuss how to create child libraries, starting with an example. Suppose we want to use the abstract data type QUEUE_PACKAGE from the previous section, but it turns out that we also need an operation LENGTH which gives the number of elements in a queue. There is no such operation defined in the package QUEUE_PACKAGE, and one possible solution would be to change the package and add the necessary operation. There is one big disadvantage to this, however. Imagine that the package QUEUE_PACKAGE has been in existence for some time and that both we and others have used it in many other compilation units. If we change QUEUE_PACKAGE then all these compilation units would suddenly become invalid and all of them would need to be recompiled, despite the fact that none of them uses the operation LENGTH. Even worse, it could happen that a compilation unit that was correct before could become incorrect, maybe because of a name clash with the new operation.

In Ada 95 there is a better solution to this problem: we create a **child package** with the name QUEUE_PACKAGE.EXTRA:

```
package QUEUE_PACKAGE.EXTRA is
  function LENGTH(Q : QUEUE) return NATURAL;
end QUEUE_PACKAGE.EXTRA;
```

It can be seen that this package is a child of QUEUE_PACKAGE from the point in its name. The first part of the package name is the name of the parent package and the second part, after the point, is the name of the child. It should be noted that both the parent package and the child package must be so-called **library units**, that is, they must appear on the outermost level of the program.

One special aspect of a child package is that both in its private part (if there is one) and in its body there is access to the declarations that were made in the private part of the parent package. This means that when we write the body of QUEUE_PACKAGE.EXTRA we know the exact implementation of queues and can make use of it:

```
package body QUEUE_PACKAGE.EXTRA is
  function LENGTH(Q : QUEUE) return NATURAL is
  begin
    return Q.NUMBER;
  end;
end QUEUE_PACKAGE.EXTRA;
```

We would not have been allowed to do this if the new package had been a normal package which referred to QUEUE_PACKAGE with a **with** clause. In that case, it would not have been known that the type QUEUE was a record type with a component NUMBER.

To use the new child library we can now write:

```
with QUEUE_PACKAGE.EXTRA;
procedure QUEUE_USER is
  Q: QUEUE_PACKAGE.QUEUE;
begin
  ...
  if QUEUE_PACKAGE.EXTRA.LENGTH(K) > 100 then
  ...
end QUEUE_USER;
```

The **with** clause ensures that *both* packages QUEUE_PACKAGE and QUEUE_PACKAGE.EXTRA are accessible. If we had only written

```
with QUEUE_PACKAGE;
```

then *only* the package QUEUE_PACKAGE would have been accessible and the user's program would have had not the least knowledge of the existence of the child package. This means that all the compilation units that include only QUEUE_PACKAGE in their **with** clause remain completely unaffected by our definition of a child package, and they do not need recompilation. The rules for **with** clauses are formulated in this way so that it is always possible to see directly from the **with** clause of a compilation unit which library units are required.

If you want to use **use** clauses to make the declarations in the package's specification directly visible, this too is possible. We can write:

```
with QUEUE_PACKAGE.EXTRA;
use QUEUE_PACKAGE; use EXTRA;
procedure QUEUE_USER is
   Q : QUEUE;
begin
   ...
   if LENGTH(K) > 100 then
   ...
   end QUEUE_USER;
```

Note that if we had written instead:

```
with QUEUE_PACKAGE.EXTRA;
use QUEUE_PACKAGE.EXTRA;
```

then the declarations in QUEUE_PACKAGE.EXTRA would have been directly visible, but not the declarations of the parent library, QUEUE_PACKAGE.

When you are using a child library, you can think logically of its declaration being placed right at the end of the specification of the parent library, after the private part. This means that if we had written:

```
with QUEUE_PACKAGE.EXTRA;
use QUEUE_PACKAGE;
```

then the delcarations in QUEUE_PACKAGE would naturally have been directly visible. The **package name** EXTRA would itself have also been visible, but nothing which was declared *within* the package QUEUE_PACKAGE.EXTRA, in its specification, would have been directly visible.

A child package can, in its turn, have children. For example, it is possible to construct a new package, QUEUE_PACKAGE.EXTRA.MORE:

```
package QUEUE_PACKAGE.EXTRA.MORE is
   function FIRST (Q : QUEUE) return CHARACTER;
   function LAST  (Q : QUEUE) return CHARACTER;
end QUEUE_PACKAGE.EXTRA.MORE;
```

This package specifies two functions which enable the user to see which elements are first and last in the queue. If you want to use this package in your program, you use the clauses:

```
with QUEUE_PACKAGE.EXTRA.MORE;
use QUEUE_PACKAGE; use EXTRA; use MORE;
```

It is also possible to create several child packages with the same parent. For example, we can define another child package to QUEUE_PACKAGE:

```
package QUEUE_PACKAGE.EXTRA2 is
   procedure PUT(Q : QUEUE);
end QUEUE_PACKAGE.EXTRA2;
```

This package contains a procedure which prints out the contents of a queue. The two child packages EXTRA and EXTRA2 are totally independent of one another and do not even know of one another's existence. However, a package can refer to a relative in a **with** clause, on condition that the relative's specification has been compiled in advance. (There are certain limitations for a so-called private child; see below.) If, for example, we had wanted to make use of EXTRA in either the specification or the body of EXTRA2, we could have included the clause:

```
with QUEUE_PACKAGE.EXTRA;
```

In Ada 95, in fact, all packages (which are library units) are child packages. If you define an ordinary package, one whose name does not include a parent name, then it is actually considered to be a child package of the STANDARD package. In this way, packages form a tree structure, with STANDARD as the tree's root.

In the example with QUEUE_PACKAGE we have seen that child libraries can be used to construct new operations for abstract data types. In Chapter 14, which takes up object-oriented programming, we will show how child packages can be used in conjunction with **expandable types** (called **tagged types**) to build up abstract data types with yet further properties.

The second large area of use for child packages is in the construction of **subsystems**. When a large program is to be written, consisting of many separately compiled packages and subprograms, it is necessary to be able to divide the program up into a number of clearly delimited subsystems. Each subsystem should have clearly defined tasks, and there should be clear **interfaces** between the various subsystems. Each subsystem consists internally of a number of packages that belong together. The packages *within* a particular subsystem need to know about one another and to be able to refer to one another using **with** clauses. Each subsystem, on the other hand, needs to be encapsulated so that the packages used internally to the subsystem are not visible *outside* the subsystem.

You want only one (or a small number) of the packages of a subsystem to make up the interface and be outwardly visible.

This can be achieved by using what are called **private child units**, and we can look at an outline example. Suppose that we want to construct a subsystem for graphic presentation. First we declare a package: GRAPHICS_ PACKAGE, which will be parent to all the packages in the subsystem:

```
package GRAPHICS_PACKAGE is
   ...
private
-- Common internal declarations for the subsystem
   ...
end GRAPHICS_PACKAGE;
```

In the private part there can be declarations of types and so on which are common to all the packages of the subsystem. By subsystem is meant all the packages which have a common ancestor, as well as the parent itself. In our example, the subsystem consists of GRAPHICS_PACKAGE and all the packages that have GRAPHICS_PACKAGE as parent or ancestor.

We can construct a special child library called INTERFACE, which contains the subsystem's interface with other subsystems:

```
package GRAPHICS_PACKAGE.INTERFACE is
   ...
end GRAPHICS_PACKAGE.INTERFACE;
```

(It is not essential to have a special package for the interface: it could equally be placed directly in the package GRAPHICS_PACKAGE.)

The actual implementation of subsystems is accomplished with the help of a number of internal help packages, which we can call INTERN_1, INTERN_2, etc. These packages are specified as follows:

```
private package GRAPHICS_PACKAGE.INTERN_1 is
   ...
end GRAPHICS_PACKAGE.INTERN_1;
```

Note that the declaration of package INTERN_1 starts with the word **private**: INTERN_1 is a *private* child library of GRAPHICS_PACKAGE. The declarations that are made in the private part of the parent package are always visible to the (whole) specification and body of a private child library.

A private child library can never be made visible outside the subsystem by using a **with** clause. Nor is a private child library visible in the *specification* of a non-private package which is included in the subsystem. In this example, this means that the packages INTERN_1, INTERN_2, etc. can be made visible in the bodies (but not in the specifications) of GRAPHICS_PACKAGE and

GRAPHICS_PACKAGE.INTERFACE. The body of the latter, for instance, could have the following outline:

```
with GRAPHICS_PACKAGE.INTERN_1,
     GRAPHICS_PACKAGE.INTERN_2, ... ;
package body GRAPHICS_PACKAGE.INTERFACE is

  ...

end GRAPHICS_PACKAGE.INTERFACE;
```

The only packages belonging to the graphics system which are outwardly visible are GRAPHICS_PACKAGE and GRAPHICS_PACKAGE.INTERFACE. A user program which makes use of the graphics system could have the following form:

```
with GRAPHICS_PACKAGE.INTERFACE;
use GRAPHICS_PACKAGE.INTERFACE;
procedure USER is

  ...

end USER;
```

It is possible to rename a child package, by compiling a line such as the following:

```
package GRAPHICS renames GRAPHICS_PACKAGE.INTERFACE;
```

The package GRAPHICS will, from the user's perspective, be seen as an ordinary package; the user will not be aware that GRAPHICS is in fact a child package. Thus one can write:

```
with GRAPHICS;
use GRAPHICS;
procedure USER is

  ...

end USER;
```

Only the package GRAPHICS (that is, GRAPHICS_PACKAGE.INTER-FACE) will be accessible: the parent package GRAPHICS_PACKAGE remains unknown to the user.

8.10   Standard packages in Ada 95

In Ada 95 child libraries have been used to organize all the different standard packages. (There are approximately 65 such packages.) Three different parent packages have been defined: ADA, INTERFACES and SYSTEM. All other standard library units are children of these three packages. As was pointed out in the previous section, all library units without a parent are considered to be children of the package STANDARD. Therefore, the three parent libraries are all in their turn children of STANDARD. The library units form a tree with the following structure:

STANDARD

ADA INTERFACES SYSTEM

...   .

(For a complete definition of all library units we refer to the reference manual.) Most library units, the packages TEXT_IO, CALENDAR and NUMERICS, for instance, are to be found in the subtree under ADA.

In Ada 83 there are no child packages and no tree structure. All packages have simple names. We write, for example:

with TEXT_IO;

In Ada 95 we should in fact write:

with ADA.TEXT_IO;

since TEXT_IO is a child package of ADA. However, Ada 95 is meant to be upward compatible with Ada 83. This means that a legal Ada 83 program should also be a legal Ada 95 program. Therefore, in Ada 95 declarations are added to rename the library units that were defined in Ada 83. One example of such a renaming declaration is:

package TEXT_IO **renames** ADA.TEXT_IO;

The following library units have also been renamed so that they can be referred to with a simple name: CALENDAR, SEQUENTIAL_IO, DIRECT_IO, IO_EXCEPTIONS, UNCHECKED_CONVERSION, UNCHECKED_DEALLO-CATION and MACHINE_CODE.
▲

EXERCISES

8.1   Write a package that contains the temperature constants:

boiling point of oxygen (at 1 atm)	=	−182.97 °C
boiling point of sulphur (at 1 atm)	=	444.60 °C
melting point of silver (at 1 atm)	=	960.5 °C
melting point of gold (at 1 atm)	=	1063 °C

8.2   Write a package SOLID_GEOMETRY that contains aids for calculating the volumes and areas of a number of common shapes:

$V = \pi r^2 h$	volume of a cylinder with radius r and height h
$A = 2\pi r(r+h)$	surface area of a cylinder with radius r and height h
$V = \dfrac{1}{3}\pi r^2 h$	volume of a circular cone with base radius r and height k
$A = \pi r(r + \sqrt{r^2 + h^2})$	surface area of a circular cone with base radius r and height h
$V = \dfrac{4}{3}\pi r^3$	volume of a sphere with radius r
$A = 4\pi r^2$	surface area of a sphere with radius r

8.3   Write a package that contains the ordinary trigonometric functions sin, cos, tan and cot. The following Maclaurin series are given:

$$\sin(x) = x - \frac{x^3}{3!} + \frac{x^5}{5!} - \frac{x^7}{7!} + \cdots$$

$$\cos(x) = 1 - \frac{x^2}{2!} + \frac{x^4}{4!} - \frac{x^6}{6!} + \cdots$$

8.4   Write a package that deals cards randomly from an ordinary pack of cards. In the package there should be a function DEAL that returns a card when called. The package must keep track internally of what cards are dealt out, so that each card in the pack is dealt only once. There should be a procedure SHUFFLE that can be called each time the pack has to be shuffled and a new deal started. Use the package RANDOM from Section 8.7.

Use the package to write a program that lets the user play a hand of 21 with the computer. The game involves the user receiving one card at a time and then deciding whether or not to take another. The aim is to try to get the total value of the cards as close as possible to 21, without going above. An ace can count as either 1 or 14. If the user gets more than 21, he or she goes 'bust' and the computer has won. If the user sticks at less than 21 the computer can also draw one card at a time and decide whether or not to continue after each card. (One strategy the computer can adopt is to continue for as long as its cards total less than 16.) If the computer goes bust, the user wins. Otherwise the winner is the one with the higher total. If the user and the computer stick at the same totals, then the computer wins. After each hand the computer writes out the winner and asks the user if he or she would like another game.

8.5   Section 2.3 described a method of writing outsize letters on an ordinary terminal. Write a package that can be used to write such giant letters. It should be possible to write several giant letters on a horizontal line at the terminal. The package should thus keep track internally of each line of letters. The following procedures should be present in the package:

WRITE(C)   Put the character C in the first vacant place in the line of giant letters. If the current line is full it should be written out and C placed at the start of a new line.

WRITE_LINE   Write out the current line of giant letters.

8.6   Modern personal computers have built-in tools for producing graphics on the screen, but simple pictures can be drawn even on old-fashioned terminals and printers. In these cases, a picture is built up in the form of a matrix in which each element is a character. The number of rows in the matrix is the number of rows on the screen (or an arbitrary number for a printer) and the number of columns can be the maximum length of a row. Initially, all the elements of the matrix can be blank characters and then the picture can be built up by filling in certain elements in a suitable way. When the picture is ready, the entire matrix is printed out either on the screen or at the printer.

Write a graphics package that can be used to draw simple pictures in the way described. The following procedures should be present in the package:

INIT(R,C)   Set the number of rows in the picture to R and the number of columns to C. Put blank characters in the whole matrix and set the current position to row 1, column 1.

MOVE(P)   Move the current position to point P without drawing.

LINE(P)   Draw a line from the current position to point P. The new current position is then P.

CHAR(C)   Put character C at the current position.

RECT(H,B)   Draw a rectangle with height H and breadth B with its lower left-hand corner at the current position. The current position does not change.

DRAW   The picture is drawn out at the terminal.

8.7   When a program writes out several pages on a printer it is often desirable to have a title, for example, a chapter name, at the top of each page. A page number may also be required at the bottom of every page. In the package TEXT_IO there are facilities for keeping track of the current page number, but this can also be achieved by writing a package of your own.

Write a package that prints a title at the top of every page and a page number at the bottom. The title and page number should be centred. After the title line and before the page number line there should be two extra blank lines. In the packages should be the procedures:

INIT(L,P)   Set the line length to L characters and the page length to P lines. The current title is set to blank characters and the current page number is set to 1.

TITLE(TEXT)	The current title is set to TEXT.
PAGE_NR(N)	The current page number is set to N.
NU_LINE	If the end of the page has not been reached, NEW_LINE is called. If the end has been reached, the page number is printed at the bottom of the page, a new page is started and the title is printed at the top.

When the package is used in a program the procedures NEW_LINE or PUT_LINE in TEXT_IO should not be called. Instead, the procedure NU_LINE should be called.

8.8   Rational numbers can be written as fractions where both numerator and denominator are integers. Write a package that provides facilities for working with the abstract data type *rational number*. The aim is to create a rational number from two integers, and to extract both the numerator and the denominator from the rational number. In the package there should be functions for adding, subtracting, multiplying and dividing rational numbers, and procedures for reading in and writing out rational numbers.

   The package should ensure that the rational numbers given as a result are in their simplest forms: the numerator and denominator should have no common factor. Furthermore, there should never be a negative denominator.

8.9   Section 8.8 showed how the abstract data type set of characters could be built up using a package SET_PACKAGE. Write a package that can be used to build up the abstract data type set of integers instead.

   The number of possible numbers in a set of integers is so great that for practical reasons it is not possible to use the technique used in SET_PACKAGE. To represent a set of integers it is possible, for example, to use an integer array in which the integers from the set are placed.

9 Input and Output

Large parts of most programs generally consist of statements concerning reading and writing data; to write programs that communicate well with the user, it is therefore important to be aware of the facilities that help with this. In Ada, these facilities are found as subprograms in the standard package TEXT_IO and some of them have been used extensively in previous chapters. A summary of these subprograms will be given in this chapter, to provide a more complete picture of the possibilities available. First, reading and writing via the terminal will be treated in greater detail. Then, **text files** will be introduced as a generalization of input and output, enabling a program to read from and write to other external units and store data permanently in the computer's secondary storage.

9.1 Output at the terminal

We shall start by looking at the facilities for producing output at the terminal. A terminal consists of two separate units: the keyboard, which is an input device, and the screen or printer, which is an output device. All output to a terminal that occurs in a program affects only its output device; all input via a terminal affects only its input device, the keyboard.

When a key is pressed at the keyboard the character is sent to the program and read, but a terminal is usually coupled to the screen in such a way that the character is also output there. For example, if the character A is typed at the terminal keyboard, then A is usually displayed on the screen. It is important to realize that the character A is not output from the program. It is called an **echo** of what has been typed at the keyboard. What is seen on the screen thus becomes a mixture of what is written out by the program and the echoes of what the user writes at the keyboard.

9.1.1 Page and line structure

The output that occurs at the terminal consists, logically, of a number of pages, irrespective of whether it is displayed on a screen or printed on paper. Each page of output comprises a certain number of lines and each line comprises a certain number of characters. Each page ends with a **page terminator** and each line with a **line terminator**. Neither of these markers is seen in the output itself. They most often consist of unprintable control characters that are sent from the computer to the terminal. When the terminal receives a page terminator, it reacts by shifting the output on to a new page, and when it receives a line terminator it moves the output to a new line. The exact appearance of the different markers depends on the individual computer system, but the Ada programmer need not be concerned with this. Page and line terminators are sent to the terminal by subprograms in TEXT_IO.

A call to the procedure NEW_PAGE causes a page terminator to be sent to the terminal. There are no parameters to the procedure and it is called simply by writing:

```
NEW_PAGE;
```

One way to send a line terminator to the terminal, and thus get a new line in the output, is to use the procedure NEW_LINE, and this is specified in the package TEXT_IO as follows:

```
procedure NEW_LINE (SPACING : in POSITIVE_COUNT := 1);
```

The procedure has one parameter called SPACING which has type POSITIVE_COUNT. POSITIVE_COUNT is a subtype of the integer type COUNT. In TEXT_IO there are the declarations:

```
type COUNT is range 0 .. implementation-dependent_integer,
subtype POSITIVE_COUNT is COUNT range 1 .. COUNT'LAST;
```

COUNT is thus an integer type with permitted values in the interval 0 to an integer that depends on the implementation and which is often large. POSITIVE_COUNT comprises all the integers in COUNT except 0.

The parameter SPACING specifies the number of line terminators to be sent to the terminal, that is, the number of lines that the output should move forward. For example, to move the output on three lines, the call:

```
NEW_LINE(3);
```

is used.

If the parameter given is not an integer literal but a variable or an expression, then it must be of the subtype POSITIVE_COUNT. For example, it is possible to declare the variable LINE_STEP:

```
LINE_STEP : POSITIVE_COUNT;
```

and use this in the call:

```
NEW_LINE(LINE_STEP);
```

Another possibility is to make a specific type conversion:

```
NEW_LINE( POSITIVE_COUNT(N) ); -- where N has the type INTEGER
```

NEW_LINE can also be called with no parameter. In this case, the parameter SPACING automatically takes the value 1 (as seen from the specification above) and the output is moved on one line.

Page and line changes
```
        NEW_PAGE;
```
gives a new page in the output.
```
        NEW_LINE(N);
```
moves the output N lines on.
```
        NEW_LINE;
```
moves the output on one line.

Another way of sending a line terminator to the terminal and ensuring that a line change occurs, is to use the procedure PUT_LINE when text is written.

The third way of causing a line change is by stating the length of line required and thereafter letting the Ada system start a new line automatically when one line is full. The required line length can be stated by calling the procedure SET_LINE_LENGTH, which has the specification:

procedure SET_LINE_LENGTH (TO : **in** COUNT);

The call:

SET_LINE_LENGTH(60);

for example, means that the maximum line length will be 60 characters. The package TEXT_IO always keeps track of how far the current line of output has got along the line. Before each output occurs, TEXT_IO checks whether it will fit into the space remaining on the line. If there is not room for the output, then a new line is automatically generated before the output is sent. We shall show how this can be utilized in writing out a table:

```
SET_LINE_LENGTH(30);
for I in 1 .. 20 loop
   PUT(I ** 2, WIDTH => 5);
end loop;
```

These lines of program cause the squares of the numbers from 1 to 20 to be written in a table with six numbers on each row and five positions for each number. The output is as follows:

```
  1    4    9   16   25   36
 49   64   81  100  121  144
169  196  225  256  289  324
361  400
```

We see that the parameter to SET_LINE_LENGTH has type COUNT, not POSITIVE_COUNT. This means that the value 0 is also allowed as a line length. This is a special case that can be interpreted as 'there is no maximum line length'. That is, there is no limit to the length of the lines of output. (Of course, no terminal can cope with this. Some terminals 'stick' at the right-hand side if a line is too long, while others feed a new line automatically. But, from the program's point of view, lines can be indefinitely long.) If nothing is specified in the program, then the line length is assumed to be 0, that is, there is no limit to the length of a line.

If it is necessary to determine the current line length in a program, the function LINE_LENGTH can be called. It returns the current line length as its result.

function LINE_LENGTH **return** COUNT;

In an analogous way, a maximum page length can also be set by calling the procedure SET_PAGE_LENGTH.

procedure SET_PAGE_LENGTH (TO : **in** COUNT);

The call:

SET_PAGE_LENGTH(48);

for example, sets the maximum size of page to 48 lines. The package TEXT_IO keeps track of the current line position on the page and if output of more than 48 lines is attempted there is an automatic change to a new page of output.

For page lengths, the special value 0 also means there is no limit to the number of lines on a page. If no other value is given in a program then the value 0 is assumed. The function PAGE_LENGTH:

function PAGE_LENGTH **return** COUNT;

can be called to determine what size of page is currently specified.

Maximum size of line and page

SET_PAGE_LENGTH(N);

set maximum page length to N lines.

SET_LINE_LENGTH(M);

set maximum line length to M columns.

Special case: If N (or M) is 0, then a boundless maximum page (or line) length is assumed.

PAGE_LENGTH

function call that returns the current maximum page length.

LINE_LENGTH

function call that returns the current maximum line length.

There are functions that can be used to find out how far the output has progressed. The function PAGE gives the current page number as its result (numbering starts at 1). The function LINE gives the number of the line to which output is currently being sent and the function COL gives the column number for the next output position on the current line. These functions have the specifications:

> **function** COL   **return** POSITIVE_COUNT;
>
> **function** LINE   **return** POSITIVE_COUNT;
>
> **function** PAGE **return** POSITIVE_COUNT;

It is also possible for the programmer to specify the output position in terms of line and column. The procedure SET_COL can be used to move the output position to a certain column on the line.

> **procedure** SET_COL (TO : **in** POSITIVE_COUNT);

To move the output position to column C, where C is assumed to have the subtype POSITIVE_COUNT, we can write:

> SET_COL(C);

If the current column number before the call is less than C, then spaces are output until the current column number becomes C. If the current column number before the call is C, then the call of SET_COL has no effect. If the current column number before the call is greater than C then a new line is started first and then space characters are output until the current column number becomes C.

Similarly, the procedure SET_LINE can be used to move the output forward to a particular line on the page:

> **procedure** SET_LINE (TO : **in** POSITIVE_COUNT);

To move the output forward to line L, where L has subtype POSITIVE_COUNT, the call:

> SET_LINE(L);

can be made. If the current line before the call is less than L then repeated calls to the procedure NEW_LINE will be made automatically until the current line number is L. If the current line number is the same as L, then nothing happens. If the current line number is greater than L then first a new page is started and then the output is moved forward to line L using calls to NEW_LINE.

We shall write a procedure NEW_LINE_PLUS that can be called instead of NEW_LINE if automatic page numbering is required. NEW_LINE_PLUS should work as follows. If there is no page size specified (that is, the maximum number of lines has value 0 so that the number of lines on a page is unbounded), then a new line will occur as usual. Each call of NEW_LINE_PLUS will then simply result in a call to NEW_LINE and no page number will be output. If the size of page is specified, by an earlier call to SET_PAGE_LENGTH, then the last line but one on each page will be left blank and the page number will be output on the last line. If a line length is specified the page number will be output in the centre of the line, otherwise it will be written on the left of the last line.

To determine whether the page size is specified, a call to the function PAGE_LENGTH can be made and the result tested for 0. For extra clarity, the value UNBOUNDED can be tested instead, this being a constant of type COUNT, declared in TEXT_IO, with the value 0.

The page number has to be written as part of the procedure NEW_LINE_ PLUS, so a package has to be created with the resources for writing integers of type COUNT, here called COUNT_INOUT:

```
procedure NEW_LINE_PLUS is

    package COUNT_INOUT is new INTEGER_IO(COUNT);
    use COUNT_INOUT;
begin
    if LINE < PAGE_LENGTH - 2 or
       PAGE_LENGTH = UNBOUNDED then
         NEW_LINE;        -- make a normal new line
    else

        -- end of page
        -- the next to bottom line should be blank
        NEW_LINE(2);

        if LINE_LENGTH /= UNBOUNDED then
            -- position in middle of the bottom line
            SETCOL(LINELENGTH/2);
        end if;

        -- page number on the bottom line
        PUT(PAGE, WIDTH => 1);
        NEW_LINE;        -- automatically gives new page

    end if;
end NEW_LINE_PLUS;
```

Current page, line and column numbers
>   PAGE

function call that gives the current page number.
>   LINE

function call that gives the current line number.
>   COL

function call that gives the current column.
>   SET_LINE(L);

move output on to line L. Change of page occurs if necessary.
>   SET_COL(C);

moves the output on to column number C. Change of line occurs if necessary.

9.1.2   Output of characters and text

The procedure PUT, of which there are several versions, is used to write out values of various kinds at the terminal. Among these versions is one for the output of characters and one for the output of text:

>   **procedure** PUT (ITEM : **in** CHARACTER);
>   **procedure** PUT (ITEM : **in** STRING);

Both these versions of PUT have the required output as their only parameter (with the name ITEM). The type STRING is an unconstrained array type and therefore texts of different lengths can be written out. For the type STRING there is a further procedure, PUT_LINE:

>   **procedure** PUT_LINE (ITEM : **in** STRING);

This works in exactly the same way as PUT, with the difference that a new line is started after the output.

Output of characters and text
>   PUT(C);
>   PUT(S);
>   PUT_LINE(S); -- gives new line *after* the output

where C has type CHARACTER and S has type STRING.

9.1.3   Output of integers

The versions of PUT for writing characters and text are always present in the package TEXT_IO. As we saw in Section 5.6, it is not always so simple in the case of numeric and enumeration types. Since it is possible to work with many different integer, floating point and enumeration types, it is not possible for TEXT_IO to contain a version of PUT for every type imaginable. Instead, it has templates for packages for input and output of integer types, floating point types and enumeration types. Such package templates are called **generic packages**, and they are used, as demonstrated in Section 5.6, to generate individual packages. To be able to read and write integers, for example, the following (or similar) must be placed among the declarations in a program (if there is no access to the package BASIC_NUM_IO or the equivalent):

```
package INTEGER_INOUT is new INTEGER_IO(INTEGER);
use INTEGER_INOUT;
```

INTEGER_IO is the name of the generic package in TEXT_IO that contains the facilities for input and output of integers. In INTEGER_IO there is the procedure PUT for integers:

```
procedure PUT (ITEM   : in NUM;
               WIDTH : in FIELD := DEFAULT_WIDTH;
               BASE   : in NUMBER_BASE := DEFAULT_BASE);
```

The first parameter ITEM is the integer that has to be output. This parameter has type NUM, which is not a true type but only a template to be filled in when an individual package is generated. NUM can be thought of as being replaced by the type given when the package is generated. In the package INTEGER_INOUT, for example, NUM is replaced by INTEGER.

We see that the two other parameters, WIDTH and BASE, are initialized to certain values in the specification. We do not need to include them, therefore, when the procedure is called.

The parameter WIDTH states the number of output positions, or width of the field, that should be used for the output. WIDTH has type FIELD, which is a subtype of INTEGER, comprising the integers greater than or equal to 0. If more output positions than needed are specified in a call to PUT, the positions to the left of the number are filled in with blanks. If, however, the number of output positions specified is insufficient for the required output, the output will contain as many positions as needed anyway, even though the value of WIDTH is exceeded. Negative integers are written out with a minus sign in front and this should be borne in mind when the output positions are being counted. The initialization value for WIDTH, DEFAULT_WIDTH, is equal to the number of digits in the largest permitted integer plus one (to allow for a possible minus sign).

> **Output of integers**
>
> > PUT(I);
>
> or:
>
> > PUT(I, WIDTH => W);
>
> where I is an expression of an integer type and W states the number of positions to be allowed for the output, including a possible minus sign. Padding takes place with blanks to the left of the number if W is larger than is needed.
>
> If W is too small, the exact number of required positions are allowed.

The final parameter, BASE, has not yet been discussed. Integers are normally written out in ordinary decimal form, but using the parameter BASE it is possible to state that the output is required in some other form, for example, in binary form (base 2) or hexadecimal form (base 16). BASE has the type NUMBER_BASE:

subtype NUMBER_BASE **is** INTEGER **range** 2 .. 16;

Bases in the interval 2–16 may be specified. BASE is initialized to DEFAULT_BASE, which has the value 10, that is, corresponding to decimal numbers. We can write out an integer in binary form:

PUT(I, BASE => 2);

If we assume that I has the value 27, the output will have the following rather strange appearance:

2#11011#

The first 2 states that the base 2 is in force, and that what is written between the two #-signs is the number 27 in binary form. If we have the call:

PUT(I, BASE => 8);

instead, we get the output:

8#33#

The number 33 is 27 in octal form (3 times 8, plus 3). The call:

```
PUT(I, BASE => 16);
```

would give the output:

```
16#1B#
```

The number 1B is 27 written in hexadecimal form (1 times 16, plus 11). The letters A, B, C, D, E and F are used in the hexadecimal number system to denote the values 10–15 in the decimal system.

9.1.4 Output of floating point numbers

For floating point numbers, as for integers, an individual package must be created for input and output, this time using the generic package FLOAT_IO in TEXT_IO. To create an input and output package for the type FLOAT, for example, write:

```
package FLOAT_INOUT is new FLOAT_IO(FLOAT);
use FLOAT_INOUT;
```

In FLOAT_IO there is a version of PUT:

```
procedure PUT (ITEM  : in NUM;
               FORE : in FIELD := DEFAULT_FORE;
               AFT   : in FIELD := DEFAULT_AFT;
               EXP   : in FIELD := DEFAULT_EXP);
```

The first parameter, ITEM, is the floating point value that is to be output. This parameter has the type NUM, which is not a true type but a template for a type. NUM takes on the type that is specified when the package is generated. In the case of the package FLOAT_INOUT generated above, we can thus think of FLOAT replacing NUM. The three other parameters state how the output should be presented. All have the type FIELD, a subtype of INTEGER in which the allowed integer values are greater than or equal to 0.

The parameter FORE states how many character positions should be in front of the decimal point in the output. The default value, DEFAULT_FORE, is 2. AFT states how many figures should appear to the right of the decimal point. The default value, DEFAULT_AFT, is equal to the number of figures of accuracy in the current floating point type, less one because it is assumed that one of the figures is output as an integer digit. The parameter EXP states how many character positions are to be used in output of the number's exponent. The default value, DEFAULT_EXP, is 3.

If EXP is given the value 0 in the call then the output will be in the form:

iiiii.ddddd

where the is denote positions for the integral part and the ds denote the figures in the decimal part. The number of figures before and after the point are determined by FORE and AFT, respectively. If the number of places is greater than needed, the space is padded out with blanks in front of the number. If the number of places is fewer than needed, it is written out in full anyway, with as many figures in the integral part as necessary. One position should be allowed for a possible minus sign in the integral part in case the number is negative.

If EXP is given a value greater than 0, the output is in the form:

ii.dddddEnn

where the is and the ds, as before, denote figures in the integral part and the decimal part, respectively, and here the ns denote the exponent. This form of output is called **exponent form** and examples are:

−5.73E+1   4.5E2   0.0E+0

which denote the numbers −57.3, 0.045 and 0.0, respectively. A number output in exponent form always has one figure before the decimal point, preceded by a minus sign if the number is negative. If FORE has a greater value than needed, the space is filled with blanks before the number. The number of figures after the decimal point is determined, as before, by AFT. The number of positions in the exponent part (including a plus or minus sign) is determined by EXP. If EXP is larger than needed, the space is padded out with zeros.

The number is rounded up to the given number of decimal figures, irrespective of the form chosen for output.

Let us study a few examples of output. We assume that P and Q are floating point variables with values −123.4 and 0.00567, respectively:

PUT(P);   -- gives: −1.23400000E+02

PUT(Q);   -- gives: 5.67000000E3

PUT(P, AFT => 2);   -- gives: −1.23E+02

PUT(Q, FORE => 5, AFT => 1); -- gives: 5.7E3

PUT(P, EXP => 4);   -- gives: −1.23400000E+002

PUT(Q, EXP => 0);   -- gives: 0.00567000

Output of floating point numbers

> PUT(X);

Gives the exponent form in standard format.

> PUT(X, FORE => N, AFT => M, EXP => 0);

Gives the ordinary form without exponent, N positions in front of the decimal point and M positions after it.

> PUT(X, FORE => N, AFT => M, EXP => K);

Gives the exponent form with K figures in the exponent, N positions in front of the decimal point and M positions after it.

Padding occurs with spaces if FORE is greater than necessary. If FORE is too small, as many positions as necessary are used.

9.1.5 Output of values of enumeration type

As shown in Section 5.5, it is possible to write out the values of an enumeration type if an input/output package is generated using the generic package ENUMERATION_IO in TEXT_IO. If we have the enumeration type:

> **type** SIGNAL **is** (ON, OFF, NORMAL, ALARM);

we can create a package SIGNAL_INOUT:

> **package** SIGNAL_INOUT **is new** ENUMERATION_IO(SIGNAL);

ENUMERATION_IO includes a procedure PUT:

> **procedure** PUT (ITEM   : in ENUM;
>   WIDTH : in FIELD := DEFAULT-WIDTH;
>   SET   : in TYPE-SET := DEFAULTSETTING);

The parameter ITEM is the value of the enumeration type that should be output. The type ENUM is not a true type but a template; when a new package is generated, ENUM is replaced with the specified enumeration type. In the package SIGNAL_INOUT for example, we can consider ENUM being replaced by SIGNAL. Since the two other parameters have default values they do not have to be present in a call to PUT. If we have the declaration:

S : SIGNAL;

we can write, for example:

PUT(S);

Then one of the words ON, OFF, NORMAL or ALARM will be written out at the terminal.

Exactly as for integers, the second parameter, WIDTH, states how many positions are to be used for the output. The initial value, DEFAULT_WIDTH, has the value 0 and this is therefore the value assumed if no parameter WIDTH is included in the call to PUT. If WIDTH is greater than the value necessary to output the current word, the field is padded out with spaces to the right of the word; if WIDTH is too small then the word is written out in full anyway.

Output of the values of enumeration types

PUT(E);

The value of E is output, no trailing spaces.

PUT(E, WIDTH => N);

The value of E is output with N positions. If N is too big, the field is padded with spaces to the right of E's value. If N is too small, N is ignored and the whole word is written out anyway.

The third parameter, SET, can be used to control the use of upper- or lower-case letters in the output. SET is initialized to DEFAULT_SETTING, which is a variable of the type TYPE_SET:

type TYPE_SET **is** (LOWER_CASE, UPPER_CASE);

The default value of SET is UPPER_CASE, and this value is assumed if nothing else is specified; all output will thus be in upper-case letters. If some output must be in lower case, then we must write:

PUT(S, SET => LOWER_CASE);   -- gives the output: alarm

assuming that S still has the value ALARM. If all output is to be in lower-case letters, it is more convenient to change the default value thus:

SIGNAL_INOUT.DEFAULT_SETTING := LOWER_CASE;

9.2   Input from the terminal

In the package TEXT_IO are facilities for reading data written at the terminal, that is, at the terminal keyboard.

9.2.1   Page and line structure

Imagine all the characters written at the terminal forming a single long stream of characters that can be read by the program. Each key stroke generates one character in the stream. For example, if we write:

Tommy 123

at the keyboard then the sequence of characters illustrated in Figure 9.1 is created and the program that is running can then read it. The blank square denotes a blank character, that is, a space character.

Viewed logically, input from the keyboard, that is, the stream of characters, consists of a number of pages. Each page comprises a number of lines and each line, in turn, comprises a number of characters. The person writing at the keyboard states where the ends of lines and pages should occur by typing special characters. To indicate where a line should end, for example, it is normal to strike the RETURN key. It is not very common to specify pages in input from the keyboard. In normal cases, therefore, the input can be considered as comprising a single long page.

When an end-of-line character is typed, a **line terminator** is generated in the stream of characters, and if an end-of-page character is typed, then a **page terminator** is generated. If, for example, we type in the following lines:

line 1
xyz
000

from the keyboard, then the sequence of characters illustrated in Figure 9.2 will be generated, where the black squares denote line terminators.

A line or page terminator may consist of one or more characters. The Ada programmer need not be concerned about their exact appearance – it is a detail that depends on the computer in use. When the data is read into a program from the character stream, any terminators present will automatically be skipped, so they can never be read into a program, either deliberately or by accident.

Figure 9.1

Figure 9.2

Pages and lines

- Data written at the keyboard forms a long stream of characters that logically consists of a number of pages. Each page comprises a number of lines and each line comprises a number of characters.

- The end of each line is marked in the stream by a line terminator and the end of each page by a page terminator.

- The end of a line is usually caused by striking the RETURN key.

How long is a stream of characters generated by pressing the keys at the terminal? The answer is that it can be of any length. It is always possible to generate new characters in the series by typing them. Sometimes, however, it is useful to be able to indicate that a series of characters is finished, that nothing more is going to be added. This can be achieved by typing a special combination of characters, the exact form depending on the computer being used. We saw earlier that it is usual to use the CTRL key with another key to mark the end of input data. When the end of input of data is indicated, it can be considered, logically, that a special **file terminator** is placed at the end of the generated series of characters. If, for example, we write the lines:

```
12 3
456
78
```

at the keyboard and then type the combination CTRL-D (which we shall assume is used to mark the end of input data) then the series of characters can be depicted as in Figure 9.3. The file terminator is the square at the end. Note that at the end there is both a line terminator and a file terminator. Normally, when data input is finished, the RETURN key has to be pressed so that the data that has been written at the keyboard will be transferred to the computer. This generates a line terminator in the stream of characters. It is therefore natural that the end of data input is marked when a new line has been started (the RETURN key has just been pressed).

Figure 9.3

It must be noted that even if the stream of characters can be considered logically as terminated by a file terminator, this does not mean that such a marker has to be physically present in the series of characters.

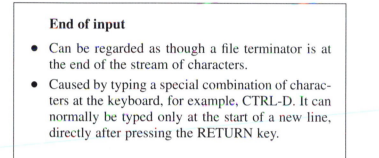

End of input

- Can be regarded as though a file terminator is at the end of the stream of characters.
- Caused by typing a special combination of characters at the keyboard, for example, CTRL-D. It can normally be typed only at the start of a new line, directly after pressing the RETURN key.

In the program, data is read in from the character stream by calls to the procedure GET. Each reading involves a small move along the stream: we can say that each reading consumes a number of characters from the stream. Reading always starts from the start of the stream. Let us assume that we have the variables I, J, K and L of type INTEGER in a program, and also the input statements:

```
GET(I);
GET(J);
GET(K);
GET(L);
```

As before, we assume that we typed in the lines:

```
12 3
456
78
```

The first call:

```
GET(I);
```

Figure 9.4

will mean that the characters '1' and '2' are consumed and that the variable I takes the value 12. Figure 9.4 illustrates this. The arrow shows how far we have come along the character stream and points to the next character waiting to be read.

The next call:

GET(J);

means that the characters ' ' and '3' are consumed and that J takes the value 3. Blank characters are always skipped automatically when numeric data or data of an enumeration type is read. The situation now is shown in Figure 9.5.

Blank characters in input

- Blank characters, that is, spaces, are always automatically skipped when data of numeric or enumeration type is read.
- Blank characters are *not* skipped when data of the type STRING and CHARACTER is read.

The arrow has moved on so that it points to the first line terminator, that is, the first line is now finished. The call:

GET(K);

Figure 9.5

means that the line terminator and the characters '4', '5' and '6' are consumed. Line and page terminators are always automatically skipped. The next character waiting in line is the line terminator for the second line (see Figure 9.6).

> **Line and page terminators in input**
>
> Line terminators and page terminators are always automatically skipped when data is read. This is true even for data of the type STRING and CHARACTER.

In TEXT_IO there is a function END_OF_LINE that can be used to find out whether the current input line is finished:

function END_OF_LINE **return** BOOLEAN;

The function returns the value TRUE if the next character waiting to be input, that is, the character the arrow is pointing to, is a line terminator or a file terminator. If, for example, we call END_OF_LINE after the call:

GET(K);

the result will be TRUE.

The final call of GET in our example:

GET(L);

consumes the line terminator for the second line and the characters '7' and '8'. The variable L will take the value 78. The arrow has moved on to the final line terminator, as shown in Figure 9.7. A call to END_OF_LINE would now return the value TRUE.

In TEXT_IO there is another function, END_OF_FILE, that can be used to determine whether the input series of characters is finished:

function END_OF_FILE **return** BOOLEAN;

Figure 9.6

Figure 9.7

This function gives the result TRUE if a file terminator is next in line to be read, or if a combination of line, page and file terminators is next. A call to END_OF_FILE after the final GET above would thus give the result TRUE.

In TEXT_IO there is also a function END_OF_PAGE, which shows whether a page is complete:

function END_OF_PAGE **return** BOOLEAN;

When called, this gives the value TRUE if the next character in line to be input is a combination of a page and line terminator, or if it is a file terminator. This function is not used much in the case of input from the keyboard.

Tests for end of line, page and file

END_OF_LINE

gives the value TRUE if the next character waiting to be read is a line terminator or a file terminator.

END_OF_PAGE

gives the value TRUE if the next character waiting to be read is a combination of a line terminator and a page terminator, or a file terminator.

END_OF_FILE

gives the value TRUE if the next character in line to be read is a file terminator or a combination of line, page and file terminators.

The procedure SKIP_LINE can be used to skip over whole lines in the input data:

procedure SKIP_LINE(SPACING : **in** POSITIVE_COUNT := 1);

The parameter SPACING states the number of lines to be skipped and it can be omitted from a call. If it is absent, one line is skipped. If the call:

    SKIP_LINE;

or:

    SKIP_LINE(1);

is made, the program skips over all the characters in the stream from the next in line until it finds a line terminator. This is also skipped and if it is followed by a page terminator, this is also skipped. The result is that after the call the next character to be read in will be the first character of the next line. If SKIP_LINE is called with a parameter N greater than one then this process will be carried out N times.

For example, if we write the numbers:

    12 3
    456

at the terminal and the program contains the calls:

    GET(I);
    GET(J);

then the value 12 is read into I and the value 3 into J, as before. If we insert a call to SKIP_LINE:

    GET(I);
    SKIP_LINE;
    GET(J);

then the value 456 would be read into J instead, because everything after the character '2' on the first line would be skipped.

There is a function SKIP_PAGE that works in a similar way, but skipping pages rather than lines. However, only one page at a time can be skipped.

Skipping to a new line or page

    SKIP_LINE;
    SKIP_LINE(N);

skips over everything up to the first character on the next line. If N > 1, it is repeated N times.

    SKIP_PAGE;

skips over everything up to the first character of the next page.

Let us study a program that reads data from the keyboard and writes out the average number of characters in the lines read in. To be able to calculate the average number of characters per line the program must count the total number of lines and characters read. For this, two variables are used, LINE_COUNT and CHAR_COUNT, both initialized to 0. In this program we are not interested in the kind of input: we shall just count the number of lines and the number of characters. Therefore it is simplest to read one character at a time to a variable CHAR of type CHARACTER. We can use the following algorithm:

(1) Set LINE_COUNT and CHAR_COUNT to 0.
(2) Repeat the following until there are no lines left (that is, the input ends):
    (2.1) Increase LINE_COUNT by 1.
    (2.2) Read the current line and add the number of characters in it to CHAR_COUNT.
    (2.3) Skip to the start of the next line.

Step (2.2) can be expanded to:

(2.2) Repeat the following until there are no more characters in the current line:
    (2.2.1) Read the next character.
    (2.2.2) Increase CHAR_COUNT by 1.

If we translate this to Ada we get:

```ada
with TEXT_IO, BASIC_NUM_IO;
use TEXT_IO, BASIC_NUM_IO;
procedure FIND_LINE_LENGTH is
  LINE_COUNT, CHAR_COUNT : INTEGER := 0;
  CHAR : CHARACTER;
begin
  PUT_LINE("Enter input. Terminate with CTRL-D");

  while not END_OF_FILE loop
    LINE_COUNT := LINE_COUNT + 1;
    while not END_OF_LINE loop
      GET(CHAR);
      CHAR_COUNT := CHAR_COUNT + 1;
    end loop;
    SKIP_LINE;
  end loop;

  PUT("The average line length is");
  PUT( FLOAT(CHAR_COUNT) / FLOAT(LINE_COUNT),
       EXP => 0, FORE => 3, AFT => 2 );
end FIND_LINE_LENGTH;
```

Note that the call to SKIP_LINE is necessary because, when the last character on the first line has been read, a line terminator is waiting to be read. If we had not skipped over this, the second loop round the outer loop statement would have started with a line terminator waiting to be read. This would have meant that the inner loop statement would not have been executed at all because the call to END_OF_LINE would have been TRUE at once. Thus no character would have been read from the terminal. Input would have stuck fast at the first line terminator and the program would have gone into an endless loop.

As in the case of output, the package TEXT_IO keeps track of the current page, line and column number in the input. Calls to GET, SKIP_LINE and SKIP_PAGE change these numbers automatically. The functions COL, LINE and PAGE, which could be used in connection with output, can also be used to determine the current position in input. If we call the function COL in a program, we get, as seen earlier, the current column in output as a result. To state that we mean the current column, line or page in input rather than output we must therefore use different versions of the functions COL, LINE and PAGE:

```
function COL  (FILE : in FILE_TYPE) return POSITIVE_COUNT;
function LINE  (FILE : in FILE_TYPE) return POSITIVE_COUNT;
function PAGE (FILE : in FILE_TYPE) return POSITIVE_COUNT;
```

These have a single **in** parameter, FILE, of type FILE_TYPE. To determine the current column in the input we can make the call:

```
COL(CURRENT_INPUT);
```

and to find the current line number we can write:

```
LINE(CURRENT_INPUT);
```

(CURRENT_INPUT is in turn a function call that returns the current input stream. We shall not go into further details here.)

It is also possible to call the procedures SET_COL and SET_LINE to move on to a particular position in the input. Again, we must use special forms of the subprograms to indicate that we mean input and not output. The alternative forms of SET_COL and SET_PAGE have the specifications:

```
procedure SET_COL  (FILE : in FILE_TYPE;
                     TO    : in POSITIVE_COUNT);
procedure SET_LINE  (FILE : in FILE_TYPE;
                     TO    : in POSITIVE_COUNT);
```

For example, we can move on to column N with the call:

```
SET_COL(CURRENT_INPUT, N);
```

Now all the characters and terminators in the input are skipped over until the next character waiting to be read is from column N of a line.

The call:

SET_LINE(CURRENT_INPUT, M);

has the same effect as calling SKIP_LINE repeatedly until the current line number is **M**.

9.2.2   Input of characters and text

To read characters of type CHARACTER, the version of GET that is used is defined as follows in TEXT_IO:

procedure GET (ITEM : **out** CHARACTER);

The only parameter is an **out** parameter of type CHARACTER. If the call:

GET(C);

is made, where C is of type CHARACTER, the next character waiting to be read will end up in C. If there is a line or page terminator next, it will be skipped. If there is a space character next in line for reading it is not skipped, but C will have the value ' ' after the call.

Sometimes we want to know the next character waiting to be read, but we do not yet want to consume the character from the input stream. Then the procedure LOOK_AHEAD can be used:

procedure LOOK_AHEAD (ITEM   : **out** CHARACTER;
                                                    END_OF_LINE : **out** BOOLEAN);

On return the out parameter END_OF_LINE is given the value TRUE if the next character of the input stream is a line terminator, page terminator or a file terminator. In that case the contents of ITEM are undefined. If the next character is not a terminator, END_OF_FILE gets the value FALSE and ITEM contains the character waiting to be read. The input stream itself is *not* affected by a call to LOOK_AHEAD.

Normally, when data is typed on the keyboard, the characters typed are not placed in the input stream until the RETURN key is pressed. (This makes it possible to correct typing errors.) However, sometimes an immediate reaction is wanted from the program as soon as a key is pressed; this is the case in text editors and game programs, for instance. In this type of program the procedure GET_IMMEDIATE can be used instead of GET. GET_IMMEDIATE exists in two variants:

```
procedure  GET_IMMEDIATE (ITEM        : out CHARACTER);
procedure  GET_IMMEDIATE (ITEM        : out CHARACTER;
                          AVAILABLE : out BOOLEAN);
```

Both variants read one character directly from the keyboard. The character read could be any kind of character, printable or non-printable, such as *esc* and *lf*. The difference between the two variants is that the first one waits until a character is available (a key is pressed) but the second one returns immediately if no character is available. In that case the out parameter AVAILABLE is set to FALSE and the value of ITEM is undefined.

To read whole texts into variables of type STRING, another version of GET can be used:

```
procedure GET (ITEM : out STRING);
```

If the call:

```
GET(S);
```

is made, where S has the type STRING, the length of S is first determined, that is, how many characters can be held in S. Many calls are then made repeatedly to the first version of GET above. The characters input are placed one by one in S, starting on the left. If S has length 0 then nothing happens.

To read a whole line at once to a variable of type STRING there is a special procedure, GET_LINE, which is sometimes convenient.

```
procedure GET_LINE(ITEM : out STRING;
                   LAST : out NATURAL);
```

We assume that S has type STRING and that the variable N has the type NATURAL. We then make the call:

```
GET_LINE(S,N);
```

When the call is made one character after another is read from the input stream and placed in S from left to right. Reading normally ends when a line terminator is met in the input stream. A call to SKIP_LINE is then made automatically; after the call to GET_LINE, the next character waiting to be read is the first character of the next line. Reading can also end if S is too short and there is no room for the current line. If S is longer than the number of characters read, then the positions in S to which nothing has been read will be undefined after the call.

After the call, the **out** parameter LAST (N in our call above), will contain the index number of the last character read in. If the indexing of S starts at 1 this simply means that, after the call, N contains the number of characters read. If no characters have been read, LAST will contain a number that is less than S's first index number.

Using GET_LINE we can write another version of the program FIND_LINE_LENGTH:

```
with TEXT_IO, BASIC_NUM_IO;
use TEXT_IO, BASIC_NUM_IO;
procedure FIND_LINE_LENGTH is
  LINE_COUNT, CHAR_COUNT : INTEGER := 0;
  NR_OF_CHARS_IN_LINE : NATURAL;
  LINE : STRING (1 .. 300);
begin
  PUT_LINE("Enter input. Terminate with CTRL-D");

  while not END_OF_FILE loop
    LINE_COUNT := LINE_COUNT + 1;
    GET_LINE(LINE, NR_OF_CHARS_IN_LINE);
      CHAR_COUNT := CHAR_COUNT
                          + NR_OF_CHARS_IN_LINE;
  end loop;

  PUT("The average line length is");
  PUT( FLOAT(CHAR_COUNT) / FLOAT(LINE_COUNT),
      EXP => 0, FORE => 3, AFT => 2 );
end FIND_LINE_LENGTH;
```

We assume that no line is longer than 300 characters. Note that a call to SKIP_LINE occurs automatically through the call to GET_LINE.

9.2.3 Input of integers

To read in integers, a special input/output package must be created using the generic package INTEGER_IO in TEXT_IO, exactly as for output. If, for example, we have declared a type:

```
type WHOLE_NUMBER is range −1000 .. 1000;
```

and want to read values into variables of this type, we must create our own package:

```
package WHOLE_NUMBER_INOUT is new
        INTEGER_IO(WHOLE_NUMBER);
use WHOLE_NUMBER_INOUT;
```

The following version of GET is found in INTEGER_IO:

```
procedure GET (ITEM   : out NUM;
                WIDTH : in FIELD := 0);
```

The first parameter is an **out** parameter corresponding to the integer variable to which input should occur. The type NUM is, as before, a template for a true type that is replaced by the type specified when a package is created. In the package WHOLE_NUMBER_INOUT, for example, we see that NUM stands for WHOLE_NUMBER. The second parameter is not generally used. A call to GET therefore generally resembles:

```
GET(W);
```

where W has the type WHOLE_NUMBER. When the call is made, any line terminators, page terminators and blanks are skipped. Then the procedure GET expects a whole number. In the input this is given as a number of characters, for example, the integer 475 is represented by the three characters '4', '7' and '5' in series.

The exact appearance of an integer to be read is specified strictly. In fact, the rules are the same as those for integer literals discussed in Section 3.3. Input continues for as long as the characters read in can be interpreted as part of an integer. If an incorrect integer is written when data is input to a program, the program usually stops and an error message is given. In Chapter 10 we shall see how to capture this kind of error in a program.

The second parameter, WIDTH, can be used if data is to be read that has been written in a special way, with a particular number of positions in the input. If the parameter WIDTH is given a value N in a call to GET, not equal to 0, then N characters will be read from the keyboard and translated into an integer. This demands that these N characters form a valid integer. Blanks in front of the integer are also counted among the N characters. If we have the call:

```
GET(W, WIDTH => 4);
```

in a program and the following is written at the keyboard:

```
-157890
```

then the variable W will have the value −157 after the call, since only four characters are read by GET. The next character waiting in line to be read after the call is '8'.

9.2.4   Input of floating point numbers

To read values into variables of floating point type the generic package FLOAT_IO in TEXT_IO must be used to create an input/output package for the particular floating point type in question. If, for example, we have made the type declaration:

```
type TEMPERATURE is digits 4;
```

we can create an input/output package for TEMPERATURE:

```
package TEMPERATURE_INOUT is new FLOAT_IO(TEMPERATURE);
```

In FLOAT_IO there is a version of GET:

```
procedure GET (ITEM    : out NUM;
               WIDTH : in FIELD := 0);
```

As in the case of input of integers, the second parameter is not generally used. The first parameter corresponds to the floating point variable that is to receive a value. If, for example, we wish to put a value in the variable T of type TEMPERATURE we write the statement:

```
GET(T);
```

Input works in the same way as for integers, except that the format rules for input of a real number differ from those for an integer. A real number for input may look the same as a real literal in a program (see Section 3.3). Data can therefore be input either in the ordinary form, with figures before and after a decimal point, or in exponent form. Furthermore, in Ada 95 we may input data without a decimal point. When the procedure GET is called it can consume all the characters in the input stream that can be part of the real number. Leading blanks and line and page terminators are skipped. The character in line to be input after a call to GET is the first character that cannot be part of a real number. If the keyboard input does not follow the rules then the program is normally stopped and an error message is given. However, this kind of error can be captured (see Chapter 10).

The WIDTH parameter works in the same way as the corresponding parameter when an integer is read. If a value of N that is not equal to 0 is given in a call, then exactly N characters are read from the keyboard and converted into a real number.

9.2.5 Input of values of enumeration type

To read the values of an enumeration type it is first necessary to create an input/output package using the generic package ENUMERATION_IO in TEXT_IO. A package for the type:

```
type COMMAND is (START, FINISH, WRITE, DECREASE, INCREASE);
```

can be created by writing, for example:

```
package COMMAND_INOUT is new ENUMERATION_IO(COMMAND);
use COMMAND_INOUT;
```

In ENUMERATION_IO there is a version of GET:

```
procedure GET (ITEM : out ENUM);
```

The only parameter here is an **out** parameter corresponding to the variable of an enumeration type to which a value will be read. If we assume that C has the type COMMAND we can now make the call:

```
GET(C);
```

When this call is made any line terminators, page terminators and blanks are skipped. Then the word that is typed at the terminal is read. The only words that may be written are the words that a variable of the enumeration type in question can take. In our example, the user must thus write one of the words START, STOP, WRITE, DECREASE or INCREASE. It does not matter whether upper- or lower-case letters are used. If something is written that is not a permitted value of the enumeration type, the program is stopped and an error message is given, unless the error is captured (see Chapter 10).

9.3 Text files

All the programs we have studied so far have read from or written to the terminal. However, it is often necessary for a program to work with other external devices connected to the computer. For example, output might be required on a line printer or a special high-quality printer instead of the terminal. Another problem is that the variables used in a program only exist while the program is being executed. If the data is to be saved permanently, so that it survives when program execution has finished, it must be stored in the computer's secondary storage, most often on disk. It is therefore important to be able to read and write data to and from secondary storage.

In computer jargon, a sequence of data elements, which can be of arbitrary length, is called a **file**. If the elements in the sequence are characters (type CHARACTER), it is called a **text file**. Programs can be written in Ada to read and write all kinds of files, but in this chapter we shall consider only text files.

Two types of text file can be distinguished:

(1)   text files that correspond to the input or output devices of the computer, such as a line-printer; and

(2)   text files that are stored in secondary storage.

In an Ada program both files are treated in the same way. They are understood logically, by a program, as a series of characters that are either to be read or to be written. Each text file exists physically in the computer system and has a special name. The format of the name depends entirely on the computer system in use. If the text file corresponds to a line-printer it may have a name such as *LPR* or */dev/printer*. A text file that is stored in secondary memory may have a name such as */u/smith/datafile* or *courseregister.text*. The rules for the format of such names do not need to agree (and generally do not agree) with the rules for identifiers in Ada.

In an Ada program all work is performed on **logical** text files. In the package TEXT_IO there is a type FILE_TYPE that can be used to declare such logical text files. If we have the usual lines:

```
with TEXT_IO;
use TEXT_IO;
```

at the start of a program then we can declare a logical text file (a file variable), for example:

```
INFILE : FILE_TYPE;
```

Thus INFILE has type FILE_TYPE. In the package TEXT_IO, FILE_TYPE is declared as a limited private type. Therefore, the programmer does not get to know what a file variable like INFILE 'really' looks like. The *only* thing that can be done with such a variable is to give it as a parameter to certain subprograms in TEXT_IO. This means that it is not possible, for example, to compare two file variables or to assign one file variable to another.

Henceforth we shall distinguish between a logical file in a program (a file variable) and a physical file in the computer system, by calling the former simply a **file** and the latter an **external file**.

Before reading or writing a file can begin in a program, it must be connected with an external file. This is accomplished by calling one of the procedures CREATE or OPEN in TEXT_IO:

```
procedure CREATE(FILE   : in out FILE_TYPE;
                 MODE : in FILE_MODE := OUT_FILE;
                 NAME : in STRING := "";
                 FORM : in STRING := "");
procedure OPEN    (FILE   : in out FILE_TYPE;
                 MODE : in FILE_MODE;
                 NAME : in STRING;
                 FORM : in STRING := "");
```

CREATE is used when a new external file is to be created and OPEN is used when work is to be performed on an existing external file.

The parameter FILE to both procedures should be a file declared as above. The parameter MODE states whether the file is to be written to or read from. In the case of text files it is not possible to both read and write a file at the same time. The type FILE_MODE has the declaration:

type FILE_MODE **is** (IN_FILE, OUT_FILE);

In Ada 95 FILE_MODE is declared as follows: ▼

type FILE_MODE **is** (IN_FILE, OUT_FILE, APPEND_FILE);

The last of these alternatives is chosen if you wish to add new text at the end of an existing file.   ▲

The parameter NAME is a text string that should contain the name of the external file. This parameter can be omitted from a call to CREATE. An empty string is then assumed for the name, and the external file created is considered to be a temporary file that will disappear when program execution finishes.

The parameter FORM is not used often. Its appearance depends on the computer system in use. (It can be used, for example, to give a password to protected external files.)

If we have the declaration:

NEW_FILE : FILE_TYPE;

we can create an external file, *my.file* for example, and connect it with the file NEW_FILE using the call:

CREATE(NEW_FILE, NAME => "my.file");

Now it is possible to write to the file NEW_FILE.

To link the file INFILE, declared earlier, to the external file */u/smith/datafile* so that it can be read, we can write:

OPEN(INFILE, IN_FILE, "/u/smith/datafile");

If an existing file is opened for writing, then any earlier contents are over-written and destroyed.

Assume the line-printer in a certain system has the name LPR. If we declare a file:

L_PRINTER : FILE_TYPE;

we can link it to the line-printer by writing:

OPEN(L_PRINTER, MODE => OUT_FILE, NAME => "LPR");

If a file is linked to an external file by a call to CREATE or OPEN, it is said to be **open**. When an attempt is made to open a file, errors can occur. For example, the file may already be open, or no external file may exist with the name specified in the call to OPEN. Possible ways of handling this kind of error are described in Chapter 10.

The function IS_OPEN can be used to test whether a particular file is open:

function IS_OPEN (FILE : **in** FILE_TYPE) **return** BOOLEAN;

To determine whether the file NEW_FILE is open, for example, we can write:

if IS_OPEN(NEW_FILE) **then**

Opening a file

- First declare a logical file:

    F : FILE_TYPE;

  where F is the name of the logical file.

- Then connect this file with a physical (external) file in one of the following ways. (S is a text string containing the name of the physical file.)

    CREATE(F, NAME => S);

  A new external file is created. The file is to be written.

    OPEN(F, MODE => IN_FILE, NAME => S);

  An existing external file is opened. The file is to be read.

    OPEN(F, MODE => OUT_FILE, NAME => S);

  An existing external file is opened. The file is to be written. The earlier contents are destroyed.

The only place in a program where the names of external files are found is in calls to CREATE and OPEN. Everywhere else, logical files are used.

An open file can either be read from or written to, and all the subprograms previously discussed in connection with reading from and writing to the terminal, such as GET, PUT, NEW_LINE, END_OF_FILE, are available. The only difference is that a file has to be given as the first parameter in any call that is not destined for the terminal. For example, to read a character from the file INFILE to a variable C:

    GET(INFILE, C);

can be written, and to write an integer I to the file NEW_FILE PUT can be called thus:

    PUT(NEW_FILE, I);

Text files, in common with input and output to the terminal, can be regarded as logically having line, page and file terminators embedded in the text, as mentioned earlier. To start a new line in the file NEW_FILE we can make the call:

    NEW_LINE(NEW_FILE);

and to test whether a line in the file INFILE is finished, the function END_OF_LINE can be called:

    if END_OF_LINE (INFILE) **then**

Reading and writing text files

- A text file has line and page structure. The same subprograms can be used as for reading from and writing to the terminal, for example, PUT, GET, NEW_LINE.
- The difference is that in all calls the name of the logical file has to be stated as the first parameter. For example:

        GET(F,N);   -- read an integer from the file F

When reading or writing a file is finished, the file has to be **closed** by calling the procedure CLOSE. To close the file NEW_FILE, for example, the call is made:

    CLOSE(NEW_FILE);

If the file has been used for writing, CLOSE takes care that the current line and page are terminated. This is achieved by automatically calling NEW_PAGE before the file is terminated. If we forget to close a file in a program, the result is not well-defined; it varies from system to system. It is probably most common for the system to close the file automatically, but to have control over the files used. The programmer should get into the habit of always closing his or her files after use.

Closing files

> CLOSE(F);

where F is a logical file.

Files should always be closed after use.

We shall study a program that creates a copy of the external file old.file. The copy will take the name copy. In the program the corresponding logical files are INF and OUTF. One line at a time is read from INF using the procedure GET_LINE and is written to OUTF using PUT_LINE.

```
with TEXT_IO;
use TEXT_IO;
procedure COPY_FILE is
   INF, OUTF       : FILE_TYPE;
   LINE            : STRING (1 .. 200);
   LINE_LENGTH     : NATURAL;

begin
   -- open the files
   OPEN(INF, MODE => IN_FILE, NAME => "old.file");
   CREATE(OUTF, NAME => "copy");
   -- copy INF to OUTF
   while not END_OF_FILE(INF)  loop
      GET_LINE(INF, LINE, LINE_LENGTH);
      PUT_LINE(OUTF, LINE(1 .. LINE_LENGTH);
   end loop;

   -- close the files
   CLOSE(INF);
   CLOSE(OUTF);
end  COPY_FILE;
```

The file OUTF will have exactly the same line structure as the file INF, that is, both files have the same number of lines and a particular line in OUTF is as long as the corresponding line in INF.

Note that INF may not be copied to OUTF using an assignment statement:

```
OUTF := INF      -- ERROR! Assignment is forbidden
```

In the program we have assumed that no line of INF is longer than 200 characters. If the maximum line length in INF is not known, then the copying program should be reformulated so that it can cope with copying a text file with lines of unlimited length. We can solve this problem by reading one character at a time instead of one line at a time, by changing the **loop** statement in the program:

```
while not END_OF_FILE(INF) loop
   while not END_OF_LINE(INF) loop
      GET(INF,  C);
      PUT(OUTF, C);
   end loop;
   SKIP_LINE(INF);
   NEW_LINE(OUTF);
end loop;
```

Here we read one character at a time, assuming the variable C has type CHARACTER, until the current line is finished. When a line in INF is finished we skip the line terminator with a call to SKIP_LINE. Each time a line in INF finishes we have to ensure that the corresponding line of OUTF also finishes. This we do by calling NEW_LINE to write a line terminator.

In the copying program we have assumed that the names of the external files are known when the program is written. We have said that the external file to be copied will have the name *old.file* and the copy will have the name *copy*. It would be better if the program were a little more general so that it could cope with copying any external file, and the copy could be given any name requested. One way of achieving this is to read in the *names* of the external files before reading them. Then the names can be given as parameters to the procedures OPEN and CREATE. To make this change in the program, first we insert the declarations:

```
FILE_NAME    : STRING (1 .. 30);
NAME_LENGTH : NATURAL;
```

Then we amend the part of the program that opens the files:

```
-- open INF
PUT_LINE("Enter name of file to be copied");
GET_LINE(FILE_NAME, NAME_LENGTH);
OPEN(INF, MODE => IN_FILE,
          NAME => FILE_NAME(1 .. NAME_LENGTH));
```

```
-- open OUTF
PUT_LINE("Enter the name of the copy");
GET_LINE(FILE_NAME, NAME_LENGTH);
CREATE(OUTF, NAME => FILE_NAME(1 .. NAME_LENGTH));
```

The statement:

```
GET_LINE(FILE_NAME, NAME_LENGTH);
```

indicates, as usual, reading from the terminal. A text string is read in and placed to the left of the variable FILE_NAME. Note that we have cut out the slice of FILE_NAME containing only the name when OPEN and CLOSE are called. If we gave the whole variable FILE_NAME as parameter we could have got 'rubbish' at the end of the file name, and this might have led to trouble for the operating system.

Instead of reading the file name in the program, the file name can be given as a parameter to the main program (see Section 6.11). Many standard programs in UNIX and MS-DOS work this way.

We shall now write another program that copies input from the terminal and stores it as a text file. This program can be used for writing information that is to be stored permanently in a text file. Here is the central portion of the program:

```
-- open OUTF
PUT_LINE("Enter the name of the new file");
GET_LINE(FILE_NAME, NAME_LENGTH);
CREATE(OUTF, NAME => FILE_NAME(1 .. NAME_LENGTH));

-- copy from the terminal to OUTF
PUT_LINE("Enter material to be stored in the file");
while not END_OF_FILE loop
   GET_LINE(LINE, LINE_LENGTH);
   PUT_LINE(OUTF, LINE(1 .. LINE_LENGTH));
end loop;

-- close OUTF
CLOSE(OUTF);
```

This differs from the previous program in that the file INF has disappeared and the parameter INF has been removed from the calls to END_OF_FILE and GET_LINE in the **loop** statement. Input is now from the terminal instead.

Files are often used to save values from calculations or measurements so that they can be analysed or processed further at some later date. In the next example we shall study a program that carries out 1000 computations of some sort and saves the results in a text file DATAFILE. The nature of the computations

is of no interest here, so we assume that they take place in the function
CALCULATION, whose internal workings we can ignore.

In the program real numbers will be written to DATAFILE. We assume,
therefore, that we have created a package FLOAT_INOUT containing facilities
for writing numbers of type FLOAT. (The home-made package BASIC_NUM_IO
is of no use here because it only includes facilities for writing to the terminal.)
The program has the following statements:

```
-- open DATAFILE

PUT_LINE("Enter the name of the new file");
GET_LINE(FILE_NAME, NAME_LENGTH);
CREATE(DATAFILE,
             NAME => FILE_NAME(1 .. NAME_LENGTH));
SET_LINE_LENGTH(DATAFILE, 100);

-- do 1000 calculations, save results in DATAFILE
for I in 1 .. 1000 loop
   VALUE := CALCULATION;       -- VALUE has type FLOAT;
   PUT(DATAFILE, VALUE);
end loop;

-- close DATAFILE
CLOSE(DATAFILE);
```

The call in the program:

```
PUT(DATAFILE, VALUE);
```

means that the value of the variable VALUE is written to the file DATAFILE.
Output to DATAFILE will be in standard exponent form. If we want to have output in some other format, for example, with one figure before the decimal point
and three after, and one blank between each number written, we can introduce
the parameters EXP, FORE and AFT:

```
PUT(DATAFILE, VALUE, EXP => 0, FORE => 2, AFT => 3);
```

In the program we have specified the maximum line length in DATAFILE to be
100 characters by making the call:

```
SET_LINE_LENGTH(DATAFILE, 100);
```

The procedure PUT automatically starts a new line each time there is insufficient
space to write the next item on the current line. If we had not specified a maximum line length, all the numbers would have gone on one, in principle, endless
line.

In the next example we shall see part of a program that reads a text file containing a number of real numbers. (This program could, for example, read a text file written by the program above.) The program calculates and writes out the mean value of the numbers in the file. We assume that we have created a package in this program that provides the facilities for reading and writing values of type FLOAT. Furthermore, we assume the declarations:

```
VALUE            : FLOAT;
VALUE_COUNT : NATURAL := 0;
SUM              : FLOAT  := 0.0;
```

The reading of the data file and calculations can then be accomplished using the statements:

```
while not END_OF_FILE(DATAFILE) loop
   GET(DATAFILE, VALUE);
   SUM := SUM + VALUE;
   VALUE_COUNT := VALUE_COUNT + 1;
end loop;

PUT("Mean value is: ");
PUT(SUM / FLOAT(VALUE_COUNT));
```

Text files can be used to build up registers of data, or databases, of various kinds. To illustrate this, we shall study a telephone list:

```
Acklin Gisela
01-345-7654
Booth Roy
021-65-4321
Cooper Sally
096-12-3214
      ⋮
```

Thus for each person there are two lines: one line for the name and one for the telephone number. We shall now work on a program that can be used to look up a person's telephone number. The program will read in a name from the terminal and then look for it in the text file *telephone.list*. If the name is present, the program will write out the corresponding telephone number. Otherwise it will give a message saying that the person in question is not on the list. We use the simplest imaginable algorithm: the program starts at the beginning of the list and reads one name at a time until either it finds the name in question, or it comes to the end of the list. To indicate that we have found the person we use the BOOLEAN variable FOUND, which has the value FALSE at the start.

Telephone lists are usually sorted alphabetically. If we assume that this is so, the search could be made more efficient by stopping when we find a person whose name comes after the sought name. If, for example, we were looking for the name Williams and found the name Wood, we would know that Williams is not present because it should come before Wood. However, here we shall do without this refinement. The program is:

```
with TEXT_IO;
use TEXT_IO;
procedure FIND_TEL_NO is
  CATALOGUE              : FILE_TYPE;
  REQ_PERS, CURR_PERS    : STRING(1 .. 50);
  TEL_NO                 : STRING(1 .. 15);
  REQ_L, CURR_L, TEL_NO_L : NATURAL;
  FOUND                  : BOOLEAN := FALSE;
begin
  -- read in the name of the required person
  PUT_LINE("What name do you require?");
  GET_LINE(REQ_PERS, REQ_L);

  -- search for the required person in catalogue
  OPEN(CATALOGUE, MODE => IN_FILE,
                  NAME => "telephone.list");

  while not FOUND and not END_OF_FILE(CATALOGUE) loop
  -- read name and telephone number
  GET_LINE(CATALOGUE, CURR_PERS, CURR_L);
  GET_LINE(CATALOGUE, TEL_NO, TEL_NO_L);

  if CURR_PERS(1 .. CURR_L) = REQ_PERS(1 .. REQ_L) then
    PUT_LINE("Telephone number: " & TEL_NO(1 .. TEL_NO_L));
    FOUND := TRUE;
    end if;
  end loop;
  CLOSE(CATALOGUE);

  if not FOUND then
    PUT_LINE("This name is not in the catalogue");
  end if;
end FIND_TEL_NO;
```

We have seen that a text file can be either read or written, but it is not possible to alternate between the two modes. Reading or writing always occurs sequentially from the start of the file: it is not possible to go back to some position in the middle of reading or writing unless certain measures are taken. The only way to go back in a text file is to go back to the *start* of the file. The procedure RESET is used to do this:

> **procedure** RESET (FILE   : **in out** FILE_TYPE;
>   MODE : **in** FILE_MODE);
> **procedure** RESET (FILE   : **in out** FILE_TYPE);

There are two versions of this procedure. In the first, apart from stating the name of the file, it is possible to state whether reading or writing is required. Thus when the file is reset it is also possible to reset the mode of the file, so that a file that was previously being written can now be read, and vice versa. In the second version, the file only returns to the start and the mode is not changed. Reading or writing is continued, as before.

If we have created a new file in a program, NEW_FILE, and written to it, we can go back to the start and read from it by writing:

    RESET(NEW_FILE, IN_FILE);

If we were reading a file, DATAFILE, earlier and want to go back to the start and read it again, we can make the call:

    RESET(DATAFILE);

To go back in a text file

    RESET(F, IN_FILE);

go back to the start of F and read it from the beginning.

    RESET(F, OUT_FILE);

go back to the start of F and write over it.

    RESET(F);

go back to the start of F. If it is open for reading, reading takes place from the start again. If it is open for writing, it is written over.

As an example of an application where files must be reset, we can study a program that can be used to change a number in the telephone list outlined earlier. The program will read in from the terminal the name of a subscriber in the list and his or her new number. The program will then amend the file *telephone.list* so that the new number is inserted. Since reading from and writing to a text file at the same time is not allowed, the work must be accomplished in two stages. In the first, *telephone.list* is read and a copy is written in a temporary new text file. If the given person is found during this copying process the new telephone number is put into the copy. Both files are then reset and the temporary text file is copied to the file *telephone.list*.

```
with TEXT_IO;
use TEXT_IO;
procedure CHANGE_TEL_NO is
   CATALOGUE, TEMPFILE    : FILE_TYPE;
   REQ_PERS, CURR_PERS  : STRING(1 .. 50);
   NEW_NO, TEL_NO        : STRING(1 .. 15);
   REQ_L, CURR_L,
   NEW_NO_L, TEL_NO_L    : NATURAL
   FOUND                 : BOOLEAN := FALSE;

begin
   -- read in the required person's
   -- name and new telephone number
   PUT_LINE("Whose telephone number has changed?");
   GET_LINE(REQ_PERS, REQ_L);
   PUT_LINE("Give the new telephone number");
   GET_LINE(NEW_NO, NEW_NO_L);

   -- open the telephone list for reading
   OPEN(CATALOGUE, MODE => IN_FILE,
                     NAME => "telephone.list");
   -- open a temporary file for writing
   CREATE(TEMPFILE);

   -- copy the telephone list to TEMPFILE
   -- and change the required telephone number

   while not END_OF_FILE(CATALOGUE) loop

      -- read name and tel number
      GET_LINE(CATALOGUE, CURR_PERS, CURR_L);
      GET_LINE(CATALOGUE, TEL_NO, TEL_NO_L);

      -- write name and tel number in TEMPFILE
      PUT_LINE(TEMPFILE, CURR_PERS(1 .. CURR_L));
      if CURR_PERS(1 .. CURR_L) = REQ_PERS(1 .. REQ_L) then
        PUT_LINE(TEMPFILE, NEW_NO(1 .. NEW_NO_L));
        FOUND := TRUE;
      else
        PUT_LINE(TEMPFILE, TEL_NO(1 .. TEL_NO_L));
      end if;
   end loop;
```

```
      if FOUND then
      -- return to the start of the files
      RESET(TEMPFILE, IN_FILE);
      RESET(CATALOGUE, OUT_FILE);

      -- copy TEMPFILE to the catalogue
      while not END_OF_FILE(TEMPFILE) loop
          GET_LINE(TEMPFILE, CURR_PERS, CURR_L);
          PUT_LINE(CATALOGUE, CURR_PERS(1 .. CURR_L));
          GET_LINE(TEMPFILE, TEL_NO, TEL_NO_L);
          PUT_LINE(CATALOGUE, TEL_NO(1 .. TEL_NO_L));
        end loop;
      else
        PUT_LINE("This name is not in the catalogue");
      end if;

      -- close the files
      CLOSE(CATALOGUE);
      CLOSE(TEMPFILE);
    end CHANGE_TEL_NO;
```

The file TEMPFILE will only be temporary because no external filename is given when it is created. If the given person is not in the directory, nothing will be changed, so we do not bother to copy TEMPFILE to CATALOGUE.

A file variable, like other variables, can be given as a parameter to subprograms. Let us write a procedure, QUICK_OPEN, which reads in an external filename from the terminal and opens the corresponding file in the program. The procedure will have two parameters: the logical file to be opened and a parameter of type FILE_MODE which states whether the file should be opened for reading or writing. If the file is to be read, QUICK_OPEN assumes that the file exists and calls OPEN. If the file is to be written, QUICK_OPEN assumes that it is dealing with a new file and calls CREATE. The procedure is easy to write using what we have seen before:

```
procedure QUICK_OPEN (THE_FILE : in out FILE_TYPE;
                      THE_MODE : in FILE_MODE) is
  FILE_NAME  : STRING(1 .. 30);
  NAME_LENGTH : NATURAL;
begin
  PUT_LINE("Give name of file to be opened");
  GET_LINE(FILE_NAME, NAME_LENGTH);
  if THE_MODE = IN_FILE then
    OPEN(THE_FILE,
         MODE => IN_FILE,
         NAME => FILE_NAME(1 .. NAME_LENGTH));
```

```
  else
    CREATE(THE_FILE,
            NAME => FILE_NAME(1 .. NAME_LENGTH));
  end if;
end QUICK_OPEN;
```

Note that the parameter THE_FILE should be an **in out** parameter, because the procedures OPEN and CREATE must be able to both read and change it. If we now have the two files INFILE and OUTFILE in our main program they can easily be opened with the call:

```
QUICK_OPEN(INFILE, IN_FILE);
QUICK_OPEN(OUTFILE, OUT_FILE);
```

In a computer system there are several important programs that work with text files. The text editor, for example, is dedicated to the task of allowing text files to be edited. Another example is a compiler. The program fed into the compiler is stored as a text file and thus the compiler reads this text file.

We have seen that the subprograms in TEXT_IO used to read from and write to the terminal work in the same way as those used for reading and writing text files. If one of these subprograms has no file parameter, it is assumed to refer to the terminal. In fact, the terminal is considered as two text files that are usually called *standard input* and *standard output*. These files are opened automatically when a program is run and are linked to the keyboard and screen, respectively. The following functions in TEXT_IO can be used to access these files, returning the logical files as their result:

```
function STANDARD_INPUT    return FILE_TYPE;

function STANDARD_OUTPUT  return FILE_TYPE;
```

The package TEXT_IO always takes care of the current input and output files. When a program starts, the current input file is set to *standard input*, that is, the keyboard, and the current output file is set to *standard output*, that is, the screen. If a call is made to one of the input or output subprograms in TEXT_IO (for example, GET or PUT) without specifying a file as the first parameter, it is assumed that the current input file or output file is intended, depending on whether the subprogram refers to reading or writing. This means that reading and writing usually occur via the terminal. However, it is possible to change the current input and output files by calling the procedures:

```
procedure SET_INPUT    (FILE : in FILE_TYPE);

procedure SET_OUTPUT  (FILE : in FILE_TYPE);
```

For example, if we want the file MY_FILE to be the current input file and the file NEW_FILE to be the current output file, we make the calls:

```
SET_INPUT(MY_FILE);
SET_OUTPUT(NEW_FILE);
```

Now if we make the call:

```
GET(C);
```

reading will occur from the file MY_FILE instead of from the terminal. In the same way the call:

```
PUT_LINE("message");
```

means that the line will be written to the file NEW_FILE instead of to the terminal.

To determine which files are the current input and output files, the functions:

```
function CURRENT_INPUT    return FILE_TYPE;
function CURRENT_OUTPUT return FILE_TYPE;
```

can be used.

In Ada 95 there is a third standard file, called *standard error*. The output to this file is normally shown on the screen. It is a good habit always to write error messages to *standard error*, since this file is not affected if *standard output* is redirected. Error messages will always be visible. The following subprograms are available for *standard error*:

```
function    STANDARD_ERROR return  FILE_TYPE;
function    CURRENT_ERROR   return  FILE_TYPE;
procedure SET_ERROR (FILE :      in  FILE_TYPE);
```

We shall finish by mentioning some further subprograms in TEXT_IO that can be of use when handling text files.

An open file is linked to a particular external file and it is open for either reading or writing. This information can be found by calling the functions NAME and MODE. For example, the call:

```
NAME(MY_FILE)
```

returns a text string containing the name of the external file that MY_FILE is linked to, and the call:

```
MODE(MY_FILE)
```

returns the result either IN_FILE or OUT_FILE, depending on whether MY_FILE is open for reading or writing. These functions have the specifications:

function NAME (FILE : **in** FILE_TYPE) **return** STRING;

function MODE (FILE : **in** FILE_TYPE) **return** FILE_MODE;

If we want to remove an external file we can use the procedure DELETE:

procedure DELETE (FILE : **in** FILE_MODE);

For example, the call:

DELETE(MY_FILE);

means that the external file that is linked to MY_FILE is simply erased.

EXERCISES

9.1   Write a program to display the values of log(x) for all values of x between 1.0 and 9.9 inclusive, in steps of 0.1 (that is, 1.0, 1.1, 1.2, ... 9.9). The values should be displayed in tabular form at the terminal. Set 10 values to a line, separated by three blank spaces. Each number should be accurate to five decimal places.

9.2   Write a program to read text from the terminal and save it in a new text file with the name *my.text.file*. The new file should have the same line structure as the text file read from the terminal. In addition, all lower-case letters should be translated into upper case in *my.text.file*.

9.3   A secret message is stored in the text file *secret.file*. This has not been stored as straightforward text but in the form of a code message so that it cannot be read easily without authorization. Each letter in the original message has been coded to another using this table:

code letter:	g u w y r m q p s a e i c b n o z l f h d k j x t v
original text:	a b c d e f g h i j k l m n o p q r s t u v w x y z

If the file contains, for example, the lines:

lnybrt jgshsbq
jrybrfygt rsqph oc

the uncoded message is:

rodney waiting
wednesday eight pm

Write a program to read the file with the secret message and write it out in plain language. The program should begin by reading in the code (the first line in the table above) from the terminal.

9.4   Write a program to read an existing text file and write out its contents at the terminal. No empty lines (containing only a line terminator) or lines full of blanks should be written out. Otherwise the output should have the same structure as the text file. The program should be applicable to any text file; the text file's name should thus be read from the terminal.

9.5   Write a program to read in two existing text files (FILE1 and FILE2) and form a new one (FILE3). The new file should contain the contents of the first followed by those of the second. The names of the external files corresponding to FILE1, FILE2 and FILE3 should be read in from the terminal.

9.6   Assume a text file contains the text of a program written in an invented programming language XYZ. Assume further that in a program written in XYZ only the following characters may appear: the lower-case letters 'a' to 'z'; the digits '0' to '9'; the left and right parentheses '(' and ')', and the space character.

Write a program to read in a text file containing a program in XYZ and write it out at the terminal. In this output any lines in the program containing illegal characters should be marked. This is achieved by writing an extra line in the output under the erroneous line, with an exclamation mark below each erroneous character.

If, for example, the file contains the text:

```
read x read y
Let z x plu? y
write z;
```

then the output at the terminal should appear as follows:

```
read x read y
Let z x plu? y
!           !
write z;
       !
```

9.7   Assume you have equipment for making automatic observations of the weather and that it performs particular measurements and stores the results on magnetic tape. From time to time you have to take the magnetic tape to read it into the computer and analyse the observations statistically.

Assume that the equipment stores data on magnetic tape in the form of a text file. Each line of the file contains the results of one complete observation. It is introduced by text in the format yymmddhhmm, which gives the date in the form year, month, day, and the time in hours and minutes, of the current observation. On the rest of the line there follows the measured values of the temperature, atmospheric pressure, humidity of the atmosphere, wind speed and wind direction. All these values are given as real numbers.

Write a program to read in a text file of weather observations from the computer's magnetic tape unit, and output the highest and lowest temperatures measured. The output should have the form:

Highest temperature: xx.xx deg. Measured xx-xx-19xx, at xx:xx
Lowest temperature: xx.xx deg. Measured xx-xx-19xx, at xx:xx

Assume that the computer's magnetic tape unit has the external name *tape0*.

9.8   A text *member.list* has been used to set up a membership register for a club. There are three lines of text in the file for each member: one line for the name, one for the address and one for the telephone number. The file is sorted so that the members appear in alphabetical order.

Write a program to insert a new member in the register. The program should read from the terminal the name, address and telephone number of the new member and then insert this information in the correct place in the file, so that the members remain in correct alphabetical order. (*Hint*: Use a temporary file.)

9.9   Write a very simple text editor. The program should read in the text file, of arbitrary external name, line by line and let the user make simple changes in the stored text. Each time a line is read from the text file it should be written at the terminal and then the program should read an editing command at the terminal. The following commands can be given:

REMOVE   The current line should be removed. Start editing the next line.

INSERT   Read a line in from the terminal and insert it in the file before the current line.

SWAP *xy*   All occurrences of character *x* on the current line should be replaced by character *y*.

NEXT   Editing the current line is finished. Start editing the next line.

After each line is completely edited it should be written to a temporary file; when all the lines are ready the program should then end by copying the temporary file back to the original text file.

9.10   Write a program that reads a text from a text file and writes it out in edited form at the terminal. The program should start by reading in the name of the text file from the terminal. It should also read in the desired page and line size. Assume that the input text file contains a number of words separated by one or more spaces or by a line terminator. In the output there should be one space between words. The line structure in the output should not be the same as that of the input file. Each line of the output should contain as many words as possible in the given line length, so that the lines are roughly the same length.

10 Exceptions

When a program is executed, unexpected situations sometimes occur. Such a situation is called an **exception.** The exception may be the result of an error of some kind, for example, dividing by zero, using an index to an array outside the allowed constraints, or giving faulty input data to a program or subprogram. An exception is not necessarily the result of an error in the program. It may be something that only happens very rarely when the program is run.

When a program is being written, the algorithm should be as clear and easy to understand as possible. If checks were inserted at each stage of the algorithm, however, for every imaginable error and other abnormal event, the algorithm would become very clumsy and hard to follow. In Ada, therefore, there is a mechanism to handle exceptional events without it showing in the program's ordinary algorithm.

10.1 Predefined exceptions

If an error occurs when a program is executed, it normally leads to the program termination and an error message, such as:

```
** MAIN PROGRAM ABANDONED -- EXCEPTION "constraint_error"
   RAISED
```

What this message is saying is that an exceptional event has occurred, in this case a 'constraint error'.

In Ada the following types of exceptions are defined:

CONSTRAINT_ERROR	Occurs when, for example, an attempt is made to assign a variable an invalid value, or to index an array outside the permitted values.
NUMERIC_ERROR	Occurs when a numeric operation cannot return a correct result. For example, the result might be greater than can be represented. A common situation is that an attempt is made to divide by 0. In Ada 95 there is no NUMERIC_ERROR, but even numeric errors generate the exception CONSTRAINT_ERROR.
PROGRAM_ERROR	Occurs in unusual circumstances, when part of the program called is not accessible, or when the final **end** in a function is reached, that is, the function has not returned a result. There are also other errors that cause this exception.
STORAGE_ERROR	Occurs if the accessible memory expires, for example, there is a recursive subprogram with a faulty terminating condition so that too many instances of the subprogram are generated.
TASKING_ERROR	Can occur in connection with parallel programs. This will not be discussed here.

These five exceptions are defined in the package STANDARD; thus they are automatically defined in all implementations of Ada.

When an exception occurs, the normal execution of the program ceases immediately. If no special precautions have been taken in the program, it will terminate abnormally with an error message stating the type of exception causing the termination.

These predefined exceptions are raised when some error occurs while a program is being executed. We also have the opportunity to define an exception by including in the program a special **raise** statement. For example, we can bring about an exception PROGRAM_ERROR with the statement:

raise PROGRAM_ERROR;

When this statement is executed the program will behave as though an error has occurred in the program. The program terminates at once with an error message, unless the exception is treated in some way.

Raise statement

> **raise** E;

where E is the name of an exception.

Normal execution terminates at once and the exception E occurs.

It is not really of much interest to raise exceptions of one of the predefined types. It is more useful, however, to raise other exceptions, as we shall demonstrate in the following sections.

10.2 Declaring exceptions

In an Ada program it is possible to work with exceptions other than the predefined ones listed in Section 10.1. It is possible to define our own exceptions. An exception TIME_UP, for example, could be declared as follows:

TIME_UP : **exception**;

This is a declaration and is placed with the other declarations – declarations of variables, for example. In form, it looks like a variable declaration, but TIME_UP is not a variable. It cannot have a value. All the declaration says is that in the program there is an exception, TIME_UP, that may happen. We can make as many declarations as we like of our own exceptions in a program. We can list several in one declaration, for example:

TABLE_EMPTY, TABLE_FULL : **exception**;

The normal rules hold for the scope of the declaration. For example, the name of an exception is not known outside the subprogram in which it is declared. (However, when an exception occurs its effects can spread outside the subprogram in which it was declared.)

Declaring exceptions

E1, E2, ... : **exception**;

where *E1, E2,* ... are the names given to the exceptions.

The declarations are placed among the other declarations.

To cause an exception to occur we can use a **raise** statement:

raise TIME_UP;

The same pattern of events occurs as with predefined exceptions. Unless we do something special, normal execution of the program ceases with an error message, in this case:

** MAIN PROGRAM ABANDONED -- EXCEPTION "time_up" RAISED

Such an error message can be much more informative than a message containing one of the predefined exceptions. A predefined exception could be caused by many different errors in a program, whereas a declared exception can only occur if a **raise** statement has been executed.

10.3   Handling exceptions

So far we have said that an exception interrupts a program so that it stops with an error message. It is, however, possible to trap exceptions in a program and take some appropriate action. If we have a program that controls an industrial process of some sort, it is not acceptable for the program to cease abruptly if an exception occurs. The program must deal with what has happened by writing a warning message to the operator or closing down a critical process, for example. It is also unacceptable for a program to cease because, for example, an operator has written input data in the wrong format or has entered an integer when the program was expecting a real number.

There are three levels of ambition in dealing with exceptions:

(1)   Take control of the exception, and try and take suitable action to enable the program to continue.

(2)   Trap, identify and pass the exception on to another part of the program.

(3)   Ignore the exception: the program will stop when the exception occurs.

The basic principle should be that the exception is controlled in the part of the program (or outside it if necessary) where its effect can most sensibly be handled. The third level is the one we have seen so far. The exceptions we have seen have been of the predefined sort and have most often occurred because of an error in the logic of our programs. To try to trap such exceptions in the program is not really worthwhile. The correct course of action is to handle what happens from outside the program, that is, correct the program so that the logic error disappears. If the Ada system gives an error message that is too scant when an error of logic occurs (that is, we cannot see where the error occurred), and if we do not have access to a debugging program, then it may be better to trap the logic error in the program ourselves. (A more meaningful error message is then possible.)

As an example of the first level of ambition, we shall study a function that calculates the tangent of an angle. We assume that we have access to a mathematical package containing the functions SIN and COS, but not TAN. It is simple to construct the function TAN:

```
function TAN (X : FLOAT) return FLOAT is
begin
    return SIN(X) / COS(X);
end TAN;
```

The problem with this function, however, is that for certain values of X (PI/2, for example), COS(X) has the value 0 and the value of TAN(X) is infinite. (Note that the parameter to TAN must be in radians and not in degrees.) If we call our function TAN with the value PI/2 then an attempt is made to divide by 0 and NUMERIC_ERROR occurs. This means that execution terminates with an error message. (In Ada 95 it is not NUMERIC_ERROR that occurs but CONSTRAINT_ERROR.)

We shall now amend the function TAN so that it traps the error and yields a 'sensible' result other than program termination. What constitutes a sensible result is open to discussion. Since we cannot store an infinitely large number we shall let it be represented by the largest possible value that a variable of type FLOAT can assume. Naturally, this is not mathematically correct. If this is unacceptable, we can do it in another way that will be discussed later.

So far we have said that a subprogram consists of a subprogram specification followed by a declarative part and a sequence of statements. In fact, there can be a further section at one end of the subprogram – a section that deals with exceptions. Let us look at TAN if we add such a section:

```
function TAN(X : FLOAT) return FLOAT is
begin
    return SIN(X) / COS(X);
exception
    when NUMERIC_ERROR =>
```

```
if (SIN(X) >= 0.0 and COS(X) >= 0.0) or
   (SIN(X) < 0.0 and COS(X) < 0.0) then
   return FLOAT'LAST;
else
   return FLOAT'LAST;
end if;

end TAN;
```

The part we have added starts with the reserved word **exception**. (This should not be confused with a declaration of an explicit exception.) The remainder of the added part is similar to the structure of a case statement. The line:

```
when NUMERIC_ERROR =>
```

means that the statements following this line should be executed if an exception of the kind NUMERIC_ERROR is raised. This is called a **handler** for the exception NUMERIC_ERROR. (In Ada 95, this line should be

```
when CONSTRAINT_ERROR =>)
```

When we execute our function TAN, NUMERIC_ERROR will occur if we try to divide by zero in the statement:

```
return SIN(X) / COS(X);
```

This statement is then aborted and the program will instead jump to the statements in the handler for NUMERIC_ERROR. This means that the **if** statement will be obeyed, and there a test will be made for the result being either plus or minus infinity. (If you think about it, you will see that the complicated logical expression following the **if** can be replaced by the rather simpler SIN(X) * COS(X) >= 0.0.) FLOAT'LAST is, as we have seen earlier, the largest possible number that can be stored in the type FLOAT. Depending on which part of the **if** statement is executed, the result of the function can be either FLOAT'LAST or LOAT'LAST.

By trapping the exception NUMERIC_ERROR program termination has been avoided. Control returns to the program that called TAN and execution continues as normal.

It is important to note that control did not return to the statement that was interrupted in the normal statement section of the function. This is not only because we have **return** statements in the exception handler for NUMERIC_ERROR – it is generally true. After the statements in the statement section of the exception handler have been executed the **end** is reached in the part of the program containing the handler. There is never a jump back to the part of the program that was interrupted.

There can be handlers for several exceptions at the end of a subprogram, both predefined and declared. We can, for example, have:

```
exception
  when TIME_UP =>
    PUT_LINE("Time to make a move");

  when CONSTRAINT_ERROR =>
    PUT_LINE("Error in index value");

  when TABLE_FULL | TABLE_EMPTY =>
    PUT_LINE("Table error");

  when others =>
    PUT_LINE("Something wrong in package PLAY");
```

We see that it is possible to have common handlers for two or more kinds of exception. In our example, TABLE_FULL and TABLE_EMPTY have a common handler. Thus the message "Table error" is output when exceptions of the kind TABLE_FULL or TABLE_EMPTY occur. We also see that there can be an **others** alternative to handle all other kinds of exception that are not already listed. An **others** alternative must appear at the end if it appears at all.

If an exception of kind E occurs and the current subprogram has no handler for exceptions of this kind (including no **others** alternative), then the exception E will be 'passed on' to the subprogram that called the current sub-program. Thus an exception of kind E will occur in the calling subprogram. If this also has no handler for exception E then the exception will be passed on further, and so on. If an exception occurs in the main program and this too has no handler for E, the program will finally be terminated by the Ada system with an error message.

It should be noted that if an exception occurs in the declarative part of a subprogram, that is, before the statements following **begin** have started to be executed, the exception is passed directly to the calling subprogram. Thus such an exception cannot be trapped in the subprogram where the exception occurs.

In Ada 95 what is called a **choice parameter** can be placed in a handler for a given exception, when you want more information about the current exception. It could look like this, for example:

```
exception
  when EXCEPTION_EVENT: others =>
    PUT_LINE(EXCEPTION_NAME(EXCEPTION_EVENT));
    PUT_LINE(EXCEPTION_MESSAGE(EXCEPTION_EVENT));
    PUT_LINE(EXCEPTION_INFORMATION(EXCEPTION_EVENT));
```

In this example, EXCEPTION_EVENT is a choice parameter. A choice parame-ter is considered as a constant of the predefined private type EXCEPTION_

OCCURRENCE. In the package ADA.EXCEPTIONS there are three predefined functions: EXCEPTION_NAME, EXCEPTION_MESSAGE and EXCEPTION_ INFORMATION, which can be called to give various information about the current exception (dependent on the installation). The three functions each have one parameter of the type EXCEPTION_OCCURRENCE and return a text result of type STRING, which can be printed as in the example given above. There is also a procedure RERAISE_OCCURRENCE which can be used to reraise a certain exception.

▲

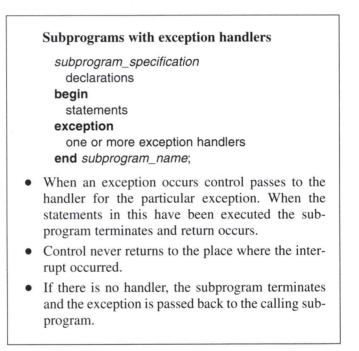

Subprograms with exception handlers

> *subprogram_specification*
>   declarations
> **begin**
>   statements
> **exception**
>   one or more exception handlers
> **end** *subprogram_name*;

- When an exception occurs control passes to the handler for the particular exception. When the statements in this have been executed the sub-program terminates and return occurs.
- Control never returns to the place where the inter-rupt occurred.
- If there is no handler, the subprogram terminates and the exception is passed back to the calling sub-program.

Exception handlers

Different forms:

> **when** *E* =>
>   statements;
> **when** *E1* | *E2* | ... | *EN* =>
>   statements;
> **when others** =>
>   statements;

where *E*, *E1*, *E2*, ... are the names of exceptions.

If there is an **others** alternative it must be last.

Let us return to the example of the function TAN. If it is not acceptable that it returns the result FLOAT'LAST in the place of infinity, we can tackle it another way. If we find that program execution breaks down as a result of trying to compute infinity, we can instead trap the error in TAN and return a suitable error message so that the programmer can more easily trace the source of the error in the program that calls TAN. Thus we settle for the second of our levels of ambition.

```
function TAN(X : FLOAT) return FLOAT is
begin
    return SIN(X) / COS(X);
exception
    when NUMERIC_ERROR =>
        PUT_LINE("The value of tangent is too big");
        raise;
end TAN;
```

In the handler for NUMERIC_ERROR, instead of trying to work out some reasonable result we have inserted an error message. On the next line we find the statement:

```
raise;
```

Any statements can go into an exception handler, even the **raise** statement. The special form of **raise** statement we have used here, where no exception name is given, is only allowed within a handler. This **raise** statement means that the exception that caused the handler to take control has occurred again, and thus the exception is passed on to the calling program.

Thus in our example the NUMERIC_ERROR exception will be passed on to the calling program. If there is no handler in this program (or the program that called it, and so on) execution of the program will terminate with an error message "numeric_error". Because we have added the error message:

The value of tangent is too big

to the function TAN, the logic fault will now be easier to find in the program.

It is not necessarily an error of logic that makes us attempt to calculate the tangent of an angle that gives an incalculable result. Let us study, for example, the following lines of program which read in the values of angles from the terminal and then calculate and write out the tangents of these angles:

```
loop
    PUT("Give a real number, or end with CTRL-D: ");
    exit when END_OF_FILE;
    GET(NUMBER);
```

```
        RES := TAN(NUMBER);
        PUT("Tangent is: "); PUT(RES); NEW_LINE;
    end loop;
```

We assume that both variables NUMBER and RES have the type FLOAT. There is no direct error in the logic of these lines, but they still do not work if we give a value such as PI/2 as input.

Thanks to the error message in TAN a good error message is sent to the operator. Now we can rewrite these lines so that the exception NUMERIC_ERROR is trapped. This then means that the program is not interrupted but can continue by asking for the next value. Our modified form of the loop is:

```
    loop
        begin
            PUT("Give a real number, or end with CTRL-D: ");
            exit when END_OF_FILE;
            GET(NUMBER);
            RES := TAN(NUMBER);
            PUT("Tangent is: "); PUT(RES); NEW_LINE;
        exception
            when NUMERIC_ERROR =>
                PUT_LINE("No tangent can be evaluated");
        end;
    end loop;
```

Note the addition of the words **begin** and **end** around the contents of the **loop** statement. These words are the start and end of a new statement in Ada that we have not yet met – a **block** statement.

The reason for introducing a block statement here is that an exception handler may be placed at the end of one. When an exception occurs within the block statement, control passes to the appropriate handler (if there is one). When the statements within the handler have been executed, execution of the whole block statement stops and the program continues with the next statement after the block statement.

If the exception NUMERIC_ERROR occurs, then the text:

No tangent can be evaluated

is written and execution continues thereafter with a new iteration of the **loop** statement. Thus the whole program is not terminated. If we had not introduced the block statement but had placed the handler for NUMERIC_ERROR at the end of the program instead, the whole program would have terminated because the exception NUMERIC_ERROR had occurred. Using the block statement thus enables us to remain in the program and continue as normal.

It should be noted that the handler can only take care of exceptions that occur within the block statement. If NUMERIC_ERROR occurs elsewhere in the program, control will not pass to this handler.

A block statement is a compound statement that has a structure reminiscent of that of a subprogram. A block statement is considered an ordinary statement and can be placed anywhere an ordinary statement can. It is executed when it is reached in the normal execution sequence of the program (thus it is not called like a subprogram). In a block statement, as in a subprogram, there can be a statement section and a section that contains exception handlers. At its most general, however, the block statement can also contain a declarative part before the statements. In this case the block statement starts with the word **declare**.

Block statement

[**declare**
   declarations]
begin
   statements
[**exception**
   one or more exception handlers]
end;

[...] can be omitted.

- Declarations made are only known inside the block statement.

- When an exception occurs, execution of the whole block terminates and the next statement is carried out.

Let us look at some examples of block statements:

```
begin
   PUT_LINE("This is program XYZ");
   PUT_LINE("Welcome");
end;

declare                -- exchange I and J
   TEMP : INTEGER;
begin
   TEMP  : = I;
   I       : = J;
   J       : = TEMP;
end;
```

```
declare
  I, J : INTEGER;
begin
  GET(I);
  GET(J);
  PUT(I ** J);
exception
  when CONSTRAINT_ERROR =>
    PUT_LINE("Exponent error");
end;
```

If we return once more to the example of the function TAN, it may be disadvantageous to pass on the exception NUMERIC_ERROR, because it can occur for so many different reasons; it can be difficult for the calling program to identify the error and realize that it occurred in TAN. Moreover, it is not always desirable to have an error message from TAN: the writer of the calling program may prefer to formulate his or her own error messages.

The solution to this dilemma is to declare an exception TAN_ERROR in TAN and to pass this on. But we cannot declare TAN_ERROR in the function TAN, because then it would not be known outside and it would not be possible to write a handler for it in the calling program. Nor is it good to declare TAN_ERROR in the calling program – TAN_ERROR belongs with the function TAN and should therefore be declared in conjunction with it.

If we assume that TAN is included as a function in a mathematical package there is a natural way of solving this problem. We declare TAN_ERROR in the specification of this package. Then TAN_ERROR is known by the program that called TAN but its declaration is still together with TAN. Thus we can have a package MATHEMATICS:

```
package MATHEMATICS is
  function SIN (X  : FLOAT) return FLOAT;
  function COS (X : FLOAT) return FLOAT;
  function TAN (X  : FLOAT) return FLOAT;
      ⋮

  TAN_ERROR : exception;
end MATHEMATICS;
```

The body of the package looks like this:

```
package body MATHEMATICS is

  function SIN (X : FLOAT) return FLOAT is
      ⋮

  end SIN;
```

```
function COS (X : FLOAT) return FLOAT is
    ⋮
end COS;

function TAN (X : FLOAT) return FLOAT is
begin
  return SIN (X) / COS (X);
exception
  when NUMERIC_ERROR =>
    raise TAN_ERROR;
end TAN;

end MATHEMATICS;
```

Now we can write a program that uses the package MATHEMATICS and that makes use of the exception TAN_ERROR:

```
with TEXT_IO, BASIC_NUM_IO, MATHEMATICS;
use TEXT_IO, BASIC_NUM_IO, MATHEMATICS;
procedure COMPUTE_TAN is
  NUMBER, RES : FLOAT;
begin
  loop
    begin
      PUT("Give a real number, or end with CTRL-D: ");
      exit when END_OF_FILE;
      GET(NUMBER);
      RES := TAN(NUMBER);
      PUT("Tangent is: "); PUT(RES); NEW_LINE;
    exception
      when TAN_ERROR =>
        PUT_LINE("The tangent is too big");
    end;
  end loop;
end COMPUTE_TAN;
```

If the value PI/2 is given as input to this program, the message:

```
The tangent is too big
```

will be output.

It is very common for a package specification to contain declarations of the exceptions that can occur in the package. Trapping problems within the package and passing on well-specified exceptions to the user gives the user the opportunity to take appropriate action. Errors most often arise during execution of a package because the user has called a subprogram wrongly. Thus, in constructing packages, we generally handle exceptions at the second of our three levels of ambition.

As a further example of packages that use this technique we shall study a package that deals with vectors. Earlier, we wrote functions that can add two vectors. Here we shall build up a small package that offers facilities for adding two vectors and for forming the scalar product of two vectors. As shown in Section 6.1, a vector can be represented by the type:

type VECTOR **is array** (INTEGER **range** < >) **of** FLOAT;

If two vectors are added the result is a new vector in which each component is the sum of their corresponding components. In calculating the scalar product of two vectors, the products of corresponding pairs of components are formed and added together. Thus the result is not a new vector but a single number. One condition governing whether it is possible to add two vectors or form their scalar product is that they both have to have the same number of components.

The specification of a package VECTOR_PACKAGE can be written:

```
package VECTOR_PACKAGE is

    type VECTOR is array (INTEGER range < >) of FLOAT;

    function ADD (V1, V2 : VECTOR) return VECTOR;
    -- add vectors V1 and V2

    function SCALAR_PROD (V1, V2 : VECTOR) return FLOAT;
    -- compute scalar product of vectors V1 and V2

    LENGTH_ERROR : exception;
    -- Occurs if the two parameters to the functions
    -- have different lengths
end VECTOR_PACKAGE;
```

In the specification we have declared an exception LENGTH_ERROR that occurs if the two parameters to ADD or SCALAR_PROD have different numbers of components. The body of VECTOR_PACKAGE can now be assembled:

```
package body VECTOR_PACKAGE is

    function ADD (V1, V2 : VECTOR) return VECTOR is
        TEMP : VECTOR(V1'RANGE);
    begin
        if V1'LENGTH /= V2'LENGTH then
            raise LENGTH_ERROR;
        end if;
        TEMP := V2;
```

```
    for I in V1'RANGE loop
       TEMP(I) TEMP(I) + V1 (I);
    end loop;
    return TEMP;
  end ADD;

  function SCALAR_PROD (V1, V2 VECTOR) return FLOAT is
    SUM   : FLOAT:=0.0;
    TEMP : VECTOR(V1'RANGE);
  begin
    if V1'LENGTH /= V2'LENGTH then
      raise LENGTH_ERROR;
    end if;
    TEMP := V2;
    for I in V1'RANGE loop
       SUM := SUM + V1(I) * TEMP(I);
    end loop;
    return SUM;
  end SCALAR_PROD;
end VECTOR_PACKAGE;
```

We use one of the concepts raised in Section 6.1. To avoid the problems that arise when two vectors have different index constraints we declare a local variable TEMP that is indexed in the same way as V1. Then we make the assignment:

```
TEMP := V2;
```

and copy the whole of V2 to TEMP. This is only feasible if V2 and TEMP (that is, V1) have the same number of components. Therefore, we first test that this is the case. If V1 and V2 have different numbers of components then we raise the exception LENGTH_ERROR:

```
raise LENGTH_ERROR;
```

10.4   Errors arising during input and output

In the package TEXT_IO the technique of generating exceptions is used if something goes wrong. In the specification of TEXT_IO the exceptions STATUS_ ERROR, MODE_ERROR, NAME_ERROR, USE_ERROR, DEVICE_ERROR, END_ERROR, DATA_ERROR and LAYOUT_ERROR are declared. The names of these exceptions are thus visible to the user of TEXT_IO, who can use them to trap errors that occur during input and output. The following summary explains when the different exceptions can occur:

STATUS_ERROR   Occurs if an attempt is made to read from or write to a file that is not open, or if an attempt is made to open a file that is already open.

MODE_ERROR   Occurs if an attempt is made to read from a file that is open for writing or to write to a file that is open for reading.

NAME_ERROR   Occurs if an attempt is made to open a file and an incorrect external name is given. The name may be in the wrong form or an external file with that name may not be found.

USE_ERROR   Occurs if an attempt is made to open a file for illegal use. This may be, for example, an attempt to open a line-printer file for reading. Another example is if CREATE is called with an external name that already exists and the system will not allow the existing file to be overwritten.

DEVICE_ERROR   Occurs if there is a technical failure on an input or output device.

END_ERROR   Occurs if an attempt is made to read something from a file and the next thing in line for reading is a file terminator.

DATA_ERROR   Occurs if a value of integer, floating point or enumeration type is read in and the input data file contains data in an incorrect form (that is, not following the rules for the type in question).

LAYOUT_ERROR   Occurs, for example, if an attempt is made to state a current line or column number for output that exceeds the maximum limits.

We shall study a procedure READ_FLOAT that can be used to read a real number from the terminal. If the user enters the real number wrongly, for example as an integer, the program will not terminate but the user will be asked to rewrite the number.

The procedure should be 'callable' in the same way as GET in a program. To read a value to a floating point variable X the call:

READ_FLOAT(X);

should therefore be made. The procedure is:

```
procedure READ_FLOAT (NUMBER : out FLOAT) is
   READY : BOOLEAN := FALSE;
begin
   while not READY loop
     begin
```

```
      GET(NUMBER);
      READY := TRUE;
    exception
      when DATA_ERROR =>
        PUT_LINE("Incorrect number. Please repeat.");
        SKIP_LINE;
    end;
  end loop;
end READ_FLOAT;
```

The procedure consists of a **loop** statement that tries to read a real number from the terminal each time round. Within the **loop** statement there is a block statement. The **loop** statement continues until a real number has been successfully read. The variable READY indicates whether the reading has been successful. At the start READY has the value FALSE. When the call:

```
GET(NUMBER);
```

is executed, the exception DATA_ERROR occurs if the user writes something wrong at the terminal. The normal execution in the block statement terminates and control passes to the handler for DATA_ERROR. The statement:

```
READY := TRUE;
```

will thus not be executed before the call to GET has been successful, that is, without a DATA_ERROR.

In the final example we show a procedure that can be used to open an existing text file for reading. The procedure reads in the name of the external file from the terminal and then tries to open it by calling the procedure OPEN in TEXT_IO. If an error occurs during the opening it is trapped and an appropriate error message is output:

```
procedure OWN_OPEN (THE_FILE : in out FILE_TYPE) is
  FILE_NAME     : STRING (1 .. 30);
  NAME_LENGTH : NATURAL;
begin
  PUT_LINE("Give the name of the file to be read");
  GET_LINE(FILE_NAME, NAME_LENGTH);
  OPEN(THE_FILE,
        MODE => IN_FILE,
        NAME => FILE_NAME(1 .. NAME_LENGTH));
exception
  when STATUS_ERROR =>
    PUT_LINE("The file is already open");
```

```
        when NAME_ERROR =>
            PUT_LINE("There is no file with that name");
        when USE_ERROR =>
            PUT_LINE("The file cannot be read");
        when others =>
            PUT_LINE("Unexpected error on opening file");
end OWN_OPEN;
```

If we assume that we have the declaration:

```
INFILE : FILE_TYPE;
```

in a program, then we can make the call:

```
OWN_OPEN(INFILE);
```

to try to open the file. It is possible to test if the opening went well by calling the function IS_OPEN:

```
if IS_OPEN(INFILE) then
    -- continue as normal
end if;
```

EXERCISES

10.1 Write a version of the function FACTORIAL that calculates $N!$ for an integer $N >= 0$. The function should give a floating point number as its result and, if the result is so great that it cannot be represented in the computer in use, the function should give as its result the largest floating point number that can be represented.

10.2 The procedure COMPUTE_ROOTS in Chapter 6 computed the roots of a quadratic equation. Rewrite this procedure so that it does not have the **out** parameter REAL_ROOTS. If a quadratic equation has no real roots, the procedure should produce the error message:

Error in COMPUTE_ROOTS. There are no real roots.

and pass the exception NUMERIC_ERROR to the calling program.

10.3 In Section 8.8 a package was constructed to describe the abstract data type queue. Add to the package so that it generates the exceptions QUEUE_FULL if an attempt is made to add more elements than the queue can hold, and QUEUE_EMPTY if an attempt is made to remove an element from an empty queue.

10.4 Write a procedure TRY_TO_GET that can be used instead of GET to read an integer from the terminal. The procedure TRY_TO_GET should have two **out** parameters. The first should be an integer parameter to hold the integer read. The second should be of type BOOLEAN. This should be given the value TRUE if the reading is successful (that is, the user writes an integer correctly) or otherwise the value FALSE.

10.5 Write a procedure that can be used to open a new text file. The procedure should read in the name of the new file from the terminal. If the user writes something incorrect, that is, no new file with that name can be opened, the procedure should produce an appropriate error message and ask the user to give another file name. This should be repeated until the new file has been opened successfully.

11 Dynamic Data Structures

For every ordinary object (variable or constant) we can assume that there is a space in the primary memory of the computer where its value is stored. It could be said that the object's name is the name of that space in memory, or store. The space in the memory is created when the object is declared and it exists during the execution of the program unit in which the object's declaration appears. Such an object is described as **static**. It cannot be created or destroyed during execution of the program unit.

In some applications, the number of objects needed is not known in advance. Then **dynamic data structures** are required, which can grow and shrink during program execution; it must therefore be possible to create new objects during execution. An example of a dynamic data structure is a list where elements can be added and removed dynamically.

This chapter reviews Ada's mechanism for creating dynamic objects. The dynamic data structures – **lists, queues, stacks** and **trees** – will be discussed.

In Ada 95 it is possible to create pointers to subprograms, which in some cases is very useful. This is demonstrated in the last section of this chapter.

11.1 Pointers and dynamic objects

To create a dynamic object during execution an **allocator** is used. This, in its simplest form, is an expression with the reserved word **new** followed by a type name. To create a dynamic object of type INTEGER, for example, we can write:

new INTEGER

It is most common to work with dynamic objects of record types. If, for example, we have declared the type PERSON:

```
type PERSON is
   record
      NAME    : STRING(1 .. 20);
      HEIGHT  : INTEGER;
      WEIGHT  : FLOAT;
   end record;
```

then we can create a new object of the type PERSON using the allocator:

new PERSON

When an allocator is used, space is reserved in memory for a new object of the type in question. Each time the allocator is executed a new object is created, or designated.

In the two foregoing examples, the contents of the space in memory is undefined. Therefore the values of the dynamic object are also undefined. It is possible to add an initialization term to the allocator to give a newly created object a value. To create a new object of type INTEGER and, at the same time, give it an initial value 5, we can write:

new INTEGER'(5)

After the type name an apostrophe is written followed by the value in brackets. The value in brackets does not need to be a constant, but it must be an expression with the same type as the new object. If N is a variable of type INTEGER, we can thus write:

new INTEGER'(2 * N)

If we want to create a new object of record or array type and initialize the object, an aggregate should be written after the apostrophe. For example, a new PERSON can be created and initialized with the allocator:

new PERSON'("Booth Abigail   ", 170, 55.0)

We know that each expression in Ada has a particular defined type. An allocator is also considered to be an expression, so what type does such an expression have? The result of an allocator is a **reference** or **pointer**, or, as generally called in Ada, an **access value**. We say that this result is of **access type**; in Ada the reserved word **access** is used to denote this pointer type. The result of the expression:

    new INTEGER

is thus a pointer to an object of type INTEGER. Similarly, the result of the expression:

    new PERSON

is a pointer to an object of type PERSON.

Allocators

    new T

or:

    new T'(*initial_value*)

where T is an arbitrary type. It creates a new object of type T. The result of the allocator is a pointer to an object of type T.

As for other types, it is possible to declare variables of access types. In the following example two access variables are declared, PI and PP:

```
type INT_POINTER   is access INTEGER;
type PERS_POINTER is access PERSON;
PI : INT_POINTER;
PP: PERS_POINTER;
```

We can now use these variables to save the pointers to the created objects. For example, we can have the statement:

```
PI := new INTEGER'(5);
```

The variable PI will now point to an object of type INTEGER. The situation is illustrated in Figure 11.1.

Figure 11.1

Similarly, we can write the statement:

PP := **new** PERSON'("Booth Abigail   ", 170, 55.0);

and then we have the situation shown in Figure 11.2.
As with other variables, an access variable can be initialized at the same time as it is declared. We could, for example, achieve the same result by declaring PP in the following way:

PP : PERS_POINTER := **new** PERSON'("Booth Abigail   ", 170, 55.0);

If an access variable is not initialized with its declaration it automatically takes the value **null**, which means that it is not pointing to anything.

Access variables

> **type** POINTER **is access** T;
> P : POINTER;

where T is any type.

The variable can be initialized at the same time as it is declared:

> **type** POINTER **is access** T;
> P : POINTER := **new** T'(*initialization_expression*);

An uninitialized access variable automatically takes the value **null**.

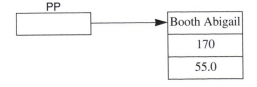

Figure 11.2

Now PP can be used to get at the new object – it points to it; it provides access to it. To change the new person's weight, for example, we can write:

PP.WEIGHT := 54.0;

and to write out the person's name we can make the call:

PUT(PP.NAME);

If the whole object that PP points to is required, the reserved word **all** can be used. For example, to change the whole record that PP is pointing to we could write:

PP.**all** := ("Booth Russell   ", 180, 75.0);

Figure 11.3 illustrates how it would then look.

To access an object

> P.**all**

means the *whole* of an object that is pointed to.

- If the object is a record type, individual components can be selected by writing:

P.*component_name*

- The access variable P is not affected.

Several access variables may point at the same object. If we declare another variable:

PP2 : PERS_POINTER;

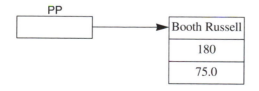

Figure 11.3

we can now write the statement:

PP2 := PP;

This means that the access value of PP is assigned to PP2 and, therefore, PP2 will point to the same object as PP. The situation is shown in Figure 11.4.

Assignment of access variables

P1 := P2;

P1 and P2 must be access variables of the same type.

- The access value of P2 is assigned to P1.

- They point at the same object.

- The value of the object is not affected.

Let us declare yet another access variable:

PP3 : PERS_POINTER := **new** PERSON;

PP3 has been initialized so that it points at a new object of type PERSON. Thus there are now two objects of type PERSON. Figure 11.5 illustrates the situation. The contents of the record that PP3 is pointing to are still undefined. If we want to copy to it the contents of the record that PP points to we can write the statement:

PP3.**all** := PP.**all**;

Observe that the word **all** must appear on both sides. If it had not been present, the access variable PP3 would have been changed to point to the same object as PP.

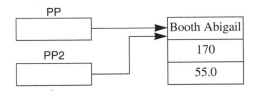

Figure 11.4

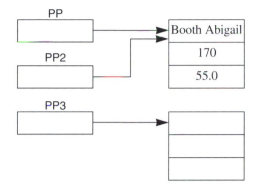

Figure 11.5

A particular access variable can only point to objects of a particular type. For example, PP can only point at objects of the type PERSON, so it would be wrong to try and write:

PP := **new** INTEGER;   -- ERROR! Different types

A dynamic object ceases to exist when execution first leaves the part of the program where the access type to the object was declared. The Ada system can automatically reuse the space thus freed in memory. Objects of the type PERSON in the foregoing example cannot, therefore, exist outside the part of the program where the type PERS_POINTER is declared.

This way of declaring the length of time a dynamic object can exist means that the problem of lingering pointers pointing to space in memory that has actually been freed can never arise. (On the other hand, during execution, it can happen that there are dynamic objects to which no pointers point.) Sometimes, however, you might want to bypass the normal rules and more closely control the demise of a dynamic object you have created; this can be done using the (generic) standard procedure UNCHECKED_DEALLOCATION. To use this you must have the **with** clause:

with UNCHECKED_DEALLOCATION;

at the start of the compilation unit. The way this works is shown in the following example. Suppose we have declared the types PERSON and PERS_POINTER as before. We can now state that we want to give back the memory which has been allocated to the type PERSON by declaring a procedure which we can call GIVE_BACK_PERSON:

procedure GIVE_BACK_PERSON **is new**
            UNCHECKED_DEALLOCATION(PERSON, PERS_POINTER);

(As you see, we have to state both the type that is being deallocated and the corresponding access type.) Now assume that we have executed the statement:

```
PP := new PERSON;
```

Then later in the program we can deallocate the memory that PP points to by making the call:

```
GIVE_BACK_PERSON (PP);
```

When you use this method of deallocating dynamically allocated memory you also take the responsibility for ensuring that there will not be any pointers to memory with undefined content.

Access may be declared to objects of any type. For example, even arrays can be allocated dynamically. Suppose we have the unconstrained array type TAB:

```
type TAB is array (INTEGER range < >) of INTEGER;
```

We can declare an access type TAB_POINTER and two access variables of the type:

```
type TAB_POINTER is access TAB;
TP1, TP2 : TAB_POINTER;
```

It is now possible to allocate two arrays dynamically, with TP1 and TP2 pointing to the allocated arrays:

```
TP1 := new TAB(1 .. 10);
TP2 := new TAB'(7, 19, 68);
```

Earlier, we saw that you must state index bounds when you declare variables of an unconstrained array type; the same rule applies when you dynamically allocate objects of an unconstrained array type. In the latter case you have to state in the allocation expression how many components there are to be in the allocated array, and that can be done either by stating the index bounds, as in the first example above, or by giving an aggregate as initial value, as in the second example. Thus, TP1 will point to an uninitialized array with 10 elements, and TP2 will point to an initialized array with three elements.

A pointer to an array can be used in the same way as an ordinary array name. (You do not need to use the word **all** to access what the pointer is pointing at.) We could, for example, write:

```
TPl (5) 94;
for I in TP2'RANGE loop
   PUT(TP2(I));
end loop;
```

We should also say a few words about the dynamic allocation of records with variants. These were first discussed in Section 7.5. The example we worked with there used a type VEHICLE, which described the following types of vehicle: PRIVATE_CAR, VAN, BUS, and UNKNOWN. Now we can declare an access type VEHICLE_POINTER and three access variables of the type:

      type VEHICLE_POINTER **is access** VEHICLE;
      VPl, VP2, VP3 : VEHICLE_POINTER;

When we declared ordinary variables which were records with variants, it was allowed, under certain conditions, to have what were called unconstrained variables, that is, variables whose variants could be changed. This is not permitted when an object which is a record with variants is dynamically allocated. Such an object is always constrained or, more explicitly, its variant may never be changed. The variant must therefore be known when allocation takes place. This can be accomplished either by directly stating the name of the variant or by having an initialization expression which contains the name of the variant:

      VP1 := **new** VEHICLE(BUS);
      VP2 := **new** VEHICLE'(PRIVATE_CAR, "A123ABC", 300, 5, HATCH);

Here, VP1 points to an uninitialized record of the variant BUS and VP2 to an initialized record of variant PRIVATE_CAR. It would be acceptable to write:

      VP3 := **new** VEHICLE;

in this case, since the variant in the type VEHICLE has a default value; VP3 will here point to an uninitialized record of the UNKNOWN variant. Note, however, that it is not possible to change the variant for this record.

    A pointer to a record with variants is used in the same way as a pointer to ordinary records. We can write, for instance,

      VP1.AIR_CONDITIONING := TRUE;
      PUT(VP2.NUMBER_OF_SEATS);

    In Ada 83 an access variable can only point to objects which have arisen as the result of an allocation expression being executed. Thus an access variable can never be made to point at a variable which has been declared in the normal way.

In Ada 95, on the other hand, you can have pointers to ordinary variables. For this to be permitted, what are called **general access types** have to be declared in a special way. For example, to declare a general access type which can point to all objects of the type FLOAT, both those declared dynamically and those declared with a variable declaration, you can write:

```
type FLOAT_POINTER is access all FLOAT;
```

It is the word **all** that states that this is a general access type. A variable of a general access type is declared in the normal way, for example:

```
FP : FLOAT_POINTER;
```

In order to be able to point to a particular variable, the variable must be made accessible, which is done by adding the reserved word **aliased** to its declaration. For example, we could write:

```
F : aliased FLOAT;
```

Then, to get a pointer to point at a particular variable we use the attribute ACCESS. The following statement, for example, makes FP point to F:

```
FP := F'ACCESS;
```

When the attribute ACCESS is used, the compiler checks that the variable and the access types are not declared in such a way that pointers to a variable which has ceased to exist can linger. (In this example, the variable F ceases to exist when execution leaves the part of the program where F was declared. Then, in order to avoid having pointers to F left, it is necessary that the type FLOAT_POINTER is not known outside that part of the program.) If, for some reason, such a check is not wanted, then the attribute UNCHECKED_ACCESS can be used instead.

A general pointer may also point to an object which has been allocated using **new**, as in the example:

```
FP := new FLOAT;
```

A general pointer like FP may not point to a constant object since it could then be changed via the pointer. For example, if we have the statement:

```
PI : constant FLOAT := 3.14;
```

then the following statement is forbidden:

```
FP := PI'ACCESS;      -- ERROR! PI is constant
```

There is a variant of the general access type which allows pointing to a constant object; the word **constant** is used in the declaration:

```
type CONSTANT_FLOAT_POINTER is access constant FLOAT;
```

With such a constant general pointer, the value of a constant object may never be changed, but the value may be read. Constant general pointers may point to both constant and non-constant objects:

```
CFP : CONSTANT_FLOAT_POINTER;
...
CFP := PI'ACCESS;
CFP := F'ACCESS;
CFP := new FLOAT;
```

General pointers are useful for constructing linked lists where the elements of the lists can be either ordinary variables or dynamically allocated objects. (An example of general pointers and linked lists is given later in this chapter.) Another area where general pointers are useful is that of making tables of texts, where the texts do not need to be of the same length, as in the following example:

```
COOL_TEXT : constant STRING := "Cooling fan is out of order";
VENT_TEXT : constant STRING := "Ventilator will not close";
EMER_TEXT : constant STRING := "Emergency cooling on";
STOP_TEXT : constant STRING := "System stopped";
type TEXT_POINTER is access constant STRING;
ERR_MESS : constant array (POSITIVE range < >) of TEXT_POINTER :=
                  (COOL_TEXT'ACCESS, VENT_TEXT'ACCESS,
                   EMER_TEXT'ACCESS, STOP_TEXT'ACCESS);
...
PUT_LINE(ERR_MESS(I).all);                                               ▲
```

11.2   Linked lists

A **linked list**, or simply a **list**, is a dynamic data structure with applications in many different areas of programming. A list of three integers is illustrated in Figure 11.6. Each element in the list contains a value (in this example an integer) and a pointer to the next element in the list. The first element of a list is usually called its **head** and that element is pointed to by a special pointer (LIST in the figure).

What is so good about lists is that they can have new elements added relatively easily – anywhere in the list. (It is most common to put new elements first or last.) It is not necessary to know while programming how many elements there will be in the list.

Figure 11.6

11.2.1 Building up a list

It is possible to build up a list in a program using arrays, but the more natural way is to make use of dynamic objects and pointers. Let us study the type declarations that have to be made to describe a linked list. We want each element in the list to consist of two parts: a link to the next element in the list and a value. An element in a list of integers can, for example, be described by the record type:

```
type LIST_ELEMENT is
  record
      NEXT   : LINK;
      VALUE  : INTEGER;
  end record;
```

The first part of the list will be a link to the next element in the list, a pointer. But the type LINK has to be declared. The declaration should be:

```
type LINK is access LIST_ELEMENT;
```

The question is simply: 'Where should it be placed among the declarations?' If we put it after the declaration of the type LIST_ELEMENT it is not so good because the type LINK is then undefined when the type LIST_ELEMENT is declared. If we put the declaration of LINK before that of LIST_ELEMENT, then LIST_ELEMENT will be undefined when LINK is declared.

The solution is to start with an **incomplete type declaration**, where it is only stated that LIST_ELEMENT is a type:

```
type LIST_ELEMENT;
```

When an incomplete type declaration has been made, the type name may then be used in other type declarations. Later (in the same part of the program) a **full type declaration** must be made. Variables of the type may not be declared until the full type declaration has been made.

Using the above, we can now describe our linked list with the declarations:

```
type LIST_ELEMENT;
type LINK is access LIST_ELEMENT;
type LIST_ELEMENT is
  record
    NEXT   : LINK;
    VALUE : INTEGER;
  end record;
```

We shall now look at how a linked list is built up using these type declarations. We start by declaring an access variable:

```
LIST : LINK;
```

This variable automatically takes the value **null** on declaration, which describes the fact that the list is empty. We can create a new element and add it to the list:

```
LIST := new LIST_ELEMENT;
```

LIST will now point at the new list element and we can easily put an integer into the list:

```
LIST.VALUE := 5;
```

The first part of the list element, the pointer to the next element in the list, automatically gets the value **null** when the element of the list is created. It now looks like Figure 11.7. It would be easier to achieve this by initializing the new element as soon as it is created:

```
LIST := new LIST_ELEMENT'(null, 5);
```

Assume that we now want to create another element in the list containing the value 3. This element should be placed first in the list. One way of achieving this is to declare a new access variable:

```
NEW_LIST : LINK;
```

Figure 11.7

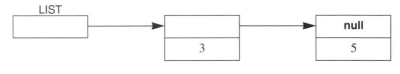

Figure 11.8

and then use the following statements:

```
NEW_LIST            := new LIST_ELEMENT;
NEW_LIST.NEXT    := LIST;
NEW_LIST.VALUE  := 3;
LIST                   := NEW_LIST;
```

The situation is illustrated in Figure 11.8.
A simpler way of adding the second element is to write:

```
LIST := new LIST_ELEMENT'(LIST, 3);
```

Perhaps the most elegant method of placing a new element into a list is to use the procedure PUT_FIRST:

```
procedure PUT_FIRST (DATA   : in INTEGER;
                                 L      : in out LINK) is
begin
   L := new LIST_ELEMENT'(L, DATA);
end PUT_FIRST;
```

If we assume that the variable LIST has the value **null** at the start, then we can build up the list in Figure 11.8 by making the calls:

```
PUT_FIRST(5, LIST);
PUT_FIRST(3, LIST);
```

Note that the parameter L in the procedure must be an **in out** parameter because it has to be both read and updated. Using this procedure it is easy to build up a list of arbitrary length by placing new elements first in the list.

11.2.2   Running through a list

If we want to run through all the elements in a list, this is easily achieved by starting at the first element and continuing until the last element is reached. The following program construct can be used to write out all the elements in a list of integers:

```
P := LIST;
while P /= null loop
   PUT(P.VALUE);
   P := P.NEXT;
end loop;
```

We have made use of another access variable P of type LINK. This construct works whether the list is empty (LIST has the value **null**) or contains elements. In the latter case, the pointer in the last element will have the value **null**.

In the next example we shall work with a register in which each element contains information about a certain person. The type declaration describes how the register should appear:

```
type PERSON;
type PERSON_LINK is access PERSON;
subtype NAME_TYPE is STRING(1 .. 20);
type PERSON is
   record
      NEXT     : PERSON_LINK;
      NAME     : NAME_TYPE;
      LENGTH   : INTEGER;
      WEIGHT   : FLOAT;
   end record;
```

We shall study a function that searches for a particular person in such a list. If the person is in the list, the function returns the pointer to the corresponding element in the list, otherwise it will return the value **null**. The function gets the required person's name as parameter and a pointer to the head of the list to be searched.

```
function FIND_PERSON (REQ_NAME  : NAME_TYPE;
                      L         : PERSON_LINK)
                               return PERSON_LINK is
   P : PERSON_LINK := L;
begin
   while P /= null and then P.NAME /= REQ_NAME loop
      P := P.NEXT;
   end loop;
   return P;
end FIND_PERSON;
```

In the function, the pointer P is made to run all through the list until it is finished (P has the value **null**) or until the required person is found.

Note that it is important to use **and then** in the Boolean expression in the **loop** statement. If the list runs out then P has the value **null**. If the value of P.NAME were evaluated then, a run-time error would result because P does not point at anything. The use of **and then** ensures that this does not happen.

11.2.3   Putting elements into a list and removing them

We have seen from the above that we can easily put a new element first in a list. To put a new element last in a list is a little more difficult because the whole list has to be run through until the end is reached. The following procedure creates a new element and puts it last in a list of integers. We assume that the types LINK and LIST_ELEMENT are declared in the same way as before.

```
procedure PUT_LAST (DATA : in INTEGER;
                    L      : in out LINK) is
  P1, P2 : LINK;
begin
  if L = null then
     -- Empty list, put in new element first
     L := new LIST_ELEMENT'(null, DATA);
  else
     P1 := L;
     while P1 /= null loop
        P2 := P1;       -- let P2 be one step after P1
        P1 := P1.NEXT;
     end loop;

     -- P2 now points at the last element
     -- Insert new element after P2
     P2.NEXT := new LIST_ELEMENT'(null, DATA);
  end if;
end PUT_LAST;
```

The case of the empty list must be treated separately because in that case the pointer L has to be changed. If the list is not empty the pointer P1 is made to run through the whole list until P1 becomes **null** and the end of the list has been reached. The pointer P2 trails one element behind P1. This means that when P1 reaches the end of the list, P2 will be pointing at the last element in the list. Therefore the new element has to be placed after the element that P2 is pointing at. (In this example, it would have been enough to have only the trailing pointer P2; in that case the expression following **while** would be P2.NEXT /= **null**.)

It is sometimes necessary to place a new element in a particular position in a linked list. Suppose, for example, we have an element in a list and a pointer P is pointing at it. Now suppose we want to put a new element with value 4 *after* this. The new element can then be created and placed in the list with a single statement:

P.NEXT := **new** LIST_ELEMENT'(P.NEXT, 4);

Figure 11.9 illustrates this. The dashed line shows the situation before the statement above is executed. If we wanted to insert a new element *in front of* a particular element that is pointed to, it would be much more trouble. Then we would need to run through the list from the beginning in order to get access to the element in front of the one pointed to.

In certain cases it is simple to remove elements from a list. The first element can be removed with the statement:

LIST := LIST.NEXT;

This is demonstrated in Figure 11.10.

It is also easy to remove the element coming after one to which there is a pointer. For example, we can remove the element that lies after the one that P points to:

P.NEXT := P.NEXT.NEXT;

It is a little more trouble to remove the last element, or the one before an element to which there is a pointer. In these cases, as in the procedure PUT_LAST, we would have to use the technique of two pointers, one lagging one step behind the other.

In Ada 95 it is possible to handle lists efficiently with the help of general pointers. The idea is based on using **pointers to pointers**. As an example of this, we will look at a procedure which investigates whether a certain element exists in a list and, if so, removes it from the list. We start with type declarations:

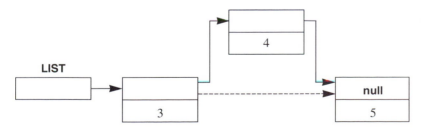

Figure 11.9

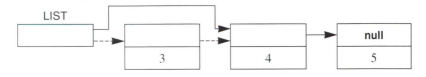

Figure 11.10

```
type LIST_ELEMENT;
type LINK is access LIST_ELEMENT;
type LIST_ELEMENT is
  record
     NEXT   : aliased LINK;
     VALUE : INTEGER;
  end record;
type LINK_POINTER is access all LINK;
```

We have now declared a general access type, LINK_POINTER, which describes pointers to pointers. We have also used the word **aliased** in the declaration of the component NEXT of an element of a list, which means that the component NEXT can be pointed to. Now we can declare a variable LIST which is, as usual, a pointer to the first node in the list:

LIST : **aliased** LINK;

We have used the word **aliased** again here, to state that the variable LIST can be pointed to. Suppose that we have built up a list of four elements containing integers 3, 6, 8 and 9, and that some time later we want to know if a particular integer, say 8, exists in the list. If the number we are looking for is found then it should be removed from the list, and to do that we can call the procedure TAKE_OUT:

TAKE_OUT (8, LIST'ACCESS);

The first parameter in this procedure is the element which is to be looked for and the second parameter is a pointer to the variable LIST. In other words, the second parameter is a pointer to a pointer to the first node of the list. If, inside the procedure TAKE_OUT, we copy the value of the second parameter to a local variable LP, then the situation when the call is made can be illustrated as in Figure 11.11. Note that LP points to the pointer LIST.

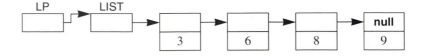

Figure 11.11

The procedure TAKE_OUT is as follows. Note that the parameter LISTP is of type LINK_POINTER, that is, it is a pointer to a pointer:

```
procedure TAKE_OUT(DATA : in INTEGER; LISTP : in out LINK_POINTER)
        is
    LP: LINK_POINTER := LISTP;
begin
    while LP.all /= null and then LP.all.VALUE /= DATA loop
        LP := LP.all.NEXT'ACCESS;
    end loop;
    if LP.all /= null then
        LP.all := LP.all.NEXT;
    end if;
end TAKE_OUT;
```

The expression after **while** tests, the first time through, whether what LP is pointing to, that is, the pointer LIST, is **null**. This is not the case, therefore there is at least one element in the list. So the test continues to see if the value in the first element is the same as the one we are looking for. Since this is not so in our example, the statement in the **while** loop will be executed once. Now the pointer LP is changed so that it points to the component NEXT in the first element of the list. Note that LP does not point at the whole of the first element in the list but only to the actual pointer NEXT.

On the second time through, what LP is pointing to, that is, the pointer NEXT in the first element of the list, is tested for equality with **null**. It is not **null**, so the value in the second node is compared with the value we are looking for. They are not the same, and so the expression in the **while** loop is executed once more. Now the situation is as in Figure 11.12.

Since the pointer NEXT in the second element of the list is not **null**, the value in the third element is examined, to see if it is the value we are looking for. This time it is, and the **while** loop ends.

If the value we are looking for is not found in the list, then the **while** statement ends when what the pointer LP is pointing to is found to be **null**. The final **if** statement checks whether the value being looked for was found in the list. If so, the corresponding element of the list is removed by changing the pointer to which LP is pointing, that is, the pointer NEXT in the element before the one to be removed. If it turns out that it is the first element in the list that has to be removed, then the pointer LIST is changed instead.

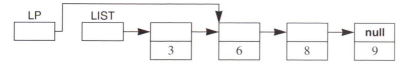

Figure 11.12

▲

This method of using pointers to pointers can be preferable to the method of trailing pointers when elements are to be inserted in or removed from linked lists. It is also a more efficient method than recursion, which is the subject of the next section.

11.2.4   Linked lists and recursion

A list can be seen as a **recursive data type**, and it can be said that a list consists of two components, a **head** and a **tail**. The head is the value in the first element of the list and the tail is a list consisting of all the elements except the first. Thus the tail is a list that is one element shorter than the original. This perspective can be extremely useful in solving certain problems involving list handling.

We saw above that it is possible to write out the contents of a list by going through the elements of the list from start to finish using a **loop** statement. This was easily done. It would have been much harder if we had wanted them written out in reverse order, with the last element written first, but this problem can be solved elegantly using recursion. We shall study a procedure that writes out a list of integers in reverse order:

```
procedure WRITE_REVERSE (LIST: in LINK) is
begin
  if LIST /= null then
    WRITE_REVERSE (LIST.NEXT);
    PUT(LIST.VALUE);
  end if;
end WRITE_REVERSE;
```

This says that a list can be written out in reverse order if we first write out its tail in reverse order and then write out its head. The list's head is accessed by writing LIST.VALUE, and LIST.NEXT is a pointer to the list's tail. An empty list has no elements and there is nothing to write for such a list.

We have already studied the problem of placing a new element at the end of a list, but it can be solved much more simply using recursion. The following algorithm is used:

If the list is empty then the new element is the list's only element and is thus placed at the start of the list, otherwise the new element should be placed at the end of the tail.

This algorithm is easily translated into this recursive procedure:

```
procedure PUT_LAST (DATA : in INTEGER;
                    LIST  : in out LINK) is
```

```
begin
  if LIST = null then
    LIST := new LIST_ELEMENT'(null, DATA);
  else
    PUT_LAST(DATA, LIST.NEXT);
  end if;
end PUT_LAST;
```

11.3   Doubly linked lists

One problem with the lists studied so far is that the whole list has to be run through – using either iteration or recursion – if an element has to be inserted or removed at the end of the list or in front of an element to which there is an access value. If it is necessary to work with a list and these operations, it can therefore be appropriate to construct a **doubly linked list**. In such a list, each element contains two access values apart from the data. One pointer points to the next element in the list, and the other points to the previous element. Figure 11.13 illustrates this concept.

Such a list is often made circular, as in Figure 11.13, by making the forward access value of the last element point to the first element and the first element's backward access value point to the last element. To describe an element in a doubly linked list of integers we can make the type declarations:

```
type LIST_ELEMENT;
type LINK is access LIST_ELEMENT;
type LIST_ELEMENT is
  record
    NEXT       : LINK;
    PREVIOUS  : LINK;
    VALUE      : INTEGER;
  end record;
```

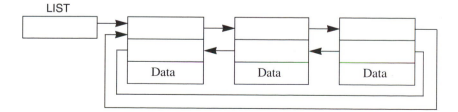

Figure 11.13

In work with linked lists, an empty list must be handled in a special way. This makes the program a little longer and more complicated. To avoid this problem it is useful to let every list have a special element at the start of the list, but which does not belong to the list itself. This is particularly useful when handling doubly linked lists. If, for example, we want to represent a list of integers that contains two elements, 4 and 9, we can do this with the list in Figure 11.14. Note that the first element, whose value is of no importance, does not belong to the logical list. If this technique of a special first element is used the empty list can be described as in Figure 11.15.

If we assume that the variable LIST has type LINK, then the structure in Figure 11.15 can be built up with the statements:

```
LIST              := new LIST_ELEMENT;
LIST.NEXT         := LIST;
LIST.PREVIOUS  := LIST;
```

It is even simpler, of course, to use a record aggregate and write instead:

```
LIST     := new LIST_ELEMENT;
LIST.all   := (LIST, LIST, 0);
```

The advantage of a doubly linked list is that it is never necessary to run through one in order to make changes. Let us look at the example of removing an arbitrary element from a list. Assume we have a list of integers containing the values 4, 7 and 9, as shown in Figure 11.16. The access value P points at the element to be removed. Now we can write a procedure REMOVE:

```
procedure REMOVE (P : in LINK) is
begin
    P.PREVIOUS.NEXT       := P.NEXT;
    P.NEXT.PREVIOUS := P.PREVIOUS;
end REMOVE;
```

LIST

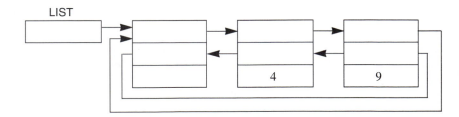

Figure 11.14

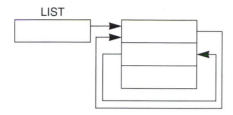

Figure 11.15

and make the call:

REMOVE(P);

The result is that the element that P is pointing at – the 'target' element – will be 'linked out' of the list. The statement:

P.PREVIOUS.NEXT := P.NEXT;

means that the forward access value in the element in front of the target will point to the one after the target. Correspondingly, the statement;

P.NEXT.PREVIOUS := P.PREVIOUS;

means that the backward access value in the element after the target element will point at the element in front of the target. (We do not need to worry about changing the access values in the target element. To do a thorough job, these could be set to **null**.)

For the next example we shall take a procedure that creates a new element and puts it at the end of a doubly linked list:

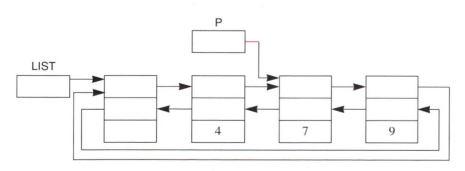

Figure 11.16

```
procedure PUT_LAST (DATA    : in INTEGER;
                     L       : in LINK) is
  PNEW : LINK := new LIST_ELEMENT'(L, L.PREVIOUS, DATA);
begin
  PNEW.PREVIOUS.NEXT := PNEW;
  PNEW.NEXT.PREVIOUS := PNEW;
end PUT_LAST;
```

The declaration:

```
PNEW : LINK := new LIST_ELEMENT'(L, L.PREVIOUS, DATA);
```

causes a new element to be created and the access value PNEW to point at it. The new element is initialized so that its forward access value points at the list's start element (the element that L points at) and its backward access value points at the element that was previously last in the list (pointed at by L.PREVIOUS).

The statement:

```
PNEW.PREVIOUS.NEXT := PNEW;
```

ensures that the forward access value in the element that was previously last in the list will point at the new element, and the statement:

```
PNEW.NEXT.PREVIOUS := PNEW;
```

ensures that the backward access value in the start element points at the new element.

A further example using doubly linked lists is this procedure, which puts a new element first in a list. The new element should be placed after the start element:

```
procedure PUT_FIRST (DATA : in INTEGER;
                      L     : in LINK) is
  PNEW : LINK := new LIST_ELEMENT'(L.NEXT, L, DATA);
begin
  PNEW.PREVIOUS.NEXT := PNEW;
  PNEW.NEXT.PREVIOUS := PNEW;
end PUT_FIRST;
```

Note that the use of a special start element in a list means that the access value L does not need to be changed in any of the procedures shown in this section. This has the advantage that we have not had to give special treatment to the insertion or removal of an element first or last in the list.

11.4   Stacks and queues

Two common data structures are **stacks** and **queues**. A queue, as we saw in Section 8.8, is a structure that works on the well-known principle 'first in, first out'. Data objects are placed at the end of the queue and taken from the front. A stack is a data structure that uses the principle 'last in, first out'. A stack can be likened to a pile of plates in a self-service cafeteria – a pile in a holder with a spring that keeps the pile at a suitable level for the customers. When a plate is placed on the pile it goes on top of those already there, and when you take a plate from the pile you have to take the top one.

   There are two operations for a stack, **push** and **pop**, which act on the element on the **top** of the stack. The operation **push** places an element of data on the top of the stack and **pop** removes the top element from the stack. Figure 11.17 illustrates this idea of the stack.

   A stack can easily be constructed using a singly linked list. The first element in the list is the top of the stack. A push operation means that a new element is put first in the list, and the pop operation removes the first element from the list. A stack can be considered as an abstract data type on which the operations push and pop can be performed. To demonstrate this we will construct a package which describes the abstract data type STACK, a stack on which objects of type CHARACTER can be placed. The specification of this package looks like this:

```
package STACK_PACKAGE is
  type STACK is limited private;
    procedure PUSH (S : in out STACK; T : in CHARACTER);
    procedure POP   (S : in out STACK; T : out CHARACTER);
    function EMPTY  (S : STACK) return BOOLEAN;
```

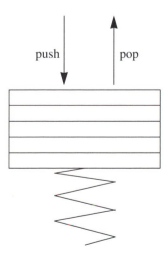

push   pop

Figure 11.17

```
private
  type STACK_ELEMENT;
  type STACK is access STACK_ELEMENT;
end STACK_PACKAGE;
```

The type is a limited private type. This means that the user of the package does not know what a stack really looks like: it is not 'visible'. The only things a user may do is declare objects of the type STACK and have parameters of type STACK in calls to subprograms.

The idea is that the user should only work on a stack through calls to the procedures PUSH and POP, as given in the package specification. Both of these have a stack as first parameter. Since the stack is updated by calls to these procedures, this first parameter is an **in out** parameter. PUSH has as **out** parameter the character that is removed from the stack. In addition to PUSH and POP, a function EMPTY is defined, and the user can call this to see if there are any objects stored on the stack.

Finally, the package has a private part that is not visible to the user. First, there is an incomplete type declaration (see Section 11.2.1) stating that STACK_ELEMENT is a type. The private type STACK is then declared as access type to an object of type STACK_ELEMENT. The complete declaration of STACK_ELEMENT could have been placed last in the package specification but, since this does not need to be known for a user program to be compiled, it is preferable to place it in the body of the package instead. In this way there are as few details as possible about the internal appearance of a stack in the package specification.

Now we can construct and compile programs that use the specification of STACK_PACKAGE. We will show an example of a program that reads in text from the terminal and writes it out in reverse order:

```
with TEXT_IO, BASIC_NUM_IO, STACK_PACKAGE;
use TEXT_IO, BASIC_NUM_IO, STACK_PACKAGE;
procedure STACK_DEMO is
  CHAR_STACK : STACK;
  CHAR        : CHARACTER;
begin
  PUT_LINE("Write in text. End with Ctrl-D");
  -- Input text and put the characters on the stack
  while not END_OF_FILE loop
    GET(CHAR);
    PUSH(CHAR_STACK, CHAR);
  end loop;
  -- Empty the stack and print the characters
  while not EMPTY(CHAR_STACK) loop
    POP(CHAR_STACK, CHAR);
    PUT(CHAR);
  end loop;
end STACK_DEMO;
```

In the program an object CHAR_STACK of type STACK is declared and the characters from the text are placed on the stack as they are read, one by one. When all the characters in the stack have been read in and put on the stack, they are removed from the stack and written in what is now the reverse of their original order.

Before the user program which is using the package can be executed, the body of the package must be compiled. In the body that detailed appearance of the character stack must be given. The complete declaration of the type STACK_ELEMENT is given here, as are the bodies of the subprograms PUSH, POP and EMPTY:

```
package body STACK_PACKAGE is
  type STACK_ELEMENT is
    record
      CH    : CHARACTER;
      NEXT : STACK;
    end record;

  procedure PUSH(S : in out STACK; C : in CHARACTER) is
  begin
    S := new STACK_ELEMENT'(C, S);
  end PUSH;

  procedure POP(S : in out STACK; C : out CHARACTER) is
  begin
    C := S.CH;
    S := S.NEXT;
  end POP;

  function EMPTY(S : STACK) return BOOLEAN is
  begin
    return S = null;
  end EMPTY;
end STACK_PACKAGE;
```

We see that the stack is quite simply a linked list in which each element contains a character, and that the type STACK is an access type for such a list. PUSH puts a new element first in the list and POP takes out the first element from the list. If the stack is empty there are no elements in the list and, in this case, the access value to the first element of the list has the value **null**.

Now let us turn to an abstract data type for a queue. In Section 8.8 we constructed a queue using arrays; here we will see how a queue can be constructed using pointers. As an example we will look at a queue where objects that describe people can be placed, a **person queue**. The specification can look like this:

```
package QUEUE_PACKAGE is
  type PERSON is
    record
      NAME      : STRING(1 .. 20);
      ADDRESS  : STRING(1 .. 30);
    end record;

  type PERSON_OUEUE is limited private;

  procedure INSERT   (Q : in out PERSON_QUEUE; PE : in PERSON);
  procedure REMOVE (Q : in out PERSON_QUEUE; PE : out PERSON);
  function EMPTY      (Q : PERSON_QUEUE) return BOOLEAN;

  QUEUE_EMPTY : exception;
private
  type QUEUE_ELEMENT;
  type LINK is access QUEUE_ELEMENT;
  type PERSON_QUEUE is
    record
      FIRST : LINK;
      LAST  : LINK;
    end record;
end QUEUE_PACKAGE;
```

The specification first describes what a person looks like – quite simply a record consisting of a name and an address. Then PERSON_QUEUE is declared to be a limited private type. A user of this package may only handle a queue by calling the subprograms that are named in the specification. The procedures INSERT and REMOVE can be used to insert and remove individuals, and the function EMPTY determines whether there are people in the queue or not.

In the private part of the specification the type PERSON_QUEUE is described. We have chosen to represent a queue by a record containing two access values, one pointing to the first element in the queue and the other pointing to the last element. Each time a user declares a variable of type PERSON_QUEUE the two access values will automatically be initialized to **null**, thereby describing an empty queue. The compiler does not need to know what an element of the queue looks like in order to compile a user's program, so in the specification we only give an incomplete declaration of the type QUEUE_ELEMENT. The complete declaration is given in the body of the package.

The body of the package contains all the details of how a queue is constructed. We have chosen to use a singly linked list, but apart from the usual pointer to the first element of the list we also have a pointer to the last element of the list. This means that we can avoid running through the whole list each time we want to add an element to the end. We have put the pointers to the first and last elements in the queue into a record; Figure 11.18 illustrates the queue.

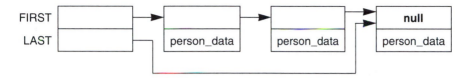

FIRST

LAST

person_data   person_data   person_data   **null**

Figure 11.18

The body of the package is as follows:

```
with UNCHECKED_DEALLOCATION;
package body QUEUE_PACKAGE is
  type QUEUE_ELEMENT is
    record
      NEXT: LINK;
      DATA : PERSON;
    end record;

procedure RETURN_QUEUE_ELEMENT is new
          UNCHECKED_DEALLOCATION(QUEUE_ELEMENT, LINK);

procedure INSERT (Q : in out PERSON_QUEUE; PE : in PERSON) is
  PNEW : LINK := new QUEUE_ELEMENT'(null, PE);
begin
  if Q.FIRST = null then
    Q.FIRST := PNEW;          -- queue is empty, put element first
  else
    Q.LAST.NEXT := PNEW;      -- change the former last
  end if;
  Q.LAST := PNEW;
end INSERT;

procedure REMOVE (Q : in out PERSON_QUEUE; PE : out PERSON) is
  TEMP : LINK := Q.FIRST;
begin
  if Q.FIRST /= null then
    PE := Q.FIRST.DATA;
    Q.FIRST := Q.FIRST.NEXT;
    if Q.FIRST = null then
      Q.LAST := null;         -- queue became empty
    end if;
    RETURN_QUEUE_ELEMENT(TEMP);
  else
    raise QUEUE_EMPTY;
  end if;
end REMOVE;
```

```
function EMPTY (Q : PERSON_QUEUE) return BOOLEAN is
begin
    return Q.FIRST = null;
end EMPTY;
end QUEUE_PACKAGE;
```

In the procedure INSERT a new element is created and will be linked last in the list, which is normally after the element to which Q.LAST points. However, the special case must be considered of the list being empty prior to insertion, in which case the new element is placed first in the list. In either case, the access value Q.LAST points to the new element after insertion.

Correspondingly, in the procedure REMOVE, when the first element of the queue is removed a check must be made to see if it leaves the list empty. In that case, the access value Q.LAST is given the value **null**. The procedure REMOVE also demonstrates how deallocation of memory is accomplished when an element is removed. Note that an extra temporary access value, TEMP, is needed to point to the element that is to be removed; this is because it is not possible to refer to an element after it has been deallocated.

11.5   Trees

In Section 11.3 we saw that each element could have two pointers. There is naturally no limit on the number of pointers in each element and these pointers do not need to point in such a way as to define a linked list. Using pointers, it is possible to build up data structures with elements that are connected arbitrarily. In this section we shall study **trees** – common data structures in which the elements are connected using pointers. A tree is illustrated in Figure 11.19.

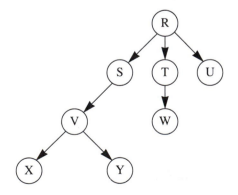

Figure 11.19

The elements of a tree are usually called **nodes.** The topmost node is called the tree's **root.** (It is usual to draw and think of a tree in an upside-down position compared with the real thing.) From the root there can be pointers to other nodes in the tree but there can never be pointers *to* the root from any of the tree's nodes. In general, there are only pointers 'downwards' from each node in the tree. To each node there is only one path from the root. (For example, in Figure 11.19 it is only possible to take path R–S–V–Y to get to the node Y.) Thus, there may only be one pointer to any one node.

If a node A points to a node B in a tree, the node B is said to be the **child** of A and A is said to be the **parent** of B. The root is the only node that is without a parent. The nodes that have no children, X, Y, W and U in our example, are usually called **leaves** and the pointers in the tree are sometimes called **arcs**.

In the tree in Figure 11.19 the nodes have up to three children. We shall limit ourselves, however, to trees in which a node can have at most two children. Such trees are common in the construction of data structures and they are generally called **binary trees**. An example of a binary tree is shown in Figure 11.20.

Trees

- A *root* is a node that no other node in the tree points to.

- To any one node there is a *unique* path from the root.

- The nodes that do not have pointers to other nodes are called *leaves*.

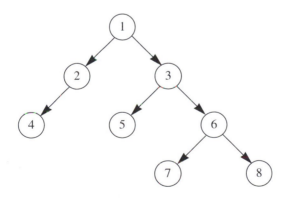

Figure 11.20

A node in a binary tree can be described by a record type:

```
type NODE;
type LINK is access NODE;
type NODE is record
   DATA : INTEGER;
   LEFT, RIGHT : LINK;
end record;
```

Each node consists of a data section describing the contents of the node and two access values that point to the node's left and right children, respectively. In our example the data part consists of an integer. If a node is lacking a child the corresponding access value is **null**. In a leaf, both the access values are **null**. The tree in Figure 11.20 can be built up as indicated in Figure 11.21. A special pointer ROOT points at the root of the tree so that the whole tree can be accessed. If we have an empty tree (a tree with no nodes) then ROOT has the value **null**.

If we want to build up a tree according to Figure 11.22 we can use the statements:

```
ROOT              := new NODE;
ROOT.DATA         := 10;
ROOT.LEFT         := new NODE;
```

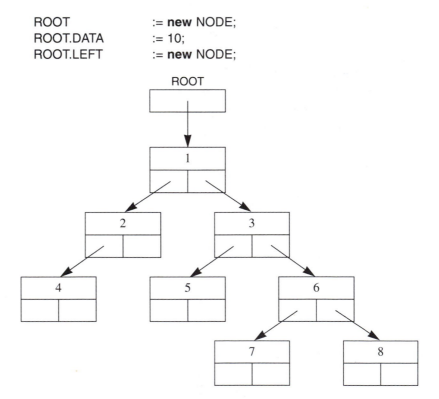

Figure 11.21

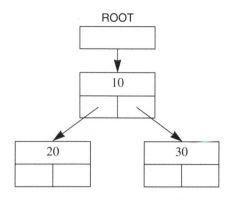

Figure 11.22

```
ROOT.RIGHT        := new NODE;
ROOT.LEFT.DATA    := 20;
ROOT.RIGHT.DATA := 30;
```

where we assume that ROOT has an access value of type LINK. Alternatively, this can be achieved in a single statement:

```
ROOT := new NODE' (10, new NODE' (20,null,null),
                       new NODE' (30,null,null) );
```

The nodes that lie to the left of the root can be considered as a new, smaller tree, with the left child of the root as its root. This tree is said to be the left **subtree** of the original tree. In the same way, the nodes to the right of the root form a right subtree. Figure 11.23 illustrates this. (For example, the left subtree in Figure 11.20 has node 2 as its root and comprises nodes 2 and 4. The right subtree has node 3 as its root and comprises nodes 3, 5, 6, 7 and 8.)

With the help of subtrees, a tree can be regarded as a recursive data type and the following definition can be given:

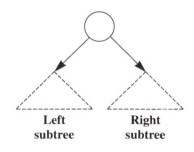

Figure 11.23

> A binary tree is either empty (has no nodes) or consists of a
> root, a left subtree and a right subtree.

This concept is useful in the design of programs for handling trees. We shall start by studying how to visit all the nodes of a given tree. We assume that we have a pointer ROOT which points at the root of the tree. When we considered linked lists it was natural to visit all the elements starting at the beginning and running through to the end, but it is not that simple with a tree. It is possible to think of several alternative ways of traversing a tree.

If we look at the tree in Figure 11.20, for example, we may think of visiting the nodes in the order, 1–2–3–4–5–6–7–8. However, to write a program for this is rather difficult. It is much simpler and more common to apply the three visiting orders – **preorder**, **inorder** and **postorder** – which are defined recursively. Let us start with the most common, inorder:

If the tree is not empty, then:

(1) Visit the tree's left subtree.

(2) Visit the tree's root.

(3) Visit the tree's right subtree.

We shall now try to apply this visiting order to the tree in Figure 11.20. First we note that the tree is not empty and so the three stages of the algorithm should be carried out. The first stage 'visit the tree's left subtree' means that the tree in Figure 11.24 should be visited. Since this is also a tree, the visiting algorithm (second instance) should be applied. The tree is not empty and so we carry out stage (1), that is, the subtree in Figure 11.25 is visited.

We now apply a third instance of the algorithm. Since the tree is not empty we carry out the first stage, 'visit the left subtree'; this means that we have to apply a fourth instance of the algorithm. This time the tree to be visited is empty because node 4 has an empty left subtree, and the fourth instance of the algorithm thus does nothing. We return to the third instance of the algorithm and carry out its second stage, 'visit the tree's root'. This means that node 4 is visited. The third stage, 'visit the tree's right subtree', starts a fifth instance of the algorithm, which does nothing because the right subtree is empty.

Figure 11.24

(4)

Figure 11.25

Now all the stages of the third instance of the algorithm have been carried out and we return to the second instance of the algorithm. We carry out the second stage, 'visit the tree's root' for the tree in Figure 11.24. Thus node 2 gets a visit.

Since the tree in Figure 11.24 has an empty right subtree nothing happens when a sixth instance of the algorithm is carried out, and we return eventually to the first instance of the algorithm. We carry out the second stage, which means that the root of the original tree, node 1, is visited.

Now we have visited nodes 4, 2 and 1, in that order, and continue by applying the algorithm in the same way to the right subtree. We eventually find that all the nodes in the tree are visited, in the order 4–2–1–5–3–7–6–8.

The following recursive procedure visits and writes out the contents of the nodes of a binary tree according to the inorder principle. The procedure needs a pointer to the root of the tree as parameter.

```
procedure IN_ORDER (P : LINK) is
begin
   if P /= null then
      IN_ORDER(P.LEFT);
      PUT(P.DATA);
      IN_ORDER(P.RIGHT);
   end if;
end IN_ORDER;
```

Definitions of the other visiting orders can be made in a similar way. The only difference is that the three stages in the algorithm already studied are rearranged. The algorithm for visiting all the nodes of a tree according to the principle of preorder can be described as follows:

If the tree is not empty, then:

(1) Visit the tree's root.
(2) Visit the tree's left subtree.
(3) Visit the tree's right subtree.

If we visit the nodes in Figure 11.20, for example, we get the visiting order 1–2–4–3–5–6–7–8 according to this principle. The procedure:

```
procedure PRE_ORDER (P : in LINK) is
begin
  if P /= null then
    PUT(P.DATA);
    PRE_ORDER(P.LEFT);
    PRE_ORDER(P.RIGHT);
  end if;
end PRE_ORDER;
```

writes out the contents of the nodes according to the principle preorder.
The definition for the third visiting order, postorder, is:

If the tree is not empty, then:

(1)   Visit the tree's left subtree.

(2)   Visit the tree's right subtree.

(3)   Visit the tree's root.

Applying this principle, the nodes in Figure 11.20 are visited in the order 4–2–5–7–8–6–3–1. The following procedure writes out the contents of the nodes of a tree according to the postorder principle:

```
procedure POST_ORDER (P : in LINK) is
begin
  if P /= null then
    POST_ORDER(P.LEFT);
    POST_ORDER(P.RIGHT);
    PUT(P.DATA);
  end if;
end POST_ORDER;
```

As we see, the algorithms for trees are naturally expressed using recursion. We shall now study a function that evaluates the **depth** of a binary tree. The function takes a pointer to the root of the tree as parameter. The depth of a tree can be defined as the number of nodes on the longest path from the tree's root to a leaf. An empty tree has depth 0 and a tree that consists of only a root has depth 1. We write the function:

```
function DEPTH (P : LINK) return NATURAL is
  L_DEPTH, R_DEPTH : NATURAL;
begin
  if P = null then
    return 0;
  else
```

```
    L_DEPTH := DEPTH(P.LEFT);
    R_DEPTH := DEPTH(P.RIGHT);
    if L_DEPTH > R_DEPTH then
      return L_DEPTH + 1;
    else
      return R_DEPTH + 1;
    end if;
  end if;
end DEPTH;
```

The simplest case is if the tree is empty. The function then returns the value 0 as its result. If the tree is not empty, the depths of the left and right subtrees are evaluated separately and saved in the variables L_DEPTH and R_DEPTH. The function DEPTH is called recursively to evaluate these depths, with access values to the respective subtrees as parameter. The function returns the depth of the deepest subtree plus 1 (the root itself) as its result.

We can now study a special form of binary tree, a **binary search tree**. The value of each node in such a tree is greater than the values of all the nodes in its left subtree and less than or equal to the values of the nodes in its right subtree. The tree in Figure 11.26 is an example of a binary search tree.

A binary search tree has the property that, if the principle of inorder is used to traverse the tree, the nodes will be visited in order of size. The nodes in our example, Figure 11.26, will be visited in the order 1–3–4–5–6–7–7–8–9.

A binary search tree can be used when information has to be found quickly. Let us study the example of a binary search tree in which each node contains information about a person. Each node stores a person's name and address. We have the type declarations:

```
subtype NAME_TYPE     is STRING(1 .. 20);
subtype ADDRESS_TYPE is STRING(1 .. 30);
```

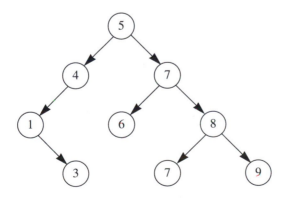

Figure 11.26

```
type NODE;

type LINK is access NODE;

type NODE is
  record
    NAME        : NAME_TYPE;
    ADDRESS     : ADDRESS_TYPE;
    LEFT, RIGHT : LINK;
  end record;
```

We can use the following function to find the node in the tree which contains the information about a particular person. The function has two **in** parameters, an access value to the tree and the name of the required person. As its result, the function returns an access value to the node in which the information about the person is stored. If the required person is not found in the tree, the function returns the value **null**.

```
function FIND (ROOT      : in LINK;
               REQ_NAME : in NAME_TYPE) return LINK is

begin
  if ROOT = null then
    return null;
  elsif ROOT.NAME = REQ_NAME then
    return ROOT;
  elsif REQ_NAME < ROOT.NAME then
    return FIND(ROOT.LEFT, REQ_NAME);
  else
    return FIND(ROOT.RIGHT, REQ_NAME);
  end if;
end FIND;
```

The search works as follows. First it checks to see whether the tree is empty and, if so, the result **null** is returned because there are no entries in the tree. If the root contains the required person then the task is easy: the result is simply the access value of the root. In other cases it must look further into one of the subtrees. The particular subtree depends on whether the required name comes alphabetically before or after the name in the root. This further searching is achieved by calling the function FIND recursively with an access value to either the right or left subtree as parameter.

To remove nodes in such a way that the tree remains a binary search tree is somewhat complicated (see Exercise 11.18). However, to insert new nodes is simple and we finish by showing a procedure for placing information about a new person into a binary search tree as described above. As parameters, the procedure takes an access value to the root of the tree and the new person's name and address. The procedure has to create a new node for the new person and insert it in the correct place in the tree.

```
procedure INSERT (ROOT         : in out LINK;
                  NEW-NAME    : in NAMETYPE;
                  NEW_DRESS : in ADDRESSTYPE) is

begin
  if ROOT = null then
    ROOT := new NODE'(NEW_NAME NEW_ADDRESS, null, null);
  elsif NEW_NAME < ROOT. NAME then
    INSERT(ROOT.LEFT, NEW_NAME, NEW_ADDRESS);
  else
    INSERT(ROOT.RIGHT, NEW_NAME, NEW_ADDRESS);
  end if;
end INSERT;
```

If the tree is empty it is easy to insert the entry in the right place. The new node is then the root of the tree and the access value ROOT is set to point at this node. Note that the parameter ROOT must be an **in out** parameter because it must be both read and updated. If the tree is not empty, a choice must be made as to whether to insert the new node in the left or the right subtree, depending on whether the person's name comes alphabetically before or after the name in the root of the tree.

11.6   Pointers to subprograms

In Ada 95 access values are allowed which point to subprograms, that is, to functions and procedures. For example, we can declare the following access type:

```
type PROC_POINTER1 is access procedure (I : INTEGER);
```

and we can declare a variable of this access type:

```
P1 : PROC_POINTER1;
```

The variable P1 can now point to procedures which have a parameter of type INTEGER. If, for instance, we have a procedure WRITE:

```
procedure WRITE(I : INTEGER);
```

then we can use the attribute ACCESS to get P1 to point to WRITE:

```
P1 := WRITE'ACCESS;
```

If we now add the following statement, the procedure WRITE will be called via P1:

```
P1(5);
```

If we want P1 to point to some other procedure, we simply assign it another access value using the attribute ACCESS. Note that P1 may not point to all procedures: it may only point to procedures which have the same parameter profile as P1's type. For example, P1 may not point to a procedure with no parameters; to be able to point to such a procedure we need a new access type and a new pointer variable:

```
type PROC_POINTER2 is access procedure;
P2 : PROC_POINTER2;
```

Now we can write, for example:

```
P2 : NEW_PAGE'ACCESS;
```

to have P2 point to the procedure NEW_PAGE. If we want to call the procedure that P2 is pointing to then we must use the reserved word **all**, since the procedure has no parameters:

```
P2.all;
```

Pointers to subprograms can be very useful. One common area of use concerns numerical computations. Many standard numeric functions are so constructed that they have a pointer to a mathematical function as one of their parameters. A standard function which carries out numeric integration, for example, has a parameter that states which mathematical function has to be integrated. As an example of this usage we will write a function FIND_ZERO which computes a zero of a mathematical function. The specification of FIND_ZERO is:

```
function FIND_ZERO (F   : FUNCTION_POINTER;
                    A, B : FLOAT;
                    EPS : FLOAT := 1.0E-10) return FLOAT;
```

The first parameter is a pointer to the mathematical function we want to find the zero of. The type FUNCTION_POINTER is declared as follows:

```
type FUNCTION_POINTER is access function (X : FLOAT)
                                            return FLOAT;
```

The two parameters A and B state the interval within which the zero should be sought. Thus we are looking for a value x in the interval $[A,B]$ such that $f(x) = 0$.

We assume that the function f is monotonous and that it has exactly one zero in the given interval. (We will write the function FIND_ZERO so that it raises the exception NO_ZERO if no zero is found for f in the interval.)

The parameter EPS states the greatest error which can be tolerated in the result.

If $f(x_1) < 0 < f(x_2)$ then the following algorithm can be used to compute the zero of f. The idea is to close in on the zero by moving the end-points x_1 and x_2 nearer and nearer to one another, subject to the condition $f(x_1) < 0 < f(x_2)$:

1. Repeat the following until the interval [X1, X2] becomes sufficiently small:
    1.1 Let XM be the midpoint of the interval [X1, X2].
    1.2 Compute the value of the function F(XM).
    1.3 If F(XM) < 0 then the zero lies to the right of XM, so set X1 to XM.
    1.4 If F(XM) > 0 then the zero lies to the left of XM, so set X2 to XM.
    1.5 If F(XM) = 0 then we have happened on the zero. Exit the algorithm and return XM as the result.
2. Give the mean of X1 and X2 as result.

We can now use the algorithm in the body of FIND_ZERO, which looks like this:

```
function FIND_ZERO (F    : FUNCTION_POINTER;
                    A, B : FLOAT;
                    EPS : FLOAT := 1.0E-10) return FLOAT is
  X1, X2, XM, FM : FLOAT;
begin
  if F(A) < 0.0 and F(B) > 0.0 then
    X1 := A; X2 := B;
  elsif F(A) > 0.0 and F(B) < 0.0 then
    X1 := B; X2 := A;        -- reverse the interval
  elsif F(A) = 0.0 then
    return A;
  elsif F(B) = 0.0 then
    return B;
  else
    raise NO_ZERO;
  end if;

  -- Now F(X1) < 0 < F(X2)
  while abs (X1 - X2) < EPS loop
    XM := (X1 + X2) / 2.0;      -- compute midpoint
    FM    := F(XM);
    if FM < 0.0 then
      X1 := XM;
    elsif FM > 0.0 then
      X2 := XM;
```

```
        else
            return XM;        -- We have happened on the zero
        end if;
    end loop;
    return (X1 + X2) / 2.0;
end FIND_ZERO;
```

In the first part of the function we ensure that the condition F(X1) < 0 < F(X2) holds. If it turns out that F(A) < 0 and F(B) > 0 then we simply set X1 to A and X2 to B. If it is the other way round, we exchange A and B. If one of the end-points A or B is a zero then we can return the result at once. Finally, if both F(A) and F(B) are greater than zero or both are less than zero, then the function can be without a zero in the interval and an exception is generated.

Now we can use the function FIND_ZERO to compute zeros for different functions. If, for example, we have two functions:

```
function F1 (X : FLOAT) return FLOAT is
begin
    return X – 1.0;
end F1;

function F2 (X : FLOAT) return FLOAT is
begin
    return 2.0 * X ** 3 – 3.0 * X ** 2 – 18.0 * X – 8.0;
end F2;
```

then the zero of the function F1 can be found using the statement:

```
X0 := FIND_ZERO(F1'ACCESS, –10.0, 10.0);
```

and the zero of F2, which lies in the interval [–1, 1], can be found using the statement:

```
X0 := FIND_ZERO(F2'ACCESS, –1.0, 1.0);
```

In the next example we will study another common use of pointers to sub-programs. We will construct a simple, but general, **command interpreter**, a program which reads commands the user types at the terminal. The interpreter must check that a command the user gives is correct and then call another program, which we can call a command program, to execute the actual command. Each command has a unique command program; when it has completed execution the current command has been obeyed and control is returned to the command interpreter, which reads the next command.

Such command interpreters form an important part of operating systems; in this example we will assume that the commands which the user gives have the same format as those used in, for example, Unix or MS-DOS. A command looks like this:

> *command_name argument$_1$ argument$_2$ ... argument$_n$*

The symbol > which comes first on the line is a prompt from the command interpreter to tell the user it is ready to receive a command. The interpreter takes the first thing the user writes in as the name of the command that has to be obeyed (such as copy or dir).

Following the command name are the arguments to the command program, written with one or more spaces between. The two most common kinds of argument are filenames and flags (or options). The number of arguments and their meaning depends on the actual command, and it is the command program that has to take care of and check these. From the point of view of the interpreter, the arguments are only pieces of text that might consist of any characters at all.

In order for the command program to be able to access its parameters the command interpreter must give them as parameters when it calls the command program, and to do this we will use the same method used by the operating system Unix. Each command program receives as parameter an array in which each element is a pointer to an argument of the command line. We will construct a package with the necessary type declarations:

```
package ARG_TYPES is
   type STRING_POINTER is access STRING;
   type ARG_ARRAY is array (NATURAL range < >) of STRING_POINTER;
end ARG_TYPES;
```

Each command program thus needs only one parameter, of type ARG_ARRAY. As an example we can look at the command program ECHO, which writes out its arguments when it is called:

```
with TEXT_IO, ARG_TYPES;
use TEXT_IO, ARG_TYPES;
procedure ECHO(ARG : ARG_ARRAY) is
begin
   for I in 1 .. ARG'LAST loop
      PUT(ARG(I).all); PUT(' ');
   end loop;
   NEW_LINE;
end ECHO;
```

The command interpreter's job is to see that the array ARG has the correct content when ECHO is called. If the user has given the command:

> echo one two three

for example, then ARG(1) should contain an access value pointing to the text one, ARG(2) an access value pointing to the text two, and ARG(3) an access value pointing to the text three. The array ARG should also have the correct length in order for ECHO to know how many arguments have been given.

We will also, in line with Unix which we are using as a model here, let the parameter array ARG have an element ARG(0), where the command interpreter puts an access value to the word the user wrote first, that is, it points to the command name. This is useful in case the command program needs to write out the command name, in an error message for example.

We can look at another example of a command program. Suppose that the user has given the command:

> print my_file

Then, we want the following command program to be called:

```
with TEXT_IO, ARG_TYPES;
use TEXT_IO, ARG_TYPES;
procedure PRINT (ARG : ARG_ARRAY) is
   F : FILE_TYPE;
   C : CHARACTER;
begin
   if ARG'LAST /= 1 then
     PUT_LINE(ARG(0).all & ": wrong number of arguments");
   else
     OPEN(F, MODE => IN_FILE, NAME => ARG(1).all);
     while not END_OF_FILE(F) loop
       while not END_OF_LINE(F) loop
          GET(F, C); PUT(C);
       end loop;
       SKIP_LINE(F); NEW_LINE;
     end loop;
     CLOSE(F);
   end if;
exception
   when NAME_ERROR => PUT_LINE(ARG(0).all &
                     ": failure to open file " & ARG(1).all);
end PRINT;
```

We can see that the program checks that it gets exactly one argument (the access value to the file name). If this is not the case the error message:

print: wrong number of arguments

is written out. Note how the access value ARG(0) has been used in generating this message.

In order for the command interpreter to know which command programs there are, it has to be given a table with the names of commands that can be accepted. In addition to the command name, the table also has to contain pointers to the command programs which are going to execute the command. We can put the command interpreter in a package with the following specification:

```
with ARG_TYPES;
use ARG_TYPES;
package COMMAND_INTERPRETER is
   type PROGRAM_POINTER is access procedure (ARG : ARG_ARRAY);
   type COMM_REC is
     record
       NAME      : STRING_POINTER;
       PROGRAM  : PROGRAM_POINTER;
     end record;
   type COMM_ARRAY is array (POSITIVE range < >) of COMM_REC;
   procedure START(COMM : COMM_ARRAY);
end COMMAND_INTERPRETER;
```

The command interpreter starts when the procedure START is called, with a COMM_ARRAY as parameter. The call is from a main program, which might have the following structure:

```
with COMMAND_INTERPRETER, BACKUP, COPY, ... ZAP;
procedure MAIN is
   COMM : constant COMMAND_INTERPRETER.COMM_ARRAY :=
                  ((new STRING'("backup"),  BACKUP 'ACCESS),
                   (new STRING'("copy"),    COPY    'ACCESS),
                   (new STRING'("delete"),  DELETE 'ACCESS),
                   (new STRING'("echo"),    ECHO    'ACCESS),
                   (new STRING'("print"),   PRINT   'ACCESS),
                   ...
                   (new STRING'("zap"),     ZAP     'ACCESS));
begin
   COMMAND_INTERPRETER.START(COMM);
end MAIN;
```

You will see how we have used the attribute ACCESS to create pointers to the various command programs.

Finally, we can study the body of the command interpreter:

```
with TEXT_IO, UNCHECKED_DEALLOCATION;
use TEXT_IO;
```

```
package body COMMAND_INTERPRETER is
  procedure DEALLOCATE is new
    UNCHECKED_DEALLOCATION(STRING, STRING_POINTER);

  -- Support procedure for binary search in command array
  procedure SEARCH_PROGRAM (SOUGHT : STRING_POINTER;
                            COMM    : COMM_ARRAY;
                            PROG    : out PROGRAM_POINTER)
                           is
    FIRST, LAST, MIDDLE : INTEGER
  begin
    FIRST := COMM'FIRST; LAST := COMM'LAST;
    while FIRST <= LAST loop
      MIDDLE := (FIRST + LAST) / 2;
      if SOUGHT.all < COMM(MIDDLE).NAME.all then
        LAST := MIDDLE - 1;
      elsif SOUGHT.all > COMM(MIDDLE).NAME.all then
        FIRST := MIDDLE + 1;
      else
        PROG := COMM(MIDDLE).PROGRAM;
        return;
      end if;
    end loop;
    PROG := null;
  end SEARCH_PROGRAM;

  procedure START(COMM : COMM_ARRAY) is
    LINE : STRING(1 .. 1000);
    LINE_LENGTH : NATURAL;
    POS, START_POS : POSITIVE;
    ARG : ARG_ARRAY(0 .. 100);
    ARG_NO : INTEGER;
    P : PROGRAM_POINTER;
  begin
    loop
      -- Read in a command line
      PUT("> ");
      exit when END_OF_FILE;
      GET_LINE(LINE, LINE_LENGTH);

      -- Pick out the arguments
      POS := 1;
      ARG_NO := -1;
      while POS <= LINE_LENGTH loop
        -- Ignore spaces
        while POS <= LINE_LENGTH and then LINE(POS) = ' ' loop
          POS := POS + 1;
        end loop;
```

```
      exit when POS > LINE_LENGTH;   -- space last

      -- Pick out next argument
      START_POS := POS;
      POS := POS + 1;
      while POS <= LINE_LENGTH and then LINE(POS) /= ' ' loop
        POS := POS + 1;
      end loop;
      ARG_NO := ARG_NO + 1;
      ARG(ARG_NO) := new STRING'(LINE(START_POS .. POS – 1));
    end loop;

    if ARG_NO >= 0 then
      -- The line contains a command
      -- Find and call the corresponding program
      SEARCH_PROGRAM(ARG(0), COMM, P);
      if P /= null then
        P(ARG(0 .. ARG_NO));
      else
        PUT_LINE(ARG(0).all & ": Unrecognized command");
      end if;

      -- Deallocate memory for argument
      for I in 0 .. ARG_NO loop
        DEALLOCATE(ARG(I));
      end loop;
    end if;
  end loop;
 end START;
end COMMAND_INTERPRETER;
```

In the procedure START there is an outer **loop** statement which is performed once per command. The iteration ceases when the user marks the end of file (for example, by writing CTRL-D). When a whole command line has been read there follows an inner **while** statement in which the arguments are picked out, one for each iteration. First, all the spaces in front of an argument are ignored and then the end of the argument in the line is sought. For each new argument encountered, space is allocated for the argument text (using **new**) such that the next access value in the array ARG points at the argument text.

When all the arguments on the line have been dealt with, ARG(0) points at the command name the user has entered and a check is carried out to see that there is a command of that name. This uses a support procedure SEARCH_PROGRAM, which performs a binary search in the table COMM, which contains all the command names and pointers to the corresponding command programs. (Note that the table in the main program MAIN must be sorted for the binary search to work.) SEARCH_PROGRAM returns in the out parameter the access value to the corresponding command program, which is subsequently used to call the command program with the relevant part of the array ARG as parameter. If the command is not found, then an error message is given instead.

When the command program has been executed the memory which had been allocated to the arguments is deallocated.

Thanks to our use of access values to the command programs, this command interpreter is very general. It is very easy to add new commands, simply by first writing a new command program and compiling it, and then by adding a new line to the table COMM in the main program and recompiling that. There is no need to recompile any other part of the program. The command interpreter itself does not need to be changed or recompiled.

There is a third area of use for pointers to subprograms which should also be mentioned here. Modern computer systems have what is known as a graphic user interface, which refers to the windows and menus that are displayed on the screen and communication of the user with the system via a mouse. A program which is to run in this sort of environment must have a special structure. The program starts by calling ready-made support functions within the windows environment to specify which windows, menus and so on will be required. Then a special wait function is called which waits until something happens, such as the user moving the mouse or hitting a key or the mouse button.

Before this wait function is called, it has to be specified what should happen when different events occur. This is done with the help of calls to the windows system's support functions, which have to be given pointers to what are called **call-back functions** as parameters. Call-back functions are functions which you write yourself and which you want to call for different events. You might, for example, write a call-back function which you want to call when the user clicks on a particular mouse button on the screen. Thus you need to use pointers to functions, which is possible in Ada 95, as we have seen. The support functions of the windows system might be written in some language other than Ada (most commonly in the program language C), but they can be linked into an Ada program. (The pragma CONVENTION should be used for a call-back function and also for the pointer type. See the reference manual for details.)

To write windows-oriented programs requires knowledge of the details of the system in use, which lies outside the scope of this book.

▲

EXERCISES

11.1 A queue of cars is to be described using a linked list. Write the part of a program that creates a list describing a queue of three cars. For each car the registration number, make and year should be stored.

11.2 Write a function to evaluate the length of a linked list.

11.3 Assume you have a linked list in which the data part of each element contains an integer. Write a function to determine whether the list is sorted.

11.4 A register of club members has been built up in the form of a linked list. Each member is represented by an element in the list, in which the name, address and telephone number are stored. The list is sorted alphabetically according to the member's name.

Write a procedure to insert a new member into the list, so that the list remains sorted.

11.5 Write a function that receives an access value to a singly linked list L as parameter. As its result the function should return the access value to a new list containing copies of all the elements of L but in reverse order.

11.6 A polynomial such as:

$$f(x) = 7.4x^5 + 3.1x^2 - 10.2x + 14.9$$

can be represented as a linked list in which every element corresponds to a term in the polynomial. The corresponding term's coefficient and degree is stored in each element. The polynomial above, for example, can be represented by the list:

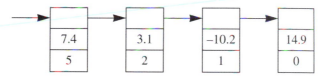

We assume that there is at most one element for any given degree and that the elements are sorted so that the highest degree comes first.

(a) Write a function that calculates the value of a polynomial for a given value of x. As parameters the function receives an access value to the list that represents the polynomial and the given value of x.

(b) Write a function that creates a new list to represent the sum of two polynomials, $P_1(x)$ and $P_2(x)$. As parameters the function gets access values to the two lists representing P_1 and P_2, and as its result it returns the access value to the new list which represents the sum of the two polynomials. The lists representing P_1 and P_2 should not be altered by the function.

(c) The **derivative** of a polynomial:

$$P(x) = a_n x^n + a_{n-1} x^{n-1} + \ldots + a_1 x + a_0$$

can be written as:

$$P'(x) = na_n x^{n-1} + (n-1)a_{n-1} x^{n-2} + \ldots + a_1$$

The derivative of the polynomial above, for example, can be written as:

$$f'(x) = 37x^4 + 6.2x - 10.2$$

Write a function that creates a new list representing the derivative of a given polynomial $P(x)$.

11.7   A **sparse matrix** is one in which most of the elements are zero. To save storage space,
such a matrix can be represented as a linked list. In the list there is one element for each
non-zero matrix element containing its line and column numbers and its value.
   Write a function that receives a sparse matrix in the normal format (a two-
dimensional array) as a parameter. Assume that all the elements in the matrix are
integers. The function should create a list to represent the sparse matrix. The result of
the function should be the access value to the list.

11.8   A **graph** is a general data structure in which a number of nodes are connected to one
another in an arbitrary manner. A graph in which the nodes contain characters can, for
example, be written:

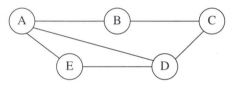

Directed graphs are those in which a particular direction is associated with each link
between two nodes. Arrows are usually drawn instead of lines:

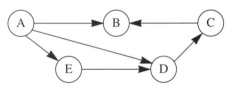

One way of representing a directed graph is to use an **access table**, where each node of
the graph is represented by an entry in a table (a one-dimensional array). Each entry
stores the data part of the corresponding node (a character in the example above) and an
access value to a linked list. The linked list describes the single paths from the given
node to other nodes in the graph, and contains one element for each path. The directed
graph in the example above can, for example, be represented by:

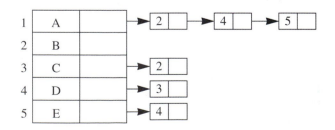

(a) Write a subprogram that inserts a path between two nodes in a directed graph as represented above. The subprogram takes the access table and two node numbers that state the two nodes that are connected.

(b) Write a subprogram that removes a connection between one node and another.

(c) An access table is not very convenient if the number of nodes in a graph must be changed or if nodes must be easily added or removed. In these situations, an access table can be replaced by a linked list in which each element contains the same information as an element of the access table above. Rewrite the subprograms in (a) and (b), representing a directed graph in this way instead.

11.9 Write a package that describes the abstract data type *integer set*. There should be subprograms in the package to carry out all the usual operations on sets. Use a linked list in the body of the package.

11.10 Write a procedure that swaps two neighbouring elements in a doubly linked list. The procedure should take as parameter an access value to the first of the two elements to be swapped.

11.11 An ordinary pack of cards can be represented using a doubly linked list in which every element corresponds to a card and contains the card's suit and colour. Write a program that builds up a list containing all 52 cards in a pack. The program should then deal the pack out randomly to four players so that they each get 13 cards. For each player the program should build up a linked list containing that player's cards. Finally, the program should write out the cards of the four players.

Assume there is a package RANDOM_PACKAGE containing a function RANDOM_NUMBER (with no parameters) which returns a floating point number x such that $0 \le x < 1$.

11.12 Rewrite the package QUEUE_PACKAGE in Section 11.4 so that a doubly linked list is used to represent the queue.

11.13 Write a function to count the number of leaves in a binary tree.

11.14 Write a function that determines whether two binary trees are equal, that is, whether they contain the same data and have the same structure.

11.15 A binary tree can be used to represent an arithmetic expression. The expression:

$$\frac{2 \times 3}{8 - 4} + 1$$

can, for example, be represented by:

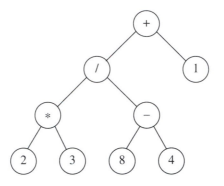

The value of the binary tree can be defined as the value obtained when the corresponding expression is evaluated.

Make the type declarations necessary to describe an arithmetic expression in this way and write a function that calculates the value of a given binary tree.

11.16 Two binary trees can be said to be **reflections** of one another if: (1) both are empty, or (2) both are non-empty, their roots contain the same information, and the right subtree of one is the reflection of the left subtree of the other, and vice versa. Write a function that determines whether two trees are reflections of one another.

11.17 Write a program that reads in a text from a text file and computes how many times different words appear in the text. Use a binary search tree to store the words read together with a counter. Each time a new word has been read from the text file, search to see whether it already appears in the search tree. If it does, increase the word's counter by one. Otherwise, create a new node for the word and insert this node in the correct place in the tree. The program should finish by writing out all the words that have appeared, in alphabetical order, together with the number of times they appeared.

11.18 It is not very difficult to insert a new node into a binary search tree. To remove a node is a little harder. The following algorithm can be applied:

Call the node to be removed P.

If P is a leaf, set the access value in P's parent that points to P, to null.

If P has a left child but no right child, let P's parent point at P's left child instead of pointing at P.

If P has a right child but no left child, let P's parent point at P's right child instead of pointing at P.

Otherwise, find the node Q in P's right subtree with the smallest value data part. Copy the data part of Q to the node P and remove node Q.

Write a procedure that removes a given node from a binary search tree.

11.19 The value of an integral

$$I = \int_a^b f(x)dx$$

can be approximated using what is known as the **trapezium rule**:

$$I \approx h \left(\frac{f(a)}{2} + f(a + h) + f(a + 2h) + \ldots + f(a + (n - 1)h) + \frac{f(b)}{2} \right)$$

The interval $[a, b]$ has been divided into n equal subintervals of length h, that is:

$$h = \frac{b - a}{n}$$

Write a function INTEGRAL which computes the integral of an arbitrary function whose argument and result have type FLOAT. A pointer to the function that is to be integrated should be given as a parameter to INTEGRAL, as should the values of A and B which define the interval of integration.

In INTEGRAL, calculations of the value of the integral are carried out repeatedly until the difference between two successive values is sufficiently small. At each new calculation, the value of n, the number of divisions, is doubled.

Use the function INTERVAL to calculate the value of the integral

$$\int_1^5 x^2 dx$$

12 Files

A **file** is an arbitrarily long sequence of data objects where all the objects have the same type (see Figure 12.1). A file can be stored in the computer's secondary storage, for example on disk, and can therefore be used to store data permanently. Earlier in the book, we discussed text files where the individual objects in a file had the type CHARACTER. In this chapter we review more general files where the data objects are allowed to be of any type. Such general files, where the objects do not have type CHARACTER, are usually called **binary files**. (The objects are actually represented in the same binary form used internally in a program.)

In Ada there are two categories of files: **sequential files,** where objects must be read and written in their correct order from start to finish; and **direct access files** or **direct files**, where an arbitrary object can be accessed without going through the file in a particular order.

Figure 12.1

12.1 Sequential files

Text files belong to the category of sequential files. Earlier we saw that the package TEXT_IO contains the facilities for handling text files; when we want to work with sequential files other than text files we shall make use of another standard package called SEQUENTIAL_IO (see Appendix C). To gain access to this package the line:

with SEQUENTIAL_IO;

must appear at the start of the program. In a text file the objects are always of type CHARACTER but in the case of other sequential files the objects can be of any type. For this reason SEQUENTIAL_IO is not a 'ready-made' package like TEXT_IO. It is a generic package (a template) that can be used to tailor input/output packages for sequential files in which the objects have exactly the required type.

Other than text files, the most common files to work with are those in which the objects have a record type. Assume we want to collect information about the weight and height of a number of people. We can store the data in a file in which each object is a record containing the person's name, weight and height. There is a record in the file for each person. We have the type declaration:

```
type PERSON is
   record
      NAME    : STRING(1 .. 20);
      WEIGHT  : FLOAT;
      HEIGHT  : INTEGER;
   end record;
```

The file's structure is made clear in Figure 12.2.

To create a package containing the facilities for handling files in which the objects have type PERSON, we write:

package PERSON_INOUT **is new** SEQUENTIAL_IO(PERSON);

Brown	Dodd	Smith		Walton
75.0	90.0	65.0		80.0
180	190	175		183

Figure 12.2

The word PERSON in brackets states that the objects will be of type PERSON. The new package will be called PERSON_INOUT. To refer to the package more conveniently, we write:

use PERSON_INOUT;

As in the case of text files, logical files are worked with in a program and file variables are declared to represent the logical files. In TEXT_IO, the type FILE_TYPE could be used to declare logical text files and SEQUENTIAL_IO also had a type called FILE_TYPE. To declare a logical file in which the objects have the type PERSON we can therefore use our new package PERSON_INOUT and write:

PERSON_FILE : PERSON_INOUT.FILE_TYPE;

Note that we have used selector notation and written PERSON_INOUT.FILE_ TYPE even though we put in a **use** clause above. The reason is that most programs also use the package TEXT_IO. If we only wrote FILE_TYPE the compiler would not know if we meant the FILE_TYPE specified in TEXT_IO or the FILE_TYPE specified in PERSON_INOUT.

General files have physical names in the computer system. For example, we can imagine that the file described earlier has the physical name person.data. To link a logical file in the program with a physical file, the procedures OPEN and CREATE, also found in the package SEQUENTIAL_IO, are used. These work in exactly the same way for general files as for text files. For example, we can create a new physical file person.data and connect it to the logical file PERSON_FILE by making the call:

CREATE(PERSON_FILE, NAME => "person.data");

Here it is assumed that the file will be used for writing. If the file had already existed, we could have opened it for reading:

OPEN(PERSON_FILE, MODE => IN_FILE, NAME => "person.data");

Reading and writing cannot proceed at the same time in sequential files: the parameter MODE must be given one of the values IN_FILE or OUT_FILE. In Ada 95, the MODE parameter can also be set to the value APPEND_FILE, which means that you wish to write at the end of an existing file. There is the possibility to go back to the beginning of a file and use it in a new way using the procedure RESET, which also exists for general sequential files. A file is closed using the procedure CLOSE:

CLOSE(PERSON_FILE);

Opening and closing files

- CREATE is used for creating a new file.
- OPEN is used for opening an existing file.
- CLOSE is used for closing a file.
- RESET is used for going back to the start of a file.
- These procedures are specified in the same way as the corresponding procedures for text files.

A file can be erased or deleted by calling the procedure DELETE. In SEQUENTIAL_IO there are also the functions IS_OPEN, MODE, NAME and FORM, which can be used to obtain information about a particular file. These subprograms work in the same way as they do for text files.

There is one important difference between text files and general files. In a general sequential file the individual objects may be of any type. Files do not necessarily contain text, therefore it is not possible to talk about pages and lines in a general file. The file only comprises a series of objects. *It is only text files that have page and line structure*, thus everything to do with pages and lines is irrelevant for a general sequential file. It is not possible, for example, to read a line, test whether a line is finished, or write on a new page. The subprograms in TEXT_IO that are concerned with lines and pages (for example, GET_LINE, END_OF_LINE and NEW_PAGE) are not found in the package SEQUENTIAL_IO.

Line and page structure

- Only *text files* have line and page structure.
- There are no lines and pages in general sequential files.
- There are no subprograms concerned with lines and pages.

For reading and writing text files the procedures GET and PUT are used. When numeric values are read and written, these procedures can make the conversion between a sequence of characters and the internal form of representation in the computer. For example, if a variable of type INTEGER is read from a text file, a number of characters are read from the text file and converted into a value of type INTEGER. In some cases, therefore, one reading from or writing to a text file can mean that several characters are read or written.

Reading and writing are in some respects simpler for general sequential files. GET and PUT are not used, but the two procedures READ and WRITE are specified in SEQUENTIAL_IO:

```
procedure READ   (FILE : in FILE_TYPE;
                  ITEM : out ELEMENT_TYPE);

procedure WRITE  (FILE : in FILE_TYPE;
                  ITEM : in ELEMENT_TYPE);
```

Here the type ELEMENT_TYPE corresponds to the type of the records in the file. In our package, PERSON_INOUT, ELEMENT_TYPE can be regarded as having been replaced by PERSON.

Assume we have declared a record variable P:

```
P : PERSON;
```

and that we have opened the file PERSON_FILE to read from it. We can then make the call:

```
READ(PERSON_FILE, P);
```

This means that a record in PERSON_FILE is read and copied to P.

Note that a call of READ reads *an entire record* from the file at once. This demands that the types of the objects in the file and the variable being read to are the same. Conversion of data never takes place. Unlike text files, it is not possible to read an individual element of data: it is not possible to read only the name from a record in the file, for example.

When a file is being read the system automatically keeps track of a **current index**. This index states the record in the file that is next in line for reading. When a file is opened (or reset) the current index is set to 1 (the first record in the file). Each time READ is called, the current index increases by 1 after the reading has occurred.

If READ is called and the current index has a value greater than the number of records in the file, then the end of the file has been reached and the exception END_ERROR occurs. To avoid this situation, as for text files, the function END_OF_FILE can be used to test whether the file has any records left to be read.

When READ is called, the exceptions MODE_ERROR and DATA_ERROR can also occur. MODE_ERROR means that an attempt has been made to read from a file that is not open for reading. DATA_ERROR arises if the objects in the file are not of the same type as the variable to which they are to be read. (There is no requirement that an Ada compiler should check for this kind of error.)

Reading sequential files

> READ(F, R);

where F is a logical file (file variable) and R is a variable of the same type as the objects in F.

- An *entire* object in the file is read and copied to P.
- The objects are read sequentially from start to finish.
- Each call gives the next object that is waiting in line.

Output works in the corresponding way. If PERSON_FILE were open for writing instead, we could make the call:

WRITE(PERSON_FILE, P);

Writing sequential files

> WRITE(F, R);

where F is a logical file (file variable) and R is a variable of the same type as the objects in F.

- A new object is written at the end of the file.
- R's value is copied to the new object.

A new record is placed at the end of the file and the value of P will be copied to this record. As with reading, one *entire* record at a time is copied when writing to a file. It is not possible to write an individual element of data to the file.

When writing, the exception MODE_ERROR can occur if the file given to WRITE is not open for writing. USE_ERROR can occur if the space available to the file in secondary storage is exceeded.

We can now look at a couple of examples. In the first, we have a program that reads in information about the weight and height of a number of people from the terminal and stores it in a new file. This new file will have the physical name *person.data*.

```
with TEXT_IO, BASIC_NUM_IO, SEQUENTIAL_IO;
use TEXT_IO, BASIC_NUM_IO;
procedure STORE_PERSON_INFO is

   type PERSON is
     record
       NAME    : STRING(1 .. 20);
       WEIGHT : FLOAT;
       HEIGHT : INTEGER;
     end record;

   package PERSON_INOUT is new SEQUENTIAL_IO(PERSON);
   use PERSON_INOUT;

   PERSON_FILE : PERSON_INOUT.FILE_TYPE;
   P : PERSON:
   L : NATURAL;

begin
   CREATE(PERSON_FILE, NAME => "person.data");

   PUT_LINE("Terminate input with CTRL-D");
   loop
     PUT("Name: ");
     exit when END_OF_FILE;
     GET_LINE(P.NAME, L);
     -- pad the name with blanks
     P.NAME(L+1 .. P.NAME'LAST) := (others => ' ');
     PUT("Weight: "); GET(P.WEIGHT);SKIP_LINE;
     PUT("Height: "); GET(P.HEIGHT); SKIP_LINE;
     WRITE(PERSON_FILE, P);
   end loop;
   CLOSE(PERSON_FILE);
end STORE_PERSON_INFO;
```

Note that the information for each person is read in the normal way, element by element from the terminal. When the information is stored in PERSON_FILE, however, it is written as an entire record at a time. In the new file the weight and height information will be stored in the same binary form as used in the program. They are not stored in the form of text as they would be in a text file, that is, the file cannot be handled by the system programs that are written to work on text files. It is not possible, for example, to edit the file using a text editor, and if an attempt should be made to write out the contents of the file using a program that lists text files, the result would be a mass of strange and indecipherable characters at the terminal.

If we would like the program to be more general we can arrange to read in the new file's name from the terminal before creating the file:

```
PUT_LINE("Enter the name of the new file");
GET_LINE(FILE_NAME, L);
CREATE(PERSON_FILE, NAME =>FILE_NAME(1 .. L));
```

In the next example we show a program that reads the above file and selects tall people (taller than 2 m). The information about tall people is stored in a new file *tall.data*. The program uses the function END_OF_FILE to see when the register comes to an end.

```
with SEQUENTIAL_IO;
procedure CHOOSE_TALL is
  type PERSON is
    record
      NAME    : STRING(1 .. 20);
      WEIGHT : FLOAT;
      HEIGHT : INTEGER;
    end record;

  package PERSON_INOUT is new SEQUENTIAL_IO(PERSON);
  use PERSON_INOUT;

  PERSON_FILE, TALL_FILE : PERSON_INOUT.FILE_TYPE;
  P: PERSON;

begin
  OPEN(PERSON_FILE, NAME => "person.data",
                           MODE=> IN_FILE);
  CREATE(TALL_FILE,   NAME => "tall.data");
  while not END_OF_FILE(PERSON_FILE) loop
    READ(PERSON_FILE, P);
    if P.HEIGHT > 200 then
      WRITE(TALL_FILE, P);
    end if;
  end loop;
  CLOSE(PERSON_FILE);
  CLOSE(TALL_FILE);
end CHOOSE_TALL;
```

12.2   Sorted files

It is very common for files to be sorted in some way, making it easier to obtain required information from the file. We can imagine, for example, that when running the program STORE_PERSON_INFO discussed in Section 12.1, the entries could be in alphabetical order so that the file *person.data* is sorted from

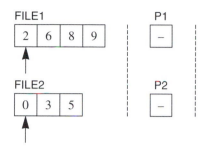

Figure 12.3

the start. The element of the record that defines the sort is called the **key**. If the file *person.data* is sorted in this way, then the element NAME is the key.

To look at methods of handling sorted files, we shall start by considering a common problem – the **merging** of files. Assume we have two sorted files of the same type, that is, the objects in the files have the same type. The task is to merge them together so that a new sorted file, containing all the records from the two files, is obtained.

We can study some diagrams that will help explain how this works. Assume we have two sorted files, FILE1 and FILE2, and for simplicity, their objects are integers. These two files should be merged into a new file that we shall call NEW_FILE. We shall also assume that we have two variables P1 and P2 to which we can read objects from FILE1 and FILE2, respectively. The initial situation is illustrated in Figure 12.3. An arrow is used to denote the current index in each file, that is, the next object waiting to be read. The variables P1 and P2 do not yet contain any file objects, as indicated by the dashes.

The first step is to read the first object from each file, as shown in Figure 12.4. The first objects from the two files are now in P1 and P2, and the pointers that mark the current indexes have moved on one place.

Now we select which of P1 and P2 contains the smaller value: P2 in this example. The contents of P2 are written to the new file NEW_FILE. This uses up the contents of P2 and we read another element of FILE2 into it. Figure 12.5 illustrates the situation.

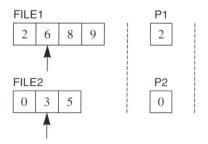

Figure 12.4

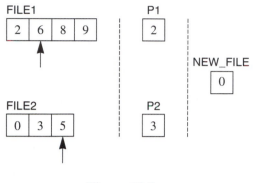

Figure 12.5

Now the smaller of P1 and P2 is chosen again and its contents are written to NEW_FILE. This time P1 is chosen and an object containing the value 2 is written to NEW_FILE. A new object (with value 6) is read from FILE1 to P1. Figure 12.6 shows the current position.

Next time P2 will be chosen and the value 3 written to NEW_FILE, as shown in Figure 12.7. P2 now holds the smaller value (5), so this is written to NEW_FILE. Since FILE2 is now finished we cannot read a new value to P2. Instead we denote that there is nothing in P2, using a dash, as shown in Figure 12.8.

The next time we try and choose the smaller of P1 and P2, we shall see that there is nothing in P2; we shall simply choose P1 and write its contents to NEW_FILE, as shown in Figure 12.9. This action will be repeated until FILE1 is also finished, and we arrive at the situation in Figure 12.9.

We can start to formulate an algorithm to describe how this merge process works:

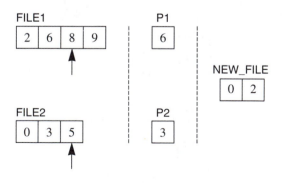

Figure 12.6

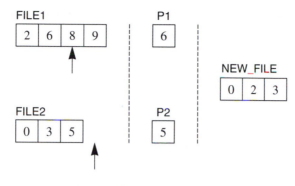

Figure 12.7

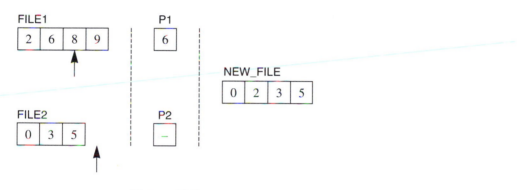

Figure 12.8

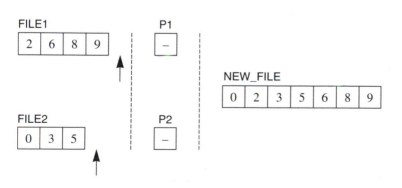

Figure 12.9

(1) Try to get a record from FILE and put it into P1.

(2) Try to get a record from FILE2 and put it into P2.

(3) Repeat the following until there is nothing left in either of FILE1 and FILE2:

(3.1) Pick out one of P1 and P2 and write it to NEW_FILE.

(3.2) Try to get a new record to replace whichever of P1 or P2 was chosen.

By the term 'try to get' we mean:

If the current file is finished, then indicate that there is nothing in the variable that belongs to that file; otherwise, read a record from the file to the corresponding variable.

We must also clarify step (3.1):

If there is something in both P1 and P2, then choose the one that should come first in a sorted file, otherwise, choose the one that contains something.

Note that step (3) guarantees that we shall never reach step (3.1) with nothing in either P1 or P2.

Using this, we can write a program that merges two registers of the kind described, *person.data1* and *person.data2*. We can assume that these files are sorted and were created using the program STORE_PERSON_INFO from the previous section.

In the program a special procedure FETCH has been written because 'try to fetch' occurs in several places in the algorithm.

```
with SEQUENTIAL_IO;
procedure MERGE is
  type PERSON is
    record
      NAME    : STRING(1 .. 20);
      WEIGHT : FLOAT;
      HEIGHT  : INTEGER;
    end record;

  package PERSON_INOUT is new SEQUENTIAL_IO(PERSON);
  use PERSON_INOUT;

  FILE1, FILE2, NEW_FILE : PERSON_INOUT.FILE_TYPE;
  P1, P2                 : PERSON;
  FOUND1, FOUND2         : BOOLEAN;
```

```
    procedure FETCH (F : in out PERSON_INOUT.FILE_TYPE;
                     P : out PERSON;
                     FOUND : out BOOLEAN) is

begin
  if END_OF_FILE(F) then
    FOUND := FALSE;
  else
    READ(F, P);
    FOUND := TRUE;
  end if;
end FETCH;

begin
  OPEN(FILE1, NAME => "person.data1",
              MODE => IN_FILE);
  OPEN(FILE2, NAME => "person.data2",
              MODE => IN_FILE);
  CREATE(NEW_FILE, NAME => "person.data.all");

  FETCH(FILE1, P1, FOUND1);
  FETCH(FILE2, P2, FOUND2);

  while FOUND1 or FOUND2 loop
    if ((FOUND1 and FOUND2) and then P1.NAME < P2.NAME)
      or not FOUND2 then
      WRITE(NEW_FILE, P1);
      FETCH(FILE1, P1, FOUND1);
    else
      WRITE(NEW_FILE, P2);
      FETCH(FILE2, P2, FOUND2);
    end if;
  end loop;
  CLOSE(FILE1);
  CLOSE(FILE2);
  CLOSE(NEW_FILE);
end MERGE;
```

We use two Boolean variables, FOUND1 and FOUND2, to indicate whether there is anything in P1 and P2, respectively.

A little trick is sometimes used to simplify this sort of program. It is easier to recognize the ends of the files if a special record is placed at the end of each file that is to be merged, indicating that the file is finished. In this end record the key is assigned such a large value that no keys with values greater than or equal to it can occur. In our example we can give the name in the end record the constant value END_NAME, which is declared as follows:

```
END_NAME : constant STRING (1 .. 20) := (others =>
                                        CHARACTER'LAST);
```

If we suppose that both FILE1 and FILE2 have such end records, the **while** statement in the program MERGE can be simplified somewhat:

```
while P1.NAME < END_NAME or P2.NAME < END_NAME loop
    if P1.NAME < P2.NAME then
        WRITE(NEW_FILE, P1);
        READ(FILE1, P1);
    else
        WRITE(NEW_FILE, P2);
        READ(FILE2, P2);
    end if;
end loop;
```

We do not need the procedure FETCH or the variables FOUND1 and FOUND2. Since we always stop when the end record has been read there is no risk of the files running out.

Even if no special end record is placed in the files, this concept can still be used by 'imagining' an end record. The procedure FETCH must be retained, but rewritten a little:

```
procedure FETCH (F : in out PERSON_INOUT.FILE_TYPE;
                 P : out PERSON) is
begin
  if END_OF_FILE(F) then
    P.NAME := END_NAME;
  else
    READ(F, P);
  end if;
end FETCH;
```

When the end of the file is reached, like 'imagining' an end record has been read, P.NAME is given the value END_NAME. The **while** statement is then written:

```
while P1.NAME < END_NAME or P2.NAME < END_NAME loop
    if P1.NAME < P2.NAME then
        WRITE(NEW_FILE, P1);
        FETCH(FILE1, P1);
    else
        WRITE(NEW_FILE, P2);
        FETCH(FILE2, P2);
    end if;
end loop;
```

F

| 11 | 23 | 14 | 37 | 9 | 80 | 59 | 40 | 20 | 36 | 67 | 15 | 75 |

Figure 12.10

We have seen ways of merging two files that are already sorted. The natural question to ask now is, how do you sort a file?

One way is to put the records in the file in order from the start. We could create a sorted file by, for example, feeding in the information to the program STORE_PERSON_INFO with the names in alphabetical order, as mentioned earlier.

One efficient way of sorting files that do not contain too many records is to read in all the records to an array in a program, sort the array and then write it back to the file. It is, however, common for files to hold many records and the accessible primary storage is not always sufficient to allow the sorting to take place in an array. Then some file sorting technique must be used, which sorts without reading in all the records to the program at once. This is usually described as **external file sorting**. This is an area of data processing where there are several methods with different degrees of sophistication. To demonstrate the concepts that can be applied, a relatively simple method will be shown here, which is far from the most efficient.

As usual, diagrams best illustrate how things work. We assume that we have to sort the file F in Figure 12.10. For simplicity, we assume that the records contain nothing but an integer key. To carry out the sort we shall use two temporary subsidiary files, Tl and T2. If we look at F, we see that it can be divided into several sequences in each of which the records are sorted. F contains the sequences [11, 23], [14, 37], [9, 80], [59], [40], [20, 36, 67] and [15, 75]. If F had been totally sorted it would have consisted of only one sequence.

The first step in the sort algorithm is that we read F, record by record, and copy alternate sequences to T1 and T2. To indicate the end of each sequence we use a special end record that contains a key value larger than any real record can take. We arrive at the situation shown in Figure 12.11. To enable T1 and T2 to have the same number of sequences, we put an empty sequence at the end of T2.

The next step is to merge pairs of sequences, one from T1 and one from T2, to file F. After this step F will appear as in Figure 12.12. F will thus have half as many sequences as it originally had.

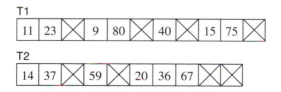

Figure 12.11

F

| 11 | 14 | 23 | 37 | 9 | 59 | 80 | 20 | 36 | 40 | 67 | 15 | 75 |

Figure 12.12

Now we can continue in this manner, sharing the sequences between T1 and T2 and then merging pairs of sequences. This process is repeated until F has only one sequence. Figure 12.13 shows the remaining stages in the process.

We shall present a program that carries out a sort according to this method. The records in the file to be sorted consist of a data part (in this example, a text string) as well as a key.

```
with TEXT_IO, SEQUENTIAL_IO;
use TEXT_IO;
procedure SORT_FILE is
  subtype KEY is INTEGER;
  subtype DATA is STRING(1 .. 30);
  type FILE_RECORD is
    record
      K : KEY;
      D : DATA;
    end record;

MAX_KEY : constant KEY := INTEGER'LAST;
MIN_KEY : constant KEY := INTEGER'FIRST;
```

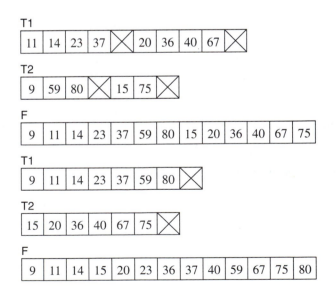

Figure 12.13

```
package REC_INOUT is new SEQUENTIAL_IO(FILE_RECORD);
use REC_INOUT;

F, T1, T2          : REC_INOUT.FILE_TYPE;
SORTED             : BOOLEAN := FALSE;
NO_OF_MERGES : NATURAL;

procedure FETCH (F  : in out REC_INOUT.FILE_TYPE;
                     R : out FILE_RECORD) is

begin
  if END_OF_FILE(F) then
    R.K := MAX_KEY;
  else
    READ(F, R);
  end if;
end FETCH;

procedure SPLIT_UP (F, T1, T2 :
                            in out REC_INOUT.FILE_TYPE) is
  R : FILE_RECORD;

  procedure  COPY_SEQUENCE
               (F, T : in out REC_INOUT.FILE_TYPE;
                R    : in out FILE_RECORD) is
    PREV_KEY  : KEY := MIN_KEY;
    FINAL_REC : FILE_RECORD;
  begin
    while R.K >= PREV_KEY and R.K < MAX_KEY loop
      PREV_KEY := R.K;
      WRITE(T, R);
      FETCH(F, R);
    end loop;
    FINAL_REC.K := MAX_KEY;
    WRITE(T, FINAL_REC);      -- end of sequence
  end COPY_SEQUENCE;

begin
  FETCH(F, R);
  while R.K < MAX_KEY loop
    COPY_SEQUENCE(F, T1, R);
    COPY_SEQUENCE(F, T2, R);
  end loop;
end SPLIT_UP;

procedure MERGE (FILE1, FILE2, FILE3 :
                      in out REC_INOUT.FILE_TYPE) is
  R1, R2 : FILE_RECORD;
```

```
      begin
        FETCH(FILE1, R1);
        FETCH(FILE2, R2);
        while R1.K < MAX_KEY or R2.K < MAX_KEY loop
          if R1.K < R2.K then
            WRITE(FILE3, R1);
            FETCH(FILE1, R1);
          else
            WRITE(FILE3, R2);
            FETCH(FILE2, R2);
          end if;
        end loop;
      end MERGE;

    begin
      OPEN(F, IN_FILE, "datafile");
      while not SORTED loop
        -- split up the sequences in F into T1 and T2
        RESET(F, IN_FILE);
        CREATE(T1); CREATE(T2);
        SPLIT_UP(F, T1, T2);

        -- merge the sequences in T1 and T2 into F
        RESET(T1, IN_FILE); RESET(T2, IN_FILE);
        RESET(F, OUT_FILE);
        NO_OF_MERGES := 0;
        while not END_OF_FILE(T1) loop
          MERGE(T1, T2, F);
          NO_OF_MERGES := NO_OF_MERGES + 1;
        end loop;
        SORTED := NO_OF_MERGES = 1;
        CLOSE(T1); CLOSE(T2);
      end loop;
      CLOSE(F);
    end SORT_FILE;
```

We have used a procedure FETCH in the program which reads from F or from one of the temporary files. When F is read, the end of the file is finally reached, and then FETCH 'imagines' that it has read a special end record.

We conclude by mentioning some improvements that could make the program more efficient. The number of times sorting has to be performed can be reduced if the file F has longer sequences from the beginning. This can be achieved by reading N records at a time from F into an array and sorting this array, using some internal sorting method, before writing them to a temporary file. The number N is chosen according to the amount of primary storage available.

Another improvement could be made by using more than two temporary files, so that several sequences could be merged at once.

A further trick is not to put the sequence that results from a merge back into F but into another set of the same number of temporary files. The sequences are placed alternately into the new temporary files. In this way, merging can be carried out 'to and fro' until only one sequence remains.

12.3   Direct files

It is not necessary to handle the records in a file sequentially in an Ada program. If instead of using the package SEQUENTIAL_IO another standard package, DIRECT_IO, is used (see Appendix D) it becomes possible to read and write records in arbitrary order.

We have already mentioned that for every open file the Ada system keeps a current index which points at the next record waiting to be read. Work with direct files offers the possibility of controlling the index. In the package DIRECT_IO there are the type declarations:

```
type      COUNT is range 0 .. implementation-dependent integer;
subtype  POSITIVE_COUNT is COUNT range 1 .. COUNT'LAST;
```

Current index has type POSITIVE_COUNT.

To set the current index to a particular value the procedure SET_INDEX is used:

```
SET_INDEX(F, 100);         -- F has type DIRECT_IO.FILE_TYPE
SET_INDEX(F, REC_NO);      -- REC_NO has type POSITIVE_COUNT
```

The value of current index can also be read by calling the function INDEX:

```
-- read the first 100 records
while INDEX(F) <= 100 loop
   READ(F, P);
end loop;
```

To determine how many records there are in a file (that is, the index number of the last record) the function SIZE can be used:

```
if SIZE(F) > 100000 then
   PUT("BIG FILE");
end if;
```

The following specifications are found in the package DIRECT_IO:

```
procedure SET_INDEX  (FILE : in FILE_TYPE;
                           TO   : in POSITIVE_COUNT);
function INDEX           (FILE : in FILE_TYPE)
                           return POSITIVE_COUNT;
function SIZE            (FILE : in FILE_TYPE
                           return COUNT;
```

Current index for direct files

- SET_INDEX(F,I) sets the current index in the file F to I.
- INDEX(F) gives the current index for the file F.
- SIZE(F) gives the number of records in the file F.

When a record is to be read or written it is possible to state which record is required. There are two versions of the subprograms READ and WRITE in the package DIRECT_IO:

```
procedure READ    (FILE   : in FILE_TYPE;
                   ITEM   : out ELEMENT_TYPE);
procedure READ    (FILE   : in FILE_TYPE;
                   ITEM   : out ELEMENT_TYPE;
                   FROM   : in POSITIVE_COUNT);
procedure WRITE   (FILE   : in FILE_TYPE;
                   ITEM   : in ELEMENT_TYPE);
procedure WRITE   (FILE   : in FILE_TYPE;
                   ITEM   : in ELEMENT_TYPE;
                   TO     : in POSITIVE_COUNT);
```

The first of each pair is identical to the READ and WRITE found in SEQUEN-TIAL_IO. The parameter F gives the file referred to and ITEM is the variable in the program that will be read to or written from. Thus direct files can be treated in exactly the same way as sequential files.

The second version of the two procedures has a third parameter FROM and TO, in READ and WRITE, respectively. This third parameter specifies the index in the file for the record that is to be read or written. Before reading or writing starts, the current index is set to the value given. To read record number l00 of file F, for example, we can write:

```
READ(F, R, 100);
```

Another example is:

```
WRITE(F, R, REC_NO);   -- REC_NO has type POSITIVE_CO'JNT
```

For all versions of READ and WRITE the current index is automatically increased by 1 after reading or writing. For example after the call:

```
READ(F, R, 100);
```

the current index has value 101.

Reading and writing direct files

READ(F, R);	read the next record in the file F to the variable R.
READ(F, R, I);	read record number I in the file F to the variable R.
WRITE(F, R);	write R to the next record in the file F.
WRITE(F, R, I);	write R to record number I in the file F.

Before reading or writing a direct file can begin, the file must be opened using CREATE or OPEN. The difference between direct and sequential files is that a direct file can be opened for *both* reading and writing. The type FILE_MODE has the declaration:

```
type FILE_MODE is (IN_FILE, INOUT_FILE, OUT_FILE);
```

If it is specified that the file should be of type INOUT_FILE when the file is opened, then the file can be both read and written. After the calls:

```
OPEN    (F1, MODE => IN_FILE,    NAME => "file1");
OPEN    (F2, MODE => INOUT_FILE, NAME => "file2");
CREATE (F3, MODE => OUT_FILE,    NAME => "file3");
```

for example, F1 can be read only, F2 can be both read and written, and F3 can be written only.

For the procedure CREATE, the MODE parameter may be omitted, and in this case the file assumes the mode INOUT_FILE.

CREATE (F4, NAME => "file4");　　-- F4 can be read and written

As with sequential files, a direct file can be reset to the beginning and the file's mode can be changed by calling RESET:

RESET (F3, INOUT_FILE);　　-- now F3 can be read and written

The remaining subprograms in SEQUENTIAL_IO, namely CLOSE, DELETE, MODE, NAME, FORM, IS_OPEN and END_OF_FILE are also found in DIRECT_IO and work in exactly the same way.

As an example of using direct files we can work with bank accounts. Let us assume that a bank has a data file in which each record contains information about a bank account. A record has to contain an account number, the account balance and information about the account holder:

```
type ACCOUNT_RECORD is
  record
    NO                 : ACCOUNT_NO;
    BALANCE            : FLOAT;
    ACCOUNT_HOLDER  : PERSON;
  end record;
```

The account file is sorted according to the account number, which can be assumed to be an eight-digit number:

```
MIN_NO  : constant := 10_000_000;
MAX_NO : constant := 99_999_999;
subtype ACCOUNT_NO is INTEGER range MIN_NO .. MAX_NO;
```

Now we shall look at an imaginary program a bank clerk may run when a client wants to make a deposit or withdrawal. The program will read in the account number from the terminal and find the record with this number in the accounts file. If the given account number is missing from the file, the program will give an error message to the clerk.

If the account number is found in the file, the program should read in from the terminal the amount that is to be deposited or withdrawn. A deposit is given as a positive amount and a withdrawal as a negative amount. The record for the account in question should be changed in the file so that the account's balance is correct after the transaction. If the proposed withdrawal is greater than the amount of money held in the account, the program should give an error message and refuse the withdrawal.

We shall use the accounts file as a direct file in this program, and both read from and write to it; that is, we let the file have the mode INOUT_FILE.

To find the required account in the accounts file we use a binary search. The algorithm for a binary search was given in Section 7.4, where we wrote a recursive function to find a particular record in an array. We shall use the same algorithm here but use iteration rather than recursion. The reason for this is that files can sometimes be very large, since they are holding many records. If recursion is used to make a binary search in a very large file, the primary store may run out since too many instances of the recursive function are made.

We use two variables, FIRST and LAST, to define the part of the file where we want to search. These variables are given the type COUNT, so that they can point at records in the file. At the start, FIRST is set to 1 and LAST is set to the index of the file's last record. Then the middle record is looked at. If the required account number is less than the account number in the middle record the search continues in the first half of the file by setting LAST to the index for the record that is one before the middle record. If the required account number is greater than the one in the middle record, the latter half is searched and FIRST is set to the index of the middle record. Now a new middle record is found, in the middle of the chosen half file. This process continues until the required record is found or until the chosen half runs out of records (that is, FIRST > LAST).

We get the program:

```
with TEXT_IO, BASIC_NUM_IO, DIRECT_IO;
use TEXT_IO, BASIC_NUM_IO;
procedure MAKE_TRANSACTION is
  type PERSON is
    record
      NAME     : STRING(1 .. 20);
      ADDRESS : STRING(1 .. 30);
    end record;
  MIN_NO  : constant := 10_000_000;
  MAX_NO : constant := 99_999_999;
  subtype ACCOUNT_NO is INTEGER
                      range MIN_NO .. MAX_NO;
  type ACCOUNT_RECORD is
    record
      NO                  : ACCOUNT_NO;
      BALANCE             : FLOAT;
      ACCOUNT_HOLDER  : PERSON;
    end record;
  package ACCOUNT_INOUT is new
                  DIRECT_IO(ACCOUNT_RECORD);
  use ACCOUNT_INOUT;
  AC_FILE                 : ACCOUNT_INOUT.FILE_TYPE;
  A                       : ACCOUNT_RECORD;
  REQUIRED_NO          : ACCOUNT_NO;
  AMOUNT               : FLOAT;
  FOUND                : BOOLEAN := FALSE;
  FIRST, LAST, REC_NO : ACCOUNT_INOUT.COUNT;
```

```
begin
  PUT("Enter account number: "); GET(REQUIRED_NO);
  OPEN(AC_FILE, INOUT_FILE, "accounts");
  -- find account record
  FIRST := 1;
  LAST   := SIZE(AC_FILE);
  while not FOUND and FIRST <= LAST loop
    REC_NO := (FIRST + LAST) / 2;
    READ(AC_FILE, A, REC_NO);    -- read middle record
    if REQUIRED_NO < A.NO then
      LAST := REC_NO - 1;    -- search in left half
    elsif REQUIRED_NO > A.NO then
      FIRST := REC_NO + 1;    -- search in right half
    else
      FOUND := TRUE;
    end if;
  end loop;

  if FOUND then
    PUT_LINE(A.ACCOUNT_HOLDER.NAME);
    PUT_LINE(A.ACCOUNT_HOLDER.ADDRESS);
    PUT("Balance: ");
    PUT(A.BALANCE, EXP => 0, FORE => 8, AFT => 2);
    NEW_LINE;
    PUT("Enter amount: "); GET(AMOUNT);
    if AMOUNT < 0.0 and A.BALANCE + AMOUNT < 0.0 then
      PUT_LINE("withdrawal not possible!");
    else
      A.BALANCE := A.BALANCE + AMOUNT;
      WRITE(AC_FILE, A, REC_NO);
      PUT("Balance after transaction: ");
      PUT(A.BALANCE, EXP => 0, FORE => 8, AFT => 2);
      NEW_LINE;
    end if;
  else
    PUT_LINE("Account number not found!");
  end if;

  CLOSE(AC_FILE);
end MAKE_TRANSACTION;
```

In the program we create a package ACCOUNT_INOUT that provides us with the facilities for directly accessing the accounts file. AC_FILE is the logical file in the program that is linked to the physical accounts file. AC_FILE has the type ACCOUNT_INOUT.FILE_TYPE. We have to use dot notation. If we had only written FILE_TYPE the compiler would not have known whether we meant

FILE_TYPE in TEXT_IO or FILE_TYPE in ACCOUNT_INOUT. For the same reason, we must state the type for FIRST, LAST and REC_NO as ACCOUNT_INOUT.COUNT and not only as COUNT, because there is also a type COUNT declared in TEXT_IO.

EXERCISES

12.1   Information about a number of people has been collected into a file *persondata* in order to carry out a statistical investigation. The following information is stored for each individual: name, height, weight, shoe size, age and civil status (married, single or widowed). To analyse the statistics, the sex of the individuals should also be known, but this was forgotten when the file was created.

Write a program that reads the file *persondata* and creates two new files *mandata* and *womandata*. The new files should store the records for all the men and women, respectively. For each person in *persondata* the program should ask the operator if the record read refers to a man or a woman.

12.2   In a scientific experiment many independent series of measurements have been made. Each series comprises 25 real numbers. The measurements are to be stored in a file where each object represents a series of measurements. Write a program that creates a file of measurements. The program should read in the values of the measurements from the terminal, and the values of the measurements from each series should be given sequentially.

12.3   A company has a register of their customers in the form of a data file. There is one record in the file for each customer, containing the customer's name and two lines of address (for example, street address and town, plus postal code). Each of these three items is at most 20 characters in length. To send out information to customers a program is required that can print self-adhesive address labels with the customers' names and addresses. A printing terminal is used loaded with special paper on which the labels are stuck contiguously, three in a row. The total width of the paper is 72 characters and each label is thus 24 characters wide. The height of each label is 5 lines.

Write a program that reads the file of customers and writes out their names and addresses on self-adhesive labels. Use only the three centre lines of each label. The program should work even if the number of customers is not an exact multiple of three.

12.4   The members of a weightlifting club spur one another on to ever greater heights (or weights) by displaying a monthly list of the best results for each member. A computer is used to keep track of the results. There is a record for each member in a file *liftresults*, holding membership number and information about the heaviest weight lifted in the current month.

Write a program that a member can run after each training session. The program should ask for the membership number and how many kilos he (or she) lifted during that session. If the result is better than earlier results the program should update the file *liftresults* so that the new result is put into the file.

(a)   Treat *liftresults* as a sequential file.

(b)   Let *liftresults* be a direct file.

12.5   A company has set up a list of its employees' room and telephone numbers in a computer file. There is a record for each employee and each record contains name, room number and telephone number. The file is sorted alphabetically.

Write a program that can add records for new employees, change existing records and remove records from the file. Name, room number and telephone number are requested. If a name is given that is not found in the file, a new record should be added in the correct place. If the given name is found, then its record should be removed if the room number is said to be zero, otherwise it should be updated. This process is repeated as often as necessary. The records in the file that are not mentioned from the terminal should be left unchanged. It may be assumed that the names are given in alphabetical order.

12.6   Write a program that merges four files into one. The records in the files are of the same type and comprise a key (an integer in the interval 1–99999) and a data array of 100 characters.

12.7   Information about the situation in a football league has been stored in a file *league*. There is one record in the file for each team in the league. A record contains the team's name, number of points, number of goals scored and number of goals let in. The records are in arbitrary order in the file.

Write a program that sorts the file *league* so that the team with most points comes first and the one with fewest comes last. If two or more teams have the same number of points they should be listed according to goal difference (number of goals scored – number of goals let in). Teams with the same number of points and the same goal difference should be listed alphabetically. (*Hint*: Do the sorting internally in the program.)

12.8   Revise the program SORT_FILE from Section 12.2 so that it uses four temporary files instead of two.

12.9   Write a program to sort a file that works on the same principle as the program SORT_FILE but which merges 'to and fro' between four temporary files T1, T2, T3 and T4. When the sequences from the files T1 and T2 are being merged the resulting sequences are placed alternately into T3 and T4. Then T3 and T4 are merged and the resulting sequences placed alternately into T1 and T2, and so on until only one sequence remains.

12.10 A company has a data file *storefile* that is used to keep track of all the articles in its warehouse. There is a record in the file for each type of article. For each article there is a record with a product code (a code of 10 characters), a description (a text of 30 characters), the number of articles in store and the price.

Write a program that can take the following commands from the terminal:

INFO artno   The program displays the information stored for the given article at the terminal.

BOUGHT artno n   The program should save in the *storefile* the information that *n* new articles of type *artno* have been bought for the warehouse stock.

SOLD artno n   The program should place into the file *storefile* the information that *n* articles of type *artno* have been sold from the warehouse stock.

12.11 When large direct files have to be searched, the number of readings made from secondary storage can be reduced if each data file has an **index table**. This table contains one element for each record in the data file. An element holds the key of the corresponding record and its position (index) in the data file. The index table is sorted so that the keys appear in order of size, but the data file does not need to be sorted.

If a record with a particular key has to be found in the data file, the index table is searched first for the index of the record in the file. Then only a single input or output action is necessary on the data file. The index table can be stored as a special file, separately from the data file itself. The program can start by reading in all the index table to an array in the program so that the search can take place internally.

Write a program for the problem formulated in Exercise 12.10, but now use an index table.

13 Generic Units

When a program or part of a program is being written it is usually advantageous to try to make it as general as possible. Then, if the conditions for a program should change, fewer changes (or even none) will be required to enable the program to work. Moreover, similar programming problems occur in many different contexts. If a general solution has been designed for one problem, it can often be used on later occasions.

Ada offers the programmer the possibility of writing general programs using **generic units.** Such a program unit can be either a subprogram or a package. A generic unit is not only *one* subprogram or *one* package, but is a description of a whole *family* of similar units. Generic units can be regarded as generalized bits of a puzzle that can be fitted together to develop a new program. Ada libraries of generic units can be built up from different sources, thereby simplifying future program development.

13.1   Definitions and instances

We shall start with a very simple program. In Section 6.3 we constructed a procedure SWAP that could be used for interchanging the values of two variables:

```
procedure SWAP (NUMBER1, NUMBER2 : in out INTEGER) is
  TEMP : INTEGER;
begin
  TEMP       := NUMBER1;
  NUMBER1  := NUMBER2;
  NUMBER2  := TEMP;
end SWAP;
```

The procedure demands that the two parameters have the type INTEGER, so it cannot be used for swapping the values of, say, two floating point variables. We shall now rewrite SWAP so that it can be used for all types of parameter. It then gets the new specification:

```
generic
  type ELEMENT is private;
procedure SWAP (A, B : in out ELEMENT);
```

Between the reserved words **generic** and **procedure** is a list of the **formal generic parameters**. In this case there is only one such parameter, the type ELEMENT. (The reason for saying that the type is private will be explained in Section 13.2.) The procedure must also have a body:

```
procedure SWAP (A, B : in out ELEMENT) is
  TEMP  : ELEMENT;
begin
  TEMP  := A; A := B; B := TEMP;
end SWAP;
```

This looks like a perfectly normal procedure, but it is not. It is a template that defines a family of procedures. In the body of SWAP a generic parameter ELEMENT is used. SWAP describes different procedures depending on the 'value' of ELEMENT. If ELEMENT has the 'value' FLOAT, for example, SWAP describes a procedure that can be used to interchange the values of two variables of type FLOAT. It is as though the word 'FLOAT' appeared in all the places where ELEMENT actually appears.

Note that a generic procedure must have a separate specification. The specification and the body may be two separate compilation units. The specification must then be compiled before the body.

Definition of a generic unit

- First make a specification:
  generic
     declaration of generic parameters
     subprogram declaration or package specification
- Then give the body of the subprogram or package.
- The specification and body may be two separate compilation units.

If the procedure SWAP is to be used in a program, the program should begin with:

with SWAP;

So far there is no 'real' procedure SWAP: there is only a template. To get a procedure we have to use the template and **generate** or **create** a version of SWAP. A particular version of a generic unit is called an **instance** of the generic unit, and it is created by making a **generic instantiation**. When an instance of a generic unit is created, the 'value' of the generic parameter has to be specified: the **actual generic parameters** are stated. To instantiate a procedure that can interchange two numbers of the type FLOAT, for example, we make the declaration:

procedure SWAP_FLOAT **is new** SWAP(FLOAT);

Here FLOAT is the actual generic parameter. Now we have a true procedure that can be called in the normal way. If the variables X and Y have the type FLOAT, for example, we make the call:

SWAP_FLOAT(X, Y);

If we also want a procedure that can swap two character variables we can instantiate a further instance of the procedure SWAP:

procedure SWAP_CHAR **is new** SWAP(CHARACTER);

This produces a new procedure that can be called with:

SWAP_CHAR(C1, C2);

where C1 and C2 have the type CHARACTER.

Instantiating generic units

Declaration is made using one of the forms:

- **procedure** *procedure_name* **is new**
  generic_procedure(actual parameters);
- **function** *function_name* **is new**
  generic_function(actual parameters);
- **package** *package_name* **is new**
  generic_package(actual parameters);

It is also possible to have generic packages. To demonstrate this we will return to the character stack package of Section 11.4, which had the specification:

```
package STACK_PACKAGE is
   type STACK is limited private:
   procedure PUSH   (S : in out STACK; T : in CHARACTER);
   procedure POP     (S : in out STACK; T : out CHARACTER);
   function    EMPTY (S : STACK) return BOOLEAN;
private
   type STACK_ELEMENT;
   type STACK is access STACK_ELEMENT;
end STACK_PACKAGE;
```

This package can only be used if you want to create stacks in which the elements are of the type CHARACTER, but it can easily be made into a generic package. We start by changing the specification:

```
generic
   type ELEMENT is private;
package STACK_PACKAGE is
   type STACK is limited private;
   procedure PUSH   (S : in out STACK; T : in ELEMENT);
   procedure POP     (S : in out STACK; T : out ELEMENT);
   function    EMPTY (S : STACK) return BOOLEAN;
private
   ...
end STACK_PACKAGE;
```

We have introduced a generic parameter ELEMENT, which we have used instead of the type CHARACTER. In the body of the package we now only need to change CHARACTER to ELEMENT wherever it occurs.

In a program which will use the generic package STACK_PACKAGE, you first insert the clause:

```
with STACK_PACKAGE;
```

We assume that we have a type PERSON:

```
type PERSON is
record
   NAME      : STRING(1 .. 20);
   ADDRESS : STRING(1 .. 30);
end record;
```

If we want two stacks, one where we can have elements of the type PERSON and one for integers, we can create two instantiations and write:

```
package INT_PACKAGE       is new STACK_PACKAGE(INTEGER);
package PERSON_PACKAGE  is new STACK_PACKAGE(PERSON);
use INT_PACKAGE, PERSON_PACKAGE;
```

Then the two stacks can be declared:

```
ISTACK  : INT_PACKAGE.STACK;
PSTACK : PERSON_PACKAGE.STACK;
```

(Point notation must be used here so that the compiler can know which of the stacks is meant.) Now we can make the calls:

```
PUSH(PSTACK, P);     -- P is of type PERSON
PUSH(ISTACK,  I);     -- I is of type INTEGER
```

Since the procedures PUSH in the two packages have different types, the compiler can determine which of them should be used.

A generic unit can have any number of parameters. It is also possible to have a generic unit without parameters. We can make use of this when several identical packages with 'memory' have to be created. As an example, we can look again at the package for generating random numbers in Section 8.7. In its final form this had the specification:

```
package RANDOM is
   subtype NUMBER is FLOAT range 0.0 .. 1.0;
   function NEXT_NUMBER return NUMBER;
   -- gives a random number greater than or
   -- equal to 0 and less than 1
end RANDOM;
```

By adding the word **generic** we can convert this into a generic package:

```
generic
package RANDOM is
   subtype NUMBER is FLOAT range 0.0 .. 1.0;
   function NEXT_NUMBER return NUMBER;
   -- gives a random number greater than or
   -- equal to 0 and less than 1
end RANDOM;
```

No changes are necessary in the body of the package. This generic package has no parameters: there is nothing between the words **generic** and **package**. Now we shall present a program that uses the generic random number generator to produce two independent series of random numbers:

```
with TEXT_IO, BASIC_NUM_IO, RANDOM;
use TEXT_IO, BASIC_NUM_IO;
procedure RANDOM_DEMO is
   package RANDOM1 is new RANDOM;
   package RANDOM2 is new RANDOM;
   X1 : RANDOM1.NUMBER;
   X2 : RANDOM2.NUMBER;
   SUM1, SUM2 : FLOAT := 0.0;
begin
   for I in 1 .. 100 loop
      X1 := RANDOM1.NEXT_NUMBER;
      X2 := RANDOM2.NEXT_NUMBER;
      SUM1 := SUM1 + X1;
      SUM2 := SUM2 + X2;
   end loop;
   PUT("Mean 1: "); PUT(SUM1 / 100.0); NEW_LINE;
   PUT("Mean 2: "); PUT(SUM2 / 100.0); NEW_LINE;
end RANDOM_DEMO;
```

Two separate random number packages are created in the program, RANDOM1 and RANDOM2, each with its own set of internal variables and each working independently of the other.

13.2   Generic parameters

When an instance of a generic program unit is created, it is as though the generic formal parameters have been replaced by the corresponding actual parameters and the generic unit has then been compiled. (For example, when the package

PERSON_STACK was compiled, ELEMENT was replaced by PERSON.) The mechanism for generic units is, however, more sophisticated than mere text substitution.

A generic unit can, and should, be compiled before it is used. A kind of partial compilation takes place. The compiler checks that the generic unit is syntactically correct and translates it as far as is possible. When an instance is later created, it is not a complete compilation that occurs – the compiler only fills in the bits that are missing.

So that the compiler will know how a formal parameter will be used in a generic unit, certain information has to be stated at the time of specification. When we generated the generic package STACK, for example, we had to state that the formal parameter ELEMENT would be a type and that the type would be private.

There are four different categories of generic parameter: **value** and **object parameters**, **type parameters**, **subprogram parameters** and **package parameters**. We will look at them one at a time.

13.2.1 Value parameters

Some generic parameters can look like ordinary subprogram parameters. They can be of two kinds: **in** parameters, which are called **value parameters**, and **in out** parameters, which are called **object parameters**. Since **in out** parameters are not common and can lead to strange side-effects, we will ignore them here and deal only with value parameters.

Let us look at an example. The stack package in the previous section implemented a stack using linked lists. It is also possible to implement stacks using arrays. We will rewrite the specification of the package:

```
generic
  type ELEMENT is private;
  MAX_NUMBER : POSITIVE := 100;
package STACK_PACKAGE is
  type STACK is limited private;
  procedure PUSH   (S : in out STACK; T : in ELEMENT);
  procedure POP    (S : in out STACK; T : out ELEMENT);
  function   EMPTY (S : STACK) return BOOLEAN;
private
  type STACK is
    record
      ELT_ARRAY : array(1 .. MAX_NUMBER) of ELEMENT;
      TOP : NATURAL := 0;
    end record;
end STACK_PACKAGE;
```

The first generic parameter is, as before, the type parameter which specifies the type of the elements in the stack. The second parameter MAX_NUMBER is a value parameter which gives the maximum size of the stack. Note that it is used in the declaration of the component ELT_ARRAY in the private part. It is possible to give a value parameter a default value, as we have done here.

Now we can create different instantiations of STACK_PACKAGE:

    package CHAR_PACKAGE   **is new**
                          STACK_PACKAGE(CHARACTER, 50);
    package PERSON_PACKAGE **is new**
                          STACK_PACKAGE(PERSON, 25);

Variables of the type CHAR_PACKAGE.STACK will have space for at most 50 elements, and variables of the type PERSON_PACKAGE.STACK will have space for 25 elements. Just as for calling a subprogram, named parameter association is allowed so we could instead have written:

    package CHAR_PACKAGE   **is new** STACK_PACKAGE(SIZE => 50,
                               ELEMENT = > CHARACTER);
    package PERSON_PACKAGE **is new** STACK_PACKAGE(ELEMENT
                            => PERSON, SIZE => 25);

A value parameter that has a default value does not have to be given a value:

    package INTEGER_PACKAGE **is new** STACK_PACKAGE(INTEGER);

Within the body of a generic program unit a generic value parameter is treated like a constant. Thus, its value may not be changed.

Generic value parameters

    parameter-name : *type* : = *default-value*

Default-value may be omitted.

13.2.2 Type parameters

The second category of generic parameters is that of type parameters. We have already seen examples of this in the generic procedure SWAP, and in the generic package STACK_PACKAGE. There, we wrote in the speckfication:

    type ELEMENT **is private**;

When a generic type parameter is specified the properties of the type are given, for the reason that the compiler must know how the type is to be used in the body of the generic program unit.

The type parameter ELEMENT has been declared to be private, which means that the only operations on objects of type ELEMENT which may be used in the body of the generic program unit are assignment and comparison.

It should be pointed out that this way of declaring type parameters must not be confused with the private types we have discussed earlier in connection with packages. A type being private in a package meant that the exact appearance of the type was only known *inside* the package. Outside the package nothing was known about the type's appearance: the type belonged exclusively to the package's private part. A private generic type parameter can be said to be private 'in the opposite direction'. In the body of the generic program unit the type's exact appearance is unknown: the only thing that is known is that only assignment and comparison are allowed. It is outside the generic program unit, in the program which creates an instantiation of the generic package, that it is known exactly what the type looks like. If, for example, the package:

```
package CHAR_PACKAGE is new STACK_PACKAGE (CHARACTER);
```

is created, then it is known that in this package ELEMENT will be the same as CHARACTER.

We will now construct a generic package as a further example of the use of private generic type parameters, this time to enable lists to be built up of any sort of element. The package should be so general that it is possible to insert and remove elements anywhere in the list. In addition, it should be possible to move both to the left and to the right within the list. This is the package's specification:

```
generic
   type ELEMENT is private;
package LIST_PACKAGE is
   type LIST is limited private;
   type DIRECTION is (THE_START, THE_END, LEFT, RIGHT);
   function    EMPTY        (L : LIST) return BOOLEAN;
   procedure  MOVE_POS     (TO : DIRECTION; L : in out LIST);
   function    POS_MISSING (L : LIST) return BOOLEAN;
   function    VALUE        (L : LIST) return ELEMENT;
   procedure  INSERT        (E : in ELEMENT; WHERE : DIRECTION;
                             L : in out LIST);
   procedure  REMOVE        (L : in out LIST);
   LIST_POS_ERROR : exception;
private
   type NODE;
   type LINK is access NODE;
   type NODE is
```

```
          record
             NEXT, PREVIOUS : LINK;
             DATA               : ELEMENT;
          end record;

       type LIST is
          record
             FIRST, LAST, POS : LINK;
          end record;
       end LIST_PACKAGE;
```

Again, we have named the generic type parameter ELEMENT. In the package the type LIST is defined as well as a number of operations that can be performed on lists. As usual, the implementation has been concealed in the package's private part. A list is built up of a series of nodes, of type NODE. Apart from data, each node contains pointers to the next and the previous node; thus this is an ordinary doubly linked list. The difference between this and doubly linked lists discussed earlier is to be seen in the type LIST. A list is described by three pointers: one points to the first node in the list, one points to the last node and the third points to a **current** node. This means that every list 'remembers' a current position in the list. The idea is that the user of the list should be able to move the current position in the list, thereby moving around in the list. To set the current position you call the procedure MOVE_POS, the parameter TO specifying the position to which the move should occur. You can say that it should move to the start or the end of the list, or to the left or the right with respect to the current position. If the list is empty, or if the current position has not been set, or if the current position is moved outside the bounds of the list, then there is no current position; the function POS_MISSING can be used to investigate this. The function VALUE gives the value of the element in the current position in the list. The procedure INSERT enables you to put a new element into the list, the parameter WHERE stating if it should be first or last, or to the left or the right of the current position. When a new element is placed in the list, it automatically assumes the current position. The procedure REMOVE takes away the element found in the current position. If there is in fact no current position but a procedure or function is called that needs a current position, such as REMOVE, then the exception LIST_POS_ERROR is raised.

As an example of how this package might be used we will construct a list of text strings which can be of different lengths. We will have pointers to the text strings as the elements of the list, starting with the type declaration:

       type STRING_POINTER is access STRING;

The next step is to create an instance of the package with the element type STRING_POINTER, and to declare a list:

```
package ST_PACKAGE is new LIST_PACKAGE(STRING_POINTER);
use ST_PACKAGE;
TEXT_LIST : LIST;
```

Now we can put text strings into the list, using for example the following statements:

```
INSERT(new STRING'("Hello"), THE_START, TEXT_LIST);
INSERT(new STRING'("Welcome"), THE_END, TEXT_LIST);
INSERT(NAME, LEFT, TEXT_LIST);
```

where we assume that NAME is of type STRING_POINTER.

To print the content of a list we can write:

```
MOVE_POS(THE_START, TEXT_LIST);
while not POS_MISSING(TEXT_LIST) loop
  PUT_LINE(VALUE(TEXT_LIST).all);
  MOVE_POS(RIGHT, TEXT_LIST);
end loop;
```

The penultimate element in the list can be removed by writing:

```
MOVE_POS(THE_END, TEXT_LIST);
MOVE_POS(LEFT, TEXT_LIST);
REMOVE(TEXT_LIST);
```

Let us look at the body of the list package, where the doubly linked list is taken care of. (The method of the extra empty node, demonstrated in Section 11.3, is not used in this package. All the nodes are 'genuine' and are included in the list.) For obvious reasons, this package body has a lot of pointer handlers, and looks like this:

```
with UNCHECKED_DEALLOCATION;
package body LIST_PACKAGE is

  function EMPTY(L : LIST) return BOOLEAN is
  begin
    return L.FIRST = NULL;
  end EMPTY;

  procedure MOVE_POS(TO : DIRECTION; L : in out LIST) is
  begin
    if TO in LEFT .. RIGHT and POS_MISSING(L) then
      raise LIST_POS_ERROR;
    end if;
```

```
      case TO is
        when THE_START  => L.POS := L.FIRST;
        when THE_END    => L.POS := L.LAST;
        when LEFT       => L.POS := L.POS.PREVIOUS;
        when RIGHT      => L.POS := L.POS.NEXT;
      end case;
  end MOV_POS;

  function POS_MISSING (L : LIST) return BOOLEAN is
  begin
    return L.POS = null;
  end POS_MISSING;

  function VALUE(L : LIST) return ELEMENT is
  begin
    if POS_MISSING(L) then
      raise LIST_POS_ERROR;
    end if;
    return L.POS.DATA;
  end VALUE;

  procedure INSERT(E: in ELEMENT; WHERE : DIRECTION;
                   L : in out LIST) is
    P1, P2 : LINK;
  begin
    if WHERE in LEFT .. RIGHT and POS_MISSING(L) then
      raise LIST_POS_ERROR;
    end if;
    case WHERE is
      when THE_START  => P1 := null; P2 := L.FIRST;
      when THE_END    => P1 := L.LAST; P2 := null;
      when LEFT       => P1 := L.POS.PREVIOUS; P2 := L.POS;
      when RIGHT      => P1 := L.POS; P2 := L.POS.NEXT;
    end case;
    -- insert new node between P1 and P2
    L.POS := new NODE'(P2, P1, E);
    if P1 = null then
      L.FIRST := L.POS; -- insert new node first in list
    else
      P1.NEXT := L.POS;
    end if;
    if P2 = null then
      L.LAST := L.POS;       -- insert new node last in the list
    else
      P2.PREVIOUS := L.POS;
    end if;
  end INSERT;
```

```
procedure FREE is new UNCHECKED_DEALLOCATION(NODE, LINK);

procedure REMOVE(L : in out LIST) is
  P : LINK := L.POS;
begin
  if POS_MISSING(L) then
    raise LIST_POS_ERROR;
  end if;
  if P.PREVIOUS = null then
    L.FIRST := P.NEXT;        -- remove the first node
  else
    P .PREVIOUS.NEXT := P.NEXT;
  end if;
  if P.NEXT = null then
    L.LAST := P.PREVIOUS;        -- remove the last node
    L.POS    := L.LAST;
  else
    P.NEXT.PREVIOUS := P.PREVIOUS;
    L.POS := P.NEXT;
  end if;
  FREE(P);
end REMOVE;
end LIST_PACKAGE;
```

A generic type parameter can also be made a private limited type, which means that not even the operations of assignment and comparison are allowed:

```
type T is limited private;
```

The next category of type parameter we will look at is that of discrete types:

```
type T is (< >);      -- T is a discrete type
```

This means that T can be presumed to be a discrete type in the body of the generic program unit, that is, an enumeration type or an integer type. As an example we will return to the package SET_PACKAGE that we worked with in Section 8.8, which described the abstract data type **sets of characters**. In that example a set was implemented as an array of type BOOLEAN, the index type being CHARACTER. It is now easy to write the set package as a generic package so that it can be indexed by an arbitrary discrete type:

```
generic
  type ELEMENT is (< >);
package SET_PACKAGE is
  type SET is private;
    ...
```

```
        function "+" (E : ELEMENT; S : SET) return SET;
        ...
     private
        type SET is array (ELEMENT) of BOOLEAN;
     end SET_PACKAGE;
```

The body of the package and the specification in general resemble those developed in Section 8.8, the difference being that the sets now have elements of the type ELEMENT instead of the type CHARACTER.

Now we can use this generic package in a program to create different kinds of sets. If we have the type declarations:

```
     type DAY is (MONDAY, TUESDAY, WEDNESDAY,
                       THURSDAY, FRIDAY, SATURDAY, SUNDAY);
     type LITTLENUMBER is range 0.. 100;
```

then we can create two instances of the set package:

```
     package DAY_PACKAGE is new SET_PACKAGE(DAY);
     package NUM_PACKAGE is new SET_PACKAGE(LITTLE_NUMBER);
```

In both these declarations the actual generic parameter is a discrete type. It would be illegal to try and create an instance of the set package and state a type that is not discrete, such as FLOAT. If we insert the line:

```
     use DAY_PACKAGE, NUM_PACKAGE;
```

then we can declare the sets:

```
        DAY_SET    : DAY_PACKAGE.SET  := EMPTY_SET;
        NUM_SET1 : NUM_PACKAGE.SET := EMPTY_SET;
        NUM_SET2 : NUM_PACKAGE.SET := EMPTY_SET;
```

We must use the selector notation to state which type of set we are referring to because the compiler cannot determine it from the context. However, selector notation is not needed in the initialization expression. There, the compiler 'understands' which of the functions EMPTY_SET should be used. The three sets can be treated in the same way as before. We can, for example, have the statements:

```
        DAY_SET := MONDAY + DAY_SET;
        NUM_SET1 := NUM_SET2 − 23;
        if NUM_SET1 <= NUM_SET2 then
```

A generic type parameter can also be specified to be a numeric type. A type parameter that will be an integer type is stated by writing:

type T **is range** < >;   -- T will be an integer type

and a type parameter that will be a floating point type is written:

type T **is digits** < >;   -- T will be a floating point type

As an example of this we shall study a generic function that can be used to evaluate the largest component in an array of floating point components:

```
generic
  type FLOAT_NR is digits < >;
  type TAB is array (INTEGER range < >) of FLOAT_NR;
function MAX (T : TAB) return FLOAT_NR;
```

Here is something new. There are two generic parameters, FLOAT_NR and TAB. When a generic parameter is declared, generic parameters declared earlier can be used. In the declaration of TAB we have stated that the elements should be of type FLOAT_NR, that is, they can be of any floating point type. The function's body is:

```
function MAX (T : TAB) return FLOAT_NR is
  M : FLOAT_NR := LOAT_NR'LAST;
begin
  for I in T'RANGE loop
    if T(I) > M then
      M := T(I);
    end if;
  end loop;
  return M;
end MAX;
```

Here we have made use of the fact that FLOAT_NR is a floating point type and used the attribute LAST, which exists for all floating point types. We also know that the parameter T is of an array type; we can therefore use the attribute T'RANGE and index T.

In the specification of MAX we have assumed that the type TAB should have an index of type INTEGER. This is an unnecessary limitation. If we want the index type to be any discrete type, we can add a further generic parameter and give the specification:

```
generic
  type INDEX is (< >);
  type FLOAT_NR is digits < >;
  type TAB is array (INDEX range < >) of FLOAT_NR;
function MAX (T : TAB) return FLOAT_NR;
```

Now we can create some instances of MAX. If we make the type declaration:

type VECTOR **is array** (INTEGER **range** < >) **of** FLOAT;

we can create an instance of MAX that looks for the largest number in an array of type VECTOR:

function MAX_NO **is new** MAX(INTEGER, FLOAT, VECTOR);

Thus we state three actual parameters. The function MAX_NO can now be called in the usual way with a parameter of type VECTOR.

Another instance of MAX can be created if we have the type declarations:

type TEMP **is digits** 5;
type DAY is (MONDAY, TUESDAY, WEDNESDAY,
                 THURSDAY, FRIDAY, SATURDAY,
                 SUNDAY);
type TEMP_MEASURES **is array** (DAY **range** < >) **of** TEMP;

The declaration:

function MAX_TEMP **is new** MAX(DAY, TEMP, TEMP_MEASURES);

then produces a function that can find the largest component in an array of the type TEMP_MEASURES.

A generic type parameter can also be specified to be an access, or pointer, type, by writing:

type T **is access** Q;   -- T is an access type

The type Q can be any type at all, even a previously specified generic type parameter.

▼

In Ada 95 there are further forms of generic type parameters which are used in connection with tagged types, and they will be discussed in the next chapter.

In Ada 95, it is permitted to specify what are called unknown discriminants for all forms of type parameters, denoted by (< >) after the name of the type. As an example, we can write:

type T (< >) **is private**;

This means that the size of a variable of type T is unknown, and that variables of type T cannot be declared within the body of the generic package without an initial value specifying the size of the variable. If you now want to instantiate the generic unit with type T replaced by type STRING, there is no risk of errors caused by the length of variables of type STRING being unknown.

▲

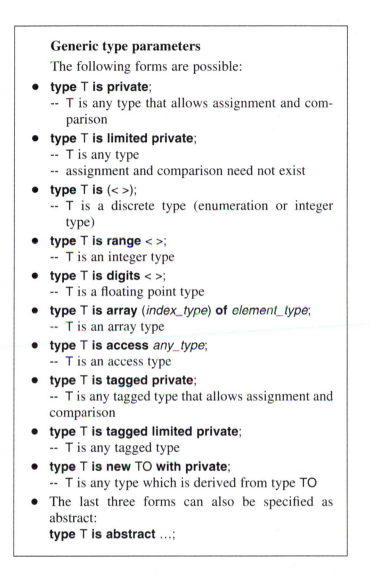

13.2.3 Subprogram parameters

The third category of generic parameter is the subprogram parameter. As a first example we shall study a problem to do with lists. Assume we have a list L:

$$L = (1_1, 1_2, 1_3, \dots , 1_n)$$

Now assume we have a function f that we want to apply to every element in L. Thus we want a list:

$$(f(1_1), f(1_2), f(1_3), \dots , f(1_n))$$

The elements in the list may, for example, be integers and the function f may be:

$$f(x) = x^2$$

In this case we want to have a list where each element is the square of the corresponding element in the original list. Another example is that we have a list where the elements are single characters. The function may then be a function that translates any upper-case letters in the list into lower case.

We shall now give a specification for a generic function APPL, which will be applicable to different kinds of lists and different functions f. As its result, APPL gives a new list where the function f has been applied to every element. We assume that a list is represented using an unconstrained array type, each element in the list being stored as a component of the array. The specification of the generic function APPL then appears as follows:

```
generic
  type ELEMENT is private;
  type LIST is array (POSITIVE range < >) of ELEMENT;
  with function F (E : ELEMENT) return ELEMENT;
function APPL (L : LIST) return LIST;
```

We have three generic parameters: ELEMENT, LIST and F. ELEMENT and LIST are type parameters and F is a subprogram parameter. A declaration of a subprogram parameter is introduced by the reserved word **with**. Afterwards a subprogram declaration is written in the normal way, and in it may be used any generic parameters that have been declared previously. In the declaration of F, for example, we have used the type parameter ELEMENT.

The body of APPL is simply:

```
function APPL (L : LIST) return LIST is
  NEW_L : LIST(L'RANGE);
begin
  for I in L'RANGE loop
    NEW_L(I) := F(L(I));
  end loop;
  return NEW_L;
end APPL;
```

Now the generic function APPL can be used in a program. Let us assume we have the type declaration:

```
type NUMBER_LIST is array (POSITIVE range < >) of INTEGER;
```

and the functions:

```
function SQUARE (X : INTEGER) return INTEGER is
begin
   return X ** 2;
end SQUARE;

function TRANSLATE (C : CHARACTER) return CHARACTER is
   DIFF : constant
        := CHARACTER'POS('a') – CHARACTER'POS('A');
begin
   if C in 'A' .. 'Z' then
      return CHARACTER'VAL(CHARACTER'POS(C) + DIFF);
   else
      return C;
   end if;
end TRANSLATE;
```

Then we are able to create two instances of APPL:

```
function QUAD is new
           APPL(INTEGER, NUMBER_LIST, SQUARE);
function LC is new
           APPL(CHARACTER, STRING, TRANSLATE);
```

Thus the function's name is given as an actual parameter. In QUAD the function F will become SQUARE. Every call to F in the body of APPL will mean a call to SQUARE. In LC, in the same way, F will be identified as the function TRANSLATE.

If the variables L1 and L2 have the type NUMBER_LIST, we can now write the statement:

```
L2 := QUAD(L1);
```

L2 will then hold the squares of all the numbers in L1. If S1 and S2 have the type STRING, the corresponding statement can be written:

```
S2 := LC(S1);
```

Then S2 will contain all the characters in S1 but the upper-case letters will have been translated into lower case.

Generic subprogram parameters can be given default values. If, for example, we have a generic procedure parameter P (without parameters) and we want to give it the default value PDEF, we write:

```
procedure P is PDEF;
```

This means that the procedure PDEF will be used in the body of the generic unit if no actual parameter is given for P.

It may not be of much use to give a special subprogram as default value. The following way of assigning a default value is more useful:

function "+" (E1, E2 : ELEMENT) **return** ELEMENT **is** < >;

First, note that a subprogram parameter can have an operator name. Here we have used the name "+". The symbol < > denotes that if no actual parameter is given when an instance of the generic unit is created then the function "+" for the type ELEMENT should automatically be used. If ELEMENT is given the type INTEGER, for example, then "+" is, of course, defined for that type and this normal "+" operator is to be used.

As a final example we shall write a generic procedure that can be used to sort all kinds of arrays, with any component type and index type. We make the specification:

```
generic
   type INDEX is (< >);
   type ELEMENT is private;
   type ARRAY_TYPE is array (INDEX range < >) of ELEMENT;
   with function "<" (E1, E2 : ELEMENT) return BOOLEAN is < >;
   procedure SORT (A : in out ARRAY_TYPE);
```

We have four generic parameters: the index type, the component type, the type of the array and a subprogram parameter "<" which is used to denote the function that compares two components in an array.

In the body of SORT we use the sort algorithm described in Section 5.9. The body is then:

```
procedure SORT (A : in out ARRAY-TYPE) is
   M : INDEX;
   T : ELEMENT;
begin
   for K in A'FIRST .. INDEX'PRED(A'LAST) loop
     -- find smallest element between K and A'LAST
     M :=K;
     for I in INDEX'SUCC(K) .. A'LAST loop
       if A(I) < A(M) then
         M := I;
       end if;
     end loop;
     -- swap elements in Kth and Mth positions
     T := A(K); A(K) := A(M); A(M) := T;
   end loop;
end SORT;
```

Note that we have written:

    INDEX'SUCC(K)

instead of:

    K + 1

The reason for this is that INDEX does not need to be an integer type and an addition operator may not be defined.

The comparison operator "<" which is used in the expression:

    F(I) < F(M)

is the function that is described in the subprogram parameter "<" in the specification.

We can show some examples of the use of SORT. Assume we have the type declarations:

```
type NO_ARRAY is array (NATURAL range < >) of INTEGER;
type PERSON is
   record
      NAME      : STRING(1 .. 20);
      ADDRESS : STRING(1 .. 30);
   end record;
type NAME_TAB is array (POSITIVE range < >) of PERSON;
type DAY is (MONDAY, TUESDAY, WEDNESDAY,
               THURSDAY, FRIDAY, SATURDAY, SUNDAY);
type TIME is digits 4;
type WEEK_TAB is array (DAY range < >) of TIME;
```

and that we have declared the variables N, P and W:

```
N  : NO_ARRAY(1 .. 50);
P  : NAME_TAB(1 .. 200);
W  : WEEK_TAB(MONDAY .. FRIDAY);
```

Two people can be compared with the function:

```
function BEFORE (P1, P2 : PERSON) return BOOLEAN is
begin
   return P1.NAME < P2.NAME;
end BEFORE;
```

Now we are ready to create three different instances of SORT:

```
procedure NO_SORT is new SORT
                    (NATURAL, INTEGER, NO_ARRAY, "<");
procedure PERS_SORT is new SORT
                    (POSITIVE, PERSON, NAME_TAB, BEFORE);
procedure TIME_SORT is new SORT
                    (DAY, TIME, WEEK_TAB);
```

In the declaration of NO_SORT we have given the subprogram parameter the value "<". Here "<" denotes the normal comparison operator for integers. Since the subprogram parameter had the default value < > in the specification, we could have left out the actual parameter, thus:

```
procedure NO_SORT is new SORT(NATURAL, INTEGER, NO_ARRAY);
```

Then the normal comparison operator for integers would be automatically assumed. In the declaration of TIME_SORT we have used this simpler form. There is no standard "<" for the type PERSON, so we have had to give the function BEFORE as an actual parameter.

The three arrays N, P and W can now easily be sorted with the calls:

```
NO_SORT(N);
PERS_SORT(P);
TIME_SORT(W);
```

Generic subprogram parameters

> **with** *subprogram_declaration*;

Default values can be given using one of the forms:

> **with** *subprogram_declaration* **is**
> *subprogram_name*;
> **with** *subprogram_declaration* **is** < >;

13.2.4 Package parameters

▼

We have now seen how we can use different kinds of generic parameters to give generic units the correct properties. In some cases there can be a great many generic parameters. In Ada 95 it is permitted to have generic packages as generic parameters to another generic unit. When we construct a generic package P2, for example, then we are allowed to have another generic package P1 as a parameter to P2, writing:

```
generic
  with package PARAM is new P1 (< >);
package P2 is
  ...
end P2;
```

As an example, we might want to construct a generic package VECTOR_
PACKAGE for handling different kinds of vectors, and it has to work for
various floating point types. Suppose that there is another generic package,
MATH_PACKAGE, containing a number of mathematical operations which
can be used when constructing VECTOR_PACKAGE. The specification of
MATH_PACKAGE is:

```
generic
  type FLOAT_PT_TYPE is digits < >;
package MATH_PACKAGE is
  ...
end MATH_PACKAGE;
```

Thus different instances of the package can be created for different floating
point types. When it comes to writing VECTOR_PACKAGE, MATH_PACKAGE
can be used as a generic package parameter.

```
generic
  with package MPACK is new MATH_PACKAGE (< >);
package VECTOR_PACKAGE is
  type VECTOR is array (POSITIVE range < >)
                  of MPACK.FLOAT_PT_TYPE
  ...
end VECTOR_PACKAGE;
```

Everything that is declared in the specification of MATH_PACKAGE is now
available in VECTOR_PACKAGE. (A **use** clause or point notation can be used.)
The generic parameters of MATH_PACKAGE are also available.

In order to instantiate VECTOR_PACKAGE you first have to have a
suitable instantiation of MATH_PACKAGE. If, for example, we want to work
with the type FLOAT we can write:

```
package MATH_FLOAT is new MATH_PACKAGE(FLOAT);
```

Then an instance of the vector package can be created:

```
package VECTOR_FLOAT is new VECTOR_PACKAGE(MATH_FLOAT);
```

> **Generic package parameters**
>
> **with package** *parameter_name* **is new**
> GEN_PACK(< >);
>
> where GEN_PACK is a generic package.

▲

13.3 Generic child packages

In Section 8.9 we discussed how to construct child packages. In this chapter we have seen how generic units can be used to construct general and reusable software. Now we are going to study how to combine these two powerful mechanisms, and the best way to do this is to use an example. Our starting point is the package QUEUE_PACKAGE, which was introduced in Section 8.8. This package described the abstract data type QUEUE, for which the type of the elements was CHARACTER. It is easy to change the package into a generic package so that it can be used to construct different sorts of queues, with different element types. At the same time we introduce a generic value parameter MAX_NUMBER which gives the maximal size of the queue. The generic package is called GEN_QUEUE_PACKAGE.

The specification is as follows:

```
generic
  type ELEMENT is private;
  MAX_NUMBER : POSITIVE := 100;
package GEN_QUEUE_PACKAGE is
  type QUEUE is limited private;
  procedure PUT_IN     (Q : in out QUEUE; E : in ELEMENT);
  procedure TAKE_OUT   (Q : in out QUEUE; E : out ELEMENT);
  function EMPTY       (Q : in QUEUE) return BOOLEAN;
private
  type ELEMENT_ARRAY is array (INTEGER range <>) of ELEMENT;
  type QUEUE is
    record
      BUF     : ELEMENT_ARRAY (1..MAX_NUMBER);
      NUMBER : NATURAL := 0;
      FIRST   : POSITIVE := 1;
      LAST    : POSITIVE := MAX_NUMBER;
    end record;
end GEN_QUEUE_PACKAGE;
```

As in Section 8.9 we add a child package containing the operation LENGTH. The specification of the child package is:

```
generic
package GEN_QUEUE_PACKAGE.GEN_EXTRA is
   function LENGTH(Q : QUEUE) return NATURAL;
end GEN_QUEUE_PACKAGE.GEN_EXTRA;
```

Note: A non-generic parent package may have either generic or non-generic child packages, but a generic parent package (as we have here) is only allowed to have generic child packages. The reserved word **generic** must therefore appear first in the child package specification.

It is not necessary to show the bodies of the two packages here; they look exactly the same as in Chapter 8. The only difference is that the type CHARACTER should be replaced everywhere by the type ELEMENT.

To demonstrate how to create instances of the packages we now construct a small program which reads integer numbers from the keyboard and puts them in a queue. When all numbers have been read the program prints out the length of the queue.

```
with TEXT_IO, BASIC_NUM_IO, GEN_QUEUE_PACKAGE.GEN_EXTRA;
use TEXT_IO, BASIC_NUM_IO;
procedure QUEUE_DEMO1 is
   package PAK1 is new GEN_QUEUE_PACKAGE(INTEGER);
   package PAK2 is new PAK1.GEN_EXTRA;
   use PAK1, PAK2;
   Q : QUEUE;
   I : INTEGER;
begin
   while not END_OF_FILE loop
      GET(I);
      PUT_IN(Q, I);
   end loop;
   PUT(LENGTH(Q));
end QUEUE_DEMO1;
```

The program needs access to the two generic packages GEN_QUEUE_PACKAGE and GEN_QUEUE_PACKAGE.GEN_EXTRA. Therefore GEN_QUEUE_ PACKAGE. GEN_EXTRA is mentioned in the **with** clause. Within the procedure an instance of GEN_QUEUE_PACKAGE must first be created. The element type is defined as INTEGER. This instance is given the name PAK1. The following rules now apply: if a generic child package has been declared for a generic parent package, then there will be one corresponding generic child package for *each instance* of the parent package. In our example this means that when we create the instance PAK1 we will automatically get a generic child package named PAK1.GEN_EXTRA. We must create an instance of this child package. In the example this instance is called PAK2. Observe that it is not possible to create instances of the generic child package GEN_QUEUE_PACKAGE.GEN_EXTRA directly. An instance of the parent package must always be created first. Also observe that PAK2 is a simple name without periods since child packages may not be declared inside subprograms. Child packages must, as mentioned in Chapter 8, be library units; that is, they must be declared in the outermost level in the program.

We shall now show a variant of the example, in which the instances are created in the outermost level and therefore become library units. First we create an instance of the generic parent package, which is given the name INT_QUEUE_PACKAGE.

```
with GEN_QUEUE_PACKAGE;
package INT_QUEUE_PACKAGE is new
   GEN_QUEUE_PACKAGE(INTEGER);
```

The next step is to create an instance of the generic child package. Since the language rules say that there is a generic child package for each instance of the parent package, there is a generic child package named INT_QUEUE_PACKAGE.GEN_EXTRA and we are going to create an instance of that package. (However, observe that GEN_QUEUE_PACKAGE.GEN_EXTRA should be mentioned in the **with** clause.)

```
with GEN_QUEUE_PACKAGE.GEN_EXTRA;
package INT_QUEUE_PACKAGE.INT_EXTRA is new
   INT_QUEUE_PACKAGE.GEN_EXTRA;
```

We give the instance of the child package the name INT_QUEUE_PACKAGE.INT_EXTRA. This name indicates that it is a child package. It is, as we know, permissible to create child packages on this level.

The four lines above constitute two separate compilation units. When these units have been compiled, two 'real' non-generic packages exist in the Ada library. These packages can be referred to in the normal way in a **with** clause. This is done in the second version of the demo program:

```
with TEXT_IO, BASIC_NUM_IO, INT_QUEUE_PACKAGE.INT_EXTRA;
use TEXT_IO, BASIC_NUM_IO, INT_QUEUE_PACKAGE; use INT_EXTRA;
procedure QUEUE_DEMO2 is
   Q : QUEUE;
   I : INTEGER;
begin
   while not END_OF_FILE loop
     GET(I);
     PUT_IN(Q, I);
   end loop;
   PUT(LENGTH(Q));
end QUEUE_DEMO2;
```

Now we shall use child packages to demonstrate an important concept, the **iterator**. Once more the generic package GEN_QUEUE_PACKAGE is our starting point. If we study the specification of this package we notice that there are operations to insert and take out elements from a queue, but we lack the possibility of running through and looking at all elements in a queue without taking out or inserting elements. Of course, the package can be extended with operations to accomplish this (see the package LIST_PACKAGE in Section 13.2.2, for instance). However, another method, which has certain advantages, is to use an iterator. An iterator is a separate variable which is linked to a data collection, to a queue or to a tree, for instance. The iterator can then be used as a tool to run through the data collection and visit all its elements. The data collection is not used directly. One advantage with iterators is that it is possible to link more than one iterator to a certain data collection at the same time. For instance, you can run through a queue from the beginning to the end at the same time as you run through it backwards from the end to the beginning. To demonstrate iterators we declare the following child package of GEN_ QUEUE_PACKAGE:

```
generic
package GEN_QUEUE_PACKAGE.ITERATOR1 is
    type QUEUE_ITERATOR1 (Q : access QUEUE) is limited private;
    function FINISHED        (QI : QUEUE_ITERATOR1) return BOOLEAN;
    procedure NEXT           (QI : in out QUEUE_ITERATOR1);
    function READ            (QI : QUEUE_ITERATOR1) return ELEMENT;
    procedure CHANGE         (QI : QUEUE_ITERATOR1; E : ELEMENT);
    procedure AGAIN          (QI : in out QUEUE_ITERATOR1);
    ITERATOR_ERROR : exception;
private
    type QUEUE_ITERATOR1 (Q : access QUEUE) is
       record
          INDEX              : POSITIVE := Q.FIRST;
          NUMBER_VISITED  : POSITIVE := 1;
       end record;
end GEN_QUEUE_PACKAGE.ITERATOR1;
```

Here a new type QUEUE_ITERATOR1 is declared. Now the idea is to declare a separate iterator of type QUEUE_ITERATOR1 each time you want to run through a queue. (A queue is a variable of type QUEUE declared in the package GEN_QUEUE_PACKAGE.)

We can postpone the investigation of the package body until later and instead start to demonstrate how everything is supposed to be used. To be able to do this we must first create suitable instances of the generic packages. Let us suppose that these instances are declared inside a procedure and that we want a queue in which the elements are of type INTEGER.

```
with GEN_QUEUE_PACKAGE.ITERATOR1;
...
    package INT_QUEUE_PAK is new GEN_QUEUE_PACKAGE(INTEGER);
    package INT_IT_PAK1 is new INT_QUEUE_PAK.ITERATOR1;
    use INT_QUEUE_PAK, INT_IT_PAK1;
```

We notice that the type QUEUE_ITERATOR1 in its declaration has some sort of parameter named Q. This is a so-called **discriminant**. Discriminants can be treated as 'ordinary' components in a record, but they may also be used to initialize record components or to specify index bounds. In Section 7.5 we also saw how discriminants could be used to construct records with variants. In Ada 95 discriminants may be either of discrete type (integer type or enumeration type) or, as we have here, of access type. When a variable is declared of a type having discriminants the discriminants must be given values (unless the discriminant has a default value, but that is not the case here).

Discriminants

> **type** *T(declaration of discriminants)* **is** ...;

Type parameters. May be of either discrete type or access type. Treated as ordinary components, but must not be changed. Can, for instance, be used to initialize other components or to specify index bounds.

When an object of the type is declared the discriminant must be given values:

OBJ : T*(values for the discriminants);*

To get a queue with an accompanying iterator we can make the variable declarations:

```
THE_Q : aliased QUEUE;
IT : QUEUE_ITERATOR1(THE_Q'ACCESS);
```

From the declaration of the type QUEUE_ITERATOR1 we can see that the discriminant should be a pointer to a QUEUE. Therefore we give a pointer to THE_Q as a parameter when the variable IT is declared. Now the iterator IT has been linked to the queue THE_Q and the component Q in IT points at THE_Q.

If we want to run through the queue we use the iterator IT. Here is an example of a part of a program which runs through the queue THE_Q and sets all elements less than zero in the queue to zero. (The variable N has the type INTEGER.)

```
while not FINISHED(IT) loop
  N := READ(IT);
  if N < 0 then
    CHANGE(IT, 0);
  end if;
  NEXT(IT);
end loop;
```

The operation FINISHED is used to test whether all elements in the queue have been visited. The operation NEXT moves the iterator to the next element in the queue. We automatically start with the first element. There is one more operation for the type QUEUE_ITERATOR1, the operation AGAIN which can be used when we want to restart from the beginning of the queue and run through it once more.

Now we should study how the iterator has been implemented. In the parent package GEN_QUEUE_PACKAGE the queue itself has been implemented using an array, a so-called circular buffer (see Section 8.8). An iterator is a record. The component INDEX holds the index of the current element in the array; INDEX is initialized to hold the index of the first element in the queue. The component NUMBER_VISITED holds the number of elements the iterator has visited so far. Since the iterator is initialized so that the first element is visited automatically, one element has been visited and NUMBER_VISITED is therefore initialized to 1. Each time the operation NEXT is called, the component NUMBER_VISITED is incremented by one, and the component INDEX is made to point at the next element in the queue. (When this is done we must be aware of the fact that the buffer is circular and therefore sometimes we must move to the beginning of the array.) The component NUMBER_VISITED is used by the operation FINISHED to check if all elements in the queue have been visited.

The package body looks as follows. Note how the iterator uses its discriminant Q to get access to the queue to which it is linked. The help function CHECK_FINISHED is called to check that we have not run too far in a queue.

```
package body GEN_QUEUE_PACKAGE.ITERATOR1 is
  function FINISHED (QI : QUEUE_ITERATOR1) return BOOLEAN is
  begin
    return QI.NUMBER_VISITED > QI.Q.NUMBER;
  end FINISHED;

  procedure CHECK_FINISHED(QI : QUEUE_ITERATOR1) is
  begin
    if FINISHED(QI) then
      raise ITERATOR_ERROR;
    end if;
  end CHECK_FINISHED;
```

```
          procedure NEXT (QI : in out QUEUE_ITERATOR1) is
          begin
            CHECK_FINISHED(QI);
            QI.NUMBER_VISITED := QI.NUMBER_VISITED + 1;
            QI.INDEX := QI.INDEX mod MAX_NUMBER + 1;
          end NEXT;

          function READ (QI : QUEUE_ITERATOR1) return ELEMENT is
          begin
            CHECK_FINISHED(QI);
            return QI.Q.BUF(QI.INDEX);
          end READ;

          procedure CHANGE (QI : QUEUE_ITERATOR1; E : ELEMENT) is
          begin
            CHECK_FINISHED(QI);
            QI.Q.BUF(QI.INDEX) := E;
          end CHANGE;

          procedure AGAIN (QI : in out QUEUE_ITERATOR1) is
          begin
            QI.INDEX := QI.Q.FIRST;
            QI.NUMBER_VISITED := 1;
          end AGAIN;
        end GEN_QUEUE_PACKAGE.ITERATOR1;
```

Iterators are often used in modern software. Their details can vary, but still the fundamental idea is the same: to use a separate variable to run through a data collection. A common variant is to let the operation NEXT return a pointer to the visited element (an empty pointer indicates that all elements have been visited), then the two operators READ and CHANGE are not needed. This variant can only be used when it is possible to access all elements in the queue via a pointer, and this may not always be the case.

The exact implementation of an iterator is dependent on the implementation of the data collection, of course. If, for instance, a queue is implemented as a linked list instead of an array, then the iterator has to use a pointer instead of an index to keep track of the current element.

Now we shall show an alternative iterator. We construct a new child package:

```
generic
  with procedure VISIT_ELEMENT (E : in out ELEMENT);
package GEN_QUEUE_PACKAGE.ITERATOR2 is
  type QUEUE_ITERATOR2 (Q : access QUEUE) is limited private;
  procedure ITERATE      (QI : in out QUEUE_ITERATOR2);
private
  type QUEUE_ITERATOR2 (Q : access QUEUE) is null record;
end GEN_QUEUE_PACKAGE.ITERATOR2;
```

The type QUEUE_ITERATOR2 is a private record type with a discriminant. Since there are no components in a record of this type we write **null record**. This has the same meaning as writing the longer

```
record
  null;
end record;
```

The only operation that is defined for the type QUEUE_ITERATOR2 is the procedure ITERATE which runs through all elements in a queue. In order for ITERATE to know what to do with every visited element, the package has a generic subprogram parameter VISIT_ELEMENT, which is called by ITERATE for each element. The body of the package becomes

```
package body GEN_QUEUE_PACKAGE.ITERATOR2 is
  procedure ITERATE (QI : in out QUEUE_ITERATOR2) is
    INDEX : POSITIVE := QI.Q.FIRST;
  begin
    for I in 1.. QI.Q.NUMBER loop
      VISIT_ELEMENT(QI.Q.BUF(INDEX));
      INDEX := INDEX mod MAX_NUMBER + 1;
    end loop;
  end ITERATE;
end GEN_QUEUE_PACKAGE.ITERATOR2;
```

Suppose that, as happened before, we want to run through a queue and set all elements that are less than zero to zero. We write a program with the following structure:

```
with GEN_QUEUE_PACKAGE.ITERATOR2;
procedure ITDEMO is
  procedure TO_ZERO (E : in out INTEGER) is
  begin
    if E < 0 then
      E := 0;
    end if;
  end TO_ZERO;

  package INT_QUEUE_PAK is new GEN_QUEUE_PACKAGE (INTEGER);
  package INT_IT_PAK2 is new INT_QUEUE_PAK.ITERATOR2 (TO_ZERO);
  use INT_QUEUE_PAK, INT_IT_PAK2;
  THE_Q : aliased QUEUE;
  IT      : QUEUE_ITERATOR2(THE_Q'ACCESS);
```

```
begin
   -- Construct the queue
   ...
   ITERATE(IT); -- Set all elements < 0 to 0
end ITDEMO;
```

An iterator of type QUEUE_ITERATOR2 is simpler to use and more elegant than an iterator of type QUEUE_ITERATOR1. The user never has to do the iteration, since it is built into the operation ITERATE. However, there are times when an iterator of type QUEUE_ITERATOR1 must be used. One such occasion is when you do not want to run through all elements at the same time. Another case is when the element visits give a common result. We could calculate the sum of all elements in an integer queue, for instance. In this case, if you want to use the second variant of iterator you must put the result in a global variable, and this should normally be avoided.

EXERCISES

13.1   Write a generic procedure ORDER that has two parameters A and B of unspecified type. After calling an instance of the procedure, A must be less than B. (Assume that A and B are of types where the operator < is defined.) Create two instances of the procedure ORDER, one to order two integers and the other to order two text strings.

13.2   Make a specification of the package RANDOM_PACKAGE so that the two constants K and M that are used in the random number generation can be stated as generic value parameters. (See Section 8.7.)

13.3   Rewrite the package QUEUE_PACKAGE from Section 11.4 so that it describes an abstract data type QUEUE in which the elements are of arbitrary type. Create instances of the package which describe the abstract data types *floating_point_queue* and *person_queue*. Then declare two floating point queues and a person queue.

13.4   Write a generic function NEXT that can be used for arbitrary enumeration types. The function should have an enumeration value as parameter and return the next value in the type when called. If the function gets the last value as parameter it should return the first value as its result. (If there is an instance of the function for the type DAYS_OF_THE_WEEK, then a call with SUNDAY as parameter should return MONDAY as result.)

13.5   Write a generic function FIND that can be used to find a certain element in an array of arbitrary type. FIND should have an array and an element value as parameters and, as result, should give the index value for the place in the array where the sought element is to be found.

13.6 Write a generic function that adds the elements in an array of arbitrary type. The function should have as generic parameter a subprogram parameter '+', which adds two elements of the component type of the array. Give the subprogram parameter an appropriate default value.

13.7 Write a generic package that handles a binary search tree where the elements are of arbitrary type. The package should contain the subprograms INSERT, REMOVE and FOUND which, respectively, inserts an element in the tree, removes an element from the tree, and investigates whether a certain element is to be found in the tree. The package should have '<' and '=' as generic parameters, where '<' determines if one element is less than another and '=' determines whether two elements are equal.

13.8 Rewrite the generic procedure SORT from Section 13.2.3 so that instead of having four generic parameters it has only one generic package parameter. This generic package should contain all the declarations that are needed in SORT, and the body of the package can be empty.

14 Object-oriented Programming

'Object-oriented' is one of the latest in-words in the computer world. You hear of **object-oriented design, object-oriented programming, object-oriented analysis** and so on. What does 'object-oriented' mean? There is no absolute definition. One way of trying to describe object-orientation is to say that it is a new approach to program development, in which a program system is built up according to the objects it involves rather than according to the functions it should perform. Another way of looking at object-orientation is from a more technical perspective and trying to describe the idea of 'object-oriented programming'. In object-oriented programming, a program is built up of a number of well-delimited units called **objects**. The whole program is built up around the following two constructs:

- *Encapsulation (information hiding)*. Everything that describes the properties of an object – both data and operations – is collected to a single place in the program. The details of a particular object are also hidden so that other objects do not need to see the details and cannot access them.

- *Inheritance*. It is possible to describe an object by referring to the properties of another object and adding to them. One idea of object-oriented programming is that objects constructed earlier should be reusable, with the help of the mechanisms of inheritance, by modifying and adapting them to current needs.

What, then is **object-oriented design**? As we discussed in Section 2.1, the design phase in the development of a program is the phase immediately prior to the implementation phase, the phase when programming takes place. Object-oriented design can therefore be said to be the activity of planning an object-oriented program – drawing the plans of a program which is planned to be object-oriented. The most important thing is to decide what objects are to be included in the program and how they should be related to one another.

Before the design phase comes the analysis phase, when you try to understand and establish what the program should do. Object-oriented analysis can thus be said to be the activity of trying to understand the world around the program, when you try to build up a model of this world. The model has to be grounded in objects, or things, which are found in the world of the program.

Of course, this is a little vague. The three activities of object-oriented analysis, design and programming merge with one another and the boundaries are not fixed. In this book we will only be discussing object-oriented programming, the most concrete of the three activities, since it is based on specific properties of programming languages.

We should mention here some important object-oriented languages. The first object-oriented language was **Simula**, which was introduced at the end of the 1960s (although the term 'object-oriented' was not then used). Another language which has been most influential is **Smalltalk**, developed during the 1970s. Smalltalk is an 'extreme' object-oriented language, where everything is in the form of objects and where, for example, there are no normal types. Much of the terminology of the object-oriented languages has its origins in Smalltalk. The object-oriented language which is currently most widely used is **C++**, which was first released commercially in 1985. C++ is a direct development of the language C with a large number of object-oriented language constructs added.

In Ada 83 there is every opportunity to practise encapsulation, but since the use of inheritance is impossible it has not been considered an object-oriented language. Ada 95, however, is fully object-oriented. All the program constructs needed to write object-oriented programs are to be found in Ada 95, including inheritance.

One of the difficulties with object-oriented programming is that a special terminology is used. For example, there is talk of **objects, classes** and **methods**. Further, the terminology is to some extent different in the different object-oriented languages. In this chapter we will try to come to terms with the concepts associated with object-orientation. We will discuss the basics of object-oriented programming and what the different words mean. In particular, we will describe the object-oriented constructs to be found in Ada 95.

14.1 Basic concepts

The main idea of object-oriented programming is to construct a number of **objects** and bring them together into a program. It can be said that an object in a program is a representation of a real or a conceptual thing in the program's environment. Every object has a unique identity, and objects are accessed in a program by means of names or access values (pointers). For example, an object THE_LIFT can be constructed to represent a real lift, or an object STACK can describe a data stack.

Each object has a set of **attributes** which describe its properties. There are two categories of attribute. The first is the **data attribute**. (Different object-oriented languages use different terms for a data attribute. In Ada 95, the term **component** is used, in C++ it is called a **data member**, and in Smalltalk it is an **instance variable**.) Each object has its own unique set of data attributes. Normally, they are hidden within the object so that they are not accessible from outside and can only be changed by the object itself. Data attributes are used to keep track of the object's **status**, since each object has a definite status which can be changed during execution.

As an example we can study the object THE_LIFT, whose status can be described using two data attributes, DIRECTION and FLOOR. The attribute DIRECTION can have one of the values STILL, UP or DOWN, while the attribute FLOOR can contain an integer stating which floor the lift is currently at.

The second category of attribute for an object are the **operations** that can be performed on it. (In Ada 95 such an operation is called a **primitive operation**, in C++ the term **member function** is used, and in Smalltalk they are called **methods**.) For the object THE_LIFT, for instance, there might be the operations GO_TO, STOP and WHICH_FLOOR. GO_TO is used to get the lift to go to a particular floor, STOP is used to stop the lift, and WHICH_FLOOR is used to find out which floor the lift is currently at. Figure 14.1 illustrates the object THE_LIFT; the data attributes are placed at the top and the operations at the bottom.

How is an object described in a program? This is where the idea of **class** comes in. A class is a sort of template, or pattern, which describes a collection of objects with a common construction and set of properties. Different classes can describe different sets of objects. An object which belongs to a particular class is said to be an **instance** of the class. There can be several of these.

THE_LIFT

DIRECTION
FLOOR

GO_TO
STOP
WHICH_FLOOR

Figure 14.1

Many programmers involved in object-oriented programming understand a class as a type (as it is in certain languages, such as C++). Declaring a class is then the same thing as declaring a type and, using the same analogy, objects are a sort of variable. An instance of a class C is simply a variable which has type C. This analogy between classes and types, however, is not entirely satisfactory in all languages (in Smalltalk, for instance, there are no types and a class, strangely, is itself an object), but to think in this way makes the different concepts more readily understandable.

Objects

- Represent real or devised objects. A sort of variable.

- Have two sorts of attribute: data attribute and operations. In Ada 95 these are called components and primitive operations, respectively.

Most object-oriented languages have a construct called **class**, which is a sort of combination of a module and a type declaration where the different attributes of the class are defined. Since a class can contain several data attributes, a class can be seen as a kind of record type, and since the idea is that an object belonging to a particular class can only be influenced by using the operations defined within that class, a class can be said to be an **abstract data type**, but one where an object-oriented approach is used (see discussion in Section 8.8). In Ada 83 there are excellent language constructs for describing abstract data types, so in Ada 95 the choice was made to build on these constructs rather than introduce a completely new construct. Classes are therefore described as abstract data types and objects are described as variables belonging to these types. In Ada 95, the concept of class is not used as we have described it here; instead we talk of types. There is actually a concept CLASS in Ada 95, but it must be noted that it is used in a somewhat different way; we will return to this later.

Sometimes there are components which are common for all objects that belong to a certain class. Such components are called **class variables** in Smalltalk and **static data members** in C++. For the sake of simplicity we will use the term class variables in this book. Class variables are particular, since they exist only in *one* instance and this instance is shared by all objects that belong to the class. One good example of a class variable is a variable which counts the current number of objects of a certain class. Another example can be found in the description of bank accounts. For each account there is a certain balance and a certain account-holder. Of course there must be one instance of these data for every single account, therefore they are normal components. The interest rate, however, is a class variable. There is no reason to store the interest rate in every bank account object.

An important mechanism in object-oriented programming is **inheritance**. When a new class is to be declared, it can be based on an existing class and attributes can be changed or added. The new class is said to **inherit** the properties of the old class: it is known as a **subclass** of the old class. The old class is said to be a **superclass** of the new class. Suppose that we have, as an example, a class PERSON which describes individuals. This class might contain, among other things, attributes NAME and ADDRESS. Suppose, further, that we want to describe students at a university. What we can do is to create a new class, STUDENT, which is a subclass of the class PERSON, which means that the new class automatically gets all the attributes to be found in the class PERSON. Thus we do not need to define the attributes NAME and ADDRESS. All we have to do in the subclass STUDENT is to define the new attributes we want. For example, we might want data attributes that state which courses a student has taken, and an operation that prints out the various grades they have achieved.

Classes

- Descriptions of groups of objects with the same properties. A sort of type, an abstract data type.
- A class C2 can inherit properties, i.e. attributes, from another class C1. C2 is then a subclass of C1.

A class which is a subclass to another class can in its turn be parent to further subclasses. A class can have several subclasses. This means that a **class hierarchy** can be built up, with a tree-like structure. One of the ideas behind inheritance is that when writing a program one can make use of ready-made classes inherited from what is called a **class library**. This means that less new code needs to be written and, further, the classes from the library are (it is to be hoped) more thoroughly tested and freer from errors than newly written code. (There are critics of this sort of programming, who claim that it forces the programmer to use a good deal of program that is not strictly necessary. This makes programs bigger and more incomprehensible than if inheritance were avoided in favour of using modules which contain only what is needed.)

We can finish this run-through of basic ideas with a discussion of **methods** and **messages**. The operations which can be carried out on objects are often called methods. In programming languages of a more conventional kind, such as C++ and Ada, methods are nothing more than ordinary functions and procedures. When an operation is carried out on an object, this is sometimes referred to in object-oriented terminology as 'sending a message to an object'. In a conventional language this simply means a call to a function or procedure which has been defined for the object.

Methods

- The (primitive) operations which can be carried out on an object. Correspond to functions or procedures.
- Calling such an operation is referred to as 'sending a message'.

In the object-oriented language it is common that calls to an operation are written in a special way. Assume that we have the object THE_LIFT, as earlier, and we want the lift to go to the third floor. We can write the call as follows:

THE_LIFT.GO_TO(3)

The parameter to the procedure which states which object we are dealing with has a special status, and is placed first. This fits with the terminology: to the object THE_LIFT send the message GO_TO with argument 3. This way of writing operation calls is used in C++ and Smalltalk.

This call format, however, can lead to certain difficulties when you want an operation that can operate on more than one object. Suppose that we want an operation CLOSER, which has two lifts and a floor number as arguments and returns as result the lift which is currently closer to the stated floor. To find out which of the two lifts LIFT_1 and LIFT_2 is closer to floor N, we would write:

LIFT_1.CLOSER(LIFT_2, N)

It is not natural to 'send a message' to one of the two lifts that are to be compared: both lifts have the same status and should be treated symmetrically. It would be more natural to write:

CLOSER(LIFT_1, LIFT_2, N)

and that is the format used in Ada 95. In Ada 95 all parameters to functions and procedures are used in the same way, and in Ada 95 we would call the procedure GO_TO above by writing:

GO_TO(THE_LIFT, 3)

In C++ the problem of symmetric arguments has been solved by introducing yet another construct, known as friend functions.

14.2   Objects

As was mentioned in the last section, objects are described in Ada 95 by using abstract data types. In particular, abstract data types are used in which the type is implemented as a record type. (When real-time programs, programs with several processes which execute simultaneously, are written, what are known as **task** types are also used to describe objects. We are not going to consider these here, since real-time programming lies outside the scope of this book.) We have already looked at examples in which objects are described, such as the examples in Sections 8.8 and 11.4 where abstract data types were constructed to declare objects of type QUEUE. We will look at another example here. The following package describes persons:

```
package PERSON_PACKAGE is
   type PERSON is
      record
         NAME    : STRING(1 .. 30);
         NAME_L : NATURAL := 0;
      end record;

   function    CALLED (P : PERSON) return STRING;
   procedure  CHANGE_NAME (P : in out PERSON; TO : STRING);
end PERSON_PACKAGE;
```

We can see that objects of the type PERSON have four attributes: NAME, NAME_L, CALLED, and CHANGE_NAME. The first two are data attributes. We represent a person by a name and at the same time keep track of how many letters the name has (that is, how many places of the component NAME have been filled in). The default value for the length of the name is zero, which simply means that, initially, each new person to be declared has no name. The last two attributes are operations which can be applied, respectively, to read a person's name and change a person's name. Operations like this, which are declared immediately with the type, are called **primitive operations** in Ada 95. In order for the operations to be considered primitive, both the type and the operations must be declared in a package specification. Thus the type PERSON has two primitive operations, CALLED and CHANGE_NAME.

As we pointed out in the introduction to this chapter, object-oriented programming is based on two concepts: **encapsulation** and **inheritance**. Encapsulation is necessary in order to be able to define the attributes that belong to an object in a single place in a program. We have done this for the type PERSON by putting everything in a package. But if we leave it as seen above, this is not complete encapsulation. The implementation of the primitive operations CALLED and CHANGE_NAME are certainly hidden from the user of the package, but the user can get at and change the two data attributes without going through the primitive operations. To prevent that, we must make PERSON a private type:

```
package PERSON_PACKAGE is
  type PERSON is private;
  function    CALLED           (P : PERSON) return STRING;
  procedure CHANGE_NAME  (P : in out PERSON; TO : STRING);

private
  type PERSON is
    record
      NAME    : STRING(1 .. 30);
      NAME_L : NATURAL := 0;
    end record;
end PERSON_PACKAGE;
```

To create new objects of the type PERSON, the user of the package can make the variable declarations:

```
A, B : PERSON;
```

and messages can be sent to the objects by calling the primitive operations:

```
CHANGE_NAME(A, "Hannah");
PUT(CALLED(A));
```

The implementation of the operations are hidden, as usual, in the body of the package:

```
package body PERSON_PACKAGE is
  function CALLED(P : PERSON) return STRING is
  begin
    return P.NAME(1 .. P.NAME_L);
  end CALLED;
```

```
  procedure CHANGE_NAME (P : in out PERSON; TO : STRING) is
    L : NATURAL := NATURAL'MIN(TO'LENGTH, P.NAME'LENGTH);
  begin
    P.NAME(1 .. L) := TO(TO'FIRST .. TO'FIRST + L – 1);
    P.NAME_L := L;
  end CHANGE_NAME;
end PERSON_PACKAGE;
```

The attribute MIN, which is only found in Ada 95, is used in the procedure CHANGE_NAME. Apart from this, everything could have been written in Ada 83. In fact, it is perfectly possible to write object-oriented programs in Ada 83, as long as the inheritance mechanism is not needed.

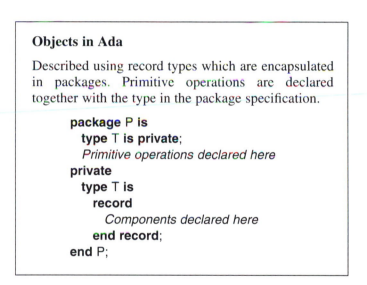

Objects in Ada

Described using record types which are encapsulated in packages. Primitive operations are declared together with the type in the package specification.

```
    package P is
      type T is private;
      Primitive operations declared here
    private
      type T is
        record
          Components declared here
        end record;
    end P;
```

Now we shall demonstrate how to implement class variables, that is, variables that are common to all objects that belong to a certain type. Let us study the bank account example discussed in the previous section. The specification of a package describing bank accounts could be

```
with PERSON_PACKAGE;
use PERSON_PACKAGE;
package BANK_PACKAGE is
  type BANK_ACCOUNT is private;
  function GET_BALANCE(B : BANK_ACCOUNT) return FLOAT;
  procedure DEPOSIT (B : in out BANK_ACCOUNT; AMOUNT : FLOAT);
  ...
  procedure CHANGE_INTEREST_RATE(NEW_INTEREST_RATE : FLOAT);
```

```
        private
          INTEREST_RATE : FLOAT;
          type BANK_ACCOUNT is
            record
              ACCOUNT_HOLDER : PERSON;
              BALANCE            : FLOAT;
            end record;
        end BANK_PACKAGE;
```

The abstract data type is BANK_ACCOUNT and it is implemented as a record type. The components that must exist for each account are ACCOUNT_HOLDER and BALANCE, and these are put into the record in the normal way. The variable INTEREST_RATE, which is a class variable, on the contrary is put outside the record type. Therefore there will only be one single variable of this kind in the package. (By placing this variable in the private part of the package specification and not in the package body, we make the variable accessible to child packages to BANK_PACKAGE, if any.) The operations GET_BALANCE and DEPOSIT are primitive operations of the type BANK_ACCOUNT (they both have a parameter of that type), but note that the procedure CHANGE_INTEREST_RATE is not a primitive operation. It is not related to a certain bank account and it does not have a bank account as a parameter. The implementation of CHANGE_INTEREST_RATE can be found in the package body:

```
        procedure CHANGE_INTEREST_RATE(NEW_INTEREST_RATE :
                 FLOAT) is
        begin
          INTEREST_RATE := NEW_INTEREST_RATE;
        end CHANGE_INTEREST_RATE;
```

An object can quite well be built of other objects, that is, it can have data attributes that are other objects. If an object of type TA has a data attribute which is of type TB, we say that 'a TA *has* a TB'. As an example of this we can look at this example of a football team:

```
        package TEAM_PACKAGE is
          type FOOTBALL_TEAM is private;
          procedure NEW_PLAYER (TEAM : in out FOOTBALL_TEAM;
                                PLAYER_NO : POSITIVE;
                                PLAYER_NAME : STRING);
          procedure PRINT_TEAM(TEAM : FOOTBALL_TEAM);

        private
          type PERSON_TABLE is array (INTEGER range < >) of PERSON;
          type FOOTBALL_TEAM is
```

```
    record
        PLAYERS : PERSON_TABLE(1 .. 11);
    end record;
end TEAM_PACKAGE;
```

(In order to make the program extracts shorter, we will omit the **with** and **use** clauses that are needed, both here and in the future.) If we now declare an object of type FOOTBALL_TEAM:

```
MILAN : FOOTBALL_TEAM;
```

it will have 11 objects of the type PERSON. The players in the team can be read in or changed:

```
PUT("Player number? "); GET(NO); SKIP_LINE;
PUT("Name? "); GET_LINE(A_NAME, L);
NEW_PLAYER(MILAN, NO, A_NAME(1 .. L));
```

and the whole team can be printed:

```
PRINT_TEAM(MILAN);
```

In the body of the package TEAM_PACKAGE, the primitive operations for the type PERSON are used:

```
package body TEAM_PACKAGE is
  procedure NEW_PLAYER(TEAM : in out FOOTBALL_TEAM;
                       PLAYER_NO   : POSITIVE;
                       PLAYER_NAME : STRING) is
  begin
    CHANGE_NAME(TEAM.PLAYERS(PLAYER_NO), PLAYER_NAME);
  end NEW_PLAYER;

  procedure PRINT_TEAM(TEAM : FOOTBALL_TEAM);
  begin
    for I in TEAM.PLAYERS'RANGE loop
      PUT(I, WIDTH => 2);
      PUT_LINE(" " & CALLED(TEAM.PLAYERS(I))):
    end loop;
  end PRINT_TEAM;
end TEAM_PACKAGE;
```

An object can thus have one or several other objects. Sometimes, an object A must know about another object B without B being a part of A. Then we say that object A needs a **reference** to object B. As an example of this we will add a number of attributes to the type PERSON so that it describes two people being married to one another:

```
package PERSON_PACKAGE is
   type PERSON is limited private;
   type PERSON_REF is access all PERSON;

   function   CALLED          (P : PERSON) return STRING;
   procedure  CHANGE_NAME (P : in out PERSON; TO : STRING);
   function   MARRIED_TO      (P : PERSON) return PERSON_REF;
   procedure  MARRIAGE        (R1, R2 : PERSON_REF);
   procedure  DIVORCE         (P1, P2 : in out PERSON);

   private
      type PERSON is
         record
            NAME              : STRING(1 .. 20);
            NAME_L            : NATURAL := 0;
            HUSB_OR_WIFE : PERSON_REF;
         end record;
end PERSON_PACKAGE;
```

A new data attribute, HUSB_OR_WIFE, has been added which is a reference to the person to whom the current person is married. The type PERSON_REF has been declared as an access value to the type PERSON. If a person is not married, then HUSB_OR_WIFE has value **null**. Three new primitive operations have been added. MARRIED_TO gives a reference to the person to whom the current person is married; note that it returns a value of the type PERSON_REF and that this value can be **null** if the person is unmarried. The two final operations are symmetric (as discussed in the previous section). The operation MARRIAGE can be called to bring about a mutual reference and DIVORCE is used to take one away. MARRIAGE has parameters of type PERSON_REF because the two people involved have to save **references** to one another, not copies.

In general, you should be careful about copying (or assigning) objects that contain access values. If, for example, we have a person EVE1 with the name 'Eve' who is married to, that is, has a reference to, another person ADAM, and we also want another person EVE2 to have the name 'Eve', then we should not make the assignment EVE2 := EVE1, for then EVE2 would refer to the same ADAM that EVE1 refers to. To avoid this happening, we have specified in the specification of the package that the type PERSON should be **limited**, which partly means (as we saw in Chapter 8) that assignment is forbidden.

The body of the package looks like this:

```
package body PERSON_PACKAGE is
  function CALLED (P : PERSON) return STRING is
    ... as before ...
  procedure CHANGE_NAME (P : in out PERSON; TO : STRING) is
    ... as before ...

  function MARRIED_TO (P : PERSON) return PERSON_REF is
  begin
    return P.HUSB_OR_WIFE;
  end MARRIED_TO;

  procedure MARRIAGE (R1, R2 : PERSON_REF) is
  begin
    R1.HUSB_OR_WIFE := R2;
    R2.HUSB_OR_WIFE := R1;
  end MARRIAGE;

  procedure DIVORCE (P1, P2 : in out PERSON) is
  begin
    P1.HUSB_OR_WIFE := null;
    P2.HUSB_OR_WIFE := null;
  end DIVORCE;
end PERSON_PACKAGE;
```

If we declare the variables:

```
ADAM, EVE : aliased PERSON;
```

then we can carry out the operations:

```
CHANGE_NAME(ADAM, "Adam");
CHANGE_NAME(EVE, "Eve");
MARRIAGE(ADAM'ACCESS, EVE'ACCESS);
PUT(CALLED(MARRIED_TO(ADAM).all));
```

The last statement produces the output 'Eve'. Of course, we could also have a dynamically allocated object:

```
A, B : PERSON_REF;
   ...
A := new PERSON; CHANGE_NAME(A.all, "Romeo");
B := new PERSON; CHANGE_NAME(B.all, "Juliet");
MARRIAGE(A, B);
```

> **Relations between objects**
>
> - An object O1 can *have* another object O2.
>   In that case O2 is a component of O1.
>
> - An object O1 can *know about* another object O2.
>   In that case O1 has a component which is a *reference* to O2.

Before we start to talk about inheritance, we should examine yet another example of objects. Suppose you have collected some simple statistics and want to present the results in the form of a histogram. We can imagine that you have collected the ages of a certain group of people and that the results have to be split up into 10-year intervals. You want to show how many people there are in the age ranges 0–9 years, 10–19 years and so on, up to 90–99 years. To do the analysis we use an object of the type HISTOGRAM:

```
package HISTO_PACK is
  type HISTOGRAM is private;
  procedure INSERT (H : in out HISTOGRAM; VALUE : INTEGER);
  procedure DRAW   (H : HISTOGRAM);
  procedure PRINT   (H : HISTOGRAM);

private
  type INTEGER_ARRAY is array (INTEGER range < >) of INTEGER;
  type HISTOGRAM is
    record
      PLACE : INTEGER_ARRAY(1 .. 10) := (others => 0);
    end record;
end HISTO_PACK;
```

A histogram has four attributes. The data attribute PLACE is an integer array with the same number of elements as there are age intervals, where you can keep track of the number of people in each age group. PLACE(1) contains, for example, the number of people between 0 and 9 years. The operation INSERT is called once for each person examined, with that person's age as parameter. The two operations DRAW and PRINT can be used to represent the results of the analysis.

The problem with this declaration of the type HISTOGRAM is that it is not flexible. You might well want to use a histogram for purposes other than to present an age structure – it is not certain that you will always want to represent values in the interval 0–100 in 10 subintervals! Therefore, we will generalize the type HISTOGRAM so that it can be used more widely, by giving the type **discriminants**. The package will now look like this:

```
package HISTO_PACK is
  type HISTOGRAM (X0 : INTEGER; NX, DX : POSITIVE) is private;
  procedure INSERT (H : in out HISTOGRAM; X : INTEGER);
  procedure DRAW   (H : HISTOGRAM);
  procedure PRINT  (H : HISTOGRAM);
  VALUE_ERROR : exception;

private
  type INTEGER_ARRAY is array (INTEGER range < >) of INTEGER;
  type HISTOGRAM(X0 : INTEGER; NX, DX : POSITIVE) is
    record
      PLACE : INTEGER_ARRAY(1 .. NX) := (others => 0);
    end record;
end HISTO_PACK;
```

We have introduced three discriminants, X0, NX and DX. X0 gives the lowest permitted measure, NX gives the number of intervals in the histogram and DX gives the width of each interval.

When you use a type with discriminants, if no default value is given then the discriminants must be given values. (In object-oriented programming, no default value should be given since it is not permitted in conjunction with expandable types (see next section).) For example, to declare a histogram Hi where the lowest possible measure is 50, the number of intervals is 20 and the width of an interval is 5, we can write;

```
H1 : HISTOGRAM(50, 20,5);
```

We could also use dynamic allocation:

```
type HISTO_POINTER is access HISTOGRAM;
H2 : HISTO_POINTER;
   ...
PUT("Give lowest value, number of intervals, interval width");
GET(V0); GET(N); GET(DV);
H2 := new HISTOGRAM(V0, N, bY);
PUT_LINE("Give measures");
while not END_OF_FILE loop
  GET(V);
  INSERT(H2.all, V);
end loop;
DRAW(H2.all);
```

The body of the histogram package looks like this (apart from the implementation of the DRAW procedure, for reasons of space):

```
package body HISTO_PACK is
  procedure INSERT (H : in out HISTOGRAM; X : INTEGER) is
    I : POSITIVE;
  begin
    if X not in H.X0 .. H.X0 + H.DX * H.NX – 1 then
      raise VALUE_ERROR;
    end if;
    I := (X – H.X0) / H.DX + 1;
    H.PLACE(I) := H.PLACE(I) + 1;
  end INSERT;
  procedure DRAW (H : HISTOGRAM) is

    ...

  procedure PRINT (H : HISTOGRAM) is
  begin
    for I in H.PLACE'RANGE loop
      PUT(H.X0 + H.DX * (I – 1), WIDTH => 3); PUT('–');
      PUT(H.X0 + H.DX * I – 1, WIDTH => 3); PUT(':');
      PUT(H.PLACE(I), WIDTH => 5);
      NEW_LINE;
    end loop;
  end PRINT;
end HISTO_PACK;
```

As an example of a type where discriminants are used to initialize components, we can declare a bank account:

```
type BANK_ACCOUNT (DEPOSIT : NATURAL) is
  record
    ACCOUNT_HOLDER : PERSON;
    BALANCE : NATURAL := DEPOSIT;
  end record;
```

To declare an account in which £100 was initially deposited, we can write:

```
K : BANK_ACCOUNT(100);
```

The discriminant DEPOSIT is treated as a component in the record, but it may not be changed. Its value is constant and is determined when the variable is declared. The component BALANCE, on the other hand, may be changed.

14.3   Inheritance

The special thing about object-oriented programming is that it contains constructs for **inheritance**. Using inheritance, you can create new types on the basis of existing types which you extend with further attributes. In the previous section we saw how two different kinds of relationships could be set up between objects: the relationships of having and knowing about (a FOOTBALL_TEAM *has* players; a PERSON *knows about* their marriage partner). With inheritance, it is possible to create yet a third set of relationships, namely those of **being**. For example, relations can be expressed such as 'an athlete *is* a person' or 'a book *is* a document'.

In Ada 95, inheritance is accomplished with the help of **expandable types**. The term used in the reference manual is **tagged types**, which highlights the fact that each object of an expandable type automatically gets a hidden component stating its exact type, and that is called the object's **tag**.

We can study a simple example for a start. This uses the type PERSON from earlier sections, but we will make it expandable by adding the reserved word **tagged**:

```
type PERSON is tagged
   record
      NAME     : STRING(1 .. 30);
      NAME_L  : NATURAL := 0;
   end record;
```

If we want to describe an athlete we can introduce the type ATHLETE:

```
type ATHLETE is new PERSON with
   record
      CLUB : STRING(1 .. 15);
   end record;
```

This new type is an **extension** of the type PERSON: we say that the type ATHLETE is **derived** from the type PERSON. Another way we can put this is that the type PERSON is the **parent type** to ATHLETE and that ATHLETE is a **child type** of PERSON. A derived type inherits all the attributes, or properties, of its parent. That means that the type ATHLETE has components NAME and NAME_L *plus* the component CLUB. If we were to declare an object of type PERSON, it would still have only the components NAME and NAME_L.

The new components, or data attributes, you give to a derived type may not have the same names as those of the parent type. For instance, it is not permitted to declare a new component called NAME in the type ATHLETE. It is, however, permitted to use the same names for inherited primitive operations. We will return to this shortly.

An expandable type can have many children. For example, we can derive another type from the type PERSON:

```
type EMPLOYEE is new PERSON with
  record
    SALARY : NATURAL;
  end record;
```

An object of type EMPLOYEE will then have components NAME, NAME_L *and* SALARY.

A derived type is, in its turn, expandable. In other words, we can derive further types from a type which is itself a derived type. For example, we can declare the type WEIGHT_LIFTER thus:

```
type WEIGHT_LIFTER is new ATHLETE with
  record
    WEIGHT_CLASS : FLOAT;
    RESULT       : FLOAT;
  end record;
```

If need be, you can derive a new type without adding new components to it; we could, for instance, describe a special sort of employee:

```
type PROGRAMMER is new EMPLOYEE with null record;
```

You should note that derived types are not the same thing as subtypes, which were discussed in Section 5.7. A derived type is a completely *new* type. If, for example, you declare two variables, one of type PERSON and the other of type EMPLOYEE, then these variables are of *different* types. To declare a subtype, on the other hand, does *not* mean that a new type is declared: it simply makes it possible to describe variables that belong to the basic type but which have certain limitations.

In general, you will want the expandable types you declare to be private and encapsulated in a package. Then, you will write declarations of the type PERSON like this:

```
package PERSON_PACKAGE is
  type PERSON is tagged private;
  function CALLED          (P : PERSON) return STRING;
  procedure CHANGE_NAME  (P : in out PERSON; TO : STRING);
  procedure PRINT_INFO     (P : PERSON);
private
  type PERSON is tagged
    record
      NAME   : STRING(1 .. 30);
      NAME_L : NATURAL := 0;
    end record;
end PERSON_PACKAGE;
```

Note that the word **tagged** appears both in the first type declaration and in the private part. For the sake of the demonstration we have added a new primitive operation, PRINT_INFO. The package's body looks like this:

```
package body PERSON_PACKAGE is
   function CALLED (P : PERSON) return STRING is
      ... as before ...
   procedure CHANGE_NAME (P : in out PERSON; TO : STRING) is
      ... as before ...
   procedure PRINT_INFO (P : PERSON) is
   begin
      PUT_LINE(P.NAME(1 .. NAME_L));
   end PRINT_INFO;
end PERSON_PACKAGE;
```

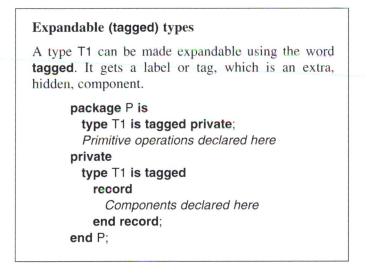

Expandable (tagged) types

A type T1 can be made expandable using the word **tagged**. It gets a label or tag, which is an extra, hidden, component.

```
package P is
   type T1 is tagged private;
   Primitive operations declared here
private
   type T1 is tagged
      record
         Components declared here
      end record;
end P;
```

Derived types can either be placed in the same package as their parent types, or be given new packages of their own. In the latter case there are two choices: you can either let the derived type know about the parent type's implementation, or you can restrict it to knowing only about the visible parts of the parent type's package. For example, if we want to place the type EMPLOYEE in a package of its own and let it know about only the visible parts of the package PERSON_PACKAGE, we should write:

```
package EMPLOYEE_PACKAGE is
   type EMPLOYEE is new PERSON with private;
   function   EARNS           (E : EMPLOYEE) return NATURAL;
   procedure  CHANGE_SALARY (E : in out EMPLOYEE; TO : NATURAL);
   procedure  PRINT_INFO      (E : EMPLOYEE);
```

```
  private
    type EMPLOYEE is new PERSON with
    record
      SALARY : NATURAL;
    end record;
  end EMPLOYEE_PACKAGE;
```

Thus we have put the derived type into an ordinary package. If we want, instead, to make the implementation of the type PERSON (that is, all that is in the private part of the package PERSON_PACKAGE) known in the new package as well, we make the new package a **child package** of PERSON_PACKAGE. Then we would write:

```
package EMPLOYEE_PACKAGE.EMPL is
  type EMPLOYEE is new PERSON with private;
  function   EARNS            (E : EMPLOYEE) return NATURAL;
  procedure  CHANGE_SALARY (E : in out EMPLOYEE; TO : NATURAL);
  procedure  PRINT_INFO      (E : EMPLOYEE);

private
  type EMPLOYEE is new PERSON with
    record
      SALARY : NATURAL;
    end record;
  end EMPLOYEE_PACKAGE.EMPL;
```

Now everything that is declared in the private part of the package PERSON_PACKAGE is known both in the private part and in the body of the package PERSON_PACKAGE.EMPL (see Section 8.9). In either case, you should notice that EMPLOYEE has to be a private type because its parent type is. Writing 'EMPLOYEE **is new** PERSON' means, as before, that EMPLOYEE is derived from PERSON and '**with private**' means that the details of this are hidden in the package's private part.

A derived type such as EMPLOYEE inherits not only its parent type's components, but also its primitive operations. If we declare the two variables:

```
P : PERSON;
COOK : EMPLOYEE;
```

we can then perform the following operations:

```
CHANGE_NAME(P, "Jane");
PUT(CALLED(P));
PRINT_INFO(P);
CHANGE_NAME(COOK, "John");
```

```
PUT(CALLED(COOK));
CHANGE_SALARY(COOK, 2000);
X := EARNS(COOK);
PRINT_INFO(COOK);
```

The operations EARNS and CHANGE_SALARY do not exist for P.

The operation PRINT_INFO is a bit special. In this case we have written a new version of the procedure in the package EMPLOYEE_PACKAGE which replaces the inherited procedure. We say that the new version **overrides** the old one. This means that when we make the call PRINT_INFO(COOK) the version declared in the package EMPLOYEE_ PACKAGE will be called. In the call PRINT_INFO(P), on the other hand, the version from the package PERSON_PACKAGE will be called.

Inheritance

A new type T2, a child type, can be derived from an expandable (tagged) type T1 and inherit all its components and primitive operations.

> **type** T2 **is new** T1 **with private**;
> *Declarations of new primitive operations and any redefinitions of inherited primitive operations*
>
> ...
> **type** T2 **is new** T1 **with**
>   **record**
>   *Declarations of further components*
> **end record**;

Let us look more closely at the body of the package EMPLOYEE_ PACKAGE.

```
package body EMPLOYEE-PACKAGE is
  function EARNS (E : EMPLOYEE) return NATURAL is
  begin
    return E.SALARY;
  end EARNS

  procedure CHANGE-SALARY (E in out EMPLOYEE; TO : NATURAL) is
  begin
    E.SALARY := TO;
  end CHANGE_SALARY;
```

```
      procedure PRINT_INFO (E : EMPLOYEE) is
      begin
        PRINT_INFO(PERSON(E));
        PUT("Salary:");PUT(E.SALARY, WIDTH => 1); NEW_LINE;
      end PRINT_INFO;
    end EMPLOYEE_PACKAGE
```

The statement PRINT_INFO(COOK); will give the printout:

```
John
Salary: 2000
```

It is worth noting that the new version of PRINT_INFO makes an internal call to the version PRINT_INFO which is in the parent package, in the statement:

```
PRINT_INFO(PERSON(E));
```

You can tell that it is the version from the parent package that is called because its parameter has the type PERSON. The expression PERSON(E) is actually nothing but a type conversion from the type EMPLOYEE to the type PERSON.

It is always permitted to make a type conversion from a derived type to a parent type (or grandparent, great-grandparent, and so on). If the variable PROG is of type PROGRAMMER, for instance, it is possible to do the type conversion PERSON(PROG). When you convert a derived type to its parent type, the components which do not exist for the parent type simply get 'chopped off'. Conversion in the other direction, from a parent type to a derived type, is not immediately possible, since new components would be needed. If you wish to make such a conversion, you have to do it by way of an aggregate where the values of the new components are stated. For example, if you want to go from the variable P of type PERSON and create a value of type EMPLOYEE, you write:

```
E := (P with SALARY => 1800);
```

This means that you have taken the values of P's components and added the new component, SALARY in this case. (The rules for what you write after the word **with** are the same as for ordinary record aggregates.) If you want to have a new value of a derived type which does not have any new components, you simply write **null record** after the word **with**. For example, we can create a value of the type PROGRAMMER:

```
PROG := (E with null record);
```

As an alternative, we can write the name of an expandable type T before the word **with**. In that case, if there are components in T that have no default value, we must also specify the values for these components in the aggregate.

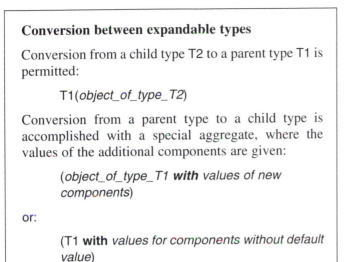

Conversion between expandable types

Conversion from a child type T2 to a parent type T1 is permitted:

T1(*object_of_type_T2*)

Conversion from a parent type to a child type is accomplished with a special aggregate, where the values of the additional components are given:

(*object_of_type_T1* **with** *values of new components*)

or:

(T1 **with** *values for components without default value*)

A derived type can also have discriminants. If the parent type has no discriminants this is very simple, as we see in this example where we give the derived type EMPLOYEE one discriminant:

```
type EMPLOYEE(STARTING_SALARY : NATURAL) is new PERSON with
   record
      SALARY : NATURAL := STARTING_SALARY;
   end record;
```

When an employee is declared, a starting salary must be stated:

```
E : EMPLOYEE(1800);
```

In the case of a parent type having discriminants but the derived type having none, it is also simple. We can declare a new derived type such as this:

```
type TEMP_EMPLOYEE is new EMPLOYEE with
   record
      START, FINISH : TIME;
   end record;
```

In this case, the derived type inherits the discriminants of the parent type. When we declare a temporary employee we must therefore give a value for the discriminant STARTING_SALARY:

```
TE : TEMP_EMPLOYEE(1600);
```

If, on the other hand, both the parent type and the derived type have discriminants, the rules that apply are a little special. We can, as an example, declare a type PERMANENT_EMPLOYEE:

```
type PERMANENT_EMPLOYEE (FIRST_SALARY : POSITIVE;
                         NO : POSITIVE) is new
               EMPLOYEE(FIRST_SALARY) with
     record
       DATE_OF_EMPLOYMENT : TIME;
     end record;
```

First, in this case the derived type does *not* inherit the discriminants of the parent type. A PERMANENT_EMPLOYEE has thus no discriminant called STARTING_SALARY. (On the other hand, it does inherit the component SALARY.) The new type only gets the discriminants that are given in the new declaration, in this example FIRST_SALARY and NO. Secondly, in the declaration of the derived type you must give values for the discriminants of the parent type. Here, for instance, we have written **new** EMPLOYEE(FIRST_SALARY). This means that the discriminant STARTING_ SALARY always has the same value as the discriminant FIRST_SALARY in the derived type. (You may, if you wish, see FIRST_SALARY as a redefinition of STARTING_SALARY.) It would also have been possible to give a constant initial value to the discriminant of the parent type, and not to link it to STARTING_SALARY, but in this example it would have been unnatural.

When you declare a variable of type PERMANENT_EMPLOYEE you must give values to the two discriminants FIRST_SALARY and NO. You can write, for example:

```
PE : PERMANENT_EMPLOYEE(1600, 1234);
```

14.4   Polymorphism and dynamic binding

In the so-called **typed programming languages**, such as Ada, Pascal and C++, types are used to monitor which operations can be carried out on the different data. If, for example, the variable X has type FLOAT and the function

```
SIN(X)
```

is called, then the compiler checks that there is a function SIN that has a parameter of type FLOAT. If such is found to be the case, the compiler generates machine code which will cause the function to be called when the program is run. Thus, which function is called is determined when the program is compiled. The call is said to be **bound** to the function SIN. In Section 6.6, we saw that in

Ada there can be **overloaded** subprograms, which means that several subprograms can have the same name but take different types of parameters. For example, if the call

PUT(X)

is made, the compiler can decide which procedure should be called by comparing the type of X with the different types of parameter which different PUT procedures take. Again, the call is bound to a particular procedure on compilation.

In Chapter 13, which dealt with **generic units**, we saw that it is possible to write program units that work for many different types. It was possible, for example, to write a package, STACK_PACKAGE, which could be used to help construct stacks of different kinds of element.

Overloading and generic program units are two forms of what is called **polymorphism** (having many forms) in the context of programming. This means that a program construct which has a certain appearance can mean different things (for example, calls to different functions) depending on the types of the operands involved. Binding means deciding exactly which form is appropriate. For both overloading and generic units, binding occurs during compilation, and this is known as **static** or **early binding**. Alternatively, **dynamic** or **late binding** can occur, and this takes place during program execution. (Dynamic binding is called **dispatching** in the reference manual to Ada 95.) In languages without typing, such as Smalltalk, only dynamic binding is used, while in other object-oriented languages, such as Ada 95 and C++, both static and dynamic binding are allowed. The polymorphism associated with static binding is usually called **ad hoc polymorphism**; if the term polymorphism is used alone it usually means polymorphism related to dynamic binding.

In the typed object-oriented languages, dynamic binding occurs in connection with inheritance. In order to discuss this further we will introduce the notion of a **type family**, which comprises all the types that have a common ancestor and the ancestor itself.† If T is a type, then T's type family consists of T and all the types which are either directly or indirectly derived from T. T is known as the **root** of the type family. The types PERSON, ATHLETE, WEIGHT_LIFTER,   EMPLOYEE,   PERMANENT_EMPLOYEE, TEMP_EMPLOYEE and PROGRAMMER, which we defined in the previous section, make up a type family with root PERSON. Note that a given type can belong to several different type families. The types EMPLOYEE, PERMA-NENT_EMPLOYEE, TEMP_EMPLOYEE and PROGRAMMER, for example, comprise another type family with EMPLOYEE as root.

---

† In the reference manual this is called **derivation class.** So as not to confuse the reader we will try to avoid the word class since it is generally used in object-oriented terminology to denote a set of objects and not a set of types.

In Ada 95 there is a distinction made between, on the one hand, **specific types** and, on the other, what are referred to as **polymorphic types**.† A specific type is a normal one that is wholly determined at compilation. Polymorphic types are found in connection with inheritance. Each type family has a polymorphic type. If a type family has root T, then the type family's polymorphic type is designated by T'CLASS (the word CLASS cannot be avoided here); this means 'any of the specific types which comprise T's type family'. If we have a parameter P, for example, whose type has been stated to be PERSON'-CLASS, then when the program is run P can have any of the specific types in PERSON's type family. P could, in this case, be ATHLETE or, equally, PROGRAMMER.

New ideas

- Polymorphism – a particular construct can be executed in different ways.
- Family of types, for a given type T – the type T itself and all the types which have T as parent, grandparent, greatgrandparent, etc.
- Specific type – common, completely known, type.
- Polymorphic type – written T'CLASS. Any of the types in T's family of types.

To demonstrate polymorphism and dynamic binding we will declare a type family that describes different kinds of vehicle. This example is related to the example in Section 7.5 which we discussed in connection with records with variants. For simplicity, we will put all the types in the same package, VEHICLE_PACKAGE, which has the following specification:

```
package VEHICLE_PACKAGE is
  type VEHICLE is tagged private;
  procedure GIVE_INFO(V : VEHICLE);

  type MOTOR_VEHICLE is new VEHICLE with private;
  procedure GIVE_INFO(M : MOTOR_VEHICLE);

  type PRIVATE_CAR is new MOTOR_VEHICLE with private;
  procedure GIVE_INFO(P : PRIVATE_CAR);
```

---

† In the reference manual, these are called **class-wide types**, but for the same reason as before, we will try to avoid using the word class.

```
        type VAN is new MOTOR_VEHICLE with private;
        procedure GIVE_INFO(VN : VAN);

        type BUS is new MOTOR_VEHICLE with private;
        procedure GIVE_INFO(B : BUS);

        type MINIBUS is new BUS with private;

    private
        type VEHICLE is tagged null record;

        type MOTOR_VEHICLE is new VEHICLE with
          record
            REG_NUMBER : STRING(1 .. 7);
          end record;

        type PRIVATE_CAR is new MOTOR_VEHICLE with
          record
            NUMBER_OF_SEATS : POSITIVE;
          end record;

        type VAN is new MOTOR_VEHICLE with
          record
            MAX_LOAD : POSITIVE;
          end record;

        type BUS is new MOTOR_VEHICLE with
          record
            NUMBER_OF_PASSENGERS : POSITIVE;
            AIR_CONDITIONING : BOOLEAN;
          end record;

        type MINIBUS is new BUS with null record;
    end VEHICLE_PACKAGE;
```

The root type is VEHICLE. This has a single child type, MOTOR_VEHICLE. (We have chosen to include this extra type so that in the future it will be possible to describe vehicles without motors, such as bicycles.) The type MOTOR_VEHICLE is in turn parent to three child types: PRIVATE_CAR, VAN and BUS. All the types in the family, apart from MINIBUS, have their own versions of the primitive operation GIVE_INFO. The type MINIBUS inherits the variant of GIVE_INFO from BUS. (For the example to operate in a more realistic situation, more primitive operations would be necessary, for example, to give values to the various components. Such operations have not been given to save space in this limited example.) In the body of the package implementations are given of the different variants of GIVE_INFO:

```
package body VEHICLE_PACKAGE is
  procedure GIVE_INFO(V : VEHICLE) is
  begin
    PUT_LINE("A vehicle");
  end GIVE_INFO;

  procedure GIVE_INFO(M : MOTOR_VEHICLE) is
  begin
    PUT_LINE("A motor-vehicle");
    PUT_LINE("Reg no: " & M.REG_NUMBER);
  end GIVE_INFO;

  procedure GIVE_INFO(P : PRIVATE_CAR) is
  begin
    GIVE_INFO(MOTOR_VEHICLE(P));
    PUT_LINE("A private car");
    PUT(P.NUMBER_OF_SEATS, WIDTH => 1);
    PUT_LINE(" seats");
  end GIVE_INFO;

  procedure GIVE_INFO(MOTOR_VEHICLE(VN : VAN) is
  begin
    GIVE_INFO(MOTOR_VEHICLE(VN));
    PUT_LINE(("A van");
    PUT(VN.MAX_LOAD, WIDTH => 1);
    PUT_LINE(" kg max load");
  end GIVE_INFO;

  procedure GIVE_INFO(B : BUS) is
  begin
    GIVE_INFO(MOTOR_VEHICLE(B));
    PUT_LINE("A bus");
    PUT(B.NUMBER_OF_PASSENGERS, WIDTH => 1);
    PUT_LINE(" passengers");
    if B.AIR_CONDITIONING then
      PUT_LINE("With air conditioning");
    end if;
  end GIVE_INFO;
end VEHICLE_PACKAGE;
```

Suppose that we have declared the following variables:

```
PC  : aliased PRIVATECAR;
VV  : aliased VAN;
MB  : aliased MINIBUS;
```

If we make the call:

GIVE_INFO(PC);   -- Static binding

we get a printout like this:

A motor-vehicle
Reg no: XYZ123K
A private car
5 seats

The variant of GET_INFO which was declared for type PRIVATE_CAR is called, and that in its turn calls the variant of GET_INFO declared for the type MOTOR_VEHICLE.

This example demonstrates **static binding**; the compiler knows which variant of GIVE_INFO should be called because the type of PC is specifically stated.

To demonstrate dynamic binding we will first make the following declarations:

type VEHICLE_POINTER **is access all** VEHICLE'CLASS;
VP : VEHICLE_POINTER;

The type VEHICLE_POINTER describes pointers which may point to objects of the polymorphic type VEHICLE'CLASS. Note that we have declared VEHICLE_POINTER as a so-called general pointer type by including the reserved word **all** in the declaration. This is not always necessary, but in most cases it is appropriate to use general pointer types when we want to point at polymorphic types. That is because some common type conversions between different pointer types are only allowed for general pointer types.

Since the variable VP is of type VEHICLE_POINTER it can point to either a vehicle, a motor vehicle, a private car, a van, a bus or a minibus. If the call:

GIVE_INFO(VP.**all**);   -- dynamic binding

is made, then on compilation it is impossible to determine which procedure GIVE_INFO should be called, and so the binding is dynamic. (Functions that can be called via dynamic binding are sometimes called **virtual functions**.) If, for example, prior to the above declaration we had written:

VP := VV'ACCESS;

then VP would point to a van and the output would be of the form:

A motor-vehicle
Reg no: M555ZZZ
A van
10000 kg max load

If we had written instead:

```
VP := MB'ACCESS;
```

then VP would point to a minibus and the output might have been:

```
A motor-vehicle
Reg no: ADA999Z
A bus
14 passengers
Has air conditioning
```

Of course, it is not natural to go this long way round simply to print out information about a van or a minibus. It is more realistic to use pointers to a polymorphic type when you have many objects belonging to the same type family. For example, to describe the vehicles owned by a car hire firm, you could use an array of pointers:

```
type VEHICLE_ARRAY is array (INTEGER range < >) of
                        VEHICLE_POINTER;
VEHICLES_OWNED : VEHICLE_ARRAY(1 .. 50);
```

Now it is possible to add to the company's stock of vehicles:

```
VEHICLES_OWNED(I) := new PRIVATE_CAR;
VEHICLES_OWNED(J) := new MINIBUS;
```

Then the following lines can be used to print out information on all the firm's cars:

```
for K in VEHICLES_OWNED'RANGE loop
  GIVE_INFO(VEHICLES_OWNED(K).all);       -- dynamic binding
end loop;
```

Compare this construction with the procedure PRINT_INFO in Section 7.5. Records with variants were used there, and it was necessary to have a case statement with an entrant for every variant. This version with dynamic binding is much simpler. Dynamic binding has yet another advantage over records with variants, namely that it is much easier to add new variants when needed. Suppose, for example, that this car hire firm extends its business into hiring out bicycles. We can make a new package which contains a type CYCLE:

```
package CYCLE_PACKAGE is
  type CYCLE is new VEHICLE with private;
```

```
    procedure GIVE_INFO(C : CYCLE);
  private
    type CYCLE is new VEHICLE with
      record
        NUMBER_OF_GEARS : POSITIVE;
      end record;
  end CYCLE_PACKAGE;
```

No changes need to be made in the existing package. If records with variants are being used, on the other hand, an entry has to be added to the **case** statement in the PRINT_INFO procedure, and everywhere else in the program with a corresponding **case** statement.

Static and dynamic binding

- Static binding – the subprogram to be called is determined on compilation. Occurs if all parameters are of a specific type.
- Dynamic binding – the subprogram to be called is determined on execution. Occurs if a primitive operation is called and one or more of its parameters are of polymorphic types.

How does dynamic binding work? It is all based on the hidden tag which exists for each expandable, or tagged, type. Each individual type within a family of types has a unique tag. When a program is being executed, the tag for an object indicates what its type is and the call is thus directed to the appropriate version of the primitive operation in question. (The exact way in which this happens depends on the implementation in use. A sort of pointer is often used to the primitive operations. With the right method, dynamic binding can be very efficient, and execution is not noticeably slower than with static binding.)

We have seen that it is possible to create and access objects of polymorphic types via pointers; however, it is not always necessary to use pointers. Parameters to procedures and functions may be of polymorphic type. The following procedure, which has parameters of the polymorphic type VEHICLE'CLASS can, for example, be used to print information for all the types in the family based on VEHICLE:

```
procedure PUT(VC : VEHICLE'CLASS) is
begin
```

```
        PUT_LINE("Information for a vehicle:");
        GIVE_INFO(VC);     -- dynamic binding
    end PUT;
```

All the following calls of PUT are correct:

```
    PUT(PC);
    PUT(VV);
    PUT(MB);
```

Polymorphic types can even be used when variables are declared, but only when a variable is initialized in such a way that its type is known when the declaration is executed. The following example is allowed:

```
    procedure P(VC : VEHICLE'CLASS) is
        TEMP : VEHICLE'CLASS := VC;
    begin
        ...
    end P;
```

Now TEMP gets the same type as VP when the call is made.

We have seen now how dynamic binding can be used when primitive operations are called. We stated earlier that the functions and procedures which are declared together with a tagged type T and which have parameters or results of type T are primitive operations for T. But a primitive operation can also have parameters, which are called **access parameters**, a kind of anonymous access value, or pointer, to objects. A function or procedure which has an access parameter to something of type T is actually considered to be a primitive operation for T. The following example demonstrates this. Suppose that the type PRIVATE_CAR has been declared as earlier and we add a new function SMALL:

```
    function SMALL(AB : access PRIVATE_CAR) return BOOLEAN is
    begin
        return AB.NUMBER_OF_SEATS < 5;
    end SMALL;
```

Here AB is an access parameter, so SMALL is a primitive operation for PRIVATE_CAR. Note that if we had declared an access type

```
    type CAR_POINTER is access PRIVATE_CAR;
```

and given AB the type CAR_POINTER, then the function SMALL would not have been a primitive operation. It is only so if the access parameter is of an anonymous access type.

Within the body of the function an access parameter is used like a normal pointer. For example, we can write AB.**all** to access the whole object that it points to, or we can, as in the example, access single components. Access parameters have a special property in that they can never have the value **null**. If we have, as an example, a variable PCAR of type CAR_POINTER and make the call SMALL(PCAR), then on execution a check is automatically made that PCAR is not **null**. If it is found to be **null**, an exception is raised. Therefore, there is never any need to check whether an access parameter is **null** in the body of a function or procedure.

Access parameters

> **procedure** P(A : **access** T) ...

A is an access parameter, a pointer to an object of type T. A's type is anonymous. A can never be **null**.

P is then a primitive operation for the type T.

In the examples of primitive operations we have seen so far there has only been one parameter, but it is possible to have primitive operations with more than one parameter. Assume, for instance, that we want a primitive operation BIGGER for the different kinds of motor vehicle, which compares two vehicles of the same type and states which of them is bigger. For cars and buses, 'bigger' means having more seats; for vans it means capable of taking a greater load. We add the following lines in VEHICLE_PACKAGE:

```
function BIGGER (M1, M2 : MOTOR_VEHICLE) return MOTOR_VEHICLE;
function BIGGER (P1, P2 : PRIVATE_CAR) return PRIVATE_CAR;
function BIGGER (V1, V2 : VAN) return VAN;
function BIGGER (B1, B2 : BUS) return BUS;
```

We add the implementations of the function BIGGER for the four types MOTOR_VEHICLE, PRIVATE_CAR, VAN, and BUS in the body of the package. For the type PRIVATE_CAR, for example, it will look like this:

```
function BIGGER (P1, P2 : PRIVATE_CAR) return PRIVATE_CAR is
begin
  if P1.NUMBER_OF_SEATS > P2.NUMBER_OF_SEATS then
    return P1;
  else
    return P2;
  end if;
end BIGGER;
```

The type MOTOR_VEHICLE causes some trouble because objects of this type have only a registration number and no other components. For the moment let us simply compare the registration numbers in the function BIGGER. Actually this is no problem, since in the real world no objects exist that are 'just' motor vehicles. A motor vehicles could always be further classified as a bus, a van or some other specific kind of motor vehicle. (In the next section, which discusses abstract types, we shall see how this problem is handled more elegantly.)

If the variables VP1 and VP2 are pointer to objects of the polymorphic type MOTOR_VEHICLE'CLASS, then we may write the following statement:

GIVE_INFO(BIGGER(VP1.**all**, VP2.**all**));

We get dynamic binding for the call of the function BIGGER.

· A function may also, as in this example, return a result of polymorphic type. The actual type of the result of a call to BIGGER depends on which variant of the function was called. If we compare two buses, the result is a bus; if we compare two vans the result is a van. This means that dynamic binding also occurs when the procedure GIVE_INFO is called.

There are two important rules concerning primitive operations with more than one parameter. These two rules guarantee that it is always possible to decide which operation is called when dynamic binding is used. There should be no ambiguity. The first rule states that it is not allowed to declare *primitive* operations where the parameters are of *different* tagged types. It is forbidden to declare a primitive function which compares buses and vans, for example:

function "<" (B : BUS; V : VAN) **return** BOOLEAN; — ILLEGAL

However if the operation is not primitive then it is allowed with parameters of different tagged types (in this case there is no dynamic binding, and therefore there can be no ambiguity). If the declaration of "<", for example, is placed outside the specification of VEHICLE_PACKAGE, then it is allowed.

The second rule states that when a primitive operation with many formal parameters of the same tagged type is called, then *all* the actual parameters must be polymorphic and of the *same* specific type. In the following call, for instance, the pointers VP1 and VP2 must point at the same kind of vehicle.

BIGGER(VP1.**all**, VP2.**all**)

Primitive operations with many parameters

There must not be formal parameters of different tagged types. All actual parameters at a call must be polymorphic and of the same specific type.

We mentioned earlier that every object in a tagged type has a hidden tag which gives its type. If you want to know what specific type a certain object has, the tag can be examined using the operator **in**. If the variable VC has, as before, the polymorphic type VEHICLE'CLASS, then you can test whether VC contains an object of type MOTOR_VEHICLE or one of its child types by writing:

if VC **in** MOTOR_VEHICLE'CLASS **then**
    ...

It is also possible to get at the tag more directly by using the attribute TAG, which can be used for both variables and types. The expression VC'TAG, for example, gives the tag for the object VC, and VAN'TAG gives the tag that objects of the type VAN get. (The type of this expression is TAG, which is defined in the package ADA.TAGS.) You can test whether VC describes a van by writing:

if VC'TAG = VAN'TAG **then**
    ...

or, more simply:

if VC **in** VAN **then**

Finally, there are a few things to be noted about the rules that apply to assignment and comparison for objects of polymorphic types. For assignment to a variable of polymorphic type, the expression on the right of the assignment sign must be of the same polymorphic type as the variable to the left, and furthermore, they must have the same tags. Suppose, for example, that the two variables VC1 and VC2 both have polymorphic type VEHICLE'CLASS. If we make the assignment

VC1 := VC2;

then a check is made on execution that the two objects are of the same specific type, or in other words that they have the same tag. If such is not the case, the exception CONSTRAINT_ERROR is generated.

If two objects are compared for equality they may have different tags, in which case the result of the comparison is FALSE. The expression

VC1 = VC2

for example, is allowed, whatever tags the two variables have.

It is permitted to convert from a polymorphic type to a specific type; on execution the expression to be converted is checked as being of the given specific type or a child type of it. Again, CONSTRAINT_ERROR is raised if an error is detected. For instance, we can write the expression BUS(VC), and a check is performed to see whether VC is one of BUS or MINIBUS.

It is also possible to convert from one polymorphic type to another. If the variable VC is of type VEHICLE'CLASS and the variable MC is of type MOTOR_VEHICLE'CLASS, then the following conversions are allowed:

```
VEHICLE'CLASS(MC)          -- safe
MOTOR_VEHICLE'CLASS(VC) -- might cause CONSTRAINT_ERROR
```

The first conversion is always safe, since the type family MOTOR_VEHICLE'-CLASS is an subset of the type family VEHICLE'CLASS. In the second conversion an error occurs if the variable VC is of type VEHICLE.

For pointer types which point to tagged types and polymorphic types, the same rules apply as for the types pointed to. If we declare the following pointer types and variables:

```
type VEHICLE_POINTER is access all VEHICLE'CLASS;
type MOTOR_VEHICLE_POINTER is access all
  MOTOR_VEHICLE'CLASS;
type MINIBUS_POINTER is access all MINIBUS'CLASS;
VP : VEHICLE_POINTER;
MP : MOTOR_VEHICLE_POINTER;
BP : MINIBUS_POINTER;
```

then you are allowed to do conversions as follows, for example:

```
BP := MINIBUS_POINTER(VP);            -- might cause
                                         CONSTRAINT_ERROR
VP := VEHICLE_POINTER(MP);            -- safe
MP := MOTOR_VEHICLE_POINTER(VP); -- might cause
                                         CONSTRAINT_ERROR
```

Testing, assigning and converting polymorphic types

Assume that OBJ is of polymorphic type and that T is a specific type.

if OBJ **in** T **then**
tests if OBJ is of type T.

if OBJ **in** T'CLASS **then**
tests if OBJ is of type T or of another type derived from T.

if OBJ1'TAG = OBJ2'TAG **then**
tests if OBJ1 and OBJ2 are of the same specific type.

if OBJ1 = OBJ2 **then**
tests if OBJ1 and OBJ2 are of the same specific type and contain the same value.

OBJ1 := OBJ2;
permitted if OBJ1 and OBJ2 are of the same specific type.

T(OBJ)
converts to type T. Permitted if OBJ is of type T or another type derived from T.
    For pointers to tagged types and polymorphic types the same rules apply as for the types pointed to. General pointer types must be used (declared with **all**).

14.5   Abstract operations and types

The primitive operation GIVE_INFO for the type VEHICLE is apparently quite meaningless since all that happens when it is used is that 'A vehicle' gets printed out. The reason for defining it is that we must make sure that there is an operation GIVE_INFO for each object belonging to any of the types in the VEHICLE type family, that is, all objects of the type VEHICLE'CLASS. If, for instance, we declare a new type TRAM as a child type to VEHICLE, but we forget to define a new GIVE_INFO operation for it, then objects of type TRAM will inherit the primitive operation GIVE_INFO from its parent type, the type VEHICLE. A prerequisite for using the method of dynamic binding is that the operation GIVE_INFO exists for all objects of type VEHICLE'CLASS, and its existence for the parent type VEHICLE ensures this. For example, if we have the declarations:

```
type VEHICLE_POINTER is access all VEHICLE'CLASS;
VP : VEHICLE_POINTER;
```

as before, and make the call:

```
GIVE_INFO(VP.all);
```

then the operation GIVE_INFO must exist for all objects that VP can possibly point to. However, there is actually no need to make up 'meaningless' primitive operations for a parent type to ensure that all objects will have this operation. Instead, what is known as **abstract primitive operations** (corresponding to what are called **pure virtual functions** in C++) can be defined. Such an operation has no implementation, so it cannot be called. The abstract operation is merely a sort of marker for a 'real' function or procedure. We will see what this looks like by rewriting the procedure GIVE_INFO for the type VEHICLE as an abstract procedure. In the visible part of the package VEHICLE_PACKAGE we will declare the procedure GIVE_INFO like this:

```
procedure GIVE_INFO(V : VEHICLE) is abstract;
```

In the body of VEHICLE_PACKAGE, now, there must *not* be an implementation of GIVE_INFO for the type VEHICLE.

Only **abstract types** (not to be confused with the concept of **abstract data types**, as discussed in Chapter 8) are allowed to have abstract primitive operations. An expandable type can be defined as abstract if the reserved word abstract is given in the declaration:

```
type T is abstract tagged
   record
   ...
   end record;
```

This also applies to the declaration of private types. The type VEHICLE, for example, can be defined as abstract:

```
package VEHICLE_PACKAGE is
   type VEHICLE is abstract tagged private;
   ...
private
   type VEHICLE is abstract tagged null record;
   ...
end VEHICLE_PACKAGE;
```

Since it is not permitted to make calls to an abstract operation, it is not permitted to declare objects of an abstract type. In our example, it would no longer be allowed to declare variables of the type VEHICLE. It is only allowed to declare objects of those types which have all the abstract operations replaced by 'real' operations which override the abstract operations. For example, you can declare an object of the type CYCLE if this type, as before, has its own version of the procedure GIVE_INFO:

> **procedure** GIVE_INFO(C : CYCLE);

When a new type is declared which is a child type of an abstract type, the new versions of the parent type's primitive operations do not have to be defined. In this case, the new type must also be defined as abstract and no objects may be declared for it. As an example of this, if we remove the definition of the procedure GIVE_INFO for the type MOTOR_VEHICLE, then this type must also be abstract and no objects of type MOTOR_VEHICLE may be declared. On the other hand, it is still allowed to declare objects of the child types of MOTOR_VEHICLE, since these have replaced the inherited abstract operation GIVE_INFO with their own versions.

Using abstract primitive operations it is possible to create an abstract parent type. It is not the idea to declare objects of this type, but the type has the function of a pattern for how the various child types should appear. The abstract parent type provides a description of the set of primitive operations which must exist for all objects belonging to any of the types in its family.

We will now give further examples of using abstract primitive operations. In the previous section we constructed a primitive operation BIGGER which compared two vehicles of the same type. One problem was to compare two objects of the specific type MOTOR_VEHICLE. Now, if we define the type MOTOR_VEHICLE as abstract we can also define the operation BIGGER for that type as abstract. If we make these changes, the visible part of the package VEHICLE_PACKAGE looks like this:

```
package VEHICLE_PACKAGE is
    type VEHICLE is abstract tagged private;
    procedure GIVE_INFO(V : VEHICLE) is abstract;

    type MOTOR_VEHICLE is abstract new VEHICLE with private;
    function BIGGER(M1, M2 : MOTOR_VEHICLE)
                            return MOTOR_VEHICLE is abstract;

    type PRIVATE_CAR is new MOTOR_VEHICLE with private;
    procedure GIVE_INFO(P : PRIVATE_CAR);
    function BIGGER(P1, P2 : PRIVATE_CAR) return PRIVATE_CAR;

    type VAN is new MOTOR_VEHICLE with private;
    procedure GIVE_INFO(VN : VAN);
    function BIGGER(VN1, VN2 : VAN) return VAN;
```

```
type BUS is new MOTOR_VEHICLE with private;
procedure GIVE_INFO(B : BUS);
function BIGGER(B1, B2 : BUS) return BUS;

type MINIBUS is new BUS with private;

private
    ...
end VEHICLE_PACKAGE;
```

The declaration of the abstract operation BIGGER for the type MOTOR_
VEHICLE now ensures that objects belonging to the type family
MOTOR_VEHICLE'CLASS will indeed have a primitive function BIGGER.

Abstract operations and types

An expandable type can be declared as abstract:

```
type T is abstract ... ;
```

No objects can be declared of an abstract type.

An abstract type can have abstract primitive operations:

```
procedure P(X : T) is abstract;
function F(X : T) return ... is abstract;
```

Abstract primitive operations have no implementation (body). Non-abstract child types must have their
own version of them.

We shall conclude this section with a slightly more advanced example
describing how to use abstract expandable types to construct iterators. This
example is an extension of the discussion in Section 13.3, where two different
techniques to construct queue iterators were shown. The starting point is the
generic package GEN_QUEUE_PACKAGE shown in Section 13.3. We declare a
child package:

```
generic
package GEN_QUEUE_PACKAGE.ITERATOR is
   type   QUEUE_ITERATOR(Q : access QUEUE) is
          abstract tagged limited private;
procedure ITERATE          (QI : in out QUEUE_ITERATOR'CLASS);
procedure VISIT_ELEMENT (QI : in out QUEUE_ITERATOR;
                         E  : in out ELEMENT) is abstract;
```

```
private
   type QUEUE_ITERATOR (Q : access QUEUE) is
        abstract tagged limited null record;
end GEN_QUEUE_PACKAGE.ITERATOR;

package body GEN_QUEUE_PACKAGE.ITERATOR is
   procedure ITERATE (QI : in out QUEUE_ITERATOR'CLASS) is
     INDEX : POSITIVE := QI.Q.FIRST;
   begin
     for I in 1.. QI.Q.NUMBER loop
        VISIT_ELEMENT(QI, QI.Q.BUF(INDEX)); -- dynamic binding
        INDEX := INDEX mod MAX_NUMBER + 1;
     end loop;
   end ITERATE;
end GEN_QUEUE_PACKAGE.ITERATOR;
```

The type QUEUE_ITERATOR has been declared as abstract. Hence the idea is that the user of the package should define his own child types of QUEUE_ ITERATOR. Two operations are defined. The procedure ITERATE runs through all elements in the current queue. For each element ITERATE calls the procedure VISIT_ELEMENT. VISIT_ELEMENT is an abstract procedure and each child type of QUEUE_ITERATOR must have its own implementation of this procedure. Since the parameter to ITERATE is of polymorphic type, dynamic binding will be used in the call to VISIT_ELEMENT. This means that different procedures VISIT_ELEMENT are called for different child types of QUEUE_ITERATOR.

   To demonstrate the use of this package we initially create an instance of the parent package GEN_QUEUE_PACKAGE and a corresponding instance of its child package GEN_QUEUE_PACKAGE.ITERATOR. The element type is set to INTEGER, since we intend to work with queues containing integers. The two instances are called INT_QUEUE_PACKAGE and INT_QUEUE_PACKAGE.IT respectively:

```
with GEN_QUEUE_PACKAGE;
package INT_QUEUE_PACKAGE is new
   GEN_QUEUE_PACKAGE(INTEGER);

with GEN_QUEUE_PACKAGE.ITERATOR;
package INT_QUEUE_PACKAGE.IT is new
   INT_QUEUE_PACKAGE.ITERATOR;
```

Now we use the instance INT_QUEUE_PACKAGE.IT and define a package containing two iterator types, one iterator that sets all queue element < 0 to zero, and one iterator that calculates the sum of all queue elements. Both these iterator types are declared as child types of the abstract type QUEUE_ ITERATOR. Since the two iterator types should not be abstract, they must have their own implementations of the operation VISIT_ELEMENT. For the iterator that calculates the sum we also declare a procedure that can be called when the sum should be calculated.

```
with INT_QUEUE_PACKAGE.IT;
use INT_QUEUE_PACKAGE.IT;
package MY_ITERATORS is
  type ZERO_ITERATOR is new QUEUE_ITERATOR with private;
  procedure VISIT_ELEMENT (QI : in out ZERO_ITERATOR;
                           E  : in out INTEGER);

  type SUM_ITERATOR is new QUEUE_ITERATOR with private;
  procedure VISIT_ELEMENT (QI : in out SUM_ITERATOR;
                           E  : in out INTEGER);
  procedure SUM_UP (QI  : in out SUM_ITERATOR;
                    RES : out INTEGER);

private
  type ZERO_ITERATOR is new QUEUE_ITERATOR with null record;

  type SUM_ITERATOR is new QUEUE_ITERATOR with
    record
      SUM : INTEGER := 0;
    end record;
end MY_ITERATORS;

package body MY_ITERATORS is
  procedure VISIT_ELEMENT (QI : in out ZERO_ITERATOR;
                           E  : in out INTEGER) is

  begin
    if E < 0 then
      E := 0;
    end if;
  end VISIT_ELEMENT;

  procedure VISIT_ELEMENT ( QI : in out SUM_ITERATOR;
                            E  : in out INTEGER) is
  begin
    QI.SUM := QI.SUM + E;
  end VISIT_ELEMENT;

  procedure SUM_UP (QI  : in out SUM_ITERATOR;
                    RES : out INTEGER) is
  begin
    QI.SUM := 0;
    ITERATE(QI);
    RES := QI.SUM;
  end SUM_UP;
end MY_ITERATORS;
```

Now a program using these packages is shown:

```
with INT_QUEUE_PACKAGE.IT, MY_ITERATORS, TEXT_IO,
     BASIC_NUM_IO;
use  INT_QUEUE_PACKAGE, INT_QUEUE_PACKAGE.IT,
     MY_ITERATORS, TEXT_IO, BASIC_NUM_IO;
procedure ITDEMO is
  THE_Q : aliased QUEUE;
  SI      : SUM_ITERATOR(THE_Q'ACCESS);
  ZI      : ZERO_ITERATOR(THE_Q'ACCESS);
  N       : INTEGER;
begin
  while not END_OF_FILE loop
    GET(N);
    PUT_IN(THE_Q, N);
  end loop;
  SUM_UP(SI, N); PUT(N); NEW_LINE;
  ITERATE(ZI);
  SUM_UP(SI, N); PUT(N); NEW_LINE;
end ITDEMO;
```

The program first creates an integer queue and a number of integers are read from the keyboard and put into the queue. After that the sum of all elements in the queue are calculated and printed out. Then all elements in the queue that are less than zero are set to zero, and finally the sum of all elements in the queue is recalculated and printed out.

This technique for constructing iterators is very flexible, since new iterators can easily be added. No knowledge of the implementation of the data structure itself is required to add a new iterator.

14.6   Heterogeneous collections of objects

It often happens that you want to collect together a number of objects that belong to the same family of types. Earlier, for example, we declared an array VEHICLES_OWNED, the elements of which were pointers to the generic type VEHICLE'CLASS. Since the objects thus accessed by the various pointers do not need to have the same specific type (that is, do not need to have the same tag), the array describes a collection of different objects. Such a collection is called a **heterogeneous collection**, in contrast to a **homogeneous collection** in which all the objects are of the same specific type.

A collection of objects does not need to be described by an array: they can also be arranged in linked lists, in tree structures, in sets and so on. In the object-oriented languages it is common to use **container types** (the more usual term is **container classes**) to construct collections of objects. Such container types are commonly held ready-made in a **type library** (more often called a **class library**) and can be used by the 'ordinary' programmer. A common method is to let the objects of a particular family of types inherit properties from an appropriate container type. Suppose, for example, that instead of an array we want to have a linked list of different kinds of vehicle. Then we can start from a package LIST_PACKAGE:

```
package LIST_PAK1 is
  type LIST_ELEMENT is tagged private;
  type LINK is access all LIST_ELEMENT'CLASS;
  procedure INSERT   ( ELEM : access LIST_ELEMENT;
                       LIST  : in out LINK);
  procedure REMOVE ( ELEM : access LIST_ELEMENT;
                       LIST  : in out LINK);
  function   NEXT     ( ELEM : access LIST_ELEMENT) return LINK;
private
  type LIST_ELEMENT is tagged
    record
      FORWARD : LINK;
    end record;
end LIST_PAK1;
```

The expandable type LIST_ELEMENT, which describes elements that can form linked lists, is now defined. We can access the first element of a list using a pointer of type LINK. The package has operations for inserting and removing elements, and for running through a list. Note that these three operations are primitive operations of the type LIST_ELEMENT, since they all have access parameters where the type pointed at is LIST_ELEMENT. The implementations of the operations are constructed as easily as possible:

```
package body LIST_PAK1 is
  procedure INSERT (ELEM : access LIST_ELEMENT;
                    LIST : in out LINK) is
  begin
    if LIST = null then
      ELEM.FORWARD := null;
      LIST := ELEM;
    else
      INSERT(ELEM, LIST.FORWARD);
    end if;
  end INSERT;

  procedure REMOVE (    ELEM : access LIST_ELEMENT;
                    LIST : in out LINK) is
  begin
```

```
     if LIST /= null then
        if LIST = ELEM then
           LIST := ELEM.FORWARD;
        else
           REMOVE(ELEM, LIST.FORWARD);
        end if;
     end if;
   end REMOVE;

   function NEXT (ELEM : access LIST_ELEMENT) return LINK is
   begin
      return ELEM.FORWARD;
     end NEXT;
   end LIST_PAK1;
```

If the type VEHICLE is now made a child type of the type LIST_ELEMENT, then all objects of the type VEHICLE'CLASS will be linkable, that is, they can be elements in linked lists. All such objects will have the component FORWARD and they will inherit the three primitive operations INSERT, REMOVE and NEXT.

So let us redeclare the type VEHICLE:

```
   type VEHICLE is new LIST_ELEMENT with null record;
```

The type VEHICLE_POINTER and the variable VP are declared as before, namely:

```
   type VEHICLE_POINTER is access all VEHICLE'CLASS;
   VP : VEHICLE_POINTER;
```

To declare a linked list of vehicles we must first declare a pointer THE_LIST which will point to the first element in the list. We also declare an extra pointer P, which is to be used later when we run through the list:

```
   THE_LIST, P : LINK;
```

Then we can insert elements in the list. If VP points to some sort of vehicle we can put it first in the list with the statement:

```
   INSERT(VP, THE_LIST);
```

Note that VP can be used as a parameter to the operation INSERT, since this operation is inherited from the parent type LIST_ELEMENT. We can also insert an object in the list without having a pointer to it:

```
INSERT(PC'ACCESS, THE_LIST); — PC is a PRIVATE_CAR
```

The following statements run through the entire list and print out information for all vehicles in the list:

```
P := THE_LIST;
while P /= null loop
   GIVE_INFO(VEHICLE_POINTER(P).all);
   P := NEXT(P);
end loop;
```

The call to GIVE_INFO makes use of dynamic binding because the list is heterogeneous.

This method of forming linked lists of vehicles has a certain elegance, but it has two problems. First, even before declaring the type VEHICLE, we must decide how it will be used so that we are sure it will inherit the properties of a suitable container type. If, instead, we wanted to build up binary trees of vehicles, then we would have to derive the type VEHICLE from a different container type. The second problem is that we are forced into making type conversions of which we cannot be certain. In the example above this is seen in the call to the procedure GIVE_INFO. The variable P is of type LINK, that is, a pointer to objects of the polymorphic type LIST_ELEMENT'CLASS. In order to call the procedure GIVE_INFO, which is only defined for the type family of VEHICLE, we have to make a conversion to the type VEHICLE'CLASS.

One way of solving the latter of these two problems would be by turning the tables and using a generic construct to make VEHICLE the parent type of LIST_ELEMENT. Ada 95 actually allows us to have generic type parameters that specify tagged types, and we can use this to add certain properties to a type after it has been declared. We construct a generic package that appears like this:

```
generic
   type BASE_TYPE is tagged private;
package LIST_PAK2 is
   type LIST_ELEMENT is new BASE_TYPE with private;
   type LINK is access all LIST_ELEMENT'CLASS;
   procedure INSERT   ( ELEM : access LIST_ELEMENT;
                        LIST  : in out LINK);
   procedure REMOVE ( ELEM : access LIST_ELEMENT;
                      LIST  : in out LINK);
   function   NEXT     ( ELEM : access LIST_ELEMENT) return LINK;
private
   type LIST_ELEMENT is new BASE_TYPE with
      record
         FORWARD : LINK;
      end record;
end LIST_PAK2;
```

The next step is to declare an instance of this package with the type VEHICLE as a generic parameter:

package VE **is new** LIST_PAK2(VEHICLE);

This means that a new type VE.LIST_ELEMENT will be declared; it will be a child type of VEHICLE and objects of the type VE.LIST_ELEMENT will have the property that they can form a linked list.

In order to make all the earlier child types of VEHICLE linkable, we must now redeclare them so that they are children of VE.LIST_ELEMENT instead of VEHICLE. We can write, for example:

type MOTOR_VEHICLE **is new** VE.LIST_ELEMENT **with private;**

A list is created by declaring a pointer THE_LIST which points to its first element, and we also declare a pointer P which can point to any kind of vehicle:

use VE;
THE_LIST, P : LINK;

Now linkable vehicles can be added to the list with the calls

INSERT(P, THE_LIST);
INSERT(MB'ACCESS, THE_LIST); -- MB is a MINIBUS

Information about all vehicles in the list can be printed using the statements:

```
P := THE_LIST;
while P /= null loop
  GIVE_INFO(P.all);
  P := NEXT(P);
end loop;
```

If we compare this with the earlier solution we see that the uncertain type conversion has disappeared.

What we have been looking at is an example of what would be done in other object-oriented languages by using **multiple inheritance**. Multiple inheritance means that a type has several parent types and thus inherits properties from various sources. In our example, if we had used multiple inheritance we would have been able to create a new type LINKABLE_VEHICLE which had both of the types VEHICLE and LIST_ELEMENT as parents. There is no multiple inheritance in Ada 95. It is judged that the need for it is slight and that all types of problem where multiple inheritance would be used can be solved using other constructions, such as the one discussed above.

It should be mentioned that there is yet another way of specifying that a generic type parameter is to be a tagged type. It is possible to write:

type T **is new** S **with private**;

This means that the generic type parameter T is to be derived (directly or indirectly) from a given type S. This method can be used if you want to construct a generic package which enables further properties to be added for all the types in a particular family of types.

The solution we now have avoids the problem of type conversion, but the problem of having to decide in advance which collection a type should go in remains. The type VE.LIST_ELEMENT must be declared before you can declare the different child types, such as PRIVATE_CAR, BUS, etc.

There is yet another alternative that we will look at now which avoids both these problems, and it is rather simple. Why should you make use of inheritance to set up collection types? It is easy to believe that inheritance must be used in all situations when you work with object-oriented programming, but such is not the case. Building up programs in a modular way can be achieved in two ways, namely **classification** and **composition**. Classification is what you use when you make use of inheritance. You try to describe your objects in a structured way by dividing them into different categories and subcategories. The vehicles we have been talking about provide a typical example of this. Composition, on the other hand, is based on putting together free-standing program modules which are independent of one another, are general, and are developed separately. An example of a general program module of this kind is the package TEXT_IO.

You can say that registration number, number of seats and so on are natural properties of a vehicle, and classification is an excellent method of describing such natural properties, but you can hardly claim that inclusion in a list is a natural property of a vehicle: vehicles have nothing to do with lists. Instead of this, it is more natural to have a special sort of object, a list handler, whose only job is to deal with lists. A list handler can be written as an independent, separate module, and now composition is the obvious method to use.

In Section 13.2.2 a generic list handler package LIST_PACKAGE was developed. A type LIST was declared together with a number of operations which could be carried out on lists. It is simple to make a list handler which can deal with lists of vehicles by creating an appropriate instance of the package and then declaring an object of type LIST. This object is then the list handler we need.

In Section 13.2.2 we demonstrated how we could build up a list of texts of different lengths by letting the list contain pointers to texts. We can use the same idea here and let the list contain pointers to vehicles. The pointers should have type VEHICLE'CLASS so that the list is able to contain all the different kinds of vehicle that are included in the VEHICLE family of types. If we have the same declaration as before:

type VEHICLE_POINTER **is access all** VEHICLE'CLASS;

we are able to create a suitable instance of the package LIST_PACKAGE and declare a list:

package LIST_PAK3 **is new** LIST_PACKAGE(VEHICLE_POINTER);
use LIST_PAK3;
THE_LIST : LIST;

To add a vehicle to the list we can write:

INSERT(MY_CAR'ACCESS, THE_START, THE_LIST);
INSERT(PCAR, THE_END, THE_LIST);

Information can be printed out for all vehicles in the list using the statements:

MOVE_POS(THE_START, THE_LIST);
while not POS_MISSING(THE_LIST) **loop**
  GIVE_INFO(VALUE(THE_LIST).**all**);
  MOVE_POS(RIGHT, THE_LIST);
end loop;

Heterogeneous collections of objects

A collection of objects of different kinds belonging to a common family of types, T'CLASS. Can be created in three ways:

(1) Let T be a child type of a container type, for example, a list type. Disadvantages: when T is declared, a decision has to be made in advance as to what sort of collection the object should be able to be part of. Uncertain type conversion becomes necessary.

(2) Let the container type be a child type of T. Can be done using generic construct. Disadvantages: all types derived from T must be child types of the container type.

(3) Do not use inheritance, but use a generic package developed separately which defines the collection wanted. Avoids the disadvantages of (1) and (2).

We see that both the problems we identified earlier have disappeared in this solution. There is no need for type conversion, and the type VEHICLE and its child classes can be developed quite separately from the type LIST. There is no need to decide in advance what data structures VEHICLE should be part of. If you should now decide to construct a stack of vehicles instead of a linked list, this is possible by using the generic package STACK_PACKAGE, which was shown in Section 13.2.1.

14.7 Storing objects in files

Input and output of data has already been discussed in terms of the standard packages TEXT_IO, SEQUENTIAL_IO and DIRECT_IO. None of these packages can be used for storing objects in files. TEXT_IO can deal with text files, files consisting of sequences of CHARACTER, that is, codes for printable symbols. Therefore, when reading or writing data internal to the program is not saved as CHARACTER, conversion always occurs when TEXT_IO is used. Of course, it is possible to use TEXT_IO to write out and read in the attributes of an object one by one, but it is not possible to deal with whole objects at a time. Nor can the packages SEQUENTIAL_IO or DIRECT_IO be used with objects. These two packages demand that all the elements which are stored in one file are of exactly the same type, but this is not the case for objects which are of polymorphic types, such as VEHICLE'CLASS.

In order to be able to store polymorphic types in files we therefore use what are called **streams**. A stream is logically seen as a sequence of **memory elements**, each of these usually being a byte (eight bits). Streams can be used to represent the content of files or other external media, for example communication channels. There are two standard packages for streams: ADA.STREAMS contains the basic declarations, and its child package ADA.STREAMS. STREAM_IO contains operations for reading streams from and writing streams to files. In the latter package there are operations including OPEN, CREATE and CLOSE for opening, creating and closing files, as well as other useful operations, such as END_OF_FILE, RESET and IS_OPEN. All these operations work in exactly the same way as the corresponding operations in the package SEQUENTIAL_IO. To make operations directly visible in a program you first write the clauses:

```
with ADA.STREAMS.STREAM_IO;
use ADA.STREAMS.STREAM_IO;
```

Now it is possible to create a file:

```
F : STREAM_IO.FILE_TYPE;
...
CREATE(F, NAME => "my.file");
```

(We have written STREAM_IO.FILE_TYPE instead of simply FILE_TYPE to avoid a collision with names for corresponding types in the package TEXT_IO.) When a file has been opened a specific stream is automatically linked to the file. A pointer to this stream can be obtained by calling the function STREAM, which returns a pointer of the type STREAM_ACCESS. Thus, you can write:

```
S : STREAM_ACCESS;
  ...
S := STREAM(F);
```

Reading and writing a file is most easily done with the attributes T'INPUT and T'OUTPUT, which exist for all types T (which are not limited). T'OUTPUT is a procedure which should have two parameters: a pointer to the relevant stream and the object which is to be written. The following statements, for example, write first an integer I and then a real number X to the stream S (that is, to the file 'my.file'):

```
INTEGER'OUTPUT(S, I);
FLOAT'OUTPUT(S, X);
```

The attribute T'INPUT, which is a function, takes the stream you wish to read from as parameter and returns the object of type T which has been read. For example, we can read the numbers which were written with the statements above thus:

```
RESET(F, IN_FILE);
I  := INTEGER'INPUT(S);
X := FLOAT'INPUT(S);
```

The attributes T'INPUT and T'OUTPUT not only read and write the values of data objects but also read and write bounds and discriminants, if any. For an object of an expandable type this means that the tag is also read or written.

To demonstrate how streams are used to read and write objects of polymorphic types we will look at two procedures, STORE_VLIST which writes a list of vehicles to a file, and GET_VLIST which reads a number of vehicles from a file and puts them into a list. The list has been constructed using the generic package LIST_PACKAGE, as shown at the end of the previous section.

```
procedure STORE_LIST(L : in out LIST; FILENAME : STRING) is
  F : STREAM_IO.FILE_TYPE;
  S : STREAM_ACCESS;
begin
  CREATE(F, OUT_FILE, FILENAME);
  S := STREAM(F);
  MOVE_POS(THE_START, L);
```

```
      while not POS_MISSING(L) loop
         VEHICLE'CLASS'OUTPUT(S, VALUE(L).all);
         MOVE_POS(RIGHT, L);
       end loop;
       CLOSE(F);
    end STORE_LIST;

    procedure GET_LIST(L : in out LIST, FILENAME : STRING) is
       F : STREAM_IO.FILE_TYPE;
       S : STREAM_ACCESS;
    begin
       OPEN(F, IN_FILE, FILENAME);
       S := STREAM(F);
       MOVE_POS(THE_START, L);
       while not END_OF_FILE(F) loop
          INSERT(new VEHICLE'CLASS'(VEHICLE'CLASS'INPUT(S)),
                                                        RIGHT, L);

       end loop;
       CLOSE(F);
    end GET_LIST;
```

Storing objects in files

Use the package ADA.STREAMS.STREAM_IO.

The same operations for opening and closing files as in SEQUENTIAL_IO.

S : STREAM_ACCESS; -- pointer to a stream

S := STREAM(F); -- gives a pointer to the stream for file F

T'CLASS'OUTPUT(S, OBJ);-- stores an object of type T'CLASS

T'CLASS'INPUT(S) -- reads and returns object of type T'CLASS

14.8   Initialization, assignment and finalizing objects

In general, you do not have to worry about the details of what is happening when you declare an object, when you assign a value to an object, or when an object ceases to exist. There are, however, situations where you as the programmer must have control over these operations in order for the object you are building to function as intended. Then you can use the package ADA.FINALIZATION and make the types of all your objects child types of one or other of the two abstract tagged abstract types CONTROLLED and LIMITED_CONTROLLED which are defined there. The idea is to use the type LIMITED_CONTROLLED if you want to create new derived types which are **limited**, and the type CONTROLLED otherwise. These two types contain some primitive operations which are called automatically in certain circumstances. The type CONTROLLED has the following primitive operations:

        procedure INITIALIZE (OBJECT : **in out** CONTROLLED);
        procedure ADJUST   (OBJECT : **in out** CONTROLLED);
        procedure FINALIZE (OBJECT : **in out** CONTROLLED);

The type LIMITED_CONTROLLED has corresponding operations, except that there is no operation ADJUST (because assignment is not permitted for limited types). The versions of INITIALIZE, ADJUST and FINALIZE that are defined for the types CONTROLLED and LIMITED_CONTROLLED contain empty bodies, which means they do nothing if called.

      Suppose now that we declare TC, a specific child type to CONTROLLED. (The example would work similarly for LIMITED_CONTROLLED, except that everything to do with assignment would be missing.)

        type TC **is new** CONTROLLED **with** … ;

We can declare our own variants of INITIALIZE, ADJUST and FINALIZE:

        procedure INITIALIZE (OBJECT : **in out** TC);
        procedure ADJUST   (OBJECT : **in out** TC);
        procedure FINALIZE (OBJECT : **in out** TC);

Let us start by thinking about what happens when variables are declared. Suppose we have the following declarations:

        A : TC;   -- The call INITIALIZE(A) is made here
        B : TC := … ;   -- copy value; ADJUST (B);

There is no initialization of A in its declaration, which means that the procedure INITIALIZE is *automatically* called with A as parameter (without it being seen in the program). If, however, a variable is initialized when declared, INITIALIZE will not be called. Instead, first the initialization value is copied to the variable, then ADJUST is called automatically.

      For initialization, you should remember that it is possible to initialize individual components of an object by initializing them in the type declaration. Discriminants can also be used, as discussed in Section 14.3.

A variable normally ceases to exist when execution leaves the part of the program in which it is declared. If, for example, A is declared in the procedure P, it will disappear when P is left. During program execution, temporary anonymous objects can be created in certain situations and disappear when no longer needed. (For example, a temporary anonymous object can be created when a function returns a result, and the object disappears when the result has been accepted by the calling subprogram.) When an object ceases to exist, 'cleaning' might sometimes be needed, for example to free memory which was allocated to the object dynamically. Therefore the procedure FINALIZE is automatically called when an object ceases to exist:

```
procedure P is
   A : TC;
begin
   ...
end;          -- FINALIZE(A) is called here
```

When assignment takes place (and other situations where copying occurs, such as passing parameters), both procedures FINALIZE and ADJUST are called automatically. Suppose we make the assignment:

```
A := B;       --FINALIZE(A); copy value; ADJUST(A);
```

First FINALIZE is called so that A's old values can be tidied away. Then, B's value is copied to A. Finally, ADJUST is called so that A's new value can be adjusted if necessary.

To demonstrate how these mechanisms can be used we will construct a VSTRING type which describes text strings of arbitarry, variable length. The package has the following specification:

```
with ADA.FINALIZATION;
use ADA.FINALIZATION;
package VSTRING_PACKAGE is
   type VSTRING is new CONTROLLED with private;
   function VSTR (S : STRING) return VSTRING;
   function STR (V : VSTRING) return STRING;
   function "=" (V1, V2 : VSTRING) return BOOLEAN;
   function "&" (V1, V2 : VSTRING) return VSTRING;
   ... further operations ...
   procedure PUT (V : in VSTRING);
   procedure GET (V : out VSTRING);

private
   type STRING_POINTER is access STRING;
   type VSTRING is new CONTROLLED with
```

```
    record
      P : STRING_POINTER;
    end record;

  procedure INITIALIZE    (V : in out VSTRING);
  procedure ADJUST        (V : in out VSTRING);
  procedure FINALIZE      (V : in out VSTRING);
end VSTRING_PACKAGE;
```

Control of initialization, assignment and finalizing

- Use the package ADA.FINALIZATION and make the type T a child type of CONTROLLED or LIMITED_CONTROLLED. If necessary, write your own versions of the primitive operations INITIALIZE, ADJUST and FINALIZE.

- Calls to INITIALIZE, ADJUST and FINALIZE take place automatically.

- INITIALIZE(OBJ) is called every time an object of type T is declared (if there is no initialization in the declaration).

- On the assignment OBJ1 := OBJ2; first FINAL-IZE(OBJ1) is called, then the value is copied, and finally ADJUST(OBJ1) is called.

- When an object ceases to exist, FINALIZE(OBJ) is called.

The type VSTRING is a child type to CONTROLLED and thus has the primitive operations INITIALIZE, ADJUST and FINALIZE. We have placed the declarations of our own variants of these procedures in the private part of the package, since they will never be called directly and should therefore not be visible. We are implementing text strings of variable length with records consisting of a pointer P to a text string which we allocate dynamically. The functions VSTR and STR are conversion functions between our variable-length text strings and 'ordinary' text strings. The functions "=" and "&" in the specification of the package are typical operations which can be carried out on strings of variable length. (You can imagine many more useful functions, such as find substrings, change substrings, and so on, but the two given here are adequate to show the general ideas involved.) There are also procedures for reading and writing strings of variable length.

The idea is that variables of type VSTRING can now be used in place of variables of type STRING. Then all the problems of texts of differing lengths can be avoided. We can do the following, for example:

```
Q, R : VSTRING;
  ...
GET(Q);
R := Q;
PUT(Q & R);
```

The body of the package looks like this:

```
with UNCHECKED_DEALLOCATION, TEXT_IO;
use TEXT_IO;
package body VSTRING_PACKAGE is
  PEMPTY: constant STRING_POINTER := new STRING'(" ");
  MAXL   : constant := 300;

  procedure INITIALIZE (V : in out VSTRING) is
  begin
    V.P := PEMPTY;
  end INITIALIZE;

  procedure ADJUST (V : in out VSTRING) is
  begin
    V.P := new STRING'(V.P.all);
  end ADJUST;

  procedure FREE is
    new UNCHECKED_DEALLOCATION (STRING, STRING_POINTER);

  procedure FINALIZE (V : in out VSTRING) is
  begin
    if V.P /= PEMPTY then
      FREE(V.P);
    end if;
  end FINALIZE;

  function VSTR (S : STRING) return VSTRING is
  begin
    return (CONTROLLED with P => new STRING'(S));
  end VSTR;

  function STR (V : VSTRING) return STRING is
  begin
    return V.P.all;
  end STR;
```

```
    function "=" (V1, V2 : VSTRING) return BOOLEAN is
    begin
       return V1.P.all = V2.P.all;
    end "=";

    function "&" (V1, V2 : VSTRING) return VSTRING is
    begin
       return (CONTROLLED with
                    P => new STRING'(V1.P.all & V2.P.all));
    end "&";

    procedure PUT (V : in STRING) is
    begin
       PUT(V.P.all);
    end PUT;

    procedure GET(V : out VSTRING) is
       S : STRING(1 .. MAXL);
       N : NATURAL;
    begin
       GET_LINE(S, N);
       V := VSTR(S(1 .. N));
    end GET;
 end VSTRING_PACKAGE;
```

In the procedure INITIALIZE, the pointer P is initialized to point to a text string of length zero, that is, an empty text string. This means that each variable of type VSTRING starts by describing an empty string unless another initialization is made on declaration. In order to avoid allocating a new empty string for every variable that is declared, we have used the pointer PEMPTY, so that all variables point to the same empty string.

The procedure ADJUST is central to this example. Suppose the variables Q and R are both of type VSTRING and that we make the assignment Q := R. If we had not used ADJUST, then after the assignment Q would have contained a pointer to the *same* text string as R, and the consequence would be that changing this text string would affect *both* variables. If, for example, Q were to be changed later, then R would also be changed, which would be misleading. In ADJUST, what happens is that Q is given a pointer to a *copy* of the text that is written in R, and in this way unnatural links between different variables are avoided.

In the procedure FINALIZE, memory is freed for the text string that is pointed to. However, the empty text string which all newly declared text string variables point to must not be freed.

The expression

```
(CONTROLLED with P => new STRING'(S))
```

which is used in the function VSTR needs a comment. The expression is an aggregate with type VSTRING. It could be seen as a conversion from the parent type CONTROLLED to the child type VSTRING. (Compare this with Section 14.3 where we discussed conversions between expandable types.)

EXERCISES

14.1 Start from the type PERSON and construct a new derived type STUDENT with suitable attributes. Then construct a new type COURSE and relate it in an appropriate way to the type STUDENT.

14.2 Create a child type of the type PERSON called CAR_OWNER, with suitable attributes. It has to be possible for a person to own more than one car. Make the necessary changes to the type VEHICLE so that the owner of a vehicle can be specified. Consider the question of a company being the owner of a vehicle: is it reasonable to make CAR_OWNER a child type of PERSON?

14.3 When object-oriented programming is being discussed, descriptions of geometric figures are often used as examples.

(a) Declare a type POINT which describes the point (x,y) in a two-dimensional plane. Then declare a type FIGURE which has a point at its centre.

(b) Declare a number of child types to FIGURE, for example CIRCLE, TRIANGLE and RECTANGLE. Give them suitable attributes to describe their sizes.

(c) Add an abstract function AREA for the type FIGURE. Then write a specific version of the operation AREA for each of the child types of FIGURE.

(d) Declare an array of pointers to arbitrary figures and then write the statements necessary to print out the areas for all the figures in the array.

14.4 In Exercise 13.7 a generic package was constructed which could be used to create binary search trees. Suppose that the package is extended with the four following operations, which are used when you want to read the information in a tree:

- TO_THE_ROOT makes the root the current node.

- NEXT_POS moves the current node to the next node in the tree (according to the inorder principle).

- POS_MISSING gives whether or not there is a current node.

- VALUE gives the value of the current node.

Using this package, write a program that builds up a binary tree containing references to vehicles of different kinds. It should be able to deal with an arbitrary number of vehicles. The program should start by reading in information about different vehicles from the terminal. For each new vehicle, the operator should state the kind of vehicle that is going to be entered. Then the program should create a vehicle of a suitable category and ask the operator to give the details of the vehicle. The program should finish by printing out information for all the vehicles, ordered according to registration number.

14.5 Extend the program in the previous exercise so that it finally saves the information for the vehicles in a file, making use of the package STREAM_IO.

14.6 (a)   Write a generic package which enables an arbitrary tagged type to be extended with an ID number. Define operations so that the ID number can be read and changed.

(b)   Change the package so that each new object that is created automatically gets a unique ID number, and remove the operation which enables the ID number to be changed. (*Hint*: Make the component which contains the ID number another object and let its type be a child type of the standard type CONTROLLED.)

▲

Appendix A

The Package TEXT_IO

```
with ADA.IO_EXCEPTIONS;
package ADA.TEXT_IO is      -- No prefix in Ada 83

   type FILE_TYPE  is limited private;
   type FILE_MODE is (IN_FILE, OUT_FILE, APPEND_FILE);

   -- APPEND_FILE is not defined in Ada 83

   type COUNT is range 0 .. implementation_defined;
   subtype POSITIVE_COUNT is COUNT range 1 .. COUNT'LAST;
   UNBOUNDED : constant COUNT := 0;        -- line and page length

   subtype FIELD            is INTEGER range 0 .. implementation_defined;
   subtype NUMBER_BASE is INTEGER range 2 .. 16;

   type TYPE_SET is (LOWER_CASE, UPPER_CASE);

   -- File Management

   procedure CREATE (FILE    : in out FILE_TYPE;
                     MODE : in FILE_MODE := OUT_FILE;
                     NAME  : in STRING := " ";
                     FORM  : in STRING := " ");

   procedure OPEN (FILE    : in out FILE_TYPE;
                   MODE : in FILE_MODE;
                   NAME  : in STRING;
                   FORM  : in STRING := " ");

   procedure CLOSE   (FILE: in out FILE_TYPE);
   procedure DELETE (FILE: in out FILE_TYPE);
   procedure RESET   (FILE: in out FILE_TYPE; MODE: in FILE_MODE);
   procedure RESET   (FILE: in out FILE_TYPE);
```

```
function MODE  (FILE: in  FILE_TYPE) return FILE_MODE;
function NAME  (FILE: in  FILE_TYPE) return STRING;
function FORM  (FILE: in  FILE_TYPE) return STRING;
function IS_OPEN(FILE: in FILE_TYPE) return BOOLEAN;
```

-- Control of default input and output files

```
procedure SET_INPUT    (FILE: in FILE_TYPE);
procedure SET_OUTPUT (FILE: in FILE_TYPE);
```

```
function STANDARD_INPUT    return FILE_TYPE;
function STANDARD_OUTPUT return FILE_TYPE;
```

```
function CURRENT_INPUT    return FILE_TYPE;
function CURRENT_OUTPUT return FILE_TYPE;
```

```
procedure SET_ERROR (FILE:  in FILE_TYPE);
function    STANDARD_ERROR return FILE_TYPE;
function    CURRENT_ERROR  return FILE_TYPE;
```

```
type FILE_ACCESS is access constant FILE_TYPE;
```

```
procedure SET_INPUT    (FILE: in FILE_ACCESS);
procedure SET_OUTPUT (FILE: in FILE_ACCESS);
procedure SET_ERROR   (FILE: in FILE_ACCESS);
```

```
function STANDARD_INPUT    return FILE_ACCESS;
function STANDARD_OUTPUT return FILE_ACCESS;
function STANDARD_ERROR   return FILE_ACCESS;
```

```
function CURRENT_INPUT    return FILE_ACCESS;
function CURRENT_OUTPUT return FILE_ACCESS;
function CURRENT_ERROR   return FILE_ACCESS;
```

```
procedure  FLUSH (FILE : in out FILE_TYPE);
procedure FLUSH;
```

-- Specification of line and page lengths

```
procedure SET_LINE_LENGTH (FILE: in FILE_TYPE; TO: in COUNT);
procedure SET_LINE_LENGTH (TO:   in COUNT);
```

```
procedure SET_PAGE_LENGTH (FILE:  in FILE_TYPE; TO: in COUNT);
procedure SET_PAGE_LENGTH (TO:    in COUNT);
```

```
function LINE_LENGTH(FILE: in FILE_TYPE) return COUNT;
function LINE_LENGTH return COUNT;
```

```
function PAGE_LENGTH(FILE: in FILE_TYPE) return COUNT;
function PAGE_LENGTH return COUNT;
```

-- Column, Line, and Page Control

```
procedure NEW_LINE  (FILE:      in FILE_TYPE;
                      SPACING: in POSITIVE_COUNT := 1);
procedure NEW_LINE  (SPACING: in POSITIVE_COUNT := 1);
procedure SKIP_LINE  (FILE:      in FILE_TYPE;
                      SPACING: in POSITIVE_COUNT := 1);
procedure SKIP_LINE  (SPACING: in POSITIVE_COUNT := 1);

function END_OF_LINE(FILE: in FILE_TYPE) return BOOLEAN;
function END_OF_LINE return BOOLEAN;

procedure NEW_PAGE (FILE: in FILE_TYPE);
procedure NEW_PAGE;

procedure SKIP_PAGE (FILE: in FILE_TYPE);
procedure SKIP_PAGE;

function END_OF_PAGE(FILE: in FILE_TYPE) return BOOLEAN;
function END_OF_PAGE return BOOLEAN;

function END_OF_FILE(FILE: in FILE_TYPE) return BOOLEAN;
function END_OF_FILE return BOOLEAN;

procedure SET_COL (FILE: in FILE_TYPE; TO: in POSITIVE_COUNT);
procedure SET_COL (TO:   in POSITIVE_COUNT);

procedure SET_LINE (FILE: in FILE_TYPE; TO: in POSITIVE_COUNT);
procedure SET_LINE (TO:   in POSITIVE_COUNT);

function COL   (FILE: in FILE_TYPE) return POSITIVE_COUNT;
function COL   return POSITIVE_COUNT;
function LINE  (FILE: in FILE_TYPE) return POSITIVE_COUNT;
function LINE  return POSITIVE_COUNT;
function PAGE (FILE: in FILE_TYPE) return POSITIVE_COUNT;
function PAGE return POSITIVE_COUNT;
```

-- Character Input-Output

```
procedure GET (FILE:  in FILE_TYPE; ITEM: out CHARACTER);
procedure GET (ITEM: out CHARACTER);
procedure PUT (FILE:  in FILE_TYPE; ITEM: in CHARACTER);
procedure PUT (ITEM: in CHARACTER);

procedure LOOK_AHEAD (FILE         : in FILE_TYPE;
                      ITEM         : out CHARACTER;
                      END_OF_LINE : out BOOLEAN);

procedure LOOK_AHEAD (ITEM         : out CHARACTER;
                      END_OF_LINE : out BOOLEAN);
```

```
procedure GET_IMMEDIATE ( FILE  : FILE_TYPE;
                                 ITEM : out CHARACTER);
procedure GET_IMMEDIATE ( ITEM : out CHARACTER);

procedure GET_IMMEDIATE (FILE : FILE_TYPE;
                         ITEM        : out CHARACTER;
                         AVAILABLE  : out BOOLEAN);
procedure GET_IMMEDIATE (ITEM        : out CHARACTER;
                         AVAILABLE  : out BOOLEAN);
```

-- String Input-Output

```
procedure GET (FILE:  in FILE_TYPE; ITEM: out STRING);
procedure GET (ITEM: out STRING);
procedure PUT (FILE:  in FILE_TYPE; ITEM: in STRING);
procedure PUT (ITEM: in STRING);

procedure GET_LINE (FILE:  in FILE_TYPE; ITEM: out STRING;
                    LAST: out NATURAL);
procedure GET_LINE (ITEM: out STRING; LAST: out NATURAL);
procedure PUT_LINE (FILE:  in FILE_TYPE; ITEM: in STRING);
procedure PUT_LINE (ITEM: in STRING);
```

   -- Generic package for Input-Output of Integer Types

```
generic
  type NUM is range < >;
package INTEGER_IO is
  DEFAULT_WIDTH: FIELD := NUM'WIDTH;
  DEFAULT_BASE: NUMBER_BASE := 10;

  procedure GET (FILE:    in FILE_TYPE;
                 ITEM:    out NUM;
                 WIDTH:  in FIELD := 0);
  procedure GET (ITEM:    out NUM; WIDTH: in FIELD := 0);

  procedure PUT (FILE:    in FILE_TYPE;
                 ITEM:    in NUM;
                 WIDTH:  in FIELD := DEFAULT_WIDTH;
                 BASE:    in NUMBER_BASE := DEFAULT_BASE);
  procedure PUT (ITEM:    in NUM;
                 WIDTH:  in FIELD := DEFAULT_WIDTH;
                 BASE:    in NUMBER_BASE := DEFAULT_BASE);

  procedure GET (FROM:   in STRING;
                 ITEM:    out NUM;
                 LAST:    out POSITIVE);
  procedure PUT (TO:      out STRING;
                 ITEM:    in NUM;
                 BASE:    in NUMBER_BASE := DEFAULT_BASE);
end INTEGER_IO;
```

-- Generic package for Input-Output of Modular Types

generic – This package is not defined in Ada 83
  type NUM **is mod** < >;
package MODULAR_IO **is**
  DEFAULT_WIDTH: FIELD := NUM'WIDTH;
  DEFAULT_BASE: NUMBER_BASE := 10;

  procedure GET (FILE: **in** FILE_TYPE;
                 ITEM: **out** NUM;
                 WIDTH: **in** FIELD := 0);
  procedure GET (ITEM: **out** NUM; WIDTH: **in** FIELD := 0);

  procedure PUT (FILE: **in** FILE_TYPE;
                 ITEM: **in** NUM;
                 WIDTH: **in** FIELD := DEFAULT_WIDTH;
                 BASE: **in** NUMBER_BASE := DEFAULT_BASE);
  procedure PUT (ITEM: **in** NUM;
                 WIDTH: **in** FIELD := DEFAULT_WIDTH;
                 BASE: **in** NUMBER_BASE := DEFAULT_BASE);

  procedure GET (FROM: **in** STRING;
                 ITEM: **out** NUM;
                 LAST: **out** POSITIVE);
  procedure PUT (TO: **out** STRING;
                 ITEM: **in** NUM;
                 BASE: **in** NUMBER_BASE := DEFAULT_BASE);
end MODULAR_IO;

-- Generic package for Input-Output of Real Types

generic
  type NUM **is digits** < >;
package FLOAT_IO **is**

  DEFAULT_FORE: FIELD := 2;
  DEFAULT_AFT: FIELD := NUM'DIGITS – 1;
  DEFAULT_EXP: FIELD := 3;

  procedure GET (FILE: **in** FILE_TYPE;
                 ITEM: **out** NUM;
                 WIDTH: **in** FIELD := 0);
  procedure GET (ITEM: **out** NUM; WIDTH: **in** FIELD := 0);

  procedure PUT (FILE: **in** FILE_TYPE;
                 ITEM: **in** NUM;
                 FORE: **in** FIELD := DEFAULT_FORE;
                 AFT: **in** FIELD := DEFAULT_AFT;
                 EXP: **in** FIELD := DEFAULT_EXP);

```
        procedure PUT (ITEM:    in NUM;
                       FORE:    in FIELD := DEFAULT_FORE;
                       AFT:     in FIELD := DEFAULT_AFT;
                       EXP:     in FIELD := DEFAULT_EXP);


        procedure GET (FROM:    in STRING;
                       ITEM:    out NUM;
                       LAST:    out POSITIVE);
        procedure PUT (TO:      out STRING;
                       ITEM:    in NUM;
                       AFT:     in FIELD := DEFAULT_AFT;
                       EXP:     in FIELD := DEFAULT_EXP);


    end FLOAT_IO;


    generic
      type NUM is delta < >;
    package DECIMAL_IO is
      DEFAULT_FORE: FIELD := NUM'FORE;
      DEFAULT_AFT:   FIELD := NUM'AFT;
      DEFAULT_EXP:   FIELD := 0;


      procedure GET (FILE:    in FILE_TYPE;
                     ITEM:    out NUM;
                     WIDTH:   in FIELD := 0);
      procedure GET (ITEM:    out NUM; WIDTH: in FIELD := 0);


      procedure PUT (FILE:    in FILE_TYPE;
                     ITEM:    in NUM;
                     FORE:    in FIELD := DEFAULT_FORE;
                     AFT:     in FIELD := DEFAULT_AFT;
                     EXP:     in FIELD := DEFAULT_EXP);
      procedure PUT (ITEM:    in NUM;
                     FORE:    in FIELD := DEFAULT_FORE;
                     AFT:     in FIELD := DEFAULT_AFT;
                     EXP:     in FIELD := DEFAULT_EXP);
      procedure GET (FROM:    in STRING;
                     ITEM:    out NUM;
                     LAST:    out POSITIVE);
      procedure PUT (TO:      out STRING;
                     ITEM:    in NUM;
                     AFT:     in FIELD := DEFAULT_AFT;
                     EXP:     in FIELD := DEFAULT_EXP);
    end FIXED_IO;
```

```
generic        -- This package is not defined in Ada 83
   type NUM is delta < > digits < >;
package DECIMAL_IO is
  DEFAULT_FORE: FIELD := NUM'FORE;
  DEFAULT_AFT:   FIELD := NUM'AFT;
  DEFAULT_EXP:   FIELD := 0;

  procedure GET (FILE:    in FILE_TYPE;
                 ITEM:    out NUM;
                 WIDTH: in FIELD := 0);
  procedure GET (ITEM:    out NUM; WIDTH: in FIELD := 0);

  procedure PUT (FILE:    in FILE_TYPE;
                 ITEM:    in NUM;
                 FORE:    in FIELD := DEFAULT_FORE;
                 AFT:     in FIELD := DEFAULT_AFT;
                 EXP:     in FIELD := DEFAULT_EXP);
  procedure PUT (ITEM:    in NUM;
                 FORE:    in FIELD := DEFAULT_FORE;
                 AFT:     in FIELD := DEFAULT_AFT;
                 EXP:     in FIELD := DEFAULT_EXP);

  procedure GET (FROM:    in STRING;
                 ITEM:    out NUM;
                 LAST:    out POSITIVE);
  procedure PUT (TO:      out STRING;
                 ITEM:    in NUM;
                 AFT:     in FIELD := DEFAULT_AFT;
                 EXP:     in FIELD := DEFAULT_EXP);
end DECIMAL_IO;

  -- Generic package for Input-Output of Enumeration Types

generic
   type ENUM is (< >);
package ENUMERATION_IO is
  DEFAULT_WIDTH:    FIELD := 0;
  DEFAULT_SETTING: TYPE_SET := UPPER_CASE;

  procedure GET (FILE:    in FILE_TYPE; ITEM: out ENUM);
  procedure GET (ITEM:    out ENUM);

  procedure PUT (FILE:    in FILE_TYPE;
                 ITEM:    in ENUM;
                 WIDTH: in FIELD := DEFAULT_WIDTH;
                 SET:     in TYPE_SET := DEFAULT_SETTING);
```

```
        procedure PUT (ITEM:    in ENUM;
                       WIDTH:   in FIELD := DEFAULT_WIDTH;
                       SET:     in TYPE_SET := DEFAULT_SETTING);

        procedure GET (FROM:    in STRING;
                       ITEM:    out ENUM;
                       LAST:    out POSITIVE);
        procedure PUT (TO:      out STRING;
                       ITEM:    in ENUM;
                       SET:     in TYPE_SET := DEFAULT_SETTING);
     end ENUMERATION_IO;
```

-- Exceptions

```
STATUS_ERROR:   exception renames IO_EXCEPTIONS.STATUS_ERROR;
MODE_ERROR:     exception renames IO_EXCEPTIONS.MODE_ERROR;
NAME_ERROR:     exception renames IO_EXCEPTIONS.NAME_ERROR;
USE_ERROR:      exception renames IO_EXCEPTIONS.USE_ERROR;
DEVICE_ERROR:   exception renames IO_EXCEPTIONS.DEVICE_ERROR;
END_ERROR:      exception renames IO_EXCEPTIONS.END_ERROR;
DATA _ERROR:    exception renames IO_EXCEPTIONS.DATA _ERROR;
LAYOUT_ERROR:   exception renames IO_EXCEPTIONS.LAYOUT_ERROR;
```

private
   -- implementation-dependent
end ADA.TEXT_IO;

Appendix B

The Package BASIC_NUM_IO

Given below is the specification of the package BASIC_NUM_IO, which can be used to simplify access to the procedures GET and PUT for the standard types INTEGER and FLOAT. The two packages STANDARD_INTEGER_IO and STANDARD_INTEGER_IO have been created using the generic packages INTEGER_IO and FLOAT_IO, which are to be found in TEXT_IO. Using the **renames** construct, the names STANDARD_INTEGER_IO.GET and so on have been renamed so that the user of BASIC_NUM_IO can simply write GET and PUT.

```
with TEXT_IO;
package BASIC_NUM_IO is

    package STANDARD_INTEGER_IO is new
                                    TEXT_IO.INTEGER_IO(INTEGER);

DEFAULT_WIDTH : TEXT_IO.FIELD := INTEGER'WIDTH;
DEFAULT_BASE  : TEXT_IO.NUMBER_BASE := 10;

    procedure GET (ITEM    : out INTEGER;
                   WIDTH   : in TEXT_IO.FIELD := 0)
                   renames STANDARD_INTEGER_IO.GET;

    procedure PUT (ITEM    : in INTEGER;
                   WIDTH   : in TEXT_IO.FIELD := DEFAULT_WIDTH;
                   BASE    : in TEXT_IO.NUMBER_BASE := DEFAULT_BASE)
                   renames STANDARD_INTEGER_IO.PUT;

    package STANDARD_FLOAT_IO is new TEXT_IO.FLOAT_IO(FLOAT);
DEFAULT_FORE           : TEXT_IO.FIELD := 2;
DEFAULT_AFT : TEXT_IO.FIELD := FLOAT'DIGITS – 1;
DEFAULT_EXP : TEXT_IO.FIELD := 3;
```

```
procedure GET  (ITEM    : out FLOAT;
                WIDTH   : in TEXT_IO.FIELD := 0)
                renames STANDARD_FLOAT_IO.GET;

procedure PUT  (ITEM    : in FLOAT;
                FORE    : in TEXT_IO.FIELD := DEFAULT_FORE;
                AFT     : in TEXT_IO.FIELD := DEFAULT_AFT;
                EXP     : in TEXT_IO.FIELD := DEFAULT_EXP)
                renames STANDARD_FLOAT_IO.PUT;
end BASIC_NUM_IO;
```

Appendix C

The Package
SEQUENTIAL_IO

```ada
with ADA.IO_EXCEPTIONS;
generic
  type ELEMENT_TYPE is private;
package ADA.SEQUENTIAL_IO is      -- No prefix in Ada 83

  type FILE_TYPE is limited private;

  type FILE_MODE is (IN_FILE, OUT_FILE, APPEND_FILE);

  -- APPEND_FILE is not defined in Ada 83

  -- File management

  procedure CREATE (FILE  : in out FILE_TYPE;
                    MODE : in FILE_MODE := OUT_FILE;
                    NAME : in STRING := " ";
                    FORM : in STRING := " ");

  procedure OPEN   (FILE  : in out FILE_TYPE;
                    MODE : in FILE_MODE;
                    NAME : in STRING;
                    FORM : in STRING := " ");

  procedure CLOSE  (FILE  : in out FILE_TYPE);
  procedure DELETE (FILE  : in out FILE_TYPE);
  procedure RESET  (FILE  : in out FILE_TYPE; MODE: in FILE_MODE);
  procedure RESET  (FILE  : in out FILE_TYPE);

  function MODE    (FILE  : in FILE_TYPE) return FILE_MODE;
  function NAME    (FILE  : in FILE_TYPE) return STRING;
  function FORM    (FILE  : in FILE_TYPE) return STRING;

  function IS_OPEN (FILE  : in FILE_TYPE) return BOOLEAN;
```

-- Input and output operations

procedure READ   (FILE: **in** FILE_TYPE; ITEM: **out** ELEMENT_TYPE);
procedure WRITE (FILE: **in** FILE_TYPE; ITEM: **in** ELEMENT_TYPE);

function END_OF_FILE(FILE: **in** FILE_TYPE) **return** BOOLEAN;

-- Exceptions

STATUS_ERROR: **exception renames**
IO_EXCEPTIONS.STATUS_ERROR;
  MODE_ERROR: **exception renames** IO_EXCEPTIONS.MODE_ERROR;
  NAME_ERROR: **exception renames** IO_EXCEPTIONS.NAME_ERROR;
  USE_ERROR: **exception renames** IO_EXCEPTIONS.USE_ERROR;
  DEVICE_ERROR: **exception renames**
IO_EXCEPTIONS.DEVICE_ERROR;
  END_ERROR: **exception renames** IO_EXCEPTIONS.END_ERROR;
  DATA_ERROR: **exception renames** IO_EXCEPTIONS.DATA_ERROR;

private
  -- implementation-dependent
end ADA.SEQUENTIAL_IO;

Appendix D

The Package **DIRECT_IO**

```
with ADA.IO_EXCEPTIONS;
generic
  type ELEMENT_TYPE is private;
package ADA.DIRECT_IO is        -- No prefix in Ada 83

  type FILE_TYPE is limited private;

  type FILE_MODE is (IN_FILE, INOUT_FILE, OUT_FILE);
  type COUNT        is range 0 .. implementation_defined;
  subtype POSITIVE_COUNT is COUNT range 1 .. COUNT'LAST;

  -- File management

  procedure CREATE (FILE:    in out FILE_TYPE;
                    MODE:    in FILE_MODE := INOUT_FILE;
                    NAME:    in STRING := " ";
                    FORM:    in STRING := " ");

  procedure OPEN   (FILE:    in out FILE_TYPE;
                    MODE:    in FILE_MODE;
                    NAME:    in STRING;
                    FORM:    in STRING := " ");

  procedure CLOSE  (FILE:    in out FILE_TYPE);

  procedure DELETE (FILE:    in out FILE_TYPE);
  procedure RESET  (FILE:    in out FILE_TYPE; MODE: in FILE_MODE);
  procedure RESET  (FILE:    in out FILE_TYPE);

  function MODE     (FILE:    in FILE_TYPE) return FILE_MODE;
  function NAME     (FILE:    in FILE_TYPE) return STRING;
  function FORM     (FILE:    in FILE_TYPE) return STRING;

  function IS_OPEN  (FILE:    in FILE_TYPE) return BOOLEAN;
```

-- Input and output operations

procedure READ   (FILE: **in** FILE_TYPE;
                       ITEM: **out** ELEMENT_TYPE;
                       FORM: **in** POSITIVE_COUNT);

procedure READ   (FILE: **in** FILE_TYPE; ITEM: **out** ELEMENT_TYPE);

procedure WRITE   (FILE: **in** FILE_TYPE;
                       ITEM: **in** ELEMENT_TYPE;
                       TO: **in** POSITIVE_COUNT);

procedure WRITE   (FILE: **in** FILE_TYPE; ITEM: **in** ELEMENT_TYPE);

procedure SET_INDEX (FILE: **in** FILE_TYPE; TO: **in** POSITIVE_COUNT);

function INDEX (FILE: **in** FILE_TYPE) **return** POSITIVE_COUNT;
function SIZE   (FILE: **in** FILE_TYPE) **return** COUNT;

function END_OF_FILE (FILE: **in** FILE_TYPE) **return** BOOLEAN;

-- Exceptions

STATUS_ERROR:**exception renames**
IO_EXCEPTIONS.STATUS_ERROR;
  MODE_ERROR: **exception renames** IO_EXCEPTIONS.MODE_ERROR;
  NAME_ERROR: **exception renames** IO_EXCEPTIONS.NAME_ERROR;
  USE_ERROR: **exception renames** IO_EXCEPTIONS.USE_ERROR;
  DEVICE_ERROR:**exception renames** IO_EXCEPTIONS.DEVICE_ERROR;
  END_ERROR: **exception renames** IO_EXCEPTIONS.END_ERROR;
  DATA_ERROR: **exception renames** IO_EXCEPTIONS.DATA_ERROR;
private
  -- implementation-dependent
end ADA.DIRECT_IO;

Appendix E

Mathematical Functions

```
generic
  type FLOAT_TYPE is digits < >;
package ADA.NUMERICS.GENERIC_ELEMENTARY_FUNCTIONS is
function SQRT       (X: FLOAT_TYPE'BASE)                return FLOAT_TYPE'BASE;
function LOG        (X: FLOAT_TYPE'BASE)                return FLOAT_TYPE'BASE;
function LOG        (X, BASE: FLOAT_TYPE'BASE)   return FLOAT_TYPE'BASE;
function EXP        (X: FLOAT_TYPE'BASE)                return FLOAT_TYPE'BASE;
function "**"       (LEFT, RIGHT: FLOAT_TYPE'BASE)
                                                        return FLOAT_TYPE'BASE;

function SIN        (X: FLOAT_TYPE'BASE)                return FLOAT_TYPE'BASE;
function SIN        (X, CYCLE: FLOAT_TYPE'BASE) return FLOAT_TYPE'BASE;
function COS        (X: FLOAT_TYPE'BASE)                return FLOAT_TYPE'BASE;
function COS        (X, CYCLE: FLOAT_TYPE'BASE) return FLOAT_TYPE'BASE;
function TAN        (X: FLOAT_TYPE'BASE)                return FLOAT_TYPE'BASE;
function TAN        (X, CYCLE: FLOAT_TYPE'BASE) return FLOAT_TYPE'BASE;
function COT        (X: FLOAT_TYPE'BASE)                return FLOAT_TYPE'BASE;
function COT        (X, CYCLE: FLOAT_TYPE'BASE) return FLOAT_TYPE'BASE;

function ARCSIN     (X: FLOAT_TYPE'BASE)                return FLOAT_TYPE'BASE;
function ARCSIN     (X, CYCLE: FLOAT_TYPE'BASE) return FLOAT_TYPE'BASE;
function ARCCOS     (X: FLOAT_TYPE'BASE)                return FLOAT_TYPE'BASE;
function ARCCOS     (X, CYCLE: FLOAT_TYPE'BASE) return FLOAT_TYPE'BASE;

function ARCTAN     (Y: FLOAT_TYPE'BASE; X: FLOAT_TYPE'BASE := 1.0)
                                                        return FLOAT_TYPE'BASE;
function ARCTAN     (Y: FLOAT_TYPE'BASE; X: FLOAT_TYPE'BASE := 1.0;
                     CYCLE: FLOAT_TYPE'BASE)     return FLOAT_TYPE'BASE;
function ARCCOT     (X: FLOAT_TYPE'BASE; Y: FLOAT_TYPE'BASE := 1.0)
                                                        return FLOAT_TYPE'BASE;
function ARCCOT     (X: FLOAT_TYPE'BASE; Y: FLOAT_TYPE'BASE := 1.0;
                     CYCLE: FLOAT_TYPE'BASE)     return FLOAT_TYPE'BASE;
```

```
function SINH      (X: FLOAT_TYPE'BASE)      return FLOAT_TYPE'BASE;
function COSH      (X: FLOAT_TYPE'BASE)      return FLOAT_TYPE'BASE;
function TANH      (X: FLOAT_TYPE'BASE)      return FLOAT_TYPE'BASE;
function COTH      (X: FLOAT_TYPE'BASE)      return FLOAT_TYPE'BASE;
function ARCSINH  (X: FLOAT_TYPE'BASE)      return FLOAT_TYPE'BASE;
function ARCCOSH (X: FLOAT_TYPE'BASE)      return FLOAT_TYPE'BASE;
function ARCTANH  (X: FLOAT_TYPE'BASE)      return FLOAT_TYPE'BASE;
function ARCCOTH (X: FLOAT_TYPE'BASE)      return FLOAT_TYPE'BASE;

end ADA.NUMERICS.GENERIC_ELEMENTARY_FUNCTIONS;
```

Appendix F

Character Codes

Table G.1 LATIN_1 character codes
Only the first 128 characters in the table are defined in the ASCII standard

0	nul	32		64	@	96	`	128		160	nbsp	192	À	224	à
1	soh	33	!	65	A	97	a	129		161	¡	193	Á	225	á
2	stx	34	"	66	B	98	b	130		162	¢	194	Â	226	â
3	etx	35	#	67	C	99	c	131		163	£	195	Ã	227	ã
4	eot	36	$	68	D	100	d	132	ind	164	¤	196	Ä	228	ä
5	enq	37	%	69	E	101	e	133	nel	165	¥	197	Å	229	å
6	ack	38	&	70	F	102	f	134	ssa	166	¦	198	Æ	230	æ
7	bel	39	'	71	G	103	g	135	esa	167	§	199	Ç	231	ç
8	bs	40	(	72	H	104	h	136	hts	168	¨	200	È	232	è
9	ht	41	)	73	I	105	i	137	htj	169	©	201	É	233	é
10	lf	42	*	74	J	106	j	138	vts	170	ª	202	Ê	234	ê
11	vt	43	+	75	K	107	k	139	pld	171	<	203	Ë	235	ë
12	ff	44	,	76	L	108	l	140	plu	172	¬	204	Ì	236	ì
13	cr	45	-	77	M	109	m	141	ri	173	—	205	Í	237	í
14	so	46	.	78	N	110	n	142	ss2	174	®	206	Î	238	î
15	si	47		79	O	111	o	143	ss3	175	–	207	Ï	239	ï
16	dle	48	0	80	P	112	p	144	dcs	176	°	208	Ð	240	ð
17	dc1	49	1	81	Q	113	q	145	pu1	177	±	209	Ñ	241	ñ
18	dc2	50	2	82	R	114	r	146	pu2	178	²	210	Ò	242	ò
19	dc3	51	3	83	S	115	s	147	sts	179	³	211	Ó	243	ó
20	dc4	52	4	84	T	116	t	148	cch	180	´	212	Ô	244	ô
21	nak	53	5	85	U	117	u	149	mw	181	µ	213	Õ	245	õ
22	syn	54	6	85	V	118	v	150	spa	182	¶	214	Ö	246	ö
23	etb	55	7	87	W	119	w	151	epa	183	·	215	×	247	÷
24	can	56	8	88	X	120	x	152		184	¸	216	Ø	248	ø
25	em	57	9	89	Y	121	y	153		185	¹	217	Ù	24	ù
26	sub	58	:	90	Z	122	z	154		186	º	218	Ú	250	ú
27	esc	59	;	91	[	123	{	155	csi	187	>	219	Û	251	û
28	fs	60	<	92	\	124	|	156	st	188	¼	220	Ü	252	ü
29	gs	61	=	93	]	125	}	157	osc	189	½	221	Ý	253	ý
30	rs	62	>	94	^	126	~	158	pm	190	¾	222	Þ	254	þ
31	us	63	?	95	_	127	del	159	apc	191	¿	223	ß	255	ÿ

Table G.2 Symbolic names in the package ADA.CHARACTERS.LATIN_1.

160	*no_break_space*	192	*uc_a_grave*	224	*lc_a_grave*
161	*inverted_exclamation*	193	*uc_a_acute*	225	*lc_a_acute*
162	*cent_sign*	194	*uc_a_circumflex*	226	*lc_a_circumflex*
163	*pound_sign*	195	*uc_a_tilde*	227	*lc_a_tilde*
164	*currency_sign*	196	*uc_a_diaeresis*	228	*lc_a_diaeresis*
165	*yen_sign*	197	*uc_a_ring*	229	*lc_a_ring*
166	*broken_bar*	198	*uc_ae_diphthong*	230	*lc_ae_diphthong*
167	*paragraph_sign*	199	*uc_c_cedilla*	231	*lc_c_cedilla*
168	*diaeresis*	200	*uc_e_grave*	232	*lc_e_grave*
169	*copyright_sign*	201	*uc_e_acute*	233	*lc_e_acute*
170	*feminine_ordinal_indicator*	202	*uc_e_circumflex*	234	*lc_e_circumflex*
171	*left_angle_quotation*	203	*uc_e_diaeresis*	235	*lc_e_diaeresis*
172	*not_sign*	204	*uc_i_grave*	236	*lc_i_grave*
173	*soft_hyphen*	205	*uc_i_acute*	237	*lc_i_acute*
174	*registered_trade_mark_sign*	206	*uc_i_circumflex*	238	*lc_i_circumflex*
175	*macron*	207	*uc_i_diaeresis*	239	*lc_i_diaeresis*
176	*ring_above*	208	*uc_icelandic_eth*	240	*lc_icelandic_eth*
177	*plus_minus_sign*	209	*uc_n_tilde*	241	*lc_n_tilde*
178	*superscript_two*	210	*uc_o_grave*	242	*lc_o_grave*
179	*superscript_three*	211	*uc_o_acute*	243	*lc_0_acute*
180	*acute*	212	*uc_o_circumflex*	244	*lc_o_circumflex*
181	*micro_sign*	213	*uc_o_tilde*	245	*lc_o_tilde*
182	*pilcrow_sign*	214	*uc_o_diaeresis*	246	*lc_o_diaeresis*
183	*middle_dot*	215	*multiplication_sign*	247	*division_sign*
184	*cedilla*	216	*uc_o_oblique_stroke*	248	*lc_o_oblique_stroke*
185	*superscript_one*	217	*uc_u_grave*	249	*lc_u_grave*
186	*masculine_ordinal_indicator*	218	*uc_u_acute*	250	*lc_u_acute*
187	*right_angle_quotation*	219	*uc_u_circumflex*	251	*lc_u_circumflex*
188	*fraction_one_quarter*	220	*uc_u_diaeresis*	252	*lc_u_diaeresis*
189	*fraction_one_half*	221	*uc_y_acute*	253	*lc_y_acute*
190	*fraction_three_quarters*	222	*uc_icelandic_thorn*	254	*lc_icelandic_thorn*
191	*inverted_question*	223	*lc_german_sharp_s*	255	*lc_y_diaeresis*

Appendix G

The Package ADA.CHARACTERS. HANDLING

package ADA.CHARACTERS.HANDLING **is**

-- CHARACTER classification functions

function IS_CONTROL	(ITEM : CHARACTER)	**return** BOOLEAN;
function IS_GRAPHIC	(ITEM : CHARACTER)	**return** BOOLEAN;
function IS_LETTER	(ITEM : CHARACTER)	**return** BOOLEAN;
function IS_LOWER	(ITEM : CHARACTER)	**return** BOOLEAN;
function IS_UPPER	(ITEM : CHARACTER)	**return** BOOLEAN;
function IS_BASIC	(ITEM : CHARACTER)	**return** BOOLEAN;
function IS_DIGIT	(ITEM : CHARACTER)	**return** BOOLEAN;
function IS_DECIMAL_DIGIT	(ITEM : CHARACTER)	**return** BOOLEAN;

   renames IS_DIGIT;

function IS_HEXADECIMAL_DIGIT	(ITEM : CHARACTER)	**return** BOOLEAN;
function IS_ALPHANUMERIC	(ITEM : CHARACTER)	**return** BOOLEAN;
function IS_SPECIAL_GRAPHIC	(ITEM : CHARACTER)	**return** BOOLEAN;

-- Conversion functions for CHARACTER and STRING

function TO_LOWER	(ITEM : CHARACTER)	**return** CHARACTER;
function TO_UPPER	(ITEM : CHARACTER)	**return** CHARACTER;
function TO_BASIC	(ITEM : CHARACTER)	**return** CHARACTER;
function TO_LOWER	(ITEM : STRING)	**return** STRING;
function TO_UPPER	(ITEM : STRING)	**return** STRING;
function TO_BASIC	(ITEM : STRING)	**return** STRING;

-- Classification of and conversion between CHARACTER and ISO_646

subtype ISO_646 **is**
       CHARACTER **range** CHARACTER'VAL(0) .. CHARACTER'VAL(127);

```
function IS_ISO_646  (ITEM : CHARACTER) return BOOLEAN;
function IS_ISO_646  (ITEM : STRING)       return BOOLEAN;
function TO_ISO_646 (ITEM        : CHARACTER;
                     SUBSTITUTE : ISO_646 := '  ') return ISO_646;

function TO_ISO_646 (ITEM        : STRING;
                     SUBSTITUTE : ISO_646 := '  ') return STRING;
```

-- Classification of and conversion between WIDE_CHARACTER and CHARACTER

```
function IS_CHARACTER  (ITEM : WIDE_CHARACTER) return BOOLEAN;
function IS_STRING        (ITEM : WIDE_STRING)       return BOOLEAN;
function TO_CHARACTER (ITEM           : WIDE_CHARACTER;
                       SUBSTITUTE  : CHARACTER := '  ')
                                      return CHARACTER;
function TO_STRING        (ITEM           : WIDE_STRING;
                           SUBSTITUTE  : CHARACTER := '  ')
                                      return STRING;
function TO_WIDE_CHARACTER (ITEM : CHARACTER)
                                      return WIDE_CHARACTER;
function TO_WIDE_STRING (ITEM : STRING) return WIDE_STRING;

end ADA.CHARACTERS.HANDLING;
```

Table Index

Index